JEW
TRAVEL
2003
International Edition

Published in association with
the *Jewish Chronicle*, London

Edited by
MICHAEL ZAIDNER

VALLENTINE MITCHELL
LONDON • PORTLAND, OR

First published in 2003 in Great Britain by
VALLENTINE MITCHELL & CO. LTD
Crown House, 47 Chase Side, Southgate
London N14 5BP

and in the United States of America by
VALLENTINE MITCHELL
c/o ISBS,
5824 N.E. Hassalo Street
Portland, Oregon 97213-3644

ISBN 0 85303 465 6
ISSN 0075 3750

Printed in Great Britain by
Creative Print and Design (Wales), Ebbw Vale

Contents

Publisher's Note

WE NEED YOUR ASSISTANCE TO KEEP
THIS GUIDE UP TO DATE

The Editor and the Publishers have made every effort to ensure that this guide is as accurate and up to date as possible.

As in previous years, an update form is included at the back of this book for those who become aware of additions they would like to be considered for inclusion. In addition, of course, we wish to be notified of any errors that may have occurred in the preparation of this book.

Any information may be sent to:

The Editor
Jewish Travel Guide
Crown House
47 Chase Side
Southgate
London N14 5BP

Tel: +44(0)20 8920 2100
Fax: +44(0)20 8447 8548
Email: mzaidner@vmbooks.com
Website: www.vmbooks.com

Potential advertisers, or those who wish to stock and sell copies of the *Jewish Travel Guide*, may use any of the above means to contact us for details of advertising rates and trade terms.

Preface

I read earlier this year that editing a guidebook is like the painting of the Forth Bridge – that is to say, as soon as one has finished it is time to start on the next edition. This is indeed quite true.

As in previous years there has been a complete updating, as far as is possible, of all entries in the book.

In last year's editorial I referred to the effect of the introduction of the Euro on travellers. Apart from the problems of consequent price rises, the change went through quite easily and, in practice, there were few problems. For the benefit of travellers from outside Europe, I have updated the note I then included, as more information has now become available of the situation both in Europe and in the various overseas territories of the relevant European countries.

The world of email has meant that an increasing number of readers have been in touch regarding proposals to add new or to update existing entries. The object of this guide is to provide a service to its readers. If you feel that there is any additional information that should be included, please send an email to mzaidner@vmbooks.com.

A feature of recent years has been the increase in the number of Jewish museums throughout the world. Of particular interest among this year's new locations listed in this guide, which should be considered by travellers, are the Museum of the History and Culture of the Jews of Cracow in Poland and Pier 51 in Halifax, Canada. In addition, Jewish museums are currently being constructed in Copenhagen (which should open in late 2003) and in Warsaw (which hopes to open around 2006).

Again, I would draw your attention to the following notes:

- **It is in the interest of all travellers, if they are uncertain, to consider checking in advance on the existence, or the current kashrut status, of an establishment. Please also bear in mind that throughout the world telephone area codes are still changing on a regular basis.**

- **No responsibility can be accepted for any errors or omissions, or indeed for any claims of kashrut or other claims made by an establishment either listed or advertising in this guide.**

Finally, I would like to thank Donna Quy for her help in maintaining the database, from which this guide is compiled, and my wife Joyce, who thought I had retired, for her continued patience.

Michael Zaidner
November 2002

An Update on the Euro €

The use of Euro as a currency started on 1 January 2002 and is now a fact of life in the countries involved.

The twelve members of the European Monetary Union are:

Austria	Germany	Luxembourg
Belgium	Greece	The Netherlands
Finland	Ireland	Portugal
France	Italy	Spain

The situation regarding the overseas territories of the relevant members of the European Monetary Union is now clearer.

The French overseas territories, in both the Caribbean and Polynesia, all use the Euro. Most Francophone countries in Africa have also, in practice, adopted the Euro.

The Netherlands Antilles in the Caribbean still prefer to use US dollars.

In addition, the following European countries, while not members of the European Union, have adopted the Euro:

Andorra	San Marino
Monaco	Vatican City

Travellers should be aware that there is still no change in the situation in respect of Denmark, Norway, Switzerland, Sweden or the United Kingdom. They all continue to retain their existing currencies.

ALBANIA

There have been Jews living on the territory now known as Albania since Roman times and there are remains in Dardania (in the north of the country) of an ancient synagogue. The community was re-established by Jews from Iberia escaping the Spanish Inquisition in the fifteenth and early sixteenth centuries.

The number of Jews in Albania never increased significantly, and, in 1930, there were only 204 Jews in the country. However, this number was soon augmented by refugees escaping the Nazis. The local population was not, on the whole, hostile to the Jews and helped most of them to hide during the war when Italy, and then Germany, occupied the country.

The strict communist regime which followed the war led to the isolation of the Jewish community until the fall of communism. In 1991, almost the entire community, about 300, was airlifted to Israel. The few Jews who remained in Albania live in the capital, Tirana.

The Albanian Israel Friendship Society will be happy to provide any further information.

GMT + 1 hour	**Total Population 3,738,000**
Country calling code (355)	**Jewish Population Under 100**
Emergency Telephone (Police – 2445) (Fire – 23333) (Ambulance – 22235)	**(Electricity voltage – 220)**

Tirana

CONTACT INFORMATION
Albanian-Israel Friendship Society
Rruga 'Barrikatave' 226   (42) 22611

ALGERIA

Jews first settled in Algeria soon after the start of the Diaspora following the destruction of the Second Temple. A later influx occurred when Jews were escaping from Visigothic Spain.

In the twelfth and thirteenth centuries, Islamic conversion was forced on the Jews. Many Jews, however, crossed the Mediterranean from Spain during the time of the Inquisition, and these included some famous scholars. In 1830 the French occupied the country and, in due course, granted the Jews French citizenship.

Algerian Jews suffered anti-semitism from both the local Muslim population and the wartime Vichy government. After the Allied landings in 1942, the anti-Jewish laws were slowly lifted. In the late 1950s, 130,000 Jews lived in Algeria, but after the civil war, which led to independence from France in 1962, most of the community moved to France, with some to Israel, leaving very few behind. The present-day community, centred in Algiers, has a synagogue but no resident rabbi.

GMT + 1 hour	**Total Population 29,050,000**
Country calling code (213)	**Jewish Population Under 100**
Emergency Telephone (Police – 24445) (Fire – 23333) (Ambulance – 2235)	**(Electricity voltage – 117/220)**

Algiers

COMMUNITY ORGANISATIONS
Association Consistoriale Israélite d'Alger
6 rue Hassena Ahmed   (2) 62-85-72

SYNAGOGUES
6 rue Hassena Ahmed   (2) 62-85-72

Blida

COMMUNITY ORGANISATIONS
Consistoire d'Algerie
29 rue des Martyrs   (3) 49-26-57

ANDORRA

Andorra, which is governed by two co-princes - the Bishop of Urgel in Spain and the President of France, does not have a Jewish history. There are currently, however, around 15 Jewish families.

A synagogue was established inh 1997 in Escaldes and is the first in Andorra's 1,100-year history. While its liturgy leans towards Sephardism, it is also influenced by its Ashkenazi members. There is a community centre in Escaldes.

GMT +1 hour	**Total Population 66,000**
Country calling code (376)	**Jewish Population Under 100**
Emergency Telephone (Police – 825 225) (Fire – 118) (Ambulance – 118)	

CONTACT INFORMATION
Dr David ben-Chayil or Dr David Bezold
Francesco B.P. 244, Andorra la Vella   333 567
                    Email: bezold@andorra.ad
For visits to the synagogue contact Isaac Benisty
Telephone 860 758

ARGENTINA

The first Jewish arrivals (Conversos, or 'secret Jews') came in the sixteenth and seventeenth centuries from Portugal and Spain. They assimilated quickly. A more significant Jewish immigration occurred in the middle of the nineteenth century, from western Europe, and at the end of the nineteenth century many Jews arrived from eastern Europe, taking advantage of the 'open-door' policy towards immigrants. The new arrivals set up some Jewish agricultural settlements, under the auspices of the Alliance Israelita Universelle, and on the whole mixed with the local population.

The largest Jewish community is in Buenos Aires, with smaller communities in provincial centres. There are also some Jewish families remaining in the Jewish agricultural colonies, with Moiseville, Rivera and General Roca being the three most important.

There are Jewish newspapers, restaurants and other institutions. The Delegation of Argentine Jewish Associations (DAIA) represents all Jewish organisations

GMT -3 hours	**Total Population 35,672,000**
Country calling code (54)	**Jewish Population 200,000**
Emergency Telephone (Police – 101) (Fire – 100) (Ambulance – 107)	**(Electricity voltage – 226)**

Bahia Blanca

CONTACT INFORMATION
Beit Jabad
Chiclana 763 8000   (291) 4453-6582
                    Fax: (291) 4456-5596
For details of Mikvah please phone.

Buenos Aires

The first recorded Jewish event in Buenos Aires was a wedding in 1860. Around 200,000 Jews live in Buenos Aires. There are fifty or so synagogues in the city and kosher food is widely available. The most interesting synagogues for visitors are in Once although fewer Jews live there now.

BAKERIES
Confitería Aielet
Aranguren 2911, Flores   (11) 4637-5419
Confitería Ganz
Paso 752, Once   (11) 4961-6918
Confitería Helueni
Tucumán 2620, Once   (11) 4961-0541
Confitería Mari Jalabe
Bogota 3228, Flores   (11) 4612-6991
Panadería Malena
Av. Pueyrredón 880, Once   (11) 4962-6290

BOOKSELLERS
Kehot Lubavitch Sudamericana
San Luis 3281 1186   (11) 4865-0625
                    Fax: (11) 4865-0625
                    Email: kehot@iname.com
                    Web site: www.kehot-lubavitch.com.ar

Librería Editorial Sigal
Av. Corrientes 2854 C1193AAN
(11) 4861-9501; 4865-7208
Fax: (11) 4962-7931; 4865-7208
Email: libreriasigal@runbox.com
Web site: www.libreria-sigal.com

COMMUNITY ORGANISATIONS

AMIA (Central Ashkenazi community)
Pasteur 633   (11) 4953-9777; 4953-2862
The community centre has now been reopened
following the terror bomb attack in 1994.

Asociacion Israelita Sefaradi Argentina (AISA)
Paso 493   (11) 4952-4707

DAIA (Political representative body of Argentine Jewry)
Pasteur 633, 7th Floor   (11) 4378-3200
Fax: (11) 4378-3200
Email: daia@daia.org.ar

CONTACT INFORMATION

Asociacion Shuva Israel
Paso 557, Once   (11) 4962-6255

Beit Jabad Belgrano
O'Higgins 2358, Belgrano 1428   (11) 4781-3848
Fax: (11) 4783-4573
Email: shlomo@overnet.com.ar

Beit Jabad Villa Crespo
Serrano 69   (11) 4855-9822

Chabad Lubavich Argentina
Agüero 1164, Flores 1425   (11) 4963-1221

Congregacion Israelita de la Republica Argentina
Libertad 785, Centro   (11) 4372-2474
Fax: (11) 4372-2474
The total number of synagogues in Buenos Aires
where there is a minyan at least Friday night
and Shabbat morning exceeds fifty. Call any of
the above numbers to locate the synagogue
nearest you.

EMBASSY

Embassy of Israel
Avenida de Mayo 701-10° 1084   (11) 4345-6207/08
Fax: (11) 4345-6207
Email: cidipal@israel-embassy.org.ar

GROCERIES

Almacén Behar
Campana 347, Flores   (11) 4613-2033

Almacén Shalom
San Luis 2513, Once   (11) 4962-3685

Autoservicio Ezra
Ecuador 619, Once   (11) 4963-7062

Autoservicio Siman Tov
Helguera 474, Flores   (11) 4611-4746

Azulay
Helguera 507, Flores

Battías
Paso 706, Once

Kahal Jaredim
Argerich 386, Flores   (11) 4612-4590

Kaler
San Luis 2810, Once

Kol Bo Brandsen
Brandsen 1389, Barracas

Kol Bo I
Ecuador 855, Once   (11) 4961-3838

Kol Bo II
Viamonte 2537, Once   (11) 4961-2012

Kosher Delights
La Pampa 2547, Belgrano   (11) 4788-3150

La Esquina Casher
Aranguren 2999, Flores   (11) 4637-3706

La Quesería
Viamonte 2438, Once   (11) 4961-3171

La Tzorja
Ecuador 673, Once   (11) 4961-1096

Lidia's Macolet
Ecuador 586, Once   (11) 4863-5595
Fax: (11) 4932-4443

Yehuda Kosher Foods
Moldes 2452, Belgrano   (11) 4637-1465

KASHRUT INFORMATION

The Central Rabbinate of the Vaad Hakehillot
Ecuador 1110, Once   (11) 4961-2944
The Orthodox Ashkenazi Chief Rabbi of Argentina is
Rabbi Shlomo Benhamu Anidjar.

LIBRARIES

Sociedad Hebraica Argentino
Sarmiento 2233   (11) 4952-5570
Also has an art gallery.

YIVO Library
Pasteur 633, Third floor   (11) 445-2474

MEDIA

Newspapers
Comunidades
Die Presse
Kesher Kehilari
Mundo Israelita

MIKVAOT

Helguera 270, Once   (11) 4612-0410
Moldes 2431, Belgrano   (11) 4786-8046
Email: ajdut@netcomputer.com.ar

MUSEUM

Museo Judio de Buenos Aires
Libertad 769   (11) 4372-2474
                            Fax: (11) 4372-2474
Email: adaszko@mail.retina.ar.
Hours: Tuesday and Thursday 4pm to 7pm.

RESTAURANTS

Confiterie Helueni
Tucuman 2620, Once   (11) 4961-0541

Dairy
Soultani Café
San Luis 2601, Once   (11) 4961-3913

Meat
Al Galope
Tucumán 2633, Once   (11) 4963-6888

Mama Jacinta
Tucuman 2580 C-P 4052   (11) 4962-9149
                            Fax: (11) 4962-7535
Supervision: Gran Rasino Josef Chehebar.

McDonald's
Shopping Abasto, (Corrientes and Anchorena), Once
Supervision: Rav Oppenheimer - Ajdut Israel
There are two McDonalds. Only one is kosher.

Sucath David
Tucuman 2349   (11) 4952-8878
                            Fax: (11) 4953-9656
Email: sucathdavid@sinectis.com.ar

SYNAGOGUES

Ashkenazi
Baron Hirsh
Billinghurst 664   (11) 4862-2624

Beit Jabad Once "LITVISHE SHUL"
Jose Evaristo Uriburu 348   (11) 4952-7968
                            Fax: (11) 4952-7968
Email: aharon@radar.com.ar

Bet Rajel
Ecuador 522   (11) 4862-2701

Brit Abraham
Antezana 145   (11) 4855-6567

Etz Jaim
Julian Alvarez 745   (11) 4772-5324

Torah Vaaboda
Julian Alvarez 667   (11) 4854-0462

Zijron le David
Azcuenaga 736   (11) 4953-0200

Conservative
Beit Hilel
Araoz 2854, Palermo   (11) 4804-2286

Colegio Wolfson, Comunidad Or-El
Amenabar 2972   (11) 4544-5461

Comunidad Bet El
Sucre 3338   (11) 4552-2365

Dor Jadash
Murillo 649, Villa Crespo   (11) 4854-4467

Nueva Comunidad Israelita
Arcos 2319   (11) 4781-0281

Or Jadash
Varela 850, Flores   (11) 4612-1171

German Orthodox
Ajdut Yisroel
Moldes 2449   (11) 4783-2831
                            Fax: (11) 4781-6725
Email: ajdut@netcomputer.com.ar

Progressive
Benei Tikva
Vidal 2049   (11) 4795-0380

Reform
Templo Emanu-El
Tronador 1455   (11) 4552-4343
                            Fax: (11) 4555-4004
Email: kol_emanuel@name.com

Sephardi Orthodox
Aderet Eliahu
Ruy Diaz de Guzman 647   (11) 4303-1320
                            Fax: (11) 4303-1320

Agudat Dodim
Avellaneda 2874   (11) 4611-0056

Bajurim Tiferet Israeil
Helguera 611   (11) 4611-3376

Comunidad Israelita Sefaradi de Buenos Aires
Camargo 870   (11) 4855-6945
                            Fax: (11) 4855-9377
Email: acisba@continuidad.com.ar

Etz Jaim
Carlos Calvo 1164   (11) 4302-6290

Jaike Grimberg
Campana 460   (11) 4672-2347

Kehal Jaredim
Helguera 270, Once   (11) 4612-0410

Od Yosef Jai
Tucuman 3326   (11) 4963-2349

Or Misraj
Ciudad de la Paz 2555   (11) 4784-5945

Shaare Sion
Helguera 453   (11) 4637-5897
                            Fax: (11) 4637-1301
Email: editorial@shaaresion.org.ar
Web site: www.shaaresion.org.ar

Shaare Tefila
Paso 733   (11) 4962-2865

Shalom
Olleros 2876   (11) 4552-2720

Shuba Israel
Ecuador 627   (11) 4862-0562

Sinagoga Rabino Zeev Gringberg
Canalejas 3047   (11) 4611-3366

Sucath David
Tucuman 2750 (11) 4962-1091
Fax: (11) 4962-1264
Email: perspect@satlink.com
Web site: www.judaicasite.com

Templo la Paz (Chalom)
Olleros 2876 (11) 4552-6730

Yeshurun
Republica de la India 3035 (11) 4802-9310

Yesod Hadat
Lavalle 2449 (11) 4961-1615

Concordia

CONTACT INFORMATION
Beit Jabad Concordia
Entre Rios 212 3200 (45) 421-1934
Fax: (45) 421-7898

Cordoba

CONTACT INFORMATION
Jabad Lubavitch Cordoba
Sucre 1380, Barrio Cofico 5000 (351) 4471-0223
Fax: (351) 4411-9721
Email: jturk@elsitio.net

GROCERIES
Almacén
Sucre 1378, Barrio Cofico 5000 (351) 471-0223

Rosario

CONTACT INFORMATION
Beit Jabad Rosario
S. Lorenzo 1882 P.A. 2000 (341) 425-2899

GROCERIES
La Granja Kasher
(341) 449-6210

Tucuman

CONTACT INFORMATION
Beit Jabad Tucuman
Lamadrid 752 4000 (381) 424-8892
Fax: (381) 4248893
Email: jabadtucuman@amet.com.ar

GROCERIES
Almacén y Carnicería
9 de Julio 625 (381) 431-0227

Beit Jabad Tucuman
Lamadrid 752 4000 (381) 424-8892
Fax: (381) 4248893
Email: jabadtucuman@amet.com.ar

AUSTRALIA

The first Jews in Australia arrived with the first convict ships from the United Kingdom in 1788 and regular, organised worship started in the 1820s. The first free Jewish settler arrived with her husband, a deported convict, in 1816. The community grew in the nineteenth century, with the first synagogue being established in the mid-1840s. Events such as the gold rush and pogroms in eastern Europe were catalysts for more Jewish immigration.

The Jewish contribution to Australian life has been prominent, with the commander of the ANZAC forces in the First World War being a practising Jew, Sir John Monash. The twentieth century saw some 7,000 Jewish refugees from Nazi Europe settling in Australia, and the community contains the largest percentage of Holocaust survivors in the world. They are a major influence on the present community, which is expanding and comparatively religious. There have also been two Jewish Governors-General; one being Sir Issac Issacs, who was the first Australian - born to hold that position.

The community is led by the Executive Council of Australian Jewry. 75 per cent of primary and 55 per cent of secondary Jewish school children attend Jewish schools and there is a low level of inter-marriage. Melbourne has the largest community (42,000), with 35,000 in Sydney. There are Jewish newspapers, radio programmes of Jewish interest and museums on Jewish themes.

GMT +7 to +10 hours	**Total Population 19,105,000**
Country calling code (61)	**Jewish Population 100,000**
Emergency Telephone (Police – 000) (Fire – 000) (Ambulance – 000)	**(Electricity voltage – 240/250)**

AUSTRALIAN CAPITAL TERRITORY

Canberra

EMBASSY
Embassy of Israel
6 Turrana Street, Yarralumla 2600   (262) 73-1309
Fax: (262) 73-4279
Email: israelembassy@israemb.org

SYNAGOGUES
The A.C.T. Jewish Community Synagogue
National Jewish Memorial Centre, cnr Canberra Ave
& National Circuit, Forrest 2603   (262) 951-052
Fax: (262) 958-608
Web site: www.actjewish.org.au
Postal address: POB 3105, Manuka 2603

NEW SOUTH WALES

Newcastle

SYNAGOGUES
122 Tyrrell Street 2300   (49) 26-2820
Contact: Dr L.E. Fredman, 123 Dawson St, Cooks Hill, 2300 N.S.W.

Sydney

The first Jewish convict settlers were generally illiterate in both English and Hebrew, and there was no Jewish organisation until a Chevrah Kadishe was formed in 1817 and services were held under the leadership of a former convict Joseph Marcus.

Most of Sydneyís Jews are now settled outside the city in two suburban areas: the eastern suburbs, including Bondi, and the North Shore.

BAKERIES
Carmel Cake Shop
14 O'Brien Street, Bondi
Supervision: NSW Kashrut Authority

BOOKSELLERS
Gold's World of Judaica
9 O'Brien Street, Bondi 2026   (2) 9300-0495
Fax: (2) 9389-7345
Email: goldsyd@matra.com.au

Shalom Gift and Book Shop
323 Pacific Highway, Lindfield 2070   (2) 9416-7076
Fax: (2) 9416-7076

BUTCHERS
Eilat
173 Bondi Road, Bondi   (2) 9387-8881
Supervision: NSW Kashrut Authority

Hadassa
17 O'Brien Street, Bondi   (2) 9365-4904
Fax: (2) 9130-4760
Supervision: NSW Kashrut Authority

COMMUNITY ORGANISATIONS

Executive Council of Australian Jewry
146 Darlinghurst Road, Second floor, Darlinghurst
2010   (2) 9360-5415
                        Fax: (2) 9360-5416
                        Email: ecaj@tig.com.au

EMBASSY

Consul General of Israel
37 York Street, Level 6. 2000   (2) 9264-7933
                        Fax: (2) 9290-2259
                        Email: sydney@israel.org

HOSPITAL

Wolper Jewish Hospital
8 Trelawney Street, Woollahra   (2) 9328-6077

KASHRUT INFORMATION

Kosher Consumer Association
                        (2) 9337-6657
                        Fax: (2) 9371-0348

NSW Kashrut Authority
4/58 Hall St, Bondi Beach 2026   (2) 9365-2933
                        Fax: (2) 9365-0933
                        Email: rabbig@ka.org.au
                        Web site: www.ka.org.au

MEDIA

Newspaper
Australian Jewish News
146 Darlinghurst Road, Darlinghurst 2010
                        (2) 9360-5100
                        Fax: (2) 9332-4207
                        Email: valhadeff@jewishnews.net.au
                        Web site: www.ajn.net.au

MIKVAOT

117 Glenayr Avenue, Bondi   (2) 9130-2509

MUSEUM

Sydney Jewish Museum
148 Darlinghurst Road, Darlinghurst 2010
                        (2) 9360-7999
                        Fax: (2) 9331-4245
                        Email: sydjmus@tmx.mhs.oz.au
Has won many awards for its work documenting
Sydney's Jewish history and the Holocaust and has a
kosher (dairy) restaurant.

RELIGIOUS ORGANISATIONS

Sydney Beth Din
166 Castlereagh Street, NSW 2000   (2) 9267-2477
                        Fax: (2) 9264-8871
                        Email: admin@greatsynagogue.org.au

RESTAURANTS

Dairy
Red Tomato Café
50 Mitchell St, N Bondi 2026   (2) 9300-0707
                        Fax: (2) 9130-4477

Toovya the Milkman
379 Old South Head Road, North Bondi 2026
                        (2) 9130-4016
Supervision: NSW Kashrut Authority
Not Cholov Yisrael. Vegetarian and vegan food. Eat in
or take away. Delivery to eastern suburbs, including
to hotel room. Hours: Sunday to Thursday, 5 pm to
10 pm; Saturday, after Shabbat to midnight. Nearest
metro: 387 bus from Bondi junction to the door.

Meat
Beaches Kosher Restaurant
11 O'Brien Street 2026   (2) 9365-5544
                        Fax: (2) 9365-5577
NSW Kashrut Authority. Lunch is only Pareve.
Delivery to all Sydney addresses.

Café Maccabee
Corner Darlinghurst and Burton Street,
Darlinghurst   (2) 9360-7999
                        Fax: (2) 9331-4245
                        Email: ceo@sjm.com.au

Katzy's Food Factory
Shop 2, 113-115 R6010Hall Street,
Bondi Beach   (2) 9130-6743
                        Fax: (2) 91306742
Supervision: NSW Kashrut Authority
Also take-away.

Lewis' Continental Kitchen
2 Curlewis Street, Bondi 2026   (2) 9365-5421
                        Fax: (2) 9300-0037
                        Email: judith@lewiskosher.com
                        Web site: www.lewiskosher.com
Supervision: NSW Kashrut Authority Inc.
Glatt Kosher. Specialise in assisting tourists with their
meals in Australia.

Savion Restaurant
38 Wairoa Ave   (2) 9130-6357
Supervision: NSW Kashrut Authority

Tibby's Kosher Restaurant at Jaffa
61-67 Hall Street, Bondi Beach 2026   (2) 9130-5051
Supervision: NSW Kashrut Authority
Open Saturday to Thursday for dinner. Continental,
Chinese, Sephardi and Israeli food. Glatt kosher.

SYNAGOGUES

Adath Yisroel
243 Old South Head Road, Bondi   (2) 9300-9447

Bondi Mizrachi Synagogue
101/60 Blair Street, North Bondi 2026   (2) 9130-7221
                        Fax: (2) 9130-7221
                        Email: mizrachisydney@bigpond.com
                        Web site: mizrachi.org.au
Synagogue location is 339 Old South Head Road,
Bondi 2026

Coogee Synagogue
121 Brook Street, Coogee   (2) 9315-8291

Cremorne & District
12a Yeo Street, Neutral Bay   (2) 9908-1853
Fax: (2) 9908-1852

Illawarra Synagogue
502 Railway Parade, Allawah   (2) 9587-5643
Email: georgefoster1@compuserve.com

Kehillat Masada
9-15 Link Road, St Ives 2075   (2) 9988-4417
Fax: (2) 9449-3897
Email: kmasada@dingoblue.net.au

Paramatta Synagogue
116 Victoria Road, Paramatta   (2) 9683-5381

Sephardi Synagogue
40-42 Fletcher Street, Bondi Junction   (2) 9389-3355
Fax: (2) 9369-2143

Shearit Yisrael
146 Darlinghurst Road, Darlinghurst 2010
(2) 9365-8770

South Head & District Synagogue
666 Old South Head Road, Rose Bay 2029
(2) 9371-7300
Fax: (2) 9371-7416
Email: admin@southhead.org
Web site: www.southhead.org

Strathfield & District Synagogue
19 Florence Street, Strathfield 2135   (2) 9642-3550
Fax: (2) 9642-4803

Western Suburbs Synagogue
20 Georgina Street, Newtown

Conservative
Temple Emanuel
7 Ocean Street, Woollahra 2025   (2) 9328-7833
Fax: (2) 9327-8715
Email: info@emanuel.org.au
Web site: www.emanuel.org.au
"Look forward to welcoming visitors from abroad."

Liberal
North Shore Temple Emanuel
28 Chatswood Avenue, Chatswood 2067
(2) 9419-7011
Fax: (2) 9413-1474
Email: nste@nste.org.au

Orthodox
Great Synagogue
166 Castlereagh Street   (2) 9267-2477
Fax: (2) 9264-8871
Email: admin@greatsynagogue.org.au
Web site: www.greatsynagogue.org.au
Houses the Rabbi L.A. Falk Memorial Library and the A.M. Rosenblum Jewish Museum. (Entrance for services: 187 Elizabeth Street.) There are synagogue tours on Tuesdays and Thursdays.

Maroubra Synagogue (K.M.H.C.)
635 Anzac Parade, Maroubra 2035   (2) 9344-6095
Fax: (2) 9344-4298
Email: maroubrasyn@bigpond.com

North Shore Synagogue
15 Treatts Road, Lindfield   (2) 9416-3710
Fax: (2) 9416-7659
Email: nss@bigpond.com

The Central Synagogue
15 Bon Accord Avenue, Bondi Junction (2) 9389-5622
Fax: (2) 9389-5418
Email: central@centralsynagogue.com.au
Web site: www.centralsynagogue.com.au

Yeshiva
36 Flood Street, Bondi 2026   (2) 9387-3822
Fax: (2) 9389-7652
Email: info@yeshiva.org.au

Sefardim
Beth Yosef
Ground Floor, 243 Old South Head Road, Bondi

TOURS OF JEWISH INTEREST

(2) 9328-7604
For information about tours of Jewish Sydney, contact the Great Synagogue at the number listed above or Karl Maehrischel at this number.

QUEENSLAND

Brisbane

COMMUNITY ORGANISATIONS
Jewish Communal Centre
2 Moxom Road, Burbank 4156   (7) 3349-9749

GROCERIES
Tarlington Trading
(7) 3216-7505
Fax: (7) 3274-0058
Email: tarling@ribbonet.com.au

MIKVAOT
Queensland Mikvah
46 Bunya Street, Greenslopes 4120   (7) 3848-5886

RELIGIOUS ORGANISATIONS
Chabad House of Queensland
43 Cedar Street, Greenslopes 4120   (7) 3848-5886
Fax: (7) 3848-5886
Email: kthomas@onenet.au

SYNAGOGUES
Brisbane Hebrew Congregation
98 Margaret Street 4000   (7) 3229-3412

Givat Zion
43 Bunya Street, Greenslopes 4000   (7) 3397-9025
Fax: (7) 3397-9025

South Brisbane Hebrew Congregation
46 Burya Street, Greenslopes 4120   (7) 3397-9025
Fax: (7) 3397-9025
Email: slatwall@ozemail.com.au

Progressive
Beit Knesset Shalom
13 Koolatah Street, Camp Hill 4152   (7) 3398-8843
Email: bks@hotmail.com

Gold Coast

BAKERIES
Goldstein's Bakery
509 Olsen Avenue, Ashmore City 4214   (7) 5539-3133
Fax: (7) 5597-1064
Supervision: Rabbi Gurevitch, Gold Coast Hebrew
Congregation
Under the umbrella of the NSW Kashrut Authority.
Challah and kosher breads available at fourteen
stores along the Gold Coast, including Surfers
Paradise shop. (Tel) 5531-5808.

COMMUNITY ORGANISATIONS
Association of Jewish Organisations
31 Ranock Avenue, Benown Waters 4217
(7) 5597-2222

SYNAGOGUES
Temple Shalom
25 Via Roma Drive, Isle of Capri 4217   (7) 5570-1716
Orthodox
Gold Coast Hebrew Congregation
34 Hamilton Avenue, Surfers Paradise 4215
(7) 5570-1851
Fax: (7) 5570-1851
Email: gchebrewcong@ausinfo.com.au

SOUTH AUSTRALIA

Adelaide

BAKERIES
Bakers Delight
Frewville Shopping Centre, Glen Osmond Road

GROCERIES
Kosher Imports
c/o Hebrew Congregation, 13 Flemington Street,
Glenside 5065   (8) 8338-2922
Fax: (8) 8379-0142
Email: jewish@ozemail.com.au
Web site: www.adelaidejewish.com
Kosher and Judaica products available.

SYNAGOGUES
Orthodox
Adelaide Hebrew Congregation
13 Flemington Street, Glenside 5065   (8) 8338-2922
Fax: (8) 8379-0142
Email: jewish@ozemail.com.au
Web site: www.adelaidejewish.com
Mikva on premises. Mailing address: PO Box 320,
Glenside 5065.

Progressive
Beit Shalom
41 Hackney Road, Hackney 5000   (8) 8362-8281
Fax: (8) 8362-4406
Email: bshalom@senet.com.au
Web site: www.user.senet.com.au/~bshalom
Mailing address: PO Box 47, Stepney 5069.

TASMANIA

Established as a penal colony in 1803. Jewish
names first appeared in 1819. One being Ikey
Solomons a famous Jewish convict who was said
to be the model for Dicken's Fagin in Oliver Twist.
    The community remained small. The
Launceston synagogue was closed in 1871 and not
reopened until 1939.

Hobart

CONTACT INFORMATION
Jewish Centre
Chabad House, 93 Lord Street,
Sandy Bay 7005   (3) 6223-7116
Fax: (3) 6223-7116
Contact in advance for Shabbat meals and mikveh.

SYNAGOGUES
Progressive
Hobart Hebrew Congregation
PO Box 128, Hobart 7001   (3) 6234-4720
Email: shule@hobart.org
The oldest synagogue in Australia, having been
consecrated in July 1845. Open 9.30 am Saturdays
and one Friday per month 6.15 pm. Other days by
arrangement.

Launceston

CONTACT INFORMATION
Chabad House of Tasmania
5 Brisbane Street, Launceston 7250   (3) 6334-0705
Email: ghgoldsteen@netspace.net.au
For all enquiries please call or fax the Hon. Manager
Mr Gershon Goldsteen at (3) 6344 9960 or email him
as above.

SYNAGOGUES

PO Box 66, St John Street 7250   (3) 6343-1143
The synagogue in St John Street is the second oldest in Australia, founded in 1846. It is shared by Reform and Orthodox congregation and still has the original "convict benches".

VICTORIA

Ballarat

SYNAGOGUES

211 Drumond Street North 3350   (353) 32-6330

Melbourne

With 42,000 Jews, Melbourne has the largest Jewish community in the country, and the largest Jewish school in the world (the Mount Scopus).

BAKERIES

Big K Kosher Bakery
316 Carlisle Street,, Balaclava 3183   (3) 9527-4582
Supervision: Rabbi A.Z. Beck, Adass Israel

Glicks Cakes and Bagels
330a Carlisle Street, Balaclava 3183   (3) 9527-2198
Supervision: Melbourne Kashrut

Greenfield Cakes
7 Willow Street, Elsternwick   (3) 9528-4261
Supervision: Rabbi A.Z. Beck, Adass Israel
At same location is King David Kosher Meals on Wheels (Refuah), hospital meals, airline and TV dinners.

Haymishe Bakery
320 Carlisle Street, Shop 4 3183   (3) 9527-7116
Supervision: Rabbi A.Z. Beck, Adass Israel

Kosher Delight Bakery
75 Glen Eira Road, Ripponlea   (3) 9532-9994
Supervision: Rabbi A.Z. Beck, Adass Israel

Lowy's Cakes & Catering
59 Gordon Street, Elsternwick   (3) 9530-0246
Supervision: Rabbi A.Z. Beck, Adass Israel

Meal-Mart
251 Inkerman Street, St Kilda 3182   (3) 9525-5077
    Fax: (3) 9525-4230
Supervision: Rabbi A.Z. Beck, Adass Israel
Pies, salads, pre-cooked and frozen foods.

BOOKSELLERS

Golds World of Judaica
3 - 13 William Street, Balaclava 3183   (3) 9527-8775
    Fax: (3) 9527-6434
    Email: info@golds.com.au
    Web site: www.golds.com.au

BUTCHERS

Continental Kosher Butchers
155 Glenferrie Road, Malvern 3144   (3) 9509-9822
    Fax: (3) 9509-9099
    Email: ckb@bigpond.net.au
Supervision: Rabbi J.S. Cohen and Rabbi M. Gutnick, Melbourne Kashrut.

Melbourne Kosher Butchers
251 Inkerman Street, East St Kilda 3182
    (3) 9525-5077
    Fax: (3) 9525-4230
Supervision: Rabbi A.Z. Beck, Adass Israel
Sell other kosher products as well. Hours: Monday, 10 am to 5:30 pm; Tuesday to Thursday, 7 am to 5:30 pm; Friday, 7 am to 3 pm. Winter 2 pm.

Solomon Kosher Butchers
140-144 Glen Eira Road, Elsternwick 3185
    (3) 9532-8855
    Fax: (3) 9532-8896
Supervision: Rabbi Y.D. Groner, Agudas Chabad Kashrut Committee
Hours: Monday to Thursday, 7 am to 5:30 pm; Friday, 7 am to 3 pm.

Yumi's Kosher Seafoods
29 Glen Eira Road, Ripponlea 3183   (3) 9523-6444
    Fax: (3) 9532-8189
    Email: yumis@bigpond.com
Supervision: Rabbi A.Z. Beck, Adass Israel
Also suppliers of kosher fresh fish.

CHOCOLATE SHOPS

Kosher

Alpha Kosher Chocolates
17 William Street, Balaclava   (3) 9527-2453
Australia's only kosher chocolate factory. Handmade chocolates of export quality. Visitors welcome. Open Sunday mornings.

COMMUNITY ORGANISATIONS

Jewish Community Council of Victoria Inc.
306 Hawthorn Road, South Caulfield 3162
    (3) 9272-5566
    Fax: (3) 9272-5560
    Email: jccv@netspace.net.au
Head body of Melbourne Jewish community.

CONTACT INFORMATION

Mizrachi Hospitality Committee
81 Balaclava Road, Caulfield 3161   (3) 9525-9833
    Fax: (3) 9527-5665
    Email: mizrachi@iprimus.com.au
Mailing address: P.O.Box 2247. Caulfield Junction. VIC 3161.

DELICATESSEN

E.S. Delicatessen
74 Kooyong Road, Caulfield 3161   (3) 9576-0804
Supervision: Melbourne Kashrut

Eshel Take-Away Foods & Catering
59 Glen Eira Road, Ripponlea 3161   (3) 9532-8309
Fax: (3) 9532-8089
Supervision: Rabbi A.Z. Beck, Adass Israel

GROCERIES
Benedikt Imports
40 Pakington Street, St Kilda 3182   (3) 9534-8192
Importers of kosher foods and wines.

Dainty Foods (Kravsz)
62 Glen Eira Road, Ripponlea 3183   (3) 9523-8463
Grocers/Importers.

Gefen Liquor Store
144 Chapel Street, Balaclava 3183   (3) 9531-5032
Fax: (3) 9525-7388
Hours: Monday to Thursday, 9 am to 5 pm; Friday, 9
am to 4 pm. Public transport access: #3 tram to
corner of Carlisle and Chapel Streets or Sandringham
line train to Balaclava Station.

Milecki's Balaclava Health Food
277 Carlisle Street, Balaclava 3183   (3) 9527-3350
Open every day except Shabbat and all Jewish
holidays. Hours: 9 am to 9 pm. Close to rail station
and on tram line.

Rishon Foods Party Ltd.
23 Williams Street, Balaclava 3183   (3) 9527-5142

Singers
57 Kooyong Road, Caulfield 3162   (3) 9509-2387
Fax: (3) 9509-2387

Tempo Kosher Supermarket
391 Inkerman Street, St Kilda 3183   (3) 9527-5021
Manufacturers of a range of kosher foods, including
cheese, butter and juice drinks.

HOTELS
Quest Kimberley Caulfield
441 Inkerman Street, Balaclava 3183   (3) 9526-3888
Fax: (3) 9525-9691
Strictly Glatt kosher.

JUDAICA
The Antique Silver Co.
253 Carlisle Street, Balaclava 3183   (3) 9525-8480
Fax: (3) 9525-8479
Large selection of Judaica and ritual objects.

KASHRUT INFORMATION
Melbourne Kashrut
81 Balaclava Road, Caulfield 3161   (3) 9525-9895
Fax: (3) 9527-5665
Email: melbkash@iprimus.com.au
Mailing address: PO Box 2247 Caulfield Junction,
Victoria 3161. Provides Kashrut information.

LIBRARIES
**Kadimah Jewish Cultural Centre & National
Library**
7 Selwyn Street, Elsternwick 3185   (3) 9523-9817
Hours: 9.30 am-2.30 pm

Makor Jewish Community Library
306 Hawthorn Road, South Cantfield 3162
(3) 9272-5611
Fax: (3) 9272-5629
Email: jlibrary@vicnet.net.au
Web site: www.vicnet.net.au/~jlibrary

MEDIA
Newspapers
Jewish News
PO Box 1000, South Cantfield
Publish weekly newspaper.

Yidishe Gesheften
(3) 9532-7323
Fax: (3) 9523-0106
Jewish advertising monthly.

MIKVAOT
Caulfield Mikva
9 Furneaux Grove, East St Kilda 3183
(3) 9528-1116/9525-8585
Contact: Mrs C Sofer.

Lubavitch Mikva
38 Empress Road, East St Kilda 3183   (3) 9527-7555
Fax: (3) 9525-8838
Email: ktrubin@wavenet.net.au

MUSEUMS
Jewish Holocaust Centre
15 Selwyn Street, Elsternwick 3185   (3) 9528-1985
Fax: (3) 9528-3758
Email: hc@sprint.com.au
Hours: Monday and Wednesday 10.00 am to 4.00
pm, Tuesday, Thursday and Friday 10.00 am to 2.00
pm, Sunday 11.00 to 3.00pm.

Jewish Museum of Australia
26 Alma Road, St Kilda 3182   (3) 9543-0083
Fax: (3) 9543-0844
Email: info@jewishmuseum.com.au
Web site: www.jewishmuseum.com.au

RELIGIOUS ORGANISATIONS
Council of Orthodox Synagogues of Victoria
C/- Level 10, 5 Queens Road 3004   (3) 9864-4622
Fax: (3) 9864-4666
Email: yaron@jewishnews.net.au

Melbourne Beth Din
Synagogue Chambers, 572 Inkerman Road,
North Caulfield 3161   (3) 9527-8337
Fax: (3) 9527-8072

Orthodox Rabbinate of Australia
ISB on Accord Avenue, Bondi Junction 2022
(3) 9389-5622
Fax: (3) 9389-5418

Rabbinical Council of Victoria
c/o Honorary Secretary, Rabbi Mordechai Gutnick,
7 Meadow St., East St Kilda 3183   (3) 9525-9542
Fax: (3) 9525-9546

Progressive
Victorian Union for Progressive Judaism
78 Alma Road, St Kilda 3182   (3) 9510-1488
Fax: (3) 9521-1229
Email: vupj@tbi.org.au

RESTAURANTS
Dairy
Sheli's Coffee Shop
306 Hawthorn Road, South Caulfield   (3) 9272-5607
Meat
Delishes Restaurant
8-10 Glen Eira Ave., Rippon Lea   (3) 9523-1801

Klein's Kosher Gourmet
19 Glen Eira Road, Ripponlea   (3) 9528-1200
Fax: (3) 9528-1300

Kosher Express
263-265 Carlisle St, Balaclava   (3) 9527-9911
Fax: (3) 9527-9922
Supervision: Mehadrin Melbourne

Lamzini's
219 Carlisle Street, St. Kilda   (3) 9527-1283
Supervision: Melbourne Kashrut

SYNAGOGUES
Independent
Bet Hatikva Synagogue
233 Nepean Highway, Gardenvale 3185
(3) 9576-9755

Liberal
Bentleigh Progressive Synagogue
549 Centre Road 3204   (3) 9563-9208
Fax: (3) 9557-9880
Email: suzpol@techno.net.au

Leo Baeck Centre
33-37 Harp Road, East Kew 3102   (3) 9819-7160
Fax: (3) 9859-5417
Email: lbc@netspace.net.au
Web site: www.leobaeckcentre.org.au
PO Box 430 East Kew 3102

Temple Beth Israel
P O Box 128, St Kilda 3182   (3) 9510-1488
Fax: (3) 9521-1229
Email: info@tbi.org.au
Web site: www.tbi.org.au

Orthodox
Brighton Hebrew Congregation
132-136 Marriage Road, East Brighton 3187
(3) 9592-9179
Fax: (3) 9593-1682
Email: brightonshule@iprimus.com.au
Office hours: Monday to Friday 9 am-1 pm. PO Box
202 Bentleigh 3204. Visitors welcome.

Burwood Hebrew Congregation
38 Harrison Avenue 3125   (3) 9808-3120

Caulfield Hebrew Congregation
572 Inkerman Road, Caulfield 3161   (3) 9525-9492
Fax: (3) 9527-8463
Email: admin@caulfieldshule.com
Web site: www.caulfieldshule.com

Chabad House
Duver Heights   (3) 9387-3822

East Melbourne City Synagogue
488 Albert St. East Melbourne 3002   (3) 9662-1372
Fax: (3) 9662-1843
Email: office@melbournecitysynagogue.com
Web site: www.melbournecitysynagogue.com
The only synagogue in the inner city area. Within
walking distance of all City hotels. A historically
significant synagogue classified by the National Trust
of Victoria.It celebrated its 125 year anniversary in
2002.

Elwood Talmud Torah Congregation
39 Dickens Street, Elwood 3184   (3) 9531-1547

Kew Synagogue
53 Walpole Street, Kew 3101   (3) 9853-9243
Fax: (3) 9853-1354
Email: kewshul@iprimus.com.au

Kollel Beth Hatalmud
362a Carlisle Street, East St Kilda 3183 (3) 9527-6156
Fax: (3) 9527-8034
Email: kbt@blaze.net.au

Melbourne Hebrew Congregation
Cnr. Toorak & St Kilda Roads, S. Yarra 3141
(3) 9866-2255
Fax: (3) 9866-2022
Email: mhc@bigpond.com

Mizrachi
81 Balaclava Road, Caulfield 3161   (3) 9525-9833
Fax: (3) 9527-5665
Email: mizrachi@iprimus.com.au
Communication: P O Box 2247, Caulfield Junction,
VIC 3161.

Moorabbin & District Synagogue
960 Nepean Highway, Moorabbin 3189
(3) 9553-3845

North Eastern Malvern Chabad
Glenferrie Road, Malvern

South Caulfield Synagogue
47 Leopold Street, South Cantfield 3162
(3) 9578-5922
Fax: (3) 9578-5299

St Kilda Hebrew Congregation Inc.
12 Charnwood Grove, St Kilda 3182   (3) 9537-1433
Fax: (3) 9525-3759
Web site: www.stkildashule.org.au

The Sassoon Yehuda Sephardi Synagogue
79 Hotham Street, East St Kilda 3183   (3) 9527-8863
Email: amar@netspace.net.au
Sephardi Kiddush follows Saturday service. Monday,
Thursday and Sunday services followed by breakfast.

Yeshiva Shule
92 Hotham Street, East St Kilda 3183   (3) 9522-8222
Fax: (3) 9522-8266

TOURIST SITE
North Eastern Jewish War Memorial Centre Inc.
6 High Street, Doncaster 3108   (3) 9816-3516
Fax: (3) 9857-4430
Email: nejc@one.au

WESTERN AUSTRALIA

Perth

BUTCHERS
W.A. Kosher Butcher & Bakery
4 Bayley St., Dianella   (8) 9276-2525

COMMUNITY ORGANISATIONS
Council of Western Australian Jewry
J.P. PO Box 763 6062

KOSHER FOOD
Aviv Catering
The Jewish Centre, 61 Woodrow Avenue,
Yokinea 6060   (8) 9276-6030
Fax: (8) 9276-6030
Supervision: Kashrut Authority of Western Australia
Open 10am-2pm

Kosher Food Centre
Freedman Road (cnr. Plantation St.), Menora
(8) 9271-1133

SYNAGOGUES
Orthodox
Chabad House
396 Alexander Drive, Dianella 6062   (8) 9275-4912

Dianella Shule
68 Woodrow Avenue, Yokine 6060   (8) 9375-1276

Northern Suburbs Congregation
4 Vernon Street, Noranda 6062   (8) 9275-5932

Perth Hebrew Congregation
Freedman Road, Menora 6050   (8) 9271-0539
Email: phc@theperthshule.asn.au
Web site: www.theperthshule.asn.au
Also has a mikvah.

Reform
Temple David
34 Clifton Crescent, Mt Lawley 6050   (8) 9271-1485

AUSTRIA

The arrival of Jews in this area of Europe (probably with the Romans) was more than a 1,000 years ago. The community was expelled from Austria between 1420 and 1421, but Jews were allowed to return in 1451. The Jews were granted their own quarter of Vienna in 1624, but were expelled again in 1670. The economy declined after the expulsion, and so they were asked to return.

It was not until 1782 that the situation became more stable when Joseph II began lifting the anti-Jewish decrees that his mother, Maria Theresa, had imposed on her Jewish subjects. The Jews received equal rights in 1848 and, in 1867, legal and other prohibitions were lifted.

Anti-semitism did continue, however, and many influential anti-semitic publications were available in Vienna and were keenly read by many people, including the young Adolf Hitler. After the First World War, Austria lost its empire (which included Czech lands and Galicia, which had a very large Jewish community), and the Jewish population fell accordingly. At the time of the Nazi take-over in 1938, 200,000 Jews lived in the country. Some 70,000 were killed in the Holocaust, the rest having escaped or hidden.

Today there are several synagogues in Vienna. The city has an active Ultra-Orthodox community and kosher food is available. There are prayer rooms in some provincial cities.

Visitors to Vienna should not miss the new Jewish Museum opened in 2001. It combines Rachel Whiteread's memorial, the museum of medieval Jewish life and details of the excavation of a medieval synagogue built around the middle of the thirteenth century.

GMT +1 hour	Total Population 8,086,000
Country calling code (43)	Jewish Population 10,000
Emergency Telephone (Police – 133) (Fire – 122) (Ambulance – 144)	(Electricity voltage – 220)

Baden

CEMETERIES

Jewish Cemetery
Halsriegelstrasse 4   (2252) 85405
Contains some 3,000 graves. (Keys to be obtained from the Jewish Community.)

SYNAGOGUES

Orthodox
Judische Gemeinde Baden
Grabengasse 14, POB 149 A-2500   (2252) 210-6767
Fax: (2252) 217-0768
Email: synagogenverein@gmx.at
Web site: www.synagogenverein.at
Kosher meals are provided by the Jewish community on Shabbatot and Chagim.

Eisenstadt

CEMETERIES

Old Cemetery
The old cemetery, closed around 1875, contains the grave of Rav Meir Eisenstaat (Maharam Esh), who died in 1744. To this day it is the scene of pilgrimages, particularly on the anniversary of his death. Keys to the cemetery are with the porter of the local hospital, which adjoins the old cemetery.

MUSEUM

Austrian Jewish Museum
Unterbergstrasse 6   (2682) 65145
Fax: (2682) 65145; 65144
Email: info@oejudmus.or.at
The museum now also comprises the restored private synagogue of Samson Wertheimer, Habsburg court Jew and Chief Rabbi of Hungary (1658–1724). The museum is open daily except Monday from 10 am to 5 pm. The Eruv Arch, spanning Unterbergstrasse, is at the end near the Esterhazy Palace. The road chain was used in former times to prevent vehicular traffic on Shabbat and Yom Tov.

Graz

Graz is considered one of the oldest Jewish communities in Austria. There has been a self-contained Jewish quarter in Graz since 1142. In November 1938 (Kristallnacht) the synagogue was burnt and the Jews community was expelled.

The new synagogue, consecrated in November 2000, was partially rebuilt using bricks from the old synagogue.

Graz has been designated a European City of Culture for the year 2003.

SYNAGOGUES

Jewish Religious Community Synagogue
David-Herzog-Platz 1 A-8020   (316) 712-468
Fax: (316) 720-433
Email: office@ikg-graz.at
Web site: www.ikg-graz.at

Innsbruck

COMMUNITY ORGANISATIONS
Community Centre
Sillgassse 15   (512) 586-892

Kobersdorf

CEMETERIES
Jewish Cemetery
Waldgasse
The keys of the cemetery on the Lampelberg are
with Mr Piniel, Waldgasse 25 (one of the two houses
to the left of the cemetery) and Mr Grässing,
Haydngasse 4.

Linz

COMMUNITY ORGANISATIONS
Community Centre
Bethlehemstrasse 26   (732) 779-805

Salzburg

The Salzburg community dates back to 803 when
Archbishop Arno summoned a Jewish doctor to
set up a practice in the town.

COMMUNITY ORGANISATIONS
Lasserstrasse 8 A-5020   (662) 872228
                            Fax: (662) 872228
                   Email: office@ikg-salzburg.at
                  Web site: www.ikg-salzburg.at
Community synagogue and mikva are to be found at
the same address.

Vienna

Vienna was in the past the most important centre
for Central European Jews. From 180,000 Jews in
the 1930s, there are about 1,000 Jews (mainly
elderly) in Vienna today. Professor Freud's clinic is
a popular attraction, and the Jewish Museum of
Vienna gives much information on the history of
the Jews.

BAKERIES
Engländer
Hollandstrasse 10 1020   (1) 214-5617
Supervision: Rabbi Abraham Yonah Schwartz

BED AND BREAKFAST
Pension Lichtenstein
Grosse Schiffgasse 19 1020   (1) 216-8498
                            Fax: (1) 214-7690
          Web site: www.pension-lichtenstein.at
The pension consists of 'suites'. It is within walking
distance of the old Jewish quarter of Vienna in one
direction, and 5-20 minutes from some small
synagogues and a kosher bakery in the other
direction. Visits should be arranged in advance as
there is no front desk reception; the key is kept in the
owner's office around the block.

BOOKSELLERS
Chabad-Simcha-Center
Hollandstrasse 10 1020   (1) 216-2924

Chai Vienna
Praterstrasse 40 1020   (1) 216-4621
                            Fax: (1) 216-4621

BUTCHERS
B. Ainhorn
Stadtgutgasse 7 1020   (1) 214-5621
Supervision: Rabbi David Grunfeld
Also supplies "Fast Food".

Rebenwurzel
Grose Mohrengasse 19 1010   (1) 216-6640
Supervision: Rabbi Chaim Stern

Sephardi Butcher
Volkertmarkt 1020   (1) 214-9650

CEMETERIES
Floridsdorfer Cemetery
Ruthnergasse 28 1210
Those wishing to visit must first obtain a permit from
the community centre.

Rossauer Cemetery
Seegasse 9 1090
This is the oldest Jewish cemetery in Vienna, dating
from the sixteenth century. It has now been restored
after being devastated by the Nazis and is open daily
from 8 am to 3 pm. Access is via the front entrance of
the municipal home for the aged at Seegasse 9-11,
but a permit must first be obtained from the
community centre.

Vienna Central Cemetery
Simmeringer Haupstr.244 A-1110
                   (1) 531 04 904, 767 6252
The Jewish section (the only one still in use) is at Gate
4 and there is an older Jewish part at Gate 1.

Währinger Cemetery
Semperstrasse 64a 1180
Those wishing to visit must first obtain a permit from
the community centre.

CONTACT INFORMATION
Jewish Community Centre
Seitenstettengasse 4
(1) 531 04104
Fax: (1) 531 04108
Email: office@ikg-wien.at
Jewish Welcome Service Vienna
Stephansplatz 10 1010
(1) 533-2730
Fax: (1) 533-4098
Email: jewish.welcome@verkehrsbuero.at
Web site: www.jewish-welcome.at
Open: Monday to Friday 9.00 am to 5.30 pm.

DOCUMENTATION CENTRES
Documentation Centre of Austrian Resistance
Old City Hall, Wipplingerstrasse 8 1010
(1) 534-3601 779
Fax: (1) 534-3699 01771
Email: office@doew.at
Web site: www.doew.at
Hours of opening: Monday to Thursday 9 am to 5 pm.

Documentation Centre of Union of Jewish Victims of the Nazis
Salztorgasse 6 A-1010
(1) 533-9131
Fax: (1) 535-0397

EMBASSY
Embassy of Israel
Anton-Frankgasse 20 1180
(1) 476-460

GROCERIES
Gross-Import-Wien
Nicklegasse 1 A-1020
(1) 214-0607
Fax: (1) 214-7690

Koscherland
Kleine Sperlgasse 7
(1) 212-8169

Kosher Supermarket & Shutnes Laboratory
Hollandstrasse 7 1020
(1) 269-9675
Supervision: Rabbi Abraham Yonah Schwartz

Ohel Moshe
Hollandstrasse 10 A-1020
(1) 216-9675
Supervision: Rabbi Abraham Yonah Schwartz

Rafael Malkov
Tempelgasse 6, Ferdinandstrasse 2 A-1020
(1) 214-8394

Vinothek Gross
Taborstrasse 15 1020
(1) 212-6299

HOTELS
Hotel Stefanie
Taborstrasse 12 1020
(1) 211-500
Fax: (1) 211-50160
Email: stefanie@schick-hotels.com
Web site: www.schick-hotels.com
Four-star hotel with kosher breakfast on request.

MEDIA
Newspaper
Die Gemeinde
(1) 531 04 271
Fax: (1) 531 04 279
Monthly.

MIKVAOT
Agudas Yisroel
Tempelgasse 3 1020
(1) 214-9973
Machsike Haddas
Fleischmarkt 22 1010
(1) 512-5262

MONUMENT
Nameless Library
Judenplatz
Rachel Whiteread's monument, opened in 2001, depicts shelves of 9,000 books with their spines turned to the inside. The names of the concentration camps in which Austrian Jews were killed are engraved around the base. Underneath the memorial one can view the ruins of a synagogue razed in 1421.

MUSEUMS
Jewish Museum Vienna
Dorotheergasse 11 A-1010
(1) 535-0431 ext. 112
Fax: (1) 535-0424
Email: susanna.koncar@jmw.at
Web site: www.jmw.at
Hours: Sunday to Friday, 10 am to 6 pm; Thursday, 10 am to 8 pm. Cafeteria and bookshop on site. The cafeteria is not under supervision.

Museum Judenplatz
Judenplatz 8 A-1010
(1) 535-0431
Fax: (1) 535-0424
Email: info@jmw.at
Web site: www.jmw.at
A memorial for the Austrian victims of the Holocaust. A place of remembrance was created that is unique in Europe. It combines Rachel Whiteread's memorial (Nameless Library, see above) and the excavations of a medieval synagogue with the Museum on Medieval Jewish Life to form a commemorative whole.
Opening hours 10am to 6pm, Friday 10am to 2pm. Special guided tours for groups by prior arrangement only.

Sigmund Freud Museum
Berggasse 19 1090
(1) 319-1596
Fax: (1) 317-0279
Email: sekretariat@freud-museum.at
Web site: www.freud-museum.at
Hours: 9.00am to 5.00pm, July to September 9am - 6pm

RESTAURANTS
Dairy
Milk 'n' Honey
Kleine Sperlgasse 7
(1) 219-6886
Meat
Restaurant Alef - Alef
Seitenstettengasse 2 A-1010
(1) 535-2530
Fax: (1) 5352-53033
Web site: www.alef-alef.at

Snack Bar
Berl Ainhorn Koscher Fleisch und Imbiss
Gross Stadtgutgasse 7 1020
(1) 214-5621

SITE
Mauthausen Memorial Site

(1) 723-82269

Fax: (1) 723-83696

Those wishing to visit the site should contact the Jewish Welcome Service.

SYNAGOGUES
Orthodox
Agudas Yeshurun
Riemergasse 9 1010

Agudas Yisroel
Tempelgasse 3 1020   (1) 214 9262
Grünangergasse 1 1010   (1) 512-8331

Machsike Haddas
GroBe Mohreng. 19 A-1020   (1) 216 0679

Misrachi
Judenplatz 8 1010   (1) 532-8301
Fax: (1) 214-8010
Email: daleno@utanet.at

Ohel Moshe
Lilienbrunngasse 19 1020   (1) 216-8864

Rambam Syn. im Maimonides Zentrum
Bauernfeldgasse 4 A-1190

Seitenstettengasse Synagogue
Seitenstettengasse 4 1010   (1) 531-040
Fax: (1) 531-04108
Email: office@ikg-wien.at
Web site: www.ikg-wien.at
Built in 1824-26 and partly destroyed during the Nazi period, this beautiful synagogue was restored by the community in 1988. For information about guided tours, contact the Community Centre offices.

Sephardi Centre
Tempelgasse 7 1020   (1) 214 3097

Shomre Haddas
Glasergasse 17 1090

Thora Etz Chayim
Grosse Schiffgasse 8 1020   (1) 214-5206
Fax: (1) 216-2032
Email: Samikern@csi.com

Progressive
Or Chadasch
Rosentalgasse 5-7/4/3 1140   (1) 967 1329
Fax: (1) 914 5245

AZERBAIJAN

Azerbaijan has a remarkable Jewish history, which can be better explored now that the country is independent from the Soviet Union. The Tats (mountain Jews) believe that their ancestors arrived in Azerbaijan at the time of Nebuchadnezzar. They lived in several mountain villages, and adopted the customs of their non-Jewish neighbours. They spoke a north Iranian language, known as Judeo-Tat, to which they had added some Hebrew words. The Soviets clamped down on their way of life after 1928, changing the alphabet of their language from Hebrew to Latin and then, in 1938, to Cyrillic. Some of their synagogues were also closed down. Zionist feeling is high, with almost 30,000 emigrating to Israel since 1989.

The other strand in Azerbaijan's Jewish population are the Ashkenazis who arrived in the nineteenth century from Poland and other countries to the west.

The community has some 10-15 organisations in Baku, the capital, including Zionist and youth groups. The largest synagogue in Baku is the Tat synagogue, but there are also Ashkenazi and Georgian synagogues. Synagogues are found in other towns.

GMT +5 hours	**Total Population 7,625,000**
Country calling code (994)	**Jewish Population 10,000**

Baku

EMBASSY
Embassy of Israel
Stroiteley Prospect 1

SYNAGOGUES
Mountain Jews
Dmitrova Street 39 370014   (12) 892-232-8867

Ashkenazi
Pervomoskaya Street 271   (12) 892-294-1571

Kuba

SYNAGOGUES
Kolkhoznaya Street 46

BAHAMAS

Luis de Torres, the official interpreter for Columbus, was the first Jew in the Bahamas, as well as being one of the first Europeans there. He was a Converso, a 'secret Jew' who officially had converted to Catholicism, but who practised Judaism in private. The British arrived in 1620, and eventually gained control of the islands. Although there was a Jewish attorney-general and chief justice in the islands in the eighteenth century, few Jews settled there until the twentieth century, coming from eastern Europe and the UK after the First World War, and settling in Nassau, the capital.

There are approximately 100 Jewish residents in the Bahamas. However, it is estimated that about 350,000 Jews visit the Islands each year as tourists. There are congregations in Nassau and Freeport. Both cities have Jewish cemeteries, that in Nassau being more historic.

GMT -5 hours	**Total Population 289,000**
Country calling code (1242)	**Jewish Population 300**
Emergency Telephone (Police – 919) (Fire – 919) (Ambulance – 919)	**(Electricity voltage – 120)**

Freeport

SYNAGOGUES

Freeport Hebrew Congregation
Luis de Torres Synagogue, East Sunrise Highway,
PO Box F-41761   373-9457
                                        Fax: (925) 871-5528
                           Email: hurst100@yahoo.com
Services every Friday evening at 8:30 pm from September through April, as well as Community Seder, Chanukah celebration and full-time certificated marriage officer.

Nassau

SYNAGOGUES

Progressive
Bahamas Jewish Congregation
POB CB-11002   363-2305

BARBADOS

Jewish history in Barbados starts in 1628, a year after the British first settled there. Jewish settlers came from Brazil, Surinam, England and Germany, and were mainly Sephardi. The first synagogue was established in Bridgetown (the capital) in 1654. Early settlers were engaged in cultivating sugar and coffee.

The Jewish population was well treated, and in 1831 Barbados was the first British possession in which Jews were granted full political emancipation. Despite a largely favourable climate, the community suffered losses from hurricanes, which destroyed sugar plantations, and the Jewish population fell to 70 by 1848. In 1925, no Jews remained, but a new influx (30 families escaping Nazism) came shortly after.

The synagogue was restored in 1987, and postage stamps were produced which commemorated its restoration. The Jewish population remains small, but it was a group of Barbadian Jews who founded the Caribbean Jewish Congress. The Jewish cemetery, one of the oldest in the Americas, is now back in use.

GMT -4 hours	Total Population 262,000
Country calling code (1246)	Jewish Population Under 100
Emergency Telephone (Police – 112) (Fire – 113) (Ambulance – 119)	(Electricity voltage – 110)

COMMUNITY ORGANISATIONS

Barbados Jewish Community
PO Box 651, Bridgetown   427-0703
                                Fax: 436-8807

Caribbean Jewish Congress
PO Box 1331, Bridgetown   436-8163
                                Fax: 437-4992
Email: comphosting.sunbeach.net\cjc

Synagogue Restoration Project
PO Box 256, Bridgetown   432-0840
                                Fax: 432-2147
Email: altman@caribsurf.com
Local inquiries to Henry Altman, Little Mallows,
Sandy Lane, St. James. Tel: 132-6462

SYNAGOGUES

Nidhe Israel
Synagogue Lane   427 7611
Services are held Friday evenings at 7 pm at 'True Blue', Rockley New Road, Christ Church, during the summer, and at the synagogue at 7.30 pm in winter.

BELARUS

For the adventurous traveller, who has a keen interest in Jewish history, Belarus (also known as White Russia) makes an interesting and unusual destination. Situated on the western side of the former Soviet Union, this largely flat country borders Poland and Lithuania to the west, Ukraine to the south and Russia to the east. Belarus finally achieved independence in 1991, and within its present borders are many towns and villages of Jewish interest, such as Minsk, Pinsk and Grodno. One of the most famous villages in Belarus is Lubavitch, a hamlet in the far east of the country, near the Russian border, where the world-wide Lubavitch movement had its origins.

The majority of this region's Jews died in the Holocaust and although emigration to Israel is high, the community is slowly rebuilding itself after decades of Soviet control. Americans and Israelis are contributing rabbis to help in this revival, and Jewish schools have been set up. Yiddish is used far more here than in other parts of the former USSR.

GMT +2 hours
Country calling code (375)
Emergency Telephone (Police – 03) (Fire – 03) (Ambulance – 003)

Total Population 10,179,000
Jewish Population 30,000
(Electricity voltage – 220)

Baranovichi

SYNAGOGUES
39 Svobodnaya St.

Bobruisk

SYNAGOGUES
Engels St.

Borisov

SYNAGOGUES
Trud St.

Brest

SYNAGOGUES
Narodnaya St.

Gomel

CONTACT INFORMATION
Rosa Sorkina
(23) 252-5808

SYNAGOGUES
13 Sennaya St.

Grodno

CONTACT INFORMATION
Misha Kemerov
(15) 2313-798

SYNAGOGUES
Menorah Jewish Community
Blk 43, Flat 37 230009
(15) 2313 798
Email: sh10@grsu.grodno.by

Minsk

CONTACT INFORMATION
Rabbi Nelly Shulman
(17) 2110-234
Email: nashulman@mail.ru

EMBASSY
Embassy of Israel
Partizanski Prospekt 6A 220002
(17) 2304-444

MEMORIAL
This memorial devoted to 5,000 Jews killed by the Nazis on Purim 1942 was erected in 1946 and is the only one in what was the USSR devoted to the Holocaust which displays Yiddish writing.

SYNAGOGUES
22 Kropotkin St.
(17) 255-8270
22 Kropotkin Fstreet
(17) 2558-270
13b Daumana Street
Progressive
Association of Progressive Jewish Congregations in Belarus
Per K Chyornogo 4, apt 18, Simcha 220012
(17) 2846-089
Fax: (17) 2662-928
Email: simcha@open.by

Moghilev

SYNAGOGUES
1 2nd Krutoy La.

Orsha

SYNAGOGUES
Nogrin St.

Rechitsa

SYNAGOGUES
120 Lunacharsky St.

BELGIUM

Jewish settlement in the area now called Belgium dates back to the thirteenth century, and suffered a similar fate to other medieval European Jewish communities, taking the blame for the Black Death and suffering expulsions. The Sephardim were the first to resettle in Belgium, mainly in Antwerp. After independence in 1830, conditions for the Jews improved and more Jews began to settle there. The diamond centre of Antwerp later developed rapidly, attracting many Jews from eastern Europe.

By 1939, the Jewish population had grown to 100,000, a large proportion of whom were refugees hoping to escape to America. Some succeeded, but many became trapped after the German invasion. Some 25,000 Belgian Jews were deported and killed in the Holocaust. A national monument listing the names of the victims stands in Anderlecht in Brussels.

The present Jewish population includes a large Chassidic community in Antwerp, where there are some 30 synagogues. There are also more than ten synagogues in Brussels. There are Jewish schools in Antwerp and Brussels, and Jewish newspapers.

GMT + I hour	**Total Population 10,188,000**
Country calling code (32)	**Jewish Population 38,000**
Emergency Telephone (Police – 101) (Fire – 101) (Ambulance – 101)	**(Electricity voltage – 220)**

Antwerp

Seen by some as 'the last shtetl in Europe', Antwerp is a well-known Hassidic centre. Antwerp's Jewish population (15,000) has one of the highest numbers of Ultra-Orthodox in the Diaspora. Served by 30 synagogues (many of them small shtiebels), there are also kosher restaurants and food shops.

BAKERIES

Gottesfeld
Mercatorstraat 20   (3) 230-0003

Kleinblatt
Provinciestraat 206   (3) 233-7513; 226-0018
                                    Fax: (3) 232-0920

Steinmetz
Lange Kievitstraat 64   (3) 234-0947

BOOKSELLERS

I. Menczer
Simonstraat 40   (3) 232-3026

N. Seletsky
Lange Kievitstraat 70   (3) 232-6966
                                    Fax: (3) 226-9446

Stauber
Van Leriusstraat 3   (3) 231-8031

BUTCHERS

Berkowitz
Isabellalei 9   (3) 218-5111

Farkas
Lange Kievitstraat 66   (3) 232-1385

Fruchter
Simonstraat 22   (3) 233-1811; 1557
                                    Fax: (3) 231-3903

Kosher King
Lange Kievitstraat 40   (3) 233-6749
Isabellalei 7   (3) 239-4189

Mandelovics
Isabellalei 96   (3) 218-4779

Moszkowitz
Lange Kievitstraat 47   (3) 232-6349
                                    Fax: (3) 226-0471

CONTACT INFORMATION

Machsike Hadass (Israelitische Orthodoxe Gemeente)
Jacob Jacobsstraat 22   (3) 233-5567

Shomre Hadass (Israelitische Gemeente)
Terliststraat 35 2018   (3) 232-0187
                                    Fax: (3) 226-3123
            Email: shomre-hadass@net4all.be
Web site: www.members.net4all.be/shomre-hadas

DELICATESSEN

Weingarten
Lange Kievitstraat 124   (3) 233-2828

GROCERIES

Col-Bo
Jacob Jacobsstraat 40   (3) 234-1212

Grosz-Modern
Terliststraat 28   (3) 232-4626

Herzl & Gold
Korte Kievitstraat 38   (3) 232-2365

Stark
Mercatorstraat 24   (3) 230-2520

Super Discount
Belgielei 104-108   (3) 239-0666

Superette Lamoriniere
Lamboriniere Straat 199   (3) 239-3110
                                    Fax: (3) 281-3205

MEDIA

Newspaper
Belgisch Israelitisch Weekblad
Pelikaanstraat 106-108 2018　　　　(3) 233-7094
　　　　　　　　　　　Fax: (3) 233-4810
　　　　　Email: biw@planetinternet.be

MIKVAOT

Machsike Hadass
Steenbokstraat 22　　　　　　　　(3) 239-7588

Shomre Hadass
Van Diepenbeeckstraat 42　　　　(3) 239-0965

MUSEUM

Plantin-Moretus Museum
Vrijdagmarkt (nr Groenplaats)　　(3) 233-0688
Open daily (except Monday). Contains examples of
early Jewish printing, such as the famous Polyglot
Bible.

RESTAURANTS

Dairy
Garden of Eden
Plantin En Moretuslei 10 2018　　(3) 281-4281
　　　　　　　　　　　Fax: (3) 700-4034
Open: 12 pm-2 pm and 6 pm-10 pm.

USA Pizza
118a Isabellalei　　　　　　　　(3) 281-2300
Supervision: Machzikey Hadas
Take away option.

Meat
Blue Lagoon
Lange Herentalsestraat 70　　　(3) 226-0114
Supervision: Machsike Hadass
Also sell chocolates. Five minutes from Central
station.

Hoffy's
Lange Kievitstraat 52　　　　　(3) 234-3535
　　　　　　　　　　　Fax: (3) 226-0282
　　　　　Email: hoffys@pandora.be

Jacob
Lange Kievitstraat 49　　　　　(3) 233-1124

Lamalo
Appelmanstraat 21
　　　　　　　　　　　　　　　(3) 213-2200

Vegetarian
Time Out
Lange Herentalse Straat 58 2018　(3) 281-2300
　　　　　　　　　　　Fax: (3) 281-2300

SYNAGOGUES

Great Synagogue Romi Goldmuntz
Van Den Nestlei 1　　　　　　(3) 232-0187

Sephardic Synagogue
Hovenierstraat 31　　　　　　(3) 232-5339
Built in 1913. This synagogue is located in the middle
of the Diamond district.

Orthodox
Machsike Hadass
Jacob Jacobsstraat 22　　　　　(3) 232-0021
　　　　　　　　　　　Fax: (3) 233-8797

Oosten Synagogue
Oostenstraat 43　　　　　　　(3) 230-9246

TOURS OF JEWISH INTEREST

Toerisme Antwerpen
Grote Markt 15 2000　　　　　(3) 232-0103
　　　　　　　　　　　Fax: (3) 231-1937
　　　　Email: toerisme@antwerpen.be
　　　　　　　Web site: www.dma.be

Arlon

SYNAGOGUES

Rue St Jean　　　　　　　　　(63) 217-985
Established 1863. The secretary, J.C. Jacob, can be
reached at 11 rue des Martyrs, 6700. A monument
has been erected in the new Jewish cemetery to the
memory of the Jews of Arlon deported and
massacred by the Nazis.

Brussels

The capital of Belgium is less well endowed with
kosher facilities than Antwerp, although there are
23,000 Jews living in the city. The headquarters of
the European Union of Jewish Students is based
there. The Anderlecht area has a monument to
the Belgian Holocaust victims and a memorial to
Jews who fought in the Belgian Resistance.

BAKERIES

Bornstein
62 rue de Suéde, St Gilles　　　(2) 537-1679

BOOKSELLERS

Colbo
121 rue du Brabant　　　　　　(2) 217-2620

Menorah
12 Ave. J. Voldens 1060　　　　(2) 537-5073

BUTCHERS

Lanxner
121 rue de Brabant 1030　　　　(2) 217-2620
Supervision: Rabbinate of the Jewish Orthodox
Community of Brussels
Grocery: Hours: Sun, Mon, Fri 8.30 am to 1.00 pm.
Tues 8.30 am to 6.00 pm. Wed-Thurs 8.30 am to 7.30
pm.

COMMUNITY ORGANISATIONS

Centre Communautaire Laic Juif
Yitzhak Rabin Center, 52 rue Hotel des Monnaies
(2) 543-0270

　　　　　　　　　　Fax: (2) 543-0271
　　　　　　　　　Email: info@cclj.be
　　　　　　　Web site: www.cclj.be

EMBASSY

Embassy of Israel
40 Avenue de l'Observatoire 1180   (2) 373-5500

GROCERIES

Hod Taim
51 Boulevard Jamar   (2) 527-1832

MEDIA

Newspapers
Centrale
91 Av. Henri Jaspar   (2) 538-8036
Monthly

Fax de Jerusalem
68 Ave Ducpétiaux   (2) 538-5673
Fax: (2) 534-0236
Email: alyabelgique@skynet.be
Weekly

Kehilatenou
2 rue Joseph Dupont B-1000   (2) 512-4334
Fax: (2) 512-9237
Monthly

Regards
52 rue Hotel des Monnaies   (2) 543-0280
Fax: (2) 537-5565
Email: Regards@cclj.be
Web site: www.cclj.be/Regards
Fortnightly

Radio
Radio Judaica (Jewish Radio) FM 90.2
Jewish interest programs 24-hours a day.

MIKVAOT

Machsike Hadass
67a rue de la Clinique   (2) 537-1439

MUSEUM

Jewish Museum
74 Ave de Stalingrad 1000   (2) 512-1963
Fax: (2) 513-4859
Email: info@mjb-jmb.org
Web site: www.mjb-jmb.org
Hours: Mon-Thurs 12.00 - 5.00 pm. Sunday 10.00 am to 1.00 pm. Closed Friday, Saturday and Jewish holidays.

RELIGIOUS ORGANISATIONS

Communaute Israelite de Bruxelles
2 rue Joseph Dupont B-1000   (2) 512-4334
Fax: (2) 512-9237

Machsike Hadass (Communauté Israélite Orthodoxe de Bruxelles)
67a rue de la Clinique   (2) 524-1486; 521-1289

Yechiva de Bruxelles
50 Ave Brugmann 1190   (2) 347-2143
Fax: (2) 347-2143
Email: bxlyechiva@hotmail.com

RESTAURANTS

Chez Gilles
Rue de la Clinique 21 1070   (2) 522-1828
Open from 9 am - 5 pm.

El Assado
Roosendael 154   (2) 346-3487

Restaurant Seven-Seventy
87 Avenue du Roi 1060   (2) 537-1158

Meat
Athenee Maimonide
Boulevard Poincarte 67   (2) 523-6336

SITE

National Monument to the Jewish Martyrs of Belgium
Corner rue Emile Carpentier and rue Goujons, Square of the Jewish Martyrs, Anderlecht.
This monument commemorates the Jews of Belgium who were deported to concentration camps and killed by the Nazis during the Second World War. The names of all 23,838 are engraved on the monument.

SYNAGOGUES

Brussels Airport
Situated in the transit lounge.

Liberal
Communaute Israelite Liberale de Belgique - Beth Hillel
Avenue de Kersbeek 96 1190   (2) 332-2528
Fax: (2) 376-7219
Email: cilb.asbl@chello.be

Orthodox
Adath Israel
126 rue Rogier 1030   (2) 241-1664
Near City Center

Ahavat Reim
73 rue de Thy   (2) 648-3837

Beth Hamidrash
rue du Chapeau, Anderlecht   (2) 524-1486

Beth Itshak
115 Ave du Roi 1060   (2) 538-3374; 520-1359

Communaute Israelite d'Uccle-Forest
11 Avenue de Messidor 1180   (2) 344-6094

Or Hahayim
77 rue P. Decoster 1190   (2) 344-2342

The Great Synagogue
32 Rue de la Regence 1000   (2) 512-4334
Fax: (2) 512-9237
The synagogue built in 1878 survived the occupation.

Sephardi
Synagogue Simon and Lina Haim
47 Rue du Pavilion 1030   (2) 215-0525
Fax: (2) 215-0242
This is a memorial to the Jews deported from Rhodes, Greece.

Charleroi

COMMUNITY ORGANISATIONS
Community Centre
56 rue Pige-au-Croly

Ghent

CONTACT INFORMATION
Jacques Bloch
Veldstraat 60   (9) 225-7085
                    Email: blochjb@yahoo.com
The treasurer of the community will be happy to
meet English-speaking visitors. As the community is a
very small one, there is no permanent synagogue.
Services are held on the High Holy Days.

Knokke

SYNAGOGUES
30 Van Bunnenlaan   (50) 61-0372
Also has a mikva.

Liège

COMMUNITY ORGANISATIONS
Community Centre
12 Quai Marcellis 4020

MUSEUM
Musee Serge Kruglanski
19 rue L. Fredericq 4020   (4) 438-043
                        Fax: (4) 226-0234

SYNAGOGUES
19 rue L. Frédéricq 4020   (4) 436-106

Mons

CONTACT INFORMATION
SHAPE
                    (65) 445-808; 444-809
Nearby, at Casteau, the International Chapel of
NATO's Supreme Headquarters Allied Powers
Europe, includes a small Jewish community,
established 1951, that holds regular services. Call for
further information.

Ostend

SYNAGOGUES
Philip Van Maastrichtplein 4   (59) 511-622
Services during July and August. Inquiries to Mrs
Liliane Wulfowicz, Parklaan 21, B-8400, (59) 802-405.

Waterloo

SYNAGOGUES
Traditionalist
**Communaute Israelite de Waterloo et du
Brabant Sud (CIWABS)**
140 Avenue Belle-Vue, 1410 Waterloo   (2) 354-6833
                        Fax: (2) 514-5977
Regular Services Shabbat and Festivals; English
speaking visitors very welcome; tel:32-2-351-3631
(evenings).

BERMUDA

Jews have lived in Bermuda since the seventeenth century, but the first formal congregation was not
established until the twentieth century.

The resident Jewish population is very small, but the transient population (of tourists largely from the
USA, Britain and Canada) is much greater. There is a Jew's Bay but whether this is merely named to balance
a nearby Christian Bay or has some other origin is not known.

GMT -4 hours
Country calling code (1441)
Emergency Telephone (Police – 112) (Fire – 113) (Ambulance – 115)

Total Population 60,000
Jewish Population Under 100
(Electricity voltage – 110)

Hamilton

COMMUNITY ORGANISATIONS
Jewish Community of Bermuda
PO Box HM 1793 HM05   (441) 291-1785
            Web site: www.jcb.bm

BOLIVIA

The history of the Jews of Bolivia dates back to the Spanish colonial period. Conversos (converts to Christianity who practised Judaism in secret) came with the Spaniards in the seventeenth century.

The main influx of Jews occurred in 1905, with immigrants from eastern Europe, but the number entering Bolivia was much smaller than that going to other South American countries. In 1933 there were only some 30 Jewish families. At the end of the decade, however, there was a small increase in Jewish immigration as German and Austrian Jews fled from Europe. Ironically, the Jewish community did not grow very much, even though the government granted every Jew an entry visa.

Many Jews started to leave Bolivia in the 1950s because of political instability and the apparent lack of educational opportunities. The present-day community has a central organisation known as the Circulo Israelita de Bolivia.

GMT -4 hours	**Total Population 8,140,000**
Country calling code (591)	**Jewish Population 500**
	(Electricity voltage – 110/220)

Cochabamba

COMMUNITY ORGANISATIONS
Asociacion Israelita de Cochabamba
PO Box 349, Calle Valdivieso

SYNAGOGUES
Calle Junin y Calle Colombia, Casilla 349

La Paz

SYNAGOGUES
Circulo Israelita de Bolivia
Casilla 1545, Calle Landaeta 346, PO Box 1545
(2) 32-5925
Fax: (2) 34-2738
Representative body of Bolivian Jewry. All La Paz organisations are affiliated to it. Service Shabbat morning only.

Comunidad Israelita Synagogue
Calle Canada Stronguest 1846, PO Box 2198
Affiliated to the Circulo. Friday evening services are held here.

TOURS OF JEWISH INTEREST
Centro Shalom
Calle Canada Stronguest 1846

Santa Cruz

COMMUNITY ORGANISATIONS
Centro Cruceño
PO Box 469

WIZO
Castilla 3409

BOSNIA-HERCEGOVINA

Sephardi Jews were the first to arrive in the area, in the late sixteenth century. They established a Jewish quarter in Sarajevo, and this was home for poorer Jews until the Austrians conquered the land in 1878. It was the Turks, however, who emancipated the Jews in the nineteenth century when Bosnia-Hercegovina was under Ottoman rule.

When Bosnia-Hercegovina became part of the newly formed Yugoslavia, after the First World War, the community maintained its Sephardi heritage and joined the all-Yugoslav Federation of Jewish Religious Communities. The Jewish population numbered 14,000 in 1941. This number dropped sharply after the Germans conquered Yugoslavia.

After the war the survivors were joined by many who had decided to return. The Sephardi and Ashkenazi communities became unified. La Benevolencija, founded 100 years ago, is a humanitarian organisation which supported the plight of the community and became well known in the early 1990s at the time of the civil war. After the Yugoslav civil war, many made aliyah to Israel, reducing the community still further.

Note: (Emergency - 94)
GMT +1 hour
Country calling code (387)
Emergency Telephone (Police – 664 211) (Fire – 93) (Ambulance – 94)

Total Population 3,784,000
Jewish Population 400
(Electricity voltage – 220)

Sarajevo

CEMETERIES

Kovacici
This historic Jewish cemetery is in town. Not far from the centre of town, on a hill called Vraca, there is a monument with the names of the 7,000 Jews from the area who fell victim to the Nazis.

COMMUNITY ORGANISATIONS

Sarajevo Jewish Community "La Benevolencija"
Hamdije Kresevljakovica 83 7100   (71) 663-472
                                   Fax: (71) 663-473

MUSEUMS

Jewish Museum
Mulamustafe Baseskije Street
This historic museum, placed in the oldest synagogue in Sarajevo, with priceless relics dating back to the expulsion from Spain, is temporarily closed to the public.

SYNAGOGUES

Synagogue and Community Centre
Hamdije Kresevljakovica 59   (71) 663-472
                                 Fax: (71) 663-473
                        Email: la_bene@soros.org.ba

BRAZIL

The first Jewish settlers in Brazil came with the Portuguese in 1500. They were mainly Conversos, escaping persecution in Portugal, and initially worked on the sugar plantations. In due course they played important roles as traders, artisans and plantation owners. The huge area which is called Brazil today was in the process of being conquered by the Dutch and the Portuguese. Two synagogues were opened in Recife during the 1640's and many Jews came from Holland. When the Dutch left Brazil in 1654 one of the terms of surrender allowed the Jews who had been on their side to emigrate. Many fled and some went on to found the first Jewish community in New York, then known as New Amsterdam. A seventeenth-century Mikvah was discovered in 2000 in the basement of the Tsur Israel Synagogue in Recife.

With Brazilian independence in 1822, conditions became more favourable for Jews and many came from north Africa and Europe. The majority of Jews in Brazil today, however, originate from the immigration of east European Jews in the early twentieth century. From about 6,000 Jews in 1914, the community grew to 30,000 in 1930. After 1937 Brazil refused to allow Jewish immigrants into the country, but some limited immigration managed to continue despite the restrictions.

A central organisation was established in 1951 (the CONIB), and this includes 200 various Jewish organisations. Brazilian Jews live in an atmosphere of tolerance and prosperity, and assimilation is prominent.

There are synagogues in all the major cities.

GMT -3 to -5 hours	Total Population 159,884,000
Country calling code (55)	Jewish Population 110,000
Emergency Telephone (Police – 147) (Fire – 193) (Ambulance – 192)	(Electricity voltage – 220/100)

AMAZONAS

Manaus

COMMUNITY ORGANISATIONS
Comite Israelita Amazonas
R. Leonardo Malcher, 630　　　　(92) 234-7647
　　　　　　　　　　　　　　　Fax: (92) 233-6361

BAHIA

Salvador

SYNAGOGUES
Rua Alvaro Tiberio 60　　　　　(71) 321-4204
　　　　　　　　　　　　　Fax: (71) 337-6412
Community centre and Zionist organisation are at the same address.

BRASILIA

EMBASSY
Embassy of Israel
Av. das Nacoes Sul, Lote 38　(61) 244-7675/244-7875
　　　　　　　　　　　　　　　Fax: 244-6129

SYNAGOGUES
ACIB
Entrequadras Norte 305-306, Lote A　(61) 273-8255
　　　　　　　　　　　　　　　Fax: (61) 366-3651
　　　　　　　　　　Email: goldner@tba.com.br
Community centre is at the same address.

MINAS GERAIS

Belo Horizonte

COMMUNITY ORGANISATIONS
Associacão Israelita Brasileira
Rua Rio Grande do Norte 477　　(31) 224-6673
　　　　　Email: associacaoisraelita@bol.com.br

Uniao Israelita de Belo Horizonte
Rua Pernambuco 326　　　　　(31) 224-6013
　　　　　　　　　　Email: ihim@pib.com.br

CONTACT INFORMATION
Lojinha do Beit Chabad
Av. Serzedelo Corrêa 276　　　(31) 241-2250

MIKVAOT
Rua Rio Grande do Norte 477　　(31) 221-0690

SYNAGOGUES
Av. Leonardo Malchez 630, Centro

Reform
Congregacao Israelita Mineira
Rua Rio Grande do Norte 477   (31) 3224-2129
Fax: (31) 3224-2129
Email: cim@pib.com.br

PARA

Belém

COMMUNITY ORGANISATIONS
Community Centre
Travessa Dr. Moraes 37   (91) 222-3184
Email: cip@zaz.com.br

SYNAGOGUES
Eshel Avraham
Travessa Campos Sales 733

Shaar Hashamaim
Rua Alcipreste Manoel Theodoro 842

PARANA

Curitiba

COMMUNITY CLUB AND JEWISH FEDERATION
Centro Israelita do Parana
Rua Mateus Leme 1431 80530   (41) 338-7575
Fax: (41) 338-7922

SYNAGOGUES
Orthodox
Francisco Frischmann
Rua Cruz Machado 126   (41) 224-5218
Fax: (41) 224-8172

PERNAMBUCO

Recife

COMMUNITY ORGANISATIONS
Community Centre
Rua da Gloria 215

SYNAGOGUES
Rua Martins Junior 29

RIO DE JANEIRO

Campos

COMMUNITY ORGANISATIONS
Community Centre
Rua 13 de Maio 52

Greater Rio de Janeiro

The old Jewish area is situated around Rua Alfandega. The country's first Ashkenazi Synagogue (Grande Templo Israelite) is an imposing building which was renovated in 1986.

BUTCHERS
Frigorifico
Rua Ronald Carvalho 265, Copacabana 22021-020
(21) 295-7341
Supervision: Rav Stauber

COMMUNITY ORGANISATIONS
Confederacao Israelita de Brazil (Conib)
Avenida Nilo Pecanha 50   (21) 240-0034
Fax: (21) 240-2717

Organizaco Israelita do Estado do Rio de Janeiro
Rua Tenente Possolo 8

Rabinado do Rio de Janeiro
Rua Pompeu Loureiro 40, Copacabana
(21) 2256-3587
Fax: (21) 2256-3587
Email: rabinatorio@aol.com

CULTURAL ORGANISATIONS
ASA - Associacao Scholem Aleichem
Rua Sao Clemente 155, Botafogo 22260
(21) 2539-7740
Fax: (21) 2266-1980
Email: asa@asa.org.br
Web site: www.asa.org.br
The institution is dedicated to promote cultural events (seminars, debates, video exhibitions, etc.).

EMBASSY
Consul General of Israel
Av. Copacabana 680   (21) 255-5432

GROCERIES
Kosher House
Rua Anita Garibaldi 37 lj. A, Copacabana
(21) 255-3891

MIKVAOT
Kehilat Yaakov
Rua Capelao Alvares da Silva 15, Copacabana 22041
(21) 2236-3922

MUSEUM
Museu Judaico do Rio de Janeiro
Rua Mexico 90, Andar 2003 1-141   (21) 2524-6451
Fax: (21) 240-1598
Email: museujudaico@uol.com.br
Web site: www.museujudaico.org.br

RESTAURANTS
Rua Pompeu Loureiro 40, Copacabana (21) 236-0249
Hours: 10am to 5pm Sunday to Thursday.

Meat
Kosher House
Rua Anita Garibaldi 37A, Copacabana   (21) 255-3891

SYNAGOGUES
Liberal
Associacão Religiosa Israelita
Rua General Severiano 170, Botafogo 22290
(21) 2543-6320; 2542-5598
Fax: (21) 2542-6499
Email: ari.adm@arirj.com.br

Orthodox
Agudat Israel
Rua Nascimento Silva 109, Ipanema 22421
(21) 267-5567

Beith Chabad of Rio de Janeiro
Rua Pompeu Loureiro No 40, Copacabana

Grande Templo Israelita
Rua Tenente Possolo 8, Centro 20230   (21) 232-3656

Kehilat Yaakov
Rua Capelao Alvares da Silva, Copacabana 22041

TOURS OF JEWISH INTEREST
Michel Mekler
Av. Graca Aranha 81/608, Centro 20030
(21) 220-8817
Web site: www.orbita.starmedia.com/via/~caritur

Niteroi

COMMUNITY ORGANISATIONS
Centro Israelita
Rua Visconde do Uruguai 255,24030

Sociedade Hebraica
Rua Alvares de Azevedo 185, Icarai 24220

Petropolis

RELIGIOUS ORGANISATIONS
Machane Israel Yeshiva
Rua Duarte de Silveira 1246 25600   (242) 45-4952

SYNAGOGUES
Sinagoga Israelita Brasileira
Rua Aureliano Coutinho 48 25600

RIO GRANDE DO SUL

Erechim

SYNAGOGUES
Av. Pedro Pinto de Souza 131

Passo Fundo

SYNAGOGUES
Rua General Osório 1049

Pelotas

SYNAGOGUES
Rua Santos Dumont 303

Porto Alegre

BUTCHERS
Kosher Butcher
Rua Fernandes Vieira 518   (51) 250-441

CULTURAL ORGANISATIONS
**Instituto Cultural Judaico Marc Chagall -
Projeto Memoria**
Rua Dom Pedro II, 1220/sala 216   (51) 343-5748

MIKVAOT
Rua Francisco Ferrer 170

MUSEUM
Museu Judaico
Rua João Telles 329   (51) 226-0379

RELIGIOUS ORGANISATIONS
City Rabbinate
Rua Henrique Dias 73   (51) 219-649

SYNAGOGUES
Liberal
SIBRA
Mariante 772   (51) 331-8133
Services on Shabbat only.

Orthodox
Beit Chabad
Rua Felipe Camarão 748   (51) 330-7078
Daily services.

Centro Israelita Porto Alegrense
Rua Henrique Dias 73   (51) 228-1935
Daily services.

Linath Ha-Tzedek
Rua Bento Figueredo 55   (51) 332-1065
Daily services.

Poilisher Farband
Rua João Telles 329   (51) 226-0379
Daily services.

União Israelita Porto Algrense
Rua Dr Barros Cassal 750   (51) 311-6515
Fax: (51) 311-5886
Daily services.

Sephardi
Centro Hebraico Riograndense
Rua Cel. Machado 1008
Services on Shabbat only.

SAO PAULO

Campinas

SYNAGOGUES
Beth Yacob Campinas
Rua Barreto Leme 1203   (19) 231-4908

Guaruja

SYNAGOGUES
Beit Yaacov
Av. Leomil 628   (13) 387-2033

Neve Itzhak
Av. Leomil 950   (13) 386-3167

Mogi Das Cruzes

COMMUNITY ORGANISATIONS
Jewish Society
Rua Dep. Deodato Wertheimer 421   (11) 469-2505

Santo Andre

SYNAGOGUES
Beit Chabad
Rua 11 de Junho 172   (11) 449-1568

Santos

COMMUNITY ORGANISATIONS
Club
Rua Cons. Neblas 254   (132) 32-9016

SYNAGOGUES
Beit Sion
Rua Borges 264

Sinagoga Beit Jacob
Rua Campos Sales 137

Sao Caetano do Sul

SYNAGOGUES
Sociedade Religiosa S. Caetano do Sul
Rua Para 67   (11) 442-3514

Sao Jose dos Campos

SYNAGOGUES
Beit Chabad
Rua Republica do Ira 91   (11) 3064-6322

Sao Paulo

Many Conversos came to sao Paulo to escape the Inquisition, which was centred in northern Brazil. A number rose to positions of importance.

By 1972 the Jews of Sao Paulo build the Albert Einstein hospital as a contribution to the public health service.

BAKERIES
Buffet Mazal Tov
Rua Peixoto Gomide 1724   (11) 883-7614
Fax: (11) 3064-5208

Matok Bakery
Al. Barros 921   (11) 66-7514
Supervision: Rabbi I. Dichi

Rua P. João Manoel 709   (11) 3064-6668
Supervision: Rabbi I. Dichi

BOOKSELLERS
Livraria Sêfer
Alameda Barros, 893 01232-001   (11) 3826-1366
Fax: (11) 3826-4508
Email: sefer@sefer.com.br
Web site: www.sefer.com.br
Bookseller and Judaica.

BUTCHERS
Casa de Carnes Casher
Rua Fortunato 241   (11) 221-2240
Under supervision of Rabbi Elyahu B. Valt.

Kosher Express
Rua Tupi, Higienopolis   (11) 3667-0863

Mehadrin
Rua S. Vicente de Paulo   (11) 67-9090
Under supervision of Rabbi M.A. Iliovitz.

Rua Prates 689   (11) 228-1771
Under supervision of Rabbi M.A. Iliovitz.

EMBASSY
Consul General of Israel
Rua Luis Coelho 308, 7th Floor
(11) 257-2111; 257-2814

GROCERIES

All Kosher
Rua Albuquerque Lins 1170   (11) 3825-1131

Casas Menora
Rua Guarani 114   (11) 228-6105

Chazak
Rua Afonsa Pena 348a   (11) 229-5607
Rua Haddock Lobo 1002   (11) 3068-9093

Kosher Mart
Rua Tenente Pena 187, Bom Retiro   (11) 221-7299
Web site: www.koshermart.com.br

Mazal Tov
Rua Peixoto Gomide 1724   (11) 3083-7614
Fax: (11) 3064-5208

Sta. Luzia
Al. Lorena 1471   (11) 883-5844
Look for kosher section.

Zilanna
Rua Itambé 506   (11) 257-8671

MEDIA

Newspapers
O Hebreu
Rua Cunha Gago 158 05421-000   (11) 3819-1616
Fax: (11) 3819-1616
Email: ohebreu@ohebreu.com.br
Web site: www.brasiljudaico.com.br
Monthly.

Resenha Judaica
Rua Antonio Carlos 582/5   (11) 255-8794
Weekly.

Tribuna Judaica
Rua Tanabi 299 05002-010
(11) 3871-3234/3873-3020/3862-9074
Fax: (11) 3871-3234
Email: tjudaica@uol.com.br
Weekly.

Periodical
Morasha Magazine
Rua Dr Veiga Filho 547, Higienopolis 01229-000
(11) 3825-9784
Fax: (11) 3030-5630
Email: morasha@uol.com.br
Web site: www.morasha.com

MIKVAOT

Rua Chabad 60 01417-030
Email: chabad@chabad.org.br

Beit Yaacov Synagogue
Rua Dr Veiga Filho 547, Higienopolis 01229-000
(11) 3662-2154
Fax: (11) 3662-2154
Email: morasha@uol.com.br

Congregacao Mekor Haim
Rua Sao Vicente de Paulo 276 01229-010
(11) 3662-6238; 3826-7699
Fax: (11) 3666-6960
Email: revista_nascente@hotmail.com

Congregacao Monte Sinai
Rua Piaui 624, Higienopolis 01241-000
(11) 3824-9229
Fax: (11) 3824-9229
Email: cmsinai@sanet.com.br

Micre Taharat Menachem - Perdizes
Rua Dr. Manoel Maria Tourinho 261   (11) 3865-0615
By appointment only.

RELIGIOUS ORGANISATIONS

Centro Judaico Religioso de Sao Paulo
Rua Correa De Mello 84/34   (11) 3331-5642
Office hours: 9 am to 1 pm weekdays.

Comunidade Israelita Ortodoxa de Sao Paulo
Rua Haddock Lobo 1091 1091   (11) 3062-1562
This community centre has two synagogues.

RESTAURANTS

Jacky Gourmet Café
Rua Rosa e Silva 146   (11) 3826-3537

Kosher Center
Rua Corrèa de Melo 68 01123-020   (11) 223-1175
Fax: (11) 223-3721
Supervision: Rabbi M.A. Iliovitch Shlita of Kehal
Hachareidim
Restaurant and Bakery. Hours: Sun 9.00 am-4.00 pm.
Mon-Thurs 8.00 am-6.00 pm. Fri 7.30 am-3.00 pm

Restaurante Kosher Delight
Rua Baronesa de Itu 436   (11) 3661-3106
Meat
Bero
Rua peixoto Gomide 2020   (11) 3086-2808
Fax: (11) 3086-2809
Email: berokosher@osite.com.br

Hebraica Kosher Restaurant
Rua Hungria 1000   (11) 381567188
Fax: (11) 38156980
Supervision: Rabbi Elyahu B. Valt
Buffet Mosaico inside the Hebraica Sao Paulo club.
Closed Mondays, open Saturday night 1 1/2 hours
after Shabbat.

Milk
Cantina Do Bero
Rua Pe. Joao Manoel, 881   (11) 3064-9022
Email: berokosher@osite.com.br
Open from Sunday to Thursday from 6.00 pm until
11.30 pm. Also delivers.

SYNAGOGUES

Hasidic
Uniao Ortodoxa Judaica
Rua Mamore 597   (11) 3224-8639
Fax: (11) 3224-9029

Hungarian
Adas Yereim
Rua Talmud Tora 86   (11) 282-1562; 852-9710

Liberal
Congregacao Israelita Paulista
Rua Antonio Carlos 653   (11) 256-7811
       Fax: (11) 257-1446
       Email: scrtgeral@dialdata.com.br
       Web site: www.cip.sp.com.br

Orthodox
Beit Chabad Augusta
Rua Augusta 259 01305-000   (11) 258-7173

Beit Chabad Central
Rua Chabad 54-60 01417-010   (11) 3060-9777
       Fax: (11) 3060-9778
       Email: chabad@chabad.org.br
       Web site: www.chabad.org.br

Beit Chabad Perdizes
Rua Man. Maria Tourinho, 261   (11) 3865-0615

Beit Itzchak
Rua Haddock Lobo 1279   (11) 3081-3804
       Fax: (11) 881-3064, 0302

Beit Yaacov
Rua Dr Veiga Filho 547, Higienopolis 01229-000
       (11) 3662-2154
       Fax: (11) 3662-2154
       Email: morasha@uol.com.br

Congregacao Mekor Haim
Rua Sao Vicente de Paulo 276 01229-010
       (11) 3826-7699
       Fax: (11) 3666-6960
       Email: revista_nascente@hotmail.com

Progressive
Comunidade Shalom
Rua Coronel Joaquim Ferreira Lobo 195 04544-150
       (11) 829-1477
       Fax: (11) 828-9177

Sephardi
Templo Israelita Brasileiro Ohel Yaacov
Rua Abolicao 457   (11) 606-9982
       Fax: (11) 227-6793

TRAVEL AGENCIES
Carmel Tur
Rua Xavier de Toledo 121/10   (11) 257-2244

Sharontur
Rua de Graca 235   (11) 223-8388
       Fax: (11) 220 5036
       Email: sharontur@sharontur.com.br
       Web site: sharontur.com.br
Open: 8.00 am-6.00 pm. Closed Shabat (Saturday) & Sunday. International & domestic tickets. Car rental, exchange, hotel reservations. Languages spoken: English, Hebrew, Spanish. Contact person: Mr Dov Smaletz

Vertice
Rua Sao Bento 545/10   (11) 3115-1970
       Fax: (11) 3115-1970
       Email: turismo@vertice.com.br

Sorocaba

SYNAGOGUES
Community Centre
Rua Dom Pedro II 56   (11) 31-3168

BULGARIA

Dating back to the Byzantine conquest, the community in Bulgaria was established by Greek Jews in Serdica (Sofia, the capital). The Jewish community grew when the Bulgarian state was founded in 681. Czar Ivan Alexander (1331-71) had a Jewish wife (who converted to Christianity).

The community has included eminent rabbinic commentators, such as Rabbi Dosa Ajevani and Joseph Caro, the codifier of the Shulchan Aruch, who escaped to Bulgaria after the expulsion from Spain. The various Jewish groups joined to form a unified Sephardi community in the late seventeenth century.

About 50,000 Jews lived in Bulgaria in 1939. Bulgaria joined the war on the side of Germany but, despite much pressure from the Nazis, the government and general population refused to allow Bulgarian Jews to be deported. Only Jews from Macedonia and Thrace, then occupied by Bulgaria, were deported. Despite being saved, most of the community emigrated to Israel after the war. The 10 per cent who remained were then under the control of the communists and had little contact with the outside world.

Since the fall of communism, the community has been reconstituted and now has synagogues in Sofia and Plovdiv. The community is ageing, although 100 children attend a Sunday school run by the Shalom Organisation, the central Jewish organisation for Bulgaria.

GMT +2 hours	**Total Population 8,306,000**
Country calling code (359)	**Jewish Population 3,000**
Emergency Telephone (Police – 166) (Fire – 160) (Ambulance – 150)	**(Electricity voltage – 220)**

Plovdiv

LIBRARIES
Library and House of Culture
Vladimir Zaimov St. 20   (32) 761-376

SYNAGOGUES
Tsar Kalojan St. 15
In the courtyard of a large apartment complex.

Rousse

SYNAGOGUES
Community Centre
Ivan Vazov Sq. 4   (82) 270-540

Sofia

About half of Bulgarian Jewry lives in Sofia. The Great Synagogue of 1878 ranks among the largest of Sephardi synagogues.

CEMETERIES
Jewish Cemetery
Orlandovtzi suburb
Take a tram (Nos 2, 10 or 14) to the last stop for this large Jewish cemetery.

COMMUNITY ORGANISATIONS
Social & Cultural Organisation of Bulgarian Jews
Shalom, Alexander Stambolisky St. 50   (2) 870-163
Publishes a periodical 'Evreiski Vesti' and a yearbook. It also maintains a museum devoted to "The Rescue of Bulgarian Jews, 1941–1944". At the same address are the offices of El Al, the Joint and the Jewish Agency.

EMBASSY
Embassy of Israel
1 Bulgaria Sq. NDK, 7th floor   (2) 951-5029
Fax: (2) 952-1101

RELIGIOUS ORGANISATIONS
Central Jewish Religious Council
Ekzarh Josef St. 16   (2) 983-1273
Fax: (2) 985-5085
Email: isaksaiu@mail.orbitel.bg

SYNAGOGUES
Sofia Central Synagogue
Ekzarh Josef St. 16   (2) 983-1273
Fax: (2) 985-5085
Email: isaksaiu@mail.orbitel.bg
Adjacent to the synagogue is a museum dedicated to the history of Bulgarian Jewry.

CANADA

The Jewish settlement of Canada began with the British expansion into Canada. In 1760, the Shearith Israel synagogue was founded in Montreal and in 1832 Jews received full civil rights. In the 1850s the community began to spread from Montreal to Toronto and Hamilton.

The community grew throughout the early twentieth century, from 16,000 in 1900 to 126,000 in 1921. After the Second World War, Jewish immigration increased and by 1961 the population was 260,000.

The headquarters of the Canadian Jewish Congress is in Montreal. This is the main national organisation for Canadian Jewry, and the community is provided with a full range of services, with Jewish schools, yeshivot, newspapers and the unique (in the Americas) Montreal Jewish Library. There are also several kosher restaurants.

Note: In remote areas, calls have to be made via the operator.
GMT -3 to -8 hours
Country calling code (1)
Emergency Telephone (Police – 911) (Fire – 911) (Ambulance – 911)

Total Population 30.491,000
Jewish Population 365,000
(Electricity voltage – 110)

ALBERTA

Calgary

BAKERIES
Susan's Kosher Bakery
131, 2515 - 90th Avenue SW   (403) 238-5300
                              Fax: (403) 238-3023
Supervision: Calgary Kosher
Hours of operation: Sunday 10 am to 2 pm, Tuesday to Thursday 9 am to 6 pm, Friday 8 am to 4 pm (winter 8 am to 2 pm). Closed Mondays and Shabbat.

COMMUNITY ORGANISATIONS
B'nai Brith Canada
Western Region, 1607 90Ave S.W. T2V 4V7
                              (403) 258 1848
                         Fax: (403) 258 1815
Calgary Jewish Community Council
1607 90th Av. S.W.   (403) 253-8600
                         Fax: (403) 253-7915
                        Email: cjcc@cjcc.ca
                   Web site: www.cjcc.ca
The Council issues a booklet "Keeping Kosher in Calgary".

DELICATESSEN
Izzy's Kosher Meat Market
2515 90th Av. S.W.   (403) 251-2552

MEDIA
Newspapers
Jewish Free Press
8411 Elbow Dr. SW T2V 1K8   (403) 252-9423
                         Fax: (403) 255-5640
                   Email: jewishfp@telus.net

RELIGIOUS ORGANISATIONS
Calgary Rabbinical Council
                              (403) 253-8600
                         Fax: (403) 253-7915

RESTAURANTS
Karen's Cafe
Calgary Jewish Centre, 1607 90th Av. S.W.
                              (403) 255-5311
Hours:Monday to Thursday, 10 am to 7 pm; Friday, 10 am to 1 pm. Closed on Sunday

SYNAGOGUES
Conservative
Beth Tzedec
1325 Glenmore Trail S.W. T2V 4Y8   (403) 252-8319
                   Email: info@bethtzedec.ab.ca
Orthodox
Congregation House of Jacob-Mikveh Israel
1613-92nd Av., Jerusalem Rd. SW T2V 5C9
                              (403) 259-3230
                         Fax: (403) 259-3240
                   Email: hojmi@cadvision.com
             Web site: www.cadvision.com/hojmi
Reform
Temple B'nai Tikvah
Calgary Jewish Centre, 1607 90th Av.
S.W. T2V 4V7   (403) 252-1654
                         Fax: (403) 252-1709
                   Email: temple@cadvision.com

Edmonton

COMMUNITY ORGANISATIONS
Edmonton Jewish Federation
7200 156th St. T5R 1X3   (780) 487-0585
                         Fax: (780) 481-1854
                   Email: edjfed@netcom.ca
Contact Gayle Tallman, Exec. Director, for additional information.

MEDIA
Newspapers
Edmonton Jewish Life
10342 107th Street T5J 1K2 (780) 488-7276
Fax: (780) 484-4978
Email: ejlife@shaw.ca

Edmonton Jewish News
#330, 10036 Jasper Av. T5J 2W2 (780) 421-7966
Fax: (780) 424-3951

RESTAURANTS
Dairy
King David Pizza
West Edmonton Mall (780) 486-9020

SYNAGOGUES
Conservative
Beth Shalom
11916 Jasper Av. T5K 0N9 (780) 488-6333
Fax: (780) 488-6259
Email: bshalom2@telusplanet.net

Orthodox
Beth Israel
131 Wolf Willow Road T5T 7T7 (780) 482-2840
Fax: (780) 482-2470
Email: edbeth@telusplanet.net

Chabad Lubavitch
Westridge Shopping Centre (780) 486 7244
Fax: (780) 486 7243

Reform
Temple Beth Ora
7200 156th St. T5R 1X3 (780) 487-4817
Fax: (780) 481-1854
Email: tbo@telusplanet.net
Services: the first Friday of the month

Lethbridge

SYNAGOGUES
Orthodox
Beth Israel
914 15th Street South T1J 3A5 (403) 327-8621

BRITISH COLUMBIA

Kelowna

SYNAGOGUES
Traditional
Beth Shalom Sanctuary
OJCC, 102-1 North Glenmore Road V1V 2E2
(250) 862-2305
Fax: (250) 862-2365
Email: shalom@ojcc.net
Web site: www.ojcc.net
Shabbat services last Saturday of the month, 9:30 am.

Richmond

BAKERIES
Garden City Bakery
#360-9100 Blundell Road (604) 244-7888
Supervision: Orthodox Rabbinical Council of British
Columbia

KASHRUT INFORMATION
**Orthodox Rabbinical Council of British
Columbia**
8080 Francis Road V6Y 1A4 (604) 275-0042
Fax: (604) 277-2225
Email: bckosher@direct.ca
Kashrut Director, Rabbi A. Feigelstock; Kashrut
Administrator, Rabbi Levy Teitlebaum.

SYNAGOGUES
Conservative
Beth Tikvah
9711 Geal Road V7E 1R4 (604) 271-6262
Fax: (604) 271-6270
Email: bethtikvah@lynx.net
Friday, 8 pm; Shabbat, 9:30 am. Wheelchair access.

Hasidic
Chabad of Richmond
200-4775 Blundell Road, Richmond (604) 277-6427
Fax: (604) 263-7934
Email: info@chabadrichmond.com

Orthodox
Eitz Chaim
8080 Frances Road V6Y 1A4 (604) 275-0007
Fax: (604) 277-2225
Email: annamarie@eitzchaim.net
Daily, 7 am and sunset; Shabbat, 9 am and sunset;
Sunday, 9 am. Wheelchair access.

Surrey

COMMUNITY ORGANISATIONS
**White Rock/South Surrey Jewish Community
Centre**
PO Box 75186 V4A (604) 541-9995
Monthly Shabbat services. Wheelchair access.

SYNAGOGUES
Hasidic
**The Centre for Judaism of the Lower Fraser
Valley**
2351 128th Street (604) 541-4111
Email: shfy@aol.com
Weekly Shabbat services. Wheelchair access.

Vancouver

The most famous of early Jewish settlers were the Oppenheimer brothers who settled there the year the city was founded. David Oppenheimer was the city's second mayor. The city's first synagogue was built in 1912, although of course services had been held much earlier.

BAKERIES
Sabra Bakery
3844 Oak St.   (604) 733-4912

BED AND BREAKFAST
Mrs Levin's Kosher Bed & Breakfast
Apt 101, 2772 Spruce V6H 2R2   (604) 738-2457

Shulamit Mass
5434 Manson Street V5Z 3H1   (604) 266-8965

CAFETERIA
Dairy
Cafe Sabra Too (Jewish Community Centre)
950 West 41st Avenue V5Z 2N7   (604) 257-5111
Supervision: Orthodox Rabbinical Council of British Columbia
Take-out, eat-in and catering. Dairy, pareve (meat is take-out only). Hours: Monday to Thursday, 8:30 am to 8 pm; Friday, 8:30 am to 2 pm; Sunday, 10 am to 6:30 pm.

CONTACT INFORMATION
Jewish Federation of Greater Vancouver
950 West 41st Avenue, Suite 200 V5Z 2N7
                                      (604) 257-5100
                              Fax: (604) 257-5119
            Email: shalom_vancouver@ultranet.ca
          Web site: www.shalomvancouver.org
Executive Director Daniella Givon.

Shalom BC
950 West 41st Avenue V5Z 2N7   (604) 257-5111
                              Fax: (604) 257-5119
                        Email: info@shalombc.org
                  Web site: www.shalombc.org
Jewish Information & Welcome Service, and Volunteer Centre. Publishes a "Guide to Jewish Life in British Columbia". Hours: Monday to Friday 9am to 4pm. Visitors welcome.

MEDIA
Newspaper
Western Jewish Bulletin
301, 68 East 2nd Avenue V5T 1B1 (604) 689-1520
                              Fax: (604) 689-1525

RESTAURANTS
Dairy
Chagall's
950 West 41st Avenue   (604) 263-7507
                              Fax: (604) 263-7507
Supervision: British Columbia Kosher Council
Deliveries to Hotels - Pareve available on request. Dairy, cafeteria style café and restaurant.

Sabra Kosher Bakery, Restaurant and Grocery
3844 Oak Street V6H 2M5   (604) 733-4912
                              Fax: (604) 733-4911
Supervision: Orthodox Rabbinical Council of British Columbia
Take-out, eat-in and catering. Dairy, pareve (meat is take-out only). Hours: Monday to Thursday, 8:30 am to 8 pm; Friday, 8:30 am to 2 pm; Sunday, 10 am to 6:30 pm.

Surat Sweet
1938 West 4th Avenue   (604) 733-7363
Indian vegetarian - Gujarati style.

Meat
Omnitsky Kosher B.C.
5866 Cambie Street   (604) 321-1818
                              Fax: (604) 321-1817
                  Email: omnitskykosher@aol.com
              Web site: www.escape.ca/omnitsky
Supervision: Orthodox Rabbinical Council of British Columbia
Fresh meats, poultry. Manufacturers of all beef delicatessen products under B.C.K.

SYNAGOGUES
Conservative
Beth Israel
4350 Oak Street V6H 2N4   (604) 731-1346
                              Fax: (604) 731-4989
Daily, 8 am (public holidays, 9 am) and 6 pm; Friday, 8:15 pm; Shabbat, 9:15 am and 6 pm; Sunday, 9 am and 6 pm. Wheelchair access.

Congregation Har El
North Shore Jewish Community Centre, 1305 Taylor Way, West Vancouver V7T 2Y7 (604) 925-6488
                              Fax: (604) 922-8245
Friday, 7 pm; Shabbat, 10 am (Seasonal). Visitors welcome.

Hasidic
Chabad-Lubavitch
5750 Oak Street V6M 2V9   (604) 266-1313
                              Fax: (604) 263-7934
            Email: information@lubavitchbc.com
Daily 7.00am; Shabbat 10.00am; Sunday 9.00am. Wheelchair access.

Jewish Renewal
Or Shalom
710 East 10th Avenue V5T 2A7   (604) 872-1614
                              Fax: (604) 872-4406
                    Email: orshalom@telus.net
              Web site: www.orshalom.bc.ca
Family Kabbalat Shabbat and potluck dinner monthly; Shabbat 10 am. Wheelchair access.

Orthodox
Louis Brier Home
1055 West 41st Avenue V6M 1W9   (604) 261-9376
Daily mincha, 4:30 pm; Friday, 4:15 pm; Shabbat, 9 am. Wheelchair access.

Schara Tzedeck
3476 Oak Street V6H 2L8   (604) 736-7307
                                 Fax: (604) 730-1621
              Email: office@scharatzedeck.com
              Web site: www.scharatzedeck.com
Monday and Thursday, 7 am; Tuesday, Wednesday
and Friday, 7:15 am; weekdays, sunset; Friday, 7:30
pm; Shabbat, 9 am and half hour before sunset;
Sunday, 8:30 am.

Torat Hayim Community
491 Eastcot Road   (604) 984-4168
                                 Fax: (604) 984-4168
              Email: info@hayim.com
Shabbat: 10.30 am followed by Kiddush

Reform
Temple Shalom
7190 Oak Street V6P 3Z9   (604) 266-1957
                                 Fax: (604) 266-7121
Monday and Wednesday, 7:15 am; Friday, 8:15 pm;
Shabbat, 10 am. Also has a gift shop.

Sephardi Orthodox
Beth Hamidrash
3231 Heather Street V5Z 3K4
                        (604) 872-4222; 873-2371
Daily, 7 am; Shabbat, 9 am; Sunday and public
holidays, 8:30 am; Friday, 5 pm; Shabbat, sunset.

Traditional
Shaarey Tefilah
785 West 16th Avenue   (604) 873-2700
Friday evening, call for time; Shabbat and Sunday, 9
am. Wheelchair access.

Victoria

COMMUNITY ORGANISATIONS
Victoria Jewish Community Centre
3636 Shelbourne Street   (250) 477-7184
                                 Fax: (250) 477-6283

SYNAGOGUES
Conservative
Emanu-El
1461 Blanshard V8W 2J3   (250) 382-0615
Thursday, 7 am; Shabbat, 9 am. Wheelchair access.

MANITOBA

Winnipeg

BAKERIES
City Bread
238 Dufferin Avenue R2W 2X6   (204) 586-8409

Goodies' Bake Shop
2 Donald Street R3L 0K5   (204) 489-5526

Gunn's
247 Selkirk Avenue R2W 2L5   (204) 586-6150

BUTCHERS
Omnitsky's
1428 Main Street R2W 3V4   (204) 586-8271

Tuxedo Quality Foods
1853 Grant Avenue R3N 1Z2   (204) 987-3830
Frozen only

COMMUNITY ORGANISATIONS
Asper Jewish Community Campus
C300 - 123 Doncaster Street R3N 1B2
                                 (204) 477-7400
                                 Fax: (204) 477-7405
              Email: info@jewishwinnipeg.org
              Web site: www.jewishwinnipeg.org
Home to Winnipeg Jewish Theatre, Canadian Jewish
Congress and Jewish Heritage Centre.

GROCERIES
Bathurst Street Market
1570 Main Street R2W 5J8   (204) 338-4911

MEDIA
Newspaper
Jewish Post & News
117 Hutchings Street R2X 2V4   (204) 694-3332
                                 Fax: (204) 694-3916
Weekly English language newspaper.

MIKVAOT
Community Mikvah
123 Doncaster Street R3N 2B1   (204) 477-7445

Mikva Chabad-Lubavitch
455 Hartford Avenue R2V 0W9   (204) 339-4761
                                 Fax: (204) 586-0487
              Email: aaltein@mbnet.mb.ca
Mailing address: 2095 Sinclair Street, Wpg.MB R2V
3K2.

MUSEUM
Jewish Museum of Western Canada
C116-123 Doncaster Street R3N 2B2 (204) 477-7460
                                 Fax: (204) 477-7465
              Email: heritage@jhcwc.org
              Web site: www.jhcwc.org

RESTAURANTS
Asper Jewish Community Campus Restaurant
123 Doncaster Street R3N 2B2   (204) 477-7418
                                 Fax: (204) 477-7507

Bathurst Downstairs Deli
1570 Main Steet R2W 5J8   (204) 338-4911

SYNAGOGUES
Egalitarian Conservative
Beth Israel
1007 Sinclair Street R2V 3J5   (204) 582-2353

Congregation Shaarey Zedek
561 Wellington Crescent R3M 0A5   (204) 452-3711

Orthodox
Chevra Mishnayes
700 Jefferson Avenue R2V OP6   (204) 338-8503

Lubavitch Centre
2095 Sinclair Street R2V 3K2   (204) 339-8737

NEW BRUNSWICK

Fredericton

SYNAGOGUES
Orthodox
Sgoolai Israel
Westmorland Street E3B 3L7   (506) 454-9698
                               Fax: (506) 452-8889
                          Email: samuels@unb.ca
For information on availability of kosher food, call
Rabbi Yochanan Samuels: (506) 454-2717.

Moncton

SYNAGOGUES
Orthodox
Tiferes Israel
56 Steadman Street E1C 8L9   (506) 858-0258
                               Fax: (506) 858-0259
                        Email: tifisrl@nbnet.nb.ca
Mikva on premises.

Saint John

MUSEUM
Saint John Jewish Historical Museum
29 Wellington Row E2L 3H4   (506) 633-1833
                               Fax: (506) 642-9926
                         Email: sjjhm@nbnet.nb.ca
                    Web site: www.sjjhm.tripod.com
May-mid Octoberr 10am to 4pm Monday to Friday.
Also, during July and August, Sunday 1pm to 4pm or
by appointment. This is the only Jewish museum in
the Atlantic Provinces of Canada. There are eight
display areas as well as library and archives. Guided
tours available.

SYNAGOGUES
Conservative
Shaarei Zedek
76 Carleton Street E2L 2Z4   (506) 657-4790
Community centre on premises.

NEWFOUNDLAND

St. John's

SYNAGOGUES
Conservative
**Hebrew Congregation of Newfoundland &
Labrador (Beth El)**
Elizabeth and Downing Avenues A1C 5L4
                               (709) 726-0480
                          Fax: (709) 777-6995
                      Email: mpaul@mun.ca
Mailing address: P O Box 724, St. John's A1C 5L4,
Newfoundland and Labrador, Canada.

NOVA SCOTIA

Glace Bay

SYNAGOGUES
Orthodox
1 Prince Street B1A 3C8   (902) 849-8605

Halifax

COMMUNITY ORGANISATIONS
Atlantic Jewish Council
5670 Spring Garden Road, Suite 508 B3J 1H6
                               (902) 422-7491
                          Fax: (902) 425-3722
              Email: atlanticjewishcouncil@theajc.ns.ca
                  Web site: www.theajc.ns.ca
Covers Jewish communities in Nova Scotia, New
Brunswick, Price Edward Island, Newfoundland and
Halifax. Also at this address: Canadian Jewish
Congress, Atlantic Region, Canadian Zionist
Federation, United Jewish Appeal, Canadian Young
Judea, Hadassah, Jewish National Fund, JSA (Jewish
Student Association) for Atlantic Canada.

MEDIA
Newspaper
Shalom Magazine
5675 Spring Garden Road, Suite 800 B3J 1H1
                               (902) 422-7491
                          Fax: (902) 425-3722
                   Email: jgoldberg@theajc.ns.ca

SYNAGOGUES
Conservative
Shaar Shalom
1981 Oxford Street B3H 4A4   (902) 423-5848
                               Fax: (902) 422-2580
              Email: shaar.shalom@ns.sympatico.ca

Orthodox
Beth Israel
1480 Oxford Street B3H 3Y8   (902) 422-1301
         Fax: (902) 422-7251
Mikva on premises.

TOURIST SITE
Pier 21
1055 Marginal Road, Pier 21   (902) 425-7770
         Web site: pier21.ns.ca
Known as Canada's Ellis Island, Pier 21 was Canada's "front door" to over one million immigrants. Visitors are able to re-enact the immigrant experience through various multimedia displays. In addition they can explore their family trees.

Sydney

SYNAGOGUES
Conservative
Temple Sons of Israel
P.O. Box 311, Whitney Avenue B1P 6H2
         (902) 564-4650

Yarmouth

CONTACT INFORMATION
R & V Indiq
13 Parade Street B5A 3A5
Will be happy to provide details of the local Jewish community.

ONTARIO

Belleville

SYNAGOGUES
Conservative
Sons of Jacob
211 Victoria Avenue K8N 2C2   (613) 962-1433

Brantford

SYNAGOGUES
Orthodox
Beth David
50 Waterloo Street N3T 3R8   (519) 752-8950

Chatham

SYNAGOGUES
Conservative
Children of Jacob
29 Water Street N7M 3H4   (519) 352-3544

Cornwall

SYNAGOGUES
Conservative
Beth-El
321 Amelia Street K6H 3P4   (613) 932-6373

Guelph

SYNAGOGUES
Traditional
Beth Isaiah
47 Surrey Street W. N1H 3R5   (519) 836-4338
         Email: cgdk@aol.com
Full line of Kosher products at Ultra-519-763-3827.

Hamilton

BUTCHERS
Hamilton Kosher Meats
889 King Street West L8S 1K5

COMMUNITY ORGANISATIONS
Hamilton Jewish Federation
1030 Lower Lions Club Road, Ancaster L9G 3N6
         (905) 648-0605
         Fax: (905) 648-8350
         Email: hamujajf@interlynx.net

DELICATESSEN
Westdale Deli
893 King Street West L8S 1K5   (905) 529-2605
         Fax: (905) 529-2605

MEDIA
Newspaper
Hamilton Jewish News
P.O. Box 7528, Ancaster L9G 3N6   (905) 648-0605
         Fax: (905) 648-8388

SYNAGOGUES
Conservative
Beth Jacob
375 Aberdeen Avenue L8P 2R7   (905) 522-1351
Orthodox
Adas Israel
125 Cline Avenue S. L8S 1X2   (905) 528-0039
         Fax: (905) 528-7497
Reform
Anshe Sholom
215 Cline Avenue N. L8S 4A1   (905) 528-0121
         Fax: (905) 528-2994

Kingston

COMMUNITY ORGANISATIONS
B'nai B'rith Hillel Foundation
26 Barrie Street   (613) 542-1120

SYNAGOGUES
Orthodox
Beth Israel
116 Centre Street K7L 4E6   (613) 542-5012
Fax: (613) 542-9071
Email: bethisrael@kingston.net

Reform
Temple Iyr Hamelech
331 Union Street West K7L 2R3   (613) 789-7022

Kitchener

SYNAGOGUES
Reform
Temple Shalom
116 Queen Street North N2H 2H7   (519) 743-0401

Traditional
Beth Jacob
161 Stirling Avenue South N2G 3N8 (519) 743-8422

London

COMMUNITY ORGANISATIONS
London Jewish Federation
536 Huron Street N5Y 4J5   (519) 673-3310
Email: admin@ljf.on.ca
There are no kosher establishments, but kosher
frozen meat, prepared foods and select groceries are
available at the local A&P, IGA North London market,
and Loblaws Stores. Communal inquiries to
Executive Director at the above number.

MEDIA
Newspaper
London Jewish Community News
536 Huron Street N5Y 4J5   (519) 673-3310
Fax: (519) 673-1161
Email: adain@sympatico.ca

SYNAGOGUES
Conservative
Congregation Or Shalom
534 Huron Street N5Y 4J5   (519) 438-3081
Fax: (519) 439-2994
Email: or.shalom@sympatico.ca

Orthodox
Congregation Beth Tefilah
1210 Adelaide Street North N5Y 4T6 (519) 433-7081
Fax: (519) 433-0616
Email: beth_tefilah@yahoo.com
Web site: www.bethtefilah.org
Mikva on premises.

Reform
Temple Israel
651 Windermere Road N5X 2P1   (519) 858-4400
Fax: (519) 858-2070
Email: jwitts@julian.uwo.ca

Mississauga

SYNAGOGUES
Reform
Solel Congregation
2399 Folkway Drive L5L 2M6   (905) 820-5915
Fax: (905) 820-1956

Niagara Falls

SYNAGOGUES
Conservative
B'nai Jacob
5328 Ferry Street L2G 1R7   (416) 354-3934

North Bay

SYNAGOGUES
Orthodox
Sons of Jacob
302 McIntyre Street West P1B 2Z1   (705) 497-9288
Fax: (705) 497-9812
Email: martybrown@gosympatico.ca
Friday evening services.

Oakville

SYNAGOGUES
Reform
Shaarei-Beth El
186 Morrison Road L6J 4J4   (905) 849-6000
Fax: (905) 849-1134
Email: sbe@idirect.com
Web site: www.sbe.ca

Oshawa

SYNAGOGUES
Orthodox
Beth Zion
144 King Street East L1H 1B6   (905) 723-2353

Ottawa

Ottawa is the capital of Canada and its fourth
largest city. The first Jewish settler came in 1858
when Ottawa was still known as Bytown. Ottawa
has always been strongly traditional and has a
growing community presently numbering around
13,000.

BAKERIES
Rideau Bakery
384 Rideau St   (613) 234-1019
1666 Bank St   (613) 737-3355

COMMUNITY ORGANISATIONS
Canadian Jewish Congress National Office
100 Sparks Street, Suite 650 K1P 5B7   (613) 233-8703
                                  Fax: (613) 233-8748
Email: canadianjewishcongress@cjc.ca
Web site: www.cjc.ca
Publishes the "National Synagogue Directory".
Contact to find out information on synagogues in the
city to which you are travelling.

Vaad Ha'ir (Jewish Community Council)
21 Nadolny Sachs Private K2A 1R9   (613) 798-4696
                                  Fax: (613) 798-4695
Web site: www.jewishottawa.org
Vaad Hakashruth located here for all kashrut
information.

EMBASSY
Embassy of Israel
Suite 1005, 50 O'Connor Street K1P 6L2
                                        (613) 567-6450
                                  Fax: (613) 237-8865

RESTAURANTS
Dairy
Viva Pizza
Solway JCC, 21 Nadolny Sachs Private
                                        (613) 798-9818

SYNAGOGUES
Conservative
Agudath Israel
1400 Coldrey Avenue K12 7P9   (613) 728-3501
                                  Fax: (613) 728-4468

Orthodox
Beth Shalom Congregation
151 Chapel Street K1N 7Y2   (613) 789-3501

Beth Shalom West
15 Chartwell Avenue K2G 4K3   (613) 723-1800

Machzikei Hadas
2310 Virginia Drive K1H 6S2   (613) 521-9700

Young Israel of Ottawa
627 Kirkwood   (613) 722-8394

Reform
Temple Israel
1301 Prince of Wales Drive K2C 1N2 (613) 224-1802

Owen Sound

SYNAGOGUES
Conservative
Beth Ezekiel
3531 Bay Shore Road N4K 5N3   (519) 376-8774

Pembroke

SYNAGOGUES
Beth Israel
322 William Street K8A 1P3   (613) 732-7811

Peterborough

SYNAGOGUES
Conservative
Waller Street   (705) 745-8398

Richmond Hill

SYNAGOGUES
Conservative
Beth Rayim
9711 Bayview Avenue L4C 9X7   (905) 770-7639

St Catharine's

COMMUNITY ORGANISATIONS
Community Centre
Newman Memorial Building   (416) 685-6767

SYNAGOGUES
Reform
Temple Tikvah
83 Church Street, PO Box 484 L2R 3C7
                                        (416) 682-4191

Traditional
B'nai Israel
190 Church Street L2R 4C4   (416) 685-6767
                                  Fax: (416) 685-3100

Sudbury

SYNAGOGUES
Orthodox
Shaar Hashomayim
158 John Street P3E 1P4   (705) 673-0831

Thornhill

BOOKSELLERS
Israel's Judaica Centre
441 Clark Avenue West L47 6W7   (905) 881-1010
                                  Fax: (905) 881-1016
Email: contact@israelsjudaica.com
Web site: www.israel.judaica.com
Also sells gifts.

Matana Judaica
248 Steeles Avenue West, #6 L4J 1A1 (905) 731-6543
                                  Fax: (905) 882-6196
Also sells gifts.

DELICATESSEN

Marky's Delicatessen North
7330 Yonge Street L4J 1V8 (905) 731-4800

Wok'n'Deli
441 Clarke Avenue West L4J 6W7 (905) 882-0809

RESTAURANTS
Dairy
My Zaidy's Pizza
441 Clark Avenue West L4J 6W8 (905) 731-3029

Meat
Miami Grill
441 Clark Avenue (905) 709-0096
Supervision: COR

Taste of Tikvah
7700 Bathurst Street (905) 771-0699
Supervision: COR

Thunder Bay

SYNAGOGUES
Orthodox
Shaarey Shomayim
627 Grey Street P7E 2E4 (807) 622-4867
Email: phlab@baynet.net

Toronto

There have been one and a half centuries of organised Jewish life in Toronto since its start in 1849. The Jewish population increased significantly during the 1980s, and now Toronto is home to almost half of Canada's Jews. There is a good range of Jewish facilities in the city.

BAKERIES

Bagels Galore
First Canadian Place M5X 1E1 (905) 363-4233

Carmel Bakery
3856 Bathurst Street (416) 633-5315

Dairy Treats Bakery
3522 Bathurst Street (416) 787-0309
Fax: (416) 787-1935

Richman's Kosher Bakery
4119 Bathurst Street (416) 636-9710
Fax: (416) 636-9614

BOOKSELLERS

Israel's Judaica Centre
897 Eglinton Avenue West M6C 2C1 (905) 256-2858
Email: contact@israelsjudaica.com
Web site: www.israel.judaica.com

Negev Importing Co Ltd
3509 Bathurst Street M6A 2C5
(416) 905-9356 (Toll free: 1-888-618-9356)
Fax: (416) 905-0071
Email: negev_imp@hotmail.com
Web site: www.negevjudaica.com

COMMUNITY ORGANISATIONS

Bernard Betel (Senior Centre)
1003 Steeles Avenue West M2R 3T6 (416) 225-2112
Fax: (416) 225-2097
Email: betelctr@idirect.com
Centre operates Conservative Synagogue - has two Sephardi congregations on site - Beth Yosef and Tehillat Yerushalayim.

UJA Federation of Greater Toronto
4600 Bathurst Street, Toronto M2R 3V2
(416) 635-2883
Fax: (416) 635-9565
Email: office@ujafed.org
Web site: www.jewishtoronto.net

CONTACT INFORMATION

Jewish Information Service - UJA Federation of Greater Toronto
4588 Bathurst Street, Suite 214 M2R 1W6
(416) 635-5600
Fax: (416) 636-5813
Email: jinfo@ujafed.org
Web site: www.jewishtoronto.net
Information about the Jewish community in the Greater Toronto area, Canada including synagogues, kosher restaurants, sites of interest.

DELICATESSEN

Marky's Delicatessen
280 Wilson Avenue, Downsview (416) 638-1081

Mati's Fallafel House
3430 Bathurst Street M6A 1C2 (416) 783-9505
Sells dairy products only.

EMBASSY

Consul General of Israel
180 Bloor Street West, Suite 700 M5S 2V6
(905) 640-8500
Fax: (905) 640-8555
Email: hasbara@idirect.com
Israel Government Tourist Office: 964-3784.

GIFT SHOP

Miriam's
3007 Bathurst Street (416) 781-8261
Fax: (416) 781-8261

MEDIA

Newspapers
Canadian Jewish News
10 Gateway Blvd, Suite 420, Don Mills M3C 3A1
(905) 422-2331
Fax: (905) 422-3790

Jewish Tribune
15 Hove Street, Downsview M3H 4Y8,
(905) 633-6224
Fax: (905) 633-6224
Email: jewishtribune@jewishtribune.ca

MEMORIAL

Holocaust Education & Memorial Centre
4600 Bathurst Street, Willowdale M2R 3V2
(416) 635-2883

MUSEUM

Silverman Heritage Museum
Baycrest Centre for Geriatric Care, 3560 Bathurst
Street M6A 2E1 (416) 785-2500 Ext.2802
Fax: (416) 785-4228
Email: pdickinson@baycrest.org
One of the few Judaica museums in Canada. It has an active exhibit program.

RELIGIOUS ORGANISATIONS

JEP/Ohr Somayach Centre
2939 Bathurst Street M6B 2B2 (416) 785-5899
Has a minyan.

Kashruth Council of Canada
4600 Bathurst Street, Ste 240 M2R 3V2
(416) 635-9550
Fax: (416) 635-8760
All enquiries about kashrut here.

RESTAURANTS

Dairy
Dairy Treats Cafe
3522 Bathurst Street M6A 2C6 (416) 787-0309
Fax: (416) 787-1935

Milk'n Honey
3457 Bathurst Street, Downsview M6A 2C5
(416) 789-7651
Fax: (416) 789-4788

Pizza Tova
3020 Bathurst Street (416) 781-1326
Supervision: COR

Tov Li Pizza
5972 Bathurst Street, Willowdale M2R 1Z1,
(416) 650-9800

Meat
King Solomon's Table
3705 Chesswood Drive, Downsview M3J 2P6
(416) 630-0666
Fax: (416) 630-4585
Open Monday to Thursday 12.00 noon to 10.00pm.
Sunday 4.00pm to 10.00pm. Closed Friday and
Saturday. Kashrut: COR.

Marky's Delicatessen
6233 Bathurst Street, (just South of Steel)
(416) 227-0707
Supervision: Kashruth Council of Toronto

The Chicken Nest
3038 Bathurst Street M6B 4K2 (416) 787-6378
Fax: (416) 222-6057

Windsor

COMMUNITY ORGANISATIONS

Jewish Community Council
1641 Ouellette Avenue N8X 1K9 (519) 973-1772

MEDIA

Periodical
Windsor Jewish Community Bulletin
Fax: (519) 973-1774

SYNAGOGUES

Orthodox
Shaar Hashomayim
115 Giles Blvd East N9A 4C1 (519) 256-3123
Fax: (519) 256-3124
Email: shaar@mnsi.net

Shaarey Zedek
610 Giles Blvd East N9A 4E2 (519) 252-1594

Reform
Congregation Beth-El
2525 Mark Avenue N9E 2W2 (519) 969-2422

QUEBEC

Montreal

1760 saw the arrival of the first Jews in Montreal as civilians attached to the British army. In the 1920s and 1930s the Boulevard St-Laurent was equivalent to London's East End or New York's Lower East Side. There are now just over 100,000 Jews in the city. Twenty percent of them are North African Sephardim.

BAKERIES

Biscuit Adar
5458 Westminister (514) 484-1198
Supervision: Vaad Ha'ir

Boulangerie-Adir
6795 Darligton (514) 342-1991
Supervision: Vaad Ha'ir

Cite Cashere
4747 Van Horne (514) 733-2838
Supervision: Vaad Ha'ir

Delice Cashere
4655 Van Horne (514) 733-5010
Supervision: Vaad Ha'ir

Katzberg Home Bread and Cake Delivery
5355 Jeanne Mance (514) 273-4042
Supervision: Vaad Ha'ir

Kleins Kosher Bakery
5540 Hutchison (514) 274-4633
Supervision: Vaad Ha'ir

Kosher Quality Bakery
5855 Victoria   (514) 731-7883
    Fax: (514) 731-0205
Supervision: Vaad Ha'ir
Hours: Sunday - Wednesday 6am to 9pm. Thursday 6am to 10pm. Friday 6am winter 2pm or summer 4pm.

La Biscuit Adar
1204 Beaumont   (514) 343-0272
Supervision: Vaad Ha'ir

Montreal Kosher
7005 Victoria   (514) 739-3651
Supervision: Vaad Ha'ir

2865 Van Horne, Wilderton Shopping Centre
    (514) 739-3651
Supervision: Vaad Ha'ir

2135 St. Louis, St. Laurent   (514) 747-5116
Supervision: Vaad Ha'ir

New Homemade Kosher Bakery
6915 Querbes   (514) 270-5567
Supervision: Vaad Ha'ir

6685 Victoria   (514) 733-4141
Supervision: Vaad Ha'ir

5638 Westminister   (514) 486-2024
Supervision: Vaad Ha'ir

1085 Bernard W.   (514) 276-2105
Supervision: Vaad Ha'ir

Patisserie Chez Ma Souer
5095 Queen Mary   (514) 737-2272
Supervision: Vaad Ha'ir

Pita Royal
5897 Van Horne   (514) 488-9414
Supervision: Vaad Ha'ir

Renfels Bakery
2800 Bates   (514) 733-5538
Supervision: Vaad Ha'ir

BOOKSELLERS
Kotel Book & Gift Store
6414 Victoria Avenue H3W 2S6   (514) 739-4142
    Fax: (514) 739-7330

Rodal's Hebrew Book Store & Gift Shop
4689 Van Horne Avenue H3W 1H8   (514) 733-1876
    Fax: (514) 733-2373
    Email: rodals@ican.net

Victoria Gift Shop
5875 Victoria Avenue H3W 2R6   (514) 738-1414

COMMUNITY ORGANISATIONS
Federation CJA
5151 ch, de la Côte Ste-Catherine H3W 1M6
    (514) 735-3541
Operates the Jewish Information and Referral Service (JIRS), Tel: 737-2221.

Jewish Community Council of Montreal
6825 Decarie, Suite 100 H3W 3E4   (514) 739-6363
    Fax: (514) 739-7024
    Email: semanuel@mk.ca
    Web site: www.mk.ca
Visitors requiring additional information about kosher establishments should contact the Vaad Ha'ir at the above numbers. Also apply to them for a list of kosher butchers, bakeries, caterers and restaurants.

EMBASSY
Consul General of Israel
1155 Boulevard Rene Levesque Ouest,
Suite 2620 H3B 4S5   (514) 940-8500
    Fax: (514) 940-8555
    Email: cgisrmtl@videotron.net
    Web site: www.israelca.org

LIBRARIES
Jewish Public Library
1 Carre Commings Square H3W 1M6   (514) 345-2627
    Fax: (514) 345-6477
    Email: info@jplmtl.org

MEDIA
Newspaper
Canadian Jewish News
6900 Decarie Blvd, #341 H3X 2T8   (514) 735-2612
    Fax: (514) 735-9090
    Email: montreal@cjnews.com

RESTAURANTS
Dairy
Bistrot Casa Linga
5095 Queen Mary H3W 1X4   (514) 737-2272

Cummings Jewish Centre for Seniors Cafeteria
5700 av. Westbury Ave. H3W 3E8   (514) 342-1234
    Fax: (514) 739-6899
    Email: michael@cummingscentre.org
    Web site: www.cummingscentre.org

Foxy's
5987A Victoria Avenue   (514) 739-8777
Supervision: Vaad Ha'ir

Pizza Pita
5710 Victoria Avenue   (514) 731-7482
Supervision: Vaad Ha'ir
Open 9.30 am-11.30 pm daily, Saturday night until 2.30 am.

Tatty's Pizza
6540 Darlington   (514) 734-8289
Supervision: Vaad Ha'ir

Meat
Chez Babys
Cote St. Luc Road
Supervision: Montreal Sephardic Vaad

El Morocco II
3450 Drummond Street   (514) 844-6888; 844-0203
Fax: (514) 844-1204
Email: elmorocco@spring.ca
Supervision: Vaad Ha'ir
Open for lunch and dinner until 10 pm. Located
downtown near hotels and boutiques.

Ernie's & Ellie's Place
6900 Decarie Blvd H3X 2T8   (514) 344-4444
Fax: (514) 344-0001

Supervision: Vaad Ha'ir

Exodus Restaurants
5395 Queen Mary   (514) 483-6610
Fax: (514) 483-6810
Supervision: Vaad Ha'ir

SYNAGOGUES
**Canadian Jewish Congress National
Headquarters**
Samuel Bronfman House, 1590 Docteur Penfield
Avenue H3G 1C5   (514) 931-7531
Fax: (514) 931-0548
Email: mikec@cjc.ca
**Contact to find out which of the many
synagogues in Montreal is nearest.**

Quebec City

CEMETERIES
Beth Israel Ohev Sholom
Boulevard Rene Levesque, Sainte-Foy (418) 658-6677
This is an official monument and historic site - 5 miles
from the old centre.

SYNAGOGUES
Orthodox
Beth Israel Ohev Shalom
1251 Place de Merici G1R 1Y2   (418) 688-3277

Ste. Agathe des Monts

A resort in the Laurentian Mountains known as
the "Catskills" of Montreal where members of the
Montreal community spend their summer
months.

SYNAGOGUES
Orthodox
House of Israel Congregation
31 rue Albert J8C 3A3   (819) 326-4320
Fax: (819) 326-8558
Web site: www.houseofisrael.org

SASKATCHEWAN

Moose Jaw

SYNAGOGUES
Conservative
Moose Jaw Hebrew Congregation
937 Henry Street S6H 3H1   (306) 692-1644

Regina

SYNAGOGUES
Orthodox
Beth Jacob
4715 McTavish Street S4S 6H2   (306) 757-8643
Fax: (306) 352-3499

Reform
Temple Beth Tikvah
Box 33048, Cathedral Post Office S4T 7X2
Email: templebethtikvah@hotmail.com

Saskatoon

SYNAGOGUES
Conservative
Agudas Israel
715 McKinnon Avenue S7H 2G2   (306) 343-7023
Fax: (306) 343-1244
Email: jewishcommunity@sk.sympatico.ca
Will be pleased to welcome visitors.

CAYMAN ISLANDS

In addition to a very small permanent Jewish community there are a number of Jews who spend part of the year on the Islands.

GMT -5 hours	**Total Population 38,000**
Country calling code (1345)	**Jewish Population Under 100**
Emergency Telephone (Police – 911) (Ambulance – 555)	**(Electricity voltage – 110)**

Grand Cayman

CONTACT INFORMATION
Harvey DeSouza
PO Box 72 GT, Grand Cayman, B.W.I. (345) 949-7739

CHILE

The original Jewish settlers in Chile were Conversos. Rodrigo de Organos, a Converso, was the first European to enter the country in 1535. The Inquisition, however, curtailed the growth of the community.

The first legal Jewish immigration, albeit small, occurred only after Chile's independence in 1810. In 1914 the Jewish community numbered some 500, but this increased in the late 1930s with those refugees from Nazism who were able to avoid the strict immigration laws. Anti-semitism, however, also grew, and the Comite Representativo was formed to respond to it.

There is an umbrella organisation and a large Zionist body in Chile. Most of the community is not religious, but some keep kosher and there are several synagogues in Santiago (the capital) and a few kosher shops. There are two Jewish schools and several Jewish newspapers are published.

GMT -4 hours	**Total Population 14,622,000**
Country calling code (56)	**Jewish Population 21,000**
Emergency Telephone (Police – 133) (Fire – 132) (Ambulance – 131)	**(Electricity voltage – 220)**

Arica

COMMUNITY ORGANISATIONS
Sociedad Israelita
Dr Herzl, Casilla 501

Iquique

COMMUNITY ORGANISATIONS
Comunidad Israelita
Playa Ligade 3263, Playa Brava

La Serena

COMMUNITY ORGANISATIONS
Community Centre
Cordovez 652

Rancagua

COMMUNITY ORGANISATIONS
Comunidad Israelita
Casilla 890

Santiago

The majority of Chilean Jews live in Santiago. The city has a couple of notable features in connection with its Jewish community. The Circulo Israelita Synagogue has an interesting stained glass design in its interior, and the "Bomba Israel" is a fire service, manned by volunteers who include a few rabbis. Two of their fire engines carry the Chilean and Israeli flags.

BUTCHER AND SUPERMARKET
Kosher Deli
Americo Vespucio Sur 1301   (2) 251-3145
Supervision: Jabad

COMMUNITY ORGANISATIONS
Communal Headquarters (Comite Representativo de las Entidades Judias de Chile)
Miguel Claro 196   (2) 235-8669

EMBASSY
Embassy of Israel
San Sebastian 2812, Casilla 1224   (2) 246-1570

SYNAGOGUES
Ashkenazi
Comunidad Israelita de Santiago
Serrano 214-218

German
Sociedad Cultural Israelita B'nei Jisroel
Mar Jonico No 8860   (2) 201-1623
     Fax: (2) 201-1623
     Email: bneisrael@entelchile.net

Hungarian
Maze
Pedro Bannen 0166   (2) 274-2536

Orthodox
Bicur Joilim
Av. Matte 624

Jabad Lubavitch
Gloria 62, Las Condes   (2) 228-2240

Jafets Jayim
Miguel Claro 196

Sephardi
Maguen David
Av. R. Lyon 812

Temuco

COMMUNITY ORGANISATIONS
Comunidad Israelita
General Cruz 355

Valdivia

COMMUNITY ORGANISATIONS
Community Centre
Arauco 136 E.

Valparaiso

COMMUNITY ORGANISATIONS
Comunidad Israelita
Alvarez 490, Vina del Mar   (32) 680-373

CHINA

There is archaeological evidence of a Jewish presence in China in the eighth century but it is believed that their existance as a community only dates from the twelth century. The largest established community of around 1,000 was in Kaifeng. The first Kaifeng synagogue was built in 1163.

The Treaty of Nanking in 1842 opened Shanghai to trade. In 1845 Elias Sassoon pioneered the Jewish settlement of Shanghai. Many Baghdadi Jews followed and were under the protection of the British government. In due course they were in the forefront of the development of the city. A second community was formed later, mainly by Russians and Poles fleeing religious persecution. The final influx was refugees from Nazi oppression in the period 1933-39. Almost all the community left Shanghai after the Second World War. In 1999 a community was again established.

Also included here is Hong Kong, previously listed as a separate entity but, since July 1997, again a region of China.

GMT +8 hours
Country calling code (86 (Hong Kong 852)
Emergency Telephone (Police – 110) (Fire – 119)

Total Population 1,284,100,000
Jewish Population 2,100
(Electricity voltage – 220/240)

Beijing

EMBASSY
Embassy of Israel
1 Jianguo Menwai Da Jia 100004   (10) 6505-2970/1/2
Fax: (10) 6505-0328

KOSHER FOOD
Mrs Shanen's Bagels
(10) 6435-9561
Ask for kosher bagels

SYNAGOGUES
Chabad Lubavitch of Beijing China
Kings Garden Villa, 18 Xiao Yun Road, D-5A, Chao
Yang District 00016   (10) 6468-1321
Fax: (10) 6468-1322
Email: chabadbeijing@hotmail.com
Shabbat services on Friday night and Shabbat as well
as Friday night dinners and Shabbat lunches. All are
welcome

Hong Kong

Although there were some Jewish merchants trading out of Hong Kong over the centuries, the first permanent community consisted of Jews who came from Baghdad in the early nineteenth century. The first synagogue was not established until 1901, the early settlers preferring to organise communal events from their homes. The majority of the community were Sephardi, but Nazi persecution led to more Ashkenazi settlers arriving in Hong Kong, via Shanghai. Since the Second World War many Chinese Jews have emigrated through Hong Kong to Australia and the USA, although some have remained in Hong Kong. Following the reversion to Chinese control in mid-1997, the Jewish community is still thriving, and the mood is optimistic.

The Jews have contributed greatly to the building of the infrastructure of Hong Kong and, since the 1960s, many Western Jews, attracted by the success of this major financial centre, have made their homes there. The first communal hall was founded in 1905, but a new, multi-purpose complex (the Jewish Community Centre) has been opened, which is one of the most luxurious in the world. This centre includes everything from a library and a strictly kosher restaurant to a swimming pool and sauna.

CEMETERIES
The Jewish Cemetery
Located in Happy Valley   2589-2621
Fax: 2548-4200

COMMUNITY ORGANISATIONS

Hong Kong Jewish Community Centre
One Robinson Place, 70 Robinson Road,
Mid-Levels   2801-5440
                         Fax: 2877-0917
                    Email: csw@jcc.org.hk
               Web site: www.jcc.org.hk
Two glatt kosher restaurants under the supervision of
a full-time Mashgiach. Regular Shabbat and Festival
Dinners. Kosher supermarket, full banquet facilities,
library, swimming pool and leisure facilities and a full
programme of activities and classes. Visitors are
welcome.

CULTURAL ORGANISATIONS

The Jewish Historical Society of Hong Kong
                              2807-9400
                         Fax: 2887-5235
Publishes monographs on subjects of Sino-Judaic
interest and maintains an archive. Information from
Mrs Judith Green.

EMBASSY

Consul General of Israel
Room 701Admiralty Centre, Tower 2, 18 Harcourt
Street   2529-6091
                         Fax: 2865-0220
              Email: isrcons@asiaonline.net

RESTAURANTS

Hong Kong Jewish Community Centre
One Robinson Place, 70 Robinson Road,
Mid-Levels   2801-5440
                         Fax: 2877-0917
                    Email: csw@jcc.org.hk
               Web site: www.jcc.org.hk
Two glatt kosher restaurants under full-time
Mashgiach supervision. Meals on Shabbat, take-away
and delivery service available.

Shalom Grill
2/F Fortune House, 61 Connaught Road,
Central   2851-6218; 2851-6300
                         Fax: 2851-7482
              Email: darvick@darvick.com.hk
Glatt kosher restaurants under full-time Mashgiach
supervision, Meals on Shabbat affer services, take-
away and delivery service available. There is also a
kosher supermarket, Sunday-Thursday Lunch 12.30
pm-2.30 pm. Dinner 6.30 pm-9.30 pm. Friday 12.30
pm-2.30pm.

SYNAGOGUES
Orthodox
Chabad of Hong Kong
Chabad House, Coda Plaza 3/F, 51 Garden Road
                              2523-9770
                         Fax: 2845-2772
              Email: info@chabadhk.org
           Web site: www.chabadasia.com
Shabbat Minyan & Meals in Central District.

Ohel Leah Synagogue
70 Robinson Road, Mid-Levels   2589-2621
                         Fax: 2548-4200
                  Email: mail@ohelleah.org
              Web site: www.ohelleah.org
Built in 1902 and carefully restored in 1998, the
Orthodox Ohel Leah Synagogue known by some as
the "crown jewel" of Asian Jewry still remains the
region's most vibrant centre of Jewish religious activity.
Classes, daily services, a Beth Din, and a mikva operate
on the premises. Gourmet catered shabbat meals -
Friday eve is by reservation and shabbat community
kiddush luncheon is complimentary following services.
Book nearby hotels at discounted rates through the
synagogue office.

Zion Congregation
21 Chatham Road, Kowloon   2366-6364
Corner of Mody Road (opposite to Kowloon Shangri-
La Hotel).

Sephardi
**Beit Midrash Shuva Israel and Community
Centre**
2/F Fortune House, 61 Connaught Road,
Central   2851-6218; 2851-6300
                         Fax: 2851-7482
              Email: darvick@darvick.com.hk
Daily Shacharil at 7.00 and Mincha-Ma'ariv fifteen
minutes before sunset. Shabbat services are followed
by Shabbat meals. Full day kollel.

Kaifeng

MUSEUM
Kaifeng Museum
The Kaifeng Museum documents the ancient history
of Kaifeng Jewry. The most significant artifact is a
fifteenth century etched stone with inscriptions
describing Kaifeng's Jewish history and customs
"from the times of Abraham".

Shanghai

Shanghai was opened to foreign trade in 1843. A
flourishing Jewish community built up including
Jews of many nationalities. There were three
synagogues; one of which the Ohel Rachel built in
1917 was designated in 2001 as an endangered
site. The current community is planning to raise
money for its restoration.

SYNAGOGUES
Orthodox
Shanghai Jewish Center
Shanghai-Mira Garden, Villa #2, 1720 HongQiao
Road 200336   (21) 6278-0225
                     Fax: (21) 6278-0223
              Email: rabbishalom@yahoo.com
              Web site: www.chinajewish.org
Shabbat Meals are available. Kosher Restaurant.

COLOMBIA

The first Jews in Colombia were Conversos, as was common in South America. However, they were soon discovered by the Inquisition when it was established in Colombia.

The next influx of Jews came in the nineteenth century, followed by mass immigration from eastern Europe and the Middle East after 1918. Jews were banned from entering after 1939, but this restriction was eased after 1950.

The present community is a mix of Ashkenazi and Sephardi elements, each having their own communual organisations. There are also youth and Zionist organisations. There is a central organisation for Colombian Jewry in Bogota (the capital). There are also Jewish schools and synagogues, and Jewish publications and radio programmes.

GMT -5 hours
Country calling code (57)
Emergency Telephone (Police – 112) (Fire – 119) (Ambulance – 132)

Total Population 36,612,000
Jewish Population 5,000
(Electricity voltage – 110/120)

Baranquilla

COMMUNITY ORGANISATIONS
Centro Israelita Filantropico
Carrera 43, No 85-95, Apartado Aereo 2537
(53) 342-310; 351-197

Comunidad Hebrea Sefaradita
Carrera 55, No 74-71, Apartado Aereo 51351
(53) 340-054; 340-050

Bogota

EMBASSY
Embassy of Israel
Calle 35, No 7-25, Edificio Caxdax
(1) 245-6603; 245-6712

MEDIA
Periodical
Menorah
Apartado Aereo 9081

RELIGIOUS ORGANISATIONS
Union Rabinica Colombiana
Tranversal 29, No 126-31
(1) 625-4377
Fax: (1) 274-9069
Email: centrocib@tutopia.com

SYNAGOGUES
Congregacion Adath Israel
Carrera 7a, No 94-20
(1) 257-1660; 257-1680
Fax: (1) 623-2237
Mikva on premises.

Ashkenazi
Centro Israelita de Bogota
Transversal 29, No 126-31
(1) 274-9069
Kosher meals available by prior arrangement with Rabbi Goldschmidt, 218-2500.

German
Asociacion Israelita Montefiore
Carrera 20, No 37-54
(1) 245-5264

Orthodox
Comunidad Hebrea Sefaradi
Calle 79, No 9-66
(1) 256-2629; 249-0372
Mikva on premises.

Jabad House
Calle 92, No 10, Apt. 405
Rabbi's Tel:(1)257-4920.

Cali

COMMUNITY ORGANISATIONS
Union Federal Hebrea
Apartado Aereo 8918
(2) 443-1814
Fax: (2) 444-5544
An umbrella organisation co-ordinating all Jewish activities in Cali.

SYNAGOGUES
Ashkenazi
Sociedad Hebrea de Socoros
Av. 9a Norte # 10-15, Apartado Aereo 011652
(2) 668-8518
Fax: (2) 668-8521

German
Union Cultural Israelita
Apartado Aereo 5552
(2) 668-9830
Fax: (2) 661-6857

Sephardi
Centro Israelita de Beneficiencia
Calle 44a, Av. 5a Norte Esquina, Apartado Aereo 77
(2) 664-1379
Fax: (2) 665-5419

Medellin

COMMUNITY ORGANISATIONS
Union Israelita de Beneficencia
Carrera 43B, No 15-150, Apartado Aereo 4702

COSTA RICA

The first Jews arrived in Costa Rica in the nineteenth century, from nearby islands in the Caribbean, such as Jamaica. The next wave of immigrants came from eastern Europe in the 1920s. Thereafter Costa Rica did not welcome new Jewish immigrants, and passed laws against foreign merchants and foreign land ownership. However, the Jewish community in Costa Rica established a communual organisation in 1930. There is a monthly newsletter, and a synagogue in San Jose. Most Jewish children attend the Haim Weizmann School, which has both primary and secondary classes.

It is interesting to note that the Costa Rican embassy in Israel is in Jerusalem and not Tel Aviv, where most other embassies are situated.

GMT -6 hours	**Total Population 3,464,000**
Country calling code (506)	**Jewish Population 2,500**
Emergency Telephone (Police – 911) (Fire – 911) (Ambulance – 911)	**(Electricity voltage – 110/220)**

San Jose

CONTACT INFORMATION
Centro Israelita Sionista de Costa Rica
PO Box 1473-1000   233-9222
                                        Fax: 233-9321
                        Email: cisdcr@racsa.co.cr
                Web site: www.centroisraelita.com

EMBASSY
Embassy of Israel
Edificio Centro Colon, Piso 11, PO Box 5147-1000
                        221-60-11/221-64-44
                                        Fax: 257-0867
                        Email: embofisr@sol.racsa.co.cr

GROCERIES
Little Israel Pita Rica
Frente a Shell Pavas Rd. 1055-1200   290-2083
                                        Fax: 262-5425
                        Email: pitarica@hotmail.com
                Web site: www.kosherfoodcostarica.com
The only kosher bakery and mini-market in Costa Rica. Delivers to hotels.

HOTELS
Barcelo San Jose Palacio
Apdo 458-1150   220-2034; 220-2035
                                        Fax: 220-2036
                        Email: Palacio@sol.racsa.co.cr
Hotel has separated kosher kitchen and its key in the mashgiach's (Rabbi Levkovitz) hands. The hotel is about a half hour walk to the synagogue.

Camino Real
Prospero Fernandezy, Camino Real Boulevard
                                        289-7000
                                        Fax: 289-8930
                        Email: caminoreal@ticonet.co.cr
Hotel has new separated kosher kitchen, with the key in the Mashgiach's (Rabbi Levkovitz) hands.

Melia Confort Corobici
PO Box 2443-1000   232-8122
                                        Fax: 231-5834
                Email: melia.confort.corobici@solmelia.com
There is no separate kosher kitchen, but it is fairly close to the Orthodox synagogue. The hotel has two separate storage rooms for kosher cookware.

SYNAGOGUES
Shaarei Zion

CROATIA

Jews were in the land now known as Croatia before the Croats themselves. The Croats arrived in the seventh century, the Jews some centuries before with the Romans: there are remains of a third-century Jewish cemetery in Solin (near Split).

The first Jewish communites were involved in trade with Italy across the Adriatic Sea, and also in trade along the River Danube. Their success was brief, however, and they were expelled in 1456, only returning more than 300 years later. The area became part of the newly formed Yugoslavia after the First World War, and the Jewish community became part of the Federation of Jewish Communities in Yugoslavia.

The Croatian Jews suffered greatly under the German occupation in the Second World War when the local Ustashe (Croatian Fascists) assisted the Germans. Despite their efforts, some Jews survived and even decided to rebuild their community when peace returned.

Today, after the civil war, there are synagogues in towns across the country. There are some Hebrew classes and newsletters are published. There are also many places of historical interest, such as Ulicia Zudioska (Jewish Street) in Dubrovnik.

Note: (Other emergency - 94)
GMT -1 hours
Country calling code (385)
Emergency Telephone (Police – 92) (Fire – 93)

Total Population 4,498,000
Jewish Population 2,000
(Electricity voltage – 220)

Dubrovnik

SYNAGOGUES
Zudioska Street 3
Zudioska means "Street of the Jews". This is the second oldest synagogue in Europe and is located in a very narrow street off the main street – the Stradun or Placa. The Jewish community office is in the same building. Zudioska Street is the third turning on the right from the town clock tower. Tourists help to make up a minyan in the synagogue on Friday night and High Holy Days.

Osijek

COMMUNITY ORGANISATIONS
Brace Radica Street 13   (31) 211-407
Fax: (31) 211-407
The community building contains objects from the synagogue that was destroyed during the Second World War. The community numbers about 150 members and has two cemeteries. No regular services are held. A former building of the pre-war synagogue in Cvjetkova Street is a Pentecostal church today. There is a plaque at the site of the destroyed synagogue in Zupanijska Street.

Rijeka

SYNAGOGUES
Filipovieva ul. 9, PO Box 65 51000
(51) 425-156/336-032
The community numbers about sixty. Services are held in the well maintained synagogue on Jewish holidays.

Split

COMMUNITY ORGANISATIONS
Zidovski Prolaz 1   (21) 45-672
The synagogue at Split is one of the few in Yugoslavia to have survived the wartime occupation. The Jewish community numbers about 200. There is a Jewish cemetery, established in 1578. More information from the community offices at the above number.

Zagreb

BOOKSELLERS
Voice of the Jewish Communities of Croatia
Email: jcz@oleh.srce.hr

COMMUNITY ORGANISATIONS
Jewish Community of Zagreb
Palmoticeva Street 16, PO Box 986   (1) 434-619
Fax: (1) 434-638
Email: jcz@public.stce.hr
Before the War Zagreb had 11,000 Jews. There are now only about 1,500, but they remain very active in Jewish communal life. Services are held in the community building on Friday evenings and holidays.

MONUMENT
Central Synagogue
Praska Street 7
There is a plaque on the spot of this pre-war synagogue.

Mirogoj Cemetery
There is an impressive monument in this cemetery to the Jewish victims of the Second World War.

TOURIST SITE
National Museum
The Sarajevo Haggadah, created in the 14th century in Spain, and considered one of the most precious Jewish illuminated manuscripts in the world is currently being restored. It is expected to again be placed on display in the National Museum during 2003.

CUBA

The first Jew to set foot in Cuba (1492) was Luis de Torres. Although hundreds arrived following the Spanish Inquisition, they were prohibited from practising their religion. This changed in 1898 following Cuba's liberation from Spain. With the end of Spanish colonial rule in that year, Jews from nearby areas, such as Jamaica and Florida, and Jewish veterans of the Spanish American War began to settle in Cuba. A congregation was established in 1904. Later, Turkish Sephardim formed their own synagogue. The community was then augmented by immigrants from eastern Europe who had decided to stay in Cuba, which was being used as a transit camp for those seeking to enter America. A central committee was established for all Jewish groups in the 1930s. Cuba imposed severe restrictions on immigration at that time, and the story of the German ship *St Louis* (full of Jewish refugees), which was refused entry into Cuba, is well known.

About 12,000 Jews lived on the island in 1952. Havana had by far the largest community, and 75 per cent of the Cuban community was Ashkenazi. Although the Cuban revolution did not target Jews, religious affiliations were initially discouraged and many Jews emigrated (as did many non-Jews). The remaining community has synagogues, and a Sunday school. Kosher food and Judaica are imported, mainly from Canada and Panama. Cuba broke off diplomatic relations with Israel in 1973, although in 1998/99 a number of Jews were allowed to emigrate to Israel.

GMT -5 hours   Total Population 11,509,000
Country calling code (53)   Jewish Population 600
Emergency Telephone (Police – 82 0116) (Fire – 81 115) (Ambulance – 404 551) (Electricity voltage – 110/220)

Havana

SYNAGOGUES
Conservative
Patronado de la Casa de la Comunidad Hebrea de Cuba
Calle 13 e I, Vedado   (8) 32-8953
This is also the location of a modern community centre.

Orthodox
Hadath Israel
Calle Picota 52, Habana Vieja   (8) 61-3495

CYPRUS

During the Roman Empire, Jewish merchants made their home on Cyprus. However, after a revolt that destroyed the town of Salamis, they were expelled. In medieval times, small Jewish communities were established in Nicosia, Limassol and other towns, but the community was never large.

It is interesting to note that Cyprus was seen as a possible 'Jewish Homeland' by the early Zionists. Agricultural settlements were established at the end of the nineteenth century, but they were not successful. Herzl himself tried to persuade the British government to allow Jewish rule over Cyprus in 1902, but met with failure.

Some German Jews managed to escape to Cyprus in the early 1930s. After the war, many Holocaust survivors who had tried to enter Palestine illegally were deported to special camps on the island. Some 50,000 European Jews were held there. Since the establishment of the state of Israel, the Jewish community on the island has become small; the Israeli embassy serves as a centre for community activities.

GMT +2 hours	**Total Population 766,000**
Country calling code (357)	**Jewish Population Under 100**
Emergency Telephone (Police – 112) (Fire – 112) (Ambulance – 112)	**(Electricity voltage – 240)**

Nicosia

COMMUNITY ORGANISATIONS
Committee of the Jewish Community of Cyprus
PO Box 24784 1303   (22) 694758
Fax: (22) 662077
Email: amiyes@spidernet.com.cy
Contact Mrs Z. Yeshurun for information.

EMBASSY
Embassy of Israel
4 Grypari Street   (22) 664195
Fax: (22) 666338
Email: press@nicosia.mfa.gov.il

CZECH REPUBLIC

Prague, the capital of this small central European country, has become a major tourist attraction. It is one of the few cities actively to promote its Jewish heritage, which dates from early medieval times. The oldest (still functioning) synagogue in Europe is there (the Altneuschul), as well as other interesting Jewish sites.

After the arrival of the first Jews in the country, in the tenth century, they suffered similar tragedies to those of other medieval Jewish communities forced baptism by the Crusaders and expulsions, together with some tolerance. Full emancipation was reached in 1867 under the Hapsburgs. The celebrated Jewish writer, Franz Kafka, lived in Prague and did not neglect his Judaism, unlike many other Czech Jews who assimilated and intermarried.

The German occupation led to 85 per cent of the community (80,000 people) perishing in the Holocaust. Further difficulties were faced in the communist period after the war, but since the 1989 'Velvet Revolution', Judaism is being rediscovered. The community (mostly elderly) has several synagogues around the country, a kindergarten and a journal, and there are kosher restaurants in the old Jewish quarter in Prague.

GMT +1 hour	**Total Population 10,304,000**
Country calling code (420)	**Jewish Population 5,000**
Emergency Telephone (Police – 158) (Fire – 150) (Ambulance – 155)	**(Electricity voltage – 220)**

Boskovice

MUSEUMS
Medieval Ghetto
(501) 454601; 452077
Fax: (501) 452077
Email: museum@mas.cz
Seventeenth-century Jewish town, synagogue and cemetery.

Brno

COMMUNITY ORGANISATIONS
Community Centre
tr. Kpt. Jarose 3 60200   (5) 4524-4710
Fax: (5) 4521-3803
Email: zob@zob.cz
Web site: www.zob.cz
The community president can be reached at 77-3233.

SYNAGOGUES
Skorepka 13

Holesov

MUSEUM

Schach Synagogue
Dating from 1650, this synagogue is now a museum.
Open in the mornings. At other times the curator will
show visitors around, if contacted. The old cemetery
is close by.

Karlovy Vary

Carslbad (as it was then called) was popular
among Jews as a spa and resort. The beautiful
synagogue, destroyed on Kristallnacht, is
recorded by a plaque on the wall of the Bristol
Hotel.

RESTAURANTS
Meat
Shalom
Mariauskolazenska 21   (17) 322-4921
                                Fax: (17) 322-3206

Liberec

SYNAGOGUES
Community Centre
Matousova 21, Reichenberg 46001   (48) 510-3340
Each weekday 9 am-11 am.

Mikulov

SITE
Only one synagogue, still being restored, remains of
the many which flourished here when the town was
the spiritual capital of Moravian Jewry and the seat of
the Chief Rabbis of Moravia. The cemetery contains
the graves of famous rabbis.

Olomouc

SYNAGOGUES
Community Centre
Komenskeho 7   (68) 522-3119

Pilsen

SYNAGOGUES
Smetanovy Sady 5, Pilsen   (19) 723-5749
Services Friday evenings. The Great Synagogue is
now closed.

Polna

MUSEUM
A museum was opened in 2000 in a reconstructed
seventeenth century synagogue. It charts the spread
of anti-Semitism in Central Europe.

Prague

Most of the Jews in the Czech Republic live in
Prague, which has had a thousand-year history of
Jewish settlement. The impact of the Jews in
Prague has been great, the Golem has entered
Prague folklore, and the Altneushul is the oldest
functioning synagogue in Europe. The Jewish
Quarter in the old town contains many historical
sites.
 Terezin is some forty miles from Prague and is
easily visited. On the way is the town of Lidice,
destroyed in June 1942 by the Nazis in retaliation
for the assassination of Reinhard Heydrich.

CEMETERIES
Old Jewish Cemetery
U Stare Skoly 1,3 11001   (2) 2171-1511
                                Fax: (2) 2481-9458
                       Email: office@jewishmuseum.cz
The oldest Jewish cemetery in Europe, containing the
graves of such famous rabbis & scholars as Avigdor
Karo (died 1439), Yehuda Low ben Bezalel (1609),
David Gans (1613) & David Oppenheim (1736).

CONTACT INFORMATION
Jewish Town Hall
Maislova 18
Houses the Federation of Jewish Communities in the
Czech Republic . It has the world famous Hebrew
clock.

EMBASSY
Embassy of Israel
Badeniho Street 2 7   (2) 333-25109
                                Fax: (2) 333-20092

HOTELS
President Hotel
Namesti Curieovych 100 116-88   (2) 231-4812
                                Fax: (2) 231-8247
A few minutes walk from the old Jewish quarter.

JUDAICA
Precious Legacy
Maiselova 16, Prague 1, Josefov   (2) 232-1951
                       Fax: (2) 232-0398, 472-1068
                       Email: legacy_tours@oasanet.cz

MUSEUMS

Jewish Museum in Prague
Ul Stare Skoly 1,3   (2) 2481-9456
Fax: (2) 2481-9458
Email: office@jewishmuseum.cz
Web site: www.jewishmuseum.cz
In 2001 a new set of facilities were opened. The complex includes art restoration workshops, a library, and an exhibition hall. Reservation centre: Tel: (2)231-7191. Fax: (2)231-7181.

RESTAURANTS

Dairy
Jerusalem
Brehova 5 1   (2) 232-4729
Fax: (2) 232-4729
Supervision: Chabad Lubavitch Prague
Sells a few groceries. Boxed lunches and Shabbat meals can be ordered.

Meat
Aarons Burger
Brehova 8   (2) 481-8752
Fax: (2) 786-4664

Carmel
Brehova 6   (2) 232-1749

Casablanca
Na Prikope 10 1   (2) 24-21-05-19
Fax: (2) 24-23-15-02

King Solomon
Siroka 8, Prague 1   (2) 248-18752
Fax: (2) 786-4664
Web site: www.kosher.cz

SYNAGOGUES

Orthodox
Altneuschul
Cervena ul.7 1   (2) 231-0909
Dates back to 1275.

Chabad Center Prague
3 Parizska Street, Prague 1 11000   (2) 232-0896
Fax: (2) 232-0200
Email: chabadprague@mbox.vol.cz
Web site: chabadprague.cz

Jubilee Synagogue
Jerusalemska 7

TOURS OF JEWISH INTEREST

Heritage Tours
     (2) 472-1068

Precious Legacy Tours
Maiselova 16, Prague 1, Josefov   (2) 232-0398
Fax: (2) 472-1068
Email: legacy_tours@oasanet.cz
Web site: legacytours

Wittmann Tours
Manesova 8, 120 00 Praha 2   (2) 2225-2472
Fax: (2) 2225-2472
Email: sylvie@wittmann-tours.com
Web site: www.wittmann.tours.com

Teplice

SYNAGOGUES
Community Centre
Lipova 25, Teplitz-Schönau   (417) 26-580

Terezin

MUSEUM
Theresienstadt
There is a new museum in the town dedicated to the Jews who were deported from Theresienstadt to Auschwitz. There is also a cemetery in which 11,250 individual, 217 mass graves and the crematorium are placed.

DENMARK

Jews were allowed to settle in Denmark in 1622, earlier than in any other Scandinavian country. Thereafter, the community grew, with immigration largely from Germany. The Danish king allowed the foundation of the unified Jewish community of Copenhagen in 1684, and the Jews were granted full citizenship in 1849.

In the early part of the twentieth century many refugees arrived from eastern Europe, and Denmark welcomed refugees from Nazi Germany. When the Germans conquered Denmark and ordered the Jews to be handed over, the Danish resistance managed to save 7,200 (90 per cent of the community) by arranging boats to take them to neutral Sweden. Some Jews did, however, stay behind and were taken to the transit ghetto of Theresienstadt (Terezin), and many died.

After the war, most of the Jews returned, and there is now a central Jewish organisation based in Copenhagen. There are also homes for the elderly, synagogues and a mikvahh. Kosher food is available.

GMT + 1 hour
Country calling code (45)
Emergency Telephone (Police – 112) (Fire – 112) (Ambulance – 112)

Total Population 5,284,000
Jewish Population 8,000
(Electricity voltage – 220)

Copenhagen

With a Jewish population of almost 8,000, the vast majority of Danish Jews live in the capital. The Community Centre contains most of the offices of the Jewish community, and three old-age homes are jointly run with the Copenhagen Municipality. The Great Synagogue and the cemetery dating from 1693 are interesting sites.

BAKERIES
Mrs Heimann
   3332-9443

BUTCHERS
Kosher Delikatesse
87 Lyngbyvej 2100   3918-5777
Fax: 3918-5390

COMMUNITY ORGANISATIONS
Jewish Community Centre
Ny Kongensgade 6 1472   3312-8868
Fax: 3312-3357
Email: mt@mosaiske.dk

EMBASSY
Embassy of Israel
Lundevangsvej 4, Hellerup 2900   3962-6288
Fax: 3962-1938
Email: israel@pip.dknet.dk

GROCERIES
I. A. Samson
Roerholmsgade 3 1352   3313-0077
Fax: 3314-8277
Kosher grocery, provisions and delicatessen. Catering for groups, twenty persons plus.

MIKVAOT
12 Krystalgade 1172   3393-7662; 3332-9443
Jewish Community Centre
Ny Kongensgade 6 1472   3312-8868
Fax: 3312-3357

SYNAGOGUES
Orthodox
Machsike Hadass
Ole suhrsgade 12 1354   3315-3117
Fax: 4396-9729
Email: machsike-hadas@subnet.dk
Web site: www.machsike-hadas.subnet.dk
Daily and Shabbat services.

The Great Synagogue of Copenhagen
12 Krystalgade 1172   3929-9520
Fax: 3229-2517
Email: bent_lexner@hotmail.com
Daily and Shabbat services.

HOTELS
Kosher
Hotel Villa Strand
Kystvej 12 3100   2176-8680
Fax: 4596-9137

SYNAGOGUES
Granavenget 8   4220-0731
Open from Shavuot to Succot.

Hornbaek

A resort and seaside town where many members
of the Copenhagen community spend the
summer months, or weekends. It is the area of
the coast from which the Jewish community
escaped in 1943.

STRAND HOTEL
HORNBAEK, DENMARK

Situated 48 km from Copenhagen. Suites and family rooms
(parents/child). Balcony or garden rooms. Danish–Jewish cuisine.
Mikveh and synagogue on premises. Tennis and golf nearby and a
special playground for children. Special Pesach package 16–25
April. Shavout 4–9 June. Kosher Mehadrin Machsike Hadas.

Tel: 00 45 21 76 86 80 Fax: 00 45 96 91 37
Sundays and evenings: 00 45 33 24 11 08
10/3-18/9-Season tel & fax 00 45 49 70 00 88

DOMINICAN REPUBLIC

Jewish settlement in the Dominican Republic is comparatively late; the oldest Jewish grave dates back to 1826. Descended from central European Jews, the community was not religious and many married Christians. President Francisco Henriquez y Carvajal (1916) traced his ancestry back to the early Jewish settlers.

In 1938 the republic decided to accept refugees from Nazism (one of the very few countries of the world that did so freely), and even provided areas where they could settle. As a result, there were 1,000 Jews living there in 1943. This number declined as, once again, the Jewish community assimilated and married the local non-Jewish population. Despite this, many non-Jewish husbands, wives and children take part in Jewish events.

Two synagogues and a rabbi who divides his time between them are features of Jewish life. There is also a Sunday school in Santo Domingo and a bi-monthly magazine is produced. There is a small Jewish museum in Sosua.

GMT -4 hours	Total Population 8,097,000
Country calling code (1 809)	Jewish Population 150
Emergency Telephone (Police – 999) (Fire – 999) (Ambulance – 999)	(Electricity voltage – 220/240)

Santo Domingo

COMMUNITY ORGANISATIONS
Consejo Dominicano de Mujeres Hebreas
PO Box 2189   (809) 535-6042
Fax: (809) 688-2058

EMBASSY
Embassy of Israel
Av. Pedro Henriquez Urena 80 1404
(809) 542-1635; 542-1548

SYNAGOGUES
Conservative
Centro Israelita de la Republica Dominicana
Av. Ciudad de Sarasota 21, Belle Vista (809) 535-6042
Email: lalo@codetel.net.do

Sosua

SYNAGOGUES
Liberal
Calle Alejo Martinez, El Batey   (809) 533-0168
Fax: (809) 533-0168
Services; Monthly, Last Friday and Saturday.

ECUADOR

As in most Latin American countries, Conversos comprised the earliest Jewish settlers in Ecuador. It was not until 1904 that East European Jews began to arrive, and numbers increased further following the Nazi take-over in Germany, as Ecuador granted refuge to more Jews than other neighbouring countries. About 3,000 Jews entered Ecuador in the 1930s. The Jewish population peaked in 1950 at 4,000, but this number declined owing to emigration. In recent years, some Jews have moved to Ecuador from elsewhere in South America.

There are no Jewish schools, but children do have access to Jewish education.

GMT -5 hours	Total Population 11,937,000
Country calling code (593)	Jewish Population 1,000
Emergency Telephone (Police – 101) (Fire – 102) (Ambulance – 131)	(Electricity voltage – 110/220)

Quito

COMMUNITY ORGANISATIONS
Communidad Judia del Ecuador
Calle Roberto Andrade, OE3 580 y Jaime, Roldos
Urbanizacion Einstein (Carcelen)   (2) 2483-800
Fax: (2) 2486-755
Email: aiq@uio.satnet.net

EMBASSY
Embassy of Israel
Av. Eloy Alfaro 969, Casilla 2463
(2) 547-322 & 548-431

EGYPT

For more than 2,000 years there has been a virtually continuous Jewish presence in the vicinity of Cairo and an even more ancient Jewish presence in Egypt is recounted in the Bible. After the exodus, Jews returned to Egypt during the time of Alexander the Great and at that time the Ben Ezra synagogue was built. The Bible was translated into Greek during that period. In the first century CE, the Jewish presence declined but a renaissance occurred with Moses Maimonides's arrival in Egypt in the twelfth century. Most of his books were written in Cairo and his yeshiva still exists in the Jewish quarter. From then on, the Jewish community expanded and flourished, especially with the arrival of refugees from pogroms and during the First and Second World Wars.

Before 1948 there were about 70,000 Jews in Egypt. The 1956 Suez War and the 1967 Six Day War encouraged Jewish emigration. At present, the community is small but the Jewish heritage, mostly synagogues classified as antiquities, represents an inestimable treasure worth visiting, as, for example, the recently restored Ben Ezra synagogue, home of the world-famous Genizah of some 400,000 documents (the majority of which are now in Cambridge, England).

GMT +2 hours	Total Population 67,974,000
Country calling code (20)	Jewish Population Under 100
	(Electricity voltage – 220)

Alexandria

SYNAGOGUES
Eliahu Hanavi
69 Nebi Daniel Street, Ramla Station
(3) 492-3974; 597-4438

Cairo

Cairo, has had a long and important Jewish history. The community has however declined in line with the rest of Egyptian Jewry. However, there are a number of interesting sites, such as the recently restored Ben Ezra Synagogue, where the Cairo Genizah used to be located.

COMMUNITY ORGANISATIONS
13 Rue Sabyl El Khazindar, Abbassieh
(2) 824-613 & 824-885
Web site: www.geocities.com

EMBASSY
Embassy of Israel
6 Ibn Malek St., Gizeh
(2) 3610528
Fax: (2) 3610414
Email: isremcai@mail.rite.com

SYNAGOGUES
Ben-Ezra
6 Harett il-Sitt Barbara, Mari Girges, Old Cairo
(2) 847-695
The synagogue was built in 1892 and is the oldest in Egypt. According to legend under the building is the site where Pharaoh's daughter found Moses.

Meir Enaim
55 No.13 Street, Maadi
Under the supervision of the Jewish Community of Cairo and can be visited on request.

Shaarei Hashamayim
17 Adli Pasha Street, Downtown Cairo (2) 392-9025
Fax: (2) 736-9639
Services are held on holidays. There is an interesting library across from the synagogue, which is only accessible with a key. Ask the guards.

EL SALVADOR

The Jewish connection to El Salvador is not a strong one. It is believed that some Portuguese Conversos crossed the country a few hundred years ago. After that, some Sephardis from France moved to Chaluchuapa. Other Jews came from Europe, but in smaller numbers than those settling in other Latin American countries. There were only 370 Jews in 1976, a number reduced during the civil war, when many emigrated. Some returned, however, when the war was over.

An official community was set up in 1944 and a synagogue was opened in 1950.

El Salvador is one of the few countries to have an embassy in Jerusalem, rather than Tel Aviv.

GMT -6 hours	Total Population 5,928,000
Country calling code (503)	Jewish Population 120
Emergency Telephone (Police – 123) (Fire – 123) (Ambulance – 123)	(Electricity voltage – 110)

San Salvador

EMBASSY
Embassy of Israel
85 Av. Norte, No 619   238-770; 239-221

SYNAGOGUES
Conservative
23 Blvd. del Hipodromo 626, Colonia San Benito
237-366
Friday evening services only.

Comunidad Israelita de El Salvador
Boulevard del Hipodromo 626 # 1, Colonia San
Benito, PO Box 06-182   263-8074
Fax: 264-5499
Email: cisraelita@yahoo.com
Services Friday, Shabbat Morning and Holy Days.

ESTONIA

Despite being the only country officially declared 'Judenrein' (free of Jews) at the Wannsee conference in 1942, there is a Jewish community here today. The community has always been small, and is believed to have begun in the fourteenth century. However, most Jews arrived in the nineteenth century, when Czar Alexander II allowed certain groups of Jews into the area.

The first community was established in Tallinn in 1830. By 1939, the community had grown to 4,500 and was free from restraints. After the Soviet and Nazi occupations in the Second World War the Jews returned, mainly from the Soviet Union. Now that Estonia is independent, the Jewish community is able to practise its religion freely.

GMT +2 hours	Total Population 1,454,000
Country calling code (372)	Jewish Population 2,500
Emergency Telephone (Police – 002 in Tallinn, 02 elsewhere)	
(Fire – 001 in Tallinn, 01 elsewhere) (Ambulance – 003 in Tallinn, 03 elsewhere)	(Electricity voltage – 220)

Tallinn

COMMUNITY ORGANISATIONS
Jewish Community of Estonia
Karu Street 16, PO Box 3576 10507   (6) 623-034
Fax: (6) 623-034

Email: ciljal@icom.ee
Publishes a monthly, called 'Hashaher', in Estonian and operates a radio programme on Radio 4 (Thursday 10:15pm-11:00pm). Information on vegetarian restaurants available.

SYNAGOGUES
Orthodox
16A Karu Street, PO Box 3576 10120   (6) 623-050
Fax: (6) 623-001
Email: rabbi@jewishestonia.com

ETHIOPIA

The Falashas (Ge'ez for 'stranger', applied to the Ethiopian Jews) of Ethiopia became known world-wide in the early 1980s, when many were airlifted to Israel. The origins of the Beta Israel, as they call themselves, are unclear and little is known for certain. Historians have concluded that they may have become Jewish as early as the second or third century.

As the area became known to the West through nineteenth-century explorers, some Western Jews set up schools in the country. The Jewish population was believed to have been about 50,000 in 1934. After the establishment of Israel, more interest was taken in the Ethiopian community and the Ethiopian civil war was the catalyst for Operation Moses, when 10,000 people were airlifted to Israel in 1984-85. A further 15,000 left for Israel in 1991.

GMT +2 hours	**Total Population 63,495,000**
Country calling code (251)	**Jewish Population 500**
	(Electricity voltage – 220)

Addis Ababa

COMMUNITY ORGANISATIONS
PO Box 50   (1) 111-725 & 446-471

FIJI

When Henry Marks, at the age of 20, moved to Fiji from Australia in 1881, he was the first recorded Jew on the island. Over the years, he developed a successful business across the region, and was later knighted.

Indian and other Jews later moved to Fiji but did not organise any official community. In recent years the Fiji Jewish Association has been created. The Israeli embassy organises an annual Seder.

GMT +12 hours	**Total Population 772,000**
Country calling code (679)	**Jewish Population Under 100**
Emergency Telephone (Police – 000) (Fire – 000) (Ambulance – 000)	**(Electricity voltage – 240)**

Suva

COMMUNITY ORGANISATIONS
Fiji Jewish Association
PO Box 882, Suva   387-980
                              Fax: 387-946
                    Email: contex@is.com.fj

FINLAND

When Finland was occupied by Russia in the nineteenth century, many Jewish conscripts in the Russian army settled in Finland after their discharge. They were still subject to several restrictions, but these ended after Finland's independence in 1917. In addition to these 'Cantonists', as they were known, immigrants came to Finland from eastern Europe. Finland proved a safe haven, as the government refused to hand over Finnish Jews to the Nazis, despite being allied to Germany in its war with Soviet Russia.

The community is keen to preserve a sense of Jewish identity among the young generation, who are encouraged to experience Jewish life in Israel. The community is also keen to help other Jews in the newly independent Baltic states across the sea to the south of the country. There is a central body for Jewish communities, and kosher food is available. There are also a school and synagogues.

GMT +2 hours	**Total Population 5,140,000**
Country calling code (358)	**Jewish Population 1,200**
Emergency Telephone (Police – 10022) (Fire – 112) (Ambulance – 112)	**(Electricity voltage – 220)**

Helsinki

Some 1,200 Jews (the majority of the Jewish population in Finland) live in Helsinki. The community centre is next to the synagogue. There is also a Jewish cemetery containing an area dedicated to the Jews who fought in the Finnish army in various wars, including the Russo-Finnish war.

DELICATESSEN
Community Centre
Malminkatu 26   (9) 586-0310
Fax: (9) 694-8916
Email: srk@jchelsinki.fi
Web site: www.jchelsinki.fi

EMBASSY
Embassy of Israel
Vironkatu 5A 00170   (9) 681-2020
Fax: (9) 135-6959
Email: israemb@pp.htu.fi

MONUMENT
A monument was unveiled in 2000 in a park opposite the harbour where Jewish refugees were deported in 1942 to Germany

RESTAURANTS
Kosher Deli
Malminkatu 24   (9) 685-4584
Fax: (9) 694-8916
Email: srk@jchelsinki.fi
Hours: Wednesday 1.00pm to 5.00pm, Thursday 9.00am to 5.00pm and Friday 9.00am to 2.00pm.

SYNAGOGUES
Orthodox
Jewish Community Synagogue
Malminkatu 26 00100   (9) 586-0310
Fax: (9) 694-8916
Email: srk@jchelsinki.fi
Built in 1906. Preserved in the synagogue is a wreath presented in 1944 by the then President of Finland in memory of Jews who died in the Russo-Finnish War. Services Monday and Thursday morning, 7:45 am, other weekdays 8 am; Friday evening, 7 pm (summer), 5 pm (winter); Shabbat and Sunday mornings, 9 am.

Turku

SYNAGOGUES
Brahenkatu 17   (2) 231-2557
Fax: (2) 233-4689
The secretary is always pleased to meet visitors.

FRANCE

France now boasts the largest Jewish community in Europe. The Jewish connection with France is a long one: it dates back over 1,000 years as there is evidence of Jewish settlement in several towns in the first few centuries of the Jewish Diaspora. The community grew in early medieval times, and contributed to the economy of the region. Two great Jewish commentators, Rashi and Rabenu Tam, both lived in France. However, French Jewry suffered both from the Crusaders and from other anti-semitic outbursts in the medieval period.

Napoleon's reign heralded the emancipation of French Jewry and, as his armies conquered Europe, the emancipation of other communities began. Despite this, incidents such as the Dreyfus Affair highlighted the fact that anti-semitism was not yet dead. The worst case of anti-semitism in France occurred under the German occupation, when some 70,000 Jews were deported from the community of 300,000. After the war, France became a centre for Jewish immigration, beginning with 80,000 from eastern Europe, and then many thousands from North Africa, which eventually swelled the Jewish population to nearly 700,000.

The community is well served with organisations. Paris alone has 380,000 Jews, more than in the whole of the UK. There are many kosher restaurants, synagogues in many towns throughout the country, newspapers, radio programmes and schools in several cities. In Carpentras and Cavaillon there are synagogues which are considered to be national monuments.

GMT +1 hour	**Total Population 58,607,000**
Country calling code (33)	**Jewish Population 600,000**
Emergency Telephone (Police – 17) (Fire – 18) (Ambulance – 15)	**(Electricity voltage – 220)**

NORTH EAST

Amiens

SYNAGOGUES
38 rue du Port d'Amont 8000

Bar-le-Duc

SYNAGOGUES
7 Quai Carnot

Beauvais

SYNAGOGUES
Rue Jules Isaac 60000   03.44.05.46.90

Belfort

COMMUNITY ORGANISATIONS
27 rue Strolz 90000   03.84.28.55.41
                                       Fax: 03.84.28.55.41
Publishes 'Notre Communaute' (quarterly)

SYNAGOGUES
6 rue de l'As-de-Carreau 90000   03.84.28.55.41
                                       Fax: 03.84.28.55.41

Benfeld

SYNAGOGUES
7a rue de la Dime 67230   03.88.74.47.11

Besancon

BUTCHERS
M. Croppet
18 rue des Granges 25000   03.81.83.35.93
Thursdays only.

COMMUNITY ORGANISATIONS
10 rue Grosjean 25000   03.81.80.82.82

SYNAGOGUES
23c Quai de Strasbourg 25000

Bitche

SYNAGOGUES
28 rue de Sarreguemines 57230
Services, Rosh Hashana & Yom Kippur.

Boulay

SYNAGOGUES
Rue du Pressoir 57220   03.87.79.28.34

Boulogne-sur-Mer

SYNAGOGUES
63 rue Charles Butor 62200

Bouzonville

SYNAGOGUES
3 rue des Benedictins 57320

Chalon-sur-Saone

SYNAGOGUES
10 rue Germiny 71100

Chalons-sur-Marne

SYNAGOGUES
21 rue Lochet 51000

Chambery

SYNAGOGUES
44 rue St-Real 73000
Services, Friday, 7pm and festivals.

Colmar

COMMUNITY ORGANISATIONS
3 rue de la Cigogne 68000   03.89.41.38.29
                          Fax: 03.89.41.12.96
Kosher food can be purchased in the community
centre on Wednesdays and Thursdays. Kosher
restaurant; Wednesday noon during the school
period.

SYNAGOGUES
3 rue de la Cigogne 68000   03.89.41.38.29
                          Fax: 03.89.41.12.96

Compiegne

SYNAGOGUES
4 rue du Dr.-Charles-Nicolle 60200

Dieuze

SYNAGOGUES
Av. Foch 57260

Dijon

BUTCHERS
Albert Levy
25 rue de la Manutention 21000   03.80.30.14.42

SYNAGOGUES
5 rue de la Synagogue 21000   03.80.66.46.47
Mikva on premises.

TOURIST SITE
Archaeological Museum
Has an important collection of old Jewish
tombstones.

Dunkirk

SYNAGOGUES
19 rue Jean-Bart 59140

Epernay

SYNAGOGUES
2 rue Placet 51200   03.26.55.24.44
Services, Yom Kippur only.

Epinal

SYNAGOGUES
9 rue Charlet 88000   03.29.82.25.23

Faulquemont-Crehange

SYNAGOGUES
Place de l'Hotel de Ville 57380
Services, festivals & High Holydays only.

Forbach

SYNAGOGUES
98 Av. St.-Remy 57600   03.87.85.25.57

Grosbliederstroff

SYNAGOGUES
6 rue des Fermes 57520

Hagondange

SYNAGOGUES
Rue Henri-Hoffmann 57300

Haguenau

SYNAGOGUES
3 rue du Grand-Rabbin-Joseph-Bloch 67500
03.88.73.38.30

Ingwiller

SYNAGOGUES
Cours du Chateau 67340

Insming

SYNAGOGUES
Rue de la Synagogue 57670

Lille

GROCERIES
Monoprix
Shopping Centre Euralille, rue du Molinel 59000
03.20.06.81.25

SYNAGOGUES
5 rue Auguste-Angellier 59012   03.20.51.12.52
Fax: 03.20.31.35.46
Mikva on premises. Phone 03.20.85.27.37.

Luneville

SYNAGOGUES
Orthodox
5 rue Castara 54300   03.83.74.08.07
The synagogue built in 1785 has been listed as an historic monument.

Merlebach

SYNAGOGUES
19 rue St-Nicolas 57800

Metz

BUTCHERS
Claude Sebbag
22 rue Mangin, Moselle 57000   03.87.63.33.50
Supervision: Chief Rabbi of Moselle

GROCERIES
Atac
23 rue de 20e Corps Américain, Moselle 57000

Galaries Lafayette
4 rue Winston Churchill, Moselle 57000
03.87.38.60.60

MIKVAOT
30 rue Kellerman
Mme Rivkah Elalouf, Tel: 03.87.32.38.04

RELIGIOUS ORGANISATIONS
Rabbi Bruno Fizon
27/29 en Jurue, Moselle 57000   03.87.36.43.82

SYNAGOGUES
Adass Yechouroun
41 rue de Rabbin Elie-Bloch, Moselle 57000

Main Synagogue and Community Centre
39 rue du Rabbin Elie-Bloch, Moselle 57000
03.87.75.04.44

Montbeliard

SYNAGOGUES
Rue de la Synagogue 25200

Mulhouse

SYNAGOGUES
2 rue des Rabbins 68100   03.89.66.21.22
Fax: 03.89.56.63.49
Mikva on premises. The old cemetery is also worth a visit.

Nancy

COMMUNITY ORGANISATIONS
Communal Centre
19 blvd Joffre 54000   03.83.32.10.67

MIKVAOT
53 rue Hoche   03.83.41.34.48
Mme Myriam Dahan

MUSEUMS
The Musee Historique Lorrain
64 Grand rue 54000
Whilst Jewish buildings were plundered in 1944 an important Jewish collection in the museum survived.

RESTAURANTS
Restaurante Universitaire
19 blvd Joffre 54000   03.83.32.10.67
Open weekdays at noon.

SYNAGOGUES
17 blvd Joffre 54000   03.83.32.10.67

Obernai

SYNAGOGUES
Rue de Selestat 67210

TOURIST SITE
41, rue du General-Gouraud
There are the remains of an old synagogue.

Phalsbourg

SYNAGOGUES
16 rue Alexandre-Weill 57370

Reims

SYNAGOGUES
49 rue Clovis 51100   03.26.47.68.47

Saint-Avold

CEMETERIES
The American Military Cemetery

Contains many graves of the USA servicemen who
fell in the Second World War.

SYNAGOGUES
Pl. Saint-Nabor 57500   03.87.91.16.16

Saint-Die

SYNAGOGUES
Rue de l'Eveche 88100
Services, festivals and Holy-days only.

Saint-Louis

CEMETERIES
The Hegenheim Cemetary
This cemetery dates from 1673.

COMMUNITY ORGANISATIONS
19 rue du Temple 68300   03.89.70.00.48
Kosher products available.

SYNAGOGUES
Rue de la Synagogue 68300

Orthodox
3 rue de General Cassagnou 68300   03.89.69.07.05
                                   Fax: 03.89.70.15.15
Kosher shop Tel: 03.89.70.00.48

Saint-Quentin

SYNAGOGUES
11 ter blvd Henri-Martin   03.23.08.30.72

Sarrebourg

SYNAGOGUES
12 rue du Sauvage

Sarreguemines

SYNAGOGUES
Rue Georges-V 57200   03.87.98.81.40
Mikva on premises.

Saverne

SYNAGOGUES
Rue du 19 Novembre 67700

Sedan-Charleville

SYNAGOGUES
6 av. de Verdun 08200

Selestat

SYNAGOGUES
4 rue Ste.-Barbe 67600

Sens

SYNAGOGUES
14 rue de la Grande-Juiverie 89100   03.86.95.16.65

Strasbourg

With a Jewish population of 16,000, this city,
contested by France and Germany throughout
history, currently has an important Jewish
community, with several kosher restaurants,
butchers and even a kosher vineyard. The earliest
evidence of jewish life dates from 1188. A
thirteenth century Mikvahhh was recently
discovered.

BAKERIES
Crousty Cash
4 rue Sellénick, Bas-Rhin 67000   03.88.35.68.21

BOOKSELLERS
Fraenckel
19 rue du Marechal-Foch 67000   03.88.36.38.39
                                   Fax: 03.88.37.96.60

Schne-or
15 rue de Bitche 67000   03.88.37.32.37
        Fax: 03.88.35.63.11
      Email: nfraenckel@aol.com
Also Judaica antiquities.

BUTCHERS

Buchinger
63 rue du Faubourg de Pierre 67000 03.88.32.85.03
13 rue Wimpheling 67000   03.88.61.06.98

David
20 rue Sellenick 67000   03.88.36.75.01

FB Espace Casher
2-4 Av. Foret Noire 67000   03.90.41.18.68
        Fax: 03.90.41.19.69

COFFEE SHOP

Coffee Shop
4 rue Strauss-Durkheim 67000

GROCERIES

Cash Center
22 rue Finkmatt 67000   03.88.35.12.38

Yarden
13 Blvd. de la Marne 67000 03.88.60.10.10
        Fax: 03.88.61.71.11

MEDIA

Newspaper
Echos-Unir
1a rue du Grand-Rabbin-Rene-Hirschler 67000
        03.88.14.46.50
        Fax: 03.88.24.26.69
Monthly publication.

MIKVAOT

1a rue du Grand-Rabbin-Rene-Hirschler 67000
        03.88.14.46.68

MUSEUMS

Musee Alsacien
23, quai Saint-Nicolas 67000 03.88.52.50.01
        Fax: 03.88.43.64.18
   Web site: www.musees-strasbourg.org
Has a section on Jewish Art.

Musee Judeo-Alsacien
62a, Grand Rue, Bouxwiller 67330 03.88.70.97.17
        Fax: 03.88.70.97.17
   Web site: www.sdv.fr/judaisme
Visiting hours: from Easter to mid September:
Tuesday to Friday from 10.00 am to 12 noon and 2.00
pm to 5.00 pm. Sundays from 2.00 pm to 6.00 pm.
The museum, which is housed in an old synagogue,
traces the history of the Jews of Alsace.

RELIGIOUS ORGANISATIONS

Consistoire Israelite du Bas-Rhin
23 rue Sellenick 67000   03.88.25.05.75
        Fax: 03.88.25.12.75
      Email: cibr1@libertysurf.fr

Regional Chief Rabbi, Rene Gutman
5 rue du General-de-Castelnau 67000 03.88.25.05.75
        Fax: 03.88.25.12.65
      Email: cibri1@libertysurf.fr

RESTAURANTS

Restaurant Universitaire
ORT-Laure Weil, 11 rue Sellenick 67000
        03.88.76.74.76
        Fax: 03.88.76.74.74
    Email: ort.strasbourg@ort.asso.fr

Dairy
Autre Part
60, blvd Clemenceau   03.88.37.10.02

Meat
Le King
28 rue Sellenick 67000   03.88.52.17.71

SYNAGOGUES

**There are in all more than fifteen synagogues in
Strasbourg; the following are among the largest
and oldest.**

Esplanade
17, rue de Nicosie 67000

Ets Hayim
7, rue Turenne 67000   03.88.24.38.36
        Fax: 03.88.24.38.36
      Email: etzhaim@free.fr

Synagogue de la Paix
1a rue du Grand-Rabbin-Rene-Hirschler 67000
        03.88.14.46.50
        Fax: 03.88.24.26.69
      Email: cis@media-net.fr

Thionville

SYNAGOGUES

31 av. Clemenceau 57100   03.82.54.47.89
        Fax: 03.82.53.03.76

Toul

SYNAGOGUES

Rue de la Halle 54200

Troyes

MEMORIAL

A statue of Rashi stands in place Jean Moulin.

MIKVAOT
15 rue Brunneval 03.25.73.34.44

SYNAGOGUES
5 rue Brunneval
The only half-timbered shul in France.

Valenciennes

SYNAGOGUES
36 rue de l'Intendance 59300 03.27.29.11.07

Verdun

SYNAGOGUES
Impasse des Jacobins 55100 03.83.41.34.48

Vittel

SYNAGOGUES
211 rue Croix-Perrot 88800 03.29.08.10.87
Open in July and August only.

Wasselonne

SYNAGOGUES
Rue des Bains 67310

NORTH WEST

Angers

SYNAGOGUES
12 rue Valdemaine 49100

Bischeim-Schiltigheim

SYNAGOGUES
9 Place de la Synagogue 67800 02.38.33.02.87

Brest

SYNAGOGUES
40 rue de la Republic 29200
Services, Friday, 7:30pm.

Caen

BUTCHERS
Boucherie Marcel
26 Rue de l'Engannerie 14000 02.31.86.16.25

SYNAGOGUES
46 Av. de la Liberation 14000 02.31.43.60.54

Chateauroux

CONTACT INFORMATION
Michel Touati
3 Allee Emile Zola, Montierchaume, Deols 36130
02.54.26.05.47

Deauville

RESTAURANTS
King J.J.
23 Rue Gambetta 14800 02.31.87.46.48

SYNAGOGUES
14 rue Castor 14800 02.31.81.27.06

Elbeuf

SYNAGOGUES
29 rue Gremont 76500 02.35.77.09.11

Le Havre

GROCERIES
Super U Porte Oceane
Bd Francois 1 er 02.35.21.31.35

SYNAGOGUES
38 rue Victor-Hugo 76600 02.35.21.14.59

Le Mans

SYNAGOGUES
4-6 Blvd. Paixhans 72000 02.43.86.00.96

Lorient

SYNAGOGUES
18 rue de la Patrie 56100
Services, Friday nights, festivals & Holy Days only.

Nantes

SYNAGOGUES
5 Impasse Copernic 44000 02.41.87.48.10
Fax: 02.41.37.11.79

Mikva on premises.

Orleans

SYNAGOGUES
14 rue Robert-de-Courtenay, (to the left of the
cathedral) 45000
Information on services to be had from Marcus
Sellem 02.62.89.18.

Rennes

COMMUNITY ORGANISATIONS

Centre Edmond Safra
Rue de la Heronniere, 5, Allee du Mont dol 35000
02.99.63.57.18
Services held. Telephone for times.

Rouen

SYNAGOGUES
55 rue des Bons-Enfants 76100   02.35.71.01.44
The Jewish Youth Club can provide board residence
for student travellers and holiday-makers.

TOURIST SITE

Old Jewish Quarter
Excavations in the 1970's uncovered the ruins of what
is the only known medieval Jewish structure whose
walls have survived. Now called "The house of the
Jews" it is considered to most likely have been a
yeshiva but it may in fact have been a synagogue.

Tours

COMMUNITY ORGANISATIONS
Community Centre
6 rue Chalmel 37000   02.47.05.59.07

SYNAGOGUES
37 rue Parmentier 37000   02.47.05.56.95

PARIS

The city of Paris is divided into districts
(*arrondissements*) designated by the last two
digits of the postcode. In the categories below,
establishments are listed in numerical order
according to the postcode (that is, -01, -02, -03
and so on).

The historic centre of Paris Jewish life is found
in the Marais area (fourth *arrondissement*)
although a synagogue stood on the Ile de la Cite
before Notre Dame, Jews having lived in the city
since Roman times. Another more central area is
that around rue Richer (ninth *arrondissement*),
which although not historic as such has many
kosher restaurants of varying styles and prices.

A most important new site to be visited is the
Musee d'art et d'histoire du Judaisme which
opened in December 1998.

BAKERIES

Korcarz
29 rue des Rosiers 75004   01.42.77.39.47
                                   Fax: 01.48.58.28.44
Supervision: Beth Din of Paris/Chief Rabbi Mordechai
Rottenberg

Mezel
1 rue Ferdinand Duval 75004   01.42.78.25.01
Supervision: Beth Din of Paris

Douieb
11 bis rue Geoffroy Marie 75009   01.47.70.86.09
Supervision: Beth Din of Paris

Golan
10 rue Geoffroy Marie 75009   01.48.00.94.71
Supervision: Beth Din of Paris

Korcarz
25 rue Trévise 75009   01.42.46.83.33
Supervision: Beth Din of Paris/Chief Rabbi Mordechai
Rottenberg

Les Ailes
34 rue Richer 75009   01.47.70.62.53
Supervision: Beth Din of Paris

Zazou
20 rue du Faubourg Montmartre 75009
01.47.70.81.32
Supervision: Beth Din of Paris

Mendez
3 Ter rue de la Présentation 75011   01.43.57.02.03
Supervision: Beth Din of Paris

Nathan de Belleville
67 blvd de Belleville 75011   01.43.57.24.60
Supervision: Beth Din of Paris

Charles Tr. Patissier
10 rue Corentin Cariou 75019   01.47.97.51.83
Supervision: Beth Din of Paris

Kadoche
2 av. Corentin Cariou 75019   01.40.37.00.14
Supervision: Beth Din of Paris

Le Relais Sucre
135 rue Manin 75019   01.42.41.20.98
Supervision: Beth Din of Paris

Mat'amim
17 rue de Crimée 75019   01.42.40.89.11
Supervision: Beth Din of Paris

Medayo
71 rue de Meaux 75019   01.40.03.04.20
Supervision: Beth Din of Paris

Lilo
20 rue Desnoyer 75020   01.47.97.63.20
Supervision: Beth Din of Paris

Nani
104 blvd de Belleville 75020   01.47.97.38.05
Supervision: Beth Din of Paris

BUTCHERS

Saada
17 rue des Rosiers 75004   01.42.77.76.22

Adolphe
14 rue Richer 75009   01.48.24.86.33

Berbeche
46 rue Richer 75009   01.47.70.50.58

Charlot
33 rue Richer 75009 — 01.45.23.10.34

La Charolaise Richer
51 rue Richer 75009 — 01.47.70.01.57

La Rose Blanche
43 rue Richer 75009 — 01.48.24.84.65

Chez Jacques
19 rue Bouchardon 75010 — 01.42.06.76.13

Charly Halak B. Y.
51 rue Richard Lenoir 75011 — 01.43.48.62.26

Chez Andre
69 blvd de Belleville 75011 — 01.43.57.80.38

Chez Jojo
20 rue Louis Bonnet 75011 — 01.43.55.10.29

Maurice Zirah
91 rue de la Roquette 75011 — 01.43.79.62.53

Boucherie Guy
266 rue de Charenton 75012 — 01.43.44.60.90

J V (Temim)
2 rue de Dr Goujon 75012 — 01.43.45.78.77

Berbeche
5 rue Vandrezanne 75013 — 01.45.88.86.50
6 rue du Moulinet 75013 — 01.45.80.89.10

Boucherie Claude
174 rue Lecourbe 75015 — 01.48.28.02.00

Gm Levy
83 rue de Lonchamp 75016 — 01.45.53.04.24

Kassab
88 blvd Murat 75016 — 01.40.71.07.34

Ste Delicatess
209 av. de Versailles 75016 — 01.44.40.07.59

Berbeche
39 rue Jouffroy 75017 — 01.44.40.07.59

Espaces Courses Elles
177 rue de Courcelles 75017 — 01.47.63.36.26

Krief
104 rue Legendre 75017 — 01.46.27.15.57

Andre Manin
135 rue Manin 75019 — 01.42.38.00.43

Aux Viandes Cacheres
6 av. Corentin Cariou 75019 — 01.40.36.02.41

Berbeche
15/17 rue Henri Ribiere 75019 — 01.42.08.06.06

Emsalem
17 quai de la Gironde 75019 — 01.40.36.56.64
18 rue Corentin Cariou 75019 — 01.40.36.56.64

Boucherie Smadja
90 blvd de Belleville 75020 — 01.46.36.25.36

Henrino
122 blvd de Belleville 75020 — 01.47.97.24.52

EMBASSY

Embassy of Israel
3 rue Rabelais 75008 — 01.40.76.55.00
Fax: 01.40.76.55.55
Email: info@amb-israel.fr

GROCERIES

Doueib
11 bis rue Geoffroy Marie 75009 — 01.47.70.86.09

Francois
45 rue Richer 75009 — 01.47.70.17.43

Le Haim
6 rue Paulin Enfert 75013 — 01.44.24.53.34

Keter David
5, rue Benjamin Franklin 75016 — 01.42.24.04.42
Fax: 01.42.24.04.41

Chekel
14 av. de Villiers 75017 — 01.48.88.94.97
Supervision: Beth Din of Paris
Also sells delicatessen and sandwiches. Hours: 9 am to 8 pm. Nearest Metro: Villiers. Near Champs-Elysées/Opéra.

Compt Pdts Alimentaires
111 av. de Villiers 75017 — 01.42.27.16.91

Chochana
54 av. Secretan 75019

HOTELS

Hôtel Aida Opéra
17 rue du Conservatoire 75009 — 01.45.23.11.11
Fax: 01.45.70.38.73
Email: reservation@aida-opera.com
Supervision: Beth Din of Paris.
Kosher breakfast.

Hotel Geoffroy-Marie Opera
12 rue Geoffroy-Marie 75009   01.47.70.11.85
                                Fax: 01.42.46.09.36
                        Email: hotelgmopera@wanadoo.fr
Supervision: Beth Din of Paris
Breakfast / Brunch is open to non residents.

Hotel Touring
21 rue Buffault 75009   01.48.78.09.16
                        Fax: 01.48.78.27.74
                Email: infos@hotel-touring.fr
                Web site: www.hotel-touring.fr

Pavillon De Paris
7 rue de Parme 75009   01.55.31.60.00
                        Fax: 01.55.31.60.01
                Email: mail@pavillondeparis.com
                Web site: www.pavillondeparis.com

L'Hotel de Mericourt
50 rue de la Folie Mericourt 75011   01.43.38.73.63
                        Fax: 01.43.38.66.13
                Email: demericourt.hotel@wanadoo.fr
Situated in an area with many kosher facilities.

LIBRARIES
Library Judaica of the Seminaire Israelite de France
9 rue Vauquelin 75005   01.47.07.22.94
Visit only by appointment.

MIKVAOT
176 rue du Temple 75003   01.42.71.89.28
The mikvah is located in the centre of Paris, near
Place de la République, at the rear of the building.
The staff is English-speaking.

19-21 rue Galvani 75017   01.45.74.52.80

Mayan Hai Source de Vie Haya Mouchka
2-4 rue Tristan Tzara 75018
01.40.38.18.29; 01.46.36.11.09
1 rue des Annelets 75019   01.44.84.05.36
For men and women. Telephone is an answer-
machine, for women only.

Mikve Haya Mouchka
25 rue Riquet 75019   01.40.36.40.92
                        Fax: 01.40.36.88.90
75 rue Julien Lacroix 75020
                01.46.36.39.20; 01.46.36.30.10
For men and women.

MONUMENT
Memorial To The Unknown Jewish Martyr
rue Geoffroy-l'Asnier 17 75004
The memorial is a tribute to the Jews who perished in
the Holocaust. Erected in 1956 it contains the
Archives of the Centre Documentation Juive
Contemporaine. At the centre is an "eternal flame".

MUSEUMS
Musée d'art et d'histoire du Judaisme
Hotel de Saint-Aignan, 71 rue du Temple 75003
                        01.53.01.86.60
                        Fax: 01.42.72.97.47
                Email: info@mahj.org
                Web site: www.mahj.org
Open Monday to Friday from 11 am to 6 pm and
Sunday from 10 am to 6 pm.

Musee Nissim de Camondo
63, rue de Monceau 75008   01.45.63.26.32
Reconstruction of an eighteenth century aristocratic
home. This home and its collections were
bequeathed to France in 1935 by Comte Moise de
Camondo in memory of his son Nissim, who died in
combat in 1917.

RELIGIOUS ORGANISATIONS
Communauté Israélite Orthodoxe de Paris
10 rue Pavée 75004   01.42.77.81.51
                        Fax: 01.48.87.26.29

RESTAURANTS
Dairy
Panini Folie
11 rue du Ponceau 75002   01.42.33.14.55
Supervision: Beth Din of Paris

Contini
42 rue des Rosiers 75004   01.48.04.78.32
Supervision: Beth Din of Paris

Hamman Café
4 rue des Rosiers 75004   01.42.78.04.46
Supervision: Beth Din of Paris

Cine Citta Café
7 rue d'Aguesseau 75008   01.42.68.05.03
Supervision: Beth Din of Paris

Maestro Pizza
19 rue d'Anjou 75008   01.47.42.15.60
Supervision: Beth Din of Paris

Bistrot Blanc
52 rue Blanche 75009   01.42.85.05.30
Supervision: Paris Beth Din

Casa Rina
18 Faubourg Monmartre 75009   01.45.23.02.22
Supervision: Beth Din of Paris

Cine Citta Café
58 rue Richer 75009   01.42.46.09.65
Supervision: Beth Din of Paris

Dizengoff Café
27 rue Richer 75009   01.47.70.81.97
Email: dizengoff@caramail.com
Supervision: Beth Din of Paris
Open from 12:00 am to 10:30 pm

King Salomon
46 rue Richer 75009   01.42.46.31.22
Supervision: Beth Din of Paris

Cocktail Café
82 av. Parmentier 75011   01.43.57.19.94
Supervision: Beth Din of Paris

Le New's
56 av. de la République 75011   01.43.38.63.18
Supervision: Beth Din of Paris

Gin Fizz
157 blvd Serrurier 75019   01.42.00.51.28
Supervision: Beth Din of Paris

Pizza Curial
44 rue Curial 75019   01.40.37.15.00
Supervision: Beth Din of Paris

Meat
Juliette
14 rue Duphot 75001   01.42.60.18.05
     Fax: 01.42.60.18.98
Supervision: Beth Din of Paris

La Petite Famille
32 rue des Rosiers 75003   01.42.77.00.50
Supervision: Beth Din of Paris

Centre Edmond Fleg
8 bis, rue de l'Eperon 75006   01.46.33.43.31
Supervision: Beth Din of Paris

Adolphe
14 rue Richer 75009   01.47.70.91.25
Supervision: Beth Din of Paris

Berbeche Burger
47 rue Richer 75009   01.47.70.81.22
Supervision: Beth Din of Paris

Chez David
11 rue Montyon 75009   01.44.83.01.24
Supervision: Beth Din of Paris

Douieb
11 bis rue Geoffroy Marie 75009   01.47.70.86.09
Supervision: Beth Din of Paris

Georges de Tunis
42 rue Richer 75009   01.47.70.24.64
Supervision: Beth Din of Paris

Le Gros Ventre
7/9 rue Montyon 75009   01.48.24.25.34
Supervision: Beth Din of Paris

Les Ailes
34 rue Richer 75009   01.47.70.62.53
Supervision: Beth Din of Paris

Synagogue Beth El
4 rue Saulnier 75009   01.45.23.34.89
Supervision: Beth Din of Paris
Shabbat meals by arrangement.

Zazou Burger
19 rue du Faubourg Montmartre 75009
     01.40.22.08.33
Supervision: Beth Din of Paris

Cash Food
63 rue des Vinaigriers 75010   01.42.03.95.75
Supervision: Beth Din of Paris

Dolly's Food
9 rue cité Riverain 75010   01.48.03.08.40
Supervision: Beth Din of Paris

Les Cantiques
16 rue Beaurepaire 75010   01.42.40.64.21
Supervision: Beth Din of Paris
Deliver.

Le Cabourg
102 blvd Voltaire 75011   01.47.00.71.43
Supervision: Beth Din of Paris
Hours: 12 pm to 2:30 pm and 7 pm to 11 pm.

Le Lotus de Nissan
39 rue Amelot 75011   01.43.55.80.42
Supervision: Beth Din of Paris

Le Manahattan
231 blvd Voltaire 75011   01.43.56.03.30
Supervision: Beth Din of Paris

Yun-Pana
115 Boulevard Voltaire 75011   01.43.79.20.48
Supervision: Beth Din of Paris

Brasserie du Belvedere
109 av. de Villiers 75017   01.47.64.96.55
Supervision: Beth Din of Paris

Darjeeling
1 bis, rue des Colonels Renard 75017   01.45.72.09.32
     Fax: 01.45.72.03.27
Web site: www.darjeeling-ontable.com
Supervision: Chief Rabbi Mordechai Rottenberg

Fradji
42 rue Poncelet 75017   01.47.54.91.40
Supervision: Beth Din of Paris

Le Chateaubriand
125, rue de Tocqueville 75017   01.47.63.96.90
                                     Fax: 01.47.63.42.55
Supervision: Beth Din of Paris

Nini
24 rue Saussier Leroy 75017   01.46.22.28.93
Supervision: Beth Din of Paris

La Muraille de Chine
44 rue d'Hautpoul 75019   01.42.01.20.30
Supervision: Beth Din of Paris

Mille Delices
52 avenue Secrétan 75019   01.40.18.32.32
Supervision: Beth Din of Paris

Auberge de Belleville
110 blvd de Belleville 75020   01.43.15.02.59
Supervision: Beth Din of Paris

Chez François
5 rue Ramponeau 75020   01.47.97.40.06
Supervision: Beth Din of Paris

Chez Rene et Gabin
92 blvd de Belleville 75020   01.43.58.78.14
Supervision: Beth Din of Paris

Elygel
116 blvd de Belleville 75020   01.47.97.09.73
Supervision: Beth Din of Paris

Le Petit Pelleport
135 rue Pelleport 75020   01.40.33.13.17
Supervision: Beth Din of Paris

Lumieres de Belleville
102 blvd de Belleville 75020   01.47.97.51.83
Supervision: Beth Din of Paris

SYNAGOGUES
Liberal
Union Liberale Israelite de France
24 rue Copernic 75116   01.47.04.37.27
                                     Fax: 01.47.27.81.02
                          Email: communication@ulif.com
                               Web site: www.ulif.com

Masorti
Communaute Juive Massorti de Paris
8 rue George Bernard Shaw (off rue Dupleix) 75015
                                     01.45.67.97.96
                                     Fax: 01.45.56.89.79
                            Email: RuzieDr@aol.com
        Web site: www.jtsa.edu/synagogues/adathsfr/
The Paris Jewish Masorti (Conservative) Community.
Services Friday night 6:30pm. Shabbat morning 10 am
festivals and Rosh Chodesh.

Orthodox
15 rue Notre-Dame de Nazareth 75003
01.42.78.00.30
Fax: 01.42.78.05.18

Groupe Rabbi Yehiel de Paris
25 rue Michel-Leconte 75003   01.42.78.89.17

Adath Yechouroun
25 rue des Rosiers 75004   01.44.59.82.36

Agoudas Hakehilos
10 rue Pavée 75004   01.48.87.21.54
Fax: 01.48.87.26.29
A striking Art Nouveau synagogue designed by
Hector Guimard, the creator of the world famous
Metro entrances, in 1913.

Consistorial Synagogue
14 place des Vosges 75004   01.48.87.79.45
Fax: 01.48.87.57.58
Email: templedesvosges@noos.fr
Web site: www.synadesvosges.com
Possibilities of "Shabbat meals".

Fondation Roger Fleishmann
18 rue des Ecouffes 75004   01.48.87.97.86

**Oratoire Mahziké Adath Mouvement
Loubavitch**
17 rue des Rosiers 75004

Synagogue des Tournelles
21 bis rue des Tournelles 75004
01.42.74.32.65; 01.42.74.32.80
Fax: 01.40.29.90.27
Email: david-halim@septodont.fr

Synagogue Tephilat Israël Frank-Forter
24 rue du Bourg-Tibourg 75004   01.46.24.48.94

Centre Rachi
30 blvd du Port-Royal 75005   01.43.31.98.20

Séminaire Israélite de France
9 rue Vauquelin 75005   01.47.07.21.22
Fax: 01.43.37.75.92

Centre Edmond Fleg
8 bis rue de l'Epéron 75006   01.46.33.43.31
Houses the Union des Centres Communautaires
(UCC), which can be contacted via the same
telephone number. Their fax number is
01.43.25.86.19. Tikvaténou, the Jewish youth
movement of the Consistoire, is also located here,
Tel: 01.46.33.43.24; Fax: 01.43.25.20.59.

E.E.I.F.
27 av. de Ségur 75007   01.47.83.60.33

Hékhal Moché
218-220 rue du Faubourg St-Honoré 75008
01.45.61.20.25
Located behind the Golden Tulip Hotel.

Adass Yereim
10 rue Cadet 75009   01.42.46.36.47; 01.48.74.51.78
Fax: 01.48.74.35.35

Nussach Ashkenez

Beth-El
3 bis rue Saulnier 75009   01.47.70.09.23
Fax: 01.45.23.15.75
Email: bethel@eboom.com

Beth-Israël
4 rue Saulnier 75009   01.45.23.34.89

Centre Communataire De Paris
5 rue Rochechouart 75009   01.49.95.95.92
Fax: 01.42.80.10.66

Grande Synagogue de Paris
44 rue de la Victoire 75009
01.40.82.26.26 ext. 2773 or 01.45.26.95.36
Fax: 01.45.26.95.36
Email: infos@lavictoire.org
Web site: www.lavictoire.org

Kollel Rav Lévy
37 blvd de Strasbourg 75009

Rachi Chull
6 rue Ambroise-Thomas 75009   01.48.24.86.95

Siège du Beth Loubavitch
8 rue Lamartine 75009   01.45.26.87.60
Fax: 01.45.26.24.37

Synagogue Berit Chalom
18 rue Saint-Lazare 75009
01.48.78.45.32; 01.48.78.38.80

Tiferet Yaacob
71 rue de Dunkerque 75009
01.42.81.32.17; 01.42.49.65.12

4 rue Martel 75010
9 rue Guy-Patin 75010   01.42.85.12.74

Rav Pealim (Braslav)
49 blvd de la Villette 75010   01.42.41.55.44

Synagogue Torath-Hayim
130 rue du Faubourg Saint-Martin 75010
01.40.05.98.34

UNAT La Fraternelle
13-15 rue des Petites-Ecuries 75010   01.42.46.65.02

Adath Israël
36 rue Basfroi 75011   01.43.67.89.20

Ets Haim
18 rue Basfroi 75011   01.43.48.82.42

Ora Vesimha
37 rue des Trois-Bornes 75011   01.43.57.49.84

Ozar Hatorath Shoul
40 rue de l'Orillon 75011   01.43.38.73.40
Fax: 01.43.38.36.45

Synagogue Don Isaac Abravanel
84-86 rue de la Roquette 75011   01.47.00.75.95

Chivtei Israel
12-14 Cité Moynet 75012   01.43.43.50.12
Fax: 01.43.47.36.78
Email: ravatlan@club-internet.fr

Névé Chalom
29 rue Sibué 75012   01.43.42.07.70
Fax: 01.43.48.44.50

Oratoire de la Fondation Rothschild (Maison de Retraite)
76 rue de Picpus 75012   01.43.44.72.98
Fax: 01.43.44.71.39

Avoth Ouvanim
59 av. d'Ivry 75013   01.45.82.80.73
Fax: 01.45.85.94.39

Merkaz Beth Myriam
19 rue Domrémy 75013   01.45.86.83.99
Fax: 01.45.86.83.99

223 rue Vercingétorix 75014   01.45.45.50.51
6 bis villa d'Alésia 75014   01.45.40.82.35
Fax: 01.45.40.72.89

Beith Chalom
25 villa d'Alésia 75014   01.45.45.38.71
Fax: 01.43.37.58.49

Ohel Mordekhai
13 rue Fondary 75015   01.40.59.96.56
23 bis rue Dufrénoy 75016
01.45.04.94.00; 01.45.04.66.73

Ohel Avraham
31 rue Montevideo 75016   01.45.05.66.73
Fax: 01.40.72.83.76

Beth Hamidrach Lamed
67 rue Bayen 75017   01.45.74.52.80

Centre Rambam
19-21 rue Galvani 75017   01.45.74.52.80

Synagogue ACIP
42 rue des Saules 75018   01.46.06.71.39
Fax: 01.46.06.71.39

Synagogue de Montmartre
13 rue Sainte-Isaure 75018   01.42.64.48.34

Beth Chalom
11-13 rue Curial 75019
01.40.37.65.16; 01.40.37.12.54

Beth Loubavitch
25 rue Riquet 75019   01.40.36.93.90
Fax: 01.40.36.60.15

53 rue Compans 75019   01.42.02.20.35

Chaare Tora
1 rue Henri-Turot 75019   01.42.06.41.12
Fax: 01.42.06.95.47

Collel Hamabit
7 rue Rouvet 75019   01.40.38.13.59

Heder Loubavitch
25 rue des Solitaires 75019   01.42.02.98.95
Fax: 01.42.02.04.62

Kollel Ysmah Moché
36 rue des Annelets 75019   01.43.63.73.94

Ohaley Yaacov
11 rue Henri-Murger 75019   01.42.49.25.00

Ohr Tora - AJJ
15 rue Riquet 75019   01.40.38.23.36
Fax: 01.40.36.42.23
Email: ajj@free.fr

Ohr Yossef
48, quai de la Marne 75019   01.42.45.74.20
Fax: 01.40.18.10.74

Pah'ad David
11 rue du Plateau 75019   01.42.46.47.03
Fax: 01.42.46.47.56

Synagogue Michkenot Israel
6 rue Jean-Nohain 75019   01.48.03.25.59
Fax: 01.42.00.26.87

Beth Loubavitch
93 rue des Orteaux 75020   01.40.24.10.60

Maor Athora
16 rue Ramponeau 75020   01.47.97.69.42

Ohr Chimchon Raphaël
5 passage Dagorno 75020   01.46.59.39.02
Fax: 01.46.59.14.99

Synagogue Achkenaze & Sephardi
49 rue Pali Kao 75020   01.46.36.30.10

Synagogue Bet Yaacov Yossef
5 square des Cardeurs, 43 rue Saint-Blaise 75020
01.43.56.03.11

Synagogue Michkan-Yaacov
118 boulevard de Belleville 75020   01.43.49.39.59

PARIS REGION

Alfortville

BUTCHERS
Tiness
12 Etienne Dollet, Val-de-Marne 94140
01.49.77.95.79

SYNAGOGUES
Orthodox
1 rue Blanche, Val-de-Marne 94140   01.43.78.86.43

Antony

BUTCHERS
A.B.C.
96 av de la Division Leclerc, Hauts-de-Seine 92160
01.46.66.13.43

SYNAGOGUES
Orthodox
Community Centre and Synagogue
1 rue Sdérot, Angle 1, Rue Barthélémy, Hauts-de-
Seine 92160   01.46.66.19.17

Asnieres

MIKVAOT
82 rue du R.P. Christian-Gilbert, Hauts-de-Seine
92600   01.47.99.26.59

SYNAGOGUES
Orthodox
73 bis rue des Bas, Hauts-de-Seine 92600
01.47.99.32.55

Athis-Mons

SYNAGOGUES
Orthodox
55 rue des Coquelicots, Essonne 91200
01.69.38.14.29

Aulnay-Sous-Bois

SYNAGOGUES
Orthodox
80 rue Maximilien Robespierre, Seine-Saint-Denis
93600   01.48.69.66.93

Bagneux

BAKERIES
Princiane
1 rue de l'Egalité, Parc de Garlande, Hauts-de-Seine
92220   01.47.35.90.77
Fax: 01.47.35.93.67
Email: princiane@princiane.com
Supervision: Beth Din of Paris. Orthodox Union.

BUTCHERS
Isaac
188 av Aristide Briand, Hauts-de-Seine 92220
01.45.47.00.21

Bagnolet

BAKERIES
Sonesta
27 rue Adélaide Lahaye, Seine-Saint-Denis 93170
01.43.64.92.93
Fax: 01.43.60.51.26
Supervision: Beth Din of Paris

SYNAGOGUES
Orthodox
15-17 rue D. Vienot, Seine-Saint-Denis 93170
01.43.60.39.93

Bobigny

RESTAURANTS
Dairy
Chez Daryl
22-24 rue Henri Barbusse, Seine-Saint-Denis 93000
01.48.43.79.00
Supervision: Beth Din of Paris

SYNAGOGUES
Orthodox
11-13 rue Mathurin Renaud, Seine-Saint-Denis 93000
01.48.32.68.86

Bondy

SYNAGOGUES
Orthodox
Maison Communautaire
28 av. de la Villageoise, Seine-Saint-Denis 93140
01.48.47.50.79

Boulogne sur Seine

BAKERIES
Ariel
143 avenue J.B. Clément, Hauts-de-Seine 92100
01.46.04.24.42
Supervision: Beth Din of Paris

GROCERIES
Ednale
28 rue Georges Sorel, Hauts-de-Seine 92100
01.46.03.83.37

SYNAGOGUES
Orthodox
43 rue des Abondances, Hauts-de-Seine 92100
01.46.03.90.63
Fax: 01.46.03.90.63

Champigny

SYNAGOGUES
Orthodox
Synagogue Beth-David
25 av. du Général-de Gaulle, Val-de-Marne 94500
01.48.85.72.29

Charenton-le-Pont

BUTCHERS
Mazel Tov
14 rue Victor Hugo, Val-de-Marne 94220
01.43.68.41.23

Chelles

SYNAGOGUES
Orthodox
14 rue des Anémones, Seine-et-Marne 77500
01.60.20.92.93

Choisy-le-Roi

BUTCHERS
Chez Ilane
131 Marechal de Lattre de Tassigny, Val-de-Marne
94600
01.48.52.27.74

MIKVAOT
28 av. de Newbum, Val-de-Marne 94600
01.48.53.43.70; 01.48.92.68.68

SYNAGOGUES
Orthodox
28 av. de Newburn, Val-de-Marne 94600
01.48.53.48.27

Clichy-sur-Seine

SYNAGOGUES
Orthodox
26 rue de Mozart (Espace Clichy), Hauts-de-Seine
92210
01.47.39.02.43

Créteil

BAKERIES
Caprices et Delices
5 rue Edouard Manet, Val-de-Marne 94000
01.43.39.20.20
Supervision: Beth Din of Paris

La Nougatine
20 Esplanade des Abîmes, Val-de-Marne 94000
01.49.56.98.56
Supervision: Beth Din of Paris

Les Jasmins de Tunis
C.C. Kennedy, Val-de-Marne 94000   01.43.77.50.66
Supervision: Beth Din of Paris

Quick Chaud
26 allée Parmentier, Val-de-Marne 94000
01.48.99.08.30
Supervision: Beth Din of Paris

Tov 'Mie
25 rue du Dr Paul Casalis, Val-de-Marne 94000
01.48.99.00.39
Supervision: Beth Din of Paris

BUTCHERS
Boucherie Patrick
2 rue Edouard Manet, Val-de-Marne 94000
01.43.39.29.64

La Charolaise Julien
Cte Commercial Kennedy, Loge 13 rue Gabriel Peri,
Val-de-Marne 94000   01.43.39.20.43

MIKVAOT
Rue du 8 Mai 1945, Val-de-Marne 94000
          01.43.77.01.70; 01.43.77.19.68

RESTAURANTS
Meat
Prumo Cacher
17, allee du Commerce, Val-de-Marne 94000
          01.49.80.04.25
Supervision: Beth Din of Paris

SYNAGOGUES
Orthodox
Consistorial Synagogue
rue du 8 Mai 1945, Val-de-Marne 94051
          01.43.77.01.70; 01.43.39.05.20
          Fax: 01.43.99.03.60
          Email: templedesvosges@noos.fr
          Web site: www.synadesvosges.com
Possibilities of "Shabbos meals".

Enghien

MIKVAOT
47 rue de Malleville, Val-d'Oise 95880   01.34.17.37.11

SYNAGOGUES
Orthodox
47 rue de Malleville, Val-d'Oise 95880   01.34.12.42.34

Epinay

BUTCHERS
Chalom
90 av. Joffre, Seine-Saint-Denis 93800   01.48.41.50.64

Fontainebleau

SYNAGOGUES
Orthodox
38 rue Paul Seramy, Seine-et-Marne 77300
          01.64.22.68.48

Fontenay aux Roses

SYNAGOGUES
Orthodox
Centre Moise Meniane
17 av. Paul-Langevin, Hauts-de-Seine 92660
          01.46.60.75.94

Fontenay sous Bois

MIKVAOT
Haya Mossia
177 rue des Moulins, Val-de-Marne 94120
          01.48.77.53.90; 01.48.76.83.84

SYNAGOGUES
Orthodox
79 blvd de Verdun, Val-de-Marne 94120
          01.48.77.38.67

Garges-les-Gonesse

BUTCHERS
Boucherie Berbeche
C C Pal de la Dame Blanche, Val-d'Oise 95140
          01.39.86.42.06

Chez Harry
1 rue J B Corot, Val-d'Oise 95140   01.39.86.53.81

MIKVAOT
15 rue Corot, Val-d'Oise 95140   01.39.86.75.64

SYNAGOGUES
Orthodox
Maison Communautaire Chaare Ra'hamim
14 rue Corot, Val-d'Oise 95140   01.39.86.75.64

Issy-Les-Moulineaux

SYNAGOGUES
Orthodox
72 blvd Gallieni, Hauts-de-Seine 92130
          01.46.48.34.49

La Courneuve

SYNAGOGUES
Orthodox
13 rue Saint-Just, Seine-Saint-Denis 93120
          01.48.36.75.59

La Garenne-Colombes

SYNAGOGUES
Orthodox
**Synagogue and Community Centre of
Courbevoie / La Garenne-Colombes**
13 rue L.M. Nordmann, Hauts-de-Seine 92250
          01.47.69.92.17

La Varenne St-Hilaire

SYNAGOGUES
Orthodox
10 bis avenue du chateau, Val-de-Marne 94210
01.42.83.28.75

Le Blanc Mesnil

SYNAGOGUES
Orthodox
65 rue Maxime-Gorki, Seine-Saint-Denis 93150
01.48.65.58.98

Le Chesnay

MIKVAOT
39 rue de Versailles, Yvelines 78150
01.39.54.05.65; 01.39.07.19.19

Le Kremlin-Bicetre

SYNAGOGUES
Orthodox
41-45 rue J.F. Kennedy, Val-de-Marne 94270
01.46.72.73.64

Le Perreux Nogent

SYNAGOGUES
Orthodox
Synagogue-Nogent/Le Perreux/Bry-Sur-Marne
165 bis av. du Gal-de-Gaulle, Val-de-Marne 94170
01.48.72.88.65

Le Raincy

MIKVAOT
67 blvd du Midi, Seine-Saint-Denis 93340
01.43.81.06.61

SYNAGOGUES
Orthodox
Maison Communautaire
19 allée Chatrian, Seine-Saint-Denis 93340
01.43.02.06.11

Le Vesinet

MIKVAOT
29 rue Henri Cloppet, Yvelines 78110
01.30.53.10.45; 01.30.71.12.26

SYNAGOGUES
Orthodox
Maison Communautaire
29 rue Henri-Cloppet, Yvelines 78110
01.30.53.10.45

Les Lilas

BUTCHERS
Boucherie Des Lilas
6 rue de la Republique, Seine-Saint-Denis 93260
01.43.63.89.15

Levallois Perret

RESTAURANTS
Meat
Delicates Eden
102 rue Rivay, Hauts-de-Seine 92300   01.42.70.97.06
Supervision: Beth Din of Paris

SYNAGOGUES
Orthodox
Synagogue
63, rue Louis Rouquier 92300   01 47 57 11 15

Maisons-Alfort

MIKVAOT
92-94 rue Victor-Hugo, Val-de-Marne 94700
01.43.78.95.69

SYNAGOGUES
Orthodox
68 rue Victor Hugo 94700   01.43.78.95.69

Massy

MIKVAOT
Allée Marcel-Cerdan 91300   01.42.37.48.24

SYNAGOGUES
Orthodox
2 allee Marcel-Cerdan 91300   01.69.20.94.21

Meaux

SYNAGOGUES
Orthodox
11 rue P. Barennes, Seine-et-Marne 77100
01.64.34.76.58

Melun

SYNAGOGUES
Cnr. rues Branly & Michelet 77003   01.64.52.00.05

Meudon-La-Foret

MIKVAOT
Rue de la Synagogue, Hauts-de-Seine 92360
01.46.32.64.82; 01.46.01.01.32

SYNAGOGUES
Orthodox
Maison Communautaire
Rue de la Synagogue, Hauts-de-Seine 92360
01.48.53.48.27

Montreuil

BAKERIES
Korcarz
134 bis rue de Stalingrad, Seine-Saint-Denis 93100
01.48.58.33.45
Supervision: Beth Din of Paris/Chief Rabbi Mordechai
Rottenberg

Le Relais Sucre
62 rue des Roches, Seine-Saint-Denis 93100
01.48.70.22.60
Supervision: Beth Din of Paris

Nat Cacher
21 rue Gabriel Péri, Seine-Saint-Denis 93100
01.48.58.05.25
Supervision: Beth Din of Paris

BUTCHERS
Andre Volailles
62 rue des Roches, Seine-Saint-Denis 93100
01.41.58.58.58

Boucherie Andre
64 rue des Roches, Seine-Saint-Denis 93100
01.41.58.58.58

SYNAGOGUES
Orthodox
179 bis rue de Paris, Seine-Saint-Denis 93100

Montrouge

MIKVAOT
Ismah-Israel
90 rue Gabriel-Péri, Hauts-de-Seine 92120
01.42.53.08.54

SYNAGOGUES
Orthodox
Centre Communautaire Regional Malakoff-Montrouge
90 rue Gabriel-Péri, Hauts-de-Seine 92120
01.46.32.64.82
Fax: 01.46.56.20.49

Neuilly

BUTCHERS
Neuilly Cacher
2/6 rue de Chartres, Hauts-de-Seine 92200
01.47.45.06.06

GROCERIES
King David
14 rue Paul- Chatrousse, Hauts-de-Seine 92200
01.47.45.18.19

RESTAURANTS
Meat
14 rue Paul-Chatrousse, Hauts-de-Seine 92200
01.47.45.18.19
Supervision: Beth Din of Paris
Deliver. Hours: 8 am to 10 pm.

SYNAGOGUES
Orthodox
12 rue Ancelle, Hauts-de-Seine 92200   01.47.47.78.76
Fax: 01.47.47.54.79
Web site: www.synaneuilly.com

Noisy Le Sec

SYNAGOGUES
Orthodox
Beth Gabriel
2 rue de la Pierre Feuillère, Seine-Saint-Denis 93130
01.48.46.71.79

Pantin

BUTCHERS
Levy Baroukh
5/7 rue Anatole France, Seine-Saint-Denis 93500
01.48.91.02.14

RESTAURANTS
Dairy
Chez Jacquy
24 rue du Pré-Saint-Gervais, Seine-Saint-Denis 93500
01.48.10.94.24
Supervision: Beth Din of Paris

SYNAGOGUES
Orthodox
8 rue Gambetta, Seine-Saint-Denis 93500

Ris-Orangis

SYNAGOGUES
Orthodox
1 rue Jean-Moulin, Essone 91130   01.69.43.07.83

Roissy-En-Brie

MIKVAOT
Rue Paul-Cézanne, C.Cial Bois Montmartre, Seine-et-Marne 77680   01.60.28.34.65; 01.60.29.09.44

SYNAGOGUES
Orthodox
Maison Communautaire
1 rue Paul-Cézanne, Centre Commercial Bois Montmartre, Seine-et-Marne 77680   01.60.28.36.38

Rosny-Sous-Bois

SYNAGOGUES
Orthodox
62-64 rue Lavoisier, Seine-Saint-Denis 93110
01.48.54.04.11
Fax: 01.69.43.07.83

Rueil-Malmaison

SYNAGOGUES
Orthodox
6 rue René-Cassin, Hauts-de-Seine 92500
01.47.08.32.62

Saint Germain

SYNAGOGUES
Liberal
Kehilat Gesher (Franco-American)
10 rue de Pologne 78100   01.39.21.97.19
Email: rabbenutom@compuserve.com

Orthodox
Synagogue
6 impasse Saint Leger 78103   01 34 51 26 60

Saint-Denis

SYNAGOGUES
Orthodox
51 blvd Marcel-Sembat, (next to the Gendarmerie), Seine-Saint-Denis 93200   01.48.20.30.87

Saint-Leu-La-Foret

MIKVAOT
2 rue Jules Vernes, Val-d'Oise 95320
01.39.95.96.90; 01.34.14.24.15

SYNAGOGUES
Orthodox
2 rue Jules Verne, Val-d'Oise 95320   01.39.95.96.90
Fax: 01.39.95.72.13

Saint-Ouen-L'Aumône

SYNAGOGUES
Orthodox
Maison Communautaire
9 rue de Chennevières, Val-d'Oise 95310
01.30.37.71.41

Sarcelles

BAKERIES
Louis D'or
90 av. Paul Valéry, Val-d'Oise 95200   01.39.90.25.45
Supervision: Beth Din of Paris

Natania
34 blvd Albert Camus, Val-d'Oise 95200
01.39.90.11.78
Supervision: Beth Din of Paris

Oh Delices
71 av. Paul Valéry, Val-d'Oise 95200   01.39.92.41.12
Supervision: Beth Din of Paris

Zazou
C.C. les Flanades, Val-d'Oise 95200   01.34.19.08.11
Supervision: Beth Din of Paris

BUTCHERS
Boucherie Du Coin
60 blvd Albert Camus, Val-d'Oise 95200
01.39.90.53.02

Hazout
5 av. Paul Valery, Val-d'Oise 95200   01.39.90.72.95

MIKVAOT
Mayanot Rachel
14 av. Ch.-Péguy, Val-d'Oise 95200   01.39.90.40.17

RESTAURANTS
Dairy
Marina
103 av. Paul-Valéry, Val-d'Oise 95200   01.34.19.23.51
Supervision: Beth Din of Paris

Meat
Berbeche Burger
13 av. Edouard-Branly, Val-d'Oise 95200
01.34.19.12.02
Supervision: Beth Din of Paris

SYNAGOGUES
Orthodox
Maison Communautaire
74 av. Paul-Valéry, Val-d'Oise 95200   01.39.90.59.59
Mikva on premises.

Sartrouville

SYNAGOGUES
Orthodox
Synagogue Rabbi Shimon bar Yohai et Rabbi Meir Baal Hannes
I rue de Stalingrad, Yvelines 78500   01.39.15.22.57

Savigny sur Orge

MIKVAOT
I av. de l'Armée-Leclerc, Essonne 91600
01.69.24.48.25; 01.69.96.30.90

SYNAGOGUES
Orthodox
I av. de l'Armee Leclerc, Essonne 91600
01.69.96.30.90

Sevran

MIKVAOT
25 bis du Dr Roux, Seine-Saint-Denis 93270
01.43.84.25.40
Mikva Kelim.

SYNAGOGUES
Orthodox
Synagogue Mayan-Thora
25 bis rue du Dr Roux, BP. 111, Seine-Saint-Denis
93270   01.43.84.25.40

St-Brice-Sous-Foret

SYNAGOGUES
Orthodox
Centre Communautaire Ohel Avraham
10 rue Pasteur, Val-d'Oise 95350   01.39.94.96.10

Stains

SYNAGOGUES
Orthodox
8 rue Lamartine (face n°2), Clos St-Lazare, Seine-Saint-Denis 93240   01.48.21.04.12
Provisional address: 8 av. Louis Bordes (Ancien Conservatoire Municipal).

Thiais

COMMUNITY ORGANISATIONS
Community Centre Choisy-Orly-Thiais
Voie du Four, 128 av. du Marechal de Lattre de Tassigny, Val-de-Marne 94320   01.48.92.68.68
Fax: 01.48.92.72.82

Trappes

SYNAGOGUES
Orthodox
7 rue du Port-Royal, Yvelines 78190   01.30.62.40.43

Versailles

SYNAGOGUES
10 rue Albert-Joly, Yvelines 78000   01.39.07.19.19
Fax: 01.39.50.96.34
Mikva on premises.

Villejuif

BAKERIES
Eden Eclair
30 rue Marcel Gromesnil, Val-de-Marne 94800
01.47.26.42.96
Supervision: Beth Din of Paris

SYNAGOGUES
Orthodox
106 av. de Gournay, Val-de-Marne 94800
01.46.78.76.53

Villeneuve-la-Garenne

MIKVAOT
42-44 rue du Fond-de-la Noue, Hauts-de-Seine
92390   01.47.94.89.98

SYNAGOGUES
Orthodox
Maison Communautaire
44 rue du Fond-de-la-Noue, Hauts-de-Seine 92390
01.47.94.89.98

Villiers Sur Marne

SYNAGOGUES
Orthodox
30 rue Léon-Douer, B.P. 15, Val-de-Marne 94350
01.49.30.01.47
Fax: 01.49.30.85.40

Villiers-le-Bel-Gonesse

MIKVAOT
I rue Léon Blum, Val-d'Oise 95400
01.39.94.45.51; 01.34.19.64.48

SYNAGOGUES
Orthodox
I rue Léon-Blum, Val-d'Oise 95400
01.39.94.30.49; 01.39.94.94.89

Vincennes

BUTCHERS
Boucherie Des Levy
32 rue Raymond du Temple, Val-de-Marne 94300
01.43.74.94.18
Boucherie Hayache
146 av. de Paris, Val-de-Marne 94300 01.43.28.16.04

SYNAGOGUES
Orthodox
Synagogue Achkenaze
30 rue Céline-Robert, Val-de-Marne 94300
01.43.28.82.83
Synagogue Sepharade
30 rue Céline-Robert, Val-de-Marne 94300
01.47.55.65.07

Vitry-sur-Seine

SYNAGOGUES
Orthodox
133-135 av. Rouget-de-l'Isle, Val-de-Marne 94400
01.46.80.76.54; 01.45.73.06.58
Fax: 01.45.73.94.01

Yerres

MIKVAOT
Beth Rivkah
43/49 rue R. Poincare, Essone 91330
01.69.49.62.74; 01.69.49.62.62
Fax: 01.69.79.27.70
Email: beth-rivkah@wanados.fr

SOUTH EAST

Aix-en-Provence

BUTCHERS
Zouaghi
7 rue de Sevigne, Bouches du Rhône 13100
04.42.59.93.94
Supervision: Grand Rabbinate of Marseille

SYNAGOGUES
5 rue de Jerusalem 13100 04.42.26.69.39

Aix-les-Bains

BUTCHERS
Berdah
29 Av. de Tresserve 73100 04.79.61.44.11

Eurocach
Av. d'Italie 73100

HOTELS
Kosher
Auberge de La Baye
Chemin du Tir-Aux-Pigeons, Savoie 73100
04.79.35.69.42
Strictly kosher.

MIKVAOT
Pavillon Salvador
rue du President Roosevelt 73100 04.79.35.38.08

SYNAGOGUES
Rue Paul Bonna 73100 04.79.35.28.08
Mikva on Premises

Annecy

SYNAGOGUES
18 rue de Narvik 74000 04.50.67.69.37

Annemasse

BUTCHERS
Yarden
59 av de la Liberation, Gaillard 74100 04.50.92.64.05

SYNAGOGUES
Orthodox
8 rue du Docteur Coquart 74100

Antibes-Juan-les-Pins

BUTCHERS
Berreche
12 av. Courbet 06160 04.93.67.16.77
Le Kineret
25 av. D l'Esterel 06160 04.92.93.16.01
Fax: 04.93.88.14.76

RESTAURANTS
L'Alhambra
12 bis, Avenue de l'Esterel 04.93.67.65.17
Le Relais de Belleville
47 Avenue Guy de Maupassant 06160
Maxime
6 Bd de la Pinede 06160 04.92.93.99.40

SYNAGOGUES
Villa La Monada, 30 Chemin des Sables 06160
04.93.61.59.34

Avignon

The first archaeological evidence of a Jewish presence dates from the fourth century. For years the Avignon Jewish population flourished and there were many Jewish scholars and writers who were born and lived there. The first printing venture in Hebrew was attempted in Avignon in 1446 before Gutenberg's success in 1450.

BUTCHERS

Cachere Royale
15 rue Chapeau Rouge 84000   04.90.82.47.50
Supervision: Grand Rabbinate of Marseille

HOTEL

Hotel Danieli
17 rue de la Republique 84000   04.90.86.46.82
Fax: 04.90.27.09.24
Email: reservation@hotel-danieli-avignon.com
Web site: www.hotel-danieli-avignon.com

MIKVAOT

Vaucluse   04.90.86.30.30
Mme Cohen Zardi

SYNAGOGUES

Orthodox
2 Place de Jerusalem 84000   04.90.85.21.24
Fax: 04.90.85.21.24
This circular synagogue was built in 1847 on the site of a 13th century synagogue.

Beziers

MIKVAOT

19 place Pierre-Semard
Mme Smolinski Tel: 04.67.28.44.24

SYNAGOGUES

19 Place Pierre-Semard 34500   04.67.28.75.98
Operates a Kosher Food Store.

TOURIST SITE

Ghetto
To visit the old Ghetto (Beziers was known as "the little Jerusalem"); contact Mr Benyacar (04 67 31 14 23).

Caluire- et- Cuire

SYNAGOGUES

107 Av. Fleming 69300   04.78.23.12.37

Cannes

BUTCHERS

Cannes Casher
9 rue Marceau 06400   04.93.39.85.08

Chez Sylvie
15 rue Mal. Joffre 06400   04.93.39.57.92

COMMUNITY ORGANISATIONS

20 Boulevard d'Alsace 06400   04.93.38.16.54
Fax: 04.93.68.92.81

GROCERIES

La Emounah
32 rue de Mimont 06400
Near the main synagogue.

Monoprix
Rue Marechal Fox
Has a comprehensive kosher section.

MIKVAOT

20 boulevard d'Alsace   04.93.99.79.03
Contact: Mme Annie Rebibo

RESTAURANTS

Dairy
Le Dany's
18 Rue Marechal Joffre   04.92.59.35.50

Pizza Dick
7 bis , rue de Mimont 06400   04.92.59.10.82

Meat
Le Tovel
3 rue du Dr Gerard Monod 06400   04.93.39.36.25

SYNAGOGUES

Chabad Lubavitch
22 Rue Commandant Vidal 06400   04.92.98.67.51
Fax: 04.92.98.81.29
Email: canorhabad@aol.com
Web site: www.jewish-cannes.com
Sephardi
20 Boulevard d'Alsace 06400   04.93.38.16.54
Fax: 04.93.68.92.81

Carpentras

Jews first settled in Carpentras in the 12th century. In 1343 permission was granted for the erection of a synagogue in which women were situated in the basement. A "rabbi of the women" was employed to guide them through the service; the only direct contact being a small window.

SYNAGOGUES

Place de la Mairie   04.90.63.39.97
The Synagogue originally built in 1367 and the oldest in France was reconstructed in 1741-43 and again in 1959. The French government has declared it a historic site.

TOURIST SITE
Cathedral St Siffrein
The fifteenth-century door on the south side is where Jews had to go on their way to conversion and is known as "Porte des Juifs".

Cavaillon

The Jews originally lived in Rue Hebraique. The present synagogue, classified as a historical monument, was built in 1772 and incorporates parts of the 16th century former building.

MUSEUM
Musee Judeo-Comatdin
04.90.76.00.34

The museum, a part of the synagogues, contains items dating back to the 14th century.

SYNAGOGUES
04.90.76.00.34
Fax: 04.90.71.47.06

Clermont-Ferrand

SYNAGOGUES
6 rue Blatin 63000   04.73.93.36.59

Evian

SYNAGOGUES
Adjacent to 1 av. des Grottes, 74502   04.50.75.15.63

Eze-Village

HOTELS
Hotel les Terrases d'Eze
Route de la Turbie 06360   04.92.41.55.55
Fax: 04.92.41.55.10

Supervision: Nice Beth Din.

Frejus

SYNAGOGUES
Orthodox
Rue de Progres, Frejus-Plage 83600   04.94.52.06.87

Grenoble

BUTCHERS
C. Cohen
19 rue de Turenne 38000   04.76.46.48.14

GROCERIES
Aux Delices du Soleil
49 rue Thiers 38000   04.76.46.19.60
Ghnassia
15 place Gustave Rivet 38000   04.76.87.80.90

MEDIA
Radio
Radio Kol Hachalom 100 FM
BP 342 - 38013, Isère 38000   04.76.87.21.22
Fax: 04.76.47.58.31
Email: rkh@rkhfm.com
Web site: www.rhkfm.com
24 hours a day broadcasting.

SYNAGOGUES
Rachi
11 rue Maginot, Isère 38000   04.76.87.02.80
Fax: 04.76.87.27.14
Email: rabbin38@aol.com
Mikva at same address.

Synagogue and Community Centre
4 rue des Bains, Isère 38000   04.76.46.15.14

Hyeres

SYNAGOGUES
Chemin de la Ritorte 83400   04.94.65.31.97

Izieu

MUSEUM
The Izieu Children's Home
Bouches du Rhône 01300
recording 04.79.87.20.00; booking 04.79.87.20.08
Fax: 04.79.87.25.01
Email: izieu@alma.fr
Web site: www.izieu.alma.fr
The Izieu Children's Memorial Museum is dedicated to the memory of forty-four children and their guardians, taken away on 6 April 1944 by the Gestapo under the command of Klaus Barbie. The Museum's mission is to defend dignity, justice and to contribute to the fight against all forms of intolerance. Two buildings can be visited: The House takes the visitors back to the everyday life of the children's home, the Barn presents the historical background through permanent and temporary exhibitions. Meetings, conferences and discussions are organized throughout the year.

La Ciotat

SYNAGOGUES
1 Square de Verdun 13600   04.42.71.92.56
Services, Friday 7pm (Winter), 7.30pm (Summer).
Saturday 9am.

La Seyne-sur-Mer

BUTCHERS
Elie Benamou
17 rue Batistin-Paul 83500   04.94.94.38.60

SYNAGOGUES
5 rue Chevalier-de-la-Barre 83501   04.94.94.40.28

Lyons

BAKERIES
Jo Delice
44, rue Rachais   04.78.69.22.98

Nassy Gourmand
41, Rue A Boutin, Villeurbanne 69100 04.78.85.72.88

BUTCHERS
Ittah David
267, Av. Berthelot 69008   04.78.00.82.35

William (Mr Dahan)
50, rue Tete d'Or 69006   04.78.24.10.10

COMMUNITY ORGANISATIONS
Consistoire Israelite de Lyon
13 Quai Tilsitt 69002   04.78.37.13.43
Fax: 04.78.38.26.57
Email: acil@free.fr

Consistoire Israelite Sepharade de Lyon
Yaacov Molho Community Centre, 317 Rue
Duguesclin 69007   04.78.58.18.74
Fax: 04.78.58.17.49

MEDIA
CIV News
4 rue Malherbe, Villeurbanne 69100 04.78.84.04.32

Hachaar
18 rue St. Mathieu 69008   04.78.00.72.50

La Voix Sepharade
317 rue Duguesclin 69007   04.78.58.18.74

MIKVAOT
Chaare Tsedek (N. African)
18 rue St.-Mathieu 69008   04.78.00.72.50

Orah Haim
17 rue Albert-Thomas, St-Fons 69190 04.78.67.39.78

Rav Hida (N. African)
La Sauvegarde, La Duchere 69009 04.78.35.14.44

RELIGIOUS ORGANISATIONS
Beth Din
34 rue d'Armenie, 3e   04.78.62.97.63
Fax: 04.78.95.09.47

RESTAURANTS
Dairy
Le Pinocchio
5 Rue A. Boutin, Villeurbanne 69100 04.78.68.62.95

Lippo
9 Rue Michel Servet, Villeurbanne 69100
04.78.84.15.00

Pizza Cach
13 Rue d'Inkerman, Villeurbanne 69100
04.72.74.44.98

Prestopizza
61 Rue Greuze, Villeurbanne 69100 04.78.68.08.41
Meat
Croq Sandwiches
32 Crs Emile-Zola, Villeurbanne 69100
04.78.84.16.07

La Palmeraie
27 Rue des charmettes, Villeurbanne 69100
04.78.24.37.03

La Petite Maison
35, rue P. Corneille 69006   04.78.24.99.43

Le Belvedere
14, rue Jean-Jaures, Villeurbanne 69100
04.78.54.72.31

Lippmann Henry
4 Rue Tony Tollet, Villeurbanne 69002 04.78.42.49.82
Supervision: Lyon Beth Din

Mac David
28 Rue Michel Servet, Villeurbanne 69100
04.78.03.31.62

SYNAGOGUES
Orthodox
Chaare Tsedek
18 rue Saint Mathieu (8e) (T.T.)   04 78 00 72 50
Fax: 04 78 75 89 74

Grande Synagogue
13 qui Tilsitt   04.78.37.13.43
Fax: 04.78.38.26.57
Email: acil@free.fr
Orthodox
Rav Hida
501 Sauvegarde La Duchere (9e) (T.T.) 04 78 35 14 44
Fax: 04 78 64 95 90

Sephardi
Neveh Chalom
13 rue Duguesclin 69007   04.78.58.18.74
Fax: 04.78.58.17.49

Macon

SYNAGOGUES
32 rue des Minimes 71000

Marignane

SYNAGOGUES
9 rue Pilote-Larbonne 13700

Marseilles

BAKERIES
Atteia et Fils
19 Place Guillardet, Bouches du Rhône 13013
04.91.66.33.28
Supervision: Grand Rabbinate of Marseille

Avyel Cash
28 rue St Suffren, Bouches du Rhône 13006
04.91.87.95.25
Supervision: Grand Rabbinate of Marseille

Cacher Food
31 blvd Barry, Bouches du Rhône 13013
04.91.70.13.43
Supervision: Grand Rabbinate of Marseille

Erets
205 rue de Rome, Bouches du Rhône 13006
04.91.92.88.73
Supervision: Grand Rabbinate of Marseille

L'Entremets
206 avenue de la Rose, Bouches du Rhône 13013
04.91.70.72.19
Supervision: Grand Rabbinate of Marseille

Le Parve
72 av. Alphonse Daudet, Bouches du Rhône 13013
04.91.66.95.16
Supervision: Grand Rabbinate of Marseille

BUTCHERS
Chez David
9 blvd G. Ganay, Bouches du Rhône 13009
04.91.75.04.56
Supervision: Grand Rabbinate of Marseille

Jamap
13 place Mignard, Bouches du Rhône 13009
04.91.71.11.70
Supervision: Grand Rabbinate of Marseille

Sebane
59 rue Alphonse Daudet, Bouches du Rhône 13013
04.91.66.98.76
Supervision: Grand Rabbinate of Marseille

Zennou Raphael
20 marché Capucin, Bouches du Rhône 13001
04.91.54.02.54
Supervision: Grand Rabbinate of Marseille

EMBASSY
Consul General of Israel
146 rue Paradis, Bouches du Rhône 13006
04.91.53.39.87
Fax: 04.91.53.39.94

GROCERIES
Av bon gout
28 rue St Suffren, Bouches du Rhône 13006
04.91.37.95.25

Delicash
94 blvd Barry, Bouches du Rhône 13013
04.91.06.39.04

Emmanuel
93 avenue Clot Bey, Bouches du Rhône 13008
04.91.77.46.08

King Kasher
25 rue François Mauriac, Bouches du Rhône 13010
04.91.80.00.01

Raphael Cash
299 avenue de Mazargues, Bouches du Rhône 13009
04.91.76.44.13

MEDIA
Radio
Radio JM
4, impasse Dragon 13006   04.91.37.78.78

MEMORIAL
Memorial of the Death Camps
Quai de la Tourette 13002   04.91.90.73.15

MIKVAOT
Mikve Esther
47 rue St Suffren 13006   04.91.81.45.15
**There are some eight mikvaot in marseilles.
This one is close to the main synagogue. The
Consistoire will provide details of others.**

RELIGIOUS ORGANISATIONS
Consistoire de Marseille
117 rue de Breteuil, Bouches du Rhône 13006
04.91.37.49.64; 04.91.81.13.57
Fax: 04.91.37.83.90
Email: consistoire.israelile@wanadoo.fr

RESTAURANTS
Dairy
Pizzeria Gan Eden
225, Paul Claudel 13010   04.91.75.12.72
Meat
Erets
205, rue de Rome, Bouches du Rhône 13006
04.91.92.88.73
Supervision: Grand Rabbinate of Marseille

Nathania
17 rue du Village, Bouches du Rhône 13006
04.91.42.05.31
Supervision: Grand Rabbinate of Marseille

SYNAGOGUES

Merlan
La Cerisaie, Batiment G1 13014   04.91.98.53.92

Ohel Yaakov
20 Chemin Ste-Marthe 13014   04.91.62.70.42

Ashkenazi
8 Impasse Dragon 13006

Reform
337 Rue Paradis Marseille 13008   04.91.37.54.31
                                     Fax: 04.91.37.54.31
                       Email: rabbi.liebermann@voila.fr

Sephardi
Bar Yohai
171 rue Abbe-de-l'Epee 13005   04.91.42.38.19

Beth Simha
31 av. Des Olives 13013   04.91.70.05.45

Main Synagogue
117 rue Breteuil 13006   04.91.37.49.64
                            Fax: 04.91.37.83.89

There are over forty more synagogues in Marseilles. The Consistoire de Marseilles will supply details if required.

Merkaz Netivot Chalom
27 blvd Bonifay 13004   04.91.89.40.62

Menton

SYNAGOGUES
Centre Altyner, 106 Cours du Centenaire 06500
                            04.93.35.28.29

Montpellier

BUTCHERS
Eretz
41 rue de Lunaret 34000   04.67.72.67.94

COMMUNITY ORGANISATIONS
Centre Communautaire et Cultural Juif
500 blvd d'Antigone 34000   04.67.15.08.76

GROCERIES
A.C.P.C.
45 rue Proudhon   04.67.02.10.99

SYNAGOGUES
Ben-Zakai
7 rue General-Laffon 34000   04.67.92.92.07

Mazal Tov
18 rue Ferdinand-Fabre 34000   04.67.79.09.82

Nice

The first reference to Jews in Nice was in 1342. The first cemetery was established in 1408 and synagogue in 1492.

The main synagogue, built in 1886 is worth a visit. Nice is home to the Chagall Museum which contains a permanent collection of his work including a number of stained glass mosaics.

BOOKSELLERS
Librairie Tanya
25 rue Pertinax 06000   04.93.80.21.74
                           Fax: 04.93.13.87.90
            Email: librairie.tanya@wanadoo.fr

BUTCHERS
Ghighi
32, av. Georges Clemenceau   04.93.88.69.88
K'Gel
18, rue Dante 06000   04.93.86.33.01

GROCERIES
Mickael
37 Rue Dabray 06000   04.93.88.81.23

Riviera Cacher
11 Avenue Villermont 06000   04.93.92.92.00

KASHRUT INFORMATION
                            04.93.85.82.06
A list of kosher butchers and bakers can be obtained from the Chief Rabbi.

KOSHER FOOD
Galleries Lafayette
Has a kosher food section.

MIKVAOT
22 rue Michelet 06100   04.93.51.89.80

MUSEUM
Chagall Museum
Avenue Docteur Menard 06000   04.93.53.87.20
                                 Fax: 04.93.53.87.39
The Museum presents to the public a permanent exhibition of the largest collection existing of the works of Marc Chagall

RELIGIOUS ORGANISATIONS
Centre Consistorial
22 rue Michelet 06100   04.93.51.89.80
Publishes an annual calendar and guide to Nice and district.

Regional Chief Rabbinate of Nice, Cote d'Azur and Corsica
1 rue Voltaire 06000   04.93.85.82.06

RESTAURANTS
Dairy
Le Leviathan
1 ave Georges Clemenceau   04.93.87.22.64

Meat
L'Alliance
13, rue Andrioli 06000   04.93.44.11.94

Le Dauphin Bleu
22, av. Malaussena 06000   04.93.82.98.74

SYNAGOGUES
Main Synagogue
7 rue Gustave-Deloye 06000   04.93.92.11.38
Ashkenazi
Synagogue Achkenaze
1, rue Blacas   04 93 62 38 68

Nimes

COMMUNITY ORGANISATIONS
5 rue d'Angouleme 30000   04.66.26.19.51

SYNAGOGUES
40 rue Roussy 30000   04.66.29.51.81
Mikva on premises.

Perpignan

BUTCHERS
Gilbert Sabbah
3 rue P.-Rameil 66000   04.68.35.41.23
    Fax: 04.68.51.09.83

SYNAGOGUES
54 rue Francois Arago 66000   04.68.34.75.81
    Fax: 04.68.51.13.31

Roanne

SYNAGOGUES
9 rue Beaulieu 42300   04.77.71.51.56

Saint-Etienne

SYNAGOGUES
34 rue d'Arcole 42000   04.77.33.56.31

Saint-Fons

SYNAGOGUES
17 av. Albert-Thomas 69190   04.78.67.39.78

Saint-Laurent-du-Var

SYNAGOGUES
Villa 'Le Petit Clos', 35 Av. des Oliviers 06700

Toulon

BUTCHERS
Abecassis
8 rue Vincent Courdouan, Var 83000   04.94.97.39.86
Supervision: Grand Rabbinate of Marseille

Fennech
15 av. Colbert, Var 83000   04.94.92.70.39
Supervision: Grand Rabbinate of Marseille

SYNAGOGUES
184 av. Lazare Carnot 83050   04.94.92.61.05
Mikva on premises.

Valence

SYNAGOGUES
1 place du Colombier 26000   04.75.43.34.43

Venissieux

SYNAGOGUES
10 av. de la Division-Leclerc 69200   04.78.70.69.85

Vichy

SYNAGOGUES
2 bis rue du Marechal Foch 03200   04.70.59.82.33

SOUTH WEST

Agen

SYNAGOGUES
52 rue Montesquieu 47000   05.53.66.24.20

TOURIST SITE
rue des Juifs 47000
Site of the old ghetto of the fifteenth Century.

Museum of the deportation
rue Montesquieu 47000

Arcachon

SYNAGOGUES
Orthodox
36 av Gambetta   05.56.83.63.40
    Fax: 05.56.83.63.40

Bayonne

SYNAGOGUES
35 rue Maubec 64100   05.59.55.03.95

Bordeaux

BAKERIES
Boucherie Peres
64 rue Bouquiere   05 56 52 88 18

COMMUNITY ORGANISATIONS
15 Pl. Charles-Gruet 33000   05.56.52.62.69

MIKVAOT
213 rue Ste. Catherine 33000   05.56.91.79.39

RESTAURANTS
Mazal Tov
137 cours Victor Hugo 33000   05.56.52.37.03

SYNAGOGUES
8 rue du Grand-Rabbin-Joseph-Cohen 33000
     05.56.91.79.39
     Fax: 05.56.94.05.12

La Rochelle

CONTACT INFORMATION
Pierre Guedj
20 rue Chef de Ville 17000   05.46.67.38.91
     Fax: 05.46.41.24.68

SYNAGOGUES
Orthodox
Centre Communautaire
M.C.I. 40 cours des Dames 17000   05 46 41 17 66

Libourne

SYNAGOGUES
33 rue Lamothe 33500

Limoges

SYNAGOGUES
25-27 rue Pierre-Leroux 87000   05.55.77.47.26

Montauban

SYNAGOGUES
12 rue St-Claire 82000   05.63.03.01.37

Pau

SYNAGOGUES
8 rue des Trois-Freres-Bernadac 64000
     05.59.62.37.85

Perigueuex

SYNAGOGUES
13 rue Paul-Louis-Courrier 24000   05.53.53.22.52

Poitiers

SYNAGOGUES
1 rue Guynemer 86000

Tarbes

SYNAGOGUES
Cite Rothschild
6 rue du Pradeau 65000

Toulouse

BUTCHERS
Cacherout Diffusion
37 blvd Carnot 31000   05.61.23.07.59
Lasry
8 rue Matabiau 31000   05.61.62.65.28
Maalem
7 rue des Chalets 31000   05.61.63.77.39

COMMUNITY ORGANISATIONS
Community Centre
2 place Riquet 31000   05.61.23.36.54

GROCERIES
Novogel
14 rue Edmund Guyaux 31200   05.61.57.03.19

MIKVAOT
13 rue Francisque Sarcey 31000   05.61.48.89.84

RELIGIOUS ORGANISATIONS
Grand Rabbinat du Toulouse et des Pays de la Garonne - A.C.I.T.
2 place Riquet 31000   05.62.73.46.46
     Fax: 05.62.73.46.47

RESTAURANTS
Community Centre
2 place Riquet 31000   05.62.73.56.56

SYNAGOGUES
Chaare Emeth
35 rue Rembrandt 31000   05.61.40.03.88

Ashkenazi
Adat Yechouroun
3 rue Jules-Chalande 31000   05.61.62.30.19
                                Fax: 05.61.62.86.79

Orthodox
Hekhal David
2, place Riquet 31000   05 62 76 46 46

Sephardi
Palaprat
2 rue Palaprat 31000   05.61.21.69.56

OVERSEAS REGION

Corsica

CONTACT INFORMATION
Jo Michel Reis
La Grande Corniche, Routes des Sanguinaires,
Ajaccio   9521-5752.
There are between ten and fifteen families in the
town.

SYNAGOGUES
3 rue du Castagno Bastia, Bastia 20200
Services Shabbat morning and festivals.

OVERSEAS TERRITORIES

FRENCH POLYNESIA

Tahiti

The first known Jew in Tahiti was Alexander
Salmon the son of a Rabbi from Hastings
(England), who arrived in 1841 and later married
the Queen's sister. No community developed
however until the 1960's when refugees came
from Algeria.

SYNAGOGUES
Synagogue
Rue Morenhouy, Quartier Fariipti, Papette
                              689.41.03.92
                          Fax: 689.41.03.92
                    Email: Acispo@mail.pf

GUADELOUPE

SYNAGOGUES
Bas du Fort, Gosier, Lot 1   590.90.99.09
The synagogue, community centre and
restaurant/kosher store are all located here.

MARTINIQUE

Kenafe Haarets
12 Anse Gouraud, Schoeler, Fort-de-France 97233
                              596.61.71.36
                          Fax: 596.61.66.71
A community centre is also located here, which
supplies kosher food, plus a kosher meat restaurant.

RÉUNION

CONTACT INFORMATION
Leon Benhamou
                              262.29.05.45

SYNAGOGUES
Communauté Juive de la Réunion
8 rue de l'Est, St-Denis 97400   262.23.78.33
High Holy Day services and communal seder held
here.

GEORGIA

Georgia has had a very long history of Jewish settlement, dating back to two centuries before the destruction of the Second Temple, if the archaeological findings are correct. These earliest Jewish communities may have been descended from the Babylonian exiles. Like the Jews in the other Caucasus regions (Armenia and Azerbaijan) they are known as 'mountain Jews'.

Synagogues are found in major towns. There is a school in Tbilisi (the capital) and there are some newsletters. It is worth noting that the non-Jewish population has traditionally been far less anti-semitic than the populations of some other ex-Soviet republics.

GMT +4 hours	**Total Population 5,434,000**
Country calling code (995)	**Jewish Population 9,000**
Emergency Telephone (Police – 02) (Fire – 01) (Ambulance – 03)	**(Electricity voltage – 220)**

Akhaltsikhe

SYNAGOGUES
109 Guramishvili Street

Batumi

SYNAGOGUES
6 9th March Street

Gori

SYNAGOGUES
Chelyuskin Street

Kutaisi

SYNAGOGUES
12 Gapanove Street
Near the main square.

Onni

SYNAGOGUES
Baazova Street

Poti

SYNAGOGUES
23 Ninoshivili
Tskhakaya Street

Sukhumi

SYNAGOGUES
56 Karl Marx Street

Surami

SYNAGOGUES
Internatsionalaya Street

Tbilisi

COMMUNITY ORGANISATIONS
Jews of Georgia Assoc.
Tsarity Tamari Street 8 380012   (32) 234-1057

SYNAGOGUES
Ashkenazi
65 Kozhevenny Lane
Sephardi
45-47 Leselidze Street

Tshkinvali

SYNAGOGUES
Isapov Street

Tskhakaya

SYNAGOGUES
Mir Street

Vani

SYNAGOGUES
4 Kaikavadze Street

GERMANY

It may be a surprise to many that Germany comes immediately after France and the UK in the population table of Western European Jewry. German Jews have contributed much to the culture of European Jews in general since their arrival in what is now Germany in the fourth century. The massive Jewish presence in Poland and other east European states stemmed from German Jews escaping persecution in the late Middle Ages. They took the early Medieval German language with them, which formed Yiddish, the old lingua franca of European Jews.

The Jews who stayed behind in Germany contributed much towards Jewish and German culture, with the Reform movement starting in nineteenth-century Germany, and Heine and Mendelssohn contributing to German poetry and music respectively. The Enlightenment and modern Orthodoxy also began in Germany.

The rise of Nazism destroyed the belief that the German Jews were more German than Jewish. Many managed to escape before 1939, but 180,000 were killed in the Holocaust (of the 503,000 who lived in Germany when Hitler came to power). Following the events of 1933-45, it seems incredible that any Jew should want to live in Germany again. However, the community began to re-form, mainly with immigrants from eastern Europe, especially Russia. Now there are again Jewish shops in Berlin, and kosher food is once more available. There are many old synagogues which have been restored, and several concentration camps have been kept as monuments to history. There is also a great interest in Jewish matters among some of the non-Jewish younger generation.

Visitors to Berlin should try to visit the new Jewish Museum (officially opened in September 2001). It covers the history of German Jewry through the Middle Ages and up to the present. It revives the tradition of an earlier museum opened in 1933 before the Nazis came to power.

GMT +1 hour	Total Population 82,071,000
Country calling code (49)	Jewish Population 100,000
Emergency Telephone (Police – 110) (Fire – 112) (Ambulance – 112)	(Electricity voltage – 220)

Aachen

COMMUNITY ORGANISATIONS
Bundesverband Jüdischer Studenten in Deutschland
Oppenhoffallee 50 52066   (241) 75998

Alsenz

SITE
Synagogue
Kirchberg 1 67821   (636) 23149
                            Fax: (636) 23149
Restored eighteenth-century synagogue.

Andernach

HISTORIC SITE
Rhine Valley
This Rhine Valley town contains an early fourteenth-century mikva. Key obtainable from the Town Hall.

Annweiler

TOURIST SITE
                            (623) 53333
The oldest cemetery in the Palatinate dating from sixteenth century.

Augsburg

COMMUNITY ORGANISATIONS
Community Centre
Halderstr. 8 86150   (821) 517985
There is a Jewish museum in the restored Liberal synagogue at this address.

Bad Kreuznach

COMMUNITY ORGANISATIONS
Gymnasialstr. 11 55543   (671) 26991

Bad Nauheim

RESTAURANTS
Judische Gemeinde
Karlstr. 34 61231   (6032) 5605 or 0171-9509084
                            Fax: (6032) 938956
In the Jewish Community Centre. Entry for the restaurant is from Friedenstrasse.

SYNAGOGUES
Karlstr. 34 61231   (6032) 5605; 0171-9509084
                            Fax: (6032) 5605
Synagogue is in the Jewish Community Centre.

Baden-Baden

SYNAGOGUES
Conservative
Werderstr. 2 76530   (722) 139-1021
Fax: (722) 139-1024

Bamberg

COMMUNITY ORGANISATIONS
Community Centre
Willy-Lessing-Str. 7 96047   (951) 23267

Bayreuth

COMMUNITY ORGANISATIONS
Munzgasse 2 95444   (921) 65407

Berlin

Jewish life is beginning to grow again in Berlin, formerly an important centre for German Jewry. There are many sites which testify to the tragedy that befell the community before and during the war, such as the ruined Oranienburgerstrasse Synagogue, which has been turned into a Jewish centre. The site of the Wannsee Conference, to the south west of the city, (where the Holocaust was officially planned), has been turned into a museum.

BED AND BREAKFAST
Guestrooms
Tucholskystrasse 40, Mitte 10117   (30) 281-3135
Fax: (30) 281-3122
Web site: www.adassjisroel.de
A synagogue and a kosher restaurant is in the house.

BOOKSELLERS
Literaturhandlung
Joachimstaler-Str. 13 10719   (30) 882-4250
Fax: (30) 885-4713

BUTCHERS
Kosher Butcher
Goethestr. 61 10625
The butcher sells certain groceries. Opening hours: 10 am to 5 pm (Friday until 2 pm only).

CEMETERIES
Adass Jisroel
Wittlicherstrasse 2, Weissensee 13088 (30) 925-1724
Established in 1880, this historic cemetery is still in use. Rabbi Esriel Hildesheimer, Rabbi Prof. David Zvi Hoffmann, Rabbi Eliahu Kaplan and many other wise and pious Jews are buried here.

COMMUNITY ORGANISATIONS
Community Centre
Fasanenstr. 79-80, off the Kurfurstendamm 10623
(30) 88028-250
Fax: (30) 88028-250
This has been built on the site of a famous synagogue, destroyed by the Nazis.

Ignatz Bubis-Gemeindezentrum
Tucholskystrasse 40, Mitte 10117   (30) 281-3135
Fax: (30) 281-3122
Open daily, except Shabbat, from 11 am to 10 pm. Closes Friday two hours before Shabbat.

Judische Gemeinde zu Berlin
Joachimstaler Str 13 10719   (30) 88020-0
Fax: (30) 88028-150

Judischer Kulturverein (Jewish Cultural Association)
Oranienburgerstr. 26, Berlin-Mitte 10117
(30) 282-6669; 285-98052
Fax: (30) 285-98053
Email: jkv.berlin@t-online.de
Hours: Monday-Thursday 11am to 5pm, Friday 11am to 2pm and 1 hour before evening and Sunday events. Friday for Kiddush 6-9 pm. (Summer 7 pm). (Entrance around the corner.)

Zentralrat der Juden in Deutschland
Tucholskystr. 9 10117   (30) 284-4560
Fax: (30) 284-45613
Email: info@zentralratdjuden.de

EMBASSY
Embassy of Israel
Auguste-Viktoria Strasse 74-78 14193 (30) 89045-500
Fax: (30) 89045-555
Email: botschaft@israel.de
Web site: www.israel.de

GROCERIES
Kolbo
Auguststrasse 77-78, Mitte 10117   (30) 281-3135
In addition to kosher food and wines, sifrei kodesh as well as general literature about Jewish subjects can be obtained here.

Platzl
Passauer Str.4 10789   (30) 217-7506

Schalom
Wielandstr. 43 10625   (30) 312-1131
Fax: (30) 318-09905
Opening hours: 11.00 am to 5.00 pm (Fridays until 3.30 pm).

LIBRARIES
Jewish Community
Fassenstrasse 79 10623

Jewish Library
Oranienburger Str. 28 10117   (30) 880-28-427/429

MEDIA

Newspapers

Allgemeine Judische Wochenzeitung
Postfach 04 03 69, Tucholskystrasse 9 10117
(30) 2844 5650
Fax: (30) 2844 5699
Email: ajw@Juedische-Presse.de
Fortnightly.

Hadshot Adass Jisroel
Tucholsky str. 40 10117 (30) 281-3135
Published by Adass Jisroel.

Periodicals
Judische Korrespondenz
Oranienburgerstr. 26, Berlin-Mitte 10117
(30) 282-6669; 285-98052
Fax: (30) 285-98053
Email: jkv.berlin@t-online.de
Monthly.

Judisches Berlin
Oranienburger Str. 31 10117
(30) 88028-260;88028-269
Fax: (30) 88028-266
Email: jued.berlin@jg-berlin.org
Monthly

MUSEUM

Jewish Museum
Lindenstrasse 9-14 10969 (30) 30878-5681
Fax: (30) 25993-409
Email: info@jmberlin.de
Web site: www.jmberlin.de
The building is now open and well worth visiting. The
permanent exhibition is a journey through German-
Jewish history and culture. In addition there are
relevant changing exhibitions. There is a restaurant
on the premises. Tours: fuehrungenjmberlin.de.
Opening hours: Monday from 10.00 am to 10.00 pm
Tuesday-Sunday from 10.00 am to 8.00 pm

RESTAURANTS

Meat
Restaurant Arche Noah
Fasanenstr. 79-80 10623 (30) 882 6138
Shabbat reservations and payment have to be
arranged before beginning of Shabbat. The
restaurant is located in the first floor of the
community building. Opening hours: Daily 12 noon
to 3.30 pm and 6.30 pm to 10.30pm.

SYNAGOGUES

Liberal
Pestalozzistr. 14, 1000 10625 (30) 313-8411

Orthodox
Joachimstaler Strasse 13, Mitte 16719
Daily minyan

Adass Jisroel
Tucholskystrasse 40, Mitte 10117 (30) 281-3135
Fax: (30) 281-3122
Web site: www.adassjisroel.de
Established 1869. Rabbinate, kashrut supervision and
mohel can all be reached at this number. Near its
community centre, there is a guest house, a kosher
restaurant and a shop which sells kosher products.

TOURIST INFORMATION

Staatliches Israelisches Verkehrsbureau
Stollbergstrasse 6 15 (30) 883-6759
Fax: (30) 882-4093

TOURIST SITE

Jewish Culture Edition
Leo-Baeck-House, Tucholsky Street 9 10117
(30) 28445659
Fax: (30) 28445661
Email: Verlang@Judaicum.de

Bochum

SYNAGOGUES
Alte Wittener Str. 18 44803 (234) 361563
Fax: (234) 360187

Bonn

SYNAGOGUES
Templestr. 2-4, cnr. Adenauer Allee 53113 213560
Fax: 2618366

Braunschweig

COMMUNITY ORGANISATIONS
Community Centre
Steinstr. 4 38100 (531) 45536

MUSEUM
Braunschweigisches Landesmuseum
Abt. Judisches Museum, Burgplatz 1 D-38100
(531) 1215-0
Fax: (531) 1215-2607
Email: derda@landesmuseum-bs.de
Web site: www.landesmuseum-bs.de
Founded in 1746, this museum was formerly the
oldest Jewish museum in the world. It was re-opened
in 1987 under the auspices of the Braunschweigisches
Landesmuseum. Hours Tuesday-Sunday: 10am to
5pm.

Bremen

SYNAGOGUES
Schwachauser Heerstr. 117 28211 (421) 498-5104
Fax: (421) 498-4944

Celle

MUSEUM
Im Kreise 24 29221
Formerly a beautiful synagogue, it now houses
travelling exhibits on various themes of Jewish history
and of Jewish life in Celle where a community started
between 1671 and 1691. There are now enough Jews
in the town to form a minyan. Opening hours:
Tuesday to Thursday 3.00pm to 5.00pm, Friday
9.00am to 11.00am and Sunday 11.00am to 1.00pm.
Conducted tours of the synagogue and tours on the
history of the Jews of Celle are also available by
arrangement. Inquire at the tourist Office, Celle,
telephone +49.5141.1212.

Chemnitz

COMMUNITY ORGANISATIONS
Community Centre
Stollberger Str. 28 09119   (371) 32862

Coblenz (Koblenz)

COMMUNITY ORGANISATIONS
Schlachthof Str. 5   (261) 42223

Cologne

BAKERIES
Koscher Backerei Lipowitz, Roonstr. 61, Koln 50674
(221) 801-7895

HOTELS
Leonet
Rubensstr. 33   (221) 272-300
Fax: (221) 210-893
Email: leonetkoeln@netcologne.de

RESTAURANTS
Meat
Community Centre
Roonstr 50, 50674   (221) 240-4440
Fax: (221) 240-4440
Phone in advance. Glatt kosher.

SYNAGOGUES
Liberal
Judische Liberale Gemeinde
Stammheimer Str 22, Koln-Riehl 50735
(221) 287-0424
Fax: (221) 287-0424
Email: jlg.koeln@gmx.de

Orthodox
Roonstr. 50, Köln 50674   (221) 921-5600
Fax: (221) 921-5609
Email: synagoge-koeln@netcologne.de
Web site: www.sgk.de
Daily services. There is a Youth centre, mikva, glatt-
kosher restaurant (meat), Jewish museum and library
at the same address. A kosher bakery is located
nearby.

Darmstadt

COMMUNITY ORGANISATIONS
Community Centre
Wilhelm-Glassing-Str. 26 64283   (6151) 28897

Dortmund

COMMUNITY ORGANISATIONS
**Landesverband der Judischen Gemeinden von
Westfalen**
Prinz-Friedrich-Karl-Str. 12 44135   (231) 528495
Fax: (231) 5860372
Email: lvjuedwest@aol.com

SYNAGOGUES
Prinz-Friedrich-Karl-Str. 9 44135   (231) 528497

Dresden

In November 2001 the first new synagogue, in
what was East Germany, was consecrated. It is on
the site of the Semper synagogue, Am Hasenberg
1, originally built in 1838 and destroyed one
hundred years later on Kristallnacht.
   A three-foot high Star of David, one of the two
that was on the top of the synagogue, was all that
remained. It will stand above the new
synagogue's gate.
   Up to date information may be found on
www.Synagogue-dresden.de

COMMUNITY ORGANISATIONS
**Landesverband Sachsen der Judischen
Gemeinden K.d.o.R.**
Bautzner Str 20 01099   (351) 804-5491;802-2739
Fax: (351) 804-1445
A memorial to the six million Jews killed in the
Holocaust stands on the site of the Dresden
Synagogue, burnt down by the Nazis in November
1938.

SYNAGOGUES
Fiedlerstr. 3 01307   (351) 693317

Dusseldorf

SYNAGOGUES
Zietenstr. 50 40476 (211) 469120
Fax: (211) 485156

Emmendingen

COMMUNITY ORGANISATIONS
Community Centre
Kirchstr. 11 D-79312

SYNAGOGUES
Orthodox
Juedische Gemeinde Emmendingen
Landvogtei 11, D-79312 79312 (764) 571-989
Fax: (764) 571-980
Email: juedgemam@aol.com
Web site: www.juedgemen.de

Erfurt

COMMUNITY ORGANISATIONS
Community Centre
Juri-Gagarin-Ring 16 99084 (361) 24964

Essen

COMMUNITY ORGANISATIONS
Sedanstr. 46 45138 (201) 273413
Fax: (201) 287112

Essingen

CEMETERIES
Largest cemetery in the Palatinate, where Anne
Frank's ancestors are buried; sixteenth century. Key
at the Mayor's Office.

Frankfurt

BUTCHERS
Aviv Butchery & Deli
Hanauer Landstrasse 50 60314 (69) 433013
Fax: (69) 448064
Email: avivgmbh.kosherfood@rhein-main.net
Under the supervision of the Frankfurt Rabbinate.

COMMUNITY ORGANISATIONS
Community Centre (Jgnatz-Bubis-
Gemeindezentrum)
Westendstr. 43 60325 (69) 768-0360
Fax: (69) 746874
Email: jg.ffm@t-online.de
This community produces a magazine, "Judische
Gemeinde-Zeitung Frankfurt".

Zentralwohlfahrtsstelle der Juden in
Deutschland
Hebelstrasse 6 60318 (69) 94 43 71-15
Fax: (69) 49 48 17
Email: zentrale@zwst.org

MIKVAOT
Judische Gemeinde
Westendstr 43 D-60325 (69) 7680360
Fax: (69) 746874

MUSEUM
Jewish Museum
Untermainkai 14-15, 60311 (69) 212-35000
Fax: (69) 212-30705
Email: info@juedischesmuseum.de
Web site: www.juedischesmuseum.de
Sunday, Tuesday to Saturday 10.00 am-5.00 pm.
Wednesday 10.00am-8.00pm. Closed Monday.

RESTAURANTS
Sohar's
Savignystrasse 66 60325 (69) 75 23 41
Fax: (69) 741 0116
Supervision: Rabbi Menachem Halevi Klein, Frankfurt
Rabbinate
Hours: Tuesday to Thursday and Sunday, 12 pm to 8
pm; Friday, 12 pm to Shabbat; Shabbat, 1:30 pm to 4
pm; Monday, closed. Special arrangements can be
made by phone. Friday and Shabbat meals must be
ordered in advance. Provides party service, airline
catering and delivery to hotels. Fifteen-minute walk
from synagogue, fair centre and main train station.

SYNAGOGUES
Baumweg 5-7 60316 (69) 439381
Westend Synagogue
Freiherr-vom-Stein-Str. 30 60323 (69) 726263
Email: verwaltung@jg-ffm.de
This is the city's main synagogue.

Freiburg

COMMUNITY ORGANISATIONS
Community Centre
Engels Strasse (761) 383096
Fax: (761) 382332
Services: Erev Shabbat in Summer 7.30pm in Winter
6.30pm. Shabbat morning 9.30 am. Kosher Kiddush
after services.

Friedberg

TOURIST SITE
Judengasse 20 61169
An Gothic style mikva, built in 1260 is located here. The town council has issued a special explanatory leaflet about it. It has been restored and it is now scheduled as a historical monument of medieval architecture.

Fulda

COMMUNITY ORGANISATIONS
Community Centre
Von-Schildeck-Str 36043 (66) 170252
Fax: (66) 147465
Services every Friday 6.30pm, every Shabat 9.00am

Furth

COMMUNITY ORGANISATIONS
Blumenstr. 31 90762 (91) 177-0879

TOURIST SITE
Julienstr. 2
There is a beautifully restored synagogue as well as a historic mikva.

Gelsenkirchen

COMMUNITY ORGANISATIONS
Community Centre
Von-der-Recke-Str. 9 45879 (20) 923143 & 206628

Hagen

COMMUNITY ORGANISATIONS
Potthofstr. 16 58095 (2331) 711-3289

Halle

COMMUNITY ORGANISATIONS
Grosse Markerstr. 13 06108 (345) 233-110
Fax: (345) 233-1122
Email: jghalle@gmx.net

Hamburg

COMMUNITY ORGANISATIONS
Schaferkampsallee 27 20357 (40) 440-9440
Fax: (40) 410-8430
Mikvah on premises.

SYNAGOGUES
Orthodox
Hohe Weide 34 20253 (40) 4409-4429
Email: kieseler@gmx.de

Hanover

COMMUNITY ORGANISATIONS
Community Centre
Haeckelstr. 10 30173 (311) 810-472

SYNAGOGUES
Haeckelstr. 10 30173 (311) 810-472

Heidelberg

RESTAURANTS
College Restaurant
Theaterstr.9 69117 (6221) 168-767
Kosher meals are available (by arrangement & in advance - it is not open all year round) Monday-Friday at the college restaurant, 100 yards from the College of Jewish Studies, situated at Friederichstrasse 9.

Herford

COMMUNITY ORGANISATIONS
Community Centre
Keplerweg 11 32049 (52) 212039

Hildesheim

SYNAGOGUES
Jewish Community in Hildesheim
Postfach 10 07 07, Lower Saxony D31135
(512) 1704962
Fax: (512) 1704964
Rabbi Dr Walter Homolka is responsible for all Lower Saxony.

Hof

COMMUNITY ORGANISATIONS
Community Centre
Am Wiesengrund 20 95032 (92) 815-3249

Ichenhausen

MUSEUM
Museum of Jewish History
Located in the fine baroque synagogue, not far from Ulm.

Ingenheim

TOURIST SITE
Klingenerstr. 20 76831
Sixteenth- century cemetery can be visited. Key
obtained from Klingenerstr. 20.

Kaiserslautern

COMMUNITY ORGANISATIONS
Community Centre
Basteigasse 4 67655 (63) 169720

Karlsruhe

COMMUNITY ORGANISATIONS
Knielinger Allee 11 76133 (72) 172035

Kassel

COMMUNITY ORGANISATIONS
Bremer Str. 9 34117 (56) 112960

Kiel

SYNAGOGUES
Orthodox
Wikingerstrasse 6 24143 (431) 739-9096
Fax: (431) 739-9095

Kippenheim

An extensive restoration of the synagogue, built in
1850-1852, and destroyed on Kristallnacht was
started in 1987. The exterior renovation is
complete and work is now taking place on the
interior. It is classified by the state of Burden-
Wurrtenberg as a 'cultural monument of
significance'.
**There are no other specific locations of interest
to travellers.**

Konstanz

COMMUNITY ORGANISATIONS
Community Centre
Sigismundstr. 19 78462 (75) 312-3077

Krefeld

COMMUNITY ORGANISATIONS
Wiedstr. 17b 47799 (21) 512-0648

Landau

SYNAGOGUES
Frank-Loebsches Haus, Kaufhausgasse 9 D-76829
(6341) 86472
Fax: (6341) 13294
Email: sabine.haas.landau.de

Leipzig

COMMUNITY ORGANISATIONS
Community Centre
Lohrstr. 10 04105 (341) 291028

Lubeck

SYNAGOGUES
Orthodox
Synagogue & Community Centre
St.-Annen-Str 13 23552 (451) 798-2182
Fax: (451) 7074-9207
Email: jgh_hl@gmx.de

Magdeburg

COMMUNITY ORGANISATIONS
Community Centre
Groperstr. 1a 39106 (391) 52665

Mainz

COMMUNITY ORGANISATIONS
Forsterstr. 2 55118 (6131) 613990
Fax: (6131) 611767

TOURIST SITE
Untere Zahlbacherstr. 11
The key to the twelfth-century Jewish cemetery can
be obtained at the 'new' Jewish cemetery.

Mannheim

COMMUNITY ORGANISATIONS
Community Centre
F 3-4 68159 (621) 153974

Marburg an der Lahn

COMMUNITY ORGANISATIONS
Unterer Eichweg 17 35041 (642) 132881

Michelstadt

TOURIST SITE
Michelstadt
The town has an old synagogue which is now a
museum of both Judaism and Jewish history. It is
open every day in the summer except Saturday.

Minden

COMMUNITY ORGANISATIONS
Community Centre
Kampstr. 6 32423   (57) 123437

Monchengladbach

SYNAGOGUES
Albertusstr. 54 41363   (216) 23879
                            Fax: (216) 14639
        Email: juedischegemeindemg@t-online.de

Mulheim

COMMUNITY ORGANISATIONS
Kampstr. 7 45468   835191

Munich

BAKERIES
Hofpfisterie Bakeries

BOOKSELLERS
Literaturhandlung
Fürstenstr. 17 80333   (89) 89-2800135
                        Fax: (89) 89-281601
        Email: literaturhandlung@online.de

COMMUNITY ORGANISATIONS
Community Centre
Reichenbachstr. 27 80469   (89) 202-4000
                        Fax: (89) 201-4604
                Email: info@ikg-m.de

GROCERIES
Danel Feinkost
Pilgersheimerstrabe 44 81543   (89) 669-888
                        Fax: (89) 669-820
                Email: danel@t-online.de
Will deliver to hotels or other addresses, throughout
Germany.

Viktualien-Markt, Westenriederstrabe 9 80331
                            (89) 2280-0258

MUSEUM
Judisches Museum Munchen
Maximilian Str. 36 80539   (89) 2000-9693
                        Fax: (89) 2024-4838
A very small museum.

RESTAURANTS
Community Centre
                            (89) 202 38252
Run by the community centre at Reichenbachstrasse.
Hours: 12pm - 2.30pm; 6pm - 9pm. Shabbat meals
must be ordered by Friday noon. Closed Sunday;
August.

SYNAGOGUES
Possartstr. 15 81679   (89) 474-440
Mikva on premises.

Reichenbachstr. 27 80469   (89) 202-4000
                        Fax: (89) 201-4604
Mikva on premises.

Schwabing Synagogue (Schaarei Zion)
Georgenstr. 71 80798   (89) 2602-3337
                        Fax: (89) 2602-3338
Friday evenings and Sabbath mornings only.
Liberal
Beth Shalom
                            (89) 8980-9373
                        Fax: (89) 8980-9374
        Email: obeth.shalom@hagalil.com
Please ask for address and timetable.

Neustadt

COMMUNITY ORGANISATIONS
Community Centre
Ludwigstr. 20 67433   212652

Odenbach

TOURIST SITE
Kirchhofstrasse 9   (67) 532745
There is a unusually shaped historic synagogue built in
1752 with baroque paintings in this small village.
Arrangements to visit need to be made in advance.

Offenbach

COMMUNITY ORGANISATIONS
Community Centre
Kaiserstr. 109 63065   (69) 820036
                        Fax: (69) 820026

Osnabruck

COMMUNITY ORGANISATIONS
In der Barlage, 41 49078   (541) 148420
                        Fax: (541) 143-4701
Kashrut information or visitors who wish to eat
kosher on Shabbat, please contact Rabbi Marc Sterm
at Tel: 49 541-48553.

SYNAGOGUES
Orthodox
Jewish Congregation Synagogue
In der Barlage, 41 49078 (541) 48420
Fax: (541) 434701
Email: Rabbistern@t-online.de
Web site: www.jiddischkeit.org

TOURIST SITE
The Felix-Nussbaum House
Lotter Str 2 49078 (541) 323-2207
Fax: (541) 323-2739
Email: jaehner@osnabrueck.de
About 20 minutes walk from the congregation

Paderborn

COMMUNITY ORGANISATIONS
Community Centre
Pipinstr. 32 33098 (52) 512-2596

Potsdam

COMMUNITY ORGANISATIONS
Potsdam Community Centre
Heinrich-Mann-Allee 103, Haus 16 14473
(331) 872018

Regensburg

COMMUNITY ORGANISATIONS
Community Centre
Am Brixener Hof 2 93047 (94) 157093; 21819

Saarbrucken

SYNAGOGUES
Synagogengemeinde Saar
Lortzingstr 8 66111 (681) 910-380
Fax: (681) 910-38-13

Schwerin

COMMUNITY ORGANISATIONS
Judische Gemeinde Schwerin
Schlachtermarkt 7 19055 (38) 5550-7345
Fax: (38) 5593-60989
Email: jgemeinde@gmx.net

Speyer

TOURIST SITE
(62) 353332
This town contains the oldest (eleventh-century)
mikva in Germany, Judenbadgasse. To visit it, obtain
the key by contacting the Tourist Office
(Maximilianstrasse 11). Guided tours are available.

Straubing

COMMUNITY ORGANISATIONS
Community Centre
Wittelsbacherstr. 2 94315 (94) 211387

Stuttgart

RELIGIOUS ORGANISATIONS
**Israelitische Religionsgemeinschaft
Wurttembergs**
Hospitalstr. 36 70174 (711) 228360
Fax: (711) 2283618

RESTAURANTS
Meat
Schalom Kosher Restaurant
Hospitalstrasse 36 70174 (711) 294752
Supervision: Orthodox Rav of the Stuttgart
community
Open during morning hours through to about 7.00pm
except Mondays (when its closed). Located on the
premises of the Stuttgart Jewish community centre.

Trier

COMMUNITY ORGANISATIONS
Community Centre
Kaiserstr. 25 54290 (65) 140530; 33295

Veitshochheim

Located a few miles from Wurzburg is the town of Veitshoechheim, which reconsecrated a pre-First World War I Synagogue and opened as a Jewish Museum in March 1994. Originally built in 1730, the synagogue was the community centre for local Jews, who had lived in the area for nearly three hundred years, from 1644 to 1942, when the last Jews were deported from Veitshochheim to the Nazi concentration camps.

In 1986 the stone fragments of the original interior, including the Bima and the Ahron Hakodesch, were discovered beneath the floor, where they had been buried in 1940. This find prompted local officials to transform the Synagogue back to its original function and splendour, using photographs from the 1920s as a guide.

MUSEUM

The Synagogue and Museum of Jewish Culture
Thuengersheimer Strasse 17, D- 97209
(931) 9802-764
Fax: (931) 9802-766
Email: museum@veitschoechheim.de
Web site: www.veitshoechheim.de
Recently restored. Museum hours: Thursday 3pm to 6pm, Sunday 2pm to 5pm.

Wiesbaden

RESTAURANTS

Communal Offices
Friedrichstr. 31-33 65185
(611) 933-3030
Fax: (611) 933-3039

SYNAGOGUES

Friedrichstr. 31-33 65185
(611) 933-3030
Fax: (611) 933-3039
Email: JG.WI@fonline.de

Worms

The original Rashi Synagogue, built in the 11th century and the oldest Jewish place of worship in Europe, was destroyed by the Nazis in 1938. After the Second World War, it was reconstructed and was reconsecrated in 1961. The building also contains a 12th century mikvahh and a Jewish museum. There is also an ancient Jewish cemetery, (the oldest in Europe).

There are no other specific locations of interest to travellers.

Wuppertal

COMMUNITY ORGANISATIONS

Community Centre
Friedrich-Ebert-Str. 73 42103
(202) 300233

Wurzburg

There are old Jewish cemeteries in Wurzburg, Heidingsfeld and Hochberg.

COMMUNITY ORGANISATIONS

Valentin-Becker-Str. 11 97072
(931) 151190
Fax: (931) 118184
Also guest rooms for tourists; kosher meals available.

MIKVAOT

Valentin-Becker-Str. 11 97072
(931) 151190
Fax: (931) 118184
Appointments to be made.

SYNAGOGUES

Valentin-Becker-Str. 11 97072
(931) 151190
Fax: (931) 118184

TOURIST SITE

There are old Jewish cemeteries in Wurzburg, Heidingsfeld and Hochberg.

GIBRALTAR

The first Jewish people in Gibraltar were Sephardi, who had crossed over the border from Spain before the Inquisition began in the fourteenth century. Many more followed in the ensuing centuries. When Britain took possession, Jews were initially banned, but later they were allowed in as traders and finally, in 1749, they were granted full permission to live there. The community began to flourish and the Jewish population, which now also included many North African Jews rose to 2,000.

At the end of the Second World War, some of the community returned after being evacuated to Britain. There are now fairly good Jewish facilities, namely four synagogues, and newsletters. There are no kosher hotels in Gibraltar.

Gibraltar has an Eruv. Gibraltar has had a Jewish prime minister and a Jewish mayor, both Gibraltar's highest offices.

GMT +1 hour	**Total Population 28,000**
Country calling code (350)	**Jewish Population 650**
Emergency Telephone (Police – 999) (Fire – 999) (Ambulance – 999)	**(Electricity voltage – 220/240)**

BAKERIES
J. Amar
47 Line Wall Road   73516

BUTCHERS
A. Edery
26 Public Market   75168
Fax: 42529
Email: edery@gibnet.gi
Web site: www.ederykosher.com

COMMUNITY ORGANISATIONS
Managing Board of Jewish Community
10 Bomb House Lane   72606
Fax: 40487

CONTACT INFORMATION
Solomon Levy M.B.E. J.P
3 Convent Place, PO Box 190
77789; 42818, 78047 (home)
Fax: 42527
Email: slevy@gibnet.gi
The vice president of the Jewish community is happy to provide information for Jewish travellers.

CULTURAL ORGANISATIONS
Jewish Social & Cultural Club
7 Bomb House Lane   79636
Email: asuissa@gibnet.gi
Mailing address: Avner Suissa, 20 Lime Tree Lodge, Montagu Gardens, Gibraltar.

DELICATESSEN
Uncle Sam's Deli
62 Irish Town   51236; 51226
Fax: 42516
Email: dabamick@gibnet.gi.com
Provides kosher groceries and wine. Catering and takeaway service. Full glatt kosher service. Fully licensed.

EMBASSY
Consul General of Israel
Marina View, Glacis Road, PO Box 141   77244

GROCERIES
I&D Abudarham
32 Cornwall's Lane, PO Box 216   78506
Fax: 73249
Email: djabudar@gibnet.gi
Kosher wines, meats & poultry.

HOTELS
The Rock Hotel
73000
Fax: 73513
The hotel has kosher facilities (meat and dairy) and can cater for pre-booked groups of 10 or more. Kosher take-away food can also be delivered to a room.

JUDAICA
A.Cohen
3 Convent Place, PO Box 190   52734
Email: sofergib@prontomail.com
Supplier of Mezuzot ,Tephilim and Shaatnez.

MIKVAOT
12 Bomb House Lane   77658 & 73090
Fax: 72359

RESTAURANTS
Jewish Club
Open daily from 10 am to 11 pm, except Shabbat, but arrangements can be made with this restaurant owner for Shabbat meals.

SYNAGOGUES
Abudarham
20 Parliament Lane 78506   78047
Fax: 42527

Etz Hayim
Irish Town 75955   75563
                                              Fax: 42939

Nefusot Yehuda
65 Line Wall Road 73037

Shaar Hashamayim
19 Engineer Lane 78069   74030
                                              Fax: 74029
Enquiries: Joseph de M. Benyunes PO Box 1474.

GREECE

After the Hellenistic occupation of Israel (the Jewish revolt during this occupation is commemorated in the festival of Hanukah), some Jews were led into slavery in Greece, beginning the first recorded Jewish presence in the country. The next significant Jewish immigration occurred after the Inquisition, when many Spanish Jews moved to Salonika, which was a flourishing Jewish centre until the German occupation in the Second World War. In 1832 Jews were granted equal civil rights to all other Greek citizens.

By the early 1940s, the Jewish population had grown to over 70,000, with 45,000 living in Salonika. The country was occupied in July 1941 and split among the Axis (German, Italian and Bulgarian) forces. During the occupation a relatively large number of Jews joined the partisans. Many local Christians did protect their Jewish neighbours in Athens. After the war, many of the survivors emigrated to Israel.

Today, there are Sephardi synagogues in Greece and, in Athens, a community centre and a Jewish museum. There are Jewish publications and a library in the community centre. In Aegina, Corfu and other Greek islands, ancient synagogues may be visited.

GMT +2 hours
Country calling code (30)
Emergency Telephone (Police – 100) (Fire – 199) (Ambulance – 166)

Total Population 10,552,000
Jewish Population 4,500
(Electricity voltage – 220)

Athens

Almost 3,000 Jews live in Athens. The community has access to a centre, containing a library, and the opportunity to have a kosher meal. The Jewish museum in the centre of the city details the rise and tragic fall of Greek Jewry.

Kosher meals are served at the Athens Jewish Cultural Centre upon request (contact Mrs Rachel Sasson, Tel. (1) 213 3371. Delivery to hotels in Athens can also be arranged).

COMMUNITY ORGANISATIONS
Central Board of the Jewish Communities of Greece
36 Voulis Street 10557   (210) 324-4315-18
                              Fax: (210) 331-3852
                       Email: hhkis@hellasnet.gr
                       Web site: www..kis.gr

EMBASSY
Embassy of Israel
Marathonodromou Street 1, Paleo Psychico,
POB 65140   (210) 671-9530

MUSEUM
Jewish Museum of Greece
39 Nikis Str 105 57   (210) 322-5582
                              Fax: (210) 323-1577
                       Email: jmg@otenet.gr
              Web site: www.jewishmuseum.gr
Open: Monday to Friday 9.00am to 2.30pm, Sunday 10.00am to 2.00pm, Saturday closed.

RESTAURANTS
Meat
5 Averof St 10433   (210) 520-2880
                              Fax: (210) 520-2881
                       Email: chabad@otenet.gr
Telephone for orders.

Vegetarian
Eden
Odos Flessa 3, Plaka

SYNAGOGUES
Sephardi
Beth Shalom
5 Melidoni Street 10553   (210) 325-2773; 2823; 2875
                              Fax: (210) 322-0761

TOURIST INFORMATION
Community Office
8 Melidoni Street 10553   (210) 325-2875
                              Fax: (210) 322-0761
                       Email: isrkath@hellasnet.gr

Chalkis

COMMUNITY ORGANISATIONS
Community Centre
35 Kotsou Street 34100   (2221) 80690

KASHRUT INFORMATION
(2221) 27297

SYNAGOGUES
36 Kotsou Street
This synagogue has been rebuilt and renewed many times on its original foundations. Tombstone inscriptions in the cemetery go back more than fifteen centuries. Only open on High Holy Days.

Corfu

COMMUNITY ORGANISATIONS
Community Centre
5 Riz. Voulephton St. 49100
(2661) 45650
Fax: (2661) 43791

TOURIST SITE
Velissariou St.
(2661) 38802
There was an ancient synagogue and cemetery here, destroyed by the Nazis.

Ioannina

COMMUNITY ORGANISATIONS
18 Josef Eliyia St. 45221
(2651) 25195
Contact: John Kalef-Ezra on 32390.

Larissa

SYNAGOGUES
Community Centre
29 Kentavron St. 41222
(241) 532 965

Rhodes

SYNAGOGUES
Khal Shalom Kadosh
1 Simmiou St., Dodecanese Islands
(2241) 22364
Fax: (2241) 73039
The synagogue belongs to the Jewish Community of Rhodes which counts 38 members. It was built around 1577 in the medieval City of Rhodes which used to be the Old Jewish Quarter. A photographic museum is functioning next to the synagogue. The synagogue is on the World Monuments Fund list of 100 most endangered sites. Tourists wishing to visit these sites should contact: Jewish Community of Rhodes, No. 5 Polydorou St. Old City. Tel: (0030) 241-22364 or Fax (0030) 241-73039.

Salonika

For many years around the turn of the 20th century Salonika, then part of the Ottoman Empire, Jews formed the majority of the city's inhabitants. It was known as the "Jerusalem of the Balkens". The official day off was Saturday.

CULTURAL ORGANISATIONS
The Israelite Fraternity House
24 Vassileos Irakliou St.
(231) 221030

Yad le Zikaron
24 Vassileos Irakliou St.
(231) 275701

LIBRARIES
The Centre for Historical Studies of Salonika Jews
24 Vassileos Irakliou St., 1st Floor
(231) 223231
Fax: (231) 229069

SYNAGOGUES
Monastirioton
35 Sygrou Str. 54630
(231) 524968

Trikkala

SYNAGOGUES
15 Athanassiou Diakou St

Yad Lezicaron
24 Vassileos Irakliou Str.
(231) 223231

Volos

COMMUNITY ORGANISATIONS
Xenophontos & Moisseos Streets 38333
(2421) 25302
Fax: (2421) 25302

KASHRUT INFORMATION
20 Parodos Kondulaki

SYNAGOGUES
Xenophontos & Moisseos Streets
Open primarily on High Holy Days.

TOURIST SITE
Holocaust Monument
Riga Ferreou Square.

GUATEMALA

Conversos were the first recorded Jews in the country, but, a few centuries later, the next Jewish immigration occurred with the arrival of German Jews in 1848. Later, some east European Jews arrived, but Guatemala was not keen to accept refugees from Nazism and, as a result, passed some laws which, although not mentioning Jews directly, were aimed against Jewish refugees.

Even though these laws were in place, in 1939 there were 800 Jews in Guatemala. An Ashkenazi community centre was built in 1965, but, despite accepting some Jewish Cuban refugees, the community is shrinking owing to assimilation and intermarriage.

Most Jews live in Guatemala City, and others in Quetzaltenango and San Marcos.

GMT -6 hours	Total Population 10,517,000
Country calling code (502)	Jewish Population 1,000
Emergency Telephone (Police – 110) (Fire – 110) (Ambulance – 125)	(Electricity voltage – 110)

Guatemala City

COMMUNITY ORGANISATIONS
Communidad Judia Guatemalteca
Apartado Postal 502   (2) 311-975
Fax: (2) 325-683

EMBASSY
Embassy of Israel
13 Av. 14-07, Zona 10   (2) 371305

SYNAGOGUES
Ashenkenazi
Centro Hebreo, 7a Av. 13-51, Zona 9   (2) 367643
Sephardi
Maguen David
7a Av. 3-80, Zona 2   (2) 232-0932

HAITI

Christopher Columbus brought the first Jew to Haiti – his interpreter, Luis de Torres, a Converso who had been baptised before the voyage. Thereafter more Jews settled but the community was destroyed in an anti-European revolt by Toussaint L'Ouverture in 1804. A hundred or so years later, Jews from the Middle East and some refugees from the Nazis settled in Haiti, but many subsequently emigrated to Israel.

The remaining community has benefited from the help of the Israeli embassy, and services are held in the embassy or in private homes. There is no central Jewish organisation, and the community is too small to support other Jewish facilities.

GMT -5 hours	Total Population 7,492,000
Country calling code (509)	Jewish Population Under 100
Emergency Telephone (Police – 114) (Ambulance – 118)	(Electricity voltage – 110)

Port au Prince

CONTACT INFORMATION
Religious services are held at the home of the Honorary Israeli Consul, Mr Gilbert Bigio.

HONDURAS

During the Spanish colonial period, some Conversos did live in Honduras, but it was only in the nineteenth century that any significant Jewish immigration occurred. In the early twentieth century, refugees from Nazism followed a handful of immigrants from eastern Europe. Honduras was one of the small number of countries to aid refugees from Nazism, and many Jews owe their lives to the help of Honduran consulates which issued visas in wartime Europe.

Tegucigalpa (the capital) contains the largest Jewish population, but the only synagogue in the country is in San Pedro Sula (services are held in private homes in Tegucigalpa). There is also a Sunday school and WIZO branch.

GMT -6 hours
Country calling code (504)
Emergency Telephone (Police – 119) (Fire – 198) (Ambulance – 37 8654)

Total Population 6,338,000
Jewish Population Under 100
(Electricity voltage – 110/220)

San Pedro Sula

CONTACT INFORMATION
530157
Services Friday and Shabbat at synagogue and community centre.

Tegucigalpa

CONTACT INFORMATION
315908
Services usually held in private homes. Contact secretary at above number.

EMBASSY
Embassy of Israel
Palmira Building, 5th Floor   324232; 325176

Balatonfured

GUEST HOUSE
Holiday center Udulo, Liszt Ferenc utca 6 8734-3404
Open May to September. It is also a restaurant and there is a synagogue on the premises.

HUNGARY

There were Jews living in Hungary in Roman times, even before the arrival of the Magyars (ancestors of the present-day Hungarians). The Jews suffered during the Middle Ages, when there was some anti-semitism, but conditions improved under Austro-Hungarian rule, and Judaism was recognised as being on a legal par with Christianity in 1896.

Hungary lost a considerable amount of territory after the First World War, and as a result many of its original Jewish communities (such as Szatmar) found themselves within other countries. Anti-semitism reached a peak in March 1944, when, during the German occupation, most Jewish communities began to be transported to Auschwitz. A number of those who were deported survived when Auschwitz was liberated by the Red Army in January 1945.

After the war, Hungary had the largest Jewish community in central Europe. Inevitably, the community dwindled through emigration (especially after the 1956 uprising) and assimilation. Communism in Hungary was far more lenient than in other Warsaw Pact countries, and synagogues were allowed to operate. Since 1989, religious interest has increased, and the government has recently renovated the Dohany Synagogue, the second biggest synagogue in the world and the largest in Europe. The Jewish population is still the largest in the region, although most are not religious. The Hungarian national tourist office has published 'Shalom', an excellent guide to Jewish Hungary.

GMT + 1 hour	**Total Population 10,153,000**
Country calling code (36)	**Jewish Population 60,000**
Emergency Telephone (Police – 107) (Fire – 105) (Ambulance – 104)	**(Electricity voltage – 220)**

Budapest

Once known in the nineteenth century as 'Judapest', this city contains the majority of Hungarian Jews. At its prewar peak its Jewish population was around 200,000. There are several functioning synagogues, from Orthodox to 'neolog' (Hungarian reform). The recently restored Dohany synagogue was built to accommodate 3,000 in prayer.

BAKERIES
Frohlich
Dob u. 22, Budapest 1074   (1) 267-2851

Kosher Bakers
Kazinczy u. 28, 1074 Budapest   (1) 342-0231

BOOKSELLERS
Judaica Art
13 Wesselenyi utca.
                    Web site: www.makkabi.hu

COMMUNITY ORGANISATIONS
Central Board of the Federation of Jewish Communities in Hungary
VII, Sip utca 12   (1) 342-1355
                    Fax: (1) 342-1790
                    Email: bzsh@mail.matav.hu

EMBASSY
Embassy of Israel
Fullank Utca 8 1026   (1) 2000-781

GROCERIES
Koser Bolt
Dob utca 12, 1072 Budapest   (1) 267-5691
Kosher products, bread, etc.

The Orthodox Central Synagogue
VII, Kazinczy utca 27
Kosher milk and cheese are available here three mornings a week.

HOTELS
Kosher
King's Hotel
Nagydiofa u. 27-29, 1075 Budapest 1074
                    (1) 352-7617
                    Fax: (1) 352-7675
Strictly kosher hotel with a restaurant.

MEDIA
Newspaper
Uj Elet (New Life)
Central Board Hotel

MIKVAOT
VII Kazinczy utca 16 1074

MUSEUM
Hungarian Jewish Museum and Archives
Dohany u.2 1077   (1) 343-6756
                    Fax: (1) 343-6756
                    Email: bpjewmus@mail.c3.hu
                    Web site: www.c3.hu/~bpjewmus

Religious Organisations

The Central Rabbinical Council
VII, Sip utca 12   (1) 142-1180
Rabbi Schweitzer is Chief Rabbi of Hungary and
Director of the Rabbinical Seminary.

Restaurants

Meat
King's Hotel
Nagydiofa Utca 25-27   (1) 352-7675
Supervision: Orthodox   Community

Synagogues

Dohany Street Synagogue
VII Dohany Utca 4-6   (1) 342-2353
Built in 1859, it is the largest in Europe and the
second largest in the world. In its grounds lie buried
Hungarian Jewish victims of the Nazis. There is also a
commemorative plaque to Hanna Senesh, the Jewish
parachutist who was captured and tortured before
being shot by the Nazis. A plaque commemorating
Theodor Herzl, the founder of Zionism is in the
Jewish Museum.

Heroes Synagogue
VII Wesselenyi utca 5   (1) 342-2353
Orthodox
The Orthodox Central Synagogue
Kazinczy u 27   (1) 351-0526
                               Fax: (1) 322-7200

Tourist Information

Jewish Information Service
                                    (1) 166-5165
                               Fax: (1) 166-5165

Tours

Jewish heritage in Budapest
Dohany Utca 2   (1) 317-2754
                 Email: hukonc@enternet.hu
                 Web site: www.ticket.info.hu
A walking tour of Jewish Budapest, arranged by the
Municipality

Tours of Jewish Interest

Chosen Tours
                                    (1) 185-9499
                               Fax: (1) 166-5165
Tours of Jewish sites are provided by telephone
arrangement.

Sopron

Museum

The Old Synagogue Museum
ul utca 22-24 H-9400   (99) 311327
                              Fax: (99) 311347
                Email: smuzeum@mail.c3.hu
A department of the Sopron Museum. A medieval
synagogue, originally a private one, situated on the
ground floor of a baroque house, restored as a
museum in 1976. Open from 1 May to 1 October,
daily between 9am and 5pm. Closed Tuesdays.

Synagogues

Orthodox
Jewish Orthodox
Kiss Janos u. 3. H-9400   (99) 313-508

Tourist Site

ul utca 11
A second medieval synagogue which formerly housed
the museum is undergoing restoration.

The Neologue Cemetery
Dating from the nineteenth-century. There is a
memorial wall dedicated to the 1,600 local victims of
the Holocaust.

INDIA

The Jewish population of India can be divided into three components: the Cochin Jews, the Bene Israel and the Baghdadi Jews. The Cochin Jews are based in the south of India in Kerala. This community can be further divided into Black (believing themselves to be the original settlers) and White (of European or Middle Eastern origin), the Paradesi. Most of the community has emigrated, but there is still a synagogue in Cochin that is a major tourist attraction.

The Bene Israel believe they are descended from Jewish survivors of a ship wrecked on its voyage from ancient Israel during the period of King Solomon. No reliable documentary evidence, however, exists to support this claim. More reliable evidence dates settlement to around the tenth century. The Bene Israel follow only certain Jewish practices, such as kosher food and Shabbat, and also adhere to certain Muslim and Hindu beliefs; for example, they abstain from eating beef. In the eighteenth century, they settled in Bombay and now form the largest group of Indian Jews.

Baghdadi Jews, immigrants from Iraq and the other Middle Eastern countries, arrived in India in the late eighteenth century, and followed British Colonial rather than local custom. Many emigrated to Israel in the 1950s and 1960s.

During the Indo-Pakistan war of 1972, the leading Indian military figure was General Samuels. In 1999 Lt-Gen J.F.R. Jacob was appointed Governor of Punjab State.

There is a central Council of Indian Jewry, based in Mumbai, where most of the Indian Jews live. Kosher food is available, and there are three Jewish schools in the city. Relations with Israel have recently improved and it is now a major trade partner.

GMT +5 1/2 hours	Total Population 1,013,662,000
Country calling code (91)	Jewish Population 5,000
	(Electricity voltage – 220)

Alibag

SYNAGOGUES
Magen Aboth Synagogue
Alibag
Established in 1848 the synagogue is in what is known as "Israel" alley to the south-east of the town.

Cochin

COMMUNITY ORGANISATIONS
Association or Kerala Jews
Thekkumbhagom Synagogue, Jews Street
366-247; 362-454

Fax: 363-747

CONTACT INFORMATION
Inquiries
Princess Street, Fort   24228; 24988

SYNAGOGUES
Chennamangalam
Jew Street, Chennamangalam
Built in 1614 and restored in 1916, this synagogue has been declared a historical monument by the Government of India. A few yards away is a small concrete pillar into which is inset the tombstone of Sara Bat-Israel, dated 5336 (1576).

Paradesi
Jew Town, Mattancherry 2
The only Cochin synagogue that is still functioning. Built in 1568.

Ernakulam

TOURIST SITES
Kadavumbagom Synagogue
Built in 1200 and rebuilt in 1690.

Thekkumbagon Synagogue
(484) 390-187
Email: anithamsamson@yahoo.co.in
Built in 1580 and rebuilt in 1939.

Khamasa

SYNAGOGUES
Magen Abraham
Bukhara Mohalla, opp. Parsi Agiari 380001
(79) 535-5224

Kolkata

COMMUNITY ORGANISATIONS
Jewish Association of Kolkata
1&2 Old Court House Corner   (33) 224861
General inquiries to this telephone number.

SYNAGOGUES

Bethel Synagogue
26/1 Pollack Street

Magen David Synagogue
109a Peplabi Rash, Bihari Bose Road, 1, (formerly Canning Street)

Neveh Shalome Synagogue
9 Jackson Lane, 1

Mumbai

EMBASSY

Consul General of Israel
50 Kailash, G. Deshmukh Marg, 26   (22) 386-2793

GROCERIES

ORT India
68 Worli Hill Estate, PO Box 6571 400018
                              (22) 496-2350; 8423; 8457
            Fax: (22) 496-2350; 491-3203
            Email: ortbbay@bom5.vsnl.net.in
                    Web site: www.ortindia.com
The Jewish Education Resource Centre provides kosher food from its bakery and kitchen to all travellers. ORT India also arranges conducted tours to places of Jewish interest in Mumbai and to ancient synagogues in the Konkan region of Maharashtra State.

SYNAGOGUES

Beth El Synagogue
Mirchi Galli, Mahatma Gandhi Road, Panvel 410206

Etz Haeem Prayer Hall
2nd Lane, Umerkhadi 400009   (22) 377-0193

Gate of Mercy (Shaar Harahamim)
254 Samuel Street, Nr Masjid Railway Station 400003
                              (22) 345-2991
This is the oldest Bene Israel synagogue in use in India, established in 1796 and known as the Samaji Hasaji Synagogue or Juni Masjid until 1896 when its name was changed to Shaar Harahamim.

Knesseth Eliahu Synagogue
V.B. Ghandi Road (Forbes Street), Fort 400001
                              (22) 283-1502
The synagogue was constructed in 1884. Freddie Sofer welcomes visitors to join him for lunch after Shabbat service.

Kurla Bene Israel Prayer Hall
275 S. G. Barve Road (C.S.T. Road), Kurla, West Bombay 400070   (22) 511-8795

Magen David Synagogue
J.J.Nagpada, Byculla 400008   (22) 300-6675
The synagogue built in 1861 with the assistance of the Sasson family has a gothic character.

Magen Hassidim Synagogue
8 Mohammaed Shahid Marg, (formerly Moreland Road), Agripada 400011   (22) 309-2493
Most marriages and bar mitzvahs are held here; it can seat 1000. Only Bene Israel carpenters were used, and they gave their services free.

Rodef Shalom Synagogue
Sussex Road, Byculla 400027

Shaar HaRahamim Synagogue
Tembi Naka, opp. Civil Hospital, Thane 400601
                              (22) 853-4817
Established in 1796, it is the oldest Bene Israel synagogue in India.

Shaare Rason Synagogue
90 Tantanpura Street, 3rd Road, Don Tad, Israel Mohalla, Khadak 400009

Tifereth Israel Synagogue
92 K. K. Marg, Jacob Circle 400011   (22) 305-3713

TOURS OF JEWISH INTEREST

ORT India
68 Worli Hill Estate, PO Box 6571 400018
                              (22) 496-2350; 8423
                    Fax: (22) 364-7308
            Email: jhirad@giasbm01.vsnl.net.in
The Travel and Tourism Department arranges tours in Bombay & Raighad District.

TOV Jewish India Tours
96 Penso Villa, 1st Floor, Mbraut Rd, Shivaji Park 400028   (22) 445-0134
                    Fax: (22) 431-9391
            Email: greenforesthills@sify.com
Tours of Jewish India.

New Delhi

SYNAGOGUES

Judah Hyam Synagogue
A/7 Nirman Vihar, Patparganj 110092   (11) 224-3136
The Judah Hyam Annexe houses a library and centre for Jewish and inter-faith studies.

2 Humayun Road 110003   (11) 463-5500

Paravur

SYNAGOGUES

Parur Synagogue
Built in 1165, the synagogue was rebuilt in 1616 by the local Jewish community with the help of David Kastiel, who was not a Paradesi Jew, but a man of local origin. Paradesi Jews were associated with Mattancherry and their synagogue was built in 1568.

Pune

SYNAGOGUES
Ohel David Synagogue
9 Dr Ambedkar Road 411001   (20) 613-2048
Email: oheldavid@ip.eth.net
The synagogue was built by David Sasoon in 1867. His grave is in the synagogue grounds.

Succath Shelomo
93 Rasta Peth 411011
Inquiries to Hon. Sec. 247/1 Rasta Peth, Trupti Apt.,
Pune 411011 or Dr S. B. David 9 Bund Garden Road,
Pune 411001

TOURS OF JEWISH INTEREST
Tov Jewish India Tours
118 Citadel Palace Orchard, rdindhari, Green Forest Hills 411028   (20) 693-1488
Fax: (20) greenforesthills

Thane

KASHRUT INFORMATION
Pearl Farm, A/1 Dhobi Alley, Sulabha, Maharashtra 400601   (22) 536-0539
Kosher goat meat and fish.

IRAN

Iran, formerly known as Persia, has an ancient connection with Jews. The first Jewish communities in Persia date from the time of the First Temple. King Cyrus, the Persian king who conquered Babylon, allowed the Jews to return to Israel from their exile. Not all returned, however, and some settled in Persia. The Persian community grew over time, suffering oppression after the Islamic conversion in 642. Certain segments of the Jewish community also grew in wealth in early medieval times.

In the twentieth century, there was a brief period of hope for the Jews in Iran when the country became more western-oriented after 1925. However, the 1979 revolution quashed the hope for a more tolerant Iran, and many thousands of Jews decided to emigrate. Association with Zionism became a capital offence and a number of Jews have been executed since 1979. The Jews are seen as 'dhimmi', (subordinates), to Islam, and as such are allowed some religious practices, but are so closely watched that maintaining a Jewish life is difficult. The tombs of Esther and Mordechai (from the Purim story) are in Hamadan, south-west of the capital Tehran. Iran currently has the largest Jewish community in the Middle East outside Israel.

Kosher food has become expensive and is difficult to obtain.

GMT +3 1/2 hours
Country calling code (98)

Total Population 60,694,000
Jewish Population 18,000
(Electricity voltage – 220)

Isfahan

SYNAGOGUES
Shah Abass Street

Tehran

SYNAGOGUES
Haim
Gavamossaltaneh Street

Meshedi
Kakh Shomali Avenue, opp. Abrishami School

The Iraqi
Anatole France Street

TOURIST SITE
Jewish Quarter of Tehran, Mahalleh, off Sirus Avenue

IRISH REPUBLIC

The first report of Jews in Ireland records that in 1079 'five Jews came over the sea'. The small community was expelled in 1290, along with the Jews from the rest of the British Isles. The community slowly grew again after Jews were allowed to return and a few conversos settled in Dublin. There was never a strong community, however, and only in 1822 did a significant influx of Jews occur when immigrants came from England and eastern Europe.

Immigration continued and large numbers arrived from the Russian Empire after 1881. Some settled in Ireland intentionally but others believed that they had landed in America, deceived by the ships captains. In 1901, the community was 3,800 strong. The highest figure for the Jewish population of Ireland has been estimated at 8,000.

Robert Briscoe (1894-1969) who played an important role in the struggle for Irish independence was twice Lord Mayor of Dublin.

Currently, most Jews live in Dublin although the community is now shrinking.

GMT +0 hours	**Total Population 3,626,000**
Country calling code (353)	**Jewish Population 1,200**
Emergency Telephone (Police – 999) (Fire – 999) (Ambulance – 999)	**(Electricity voltage – 220)**

Cork

SYNAGOGUES
Orthodox
10 South Terrace   (21) 487-0413
Fax: (21) 487-6537
Email: rosehill@iol.ie
Services: For information contact Fred Rosehill (353) 21 487-0413.

Dublin

The centre of Irish Jewry, Dublin's position on the east coast meant that many Jews settled there in the flight from Eastern Europe in the nineteenth century. The Jewish Museum in Dublin, opened by the then President of Israel, Irish-born Chaim Herzog, in 1985 during a state visit to Ireland, gives much information on the town's Jewish history.

Dublin was also the home of possibly the world's most famous fictional Jew, Leopold Bloom of James Joyce's 'Ulysses'.

BAKERIES
Hemmingway's Deli
Ballsbridge Terrace 4

Rowan's Deli
Main Street, Rathfarnham 14

CONTACT INFORMATION
Vegetarian Society of Ireland
PO Box 3010, Ballsbridge 4
Email: vegsoc@ireland.com
Web site: www.vegetarian.ie
The society will provide details of establishments which cater for vegetarians.

DELICATESSEN
The Big Cheese
St Andrew's Lane 2   (1) 671-1399
Fax: (1) 490-9917
Has a Kosher section and is open on Sunday Morning

EMBASSY
Embassy of Israel
Carrisbrook House, 122 Pembroke Road,
Ballsbridge 4   (1) 668-0303
Fax: (1) 668-0418
Email: info@embisrael.iol.ie

MIKVAOT
Terenure Hebrew Congregation, Rathfarnham Road
(1) 490-5348

MUSEUM
Irish Jewish Museum
3-4 Walworth Road 8   (1) 490-1857
Fax: (1) 490-1857
Open Tuesday, Thursday and Sunday. May to September 11 am to 3.30 pm; October to April 10.30 am to 2.30 pm. Group visits by arrangement. (1) 490-1857.

RELIGIOUS ORGANISATIONS
Board of Shechita
1 Zion Road 6   (1) 492-3751
Email: irishcom@iol.ie

The Chief Rabbinate of Ireland
Herzog House, 1 Zion Road 6   (1) 492-3751
Fax: (1) 492-4680
Email: irishcom@iol.ie

RESTAURANTS
Vegetarian
Blazing Salads
25c Powerscourt Town House 2   (1) 671-9552

Café Paradiso
16 Lancaster Quay, Cork City   (1) 277-939

Cornucopia
19 Wicklow St. 2   (1) 677-7583

Juice
South Great Georges St. 2   (1) 475-7856

SYNAGOGUES
Orthodox
Machzikei Hadass
Rathmore Villas, Rear of 77 Terenure Road
North 6W   (1) 492-3751
Email: machadass@jerusalemail.com
Web site: www.jpostmail.com/jpost/users/machadass

Terenure Hebrew Congregation
Rathfarnham Road, Terenure 6

The Jewish Home of Ireland
Denmark Hill, Leinster Road West, Rathmines,
Dublin 6   (1) 497-6258
Fax: (1) 497-2018
Email: thejewishhomeofirl@tinet.ie
Services are held Friday evening at start of Sabbath
and Sabbath morning. Kosher meals may be had in
the home's dining room. Forty-eight hours notice is
required.

Progressive
7 Leicester Avenue, Rathgar, Po Box 3059 6
(1) 490-7605
Email: djpc@ulps.org
Friday evening at 8.15pm, first Sabbath in the month
and Festivals at 10.30am.

ISRAEL

General Information
Israel, the Promised Land of the Bible, is today a modern, thriving, bustling and vibrant country. For centuries, the sites of many of the most stirring events in the history of mankind lay dormant beneath shifting sands and crumbling terraces, until the land was reclaimed by the People of Israel returning from exile. In today's Israel, cities, towns and villages, fertile farms and green forests, sophisticated industries and well-developed commercial enterprises have replaced barren hillsides, swamps and desert wilderness.

Climate
Israel enjoys long, warm, dry summers (April–October) and generally mild winters (November–March), with somewhat drier, cooler weather in hilly regions, such as Jerusalem and Safed. Rainfall is relatively heavy in the north and centre of the country with much less in the northern Negev and almost negligible amounts in the southern areas. Regional conditions vary considerably, with humid summers and mild winters on the coast; dry summers and moderately cold winters in the hill regions; hot, dry summers and pleasant winters in the Jordan Valley; and year-round semi-desert conditions in the Negev.

Languages
Hebrew, the language of the Bible, and Arabic, are the official languages of Israel. Hebrew, Arabic and English are compulsory subjects at school. French, Spanish, German, Yiddish, Russian, Polish and Hungarian are widely spoken. Local and international newspapers and periodicals in a number of languages are readily available. All street and most commercial signs are in Hebrew and English and often in Arabic.

Passports and Visas
Every visitor to Israel must hold a valid passport; valid for a minimum of six months beyond the intended date of arrival. Stateless persons require a valid travel document with a return visa to the country of issue. Visitors may remain in Israel for up to three months from the date of arrival, subject to the terms of the visa issued. Visitors who intend to work in Israel must apply to the Ministry of the Interior for a special visa (B/1).

Electrical Appliances
The electric current in Israel is 220 volts AC, single phase, 50 Hertz. Most Israeli sockets are of the three-pronged variety but many can accept some European two-pronged plugs as well. Electric shavers, travelling irons and other small appliances may require adapters and/or transformers which can be purchased in Israel.

Health Regulations
There are no vaccination requirements for visitors entering Israel.

Pets
Dogs or cats accompanying visitors must be over four months old, inoculated against rabies and bear a valid official veterinary health certificate from the country of origin.

Accommodation

Kashrut
In Israel, kosher means under official rabbinical supervision. Most hotels (but not all) do adhere. Kosher restaurants, hotels and youth hostels are by law required to display a kashrut certificate. As far as we are aware all establishments listed are kosher.

Hotels
Israel has over 300 hotels, offering a wide choice of accommodation to suit all tastes, purposes and budgets, ranging from small, simple facilities to five-star luxury establishments, with prices varying according to grade and season. Hotel rates are generally quoted in US dollars and do not include the 15 per cent service charge.

Kibbutz Hotels
The kibbutz (collective settlement) is an Israeli social experience, in which all property is collectively owned and members receive no salaries but are provided with housing, education for their children, medical services, social amenities and all other necessities. Most of the 280 kibbutzim throughout Israel are essentially agricultural settlements but many are moving to a more industrially orientated economy.

Several kibbutzim, mostly in northern and central Israel, have established hotels on their premises, providing visitors with a close view of this world-renowned lifestyle. They offer guests the opportunity of a relaxed, informal holiday in delightful rural surroundings. Some present special evening programmes about the kibbutz experience.

For further information and a special tour of Israel's kibbutzim and kibbutz hotels, contact any Israel Government Tourist Office (IGTO), or the tourist information offices (TIO) in Israel, or Kibbutz Hotels, I Smolinskin St., Tel Aviv. Tel.: 03-527 8085. Fax: 03-523 0527.

Youth Hostels

The Israel Youth Hostels Association (IYHA), affiliated with the International Youth Hostels Association, operates some 32 youth hostels throughout the country for guests of all ages. All offer dormitory, usually single sex, accommodation and most also provide meals and self-service kitchen facilities. Some hostels also provide family accommodation for parents accompanied by at least one child. Individual reservations should be booked directly at specific hostels and group reservations with the IYHA.

The IYHA also arranges individual 14-, 21- or 28- day package tours, called 'Israel on the Youth Hostel Trail'. These include nights in any of 25 hostels with breakfast and dinner, unlimited bus travel, a half-day guided tour, free admission to National Parks, a map and other informative material.

Currency and Bank Information

The currency of Israel is the New Israeli Sheqel (NIS) (plural sheqalim). Each sheqel is divided into 100 agorot (singular agora). Bank notes circulate in denominations of NIS 200, 100, 50 and 20 sheqels and coins in denominations of 5 sheqels, 10 sheqels, 1 sheqel and 50 and 10 agorot. One may bring an unlimited amount of local and foreign currency into Israel in cash, travellers' cheques, letters of credit, or State of Israel Bonds. Foreign currency may be exchanged at any bank and at many hotels.

Most banks are open from Sunday to Thursday from 08:30 am to 12:00 midday, and from 4:00 pm to 6:00 pm on Sunday, Tuesday and Thursday. On the eve of major Jewish holidays, banks are open from 08:30 am to 12.00 midday. Bank branches in major hotels usually offer convenient additional banking hours.

Shopping

Colourful oriental markets and bazaars may be found in the old city of Jerusalem and in several other towns and villages; bargaining is often expected. The unique variety of goods available includes handmade items of olive wood, mother-of-pearl, leather and straw, as well as hand-blown glass and exotic clothing. In all cities and towns there are shopping malls which are open from 08:00 pm to 10:00 pm. There are duty-free shops at Ben Gurion, Eilat and Ovda International Airports.

Opening Hours:

Most shops are open daily, Sunday to Thursday, from 9:00 am to 7:00 pm, although some close for a mid-day break between 1:00 pm and 4:00 pm. On Fridays and the eve of major Jewish holidays, shops close early in the afternoon. Some Muslim-owned establishments are closed on Fridays and some Christian shops on Sundays

Radio and Television

Radio programmes are broadcast daily in English, Arabic, French, Yiddish, Russian and other languages. There are three daily news programmes in English and French. Many programmes shown on Israeli TV are in English with Hebrew, Arabic and Russian subtitles.

The Israel Broadcasting Authority news in English is screened nightly on Channel 1 at 6.00 pm

Facilities for the handicapped

Many hotels and public institutions in Israel (including Ben Gurion International Airport) provide ramps, specially equipped lavatories, telephones and other conveniences for the handicapped.

Milbat, the Advisory Centre for the Disabled at Sheba Medical Center in Tel Aviv (Tel: 03-530 3739), will be pleased to answer visitors' questions.

The Yad Sarah Organisation with branches located throughout Israel provides wheelchairs, crutches and other medical equipment on loan, free of charge (a small deposit is requested). For more specific information, contact the organisation's main office in Jerusalem, Tel: 02-624 4242.

Travellers to Israel, especially those with specific medical/paramedical needs, can turn to Traveller Hotline operated by Ezer Mizion, the Israel Health Support Fund. This volunteer organisation provides all paramedical information and needs free of charge to the traveller, via the International Office (02-537 8070) and Travellers Hotline (020-500 2111). Transport and other arrangements can be organised prior to arrival and special inquiries/needs can be seen to while in Israel.

Organised Tours

Numerous organised tours, mostly in air-conditioned buses or minibuses, are conducted by licensed tour operators. Itineraries and prices are determined in accordance with the Ministry of Tourism guidelines to ensure a full sightseeing programme in maximum comfort. Half-day, full-day and longer tours are available, some combining air with road travel. Tours depart regularly from major cities as well as from popular resort areas during the peak season. All organised tours are accompanied by experienced, licensed multilingual guides identified by an official emblem bearing the words Licensed Tourist Guide.

Smaller groups may hire a licensed driver-guide and a special touring limousine or minibus, identified by the red Ministry of Tourism emblem.

Full details of itineraries, prices and schedules are available at travel agencies, tour companies, IGTOs and TIOs.

Major public institutions and organisations such as WIZO, Hadassah, universities and the Knesset (Parliament) conduct guided tours of their facilities. Walking tours of the larger cities are arranged by the municipalities.

Visitors should be aware that certain tourist sites such as the Tomb of the Patriachs and Jericho are now within the boundaries of the Palestinian Authority. They should consult the local tourist offices in Israel concerning travel to those areas.

When visiting religious sites always take care to be modestly dressed; if not you may be refused entry.

Buses
Buses are the most popular means of urban and inter-city transport throughout Israel. The Egged Bus Cooperative operates nearly all inter-city bus lines and also provides urban services in most cities and towns. (The greater Tel Aviv area is serviced by the Dan Cooperative and independent bus companies operate in Beer Sheva and Nazareth.) Fares are reasonably priced and service is regular. Most bus lines do not operate on the Sabbath (Friday evening to Saturday evening) and on Jewish holidays. Students are eligible for discount fares on inter-urban bus routes on presentation of an International Student Card. Special monthly tickets are available for Dan and Egged urban bus lines. Overseas visitors can purchase Israbus passes valid on all Egged bus lines for periods of 7, 14, 21 and 30 days. Tickets can be obtained at any Egged bus station.

Taxis
These are both shared taxis (sheruts) and normal taxis. Taxis are required to operate a meter.

Traffic Regulations
A valid International Driving Licence is recognised and preferred, although a valid national driving licence is also accepted, provided it has been issued by a country maintaining diplomatic relations with Israel and recognising an Israeli driving licence.

An excellent system of roads connects all towns. Traffic travels on the right and overtakes on the left. It is compulsory for the driver and all passengers to wear seat belts. Drivers coming from the right have priority, unless indicated otherwise on the road signs, which are international. Distances on road signs are always given in kilometres (1 km is equal to 0.621 miles).

The speed limit is 50 km (approx. 31 miles) per hour in built-up areas; 80-90 km (approx. 50-56 miles) per hour on open roads.

Special Programmes For Tourists
Plant a Tree With Your Own Hands
Tree-planting centres have been established by the Jewish National Fund at several locations throughout Israel. For a nominal contribution, visitors may plant trees and receive a certificate and pin to mark the event. For further information, contact the Jewish National Fund, PO Box 283, 91002 Jerusalem, Tel: 02-670 7402, or 96 Hayarkon Street, 63432 Tel Aviv, Tel: 03-523 4367, Fax: 03-5246084.

GMT +2 hours	**Total Population 6,100,000**
Country calling code (972)	**Jewish Population 5,000,000**
Emergency Telephone (Police – 100) (Fire – 102) (Ambulance – 101)	

Afula

RESTAURANTS
La Cabania
Ha'atzmaut Square   (4) 659-1638

San Remo
4 Ha'atzmaut Square   (4) 652-2458

Akko

HOTELS
Palm Beach
P.O. Box 2192 24101   (4) 981-5815
                                       Fax: (4) 991-0434
Hotel, Restaurant and Convention Centre.

Palm Beach Sport E Spa Hotel
Sea Shore 24101   (4) 987-7777
Fax: (4) 9910434
Email: palmbech@netvision.net.il
Web site: www.palmbeach.co.il

MUSEUMS
Akko Municipal Museum
Old City   (4) 991-8251
Fax: (4) 981-6686

RESTAURANTS
Vegetarian
Amirei Hagalil
Akko-Safed Road, nr. Moshav Amirim 20115
(4) 698-9815/6

TOURIST INFORMATION
Eljazar Street, opposite Mosque
(4) 177-022-7764; 999-1764

YOUTH HOSTELS
Acre Youth Hostel
(4) 991-1982
Fax: (4) 991-1982

Arad

HOTELS
Arad
6 Hapalmach Street   (8) 995-7040
Fax: (8) 995-7272

Margoa
Mo'av Street, POB 20 89100   (8) 995-1222
Fax: (8) 995-7778
Email: margoa@mail.inter.net.il

Nof Arad
Moav Street   (8) 995-7056
Fax: (8) 995-4053

YOUTH HOSTELS
Blau-Weis
(8) 995-7150
This organisation is located in the centre of town.

Ashdod

HOTELS
Miami
12 Nordau Street   (8) 852-2085
Fax: (8) 856-0573

TOURIST INFORMATION
4 Haim Moshe Shapira Street, Rova Daled
(8) 864-0485/090

Avihail

MUSEUMS
Beit Hagedudim (History of Jewish Brigade W.W.I)
(9) 882-2212
Fax: (9) 862-1619

B'nei Berak

HOTELS
Wiznitz
16 Damesek Elizier Street   (3) 777-1413

RESTAURANTS
Dairy
Dairy Capit
34 Rabbi Akiv St   (3) 579-6927

Beersheba

HOTELS
Desert Inn
Tuviyahu Av.   (8) 642-4922
Fax: (8) 641-2722

MUSEUMS
Man in the Desert Museum
Situated five miles north-east of the city.

Negev Museum
Ha'atzmaut Street, cnr of Herzl Street   (8) 623-4438
Fax: (8) 623-9105

TOURS OF JEWISH INTEREST
Bedouin Market
The market is held every Thursday but it has been affected negatively by tourism and modernization. Permanent Bedouin encampments can be seen south of town.

Caesarea

HOTELS
Dan Caesarea Golf Hotel
PO Box 1120 30600   (4) 626-9111
Fax: (4) 626-9122
Email: caesarea@danhotels.com
Web site: www.danhotels.com

RESTAURANTS
Caesarean Self Service
Paz Petrol Station   (4) 633-4609

Dan

MUSEUM
Natural History and Archaeology
Beit Ussishkin Nature Reserve 12245   (4) 694-1704
Fax: (4) 695-1480
Email: ussishkin@kdan.co.il

Dead Sea

HOTELS
Caesar Premier
(8) 668-9666
Fax: (8) 652-0303
Contact the Caesar Group sales office in Tel Aviv for information, Tel: (03) 696-8383; Fax: (03) 696-9896.

Crown Plaza
(8) 659-1919

Grand Nirvana
(8) 668-9444
Fax: (8) 668-9400
Email: info@nirvana.co.il

Hod
(8) 658-4644

Hyatt Regency
(8) 659-1234

Moriah Gardens
(8) 659-1591
Fax: (8) 658-4238

Radisson Moriah Plaza
(8) 659-1591

Degania Alef

MUSEUMS
Beit Gordon
(4) 675-0040
Fax: (4) 670-9514

Eilat

HOTELS

Ambassador
Coral Beach, PO Box 390 88103   (8) 638-2222
Fax: (8) 638-2200
Email: info@ambassador.co.il
Web site: www.ambassador.co.il

Americana Eilat
PO Box 27, North Beach 88000   (8) 633-3777
Fax: (8) 633-4174
Email: info@americanahotel.co.il
Web site: www.americanahotel.co.il

Caesar
North Beach   (8) 630-5555
Fax: (8) 633-3497

Club-In Villa Resort
Rte. 90 (Eilat-Taba Road), Box 1505
Coral Beach 88000   (8) 633-4555
Fax: (8) 633-4519

Dalia
North Beach   (8) 633-4004
Fax: (8) 633-4072

Dan Eilat
Promenade, North Beach   (8) 636-2222
Fax: (8) 636-2333

Edomit
New Tourist Center   (8) 637-9511
Fax: (8) 637-9738

King Solomon's Palace
Promenade, North Beach   (8) 633-3444
Fax: (8) 633-4189
Email: cro@isrotel.co.il
Web site: www.isrotel.co.il

Marina Club
North Beach   (8) 633-4191
Fax: (8) 633-4206

Orchid
Rte. 90 (Eilat-Taba Road), Box 994 88000
(8) 636-0360
Fax: (8) 637-5323

Princess
Rte. 90 (Eilat-Taba Road), Box 2323 88000
(8) 636-5555
Fax: (8) 637-6333

Radisson Moriah Plaza
Promenade, North Beach   (8) 636-1111
Fax: (8) 633-4158

Red Rock
North Beach   (8) 637-3171
Fax: (8) 637-1705

Royal Beach
North Beach   (8) 636-8888
Fax: (8) 636-8811
Email: cro@isrotel.co.il
Web site: www.isrotel.co.il

The Neptune Hotel
North Beach   (8) 636-9369
Fax: (8) 633-4389

RESTAURANTS
Café Royal
King Solomon's Palace Hotel, North Beach
(8) 667-6111

Chinese Restaurant
Shulamit Gardens Hotel, North Beach   (8) 667-7515

Dolphin Baguette
Tourist Centre

Egged
Central Bus Station (8) 667-5161

El Morocco
Tourist Centre

Golden Lagoon
New Lagoona Hotel, North Beach (8) 667-2176

Halleluyah
Building 9, Tourist Centre (8) 667-5752

Dairy
La Trattoria
Radisson Moriah Plaza Hotel, North Beach
(8) 636-1111

Meat
El Gaucho
Arrava Road. (Rte. 90) (8) 633-1549

Shipudei Habustan
The Dan Eilat Promenade (8) 636-2294

Tamarind
North Shore 88103 (8) 638-0000

TOURS OF JEWISH INTEREST
Orionia
(8) 667-2902

Pirate
(8) 667-6549

YOUTH HOSTELS
Eilat
(8) 637-0088

Galilee

HOTELS
Ayelet Hashahar
Upper Galilee, Katzrin 12200 (4) 693-2611
Fax: (4) 693-4777

Hacienda
Ma'a lot (4) 957-9000
Fax: (4) 997-4404

Rakefet
Mishgav, Western Galilee (4) 980-0403
Fax: (4) 980-0317

MUSEUMS
Bar-David Museum of Jewish Art
Kibbutz Bar'am, off Route 899 (4) 698-8295
Fax: (4) 698-7505
Web site: www.galil-elion.org.il

Sculpture Gallery for Peace and Co-existence
Kawkab Abu Elhija, Gush Segev, Lower Galilee
(4) 852-5251
Fax: (4) 852-9166
Email: bhagefen@netvision.il
Web site: www.haifa.gov.il/beit-hagefen/index

Tel Hai Sculpture Garden
Tel Hai, Upper Galilee Region (4) 694-3731
Fax: (4) 695-0697

The Museum of Photography
Tel Hai Industrial Park (4) 695-0769
Fax: (4) 695-0771
Web site: www.iscar.com

The Open Museum
Tefen Industrial Park, Migdal Tefen (4) 987-2977
Fax: (4) 987-2861
Web site: www.iscar.com

RESTAURANTS
Lev Hagolan
30 Dror. Street, Katzrin (4) 961-6643

Orcha
Commercial Centre, Katzrin (4) 696-1440

YOUTH HOSTELS
Karei Deshe (Tabgha)
Yoram (4) 672-0601
Fax: (4) 672-4818

Eleven miles north of Tiberias.

Golan Heights

LEISURE
Hamat Gader
The Golan Heights rise steeply fron the Sea of Galilee to the Mount Avital plateau. The Hamat Gader were thought to be the nicest spa baths in the whole Roman world, according to the Byzantine empress Eudocia. There are impressive ruins including the extensive Roman and Byzantine spa, which served as a grand bathing resort for six centuries, and an ancient synagogue. Four mineral springs and a freshwater spring emerge at Hamat Gader and so it is used today as a modern bathhouse. There is also an alligator farm where dozens of alligators and crocodiles can be seen lazing around.

MUSEUM
The Golan Archeological Museum
Katzrin (4) 696-9636
Fax: (4) 696-9637

NATURE RESERVE
Gamla Nature Reserve
(4) 682-2282
Fax: (4) 682-2285
Fifteen kilometres southeast of Katzrin.

RESTAURANTS
Hamat Gader Restaurant
(4) 675-1039

Gush Etzion

RESTAURANTS

Cravings Café
Dekel Shopping Center, Efrat　　　(2) 993-3188

Pizzeria Efrat
Te'ena Shopping Center, Efrat　　　(2) 993-1630

Meat
The Oak Tree Restaurant
Judaica Center, Gush Etzion Junction　　(2) 993-4370
　　　　　　　　　　　　Fax: (2) 993-4949
　　　　　Email: judaica1@netvision.net.il
Available for groups and events.

TOURS OF JEWISH INTEREST

Gush Etzion Judaica Center
Gush Etzion Junction
　　　　　(2) 993-4040; Tourism Dept. 993-8388
　　　　　　　　　　　　Fax: (2) 993-4949
　　　　　Email: judaica1@netvision.net.ill
　　　　　　　Web site: www.judaica.org.il
Display and sales hall that features the items of over
200 items of Israeli Judaica. Can be combined with a
visit to Kibbutz Kfar Etzion to see an audio visual
show that movingly describes the history of Gush
Etzion.

Hadera

MUSEUMS

The Khan Museum
74 Hagiborim Street, POB 3232 38131
　　　　　　　　　(4) 632-2330; 632-4562
　　　　　　　　　　　　Fax: (4) 632-2072
Hours: Sunday to Thursday, 8 am to 1 pm; Friday, 9
am to 12 pm; Sunday and Tuesday, 4 pm to 6 pm.

Haifa

HOTELS

Dan Carmel
85 Hanassi Avenue　　　　　(4) 830-3030
　　　　　　　　　　　　Fax: (4) 830-3040
　　　　　　Email: dancarmel@danhotels.com
　　　　　　　Web site: www.danhotels.com

Dan Panorama
107 Hanassi Avenue　　　　　(4) 835-2222
　　　　　　　　　　　　Fax: (4) 835-2235
　　　　Email: panorama-haifa@danhotels.com

Dvir
124 Yafe Nof Street　　　　　(4) 838-9131
　　　　　　　　　　　　Fax: (4) 838-1068

Nof Haifa
101 Hanasi Avenue　　　　　(4) 835-4311
　　　　　　　　　　　　Fax: (4) 838-8810
　　　　　　　　Email: s1@actcom.co.il
　　　　　　　Web site: nof-hotels.co.il

Shulamit
15 Kiryat Sefer Street 34676　　(4) 834-2811
　　　　　　　　　　　　Fax: (4) 825-5206

MUSEUMS

Beit Pinchas Biological Insititute
124 Hatishbi Street　　　　　(4) 837-2390
　　　　　　　　　　　　Fax: (4) 837-7019
　　　　　Email: biolinst@netvision.net.il
Includes nature museum, zoo and botanical garden.
Entrance via Gan Ha'em. Hours: Sunday to Thursday,
Winter, 8 am to 4 pm, July to August, 8 am to 7 pm;
Friday and holiday eves, 8 am to 2 pm; Saturday, 9 am to
5 pm; Winter, 9 am to 4 pm.

Israel Edible Oil Industry Museum
Shemen Factory, 2 Tovim Street, POB 136 31000
　　　　　　　　　　　　(4) 865-4237
　　　　　　　　　　　　Fax: (4) 862-9237

Israel Railways Museum
Haifa East Railway Station　　　(4) 856-4293
　　　　　　　　　　　　Fax: (4) 856-4310
　　　　　　　Email: paulc@rail.org.il

Mane Katz Museum
89 Yafe-Nof Street 34641　　　(4) 838-3482
　　　　　　　　　　　　Fax: (4) 836-2985

**Museum of Clandestine Immigration & Navy
Museum**
204 Allenby Street 35472　　　(4) 853-6249
　　　　　　　　　　　　Fax: (4) 851-2958
Open: Sunday-Thursday 08.30 am - 16.00 pm.

Museum of Haifa
26 Shabbtai Levy Street 33043　　(4) 852-3255
　　　　　　　　　　　　Fax: (4) 855-2714
　　　　　Email: haifa4@netvision.net.il
　　　　　　　Web site: www.haifa.gov.il
Includes Museums of Ancient Art, Modern Art and
Music & Ethnology. Hours: Sunday, Monday, Wednesday,
Thursday, 10 am to 4 pm; Tuesday, 4 pm to 7 pm; Friday
and holidays, 10 am to 1 pm; Saturday, 10 am to 2 pm.

Museum of Pre-History
124 Hatishbi Street, Entrance from Gan Ha'em
　　　　　　　　　　　　(4) 837-1833
　　　　　　　　　　　　Fax: (4) 855-2714

Reuben & Edith Hecht Museum
Haifa University 31905　　　　(4) 825-7773
　　　　　　　　　　　　Fax: (4) 824-0724
　　　Email: mushecht@research.haifa.ac.il
　　　　Web site: www.mushecht.haifa.ac.il
Hours: Sunday, Monday, Wednesday, Thursday, 10 am
to 4 pm; Tuesday, 10 am to 7 pm; Friday, 10 am to 1 pm;
Saturday, 10 am to 2 pm. Admission free. Kosher
restaurant.

**The Israel National Museum of Science,
Planning and Technology.**
The Historic Technion Building, Balfour Street, Hadar
Ha carmel　　　　　　　　(4) 862-8111
　　　　　　　　　　　　Fax: (4) 867-9103
　　　　　Email: museum@mustsee.org.il
　　　　　　Web site: www.mustsee.org.il

The National Maritime Museum
198 Allenby Road (4) 853-6622
Fax: (4) 853-9286
Hours: Sunday, Monday, Wednesday, Thursday, 10 am
to 4 pm; Tuesday, 4 pm to 7 pm; Friday and holidays,
10 am to 1 pm; Saturday, 10 am to 2 pm.

Tikotin Museum of Japanese Art
89 Hanassi Avenue, Mount Carmel 34642
(4) 838-3554
Fax: (4) 837-9824
Hours: Monday, Wednesday, Thursday, 10 am to 5
pm; Tuesday, 10 am to 2 pm and 5 pm to 8 pm; Friday
and holiday eves, 10 am to 1 pm; Saturday, 10 am to 2
pm.

University of Haifa Art Collection
University of Haifa, Mount Carmel (4) 824-0660
Fax: (4) 824-0309

RESTAURANTS

Banker's Tavern
2 Habankim Street (4) 852-8439
Lunch only. Closed Shabbat.

Ben Ezra
71 Hazayit Street (4) 884-2273

Egged
Central Bus Station (4) 851-5221
Self-service.

Gan Rimon
10 Habroshim Street (4) 838-1392
Lunch only.

Ha'atzmaut
63 Derech Ha'atzmaut (4) 852-3829

Hamber Burger
61 Herzl Street (4) 866-6739

Hamidrachov
10 Nordau Street (4) 866-2050

Paznon
Hof Carmel (4) 853-8181

Rondo
Dan Carmel Hotel, 87 Hanassi Blvd (4) 838-6211

Technion
Neve Shaanan (4) 823-3011
Self service. Lunch only.

The Chinese Restaurant of Nof
Nof Hotel, 101 Hanassi Blvd (4) 838-8731

The Second Floor
119 Hanassi Blvd (4) 838-2020

Tsemed Hemed
Herbert Samuel Square (4) 824-2205

Dairy
Milky Pinky (Milk Bar)
29 Haneviim Street (4) 866-4166

Wissotsky Tea House
2 Mahanaim, Carmel Centre

Meat
Mac David
131 Hanassi Blvd (4) 838-3684
1 Balfour Street

TOURIST INFORMATION
106 Sderot Hanassi (4) 837-4010
What's on in Haifa
(4) 864-0840

TOURS OF JEWISH INTEREST
(4) 867-4342
Bahai shrine and gardens, Druse villages, Muchraka,
the Moslem village of Kabair, the Carmelite
monastery and Elijah's cave, Wednesday, 9:30am.

Mt Carmel, Druse villages, Kibbutz Ben Oren and Ein
Hod artists' colony: Sundays, Mondays, Tuesdays,
Thurdays, Saturdays, 9:30am.

YOUTH HOSTELS
Carmel
(4) 853-1944
Fax: (4) 853-2516
Shlomi
Hanita Forest (4) 980-8975

Hanita

MUSEUMS
Tower & Stockade Museum
Route 8990 (4) 985-9677
Fax: (4) 985-9677

Haon

HOLIDAY VILLAGE
Kibbutz Haon
Jordan Valley (4) 675-7555/6

Hazorea

MUSEUMS
Wilfrid Israel House of Oriental Art
(4) 989-9566
Fax: (4) 989-0942

Herzlia

HOTELS
Dan Accadia
Herzlia on Sea (9) 959-7070
Fax: (9) 959-7092
Email: danhtls@danhotels.co.il

Tadmor
38 Basel Street   (9) 952-5000
Fax: (9) 957-5124
Email: hotel@tadmor.co.il

The Sharon
Herzlia on Sea 46748   (9) 952-5777
Fax: (9) 956-8741
Email: hasharon@netvision.net.il
Web site: www.sharon.co.il

MUSEUMS
Herzlia Museum of Art
4 Habanim Street 46379   (9) 950-2301
Fax: (9) 950-0043
Email: herz_mus@netvision.net.il
Web site: www.adgo.co.il/herzliya_museum

RESTAURANTS
Dona Flor
22 Hagalim Blvd., Herzlia Pituach   (9) 950-9669

Tadmor Hotel School
38 Basel Street 46660   (9) 952-5050
Fax: (9) 957-5124
Email: hotel@tadmor.co.il

Meat
Steak.com
27 Rehov Maskit, Herzliya Pituah   (9) 956-1145

TOURIST INFORMATION
English-Speaking Residents Association
PO Box 3132 46104   (9) 950-8371
Fax: (9) 954-3781
Email: esra@trendline.co.il

Jaffa

MUSEUMS
**The Antiquities Museum of Tel Aviv-Yafo
(Jaffa Museum)**
10 Mifratz Shlomo Street, Old Jaffa 68038
(3) 682-5375
Fax: (3) 681-3624
Part of Eretz Israel Museum Tel Aviv. Opening hours:
Sunday-Thursday 9 am to 1 pm.

TOURS OF JEWISH INTEREST
Tel Aviv-Yafo Tourism Association
Ramat Gan
Walk takes 2.5 hours, starting at Clock Square near
Yefet Street, in the centre of Jaffa. Free.

Jerusalem

ACCOMMODATION INFORMATION
Good Morning Jerusalem
9 Coresh Street 94146   (2) 623-3459
Fax: (2) 625-9330
Email: gmjer@netvision.net.il
Web site: www.accommodation.co.il
Lists rooms and apartments available for tourists.

BED AND BREAKFAST
Le Sixteen
16 Midbar Sinai Street, Givat Hamivtar 97805
(2) 532-8008
Fax: (2) 581-9159
Email: le16@le16-bnb.co.il
Web site: www.le16-bnb.co.il
Member of the Jerusalem Home Accommodation
Association. Can provide guest studios with kosher
dairy kitchenettes.

CONTACT INFORMATION
Jeff Seidel's Jewish Student Information Centre
5 Bet-El, Jewish Quarter, Old City   (2) 628-2634
Fax: (2) 628-8338
Email: jseidel@jeffseidel.com
Web site: www.jeffseidel.com

**Jeff Seidel's Student Centre for Hebrew
University Students**
14 Lechi   (2) 581-2240
Email: jseidel@jeffseidel.com

Jewish Student Information Centre
Hebrew University Off-Campus Center,
5/4 Etzel Street, French Hill   (2) 581-4939
Email: jseidel@netmedia.net.il

GUEST HOUSE
Bet Shmuel
6 Shamma Street 94101   (2) 620-3473; 620-3465
Fax: (2) 620-3467
Single and family guest rooms with a capacity of 240
beds; conference facilities and banquet services;
restaurant and coffee shop; international culture and
education centre with a central location.

HOLIDAY VILLAGE
Youth Recreation Centre Holiday Village
Yefei Nof, Jerusalem Forest   (2) 641-6060

HOTELS
Ariel Hotel Jerusalem
31 Hebron Road   (2) 568-9999
Fax: (2) 673-4066
Email: info@arieljrm.co.il
Walking distance from Old City.

Caesar
208 Jaffa Road   (2) 500-5656
Fax: (2) 538-2802
Email: caesarjm@netvision.net.il

Central
6 Pines Street (2) 538-4111
Fax: (2) 5381-480

Four Points
4 Vilnai Street 96110 (2) 655-8888
Fax: (2) 651-2266
The hotel is located in the hotel area at the entrance
to the city and is within walking distance of the Israel
Museum and the Knesset.

Hyatt Regency Jerusalem
32 Lehi Street (2) 533-1234
Fax: (2) 581-5947
Email: hyattjrs@trendline.co.il
Web site: www.hyattjer.co.il

Inbal
Liberty Bell Park, 3 Jabotinsky Street 92145
(2) 675-6666
Fax: (2) 675-6777
Email: rsv@inbal-hotel.co.il
Web site: www.inbal-hotel.co.il

Isrotel Tower Jerusalem
204 Jaffa Street 94383 (2) 500-7777
Fax: (2) 500-7772
Email: towerjerusalem@isrotel.co.il
Web site: www.isrotel.co.il

Jerusalem Hilton
7 King David Street 94101 (2) 621-1111
Fax: (2) 621-1000

Jerusalem Tower
23 Hillel Street (2) 620-9209
Fax: (2) 625-2167
Email: towerhotels@012.net.il

King David
23 King David Street 94101 (2) 620-8888
Fax: (2) 620-8882
Email: kingdavid@danhotels.com

King Solomon
32 King David Street (2) 569-5555
Fax: (2) 624-1174
Email: solhotel@netvision.net.il

Lev Yerushalayim
18 King George Street (2) 530-0333
Fax: (2) 623-2432

Menorah
44 Jaffa Road (2) 622-3122
Fax: (2) 625-0707

Mount Zion
17 Hebron Road (2) 568-9555
Fax: (2) 673-1425
Email: hotel@mountzion.co.il

Palatin
4 Agripas Street (2) 623-1141
Fax: (2) 625-9323
Email: info@hotel-palatin.co.il
Web site: www.hotel-palatin.co.il

Radisson Moriah Plaza Jerusalem
39 Keren Hayessod Street 94188 (2) 569-5695
Fax: (2) 623-2411

Reich
1 Hagai Street, Bet Hakerem (2) 652-3121
Fax: (2) 652-3120

Renaissance Jerusalem Hotel
Ruppin Bridge, at Herz Blvd 91033 (2) 659-9999
Fax: (2) 651-1824
Email: renjhot@netvision.net.il
Contact: Eli Velter.

Sheraton Jerusalem Plaza
47 King George Street (2) 629-8666
Fax: (2) 623-1667

Windmill
3 Mendele Street (2) 566-3111
Fax: (2) 561-0964

MUSEUMS

Ammunition Hill Memorial & Museum, Ramat Eshkol
Levy Eshkol Boulevard 91181 (2) 582-8442
Fax: (2) 582-9132

Bible Lands Museum Jerusalem
25 Granot Street, POB 4670 91046 (2) 561-1066
Fax: (2) 563-8228
Email: contact@blmj.org
Web site: www.blmj.org
The home of one of the most important collections of
ancient artifacts displaying rare works of art from the
dawn of civilisation to the Byzantine period. Gift
shop, special exhibitions,weekly lectures and
concerts. Daily guided tours in English and an audio
guide are available. Groups by advance reservation.
Open daily except Shabbat and Holidays. Call or
email the museum for hours and program details.
"Kosher restaurant". Daily English guided tours.

Herzl Museum
Herzl Blvd, Mount Herzl (2) 651-1108

Israel Museum
Ruppin Blvd (2) 670-8985
Fax: (2) 563-1832
Web site: www.imj.org.il
Includes Bezalel National Museum, Samuel Bronfman
Biblical & Archaeological Museum, Shrine of the Book
& the Rockefeller Museum in East Jerusalem.

L.A. Mayer Museum for Islamic Art
2 Hapalmach Street 92542 (2) 566-1291/2
Fax: (2) 561-9802

Museum of Italian Jewish Art
27 Hillel Street 94581 (2) 624-1610
Fax: (2) 625-3480
Web site: www.itcham.org.il/museum/

Museum of Natural History
6 Mohilever Street (2) 563-1116
Fax: (2) 566-0666

Nahon Museum of Italian Jewish Art
27 Hillel Street 94581   (2) 624-1610
Fax: (2) 625-3840
Email: jija@netvision.net.il
Web site: www.jija.org
This special museum collects and preserves objects pertaining to the life of the Jews in Italy from the Middle Ages to the present day. The main attraction is the ancient synagogue of Conegliano Veneto, a township some 60 km from Venice relocated in its entirely to Israel. Hours: Sunday, Tuesday, Wednesday, 9.00am to 5.00pm, Monday, 9.00am to 2.00pm, Thursday, Friday, 9.00am to 1.00pm. For guided tours contact the numbers above.

Old Yishuv Court Museum
6 Or Hayim Street 91016   (2) 628-4636
Fax: (2) 628-4636
The museum is located in the heart of the Jewish Quarter in the Old City of Jerusalem in a sixteenth-century building. It displays the story of the Jewish community from the periods under Ottoman rule, through the final days of the British Mandate. Hours Sunday to Thursday, 9 am to 2 pm.

S.Y. Agnon's House
16 Joseph Klausner Street, Talpiot 93388
(2) 671-6498
Email: agnon-h@inter.net.il
Hours: Sunday to Thursday, 9 am to 1 pm.

Siebenberg House of Archaeological Museum
7 Hagittit Street, Jewish Quarter   (2) 628-2341

The Chagall Windows at the Hadassah Medical School
The Hebrew University, Hadassah   (2) 641-6333
Fax: (2) 641-6333

The Sir Isaac & Lady Wolfson Museum, Hechal Shlomo
4th Floor, 58 King George Street   (2) 624-7908
Fax: (2) 623-1810
Email: hechalshlomo@hotmail.com

Tourjeman Post Museum
4 Hail Hahandassa Street   (2) 628-1278
Fax: (2) 627-7061

Tower of David Museum of the History of Jerusalem
Jaffa Gate   (2) 626-5333
Fax: (2) 628-3418
Email: shivuk@tower.org.il
24-hour information line: 972-2-6265310

Yad Vashem, The Holocaust Martyrs' and Heroes' Remembrance Authority
Har Hazikaron, PO Box 3477 91034   (2) 644-3400
Fax: (2) 644-3443
Email: general.information@yadvashem.org.il
Web site: www.yadvashem.org.il
Open 9 am-5 pm Sunday-Thursday, 9 am-2 pm Friday and eves of holidays, closed on Saturday and all Jewish holidays.

ORGANISATIONS

Ezer Mizion "Help from Zion"
25 Yirmiyahu St. 94467   (2) 537-8070
Fax: (2) 538-3315
Email: ezerm@netvision.net.il
Web site: www.ezer-mizion.org.il
Opening hours are 8.00 am - 8.00 pm. Mailing address (midweek) - POB 41130 Jerusalem 91410.

Travelers Aid of Israel
PO Box 2828   (2) 582-0126
Fax: (2) 623-2742
Email: wolfilaw@netvision.net.il
Legal counselling, social and human services, accident victims legal assistance, immigrant assistance, interest free-loans, stranded travellers, medical assistance, crime-victim assistance, homelessness, emergency assistance.

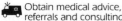

Yad Sarah
P.R. Department, Kiryat Weinbergl Blvd. 95141
(2) 644-4242
Email: infor@yadsarah.org.il
Web site: www.yadsarah.org.il
Yad Sarah home care organization lends, free against a returnable deposit, regular and high-tech medical rehab. equipment. Visitors in wheelchairs can use the Yad Sarah special transportation vans, at a low fee. By pre-arrangement you can have the van and driver waiting at Ben Gurion airport. Minimum two weeks notice please for this service. Yad Sarah has 85 branches in Israel.

RESTAURANTS

Casa Italiana
6 Yoel Salamon Street

Clafouti
2 Hasoreg Street | (2) 624-4491

Dagrill
21 King George Street | (2) 622-2922

Pampa
3 Rehov Yosef Rivlin | (2) 623-1455

Ye Olde English Tea Room
68 Jaffa Road | (2) 537-6595

Dairy
Bagel Nash
14 Ben-Yehuda Street | (2) 622-5027

Besograyim
45 Ussishkin Street | (2) 624-5353

Café Rimon
4 Luntz Street (off Midrehov) | (2) 624-3712

Chamomille
6 Yoel Solomon Street | (2) 625-2750

Dagim Beni
1 Mesilat Yesharim Street | (2) 622-2403

Daglicatesse
1 Rachel Imenu | (2) 563-2657

La Pasta
16 Rivlin Street | (2) 622-7687

Little Italy
38 Keren Hayesod Street | (2) 561-7638

Mamma Mia
38 King George Street 94262 | (2) 624-8080
Fax: (2) 623-3336
Located in the centre of town in an old (1899) restored building. Air-conditioned. Hours: Sunday to Thursday, 12 pm to midnight, Friday 12 pm to 4 pm; Saturday, from the end of Shabbat.

Michael Andrew
12 Emil Bota | (2) 624-0090

Of Course!
Zion Confederation House, Emile Botta Street
(2) 624-5206

Off The Square
8 Ramban Street

Poire et Pomme
The Khan Theatre, 2 Remez Square | (2) 671-9602

Primus
3 Yavetz Street | (2) 624-6565

Rienzi
10 King David Street | (2) 622-2312

Rimon
4 Lunz Street | (2) 622-2772

Theatre Lounge
Jerusalem Theatre, 20 Marcus Street | (2) 566-9351

Zeze
11 Bezalel Street | (2) 623-1761
Meat
Burger Ranch
18 Shlomzion Hamalka Street | (2) 622-2392
3 Lunz Street | (2) 622-5935

El Gaucho
22 Rivlin Street | (2) 624-1227
Fax: (2) 623-2660

El Marrakesh
4 King David Street | (2) 622-7577

El Morocco
43 Yirmiyahu Street, Centre One | (2) 500-1670
Fax: (2) 538-3496

Hanevi'im
54 Hanevi'im Street, Jerusalem | (2) 624-7433

Kinor David
19 King David Street

Marvad Haksamim
16 King George Street

Marziano & Toledano
15 Rehov Yad Harutzim | (2) 672-8672

Norman's Steak 'n Burger
27 Emek Refaim Street | (2) 566-6603
Fax: (2) 673-1768
Email: burger@normans.co.il
Web site: www.normans.co.il
American steakhouse. Reservations recommended. Easy walking distance from main hotels. Hours: Sunday to Thursday, 12 pm to 11 pm; Friday, closed; Saturday, from after Shabbat.

Rungsit
2 Jabotinsky Street | (2) 561-1757

Shaul's Shwarma Centre
14 Ben-Yehuda Street | (2) 622-5027

Shemesh
21 Ben-Yehuda Street | (2) 622-2418

Shipodei Hagefen
74 Agrippas Street | (2) 622-2367

Yemenite Step
12 Yoel Salamon Street (2) 624-0477

Yo-si Peking
5 Shimon Ben-Shetach Street (2) 622-6893

Pizzerias

Pizzeria Rimini
43 Jaffa Road (2) 622-5534
15 King George Street (2) 622-6505
7 Paran Street, Ramat Eshkol

Pizzeria Trevi
8 Leib Yaffe Street (2) 672-4136

Vegetarian

Belinda
20 King George Street (2) 624-5717
 Fax: (2) 561-1176
 Email: belindacatering@hotmail.com

Chamomile
6 Yoel Solomon St. (2) 625-2750

Village Green
33 Jaffa Street (2) 625-3065
 Fax: (2) 625 3062

Take away

SYNAGOGUES

Great Synagogue
60 King George Street

Yeshurun
44 King George Street (2) 624-3942
 Fax: (2) 622-4528
 Email: netypjer@netvision.net.il

TOURIST INFORMATION

ISSTA
5 Eliashar Street (2) 622-5258

Ministry of Tourism
24 King George Street (2) 675-4811

Tourism Coordinator with the Palestinian Authority
Israel Ministry of Tourism, PO Box 1018,
Jerusalem 91009 (2) 675-4903
 Fax: (2) 624-0571
 Email: zvin@tourism.gov.il

TOURS OF JEWISH INTEREST

American P'eylim Student Union
10 Shoarim Street (2) 653-2131
Free tours of Jewish Quarter and free
accommodation, in the hostel quarters.

Knesset (Parliament)
 (2) 675-3416
 Fax: (2) 561-1201
Sunday & Thursday 8.30am and 2.30pm

**Society for the Protection of Nature in Israel:
Israeli Nature Trails**
13 Helen Hamalka Street 95101 (2) 624-4605
 Fax: (2) 625-4953
 Email: spnijeru@inter.net.il

YOUTH HOSTELS

Bet Bernstein
1 Keren Hayesod Street (2) 625-8286
80 rooms.

Davidka
67 HaNevi'im Street, PO Box 37110 (2) 538-4555
 Fax: (2) 538-8790
Seventy-five rooms; 4-6 bedded.

Ein Karem
 (2) 641-6282
Ninety-seven rooms. Ten minutes from the Louise
Waterman-Wise Hotel in Bayit Vegan

Israel Youth Hostels Association
Youth Travel Bureau, Jerusalem International
Convention Center, POB 6001, Jerusalem 91060
 (2) 655-8442
 Fax: (2) 655-8431
 Email: iyha@iyha.org.il
 Web site: www.iyha.org.il
There are thirty-one youth hostels in Israel for
students, youth groups and adults, which are
supervised by the Israel Youth Hostels Association (a
member of the International Youth Hostels
Federation). All hostels offer the standard facilities of
dormitories, kosher dining rooms, etc. Most hostels
also have a guest house section, with double and
family rooms and private facilities. Most are air-
conditioned.

Jerusalem Forest
 (2) 675-2911
One hundred and forty rooms.

Moreshet Yahadut
 (2) 628-8611
Old city, 75 rooms.

Kfar Giladi

MUSEUMS

Beit Hashomer
 (4) 694-1565
 Fax: (4) 695-1505

Kfar Vitkin

YOUTH HOSTELS

Emer Hefer
 (9) 866-6032
Twenty-five miles north of Tel Aviv.

Kibbutz Harduf

RESTAURANTS
Vegetarian
Jutka's Restaurant

(4) 905-9229
Fax: (4) 986-1106

Kibbutz Yotvata

LEISURE
Biblical Wildlife Reserve Hai Bar Arava
The reserve is situated thirty-seven miles north of
Eilat. Biologoists have settled every breed of animal
that is mentioned in the Bible. Animals include herd of
Somalian wild asses, oryx antelope, ibex, ostriches,
desert foxes, lynx, hyenas and the last desert leopard
in the Negev, living out her days on the reserve.
Guided tours start at 9 am and 10.30 am, noon and
1.30 pm.

RESTAURANTS
Dairy
Dairy Restaurant

(8) 635-7449

Korazim

HOLIDAY VILLAGE
Amnon Bay Recreation Centre

(4) 693-4431

Vered Hagalil Guest Farm

(4) 693-5785
Fax: (4) 693-4964
Email: vered@veredhagalil.co.il

Lod

MUSEUMS
Museum of Jewish Ethnic Heritage
20 David Ha'melech Boulevard, Lod   (8) 924-1160
Fax: (8) 924-9466
Email: zmalachi@post.tau.ac.il
P.O.B 383 Lod, 71101.

TOURIST INFORMATION
Ministry of Tourism
Ben Gurion International Airport   (8) 971-1485

Lohamei Hagetaot

MUSEUMS
Ghetto Fighters' House, Holocaust &
Resistance Museum
M.P. (Mobile Post) 25220   (4) 995-8080
Fax: (4) 995-8007
Email: simstein@gfh.org.il
Web site: www.gfh.org.il
Hours: Sunday-Thursday 9.00am to 4.00pm. Friday
9.00am-1.00pm, Saturdays and holidays: Main
museum closed. Yad Layeled open: 10.00am-5.00pm.

Maagan

HOLIDAY VILLAGE
Maagan Holiday Village
Sea of Galilee 15160   (4) 665-4400
Fax: (4) 665-4455
Email: maaganhv@netvision.net.il

Maayan Harod

YOUTH HOSTELS
Hankin

(4) 658-1660
Seven miles east of Afula.

Mahanayim

TOURIST INFORMATION
Zomet Mahanayim   (4) 693-5016

Moshav Shoresh

HOTELS
Shoresh Hotel
Harey Yehuda   (2) 533-8338
Fax: (2) 534-0262
Email: info@shoresh.co.il
Web site: www.shoresh.co.il

Nahariya

HOTELS
Carlton
23 Ha'agaaton Blvd   (4) 900-5555
Fax: (4) 982-3771
Email: carlton2@netvision.net.il
Web site: www.carlton-hotel.co.il

Rosenblatt
59 Weizmann Street   (4) 992-0069
Fax: (4) 992-8121

LEISURE
Rosh Hanikra
Rosh Hanikra is situated four miles north of Nahariya, on the Lebanese border, and has an extensive system of caves which the sea has washed out of the soft chalk. There is also a lookout point with an adjacent restaurant which reveals a gorgeous panorama of the coast.

MUSEUMS
Nahariya Municipal Museum
Hagaaton Blvd   (4) 987-9863
                                      Fax: (4) 992-2303

RESTAURANTS
Cafe Tsafon
10 Gaaton Blvd   (4) 992-2567

TOURIST INFORMATION
Israel Camping Union
POB 53   (4) 992-5392

Nazareth

RESTAURANTS
Iberia
Rassco Centre, Nazareth Elite   (4) 655-6314
Nof Nazareth
23 Hacarmel Street, Nazareth Elite   (4) 655-4366

Negev

RESTAURANTS
Bulgarian
112 Keren Kayemet Street, Beersheba   (8) 623-8504

YOUTH HOSTELS
Bet Noam
Mitzpeh Ramon   (8) 658-8433
                                      Fax: (8) 658-8074

Bet Sara
Ein Gedi   (8) 658-4165
1.5 miles north of Kibbutz Ein Gedi on Dead Sea.

Blau-Weiss
Arad   (8) 995-7150
Centre of town.

Hevel Katif: Hadarom
                                           (8) 684-7597
                                      Fax: (8) 684-7680
For more detailed information, apply either to the Israel Youth Hostels Assoc. or to the nearest Israel Government Tourist Office.

Isaac H. Taylor
Masada   (8) 658-4349
28 miles from Arad.

Netanya

HOLIDAY VILLAGE
Green Beach Holiday Village
                                           (9) 865-6166
                                      Fax: (9) 835-0075

HOTELS
Arches
4 Remez Street 42271   (9) 860-9860
                                      Fax: (9) 860-9866
               Email: arches-hotel@correy.com

Galei Hasharon
42 Ussishkin Street 42273   (9) 834-1946
                                      Fax: (9) 833-8128

Galil
26 Nice Blvd   (9) 862-4455
                                      Fax: (9) 862-4456

Ginot Yam
9 David Hamelech Street   (9) 834-1007
                                      Fax: (9) 861-5722

Goldar
1 Usishkin Street   (9) 833-8188
                                      Fax: (9) 862-0680
               Email: order@goldar.co.il

Grand Yahalom
15 Gad Machnes Street   (9) 862-4888
                                      Fax: (9) 862-4890

Green Beach
PO Box 230   (9) 865-6166
                                      Fax: (9) 835-0075

Jeremy
11 Gad Machnes Street   (9) 862-2651
                                      Fax: (9) 862-2651

King Koresh
6 Harav Kook Street   (9) 861-3555
                                      Fax: (9) 861-3444

King Solomon
18 Hamaapilim Street   (9) 833-8444
                                      Fax: (9) 861-1397

MacDavid
7a Ha'atzmaut Street   (9) 861-8711

Margoa
9 Gad Machnes Street   (9) 862-4434

Maxim
8 King David Street   (9) 862-1062
                                      Fax: (9) 862-0190

Metropol Grand
17 Gad Machnes Street   (9) 862-4777
                                      Fax: (9) 861-1556

Orly
20 Hamaapilim Street   (9) 833-3091
                                      Fax: (9) 862-5453

Palace
33 Gad Machnes Street   (9) 862-0222
                                    Fax: (9) 862-0224
                            Email: palacent@012.co.il

Park
7 David Hamelech Street   (9) 862-3344
                                    Fax: (9) 862-4029

Residence
18 Gad Machnes Street   (9) 862-3777
                                    Fax: (9) 862-3711

The Seasons
1 Nice Blvd   (9) 860-1555
                                    Fax: (9) 862-3022
                        Email: seasons@netmedia.net.il

Synagogues

Congregation Agudath Achim
45 Jabotinsky Street

Netanya Cultural Center
4 Raziel Street   (9) 861-1687
                                    Fax: (9) 861-7555
                    Email: Rina@netanya-cultural.co.il
Orthodox
New Synagogue of Netanya
7 MacDonald Street   (9) 861-4591

Young Israel Congregation of North Netanya
39 Shlomo Hamelech Street   (9) 862-6472

Tourist Information
Kikar ha'Atzmaut   (9) 882-7286

Petach Tikva

Museums

Beit Yad Labanim
30 Arlozorov Street   (3) 922-3450
                                    Fax: (3) 922-3450

Qatzrin

Museums

Golan Archaeological Museum
                                         (4) 696-9636
                                    Fax: (4) 696-2412
                        Email: museum@golan.org.il

Ra'anana

Restaurants

Dana
198 Achuza   (9) 790-1452

Lady D
158 Achuza   (9) 791-6517

Limosa
5 Eliazar Jaffe   (9) 790-3407

Pica Aduma
87 Achuza   (9) 791-0508

Ramat Gan

Museums

Museum of Israeli Art
146 Abba Hillel Street 52572   (3) 752-1876
                                    Fax: (3) 752-7377
                    Email: meirmusun@mail.inter.net.il

Pierre Gildesgame Maccabi Sports Museum
Kfar Hamaccabiah   (3) 671-5729
                                    Fax: (3) 574-6565
                        Email: lod@netvision.net.il

Yechiel Nahari Museum of Far Eastern Art
18 Hibat Zion Street   (3) 578-1216
                                    Fax: (3) 619-5837

Ramat Hanegev

Tourist Information
Zomet Mashabay Sadeh   (8) 655-7314

Ramat Yohanan

Youth Hostels
Yehuda Hatzair
                                         (4) 844-2976
                                    Fax: (4) 844-2976
Eleven miles north-east of Haifa.

Rehovot

Museums

Havayeda - Science Through Fun Science Park
5 Yechezkai Habibi Street 76000   (8) 945-2949
                                    Fax: (8) 945-2949
                        Web site: www.weizmann.ac.il

Weizmann Institute of Science
Yad Haim Weizmann, Marcus Sieff Blvd 76100
                                         (8) 934-4499
                                    Fax: (8) 934-4960
                        Web site: www.weizmann.ac.il

Restaurants
Rehovot Chinese Restaurant
202 Herzl Street   (8) 947-1616

Rosh Hanikra

Youth Hostels
Rosh Hanikra
                                         (4) 998-2516
Near the grottos.

Rosh Pina

YOUTH HOSTELS
Hovevei Hateva
(4) 693-7086
Sixteen miles north of Tiberias

Safed

HOTELS
David
Mount Canaan
(4) 692-0062

Nof Hagalil
Mount Canaan
(4) 692-1595

Pisgah
Mount Canaan
(4) 692-0105

Rimon Inn
Artists Colony
(4) 692-0665/6

Ron
Hativat Yiftah Street
(4) 697-2590

MUSEUMS
Beit Hameiri Institute(History & Heritage of Safed)
Keren Hayesod Street 13110
(4) 697-1307
Fax: (4) 692-1902

Israel Bible Museum
Citadel Hill
(4) 699-9972
Fax: (4) 699-9972

Near Ron Hotel

Museum of Printing
Artists' Quarter
(4) 692-3022

TOURIST INFORMATION
50 Jerusalem Street
(4) 692-0961/633

YOUTH HOSTELS
Bet Benyamin
(4) 692-1086
Fax: (4) 697-3514

In southern part of town.

Tel Aviv

ACCOMMODATION INFORMATION
Kibbutz Hotels Chain: Head Office
1 Smolanskin Street, POB 3193 61031   (3) 524-6161
Fax: (3) 527-8088
Email: batya@kibbutz.co.il
Web site: www.kibbutz.co.il

CONTACT INFORMATION
Jewish Student Information Centre
Tel Aviv University Off-Campus Center, 82/10
Levanon Street, Ramat Aviv
Email: jseidel@netmedia.net.il

HOTELS
Adiv
5 Mendele Street
(3) 522-9141

Ambassador
56 Herbert Samuel Street
(3) 510-3993
Fax: (3) 517-6308

Armon Hayarkon
268 Hayarkon Street
(3) 605-5271
Fax: (3) 605-8485

Avia
Ben Gurion Intl Airport Area
(3) 539-3333
Fax: (3) 539-3319

Basel
156 Hayarkon Street
(3) 520-7711
Fax: (3) 527-0005

Bell
12 Allenby Street
(3) 517-7011
Fax: (3) 517-4352

Carlton Tel Aviv
10 Eliezer Peri Street
(3) 520-1818
Fax: (3) 527-1043
Email: request@carlton.co.il

City
9 Mapu Street
(3) 524-6253
Fax: (3) 524-6250

Dan Panorama
Charles Clore Park
(3) 519-0190

Dan Tel Aviv
99 Hayarkon Street
(3) 520-2525
Fax: (3) 524-9755
Email: dantelaviv@danhotels.com

Grand Beach
250 Hayarkon Street
(3) 543-3333
Fax: (3) 546-6589
Email: reservation@grandbeach.co.il
Web site: www.grandbeach.co.il
Synagogue on premises.

Howard Johnson - Shalom
216 Hayarkon Street
(3) 524-3277
Fax: (3) 523-5895
Email: h_shlom@netvision.net.il

Maxim
86 Hayarkon Street, P.O.B. 3442 63903
(3) 517-3721/5
Fax: (3) 517-3726

Metropolitan
11-15 Trumpeldor Street 63803
(3) 519-2727
Fax: (3) 517-2626
Email: reserve@metrotlv.co.il
Web site: www.hotelmetropolitan.co.il

Ramat Aviv
151 Namir Road
(3) 699-0777
Fax: (3) 699-0997

Renaissance Tel Aviv
121 Hayarkon Street 63453   (3) 521-5555
Fax: (3) 521-5588
Email: reserv@renaissance-tlv.co.il

Sheraton Moriah
155 Hayarkon Street   (3) 521-6666
Fax: (3) 527-1065
Email: shermor@inter.net.il

Sheraton Tel Aviv Hotel & Towers
115 Hayarkon Street   (3) 521-1111
Fax: (3) 523-3322
Email: shtelviv@netvision.net.il

Tal
287 Hayarkon Street   (3) 542-5500
Fax: (3) 542-5501

Tel Aviv Hilton
Independence Park 63405   (3) 520-2222
Fax: (3) 527-2711
Email: fom_tel-aviv@hilton.com

Yamit Park Plaza
79 Hayarkon Street   (3) 517-7111
Fax: (3) 517-4719
Email: yamit@netvision.net.il

MUSEUMS

Beit Bialik
22 Bialik Street   (3) 525-3403
Fax: (3) 525-4530

Ben Gurion House
17 Ben Gurion Boulevard   (3) 522-1010
Fax: (3) 524-7293

Eretz Israel Museum
2 Haim Levanon Street 69975   (3) 641-5244
Fax: (3) 641-2408

Hagana Museum
23 Rothschild Blvd. 65122   (3) 560-8624
Fax: (3) 566-1208

Helena Rubenstein Pavilion for Contemporary Art
6 Tarsat Street   (3) 528-7196

Jabotinsky Museum
38 King George Street 62398   (3) 528-7320
Fax: (3) 528-5587
Email: jabo@actcom.co.il
Web site: www.jabotinsky.org
Hours: Sunday to Thursday, 8 am to 4 pm.

Lehi Museum
8 Stern Street 66085   (3) 682-0288
Fax: (3) 681-9264

Museum of the Jewish Diaspora (Beth Hatefutsoth)
Klausner Street, Ramat Aviv   (3) 646-2020
Fax: (3) 646-2134
Email: bhmuseum@post.tav.ac.il
Web site: www.bh.org.il

Tel Aviv Museum of Art
27 Shaul Hamelech Boulevard 61332   (3) 696-1297
Fax: (3) 695-8099
Hours: Monday and Wednesday 10 am - 4 pm,
Tuesday and Thursday 10 am to 10 pm , Friday 10am
to 2 pm and Saturday, 10 am to 4 pm Public
transport: buses 9, 11 18, 28, 70, 82, 90, 91, 111.
Parking facilities.

RESTAURANTS

Dairy

Apropo
Alexander Hotel, 3 Havakuk Street   (3) 544-4442

Felafelim Shop
86 Rehov Ibn-Gvirol   (3) 524-6781

Hungarian Blintzes
35 Yirmiyahu Street   (3) 605-0674

Meat

China Lee
102 Hayarkon Street   (3) 524-6119

Olive Leaf
Sheraton Tel Aviv Hotel and Towers, 115 Hayarkon Street   (3) 521-9300
Fax: (3) 521-9301
Web site: www.sheraton-telaviv.com
Innovative cuisine with Mediterranean flavours.

Shaul's Inn
11 Elyashiv Street, Kerem Hatemanim   (3) 517-3303
Fax: (3) 517-7619
Oriental and Yemenite food. Popular and exclusive
sections. Hours: 12 pm to 12 am.

SYNAGOGUES

Bilu
122 Rothschild Blvd.

Great
314 Dizengoff Street

Ihud Shivat Zion
86 Ben-Yehuda Street
Central European rite.

Tiferet Zvi
Hermann Hacohen Street

Ashkenazi

Main Synagogue
110 Allenby Road

Progressive

Kedem
20 Carlebach Street

Sephardi

Ohel Mis'ad
5 Shadal Street

TOURIST INFORMATION

Shop # 6108, 6th Floor, New Central Bus Station
(3) 639-5660
Fax: (3) 639-5659

ISSTA
109 Ben Yehuda Street

The Ministry of Tourism
6 Wilson Street   (3) 556-2339
The Ministry of Tourism publishes a guide called 'The
Best of Israel', detailing shops participating in the VAT
refund scheme and recommended restaurants.

TRAVEL AGENCIES
Interom Tourism Ltd.
                                             (3) 924-6425
                                        Fax: (3) 579-1720

Tiberias

HOTELS

Ariston
19 Herzl Blvd   (4) 679-0244
                                        Fax: (4) 672-2002

Astoria
13 Ohel Ya'akov Street   (4) 672-2351
                                        Fax: (4) 672-5108

Caesar
103 The Promenade   (4) 672-7272
                                        Fax: (4) 679-1013

Carmel Jordan River
Habanim Street   (4) 671-4444
                                        Fax: (4) 672 2111

Gai Beach
Derech Hamerchatzaot   (4) 670-0700
                                        Fax: (4) 679-2766

Galei Kinnereth
1 Kaplan Street   (4) 672-8888
                                        Fax: (4) 679-0260

Golan
14 Achad Ha'am Street   (4) 679-1901
                                        Fax: (4) 672-1905

Kinar
N.E. Sea of Galilee   (4) 673-8888
                                        Fax: (4) 673-8811
                        Email: kinarmamag@kinar.co.il

Lavi Kibbutz Hotel
Lower Galilee 15267   (4) 679-9450
                                        Fax: (4) 679-9399
                             Email: hotel@lavi.co.il
                           Web site: www.lavi.co.il

Pagoda
Lido Beach, PO Box 253 14102   (4) 672-5513
                                        Fax: (4) 672-5518
                             Email: liz@kinneret.co.il
Open Sunday to Thursday 12.30-11.30pm. Saturday -
opens for dinner only.

Quiet Beach
Gedud Barak Street   (4) 679-0125
                                        Fax: (4) 679-0261

Tzameret Inn
Plus 2000 Street   (4) 679-4951
                                        Fax: (4) 673-2444

Washington
13 Zeidel Street   (4) 679-1861
                                        Fax: (4) 672-1860

TOURIST INFORMATION
HaBanim Street, The Archaeological Park
                                             (4) 672-5666

YOUTH HOSTELS
Taiber
                                             (4) 675-0050
                                        Fax: (4) 675-1628
2.5 miles south of Tiberias.

Zichron Ya'achov

MUSEUMS
Nili Museum & Aaronson House
40 Hameyasdim Street 30950   (4) 639-0120
                                        Fax: (4) 639-0119

RESTAURANTS
Dairy
Habayit Bayekev
Carmel Mizrachi Winery, Rehov Hayayin   (4) 629-0977
                                        Fax: (4) 629-0957

TOURS OF JEWISH INTEREST
American P'eylim Student Union
10 Shoarim Street   (4) 653-2131
Free tours of Jewish Quarter and free
accommodation, in the hostel quarters.

Jerusalem Youth Centre
9 Shonei Halachot Street   (4) 628-5623
Free accommodation.

ITALY

Italy has an ancient connection with the Jews, and was home to one of the earliest Diaspora communities. Before the Roman invasion of ancient Israel, Judah Maccabee had a representative in Rome, and one of the reasons for the invasion was the Romans' desire to access the salt supply from the Dead Sea. There were Jewish communities in Italy after the destruction of the Second Temple, as Italy was the trading hub of the Roman empire. After Christianity became the official religion in 313CE, restrictions began to be placed on the Jewish population, forcing the community to migrate from town to town across the country.

In the medieval period, there was a brief flourishing of learning, but the Spanish conquered southern Italy in the fifteenth century, expelling the Jews from Sicily, Sardinia and, eventually, Naples. The first ever ghetto was established in Venice in 1516. Later in the century descendants of those expelled from Spain and Portugal arrived. Conquest by Napoleon led to the emancipation of Italian Jewry, and full equal rights were granted in 1870.

Ironically, the Italian Fascist party contained some Jewish members, as Mussolini was not anti-semitic and, even under pressure from Hitler, did not instigate any major anti-semitic policy. The situation changed after Germany's occupation of the north in 1943. Eventually, almost 8,000 Italian Jews were killed in Auschwitz, although the local population hid many of those who survived.

Today there is a central organisation which provides services for Italian Jews. There are kosher restaurants in Rome, Milan and other towns. There are also Jewish schools.

GMT + I hour	**Total Population 57,523,000**
Country calling code (39)	**Jewish Population 30,000**
Emergency Telephone (Police – 112) (Fire – 115) (Ambulance – 116)	**(Electricity voltage – 220)**

Ancona

COMMUNITY ORGANISATIONS
Community Offices
Via Fanti 2 bis   (71) 202638

MIKVAOT
Via Astagno

Asti

MUSEUM
Via Ottolenghi 8, Torino   (141) 539281

SYNAGOGUES
Via Ottolenghi 8, Torino

Bologna

CAFETERIA
Comunita Ebraica Bologna
Via Gombruti 9 40123   (51) 232-066
                                   Fax: (51) 229-474
              Email: comebrbol@libero.it
Supervision: Rabbi Alberto Sermoneta
Lunch Sunday to Friday; dinner Friday; closed mid-July and August.

COMMUNITY ORGANISATIONS
Via Gombruti 9 40123
          (51) 232-066 & 227-931 (office of Rabbi)
                          Fax: (51) 229-474
                 Email: comebrbol@libero.it
      Web site: www.menorah.it/ceb/indice.htm

MIKVAOT
Mikveh Chaya Mushkah
Via Oreste Regnoli 17/1   (51) 623-0316

MUSEUM
Museo Ebraico
Palazzo Pannolini, via Valdonica, 1/5 40124
                                  (51) 2911280
                          Fax: (51) 235430
              Email: info@museoebraicobo.it
           Web site: www.museoebraicobo.it
The Jewish Museum of Bologna is located in Via Valdonica, in the area of the former ghetto. It was established as a means of conserving the Jewish cultural heritage that for centuries has been deeply rooted in Bologna and in the Emila Romagna region. It has a bookshop specialising on Jewish matters. Jewish itineraries.

SYNAGOGUES
Via Mario Finzi

Casale Monferrato

SYNAGOGUES
Community Offices
Vicolo Salomone Olper 44 (142) 71807
Fax: (142) 76444
Email: qqcasale@mail.dex-net.com
Web site: www.menorah.it/qqcasale/indice.htm
The synagogue, built in 1595 is one of the most
interesting in North Italy. It also contains a Jewish
museum. Casale-Monferrato is on the Turin-Milan
road, and can be reached by turning off it about
thirteen miles beyond Chivasso. Casale may also be
reached with tollway A26 (exit Casale north or south,
whichever comes first). It is better to make advance
appointments for visiting either the synagogue or
Museum. Closed in the months of January, February
and August.

Cuneo

SYNAGOGUES
Via Mondovi (171) 692-007
A beautiful synagogue; parts dating from the fifteenth
century. Services are now only held on Yom Kippur.
In 1799 a special Purim was established after the
synagogue was saved from destruction by a shell.

Ferrara

COMMUNITY ORGANISATIONS
Community of Ferrara
Via Mazzini 95 44100 (532) 24 70 04
Fax: (532) 24 70 04

MIKVAOT
Via Mazzini 95 (532) 24 70 04

MUSEUM
Jewish Museum of Ferrara
Via Mazzini 95 44100 (532) 21 02 28
Fax: (532) 21 02 28
Email: museoebraico@comune.fe.it
Web site: www.comune.fe.it/museoebraico
Guided tours in English on Sunday to Thursday 10.00
am, 11.00 am, 12.00 pm. Closed on Fridays and
Saturdays.

SYNAGOGUES
Via Mazzini 95 (532) 24 70 33

Florence

Although there is a belief that Jewish merchants
lived in the city during Roman times there is no
real evidence to substantiate this.
The known community was established in 1437
when Jewish financiers were invited to the city.
The Medici family protected the community.
Following their leaving in 1494 the Jews were
expelled. In due course they returned and a
ghetto was established in 1571. Emancipation was
only achieved with the entry of Napoleon in 1799.

BAKERIES
Forno dei Ciompi
Piazza dei Ciompi (55) 241-256

BUTCHERS
Bruno Falsettini
Mercato Coperto di S., Ambrogio (55) 248-0740
8 am to 10 am. Order in advance in advance
specifying kosher.

Gionvannino
Via dei Macci 106 (55) 248-0734
7.30 am to 1.00 pm. Order in advance specifying
kosher.

COMMUNITY ORGANISATIONS
Community Offices
Via L.C. Farini 4, Firenze 50121 (55) 245252
Fax: (55) 241811
Email: comebrfi@fol.it
Web site: www.fol.it/sinagoga
Open from Sunday to Friday from 9.30 am to 12.30
pm (Sunday closed in July and August).

HOTELS
Regency
Massimo D'Azeglio 3 (55) 245247
Fax: (55) 2346735
Email: info@regency-hotel.com
Web site: www.regency-hotel.com
Located in the square, near the synagogue.

MIKVAOT
Via L.C. Farini 4, Firenze 50121 (55) 245252
Fax: (55) 241811
Email: comebrfi@fol.it
Web site: www.fol.it/sinagoga

MUSEUM
Jewish Museum
Via L.C. Farini 4, Firenze 50121   (55) 245252
Fax: (55) 241811
Email: comebrfi@fol.it
Web site: www.fol.it/sinagoga
There is also a religious and artistic souvenir shop.
Open Sunday - Thursday. Groups are kindly
requested to book in advance. For further
information and booking, please contact the
Administation Office. (055) 2346054.

RESTAURANTS
Vegetarian Kosher
Ruth's
Via Farini 2/A   (55) 248-0888
Bookings required for Shabbat meals and groups.
Take-away.

SYNAGOGUES
Orthodox
Via L.C. Farini 4, Firenze 50121   (55) 245252
Fax: (55) 241811
Email: comebrfi@fol.it
Web site: www.fol.it/sinagoga
After service there is a public Kiddush. Services on
Shabbat and holidays, not daily. The synagogue is
open for tourists from Sunday to Thursday (hours
vary). Groups should book in advance.

Via De Banchi   (55) 212-474
After the service there is a public Kiddush. For the
timetable of services ask in the Community Office.

Genoa

SYNAGOGUES
Synagogue and Community Offices
Via Bertora 6 16122   (101) 839-1513
Fax: (101) 846-1006
Email: comgenova@tin.it
Every Friday and Shabbat morning.

Gorizia

SYNAGOGUES
Via Ascoli 19, Gradicia   (3831) 532115

Leghorn

BUTCHERS
Corucci
Banco 25, Mercato Centrale, Livorno   (586) 884596

MIKVAOT
Community Offices
Piazza Benamozegh 1, Livorno   (586) 896290

MUSEUM
Jewish Museum
via Micali 21, Livorno   (586) 893361
Visits only by appointment.

SYNAGOGUES
Community Offices
Piazza Benamozegh 1, Livorno   (586) 896290
Fax: (586) 896290

Mantua

SYNAGOGUES
Via G. Govi 11, Mantova   (379) 321490

Merano

MUSEUM
Jewish Museum
Via Schiller 14   (473) 236127
Fax: (473) 206210
Email: meranoebraica@hotmail.com
Hours: Tuesday and Wednesday 3 pm-6 pm.
Thursday 9 am-12 am. Friday 3 pm-5 pm.

SYNAGOGUES
Community Offices
Via Schiller 14   (473) 236127
Fax: (473) 206210
Email: meranoebraica@hotmail.com

Milan

Home for the second largest community in Italy,
(10,000). The Ambrosiana Museum (Piazza Pio
XI) contains a number of Hebrew books,
manuscripts and other Judaica.

COMMUNITY ORGANISATIONS
Sally Mayer 2   (2) 483-02806
Fax: (2) 483-04660

DOCUMENTATION CENTRE
Contemporary Jewish Documentation Centre
Via Eupili 8   (2) 316338
Fax: (2) 336-02728

GROCERIES
Eretz
Largo Scalabrini 5   (2) 423-6891
Fax: (2) 423-4753
Hours: 9 am to 7:30 pm. Buses, 50, 95, 13, 61,
subway 1 (red), stop, Bande-Nere.

MIKVAOT
Central Synagogue
Via Guastalla 19   (2) 551-2101
Fax: (2) 5519-2699

Chaya Mushka
35 Carlo Poerio

Persian
Angelo Donati Beth Hamidrash
Via Sally Mayer 4-6

RESTAURANTS
Eshel Isroel
Via Benvenuto Cellini 2   (2) 545-5076
Supervision: Rav G. H. Garelik
Open weekdays.

Mifgash Jewish Center
via Montecuccoli 35 20146   (2) 4156199
Fax: (2) 41291105
Email: sissirattan@libero.it

Dairy
Restaurant Pizzeria Dairy
viale San Gimignano 10 20146   (2) 416368
Fax: (2) 416368
Email: info@carmelbylolita.com
Web site: www.carmelbylolita.com
Supervision: Rav S. Behor
Hours 12.00 noon to 2.30pm and 6.00pm to
11.30pm.

Meat
Glat Kosher Beit Yoshef
via Montecuccoli 35 20146   (2) 4156199
Fax: (2) 41291105
Email: sissirattan@libero.it
Re Salomone
Via Washington, 9   (2) 469-4643
Fax: (2) 43318049
Email: resalomone@tiscalinet.it
International Meat restaurant with mediterranean,
Italian and oriental food and take-away.

SYNAGOGUES
Beth Shlomo
Galleria Vittorio Emanuele, (Via Ugo Foscolo 3.)
20121   (2) 8646-6118
Fax: (2) 2901-9561
Email: fweb.shlomo@bethshlomo.it
Web site: www.bethshlomo.it
Services are held on Friday evening, Shabbat, Sunday
morning and Holy Days.

Central Synagogue
Via Guastalla 19   (2) 551-2101
Fax: (2) 5519-2699

Merkos L'Inyonei Chinuch
Via Carlo Poerio 35 20129   (2) 295-31213

New Home for Aged
Via Leone XIII   (2) 498-2604
Services on Sabbaths and festivals. Kosher food
available upon reservation.

New Synagogue
Via Eupili 8
Service on Sabbaths and festivals.

Lubavitch
Ohel Yacob
Via Benvenuto Cellini 2   (2) 545-5076
Orthodox Sephardi
Via Guastalla 19   (2) 551-2029
Fax: (2) 551-92699
Rabbi Dr Laras is the Chief Rabbi.

Modena

BUTCHERS
Macelleria Duomo
Mercato Coperto (Covered Market), Stand 25
(59) 217269

SYNAGOGUES
Community Offices
Piazza Mazzini 26   (59) 223978

Naples

SYNAGOGUES
Via Cappella Vecchia 31, Napoli   (81) 764-3480
Email: c.l.na@virgilio.it

Padua

MIKVAOT
Via S. Martino e Solferino 9, Padova   (49) 871-9501

SYNAGOGUES
Community Offices
Via S. Martino e Solferino 9, Padova   (49) 875-1106

Parma

SYNAGOGUES
Vicolo Cervi 4

TOURIST SITE
Biblioteca Palatina
Palazzo della Pioltta 1-43100   (521) 282-217
Fax: (521) 235-662
The collection of 1700 Hebrew manuscripts, derived
from the collection of Giovanni Bernardo Rossi
(1742-1831) the first bibliographer of Hebrew
incunabula is said to be the greatest collector of
Judaica put together by a Christian scholar.

Perugia

SYNAGOGUES
P. della Republica 77   (75) 21250

Pisa

SYNAGOGUES
Community Offices
Via Palestro 24   (50) 542580
Services are held on festivals and Holy Days. During the week the resident beadle will be glad to show visitors round the synagogue, which is famed for its beauty. It is very near the Teatro Verdi.

Riccione

HOTELS
Vienna Touring Hotel
                                   (54) 160-1245
In the summer, kosher food is obtainable. Provides vegetarian food and particularly welcomes Jewish guests.

Rome

About half of Italian Jewry (some 15,000) live in Rome. As there has been such a long period of Jewish settlement, a Nusach Italki (Italian prayer ritual) has developed, which is practised in some synagogues in the town. Kosher restuarants and kosher food are available. Titus' Arch, depicting the destruction of Jerusalem by the Romans, is in the city, and Jews were forbidden to walk under it. The ghetto of Rome is behind the Great Synagogue. A visit worth considering is to the ancient Jewish burial sites along the Appian Way. Check about tour arrangements with the Jewish Community offices, Tel: 580-3667.

BAKERIES
Limentani Settimio
Via Portico d'Ottavia 1

BED AND BREAKFAST
Pension Carmel
via Goffredo Mameli 11 00153   (6) 580-9921
                                Fax: (6) 581-8853
Email: reservation@hotelcarmel.it
Kosher pension situated in the old district of Trastevere, ten minutes from the main synagogue.

BUTCHERS
Massari
Piazza Bologna 11   (6) 429120

Sion Ben David
Via Filippo Turati 110   (6) 733358

Terracina
Via Portico d'Ottavia 1b   (6) 654-1364

COMMUNITY ORGANISATIONS
Unione Comunita Ebraiche Italiane (Union of Italian Jewish Communities)
Lungotevere Sanzio 9   (6) 580-3667; 580-3670
                                Fax: (6) 589-9569
Information on Italian Jewry, its monuments and history may be obtained from here.

DELICATESSEN
Kosher Bistrot
Terracina Angelo, via Santa Maria del Pianto 68-69
                                     (6) 686-4398
Supervision: Chief Rabbinate of Rome

EMBASSY
Embassy of Israel
Via Michelle Mercati 14 00197   (6) 322-1541

Embassy of Israel to The Holy
Via M. Mercati 12 00197   (6) 3619-8690
                                Fax: (6) 3619-8626

GROCERIES
Sabra
Via S. Ambrogio 6

MEDIA
Newspaper
Shalom
Lungotevere Cenci 1   (6) 687-6816
                                Fax: (6) 686-8324
Email: shalom.mensile@flashnet.it
Web site: www.shalom.it
Monthly.

MIKVAOT
Lungotevere Cenci (Tempio) 9

MUSEUMS
Museum of the Italian Resistance
Via Tasso 145   (6) 700-3866
The museum was extended in 2001 with new displays dedicated to the fate of Roman Jews between 1938 and 1944.

The Jewish Museum
Lungotevere Cenci   (6) 6840-0661
                                Fax: (6) 6840-0684
Email: museo.ebraico@romacer.org
The main synagogue building contains a permanent exhibition covering the 2000 year history of the Italian Jewish community. Another link with this long history is the Rome Ghetto almost adjoining. It is a maze of narrow alleys dating from Imperial Roman times, within which, until 1870, al Roman Jews were confined under curfew. A striking monument has been erected to the memory of 335 Jewish and Christian citizens of Rome who were massacred in 1944 by the Nazis in the Fosse Ardeatine: It lies just outside the Porta San Paolo.

RELIGIOUS ORGANISATIONS

The Italian Rabbinical Council
Headquarters, Lungotevere Sanzio 9
(6) 580-3667; 580-3670

RESTAURANTS

Kosher Bistrot
via S. Maria del Pianto, 68-69 00186   (6) 686-4398
Fax: (6) 6880-1364

La Taverna del Ghetto
Via Portico de Ottivia 8   (6) 880-9771

Macelleria Terracina
via S. Maria del Pianto, 62 00186   (6) 6880-1364

Dairy
Piazza Cenci 70 00186   (6) 6813-4481
Supervision: Chief Rabbinate of Rome
Open at noon.

Zi Fenizia
via Santa Maria del Pianto 64-65 00186   (6) 689-6976
Kashrut certificate is for cheese.

Meat
Da Lisa
via Foscolo 16/18   (6) 704-95456
Fax: (6) 704-95456

Kasher Pizza
Via Luigi Magrini 12   (6) 5590-790

La Taverna Del Ghetto
Via Portico D'Ottavia 8   (6) 6821-2309
Fax: (6) 6880-9771

Oriental Foods Kosher
Via Livorno, 8-10   (6) 440-4840
Fax: (6) 440-4840

Simcha Labi
Via Imperia 2, CAP 00161   (6) 4423--0332
Supervision: Chabad Rabbi

SYNAGOGUES

Orthodox
The Great Synagogue
Lungotevere Cenci (Tempio)   (6) 684-0061
Fax: (6) 684-0000684
Email: info@romacer.org

Orthodox Ashkenazi
Via Balbo 33

TOURS OF JEWISH INTEREST

G. Palombo
Via val Maggia 7   (6) 810-3716; 993-2074
Guides can be contacted also through the Jewish
Museum, Tel 0668400661.

Ruben E. Popper
12 Via dei Levii   (6) 761-0901
Fax: (6) 761-0901
Telephone number is afternoons only.

Sardinia

There is no Sardinian Jewish community today,
but the island is of more than passing Jewish
interest. In 19 CE, the Emperor Tiberius exiled
Jews to Sardinia. There was a synagogue at
Cagliari, the islandís capital, at least as early as
599, for in that year a convert led a riot against it.
Sardinia eventually came under Aragonese rule,
and when the edict of expulsion of the Jews from
Spain was issued in 1492, the Jews of the island
had to leave. Since then there has been no
community.

**There are no specific locations of interest to
travellers.**

Senigallia

SYNAGOGUES
Via dei Commercianti

Sicily

Although there are very few Jews in Sicily today,
there is a long and varied history of Jewish
settlement on the island stretching back to at least
the sixth century and possibly according to some
scholars to the first or second centuries.

By the late Middle Ages, the community
numbered 40,000. In 1282, Sicily came under
Spanish rule. A century or so later, there was a
wave of massacres of Jews, and another in 1474.
These culminated in the introduction of the
Inquisition in 1479, and the expulsion of the Jews
in 1492.

**There are no specific locations of interest to
travellers.**

Siena

SYNAGOGUES
Vicolo delle Scotte 14   (577) 284647
The committee has issued a brochure in English,
giving the history of the community which dates back
to medieval times. The synagogue dates from 1750.
Services are held on the Sabbath and High Holy-days.
Further information from Burroni Bernardi, Via del
Porrione. M. Savini, via Salicotta 23. Tel: 283140
(close to the synagogue).

Spezia

SYNAGOGUES
Via 20 Settembre 165

Trieste

COMMUNITY ORGANISATIONS

Community Offices
Via San Francesco d'Assisi 19 34133   (40) 371466
Fax: (40) 371226
Chief Rabbi: Rav Dr. Avraham Umberto Piperno. Tel: 3722681.

SYNAGOGUES
Via Donizetti 2   (40) 631898

TOURS OF JEWISH INTEREST

Smile Service
via Martiri della Liberta' 17 34134   (40) 375-5638
Fax: (40) 375-5638
Email: smile@com.area.trieste.it
This service agency organises tours around the Jewish sites of Friuli Venezia-Giulia.

Turin

BOOKSELLERS

Biblioteca "E. Artom"
P.tta Primo Levi 12, Torino 10125   (11) 669-9097

Libreria Claudiana
Via Principe Tommaso 1, Torino 10125 (11) 669-2458
Fax: (11) 669-2458

COMMUNITY ORGANISATIONS

Community Centre

P.tta Primo Levi 12, Torino 10125   (11) 658-585
Fax: (11) 669-1173
Email: comebrato@libero.it

GROCERIES

Panetteria Bertino
Via B. Galliari 14, Torino 10125   (11) 669-9527

MIKVAOT

P.tta Primo Levi 12, Torino 10125   (11) 658-585
Fax: (11) 669-1173
Email: comebrato@libero.it

RESTAURANTS

Salomon e Augusto Segre - Jewish rest home
Via B. Galliari 13, Torino 10125   (11) 658-585
Only by reservation

SYNAGOGUES

P.tta Primo Levi 12 10125   (11) 658-585
Fax: (11) 669-1173
Email: comebrato@libero.it
Daily 6.50 am and sunset; Shabbat 9 am and half an hour before sunset (winter) or 6.30 pm (summer); on Shabbat (in winter) between Minchah and Maariv a Seudat Shelishit is held.

TOURIST SITE

Mole Atonellianta
Now the National Cinema Museum, it was originally built in the nineteenth Century and was meant to be the grandest synagogue in Europe but was never completed.

Urbino

SYNAGOGUES
Via Stretta

Venice

Jews settled in Venice early in the tenth century and became an important factor in the economic life of the city. In 1516 however the authorities banished the Jews to the Ghetto Nuovo (new foundry), district so establishing the first ghetto. The high walls surrounding the area still exist.

The 14th-century Jewish cemetery (the second oldest in Europe after the one in Worms) has recently been restored and was reopened in 1999 for guided tours (for details call the Jewish Museum).

COMMUNITY ORGANISATIONS

Community Offices
2899 Cannaregio , Ghetto Nuovo 30121(41) 715-012
Fax: (41) 524-1862
Email: com.ehza.ve@lihero.it

GIFT SHOP

David's
Campo del Ghetto Nuovo 2880   (41) 716278
Email: dcuriel@iol.it
Jewish articles & religious appurtenances are available.

Mordehai Fusetti
Ghetto Nuovo 1219   (41) 714024
Jewish articles & religious appurtenances are available.

GUEST HOUSE

Jewish Rest Home
2874 Cannaregio, Ghetto Nuovo 30121   (41) 716002
Fax: (41) 714394
Kosher meals and accommodation can be had. Early booking is advised.

HOTEL

Kosher
Locanda del Ghetto
2892 Cannaregio , Campo del Ghetto Novo
30121   (41) 275-9292
Fax: (41) 275-7987
Email: ghetto@veneziahotels.com
Web site: www.veneziahotels.com

HOTELS
Buon Pesce
50 S. Nicolo , Lido island   (41) 526-8599
Fax: (41) 526-0533
Email: info@hotelbuonpesce.com
Open February to November.

LIBRARIES
Jewish Library and Archives "Renato Maestro"
2899 Cannaregio
Ghetto Nuovo 30121   (41) 718833
Fax: (41) 5241862
Email: renatomaestro@libero.it

MIKVAOT
Jewish Rest Home
2874 Cannaregio , Ghetto Nuovo   (41) 715-118
Fax: (41) 718-474
Email: chiefrabbivenice@virgilio.it
Booking 24 hours in advance.

MUSEUM
Jewish Museum
Cannaregio, Ghetto Nuovo 2902/B   (41) 715-359
Fax: (41) 723-007
Jewish Museum (Open Sunday through Friday from
10.00am to 4.30pm from October to May and from
10.00am to 7.00pm from June to September). Closed
on Saturdays and Jewish holidays. Guided visits to the
synagogues in English start every hour from the
Jewish Museum. Sandwiches and drinks are available.

RESTAURANTS
Meat
Gam-Gam
1122 Cannaregio , Sottoportico di Ghetto Vecchio
(41) 715284
Fax: (41) 715284
Email: jewishvenice.org
Shabbat arrangements available. Open lunch and
dinner. Glatt kosher.

Jewish Rest Home
2874 Cannaregio, Ghetto Nuovo   (41) 716-002
It is necessary to book in the morning.

SYNAGOGUES
Orthodox
Chabad of Venice
Cannaregio, Ghetto Nuovo 2915   (41) 715284
Fax: (41) 715284
Email: guide@jewishvenice.org
Web site: www.jewishvenice.org
Shabbat and Holiday hospitality available.

Schola Levantina
1228 Cannaregio , Ghetto Vecchio   (41) 715-012
Fax: (41) 5241-862
Shabbath services are held during winter. Friday
about one hour before sunset and Saturday at
9.00am; on Saturday at 4.00pm (later in spring and
summer). Tefillah Mincha and Seuda Shelishit.

Schola Spagnola
1149 Cannaregio , Ghetto Vecchio   (41) 715-012
Fax: (41) 524-1862
Shabbath services are held here during summer.
Friday about one hour before sunset and Saturday at
9.00am; on Saturday at 4.00pm (later in spring and
summer). Tefillah Mincha and Seuda Shelishit.

Vercelli

COMMUNITY ORGANISATIONS
Community Offices
Via Oldoni 20

SYNAGOGUES
Via Foa 70

Verona

COMMUNITY ORGANISATIONS
Community Centre
Via Portici 3   (45) 800-7112
Fax: (45) 596627
Email: comebraica@libero.it

SYNAGOGUES
Via Portici 3

Viareggio

CONTACT INFORMATION
Mr Sananes
via Pacinotti 172/B   (584) 961-025
Private office: Tirreno Tour, 26 Viale Carducci, Tel:
30777, during daytime.

JAMAICA

During the time of Spanish colonisation, Jamaica witnessed many Conversos arriving from Portugal. After the British took over in 1655, many of these could again practise Judaism openly. Soon, other Jews, mainly Sephardim, followed from Brazil and other nearby countries. The community received full equality in 1831 (before a similar step was taken in England).

The Jews played an important role in Jamaican life, and in 1849 the House of Asembly did not meet on Yom Kippur! However, assimilation and intermarriage took their toll and in 1921 the Ashkenazi and Sephardi synagogues combined. There is now only one synagogue on the island, but there are remains of old synagogues in Kingston, Port Royal and other towns.

Community life includes WIZO, B'nai B'rith and a school (the Hillel Academy). The community lost members after the Cuban revolution, because many feared a similar revolution in Jamaica. However, this was not the case.

GMT -5 hours	**Total Population 2,590,000**
Country calling code (1 809)	**Jewish Population 300**
Emergency Telephone (Police – 119) (Fire – 110) (Ambulance – 110)	**(Electricity voltage – 110)**

Kingston

SYNAGOGUES

Shaare Shalom
Duke Street & Charles Street   (876) 927-7948
                                            Fax: (876) 978-6240
Services, Friday, 5:30 pm (all year), Shabbat, 10 am;
festivals, 9 am all year round.

JAPAN

After Japan became open to Western ideas and Westerners in the mid-nineteenth century, a trickle of Jewish immigrants from the Russian Empire, the UK and the USA began to make their homes there. The first Jewish communtiy at Yokohama was founded in 1860. Many were escaping anti-semitism and by 1918 there were several thousand in the country.

Individual Japanese, despite being allied to Nazi Germany, did not adopt the anti-Semitic attitude of the Nazis, and the Japanese consul in Kovno Lithuania even helped the Mir Yeshivah escape from occupied Europe in 1940.

The post-war American occupation of the country brought many Jewish servicemen, and the community was also augmented by Jews escaping unrest in China. In recent years, there have been some Jewish 'gaijin', or (foreign workers).

In Tokyo there is a synagogue, which provides meals on Shabbat, a Sunday school, and offices for the Executive Board of the Jewish Community of Japan, which is the central body.

GMT +9 hours	Total Population 125,638,000
Country calling code (81)	Jewish Population 1,500
Emergency Telephone (Police – 110) (Fire – 119) (Ambulance – 119)	(Electricity voltage – 110)

Hiroshima

TOURIST SITE
Holocaust Education Centre
866 Nakatsuhara, Miyuki, Fukuyama 720
(849) 558001
Fax: (849) 558001
Email: hecjpn@urban.ne.jp
Web site: www.urban.ne.jp/home/hecjpn/
Open Tuesday, Wednesday, Friday and Saturday,
10:30 am to 4:30 pm.

Kobe

SYNAGOGUES
Orthodox Sephardi
Ohel Shelomoh (Jewish Community of Kansai)
4-12-12 Kitano-cho, Chuo-ku 650-0002
(78) 221-7236
Fax: (78) 242-7254
Email: j.yohay@seifu.ac.jp
Web site: chabonline.com/kobe
Shabbat meals; kosher provisions;mikvah by
arrangement.

Nagasaki

Nagasaki
Now there are no known Jews living in Nagasaki. As a centre of foreign trade in the mid-19th century it had a community. The old Jewish cemetery is located at Sakamoto Gaijin Bochi. The site of the first synagogue in Japan is Umegasaki Machi.
There are no specific locations of interest to travellers

Tokyo

COMMUNITY ORGANISATIONS
8-8 Hiroo, 3-chome, Shibuya-ku 150   (3) 3400-2559
Fax: (3) 3400-1827
Email: jccmanager@gol.com
Web site: www.jccjapan.co.jp

EMBASSY
Embassy of Israel
3 Niban-cho, Chiyodaku   (3) 3264-0911

RESTAURANTS
Japan Jewish Community Center
8-8 Hiroo, 3-chome, Shibuya-ku 150   (3) 3400-2559
Fax: (3) 3400-1827
Email: jcc@crisscross.com
They sell prepared foods and kosher wine, as well as serve meals on Friday evening and Shabbat. Reservation strongly recommended.

SYNAGOGUES
Beth David Synagogue
8-8 Hiroo, 3-chome, Shibuya-ku 150   (3) 3400-2559
Fax: (3) 3400-1827
Services are held Friday evening at 6:30 pm (7 pm during summer); Shabbat morning, 9:30 am; and on Holy-days and festivals. Advance notification requested. Mikvah on premises.

KAZAKHSTAN

Essentially this community began when the Soviets rescued several thousand Jews at the time of the Nazi invasion of the Soviet Union in 1941. Others joined after the war. The community is mainly based in Almaty, the capital, and also in Chimkent. Some 2,000 Bukharan and Tat Jews also live in the country.

The central organisation is the Mitzvah Association, which heads various Jewish groups. It even has a chair on the All-Peoples Assembly of Kazakhstan. There is a high rate of emigration to Israel.

GMT +6 hours
Country calling code (7)
Emergency Telephone (Police – 03) (Fire – 03) (Ambulance – 03)

Total Population 16,223,000
Jewish Population 10,000
(Electricity voltage – 220)

Almaty

COMMUNITY ORGANISATIONS
206 e Raimbek St.   (3272) 439-358
                                Fax: (3272) 507-770
                          Email: info@chabad.kz
Also has a store, kosher butcher, library and mikvah.

SYNAGOGUES
Orthodox
206 e Raimbek St.   (3272) 439-358
                                Fax: (3272) 507-770
                      Email: synagogues@chabad.kz

Astana

SYNAGOGUES
Jewish Center of Astana
11 Respublki Street, #3 473000   (3172) 216-913
                          Email: astana@chabad.kz

Chimkent

SYNAGOGUES
Sephardi
Svobody Street, 47th Lane

KENYA

Kenya could have been the site of the first Jewish state for two thousand years as this offer was made to the Zionists in 1903. It was, however, rejected in 1905. There were some Jews living in Kenya at that time, and a synagogue was built in 1912. Many more Jews came here after the Second World War as Holocaust survivors, and recently some Israelis have worked on a short-term basis in the country.

Kenya was an ally to Israel in its rescue of the Jews from Entebbe in Uganda. Jews have contributed much to the hotel industry and professional life of the country.

Regular services are held every Saturday in the Nairobi Hebrew Congregation, and there is a Community Centre next to the synagogue. The centre, the Vermont Memorial Hall, offers educational and social events.

GMT +3 hours
Country calling code (254)
Emergency Telephone (Police – 999) (Fire – 999) (Ambulance – 999)

Total Population 33,144,000
Jewish Population 400
(Electricity voltage – 220/240)

Nairobi

COMMUNITY ORGANISATIONS
Community Centre
Vermont Memorial Hall
Open Monday, Tuesday, Friday 9 am to 1 pm;
Wednesday 2.30 pm to 5.30 pm; Services Friday
evening at 6.30 pm; Saturday morning at 8 am. All
festivals. Kosher chickens available.

SYNAGOGUES
Nairobi Hebrew Congregation
cnr. University Way & Uhuru Highway, P.O.Box 25233
(2) 577871

                                Fax: (2) 577871
             Email: azfactor@africaonline.co.ke

KYRGYZSTAN

This central Asian ex-Soviet republic has only a short history of Jewish settlement. The community originated from migrants after the Russian Revolution and evacuees from the German advance into the Soviet Union in the Second World War. As a result, community members are almost all Russian speakers and are assimilated into the Russian minority of the country.

Before the collapse of the Soviet Union, there was no organised community. Following 1991, there is a synagogue in Bishkek (the capital), where there is also a Jewish library and an Aish HaTorah centre. The main umbrella group is the Menorah Society of Jewish Culture.

GMT +5 hours
Country calling code (996)
Emergency Telephone (Police – 03) (Fire – 03) (Ambulance – 03)

Total Population 4,856,000
Jewish Population 2,500
(Electricity voltage – 220)

Bishkek

SYNAGOGUES
193 Suymbaeva (Karpinsky) Street   (3312) 681966
Fax: (3312) 681966
Email: chabad@netmail.kg

LATVIA

The Jews in the medieval principalities of Courland and Livonia represent the earliest Jewish settlement in Latvia. Tombstones from the fourteenth century have been found. After the Russian take-over, Jews were only allowed to live in the area if they were considered 'useful', or had lived there before the Russians took control, because the area was outside the 'Pale of Settlement' that the Russian Empire had designated for the Jews.

The Jews contributed much to Latvia's development, but this was never recognised by the government, which tried to restrict their influence in business matters. Religious Jewish life, however, was strong. When the Nazis invaded Latvia, 90 per cent of the 85,000 Jews were systematically murdered by them and their Latvian collaborators.

The bulk of today's community originates from immigration into Latvia after the war, although 3,000 Holocaust survivors did return to Latvia. Before the collapse of communism, there was much Jewish dissident activity. There is a Jewish school and a Jewish hospital. There are some Holocaust memorial sites, in Riga (the capital), and also in the Bierkernieki Forest, where 46,000 Holocaust victims were shot.

GMT +2 hours
Country calling code (371)
Emergency Telephone (Police – 02) (Fire – 01) (Ambulance – 03)

Total Population 2,474,000
Jewish Population 10,000
(Electricity voltage – 220)

Daugavpils

COMMUNITY ORGANISATIONS
Jewish Community
Saules Street 47
Fax: (54) 8254-24658

SYNAGOGUES
Suvorov Street
Gogol Street

Liepaja

COMMUNITY ORGANISATIONS
Jewish Community
Kungu Street 21   (34) 25336

Rezhitsa

SYNAGOGUES
Kaleyu St.

Riga

CULTURAL ORGANISATIONS
Latvian Society for Jewish culture
Skolas 6 LV1322   (2) 289-580
Fax: (2) 821-494

EMBASSY
Embassy of Israel
Elizabetes Street 2a LV1340   (2) 732-0980
Fax: (2) 783-0170
Email: press@rig.mfa.gov.il

MUSEUM
The Jewish Museum of Riga
6 Skolas Street LV-1322
The museum is small but has many moving exhibits and photos. A short video is shown depicting the tragedy of the Holocaust in Latvia.

SYNAGOGUES
Orthodox
Chabad Lubavitch Latvia
141 Lacplesa St., LV-1003   (2) 720 4022
Fax: (2) 783 0444
Email: chabad@mailbox.riga.lv
Visitors welcomed for Shabbat and holiday meals.
Take-out by order.

Riga Central Synagogue
6/8 Peitavas Street, L.V. 1050   (2) 721-4507
Fax: (2) 721-4507
Email: rerd@inbox.lv
Web site: www.jrcr.com
Hot kosher meals may be ordered in advance. Also has a mikva.

LITHUANIA

The history of Lithuania Jewry is as old as the state of Lithuania itself. There were Jews in the country in the fourteenth century, when Grand Duke Gedeyminus founded the state. The community eventually grew, and produced many famous yeshivas and great commentators, such as the Vilna Gaon. The community began to emigrate (particularly to South Africa) at the beginning of the nineteenth century; even so in 1941 there were still 160,000 Jews in the country. Ninety-five per cent of these were murdered in the Holocaust, by the local population as well as the Nazis.

The remaining post-war community included some who had hidden or had managed to survive by other means and some Jews from other parts of the Soviet Union. Interestingly, the Lithuanian Soviet Socialist Republic was more tolerant of Jewish activity than some of the neighbouring republics, such as Latvia. Now that Lithuania is independent, Jewish life is free once again.

The Lubavitch movement is present, and there are synagogues in Vilnius (known to many as Vilna), the capital, and Kaunas. There is also a school and it is possible to study Yiddish. There are tours available to show the old Jewish life in Lithuania. The grave of the Vilna Gaon can be visited, as well as Paneriai, otherwise known as Ponary, where thousands of Jews were shot during the Holocaust.

GMT +2 hours	**Total Population 3,701,000**
Country calling code (370)	**Jewish Population 5,000**
Emergency Telephone (Police – 02) (Fire – 01) (Ambulance – 03)	**(Electricity voltage – 220)**

Druskininkai

COMMUNITY ORGANISATIONS
Jewish Community
9/15 Sporto Street   54590

Kaunas

COMMUNITY ORGANISATIONS
26 B Gedimino Street   (7) 203717
Fax: (7) 7201135
Hours of opening: Sunday to Thursday 3 pm-6 pm.

SYNAGOGUES
11 Ozheshkienes Street

Klaipeda

COMMUNITY ORGANISATIONS
Jewish Community
3 Ziedu Skersqatvis   (6) 93758

Panevezys

COMMUNITY ORGANISATIONS
6/22 Sodu Street 5300   (54) 68848

Shiauliai

COMMUNITY ORGANISATIONS

24 Vyshinskio   (1) 26795

Vilnius

Otherwise known as Vilna, this town used to be known as the 'Jerusalem of the North'. Jews started to live in Vilnius during the middle of the sixteenth century. In due course it became a pre-eminent centre for rabbinical studies. The town still has the largest community of Lithuanian Jews, and there are many sites of historical interest, including the Vilna Gaon's grave and the State Jewish Museum.

BAKERIES

Matzah Bakery
39 Pylimo Street   (2) 61-2523

COMMUNITY ORGANISATIONS

Jewish Community of Lithuania
Pylimo St. 4 2001   (2) 61-3003
                            Fax: (2) 5212-7915
          Email: jewishcom@post.5ci.lt
               Web site: www.litjews.org
Opening hours: Monday to Thursday 10.00am to 6.00pm, Friday 10.00am to 4.00pm.

CULTURAL ORGANISATIONS

The Israel Centre of Cultures and Art in Lithuania
4 Pylimo, 2nd Floor 2001   (2) 61-1736 or 652139

MUSEUM

The Vilna Gaon Jewish State Museum
Pylimo 4, LT 2001   (2) 62-0730
                            Fax: (2) 22-7083
              Email: jmuseum@puni.osf.lt
The Tarbut School, Exhibitions and seat of Jewish Community. Opening hours Monday to Thursday 9 am to 5 pm and Friday 9 am to 4 pm.

SYNAGOGUES

Central Synagogue of Vilnius Chabad
12 Saltiniu g. St. 2006   (2) 250-387

Main Synagogue (Choral Synagogue)
39 Pylimo Street   (2) 61-2523

LUXEMBOURG

The small community in Luxembourg faced massacres and expulsions during medieval times and Jews only began to resettle here several hundred years later. Napoleon heralded the rebirth of the community when he annexed Luxembourg, and by 1823 a synagogue had been built, but the community remained small, although in 1899 another synagogue was built.

Later many refugees from the Nazis arrived in the country, bringing the number of Jews to nearly 4,000. After the Nazi take-over, 750 Luxembourg Jews were killed, but many others were saved by the local population.

The present community is generally prosperous and assimilated. The Consistoire Israelite, established by Napoleon, is recognised by the government as the representative of the community, and is also financed by the government. The Orthodox synagogue is situated fairly centrally in Luxembourg City.

GMT + I hour	Total Population 417,000
Country calling code (352)	Jewish Population 600
Emergency Telephone (Police – 133) (Fire – 112) (Ambulance – 112)	(Electricity voltage – 220)

Esch-Sur-Alzette

SYNAGOGUES
52 rue de Canal
Services held on Friday evenings.

Luxembourg City

COMMUNITY ORGANISATIONS
Consistoire Israelite de Luxembourg
45 av. Monterey 2018   452914
                                         Fax: 473772

EMBASSY
Consul General of Israel
38 BD Napoleon I er L-2210   446-557
                                         Fax: 453-676

GROCERIES
Calon
rue de Reins 3

KASHRUT INFORMATION
34 rue Alphonse munchen 2172   452366

SYNAGOGUES
45 av. Monterery   452914
                                         Fax: 250430

MACEDONIA

At the southern end of the former Yugoslavia, this new country has an ancient Jewish heritage dating back to Roman times. The Jews took advantage of the area's favourable commercial position, lying between Turkey and Western Europe, and the remains of a synagogue at Stobei dating back to the second and third centuries is evidence of a once thriving Jewish community.

Iberian Jews escaping the Inquisition settled in the area, and brought with them Sephardi customs and the Ladino language (based on Spanish). The fate of the 8,000 Macedonian Jews under Bulgarian occupation during the Second World War is in stark contrast to the fate of the Bulgarian Jews the Macedonian Jews were deported to their deaths, yet the Bulgarian Jews were saved by the defiance of the king and the people. Only ten per cent of the Macedonian community survived, of whom many have emigrated to Israel.

Today's community is mainly based in the capital Skopje, but there are no synagogues and there is little access to Jewish life. However, the community does have contact with Jews in Serbia and Greece.

GMT +1 hour
Country calling code (389)
Emergency Telephone (Police – 92) (Fire – 93) (Ambulance – 94)

Total Population 2,190,000
Jewish Population Under 100
(Electricity voltage – 220)

Skopje

COMMUNITY ORGANISATIONS
Community Offices
Borka Talevski Street 24   (91) 237-543

MALAYSIA

Malaysia is a Muslim state, and the Jewish population is tiny, barely into double figures. There is, however, a Jewish cemetery on the island of Penang, in Georgetown in Jalan Yahudi (Jewish Street). The cemetery is looked after by Selvaraj Sundram, a Hindu. Decades ago the then vibrant Jewish community hired his great-grandfather to look after the site. His family has done so ever since, funds now being provided by an anonymous German. The Jews who today live on Penang originate from refugees from Russia. There was a synagogue, but it is now closed.

GMT +8 hours
Country calling code (60)
Emergency Telephone (Police – 999) (Fire – 999) (Ambulance – 999)

Total Population 21,667,000
Jewish Population Under 100
(Electricity voltage – 220)

There are no specific locations of interest to travellers.

MALTA

There is evidence of an ancient Jewish community on Malta, as archaeologists have discovered remains from 2,000 years ago. Malta fell into Arab hands in the early Middle Ages, when there were still a few Jews on the island. The island then changed to Sicilian hands and, in 1492, the Jews were expelled.

Between the sixteenth and eighteenth centuries, the island was used as a prison for Jewish captives of the Knights of St John. They were held for ransom, but managed to find time to build a synagogue. A synagogue in Spur Street Valetta, opened in 1912, was demolished in 1995 as part of a redevelopment scheme.

GMT +1 hour	**Total Population 378,000**
Country calling code (356)	**Jewish Population 100**
Emergency Telephone (Police – 191) (Fire – 199) (Ambulance – 196)	**(Electricity voltage – 240)**

Birkirkara

COMMUNITY ORGANISATIONS

P O Box 4

445924

Valletta

SYNAGOGUES
Conservative
Jewish Community of Valetta
Flat 1, Florida Mansions, Enrico Mizzi St., MSD 02

237-309

Fax: 676-926

Email: sabra@keyworld.net

Web site:

www.angelfire.com/al/AttardBezzinaLawrenc
Morning services on the first and third Shabbat of
each calendar month and on the first days of the main
festivals, and on erev Yom Kippur & on two days of
Rosh Hashanah. Visitors are welcome.

MEXICO

Conversos were the first Jews in the country, and some achieved high positions in early Spanish colonial Mexico. As the Inquisition was still functioning here some 200 years after the sixteenth century, the number of Jewish immigrants was small. When Mexico became independent of Spain, Jews gradually began to enter the country, coming from German and other European communities.

There were both Ashkenazis and Sephardis, and they settled throughout the country. The communities grew on a parallel level, rather than together, with two languages, Yiddish and Ladino.

The current community is largely middle class and all the various factions come under the Comite Central Israelita. There are numerous synagogues and there are also kosher restaurants. The community is well equipped with Jewish schools and yeshivas.

GMT -6 to 8 hours	**Total Population 96,400,000**
Country calling code (52)	**Jewish Population 41,000**
Emergency Telephone (Police – 080) (Fire – 080) (Ambulance – 080)	**(Electricity voltage – 110)**

Acapulco

HOTELS
The Hyatt Regency
Costera Miguel Aleman 1 39869   (744) 69-1234
Fax: (744) 84-3087
Email: hyatta@netmex.com
The hotel has a synagogue and a mikva.

RESTAURANTS
Costera Miguel Aleman 1 39869   (744) 69-1234
Fax: (744) 84-3087
Email: hyatta@netmex.com
Open only during the high season (generally Nov/Dec to March/April).

Cuernavaca

SYNAGOGUES
Madero 404   (777) 186-846
At the home for the elderly.

Guadalajara

COMMUNITY ORGANISATIONS
Comunidad Israelita de Guadalajara
Juan Palomar y Arias 651   (33) 416-463
Fax: (33) 427-168
Includes kosher restaurant, mikva and two synagogues. Phone in advance.

Mexico City

Despite the fact that the first auto-da-fe at which Conversos were burnt at the stake took place in Mexico City it has been said that in 1550 there were more crypto-Jews in Mexico City than Roman Catholics. There are now many Jews, the vast majority of Mexican Jewry. With twenty-three synagogues, kosher restuarants and Jewish schools, the city is well equipped with Jewish facilities. Polanco is a Jewish area in the city with some synagogues. The first synagogue, dating from 1912, is in the downtown area.

BUTCHERS
Fuente de Templanza 17, Tecamachalco
Mehadrin.

Carniceria Sary
Tecamachalco
Mehadrin.

Pollos Mugrabi
Platon 133, Polanco
Mehadrin.

COMMUNITY ORGANISATIONS
Comunidad Monte Sinai
Tennyson 134, Polanco   (55) 280-6369
Fax: (55) 281-3969

EMBASSY
Embassy of Israel
Sierra Madre 215, PO Box 11000 10   (55) 201-1500
Fax: (55) 201-1555

GROCERIES
Casa Amiga
Horacio 1719, Col. Polanco   (55) 540-1455

Kurson Kosher
Acuezunco 15, San Miguel
(55) 905-589-9823, 9860 or 3225
Emilio Castelar , Polanco 204-G 11560   (55) 280-3500
Fax: (55) 280-3361
Email: kkurson@aol.com
Web site: www.kursonkosher.com
Will also deliver and ship to any resort in Mexico.

MEDIA
Newspapers
CDI
Centro Deportivo, Plaza de toros of Cuatro Caminos
(55) 557-3000
Spanish weekly.

Di Shtime
Pedro Moreno 149   (55) 546-1720
Yiddish weekly.

Foro de Vida Judia en el Mundo
Aviacion Commercial 16, Col. Polanco 15700
(55) 571-1114
Spanish monthly.

Kesher
Leibnitz 13-10, Colonia Anzures CP 11590
(55) 203-0446
Fax: (55) 203-9084
Email: info@kesher.org.mx
Spanish bi-weekly.

La Voz de la Kehila
Acapulco 70, 2nd Floor   (55) 211-0501
Spanish monthly.

MIKVAOT
Banos Campeche 58   (55) 574-2204
Platon 413   (55) 520-9569
Av. de los Bosques 53, Tecamachalco   (55) 589-5530
Bernard Shaw 110, Polanco   (55) 203-9964

Tevila Cuernavaca
Priv. de Antinea 4, Col. Delicias
(55) 15 08 41; 18 16 55

MUSEUM
The Holocaust Museum
Acapulco 70, Col Condesa   (55) 211-051

RELIGIOUS ORGANISATIONS
Comite Central
(55) 520-9393; 540-7376

Comunidad Maguen David
Email: mdavid@ort.org.mx
Contact for any religious questions.

Jerusalem de Mexico
Anatore France 359, Local C, Polanco   (55) 531-2269

RESTAURANTS
Meat
Aladinos
Ingenieros Militares 255   (55) 395-2959
Fax: (55) 395-9219

Hilarios
Cofre de Perote 244-B   (55) 540-0453

Jewish Sport Center
Manuel Avila Camacho   (55) 557-3000
Supervision: Rab. David E. Tabachnik

O Grill/Kosher House
37 Polanco, Mexico City   (55) 280-1638
Fax: (55) 280-1638

Restaurant Pini
Ejercito Nacional 458d
Supervision: Maguen David

Sinai
Izazaga, Near Pino Suarez   (55) 709-4906
Supervision: Maguen David

SYNAGOGUES
Agudas Achim
Montes de Oca 32, Condesa 06140   (55) 553-6430

Bet Midrash Tecamachalco
Fuente de Marcela 23, Col. Tecamachalco
(55) 251-8454

Beth Moshe
Tennyson No 134, Col. Polanco 11560
(55) 280-6369 ;6375
Fax: (55) 281-3969
Email: monsinai@ort.org.mx

Beth Yehoshua
Fuente de San Sulpicio No. 16, Col. Tecamachalco
53950   (55) 294-8617

Bircas Shumel
Plinio 311, Polanco   (55) 280-2769

Cuernavaca
Prolongacion Antinea Lote 2, Delicias

Jajam Elfasi
Fuente Del Pescador 168, Col. Tecamachalco
Shabbat services only.

Kolel Aram Zoba
Sofocles 346, Col. Polanco   (55) 280-2669; 4886;

Kolel Maor Abraham
Lafontaine 344, Col. Polanco   (55) 545-2482

Nidche Israel
Acapulco 70, Condesa   (55) 211-0575

Or Damesek
Seneca 343   (55) 280-6281

Ramat Shalom
Fuente del Pescador 35, Tecamachalco   (55) 251-3854

Shaare Shalom
Av. de Los Bosques 53, Tecamachalco   (55) 251-0973

Shuba Israel
Edgar Alan Poe 43, Col. Polanco
(55) 545-8061 & 280-1036
Conservative
Bet El
Horacio 1722, Polanco los Morales   (55) 281-2592
Fax: (55) 281-2467
Email: comunidad.betel@bigfoot.com

Beth Israel
Virreyes 114, Lomas   (55) 520-8515
Fax: (55) 520-9559
Email: bethisrael@psi.net.mx
English-speaking.

Orthodox
Beth Itzjak de Polanco
Eujenio Sue 20, Polanco   (55) 280-9296
Fax: (55) 280-0520
Email: bitzjak@prodigy.net.mx

Eliahu Fasja
Fuente de Templanza 13, Col. Tecamachalco
(55) 294-9388

Midrash Latorah
Cerrada de Los Morales 8, Col. Polanco 11510
(55) 280-0875
Fax: (55) 280-5978
Rabbi Asher Zrihen, formerly of London, will be
happy to welcome and assist visitors.

Sephardi
Maguen David
Bernard Shaw 110, Polanco   (55) 203-9964
Sephardi Synagogue
Monterey 359   (55) 564-1197;1367

Monterrey

COMMUNITY ORGANISATIONS
Centro Israelita de Monterrey
Canada 207, Nuevo León   (81) 461-128
Includes a synagogue and mikva.

Tijuana

CONTACT INFORMATION
JCC Chabad House
Centro Social Israelita de Baja California, Av. 16
Septiembre, Baja California 3000
(664) 862-692; 862-693
Fax: (664) 341-532
Email: chabadtj@telnor.net
Synagogue and mikva on premises.

SYNAGOGUES
Tijuanua Hebrew Congregation
Amado Nervo 207, Baja California

MOLDOVA

Moldova used to be a Soviet Republic bordering Romania to the west and the Ukraine to the east. When the Jews first entered what is now Moldova, the area was known as Bessarabia, and was on an important trade route between Turkey and Poland. By the time of Russian rule in 1812, there was a permanent Jewish community. The Russians included the area in the 'Pale of Settlement', which held the majority of the Jews of their empire. By the end of the nineteenth century, there were over 200,000 Jews in the region. However, the twentieth century started with the infamous progrom in the capital Chisinev, where 49 Jews were killed and much damage was done to Jewish property. Emigration began to increase. The area fell under Romanian control between 1918 and 1940, but the community continued to lead a normal life until the Second World War, when many thousands of the pre-war community of over 250,000 were killed during the German occupation.

After the war, some survivors continued to live in Moldova, and Jews from other parts of the Soviet Union joined them. There is an umbrella society for Moldovan Jews, and there are synagogues and schools. The Lubavitch movement is active in building up religious life.

GMT +2 hours
Country calling code (373)

Total Population 4,335,000
Jewish Population 15,000
(Electricity voltage – 220)

Chisinau

Most of Moldova's Jews live in Chisinau (formerly Kishinev). This city was the scene of two notorious progroms in 1903 and 1905.

RELIGIOUS ORGANISATIONS
Yeshiva of Chisinau
Sciusev 5 277001   (2) 274-362
Fax: (2) 274-331
Email: agudath@yeshiva.mldnet.com
Aside from Jewish studies, a mikva and kosher food supplies are on the premises.

SYNAGOGUES
Yakimovsky per. 8 277000   (2) 221-215
A mikvah is on the premises and kosher food can be obtained.

Teleneshty

SYNAGOGUES
4 28th June Street

Tiraspol

CONTACT INFORMATION
336-495
Fax: 322-208
Details of the Jewish Community from Dr Vaisman.

MONACO

Some French Jews lived in Monaco before 1939, and the government issued them with false papers during the war, thus saving them from the Nazis. This tiny country has also attracted retired people from France, North Africa and the UK.

There is an official Jewish body, the Association Culturelle Israelite de Monaco, and there is a synagogue, a school and a kosher food shop. Half of the total Jewish population are Ashkenazi and the other half are Sephardi, and 60 per cent of the community is retired.

GMT +1 hour	**Total Population 32,000**
Country calling code (377)	**Jewish Population 800**
Emergency Telephone (Police – 17) (Fire – 18) (Ambulance – 18)	**(Electricity voltage – 220)**

Monte Carlo

COMMUNITY ORGANISATIONS
Association Culturelle Israelite de Monaco
15 Av. de la Costa   9330-1646

SYNAGOGUES
15 Av. de la Costa, opp. Balmoral Hotel MC 98000
9330-1646
Services, Friday even. at 6.30pm and Sat. morning at 8.45am and Sat. afternoon at 5.30pm.

MOROCCO

There were Jews in Morocco before it became a Roman province (they first arrived after the destruction of the Temple in 587 BCE). Since the first century, the Jewish population settled in Morocco has increased steadily owing to several waves of immigration from Spain and Portugal following the expulsion of Jews by the Inquisition in 1492.

Under Moslem rule, the Jews experienced a general climate of tolerance, although they have suffered some persecution. During the Vichy period in the Second World War, Sultan Mohammed V protected the community. Almost 250,000 Jews have emigrated to Israel, Canada, France, Spain and Latin America, but they maintain strong links with the Kingdom.

Since ancient times, the Jewish community has succeeded in cohabiting harmoniously with the Berber and then with the Arab community. Today the present Jewish population is a living community, playing a significant role in Moroccan society although they have declined in number.

Country calling code (212)
Emergency Telephone (Police – 19) (Fire – 15) (Ambulance – 19)

Total Population 27,310,000
Jewish Population 6,000
(Electricity voltage – 110/170)

Agadir

COMMUNITY ORGANISATIONS
Community Offices
Imm. Arsalane Av. Hassan II   (8) 840091
     Fax: (8) 822268

MIKVAOT
Av. Moulay Abdallah, cnr. rue de la Foire   (8) 842339

SYNAGOGUES
Av. Moulay Abdallah, cnr. rue de la Foire   (8) 842339

Casablanca

At the beginning of the 19th century around one quarter of the city's population was Jewish. The community thrived until restrictions were imposed by the Vichy government during the Second World War.

In 1948 the Jewish population amounted to 74,000. Since then it has declined and is now considered to be around 5000.

COMMUNITY ORGANISATIONS
Community Offices
Rue Abbou Abdallah al Mahassibi
     (2) 270976 & 222861
     Fax: (2) 266953

MIKVAOT
32 rue Officier de Paix Thomas   (2) 276688

RESTAURANTS
Americano
7 Place d'Aknoul

Aux Bon Delices
261 Blvd Ziraoui, opp. Lycee Lyautey

SYNAGOGUES
Benisty
13 rue Ferhat Achad

Bennaroche
24 rue Lusitania

Em Habanim
14 rue Lusitania

Hazan
Rue Roger Farache

Ne'im Zemiroth
29 rue Jean-Jacques Rousseau

Temple Beth El
61 rue Jaber ben Hayane   (2) 267-192

El Jadida

COMMUNITY ORGANISATIONS
Community Offices
PO Box 59

Essaouira (formerly Mogador)

COMMUNITY ORGANISATIONS
2 rue Ziri Ben Atyah

SYNAGOGUES
2 rue Ziri Ben Atyah

Fez

COMMUNITY ORGANISATIONS
Community Offices
rue Dominique Bouchery

CONTACT INFORMATION
Mrs Danielle Mamane, La Boutique, Hotel Palais
Jamai, Fez   (5) 5562 2353
                        Email: boutique.palaisjamai@iam.net.ma
Mrs Mamane will be pleased to assist all Jewish
visitors.

MIKVAOT
Talmud Torah
rue Dominique Bouchery

RESTAURANTS
Meat
Centre Maimonide
24 rue Zerktouni, (adjacent to Hotel Splendide)
                        (5) 620-593
                        Fax: (5) 659-412

Supervision: Local Rabbanut

SYNAGOGUES
Beth El
rue de Beyrouth

Sadoun
ruelle 1, blvd Mohammed V.

Talmud Torah
rue Dominique Bouchery

Kenitra

COMMUNITY ORGANISATIONS
Community Offices
58 rue Sallah Eddine

MIKVAOT
58 rue Sallah Eddine

SYNAGOGUES
rue de Lyon

Marrakech

COMMUNITY ORGANISATIONS
Community Offices
PO Box 515   (4) 448754

MIKVAOT
Blvd Zerktouni (Gueliz)   (4) 448-754
                        Fax: (4) 438-676

Contact: Mme Kadoch

RESTAURANTS
Le Sepharade
31 Lotissement Hassania, Gueliz   (4) 43 98 09

Le Viennois Hotel Pulman Mansour Eddahbi
Avenue de France, Marrakech   (4) 339100

SYNAGOGUES
Beth-el
Blvd Zerktouni (Gueliz)   (4) 448-754
                        Fax: (4) 438-676

Bittoun
Medina, Rue Arset Laamach, Touareg
In course of renovation.

Rabbi Pinhas Ha Cohen
Medina Rue Arset, Laamach   (4) 389-798

Salat Laazama
Rue Talmud Torah, Mellah, Hay Essalam   (4) 403-798

Meknes

MIKVAOT
5 rue de Ghana   (5) 21968 or 22549
Tourists will be assisted if telephoning twenty-four
hours in advance of their requests.

SYNAGOGUES
5 rue de Ghana   (5) 21968 or 22549

Oujda

COMMUNITY ORGANISATIONS
Community Offices
Texaco Maroc, 36 blvd Hassan Loukili

Rabat

COMMUNITY ORGANISATIONS
1 rue Boussouni

MIKVAOT
3 rue Moulay Ismail

RESTAURANTS
Cercle de l'Alliance
3 rue Mellila   (7) 72 76 79
The Menora
Villa 5, rue Er Riyad   (7) 26 01 03

SYNAGOGUES
3 rue Moulay Ismail

Safi

SYNAGOGUES
Beth El
Rue de R'bat

Mursiand
Rue de R'bat

Tangier

COMMUNITY ORGANISATIONS
Community Centre
I rue de la Liberte   (9) 931-633
                           Fax: (9) 937-609

MIKVAOT
Shaar Raphael
27 blvd Pasteur   (9) 231304

SYNAGOGUES
27 blvd Pasteur   (9) 231304

Temple Nahon
Rue Moses Nahon

TOURIST SITE
Rue des Synagogues, off rue Siaghines.
There are a number of synagogues in the old part of
the town in this street.

Tetuan

COMMUNITY ORGANISATIONS
Community Offices
16 rue Moulay Abbas

SYNAGOGUES
Benoualid
The old Mellah

Pintada
The old Mellah

Yagdil Torah
Adj. Community Centre

MOZAMBIQUE

The small community in Mozambique originally consisted of South African Jews who were forced out of South Africa by President Kruger for supporting the British at the beginning of the twentieth century. A synagogue was opened in 1926, and there is a cemetery in Alto Maha. The biggest Jewish community is in Maputo.

GMT +2 hours   Total Population 16,917,000
Country calling code (258)   Jewish Population Under 100
Emergency Telephone (Police – 119) (Fire – 198) (Ambulance – 117)   (Electricity voltage – 220)

Maputo

COMMUNITY ORGANISATIONS
Jewish Community of Mozambique
Av. Tomas Nduda 235, PO Box 235   (1) 494413
        Email: xero_servicos@mail.garp.co.mz

MYANMAR

The first Jews came to Myanmar in the early eighteenth century from Iraq and other Middle Eastern countries. A synagogue was built in 1896. In the first years of the twentieth century Rangoon and Bassein both had Jewish mayors. The Jewish population swelled to 2,000 before 1939, but most of these fled to Britain and India before the Japanese invasion in the Second World War. Not many returned after the war (only a few hundred), and the community began to decline through intermarriage and conversion. The handful of remaining Jews are elderly and services are held only on the High Holy Days when a minyan is made up with help from the Israeli Embassy.

There is also a tribe of Jews in the north of the country (the Karens), who have their own prayer houses and who believe that they are descended from the tribe of Menashe.

Note: In Yangon [Rangoon] only	
GMT +6 1/2 hours	**Total Population 46,402,000**
Country calling code (95)	**Jewish Population Under 100**
Emergency Telephone (Police – 199) (Fire – 191) (Ambulance – 192)	**(Electricity voltage – 220/230)**

Yangon (formerly Rangoon)

EMBASSY

Embassy of Israel
49 Pyay Road   222-290; 222-709; 222-201
Fax: 222-463
Email: emisrael@datserco.com.mm

SYNAGOGUES

Musmeah Yeshua
85 26th Street   75062

NAMIBIA

Namibian Jewry began at the time when the country was a German colony, before the First World War. The cemetery at Swakopmund dates from that settlement. Keetmanschoop also had a congregation, but this no longer exists. The Windhoek synagogue is still in use, and was founded in 1924. Services are held on Shabbat and festivals.

South Africa provides some help for the community, such as a cantor on festivals, and the Cape Board of Jewish Education assists with Hebrew education. From approximately 100 Jewish families in the 1920s and 1930s, the number has dwindled.

GMT +2 hours	**Total Population 1,613,000**
Country calling code (264)	**Jewish Population Under 100**
Emergency Telephone (Police – 1011) (Fire – 2032270) (Ambulance – 2032276)	**(Electricity voltage – 220/240)**

Windhoek

SYNAGOGUES

Cnr. Tal & Post Streets, PO Box 563

NEPAL

Nepal has no Jewish history. It is however well visited by Israeli and other young Jewish tourists. Each year a large Seder is organised by the Lubavitch movement. In 2000 approximately 1,000 attended at the Radisson Hotel.

GMT +5.45 hours
Country calling code (977)

Total Population 22,591,000
Jewish Population Under 100

Kathmandu

EMBASSY
Embassy of Israel
Bishramalaya House, Lazimpat Street, G.P.O. Box 371
(1) 411-811
Fax: (1) 413-920
Email: kathmandu@israel.org

NETHERLANDS

Although some historians believe that the first Jews in Holland lived there during Roman times, documentary evidence goes back only to the twelfth century. The contemporary settlement occurred when Portuguese Marranos found refuge from the Inquisition in Holland. Religious freedom was advocated in the early seventeenth century and Jews contributed much to the Netherlands' 'golden age' of prosperity and power.

By the time of Napoleon, the community had grown to 10,000 (the largest in Western Europe), mainly by incoming Jewish traders from eastern Europe. The Jews were emancipated in 1796, but the community began to decline slowly during the nineteenth century. Of the 140,000 Jews (including 30,000 German Jewish refugees) in Holland in 1939, the Germans transported 100,000 to various death camps in Poland, but the local Dutch population tended to behave sympathetically towards their Jewish neighbours, hiding many. Anne Frank and her family are the most famous of the hidden Jews from Holland. Amsterdam witnessed a strike in February 1941, called as a protest against the Jewish deportations.

Today, there are three Jewish councils in the Netherlands, representing the Ashkenazi, Reform and Orthodox communities. There are many synagogues in Amsterdam, as well as synagogues in other towns. There are kosher restaurants in Amsterdam, which also has many historical sites; the Anne Frank House, the Portuguese Synagogue, still lit by candlelight, and the Resistance Museum.

GMT +1 hour
Country calling code (31)
Emergency Telephone (Police – 112) (Fire – 112) (Ambulance – 112)

Total Population 15,604,000
Jewish Population 28,000
(Electricity voltage – 220)

Amersfoort

SYNAGOGUES
Drieringensteeg 2, P O Box 1039-3800   720943
Email: nigamersfoort@hetnet.nl

Amsterdam

The first Jews were said to have come to the city in 1598 following the Union of Utrecht when the northern provinces proclaimed their independence from Catholic Spain and abolished religious discrimination. It soon became the centre of the Converso Diaspora. The Jewish Historical Museum and the Anne Frank house are essential visits. The Rijksmuseum contains a number of paintings of Jewish interest including 'The Jewish Bride' by Rembrandt.

BAKERIES

Thee Boom
Bolestein 45-47   (20) 642-7003
Supervision: Amsterdam Jewish Community
Hours: Sunday - Friday 9.00 am - 5.00 pm, closed on
Tuesday. Trams: 12, 25.

Maasstraat 16   (20) 662-4827
Supervision: Amsterdam Jewish Community

BOOKSELLERS

Joachimsthal's Boekhandel
Van Leijenberghlaan 116 1082 DB   (20) 442-0762
Fax: (20) 404-1843
Email: joachims@xs4all.nl

Samech Books
Gunterstein 69   (20) 642-1424
Fax: (20) 642-1424
Email: samech@dds.nl.

BUTCHERS

Marcus, Rituel
Ferd. Bolstraat.44   (20) 671-9881
Fax: (20) 642-6532
Supervision: Amsterdam Jewish Community

CHOCOLATE SHOPS

Chocolate shop Bonbon Jeannette
Hall Central Station Amsterdam, Stationsplein 15
1012 AB   (20) 421-5194
Fax: (20) 421-5194
Their bitter and dairy chocolates and bonbons are
kosher and are sanctioned by the Chief Rabbinate for
the Netherlands. Open daily, 8 am to 9 pm.

DELICATESSEN

Mouwes Koshere Delicatessan
Kastelenstraat 261 1082   (20) 661-0180

HOTELS

Golden Tulip Amsterdam Centre
Stadhouderskade 7 1054 ES   (20) 685-1351
Fax: (20) 685-1611
Email: info@gtacentre.goldentulip.nl

Hotel Doria
Damstraat 3 1012   (20) 638-8826
Fax: (20) 638-8726
Email: doria@euronet.nl
Kosher breakfast.

Hotel la Richelle
Holbeinstr 41   (20) 671-7971
Fax: (20) 671-0541

Kosher breakfast on request.

JEWISH LIBRARY

Ets Haim Library - Livraria Montezinos
Mr. Visserplein 3 1011RD   (20) 428-2596
Fax: (20) 428-2597
Email: biblio@etshaim.org
Open for research only Monday-Thursday 10.00-16.00, Friday 10.00-12.30.

LIBRARIES

Bibliotheca Rosenthaliana
Singel 425 1012 WP   (20) 525-2366
Fax: (20) 525-2311
Email: ros@uba.uva.nl
The Amsterdam University Library contains an extraordinary collection of Judaic and Hebrew writings given to the city in 1880 by the heirs of Lesser Rosenthal (1794-1868). The German occupation in the Second World War had severe repercussions for the Bibliotheca Rosenthaliana. The books were sent to Germany, where they were found by the Americans, and returned to Amsterdam in 1946. The collection now contains over 100,000 volumes, some dating back to the fifteenth century.

MEDIA

Newspaper
Nieuw Israelietisch Weekblad
Rapenburgerstr. 109 1011 VL   (20) 627-6275
Fax: (20) 624-2519
Email: niw@xs4all.nl
Web site: www.xs4all.nl/~niw

MIKVAOT

Heinzestr. 3   (20) 662-0178/671938
Mr. Visserplein 3   (20) 625-6222

MUSEUMS

Anne Frank House
Prinsengracht 263   (20) 556-7100
Fax: (20) 620-7999
Web site: www.annefrank.nl
The original hiding place of Anne Frank, where she wrote her diary. Open daily from 9am to 7pm (April 1st to September 1st daily from 9am to 9pm. January 1st and December 25th 12 noon to 5pm). Last entry thirty minutes before closing time.

Dutch Resistance Museum
Plantage Kerklaan 61 1018 CX   (20) 620-2535
Fax: (20) 620-2960
Email: info@verzetsmuseum.org
Web site: www.verzetsmuseum.org
Open all year, except January 1st, April 30th and December 25th. Permanent Exhibition: From 10 May 1940 to 5 May 1945, the Netherlands were occupied by Nazi Germany. Almost every Dutch person was affected by the consequences of the occupation. The Plancius Building, in which the museum is located, was built in 1876 as the social club for a Jewish choir.

Jewish Historical Museum
Jonas Daniël Meÿerplein 2-4 1011 RH   (20) 626-9945
Fax: (20) 624-1721
Email: info@jhm.nl
Web site: www.jhm.nl
Housed in a complex of four former synagogues. Sandwich shop serving kosher food. Open daily from 11am to 5pm. Group visits by arrangement. Next to the permanent collection on the culture and the history of the Jews in the Netherlands, there are changing exhibitions and a program of events. Until the end of 2003: 'Where Mokum is home', an exhibition especially for children of the ages of 8-12 years (Awarded with the prestigious Museum Price 2002 of the Prince Bernhard Cultural Fund).

RELIGIOUS ORGANISATIONS

Ashkenazi Community Offices/Community Center
van der Boechorststr. 26, PO Box 7967 1008 AD
(20) 646-0046
Fax: (20) 646-4357
Email: info@nihs.nl
Web site: www.nik.nl

RESTAURANTS

Nasj Viel Restaurant
Jewish Youth Center, De Lairessestraat 13, (near Concertgebouw) 1071   (20) 676-7622
Fax: (20) 673-5215
Email: info@nasjviel.nl
Supervision: Amsterdam Rabbinate
Open: Sunday - Thursday, 6.00pm - 10.00pm (kitchen closes at 9.00pm). Groups can be accommodated - reserve in advance.

Sandwichshop Sal. Meijer
Scheldestraat 45 1078 GG   (20) 673-1313
Fax: (20) 642-9020
Supervision: Amsterdam Jewish Community

Dairy
Museum Café
Jewish Historical Museum,
Jonas Daniel Meijerplein 2-4   (20) 626-9945
Fax: (20) 624-1721
Supervision: Amsterdam Jewish Community
Hours 11am to 5pm daily.

Meat
Carmel
Amstelveenseweg 224 1075 XT   (20) 675-7636
Fax: (20) 773-5960
Supervision: Amsterdam Jewish Community
Hours: 12 pm to 11:30 pm, Sunday to Thursday. Cater Shabbat meals for groups if ordered in advance. Transport: trams 6, 16, bus 15, 63, 170, 171, 172.

Jerusalem of Gold
Jodenbreestraat 148 1011 NS   (20) 6250923
Fax: (20) 6415854
Web site: www.jerusalemofgold.homepage.com
Supervision: Amsterdam Jewish Community
Hours: Noon to 10pm daily.

King Solomon Restaurant
Waterlooplein 239   (20) 625-5860

Shabbes - Tisch
Plantage Westermanlaan 9 1018 DK   (20) 623-4684
Supervision: Rabbinate of The Netherlands
Five minutes from Portuguese Synagogue. Friday
night and Shabbath only. Reservations in advance.

Vegetarian
Bolhoed
Prinsengacht 60-62   (20) 626-1803
Hours: 12 pm to 10 pm daily. Serve organic
vegetarian and vegan food.

Restaurant Betty's
Rijnstraat 75 1079 GX   (20) 644-5896

SYNAGOGUES
Liberal
Liberaal Joodse Gemeente
Jacob Soetendorpstr. 8 1079 RM   (20) 642-3562
Fax: (20) 442-0337
Email: ljgadam@ljg.nl
Web site: www.ljg.nl
Also houses the Judith Druk Library and The Centre
for Jewish Studies.

Orthodox
Gerard Doustraat Synagogue
Gerard Doustr. 238   (20) 675-0932
Fax: (20) 867-1626
Email: gd_sjoel@joods.nl
Web site: www.joods.nl/gd_sjoel
Services: Saturday and Festival mornings.

Kehilas Ja'Akow (E. Europe)
Gerrit van der Veenstraat 26 1077 ED   (20) 676-3602

Portuguese Jews' Congregation
Mr. Visserplein 3 1011 RD   (20) 624-5351
Fax: (20) 625-4680
Email: pig-amsterdam@euronet.nl
This synagogue has been completely restored and is
open from Sunday - Friday from 10 am to 4 pm. In
August 2000 Hollands unique Sephardi Judaism
collection was returned from safe keeping at The
Hebrew University at Jerusalem.

Raw Aron Schuster Sjoel
Jacob Obrechtplein
Daily services.

Sephardi
Portuguese Synagogue & Community Centre
Texelstr. 82   (20) 624-5351

TOURIST SITE
Portuguese Jewish Cemetery
Kerkstraat 7, 1191 JB, Ouderkerk aan de Amstel
(20) 496-3498
Fax: (20) 496-5496
Email: bethaim@wxs.nl
Established 1614. One of the oldest Sephardic
cemeteries still in use in Europe. Menasseh ben Israel
is buried here, as are the parents of the philosopher
Spinoza. Ten kilometres south-east of Amsterdam.

TOURS
Easy Rider Excursions
Majella 1, 1186 CE Amstelveen   (20) 489-7045
Email: maxmeron@hotmail.com
Web site: www.easyriderexcursions.nl
Walk through the jewish history of Amsterdam.
Licensed tour guides. By reservation only: 06-
11292616, from June 1st till September 30th.

Arnhem

SYNAGOGUES
Pastoorstr. 17a   (26) 442-5154
Liberal
Liberaal Joodse Gemeente Arnhem
Veluws Hof 24, Ermelo 3852 JJ   (26) 557-860
Email: elisjewa@hetnet.nl

Bussum

SYNAGOGUES
Orthodox
Kromme Englaan 1a   (35) 691-4882
Fax: (35) 538-0236

Delft

SYNAGOGUES
Beth Studentiem
Hillel House, Jewish Students Centre, Technical
University, Koornmarkt 9   (15) 212-0300

Eindhoven

RELIGIOUS ORGANISATIONS
Synagogue Inquiries
     (40) 241-2710

SYNAGOGUES
H. Casimirstr. 23   (40) 751-1253

Enschede

SYNAGOGUES
Prinsestr. 16   (53) 432-3479
     Fax: (53) 430-9725
     Email: jmhartog@vromen.nl

Liberal
Liberal Congregation Inquiries
Haaksbergen   (53) 435-1330

Groningen

SYNAGOGUES
Postbus 550 9700 AN   (50) 312-3151
     Email: NIG_Groningen@hotmail.com

Haarlem

SYNAGOGUES
Kenaupark 7   (23) 332-6899; 324-2051

Hilversum

CENTRAL ORGANISATION
Nederlandse Vegetariersbond
Larenseweg 26 1221 CM   (35) 683-4796
     Fax: (35) 683-6152
     Email: info@vegetariers.nl
     Web site: www.vegetariers.nl
Provides information on vegetarian hotels,
restaurants and guest houses.

SYNAGOGUES
Orthodox
Synagogue
Laanstr. 30   (35) 621-2044
     Fax: (35) 624-3654
     Email: ipor@wxs.nl
The Inter-Provincial Chief Rabbinate is also based at
this address. Tel: 035-623-9238.

Leiden

ORGANISATIONS
Jewish Students Centre
Levendaal 8   (71) 513-0382

SYNAGOGUES
Levendaal 14-16 2311 JL   (71) 512-5793
     Fax: (71) 512-5793

Maastricht

SYNAGOGUES
Capucijnengang 2
The present synagogue was built in 1841. It is
believed however that there had been one in the
town in the 14th century

Rotterdam

SYNAGOGUES
Liberal
**Liberaal Joodse Gemeente Rotterdam (Liberal
Jewish Community of Rotterdam)**
Mozartlaan 99 3007   (10) 461-2606
     Fax: (10) 218-0322
     Email: norbird@hetnet.nl
Mailing address: Postbox 91119, 3007 MA. Inquiries
to Secretary: 180 423474

Orthodox
Joodse Gemeente Rotterdam
A B N Davidsplein 2   (10) 466-9765
     Fax: (10) 467-5713
     Email: nig.rotterdam@zonnet.nl
Mikva on premises.

The Hague

DELICATESSEN
Jacobs
Haverkamp 220   (70) 347-4980
     Fax: (70) 347-4980

EMBASSY
Embassy of Israel
Buitenhof 47 2513 AH   (70) 376-0500
     Fax: (70) 376-0555
     Email: ambassade@israel.nl

RESTAURANTS
Vegetarian
Restaurant De Wankele Tafel
Mauritskade 79 2514 HH   (70) 364-3267

Synagogues
Liberal
Liberal Synagogue
Prinsessegracht 26   (70) 365-6892
Fax: (70) 360-3883
Email: ljg-denhaag@hetnet.nl
Web site: www.ljgdenhaag.nl

Orthodox
Beis Jisroel
Doorniksestraat 152 2587 AZ   (70) 358-6363
Fax: (70) 347-9002

Synagogue
Corn. Houtmanstraat 11,
Bezuidenhout 2593 RD   (70) 347-0222
Fax: (70) 347-9002
Email: raabinaat-haag@zonnet.nl
Mikva on premises, appointments should be made twenty-four hours in advance by telephoning 350-7621.

Tourist Site

Spinoza House
Paviljoensgracht
Spinoza House is of special interest, as is the eighteenth-century Portuguese synagogue in the Prinsessegracht, which is now used by the Liberal congregation.

Tulburg

Synagogues
Liberal
Liberal Synagogue Brabant
    (70) 365-6893
Inquiries to 013-467-5566.

Utrecht

Bakeries
De Tarwebol
Zadelstr. 19   (30) 231-4887

Restaurants
Eetkafee De Baas
Lijnmarkt 8 3511 KM   (30) 231-5185

Synagogues
Liberal
Liberal Synagogue
    (30) 644-2619
Email: batja@hetnet.nl
Inquiries to 030-603-9343

Orthodox
Springweg 164 3511 VZ   (30) 231-4742
Fax: (30) 272-2091
Email: nigutrecht@hotmail.com

Zwolle

Synagogues
Samuel Hirschstr. 8, Postbox 1468 8001   (38) 211412

OVERSEAS TERRITORIES

NETHERLANDS ANTILLES

A Samuel Cohen served as an interpreter to the Dutch Army which captured Curaçao from the Spaniards in 1634. A congregation was founded in 1651. The Jews of Curaçao enjoyed excellent relations with the Dutch West India Company who owned the island until the end of the eighteenth century.

The Sephardi synagogue in Curacao established in 1732 is the oldest synagogue building in continuous use in the western hemisphere. It has, like the one in Paramaribo (Suriname), sand covering its floor because the synagogue is modelled on after the Tabernacle used in the Sinai desert during the forty years of exile. It is also a reminder of the days of the Conversos when sand was used to muffle sounds.

Curaçao also has the oldest existing Jewish cemetery in the western hemisphere.

Aruba

Synagogues
Conservative
Congregation Beth Israel
Adriaan Lacle Blvd. #2, PO Box 5397,
Royal Plaza, Oranjestad   (297) 823272
Fax: (297) 886264
Email: ledaneps@setarnet.aw

Curaçao

Embassy
Consul General of Israel
Blauwduifweg 5, Willemstad   736-5068
Fax: 737-0707
Email: midalya@ibm.net

Kashrut Information
There is no kosher restaurant in Curacao.However many kosher items may be purchased at the "food store" of the Congregation Shaarei Tsedek.

MUSEUM

Jewish Cultural Historical Museum
Hanchi di Snoa 29, PO Box 322   461-1633
                                    Fax: 465-4141
Opening hours: Monday to Friday 9.00 to 11.45am
and 2.30 to 4.45pm. If there is a cruise ship in port
also on Sundays from 9am to noon. Closed on
Shabbaths and Holy Days. On permanent display are
a great many ritual, ceremonial and cultural objects,
many of which date back to the seventeenth and
eighteenth centuries and are still in use by the
adjacent congregation Mikve Israel-Emanuel (founded
1651, oldest in the Hemisphere).

SYNAGOGUES

Ashkenazi
Congregation Shaarei Tsedek
Leliweg 1a, PO Box 498   737-5738
                                    Fax: 736-9546

Sephardi, Reconstructionist
United Congregation Mikve'Israel Emanuel
Hanchi di Snoa 29, PO Box 322   461-1067
                                    Fax: 465-4141
                           Email: info@snoa.com
Sabbath services are Friday at 6.30pm (second Friday
in the month is a family service), Saturday at 10am.
Holy-day services at same times.

NEW ZEALAND

New Zealand Jewry is almost as old as the European presence in the country. The year 1829 marks the
beginning of Jewish settlement, and Jews played a prominent role in the development of the country in the
nineteenth century, especially in trading with Australia and Britain. Auckland Jewish community was founded
in 1841, followed by Wellington in 1843. There was also a Jewish Prime Minister, Sir Julius Vogel, in the
nineteenth century.

British Jews emigrated to New Zealand in the twentieth century, but New Zealand restricted
immigration from Nazi Europe.

Today the community has six synagogues, four on the North Island and two on the South Island. Auckland
and Wellington have Jewish day schools, and the 'Kosher Kiwi Guide' is published in Auckland. There has
been recent Jewish immigration from South Africa.

GMT +12 hours	**Total Population 3,811,000**
Country calling code (64)	**Jewish Population 5,000**
Emergency Telephone (Police – 111) (Fire – 111) (Ambulance – 111)	**(Electricity voltage – 230)**

Auckland

BAKERIES
Manhattan Bagels
                                    (9) 309-9098

COMMUNITY ORGANISATIONS
Auckland Jewish Council
80 Webb St, Wellington   (9) 384-4229
                                Fax: (9) 384-4229
Has a small shop selling kosher food.

SYNAGOGUES
Orthodox
Auckland Hebrew Congregation
108 Greys Avenue   (9) 373-2908
                                Fax: (9) 303-2147
                          Email: office@ahc.org.nz
New Zealands largest selection of kosher goods.
Open Wednesday to Friday 8.30 am to 3.30pm.
Sundays 9.00am to 11.00am.Mailing address: PO Box
68224 Newton Auckland

Progressive
Beth Shalom Progressive Synagogue
180 Manukau Road, Epsom 3   (9) 524-4139
                                Fax: (9) 524-7075
                     Email: bshalom@ihug.co.nz

Christchurch

COMMUNITY ORGANISATIONS
Christchurch Jewish Council
                                         (3) 358-8769

SYNAGOGUES
406 Durham Street   (3) 365-7412
                                Fax: (3) 355-7982
                    Email: coxst@chch.planet.org.nz

Dunedin

SYNAGOGUES
Progressive Congregation
cnr. George & Dundas Streets

Wellington

COMMUNITY ORGANISATIONS

Wellington Jewish Community Centre
80 Webb Street   (4) 384-5081
                                   Fax: (4) 384-5081
                         Email: bethel@ihug.co.nz
There are no kosher restaurants in Wellington.
Visitors who want kosher meals & kosher food should
contact the office of the Community Centre or the
Kosher Co-op, on 384-3136.

Wellington Regional Jewish Council
54 Central Terrace 5   (4) 475-7622
                        Email: zwartz@actrix.gen.nz

DELICATESSEN

Dixon Street Delicatessen
                                        (4) 384-2436
                                   Fax: (4) 384-8692
Not fully kosher but provides kosher challahs and
various American & Israeli kosher foods.

EMBASSY

Embassy of Israel
Level 13, 111 The Terrace, Equinox House, P O Box
2171   (4) 472-2368
                                   Fax: (4) 499-0632
                      Email: israel-ask@israel.org.nz
                      Web site: www.webnz.co.nz/israel

GROCERIES

Kosher Co-op
80 Webb Street   (4) 384-3136
                                   Fax: (4) 384-5081
                        Email: clemclan@ihug.co.nz
                      Web site: www.go.to/koshernz
Open on Wednesday, Friday and Sunday for kosher
meats, cheese and imported products. Goods can be
sent anywhere in New Zealand.

MEDIA

Newspapers
New Zealand Jewish Chronicle
PO Box 27-156   (4) 934-6077
                                   Fax: (4) 934-6079
                         Email: mike@rifkov.co.nz
Monthly newspaper of local, Israeli and Jewish News.

MIKVAOT

Wellington Jewish Community Centre
80 Webb Street   (4) 384-5081
                                   Fax: (4) 384-5081
                         Email: bethel@ihug.co.nz

SYNAGOGUES

Orthodox
Beth-El Synagogue
80 Webb Street   (4) 384-5081
                                   Fax: (4) 384-5081
                         Email: bethel@ihug.co.nz

Progressive
Temple Sinai
147 Ghuznee Street   (4) 385-0720
                                   Fax: (4) 385-0572
                      Email: temple@actrix.co.nz
                      Web site: www.sinai.org.nz

NORWAY

The only way Jews could enter Norway before the nineteenth century was with a 'Letter of Protection', as Danish control limited the amount of Jewish entry. The situation changed in 1851, when a Norwegian liberal poet, Henrik Wergeland, argued for the admission of Jews into the country, and the parliament eventually agreed. There were only some 650 Jews in the country after emancipation in 1891, mainly in Oslo and Trondheim. By 1920, the community numbered 1,457 and by the time of the Nazi invasion there were 1,800. Despite attempts by the Norwegian resistance to smuggle Jews to Sweden, 767 Jews were transported to Auschwitz, although 930 were able to reach Sweden. The Jewish survivors were joined after the war by Displaced Persons, especially invited by the Norwegian government.

The current situation forbids shechita, but there are no other restrictions on Jewish life. There is a synagogue in Oslo, and a kosher food shop. There is also a Jewish magazine. An old-age home was built in 1988. Trondheim, in the north of the country, has the northernmost synagogue in the world.

GMT +1 hour	**Total Population 4,445,000**
Country calling code (47)	**Jewish Population 1,500**
Emergency Telephone (Police – 112) (Fire – 110) (Ambulance – 113)	**(Electricity voltage – 220)**

Oslo

Oslo is the major centre of Norwegian Jewry, with 900 Jews living in the capital. The Resistance Museum is of interest as is the Wergeland Monument in the Var Frisler Cemetery. A monument consisting of 8 empty chairs in remembrance of the Norwegian Jews who were killed during the War is located near Akershus fortification.

COMMUNITY CENTRE
Bergstien 13 0131   2269-6570
                                Fax: 2246-6604
                          Email: kontor@dmt.oslo.no
                        Web site: www.dmt.oslo.no
Also has a kosher shop. Opening hours: Tuesday and Thursday 4.00pm to 6.00pm, Wednesday 2.00pm to 5.00pm, Friday 12 noon to 2.00pm (winter)/ 12 noon to 3.00pm (summer). Phone 2260-9166.

EMBASSY
Embassy of Israel
Parkveien 35, Oslo 0258   2101-9500
                                Fax: 2101-9530
                          Email: israel@online.no

RESTAURANTS
Kosher Food Centre
Corner Bergstien/Waldemar Thranes gate 0171
                                       2260-9166
Supervision: Rabbi Michael Melchior
There are no kosher hotels or restaurants in Oslo but there is the Kosher Food Centre. Open 4 pm to 6 pm Tuesday and Thursday, and 12.00 noon to 2 pm on Friday. Closed Shabbat.

SYNAGOGUES
Orthodox
Mosaiske Trossamfund (The Jewish Community)
Bergstien 13 0172   2269-6570
                                Fax: 2246-6604
                          Email: kontor@dmt.oslo.no
                        Web site: www.dmt.oslo.no
Postal address: postboks 2722 St. Hanshaugen, 0131 Oslo, Norway

TOURIST SITE
Ostre Gravlund Cemetary
There is a Jewish war memorial here.

Trondheim

SYNAGOGUES
Ark. Christiesgt. 1   7352-6568 or 4752-2030
                                Fax: 7353-1108
                          Email: palkom@online.no
The Worlds northernmost synagogue. The synagogue also has a museum. Postal address Postboks 2722 St. Hanshaugen, 0131 Oslo, Norway.

PANAMA

Some Jews, most of them pretending to be Christians, came to Panama during colonial times. Panama was an important crossroads for trade and, as a result, many Jews passed through the country on their journeys in the region.

In 1849, immigrant Sephardic Jews in Panama founded the Hebrew Benevolent Society, the first Jewish congregation in the Isthmus. They came from the pious congregation of the Netherlands Antilles (Curacao) to settle in Panama.

Jews from Saint-Thomas (Virgin Islands) and Curacao founded in 1876 the Kol Shearith Israel Synagogue in Panama City, and in 1890 the Kahal Hakadosh Yangacob in Colon.

By the end of the First World War, a number of Middle Eastern Jews had settled in the country and founded the Israelite Benevolent Society Shevet Ahim. During the years of the Second World War, immigrants from Europe arrived at Panama, establishing Beth-El, the only Ashkenazi community in the country. The majority of Jewish community is Sephardi (around 80 per cent).

There have been two Jewish presidents in Panama, the only country - apart from Israel of course where this has happened.

GMT -5 hours	Total Population 2,719,000
Country calling code (507)	Jewish Population 7,000
Emergency Telephone (Police – 104) (Fire – 103)	(Electricity voltage – 120)

Panama City

BAKERIES

Pita Pan
Plaza Bal Harbour, Paitilla   264-2786

BUTCHERS

Ricuras de Esther
Calle 48, Urb. Marbella   265-7190
Supervision: Shevet Ahim

Shalom Kosher
Plaza Bal Harbour, Paitilla   264-4411

Super Kosher
Calle San Sebastian, Paitilla   263-5254
                              Fax: 263-2067
          Email: mzakay@skosher.com
Supervision: Shevet Ahim Rabinate
Mailing Address POB 8242 Panama 7. Also Kosher supermarket, bakery and restaurant. Open from 8.30am to 8.30 pm Sunday to Thursday. Friday until 4.30pm.

CHOCOLATE SHOPS

Candies Bazaar
Via Argentina, 155 L-2   269-4857

Chocolatier
Calle 53,, Urb. Marbella   264-4712
                              Fax: 223-1663
          Email: chocolat@orbi.net

La Bonbonniere
Calle Juan XXIII, Paitilla   264-5704

COMMUNITY ORGANISATIONS

Consejo Central Comunitario Hebreo de Panama
P O Box 3309 4   263-8411
                    Fax: 264-7936

Jewish Centre: Centro Cultural Hebreo De beneficiencia
Calle 50 Final, PO Box 7166, 5 5   226-0455
                              Fax: 226-0869
(K) Restaurant open daily for lunch and supper. Closed Saturdays.

EMBASSY

Embassy of Israel
Edificio Grobman, Calle Manuel Maria Icaza, 5th Floor   264-8257

MIKVAOT

Beneficiencia Israelita Beth El
Calle 58E,, Urb. Obarrio   223-3383

Sociedad Israelita Shevet Ahim
Calle 44-27   225-5990
                    Fax: 227-1268

RESTAURANTS

Restaurante Don Jacobo
Centro Cultural Hebreo de Beneficiencia, Calle 50 Final   226-0455
                              Fax: 226-0869
Open daily for lunch and supper.

Dairy
Pita Pan
Plaza Bal Harbour, Paitilla   264-2786

Meat

Shalom Kosher
Plaza Bal Harbour, Paitilla 264-4411

Pizzeria

Pizzeria Italiana
Centro Cultural Hebreo de Beneficiencia, Calle 50
Final 226-0455
  Fax: 226-0869

SYNAGOGUES

Ashkenazi
Beneficiencia Israelita Beth El
Calle 58E, Urb. Obarrio 264-0058
Mikva on premises.

Orthodox Sephardi
Ahavat Sion
Calle Juan XXIII, Paitilla 265-1891
Daily Services. Mikva for women on premises.

Sociedad Israelita Shevet Ahim
Calle 44-27 225-5990
  Fax: 227-1268
Daily services.

Reform
Kol Shearith Israel
Av. Cuba 34-16 5 225-4100

PARAGUAY

Jewish settlement in this land-locked country came late for this area of South America. The few who came over from Western Europe at the end of the nineteenth century rapidly assimilated into the general population. The first synagogue was founded early in the twentieth century by Sephardism from Palestine, Turkey and Greece. Ashkenazis arrived in the 1920s and 1930s from eastern Europe and some 15,000 came to the country to escape Nazism, intending to move on into Argentina. Some of these settled in Paraguay.

Paraguay, in more recent times, has accepted Jews from Argentina who were fleeing from the military regime.

GMT -5 hours	**Total Population 5,085,000**
Country calling code (507)	**Jewish Population 900**
Emergency Telephone (Police – 00) (Fire – 00) (Ambulance – 00)	**(Electricity voltage – 220)**

Asuncion

COMMUNITY ORGANISATIONS

Consejo Representativo Israelita de Paraguay
General Diaz, 657, PO Box 756 (21) 441-744
  Fax: (21) 448-289

EMBASSY

Embassy of Israel
Calle Yegros No. 437 C/25 de Mayo, Edificio San Rafael, Piso 8, PO Box 1212
  (21) 495-097; 496-043; 496-044
  Fax: (21) 496-355

SYNAGOGUES

General Diaz, 657

PERU

The first Jews in Peru arrived with the first Europeans, as many Conversos were leaders in the Spanish army which invaded the country in 1532. After the Inquisition was set up in 1570, the Jews were persecuted, and many were burned alive. From 1870, groups of Jews came over from Europe, but tended to disappear into the general population. In 1880, a group of North African Jews settled in Iquitos and worked in the rubber industry. More Jewish immigration occurred after the First World War, and later Nazi refugees entered the country. By the end of the Second World War the Jewish population had reached 6,000, but this subsequently declined.

Almost all of the present Jewish population are Ashkenazi. Two Jewish newspapers are produced and most Jewish children go to the Colegio Leon Pinelo school, which is well known for its high standards. There is a cemetery at Iquitos built by the nineteenth-century community. The community is shrinking owing to intermarriage and assimilation.

GMT -5 hours	**Total Population 25,015,000**
Country calling code (51)	**Jewish Population 3,000**
Emergency Telephone (Police – 105) (Fire – 116) (Ambulance – 470 5000)	**(Electricity voltage – 220)**

Lima

COMMUNITY ORGANISATIONS
Asociacion Judia de Beneficencia y Culto de 1870
Libertad 375, Miraflores 18   (1) 445-1089
                                      Fax: (1) 445-1089
                    Email: AJBC1870@terra.com.pe

EMBASSY
Embassy of Israel
Natalio Sanchez 125 6to Piso, Santa Beatriz 1
                                      (1) 433-4431
                                      Fax: (1) 433-8925

GROCERIES
Minimarket Kasher
Av. Gral. Juan A. Pezet 1472, San Isidro, 27
                                      (1) 264-2187
                                      Fax: (1) 264-2187
                    Email: minimarket@terms.com.pe
Supervision: Rabbinate of the Union Israelita del Peru
Hours of opening: Monday-Thursday 9.00 am-6.00 pm, Friday 9.00 am-3.00 pm.

Pharmax
Av. Salaverry 3100, San Isadoro 27
Kosher items available.

Santa Isabel
Kosher items available.

HOTELS
Hotel Libertador
Los Eucaliptos 550, San Isidro, 27   (1) 421-6680
                                      Fax: (1) 442-3011
                    Web site: libertador.com.pe
A short walk away from the Union Israelita
Synagogue

KASHRUT INFORMATION
Chief Rabbi Abraham Benhamu
                                      (1) 442-4505
                                      Fax: (1) 442-8147
                    Email: absolben@terra.com.pe
Rabbi Benhamu is the Chief Rabbi of Peru.

KOSHER FOOD
Salon Majestic
Av. Bolivar 965, Pueblo Libre, 21   (1) 463-0031
                                      Fax: (1) 461-8912
Supervision: Chief Rabbi Abraham Benhamu
Catering for special groups and parties by prior arrangement only.

MEDIA
Newspapers
Menora
Jose Quinones 290, Miraflores 18   (1) 441-3461
                                      Fax: (1) 422-5796
                    Email: jta_bnaibrith@terra.com.pe
Daily.

Shofar
Jose Bielovucic 1350, Lince 14   (1) 440-0853
                                      Fax: (1) 440-0853
Bimonthly.

MIKVAOT
Beit Jabad
Av. Salaverry 3095, San Isidro, 27   (1) 264-6109
Ask for Sara or Sally.

Union Israelita
Ave. Gral. Juan A. Pezet 1472, San Isidro, 27
                                      (1) 264-2187
Sociedad Israelita Sefardi; Beit Jabad.

MUSEUM

Museum of the Inquisition
Junin 548, Lima 1   (1) 427-0365
Dungeon and torture chamber of the headquarters of
the Inquisition for all Spanish South America from
1570 to 1820. On the right side of the Plaza Bolivar.

SYNAGOGUES

Conservative
**Asociacion Judia de Beneficiencia y Culto de
1870**
Jose Galvez 282, Miraflores 18
                        (1) 445-1089 or445-5148
                        Fax: (1) 445-1089
            Email: fambrons@junin.itete.com.pe
Orthodox
Beit Jabad
Av. Salaverry 3095, San Isidro, 27   (1) 264-6060
                        Fax: (1) 264-5499
                Email: chabadperu@unired.net.pe
                Web site: www.lp.edu.pe/jabad
Synagogues (services daily), mikva, kosher food.

Sociedad de beneficencia Israelita Sefardi
Enrique Villar 581, Santa Beatriz, 1   (1) 471-7230
                        Fax: (1) 422-8147
            Email: absolben@terra.com.pe
Union Israelita del Peru
Av. Dos de Mayo 1815, San Isidro 27 27 (1) 421-3688
                        Fax: (1) 421-3684
        Web site: orbita.starmedia.com/~uiperu
Services are held at the Centro Sharon.

TOURIST SITE

Pilatos House
Ancash 390, Lima 1   (1) 427-5814
Seventeenth-century private mansion, now used by
the Constitutional Court. On the 2nd floor was the
synagogue of the Converso Jews.
In front of the San Francisco Monastery.

PHILIPPINES REPUBLIC

Conversos who came with the Spanish in the sixteenth century were the first Jewish presence in the region. In the late nineteenth century, western European Jews came to trade in the area, and after the Americans occupied the country in 1898, more Jews arrived from a variety of places, including the USA and the Middle East. The first synagogue was built in 1924. The Philippines accepted refugees from Nazism, but the Japanese occupied the islands during the war and the Jewish population was interned. After the war many of the community emigrated. However, a new synagogue opened in 1983, and services are also held in the US Air Force bases around the country.

GMT +8 hours
Country calling code (63)

Total Population 73,527,000
Jewish Population 100
(Electricity voltage – 220)

Manila

EMBASSY

Embassy of Israel
Trafalgar Plaza 23rd Floor, 105 H.V. dela Costa
Street, Salcedo Village, Makati City 1200
(2) 892-5329/30/31/34
                        Fax: (2) 894-1027
            Email: israelembphl@netasia.net
Postal address: POB 1697 MCPO, Makati Metro,
Manila 1299.

MIKVAOT

**Jewish Association of the Philippines (Beth
Yaacov Synagogue)**
110 H.V. de la Costa corner Tordesillas West, Salcedo
Village, Makati City, Metro Manila 1227 (2) 815-0265
                        Fax: (2) 840-2566
            Email: jap.manila@usa.net
By arrangement.

SYNAGOGUES

Orthodox, Sephardi
110 H.V. de la Costa corner Tordesillas West, Salcedo
Village, Makati City, Metro Manila 1227 (2) 815-0265
                        Fax: (2) 840-2566
            Email: jap.manila@usa.net
Services; Fri at 6.30pm, Sat at 9.30am.

POLAND

After just five years of German occupation in the Second World War, the thousand-year-old Jewish settlement in Poland, one of the largest Jewish communities in the world, had been almost totally eradicated. Jews came to Poland, in order to escape anti-semitism in Germany, in the early Middle Ages. They were initially welcomed by the rulers, and the Jews became greatly involved in the economy of the country.

Before the Second World War most Jews lived in the east and south of the country, under Russian and Austrian domination, respectively, until 1918. After 1918, Poland became an independent country once more, with over 3,000,000 Jews (300,000 in Warsaw.) The community continued to flourish before 1939, with Yiddish being the main language of the Jews. The community was destroyed in stages during the war, as Poland became the centre for the Nazi's destruction of European Jewry. After the war, the borders shifted again, and the 100,000 or so survivors mostly tried to emigrate. The few who remained endured several progroms even after the events of the Holocaust.

Today the community is comparatively small, and most of the members are elderly, but there is a functioning synagogue in Warsaw and many Jewish historical sites are scattered throughout the country. The Polish Tourist Board publishes information about the Jewish heritage in Poland.

GMT + I hour
Country calling code (48)
Emergency Telephone (Police – 997) (Fire – 998) (Ambulance – 999)

Total Population 38,650,000
Jewish Population 5,000
(Electricity voltage – 220)

Bialystok

Although there are only a few Jews living here now, before the Second World War it was more than 60 per cent Jewish, giving it the then highest concentration of Jews in any city in the world. In fact in 1912 the Jewish population of Bialystok almost equalled the total number of Jews in the then Palestine.

It is possible to visit the sites of a number of buildings of great Jewish interest.

CEMETERIES
Wschodnis Street

HISTORIC SITE
Synagogue
Branickego Street

Bielsko-Biala

ORGANISATIONS
Elzbieta Wajs
ul. Mickiewicza 26 43-300   (2) 22438

Cracow

BOOKSELLERS
Jarden
2 Szeroka Street, Miodowa 41   (12) 217166

COMMUNAL ORGANISATIONS
The Jewish Religion Congregation
2 Skawinska Street   (12) 429-5735
Mondays to Thursdays 9.00am to 2.00pm, Friday 9.00am to 12.

CULTURAL FESTIVAL
Jewish Culture Festival
                                 (12) 429-2573
Email: office@jewishfestival.art.pl
Web site: www.jewishfestival.pl
The twelth annual Jewish Culture Festival will be held between 28 June and 6 July 2003 in the restored Jewish quarter of Kasimierz.

HOTEL
Kosher
Hotel Eden
Ul. Ciemna 15, Cracow 31057   (12) 430-6565
Fax: (12) 430-6767
Email: eden@hoteleden.pl
Web site: www.hoteleden.pl

MUSEUMS
Museum of the History and Culture of the Cracow Jews
The Old Synagogue, 24 Szeroka Street (12) 422-0962
Fax: (12) 431-0545
Email: alteszul@poczta.onet.pl

ORGANISATIONS
Judaica Foundation
ul. Rabina Meiselsa 17   (12) 423-5595
Fax: (12) 423-5034
Email: uwrussek@cyf-kr.edu.pl

RESTAURANTS
Meat
Na Kazimierzu
ul Szeroka 39 31-053   (12) 229-644
                  Fax: (12) 219-909
Billed as the 'only kosher restaurant in Cracow and
the south of Poland'. Hours: 12 pm to 12 am
everyday. Traditional Shabbat courses are available on
Shabbat.

SYNAGOGUES
Isaac Synagogue
18 Kupa Street   (12) 430-55-77
             Fax: (12) 602-144-262
    Email: synagogaizaaka@eranet.pl
Contact Dominik Dybek.

Remuh
ul. Szeroka 40
Built in 1557 the synagogue is named after Rabbi
Moses Isserles the son of its founder, who is buried in
the adjacent cemetery.

For information; contact 603 860 373 (Mobile)

TOURIST SITE
Temple Synagogue
24 Miodowa Street
Built in 1862 it was used by the Germans during the
war as a stable during the War and is currently being
restored.

Gliwice

CONTACT INFORMATION
ul. Dolnych Walow 9 44100   (32) 314797

Katowice

CONTACT INFORMATION
ul. Mlynska 13 40098   (32) 537742

Legnica

CONTACT INFORMATION
ul. Chojnowska 37 59220   (76) 22730

Lodz

COMMUNITY ORGANISATIONS
Jewish Congregation
Zachodnia 78   (42) 335156

RELIGIOUS ORGANISATIONS
Jewish Chabad
         (42) 331221, 336825

Lublin

Once a major Jewish town in eastern Europe,
Lublin today has fewer than a hundred Jews. Pre-
war Lublin was a centre for Torah study, and a
large yeshivah was built only a few years before
the Second World War, and is now used as a
dental college. Majdanek Concentration Camp
lies within the city's boundary, clearly visible from
a major road leading south east. There is a
particularly moving memorial in the camp,
consisting of the ashes from the camp's
crematoria.

CONTACT INFORMATION
ul. Lubartowska 10 20080   (81) 22353

Rzeszow

SYNAGOGUES
ul Bonicza, edge of Pl. Ofiara Getta

Szczecin

CONTACT INFORMATION
ul. Niemcewicza 2 71553   (91) 221674

Warsaw

Before the war, Warsaw had approximately
300,000 Jews. Now there are only a couple of
thousand, mostly elderly. There are many sites
which can be visited, such as surving fragments of
the Ghetto walls and 'A memorial Route to the
struggle and Martyrdom of the Jews 1940-1943'
known as 'Memory Lane'. The old Jewish
cemetery, untouched by the Nazis, is very
imposing, and is still in use. The Warsaw Ghetto
fighters are included in the inscription to Tomb of
the Unknown Soldier in the centre of the city. In
2002 the Nozyk synagogue celebrated its
centenary.

EMBASSY
Embassy of Israel
ul. I Kryzwickiego 24

MIKVAOT
Nozyk Synagogue
6 Twarda Street   (22) 652-2805
            Fax: (22) 652-2805
    Email: varshe@jewish.org.pl
Contact: Sharona Kanofsky tel: 652 21 50.

MONUMENT
Monument to the Ghetto Heroes
Zamenhofa
Erected in 1948 this monument symbolises the heroic
Ghetto defiance of the 1943 uprising.

ORGANISATIONS

The Jewish Historical Institute
3/5 Tlomackie Street 00090   (22) 827-9221
Fax: (22) 827-8372
Email: zihinb@ikp.atm.com.pl
This establishment has a remarkable collection of
Judaica. It includes a library of documents on the
manuscripts stolen by the Germans from all over
Europe.

RESTAURANTS

Menora
Plac Grzybowski 2   (22) 203754

Nove Miasto Ecological Restaurant
Rynek Nowego Miasta 13/15   (22) 831-4379
Fax: (22) 831-4379
Web site: www.novemiasto.waw.pl

Panorama
Al Witsoa 31   (22) 642-0666

Salad Bar
ul. Tamka 37   (22) 635-8463

SYNAGOGUES

**Nozyk Synagogue, Jewish Community of
Warsaw, Union of Jewish Communities in
Poland.**
6 Twarda Street 00-950   (22) 6204324
Fax: (22) 6201037
Email: varshe@jewish.org.pl
The synagogue was renovated in 1977-83 and is well
worth a visit. It is the only pre-War synagogue still
standing in Warsaw. Visitors welcomed. Friday night
dinner available. Kosher store in the synagogue.

THEATRE

Jewish National Theatre
Plac Grzybowski 12/16
Performances are given in Yiddish.

TOURS OF JEWISH INTEREST

Shalom Travel Service
Twarda Street 6 00-105   (22) 652-2802
Fax: (22) 652-2803
Email: shalom@jewish.org.pl

Wrocklaw

MUSEUM

Historical Museum
Slezna Street 37   (71) 678236

PORTUGAL

Portuguese Jewry had a parallel history to Spanish Jewry until the twelfth century, when the country emerged from Spain's shadow, and Jews worked with the Portuguese kings in developing the country. However, they were heavily taxed and had to live in special areas, although they were free to practise their religion as they pleased. As a result, the community flourished.

Persecution began during the period of the Black Death, and the Church was a key instigator of the riots which broke out against the Jews. After the Inquisition in neighbouring Spain, many Jews fled to Portugal, but were expelled in 1496. Many Jews converted in order to remain in the country and helped with the economy. These became the Portuguese 'Conversos' and some of their descendants are converting back to Judaism today.

Over the last century and a half, Jews have begun to re-enter the country, and many others used it as an escape route to America during the last war. Most of the community are Sephardi, and there is a Sephardi synagogue in Lisbon. There is also a central Jewish organisation which is a unifying force for Jews in the country.

GMT +0 hours	**Total Population 9,921,000**
Country calling code (351)	**Jewish Population 800**
Emergency Telephone (Police – 115) (Fire – 115) (Ambulance – 115)	**(Electricity voltage – 220)**

Algarve

COMMUNITY ORGANISATIONS

Jewish Community of Algarve
Rua Judice Biker 11-5°., Portimão 8500-701
(282) 416-710
Fax: (282) 416-515

MUSEUM

Faro Jewish Cemetery and Museum
(282) 416-710
Fax: (282) 416-515
Only remaining vestige of the first post-Inquisition Jewish presence in Algarve. Open weekday mornings from 9:30 am to 12:30 pm. Situated opposite entrance to Faro Hospital. Enquiries to Ralf Pinto, Jewish Community of Algarve.

Belmonte

COMMUNITY ORGANISATIONS

Jewish Community of Belmonte
Apt. 18, Bairro de Santa Maina, 6250 Belmonte
(275) 912465
Fax: (275) 912465

Lisbon

Jews settled in Lisbon in the 12th century. Many Jews were prominent in court circles. In 1496 when the Jews were expelled Lisbon was chosen as a point of embarkation.

In the Alfama district, London's oldest, is the Rua de Judiara and at 8 Beco dos Barretas is the site of what is believed to be an ancient synagogue.

The first official synagogue dates from 1813. The Shaare Tikvah synagogue opened in 1904, was constructed inside a garden because legislation at that time did not permit non-Catholic places of worship to be directly on a public highway. It was classified as a "Building of Public Interest" in 1997.

COMMUNITY ORGANISATIONS

Communal Offices
Rua do Monte Olivete 16-r/c 1200-280 (21) 393-1130
Fax: (21) 393-1139
Email: secretaria@cilisboa.org
Web site: www.cilisboa.org

Jewish Club & Centre
Rua Rosa Araujo 10
(21) 572041

EMBASSY

Embassy of Israel
Rua Antonio Enes 16-4 1020-025
(21) 355-3640
Fax: (21) 355-3658
Email: israemb@mail.telepac.pt

JEWISH TOURS
Jewish Heritage Tours
Avenida 5 de Outubro, 321 1649-015   (21) 7919-954
Fax: (21) 7919-959
Email: fit.lisboa@space.pt
Web site: www.jewishheritage.pt
Tours to explore Jewish ancestral roots in Portugal
and to meet the descendants of the Conversos, the
'secret' Jews.

KOSHER FOOD
Mrs R. Assor
Rua Rodrigo da Fonseca 38.1'D   (21) 386-0396
Fax: (21) 386-6336
Email: iassor@mail.telepac.pt
Kosher meals and delicatessen are obtainable if prior
notice is given. For kosher meats, contact the
communal offices.

SYNAGOGUES
Ashkenazi
1 Avenida Elias Garcia 100

Shaare Tikvah
Rua Alexandre Herculano 59 5246   (21) 385-8604
Fax: (21) 388-4304
Email: cilisboa@mail.telepac.pt
Tours for visitors. 10.00 am until 5 pm except Friday
(until 1pm.) For groups please book in advance.

Oporto

SYNAGOGUES
Rua Guerra Junqueiro 340

OVERSEAS REGION

AZORES

SAO MIGUEL

Ponta Delgada

SYNAGOGUES
The only synagogue in the Azores. It was built in 1836
and has been out of use since the 1950's. It is
expected to reopen during the early part of 2003.

PUERTO RICO

The Jewish community in Puerto Rico is just over 100 years old, with the first Jews arriving from Cuba in
1898 after the beginning of American rule. During the Second World War, many Jewish American
servicemen went to the island, along with refugees from Nazism. The Jewish Community Centre dates
from the early war years. After the war the community grew with an influx of Cuban and American Jews.
San Juan, the capital, has the largest Jewish population, and there are two synagogues. There is also a
Hebrew school, held in the Community Centre. The first Chief Justice of Puerto Rico was Jewish.

GMT -4 hours
Country calling code (1 787)
Emergency Telephone (Police – 343 2020) (Fire – 343 2330)

Total Population 3,771,000
Jewish Population 2,500
(Electricity voltage – 120)

San Juan-Santurce

SYNAGOGUES
Shaare Zedeck
903 Ponce de Leon Av., Santurce 00907
(787) 724-4157

Orthodox
Chabad of Puerto Rico
8 Rosa Street, Isla Verde 00979   (787) 724-1680
Fax: (787) 268-7679
Email: chabadpr1@aol.com
Kosher takeout available, for menu please call 787-
727-2709.

Reform
Temple Beth Shalom
San Jorge Av. & Loiza St., Santurce 00907

ROMANIA

Romanian Jewry began at the time the Romans gave the country its name and language. In the fifteenth century, community life had begun to be organised, and settlement had spread to the town of Iasi and some Moldavian towns. Jews were welcomed from Poland and other east European countries, despite the opposition of the Church. Over the years, the community grew in size with further immigration, but emigration became the dominant factor after 1878, when the Treaty of Berlin, which demanded equal rights for Jews, was not implemented in Romania. Following Romania's acquisition of the large area of Transylvania from Hungary after 1918, the Jewish population increased once more. The Jews were finally emancipated, but harsh discriminatory decrees were passed in 1937, and Romania's alliance with Nazi Germany during the war led to 385,000 of the 800,000 Romanian Jews being killed in the Holocaust.

It is ironic that Romanian Jewry was able to function relatively normally under the harsh Ceausescu regime. He was the only Warsaw Pact leader not to sever relations with Israel in 1967, and he allowed Jewish practices to continue, even permitting the then Chief Rabbi, Dr Moses Rosen, to have a seat in the parliament. This freedom also tolerated emigration to Israel, which was seen by Ceausescu as being advantageous to Romania. Post-1989, the community still has its central body, the Federation of Jewish Communities, and there are kosher cafeterias in several cities. The community is ageing, but many synagogues are still functioning, and there are also Jewish newspapers and a Yiddish theatre. The Choral Synagogue in Bucharest is of particular interest to visitors.

GMT +2 hours	Total Population 22,520,000
Country calling code (40)	Jewish Population 12,000
Emergency Telephone (Police – 995) (Fire – 981) (Ambulance – 961)	(Electricity voltage – 220)

Arad

COMMUNITY ORGANISATIONS
Community Offices
10 Tribunal Dobra Street   (257) 281310

RESTAURANTS
Ritual
22, 7 Episcopei Street   (257) 280731

SYNAGOGUES

Muzeul Judetean
Piata George Enescu 1   (257) 280114

Neologa
10 Tribunal Dobra Street
Orthodox
12 Cozia Street

Bacau

COMMUNITY ORGANISATIONS
Community Offices
11 Alexandru cel Bun Street   (234) 134714

RESTAURANTS
11 Alexandru cel Bun Street

SYNAGOGUES
Avram A. Rosen Synagogue
31 V. Alecsandri Street

Cerealistilor
29 Stefan cel Mare Street

Botosani

COMMUNITY ORGANISATIONS
Community Offices
220 Calea Nationala   (231) 0315-14659

MIKVAOT
67 7 Aprilie Street

RESTAURANTS
69 7 Aprilie Street   (231) 0315-15917

SYNAGOGUES
Great
1a Marchian Street

Mare
18 Muzicantilor Street

Yiddish
10 Gh. Dimitrov Street

Brasov

COMMUNITY ORGANISATIONS
Community Offices
27 Poarta Schei Street   (268) 143532

RESTAURANTS
27 Poarta Schei Street   (268) 144440

SYNAGOGUES
27 Poarta Schei Street

TRAVEL AGENTS
International Tourism and Trade
Jozef Bem Str. 2, Sf. Gheorghe 4000   (268) 316 375
         Fax: (268) 351 551
         Email: it&t@honoris.ro
PO Box : 1/152

Bucharest

COMMUNITY ORGANISATIONS
Federation of Jewish Communities of Romania
Str. Sf. Vineri 9-11, Sector 3   (21) 313-2538
         Fax: (21) 312-0869
         Email: asivan@pcnet.ro
Kosher supervision on 11 restaurants in the main
Jewish communities of Romania.

Federation of Romanian Jewish Communities
24 Popa Rusu Street   (21) 211-8080
The Federation publishes a bi-monthly, 'Revista
Realitatea Evreiasca'.

DOCUMENTATION CENTRE
Romanian Jewish History Research Centre
12 Juliu Barasch Street   (21) 323-7246

EMBASSY
Embassy of Israel
1 Dimitrie Cantemir Bd.   (21) 613-2634/5/6

MIKVAOT
5 Negustori Street

MUSEUM
Museum of the Jewish Community in Romania
3 Mamoulari Street   (21) 615-0837
Hours: Wednesday and Sunday, 9 am to 1 pm.

RELIGIOUS ORGANISATIONS
Chief Rabbi of Romania
Strada Sf. Vineri 9   (21) 613-2538
         Fax: (21) 312-0869

RESTAURANTS
Jewish Community
18 Popa Soare Street   (21) 322-4067
         Fax: (21) 322-4067
         Email: fcerdas@com.pcnet.ro
This restaurant is operated by the Jewish Community.

SYNAGOGUES
Choral Temple
Strada Sf. Vineri 9, Sector 3   (21) 313-1782
         Fax: (21) 312-0869
         Email: ccmailb@dial.kappa.ro

Credinta
48 Vasile Toneanu Street

Ieshua Tova
9 Nikos Beloiannis Street   (21) 659-5675
Near the Lido and Ambassador hotels.

Sephardi
Great Synagogue
9-11 Vasile Adamache Street   (21) 615-0846

THEATRE
Jewish State Theatre
15 Iuliu Barash Str., Sector 3 74212   (21) 323-4530
         Fax: (21) 323-2746
         Email: tes@dnt.ro
      Web site: www.dnt.ro/users/tes

Cluj Napoca

COMMUNITY ORGANISATIONS
Community Offices
25 Tipografiei Street   (264) 11667

MIKVAOT
16 David Fransisc Street

RESTAURANTS
5-7 Paris Street   (264) 11026

SYNAGOGUES
Beth Hamidrash Ohel Moshe
16 David Fransisc Street

Sas Hevra
13 Croitorilor Street

Templul Deportatilor
21 Horea Street

Constanta

COMMUNITY ORGANISATIONS
Jewish Community Office and Cultural Club
3 Sarmisagetuza Street   (241) 611598

SYNAGOGUES

Great Temple
2 C. A. Rosetti Street

Small
3 Sarmisagetuza Street

Dorohoi

COMMUNITY ORGANISATIONS
Community Office
95 Spiru Haret Street   (31) 611797

RESTAURANTS
14-18 Dumitru Furtuna Street

SYNAGOGUES
Great
4 Piata Unirii Street

Galati

COMMUNITY ORGANISATIONS
Community Office
9 Dornei Street   (236) 413662

RESTAURANTS
9 Dornei Street   (236) 413662

SYNAGOGUES
Meseriasilor
11 Dornei Street

Iasi (Jassy)

COMMUNITY ORGANISATIONS
Community Office
15 Elena Doamna Street   (232) 114414

MIKVAOT
15 Elena Doamna Street

RESTAURANTS
15 Elena Doamna Street   (232) 1117883

SYNAGOGUES
Great
7 Sinagogilor Street

Schor
5 Sf. Constantin Street

Oradea

COMMUNITY ORGANISATIONS
Community Office
4 Mihai Viteazu Street   (259) 134843

MIKVAOT
5 Mihai Viteazu Street

RESTAURANTS
5 Mihai Viteazu Street   (259) 131383

SYNAGOGUES

Great
4 Mihai Viteazu Street

Neolog
22 Independentei Street

Piatra Neamt

COMMUNITY ORGANISATIONS
Community Office
7 Petru Rares Street   (33) 623815

SYNAGOGUES
Leipziger
12 Meteorului Street

Old Baal Shem Tov
7 Meteorului Street
Old historical monument.

Radauti

COMMUNITY ORGANISATIONS
Community Office
11 Aleea Primaverii, Block 14, Apt. 1   (30) 461333

SYNAGOGUES
Great
2, 1 Mai Street

Vijnitzer
49 Libertatii Street

Satu Mare

Satu Mare is the Romanian name for the town of Szatmar, where the famous Hassidic sect originated. It is in the north west of Romania, very near the border with Hungary. Before World War One, the town itself used to be in Hungary.

COMMUNITY ORGANISATIONS
Community Office
4 Decebal Street   (61) 743783

SYNAGOGUES
Great
4 Decebal Street

Sighet

COMMUNITY ORGANISATIONS
Community Office
8 Basarabia Street   (62) 511652

SYNAGOGUES
Great
8 Basarabia Street

Suceava

COMMUNITY ORGANISATIONS
Community Office
8 Armeneasca Street   (30) 213084

SYNAGOGUES
Gah Chavre
4 Dimitrie Onciu Street

Timisoara

COMMUNITY ORGANISATIONS
Community Office
5 Gh. Lazar Street   (56) 132813

MIKVAOT
55 Resita Street

RESTAURANTS
10 Marasesti Street   (56) 136924

SYNAGOGUES
Cetate
6 Marasesti Street

Fabric
2 Splaiul Coloniei

Iosefin
55 Resita Street

Tirgu Mures

COMMUNITY ORGANISATIONS
Community Office
10 Brailei Street   (65) 115001

SYNAGOGUES
21 Aurel Filimon Street

Tushnad

HOTELS
Kosher
Olt Hotel
c/o Interom Tours   972-3924-6425
                                  Fax: 972-3579-1720

Vatra Dornei

COMMUNITY ORGANISATIONS
Community Office
54 M Eminescu Street   (30) 371957

SYNAGOGUES
Vijnitzer
14 Luceafarul Street

RUSSIAN FEDERATION

In early Russian history, Jews were not allowed to settle, and the few who did were later expelled by various Czars. After 1772, however, Russia acquired a large area of Poland, in which lived a significant number of Jews. There were still restrictions against the Jews, but eventually they were allowed to settle in the 'Pale of Settlement', an area in the west of the Russian Empire. Between 1881 and 1914, 2,000,000 Jews emigrated from the Empire, escaping from anti-semitism.

Jews were only allowed into Russia itself in the mid-nineteenth century, and by 1890 there were 35,000 Jews in Moscow. Most were expelled the following year. The community grew after the Second World War, drawing Jewish immigration from Belarus and Ukraine to cities such as Moscow and Leningrad. Birobidzhan was a failed experiment to give the Jews their own 'Autonomous District', and those who moved there (in the far east, near China) soon moved away. Under communism, both religious practices and emigration to Israel, were restricted but since 1991 there has been a revival in Jewish learning. There are synagogues functioning in many cities, and there are now 100 Jewish schools. The major threat is still from anti-semitic right-wing groups, who are unfortunately increasing their activity.

GMT + 2 to +12 hours	**Total Population 146,100,000**
Country calling code (7)	**Jewish Population 300,000**
Emergency Telephone (Police – 02) (Fire – 01) (Ambulance – 03)	**(Electricity voltage – 220)**

Astrakhan

SYNAGOGUES
30 Babushkin Street

Birobidjan

Birobidjan, the size of Belgium was created in 1934 as a Jewish homeland in the wilds of Siberia. It was not a success and was effectively terminated in the 1940s. There has, however, now been a resurgence of interest in what was known as the Jewish Autonomous District.

SYNAGOGUES
9 Chapaev Street, Khabarovsk Krai

Bryansk

SYNAGOGUES
Narodov Vostoka Street

82 Lermontov Street

Lubavitch
Synagogue of Bryansk
27a Uritskovo Street 241000   (832) 445-515

Derbent

SYNAGOGUES
94 Tagi-Zade Street

Lubavitch
Jewish Community of Derbent
23 Kandelaky Street 368600   (8724) 021-731

Ekaterinburg

SYNAGOGUES
18/2 Kirov Street

14 Kuibyshev Street

Irkutsk

SYNAGOGUES
17 Karl Liebknecht Street

Kazan

The capital of Tatarstan, an autonomous Russian republic, has 10,000 Jews an Ort school and its own Jewish newspaper.

SYNAGOGUES
Lubavitch
Synagogue of Kazan
15 Profsouznaya Street 420111   (8432) 329-743

Kostrama

SYNAGOGUES
Lubavitch
Synagogue of Kostrama
16a Sennoi Peroulok 156026   (942) 514-388

Krasnoyarsk

SYNAGOGUES
Lubavitch
Synagogue of Krasnoyarsk
65 Surikova Street 660049   (3912) 223-615
Fax: (3912) 440-137
Email: jckras@hotmail.com

Kursk

SYNAGOGUES
3 Bolshevitskaya Street

Makhachkala

SYNAGOGUES
111 Yermoshkin Street

Moscow

Around 200,000 Jews now live in Moscow, and since the collapse of the USSR in 1991, the community has experienced a revival. The Choral Synagogue on Arkhipova Street, which was built in 1891 and was used during the Soviet regime, is again the focus of Jewish religious life. The Lubavitch movement has its own centre, and there has been an upsurge of interest in Jewish education.

CONTACT INFORMATION
Rabbi Pinchas Goldschmidt
Chief Rabbi of Moscow   (95) 923-4788; 924-2424

EMBASSY
Embassy of Israel
Bolshaya Ordinka 56   (95) 230-6777
Fax: (95) 238-1346

KOSHER FOOD
Spassoglinishevsky per., 10

LIBRARY
Central Library
A Jewish literature reading hall opened in 2002. The hall holds the State Library's Jewish literature collection.

MUSEUM
Poliakoff Synagogue
Bolshaya Brennaya 6

RESTAURANTS
Kosher Food
Na Gorke
Spassoglinishevsky per., 10   (95) 923-5012
The restaurant on Nikitskaya
Nikitskaya str., 47   (95) 291-4045

Meat
King David Club
Bolshoi Spasoglinishchevsky per.
(Arkhipova St) 6, door code 77   (95) 925-4601
Fax: (95) 924-4243
Email: ail@ail.msk.ru
Supervision: Rabbi Pinchas Goldschmidt, Chief Rabbi
of Moscow
This kosher food centre serves as a glatt kosher
restaurant and a mini hotel. Catering services are
available as are lunchboxes.

Na Monmartre
Vetoshny per., 9   (95) 745-5230
Fax: (95) 745-5239
Supervision: Rabbi Berl Lazar
On the 5th floor of a modern shopping centre.

SYNAGOGUES
2nd Korenyovsky Lane, Moscow Oblast

Moscow Choral Synagogue
Bolshoi Spasoglinishchevsky per.
(Arkhipova St) 10   (95) 924-2424
Lubavitch
Chabad Lubavitch
4 Novousushevsky Peroulok 103055   (95) 218-0001
Fax: (95) 219-9707
Email: lazar@glasnet.ru

Chabad Lubavitch Synagogue
6 Balshaya Bronya Street 103104   (95) 202-4530
Fax: (95) 291-6483

Darkei Shalom Synagogue
I Novovladikinsky Peroulok 103055   (95) 903-0782
Fax: (95) 903-2218

Nalchik

SYNAGOGUES
73 Rabochaya Street, cnr. Osetinskaya

Nizhny Novgorod

SYNAGOGUES
Lubavitch
Nizhny Novgorod Synagogue
5a Gruzinskaya Street 603000   (8312) 336-345
Fax: (8312) 303-759

Novosibirsk

SYNAGOGUES
23 Luchezarnaya Street
Lubavitch
Synagogue of Novosibirsk
14 Koministisheskaya   (3832) 210-698

Penza

SYNAGOGUES
15 Krasnaya Street

Perm

SYNAGOGUES
Pushkin Street
Kuibyshev Street

Rostov-na-Donu

SYNAGOGUES
Lubavitch
Synagogue of Rostov-na-Dou
18 Gazetny Peroulok 344007   (8632) 624-759
Fax: (8632) 624-119

Sachkhere

SYNAGOGUES
145 Sovetskaya Street
105 Tsereteli Street

Samara

SYNAGOGUES
3 Chapaev Street
Lubavitch
**Jewish Community Center of Samara
Synagogue**
84B Chapaevskaya St 443099   (8462) 334-064
Fax: (8462) 320-242
Email: samara@fjc.ru
The community center has a mikva, and a kosher
lemihadrin kitchen.

Saratov

SYNAGOGUES
Posadskov Street
2 Kirpichnaya Street
Lubavitch
Synagogue of Saratov
208 Posadskovo Street 410005   (8452) 249-592

St Petersburg

With 100,000 Jews, St Petersburg is witnessing a
similar Jewish revival to Moscow. There are
opportunities to pray, learn and eat kosher; this
was not the case (in general) before 1991 in the
USSR. Americans and Israelis are the main
motivators behind the revival, but St Petersburg
Jewry is also eager to learn about religion, now
that there is the freedom to do so.

COMMUNITY ORGANISATIONS

St Petersburg Jewish Association
Ryleev St, 29-31, a/b 103   (812) 272-4113

MIKVAOT

2 Lermontovsky Prospekt   (812) 114-4428
Fax: (812) 113-6209
Email: synagog@peterlink.ru

RESTAURANTS

Dining Room at Shamir School
Ligovskiy Prospekt 161-8   (812) 116-1003
Meat
Shalom
8,K. Tomchaka Street   (812) 327-5475

SYNAGOGUES

The Grand Choral Synagogue of St. Petersburg
2 Lermontovsky Prospekt 190121   (812) 114-4428
Fax: (812) 113-6209
Email: pewzner@synagogue.spb.su
This is the second street past the Mariinsky Opera &
Ballet Theatre.

TOURS OF JEWISH INTEREST

Zekher Avoteinu
Jewish Tourist and Genealogical Agency, Pr.
Netakkustiv 6-57 195027   (812) 945-0874
Fax: (812) 175-1229
Email: zekhera@hotmail.com
Web site: www.zekheravoteinu.get-2.com
The centre carries out a tour programme combining
Jewish and general sightseeing in Russia and the
former Pale of Jewish Settlement. It also does
genealogical research for the families whose
ancestors were from the Russian Empire.
Representative in USA: 6801 19th Avenue, 4C,
Brooklyn, NY 11204, USA. Tel: 1 718 236 6037.

Tshelyabinsk

SYNAGOGUES

Lubavitch
Synagogue of Tshelyabinsk
PO Box 16187 454091   (3512) 333-618
Fax: (3512) 332-468
Email: chabadural@mail.ru

Tula

SYNAGOGUES

15 Veresaevskaya Street

Vladikavkaz

SYNAGOGUES

Revolutsiya Street

Volgograd

SYNAGOGUES

Chabad of Volgograd
Novorosiyskaya 43 400087   (8442) 378-308
Email: volgograd@fjc.ru

Yekatrinburg

SYNAGOGUES

Lubavitch
Yekatrinburg Synagogue
118/93 Shekmana Street 620144   (3432) 236-440
Fax: (3432) 293-054

SINGAPORE

As Singapore developed into an important south-east Asian trading centre in the mid-nineteenth century, some Jewish traders from India and Iraq set up a community there in 1841. A synagogue was built in 1878, and another in 1904. By the time of the Japanese occupation in the Second World War, the community had grown to 5,000, and included some eastern European Jews. The Japanese imprisoned the community and took their property. After the war, emigration to Australia and the USA reduced numbers, but in recent years Israelis who worked in the country and other Jews have moved in. Ninety per cent of the community are Sephardi.

David Marshall, who had been a POW in Japan, returned to Singapore and in 1955 became Chief Minister. One of the two synagogues is used regularly, and there is a mikvahh and a newsletter. The Jewish community today is small and mainly composed of professionals.

	Total Population 3,737,000
Country calling code (65)	**Jewish Population 300**
Emergency Telephone (Police – 999) (Fire – 999) (Ambulance – 999)	**(Electricity voltage – 220/240)**

COMMUNITY ORGANISATIONS

Jewish Welfare Board
Robinson Road, PO Box 474

CONTACT INFORMATION

Rabbi Abergel
737-9112
Email: mordehai@singnet.com.sg
Contact for more detailed information on the community and availability of kosher products.

EMBASSY

Embassy of Israel
58 Dalvey Road S-1025   235-0966
Fax: 733-7008

SYNAGOGUES

Orthodox
Chesed-El
2 Oxley Rise S-0923   732-8832
Services, Monday only, Shacharit and Mincha/Maariv.

Maghain Aboth Synagogue
24/26 Waterloo Street 187950   337-2189
Fax: 336-2127
Email: jewishwb@singnet.com.sg
Daily and Shabbat services are held, except for Monday when services are held at Chesed-El Synagogue, 2 Oxley Rise, at 7:30 am. Because Singapore has equatorial times, Mincha/Maariv commences at 6:45 pm throughout the year. Shacharit: weekdays, 7:30 am, Friday night Shabbat meal served after evening service. Shabbat 09.00 am. Every Shabbat lunch is served for the community. Breakfast is currently served every morning after services. Mikvah is available for use. For details please contact 737 9112 Rabbi Mordechai Abergel. There are kosher meat, cheeses, wine and other grocery items on sale at the synagogue.

SLOVAKIA

Slovakia has passed through the control of various countries over the centuries, finally gaining independence after the peaceful splitting of Czechoslovakia in 1992. Before 1918 the region was part of Hungary and many in southern Slovakia, near the Hungarian border, still speak Hungarian.

In 1939, the Jewish population in the Slovak area of Czechoslovakia numbered 150,000. The Hungarians occupied the south of the country, and assisted the Germans in deporting Jews to Auschwitz and other camps. Many survivors emigrated after the war, but some remained, and are now rediscovering their Jewish heritage. Since independence, B'nai B'rith and Maccabi have been established, but anti-semitism has re-emerged. There are kosher restaurants in Bratislava and Kosice, and Jewish education is available once more.

GMT +1 hour	Total Population 5,383,000
Country calling code (421)	Jewish Population 5,000
Emergency Telephone (Police – 158) (Fire – 150) (Ambulance – 155)	(Electricity voltage – 220)

Bratislava

Known in German as Pressburg, Bratislava was a key centre of Judaism when Slovakia was under Hungarian rule before the First World War. Bratislava was especially famous for the number of Jewish scholars living there, including the Chatam Sofer. The preserved underground tomb of the Chatam Sofer and other rabbis is now a place of pilgramage.

BED AND BREAKFAST
Chez David
Zamocka 13, . 81101   (2) 544-13 824; 544-16 943
Fax: (2) 544-12 642
Email: recepcia@chezdavid.sk
Web site: www.chezdavid.sk
Kashrut supervision of Rabbi Baruch Myers.

COMMUNITY ORGANISATIONS
Central Union of Jewish Religious Communities in the Slovak Republic
Kozia ul. 21 81447   (2) 5441-2167; 5441-8357
Fax: (2) 5441-1106
Email: uzzno@netax.sk

MIKVAOT
Zamocka 13 81101   (2) 544-17829
Fax: (2) 544-17814
Email: chabad@mail.eurotel.sk

MUSEUMS
The Museum of Jewish Culture
Zidovska Street 81101   (2) 59349142/3/4
Fax: (2) 59349145
Contact person: Prof. PhDr. Pavol Mest'an Dr. Sc.

Underground Mausoleum
Contains the graves of eighteen famous rabbis, including the Chatam Sofer. The key is available from the community offices.

RESTAURANTS
Meat
Chez David
Zamocka 13 81101   (2) 544-13824, 544-16943
Fax: (2) 544-12642
Email: recepcia@chezdavid.sk
Web site: www.chezdavid.sk

SYNAGOGUES
Heydukova 11-13
Services held Monday, Thursday and Saturday.

Galanta

MIKVAOT
Partizanska 907

SYNAGOGUES
Partizanska 907
Daily services held.

Kosice

RESTAURANTS
Meat
Community Centre
Zvonarska Ul 5, Kaschau 04001   (55) 622-1047

SYNAGOGUES
Puskinova Ul 3, Kaschau

Beth Hamidrash
Zvonarska Ul 5, Kaschau
Daily services held.

Piestany

CEMETERIES
Old Cemetery
Janosikova Ul 606

SYNAGOGUES
Hviezdoslavova 59
Shabbat and festival services held.

SYNAGOGUES
Kapitulska Ul 7

Trnava

MONUMENT
Monument to Deportees
Halenarska Ul 32
In the courtyard of the former synagogue.

SLOVENIA

Maribor was the centre for medieval Jewish life in what is now Slovenia. Expulsion followed after the Austrian occupation in the late Middle Ages, but in 1867 the Jews in the Austrian empire were emancipated and some returned to Solvenia. The community was never large. During the Second World War the members of the small Jewish community either escaped to Italy, fought with the Yugoslav partisans, or were deported.

There is a Jewish Community of Slovenia, connected to the Croatian community. There is one synagogue in Maribor, that is classed as an historic monument and dates from the Middle Ages. There are also some sites from medieval times such as the cemeteries in Ljubljana (the capital) and Murska Sobota.

GMT + I hour
Country calling code (386)
Emergency Telephone (Police – 93) (Fire – 92) (Ambulance – 94)

Total Population 1,987,000
Jewish Population Under 100
(Electricity voltage – 220)

Ljubljana

COMMUNITY ORGANISATIONS
Jewish Community of Slovenia
Trzaska 2 1000   (61) 2521-836
Fax: (61) 2521-836
Email: jss@siol.net
Web site: www.jewishcommunity.si

SYNAGOGUES

(61) 315-884

SOUTH AFRICA

Although some believe that Jews were present in the country at around the time of the first European settlement in the area in the seventeenth century, the community only really began in the nineteenth century, when religious freedom was granted. In 1836 the explorer Nathaniel Isaacs published 'Travels and Adventures on Eastern Africa', an important contemporary account of Zulu life and customs.

The year 1841 saw the first Hebrew Congregation in Cape Town, and the discovery of diamonds in the Transvaal later in the century prompted a wave of Jewish immigration.

The main immigration of Jews into South Africa however occurred at the end of the nineteenth century, when many thousands left Eastern Europe, the majority from Lithuania (40,000 had arrived by 1910). Although the country did not officially accept refugees from the Nazis, about 8,000 Jews managed to enter the country after their escape from Europe.

Today the community is affluent and has good relations with the government. There is a South African Board of Deputies, and many international Jewish associations are present in the country. There are kosher hotels and restaurants, and Jewish museums. Kosher wine is produced at the Zaandwijk Winery.

GMT +2 hours	Total Population 43,336,000
Country calling code (27)	Jewish Population 80,000
Emergency Telephone (Police – 1011) (Fire – 1022) (Ambulance – 10222)	(Electricity voltage – 220/250)

EASTERN CAPE

East London

SYNAGOGUES
Orthodox
Shar Hashomayim
Lukin Road   (43) 722-2071

Reform
Belgravia Crescent

Port Elizabeth

MUSEUMS
Jewish Pioneers' Memorial Museum
Raleigh Streetr cnr Edward Street   (41) 373-5197
                                 Fax: (41) 374-3612
Open between 10 am and noon every Sunday. The museum has a ramp for disabled for access via wheelchairs. It is also a National Monument. For further information visitors may phone Dr Sam Abrahams (041) 583-3671.

SYNAGOGUES
Orthodox
Port Elizabeth Hebrew Congregation
Abraham Levy Centre, Barris Walk, Glendinningvale
6001   (41) 373-1332
                                 Fax: (41) 374-3612
                       Email: peheb@xsinet.co.za

Progressive
Temple Israel
Upper Dickens Street   (41) 373-6642

FREE STATE

Bloemfontein

RELIGIOUS ORGANISATIONS
United Hebrew Institutions
Community Centre, 1 Dickie Clark Street, PO Box
1152   (51) 436-2207
                                 Fax: (51) 436-6447
Mornings.

SYNAGOGUES
1 Dickie Clark Street, Dan Pienaar, PO Box 1152
9300   (51) 436-2207
                                 Fax: (51) 436-6447
Mikvah also available. Contact telephone number above.

GAUTENG

Brakpan

RELIGIOUS ORGANISATIONS
Brakpan Synagogue
cnr. Victoria Avenue and Caendish   (53) 832-5652
For further information phone Mr Waner, Tel: (011) 740-0903.

Johannesburg

The largest city in South Africa has the largest Jewish community in the country. About 70% of the country's Jews live there (a community of some 55,000) and the headquarters of many of South African Jewry's institutions are housed there. There are more than fifty synagogues in the city.

BAKERIES

Brooklyn Bagel
Shop 7, Lyndhurst Discount Centre, cnr
Modderfontein & Pretoria Rds, Lyndhurst
(11) 882-2474
Fax: (11) 882-8565
Supervision: Johannesburg Beth Din

Friends Bakery
53 Ridge Road, Glenhazel (11) 440-5094
Fax: (11) 440-5096
Supervision: Johannesburg Beth Din

Shirley's
114 William Road, Norwood (11) 728-0974
Fax: (11) 728-2807
Supervision: Johannesburg Beth Din

Shula's
173 Oxford Road, Rosebank (11) 880-6989
Fax: (11) 880-6605
Supervision: Johannesburg Beth Din

BED AND BREAKFAST

Kosher Bed and Breakfast
124 Third Avenue, Fairmount (11) 485-5006
Fax: (11) 485-5518
Supervision: Johannesburg Beth Din

BOOKSELLERS

Chabad House Books
Fairmount Shopping Centre, George Street,
Fairmount (11) 485-1957

Kollei Bookshop
Pick 'N' Pay Shopping Centre, 54 Sixth Ave., Gardens
(11) 728-1822
Fax: (11) 728-1813

BUTCHERS

Bolbrand Poultry Shoppe
74-76 George Avenue, Sandringham 2192
(11) 640-4080
Supervision: Johannesburg Beth Din

Gallo Manor Kosher Butchery
Morning Glen Shopping Centre, cnr. Braides & Kelvin
Sts, Gallo Manor (11) 802-3539
Fax: (11) 802-6546
Supervision: Johannesburg Beth Din

Gardens Kosher
cnr. Grant & 6th Avenue, Norwood 2052
(11) 483-3357
Fax: (11) 728-1562
Supervision: Johannesburg Beth Din

Maxi Discount Kosher Butcher
74 George Avenue, Sandringham 2192
(11) 485-1485; 485-1486
Fax: (11) 485-2991
Supervision: Johannesburg Beth Din

Nussbaums
434 Louis Botha Avenue, cnr. Main St., Rouxville
(11) 485-2303
Fax: (11) 640-4663
Supervision: Johannesburg Beth Din

Rishon Balfour
Checker Balfour Park, cnr. Louis Botha & Athol Sts,
Highlands North (11) 786-9626
Fax: (11) 885-1996
Supervision: Johannesburg Beth Din

Saveways Spar
Fairmount Shopping Centre, cnr. Sandler and
Livingstone St, Fairmount (11) 640-6592
Fax: (11) 640-3057
Supervision: Johannesburg Beth Din

Trevors
Bramley Gardens Shopping Centre (11) 885-3663
Fax: (11) 887-9502
Supervision: Johannesburg Beth Din

DELICATESSEN & BAKERIES

Feigel's Kosher Delicatessan
Shop 3, Queens Place, Kingswood Road,
Glenhazel 2192 (11) 887-1364
Supervision: Johannesburg Beth Din

Bramley Gardens Shopping Centre, Shop 1,
280 Corlett Drive (11) 887-9505/6
Fax: (11) 887-9507
Supervision: Johannesburg Beth Din
Hours: Friday, 7:30 am to 4:30 pm; Sunday, 8 am to 1
pm; Monday to Thursday, 10 am to 5 pm.

Kosher King
74 George Avenue, Sandringham (11) 640-6234
Supervision: Johannesburg Beth Din
Hours: Monday to Thursday, 8:30 am to 5 pm; Friday,
8 am to 3 pm; Sunday, 9 am to 1 pm.

Pick 'N Pay
Cnr. Grant Avenue & 6th Street, Norwood
(11) 483-3357
Fax: (11) 728-1562
Supervision: Johannesburg Beth Din

Saveways Spar Supermarket
Fairmount Shopping Centre, cnr. Livingstone St &
Sandler Avenue, Fairmount 2192 (11) 640-3056
Fax: (11) 640-3057
Supervision: Johannesburg Beth Din
Hours: Monday to Thursday, 8 am to 6 pm; Sunday
and public holidays, 8 am to 1 pm.

Shoshana's Bakery
Stan Tech House, cnr. Cross Road and Queens
Square, Glenhazel (11) 885-1039
Supervision: Johannesburg Beth Din

The Pie Works
74 George Avenue, Sea Point, Sandringham 2192
(11) 485-2447
Supervision: Johannesburg Beth Din
Hours: weekdays, 8 am to 5 pm; Friday, to 4 pm;
Sunday, to 2 pm.

Shop 35 Greenhill Road, Emmarentia 2195
(11) 486-1502
Fax: (11) 486-1527
Email: jossel@iafrica.com
Supervision: Johannesburg Beth Din
Hours: Weekdays, 8.00am to 5.30pm; Friday to
4.00pm; Sunday 9.00am to 2.00pm.

LIBRARIES
Kollel Library
5 Water Lane, Orchards 2198
(11) 728-1308
Fax: (11) 728-8597

MEDIA
Newspapers
The S.A. Jewish Report
Suite 175, Postnet X10039, Randburg 2125
(11) 886-0162
Fax: (11) 886-4202
Email: carro@global.co.za

Periodicals
Jewish Affairs
2 Elray Street, Raedene
(11) 645-2500
Fax: (11) 645-2559
Email: sajbod@iafrica.com
Quarterly journal of the South African Jewish Board
of Deputies.

Jewish Heritage
PO Box 3 7179, Birnham Park 2015
(11) 880-1830

Jewish Tradition
PO Box 46559, Orange Grove 2119
(11) 485-4865
Fax: (11) 640-7528
Email: isaacrez@yebo.co.za
Publication of the Union of Orthodox Synagogues of
South Africa.

South African Jewish Observer
PO Box 29189, Sandringham 2131
(11) 440-2206
Fax: (11) 786-8155
Email: mizrachi@netactive.co.za
A publication of the Mizrachi Organisation of South
Africa.

MIKVAOT
Adase Yashurun Mikvah
34 Fortesque Road, Yeoville
(11) 648-6300
By appointment only. Phone Mrs Levy. (011) 648-
6751

Glenhazel Mikvah (Be'er Rachel)
65 Nicholson Avenue, Glankay
(11) 485-1555
Email: nisaacson@africakoshersafaris.com

Sandton Mikvah
211 Rivonia Road, Morningside
(11) 883-4210

RELIGIOUS ORGANISATIONS
**The Southern African Union for Progressive
Judaism**
357 Louis Botha Avenue, Highlands North
(11) 640-6614

Union of Orthodox Synagogues of South Africa
58 Oaklands Road, Orchards 2192   (11) 485-4865
Fax: (11) 640-7528
Email: jhb@uos.co.za
The office of the chief Rabbi as well as the Beth Din
are located at the same address and phone number.

RESTAURANTS
Dairy
Brazilian Coffee Shop
Shop 174, Balfour Park Shopping Centre,
cnr. Athol Road, Highlands North   (11) 440-8822
Fax: (11) 466-1876
Supervision: Johannesburg Beth Din

Michelo's
3 Dunottar Street, (off Louis Botha Ave)
(11) 485-4626
Fax: (11) 615-3360
Supervision: Johannesburg Beth Din

Shula's
173 Oxford Road, Rosebank 2196   (11) 880-6969
Fax: (11) 880-6605
Supervision: Johannesburg Beth Din
Pareve and milk restaurant. Hours: Sunday to
Thursday, 7 am to 11 pm; Friday, to 4 pm; Motzei
Shabbat to 1 am.

Meat
D.J's Take Away
Balfour Park Shopping Centre, Shop No. 232,
Balfour Park 2090   (11) 440-1792
Supervision: Johannesburg Beth Din

Marc Chagall's
Upper Level, Balfour Park Shopping Centre, cnr.
Athol Road, Highlands North   (11) 786-0593
Fax: (11) 786-0594
Supervision: Johannesburg Beth Din

Nandos
27 Aintree Avenue Savoy   (11) 885-1496
Fax: (11) 885-1492
Supervision: Johannesburg Beth Din

On The Square
Shop No. 7, Shell Court, cnr. Craddock Avenue &
Baker Street, Rosebank 2196
(11) 880-4153; 447-4891
Supervision: Johannesburg Beth Din
Hours: Sunday to Thursday, 10 am to 3 pm; 6 pm to
10 pm; Motzei Shabbat, 1 hour after Shabbat to 12
am.

The Junction Grill
4 Dunnottar Street, Sydenham   (11) 485-2585
Fax: (11) 485-3707
Supervision: Johannesburg Beth Din

SYNAGOGUES

There are more than fifty synagogues in Johannesburg. Please contact the appropriate Religious Organisation.

TOURS INFORMATION

Africa Kosher Safaris
P O Box 51380, Raedene 2124   (11) 485-3465
        Email: yisaacson@africakoshersafaris.com

TOURS OF JEWISH INTEREST

Celafrica Tours
PO Box 357, Highlands North, 2037   (11) 887-5262
        Fax: (11) 885-3097
        Email: celeste@celafrica.com
        Web site: www.celafrica.com
The company specialises in kosher tours to southern Africa, for people needing kosher food and Shabbat arrangements.

Krugersdorp

SYNAGOGUES

Krugersdorp Synagogue
1 Cilliers Street, Monument   (11) 954-1367
        Fax: (11) 953-4905

Pretoria

EMBASSY

Embassy of Israel
3rd Floor, Dashing Centre, 339 Hilda Street,
Hatfield   (12) 342-2693

KASHRUT INFORMATION

Pretoria Council of BOD
        (12) 344-2372
        Fax: (12) 344-2059

KOSHER FOOD

Pick 'N Pay
Brooklyn Square Mall, Middle Street,
Muckleeneuk   (12) 346-8680
Kosher prepacked food under the Johannesburg Beth Din

Spar
Groenkloof Plaza, George Stonar Drive,
Groenkloof   (12) 346-5555
Kosher prepacked food under the Johannesburg Beth Din

MUSEUMS

Sammy Marks Museum
Swartkoppies Hall, Old Brokhorstspruit 0001
        (12) 802-1150
        Fax: (12) 802-1292
        Email: smarks@nfi.co.za
Hours of opening: Tuesdays - Sundays, 10.00-16.00

RESTAURANTS

JAFFA Old Age Home
42 Mackie Street, Baileys Muckleneuk 0181
(12) 346-2006
Fax: (12) 346-2008
Email: jaffa@smartnet.co.za
Hotel as well. Prior booking necessary. Kosher catering, resident mashgiach. Kosher meals, both meat and dairy, available on request.

SYNAGOGUES

Orthodox
Adath Israel Centre
246 Schroder Stresst, Groenkloof   (12) 460-7991
Fax: (12) 480-5911
Email: phc@netactive.co.za

Progressive
Temple Menorah
315 Bronkhorst Street, New Muckleneuk,
PO Box 1497   (12) 467-296

Springs

SYNAGOGUES

Springs Synagogue
40 Charterland Avenue, Selcourt   (11) 818-2572

KWAZULU-NATAL

Durban

BED AND BREAKFAST

Beit Ya'akov
75 Windmill Road, PO Box 47314,
Greyville 4023   (31) 202-7275
Fax: (31) 202-7302
Email: koby@global.co.za
Run by family who are shomer mitzvot.

BUTCHERS

Pick 'N Pay
Musgrave Centre, Berea 4001   (31) 201-4208
Bakery as well.

COMMUNITY ORGANISATIONS

Council of KwaZulu-Natal Jewry
44 Old Fort Road 4001   (31) 337-2581
Fax: (31) 337-9600
Email: cknj@letni.co.za
Mailing address: PO Box 10797, Marine Parade, 4056

Durban Jewish Club
44 Old Fort Road 4001   (31) 337-2581
Fax: (31) 337-9600
Email: cknj@letni.co.za
Mailing address: PO Box 10797, Marine Parade 4056.

RESTAURANTS

Café Shalom
Durban Hebrew Congregation, cnr. Essenwood & Silverton Roads   (31) 202-1205
Dairy
Great Synagogue cnr. Silverton & Essenwood Roads,
PO Box 50044, Musgrave Road 4062   (31) 202-1205
Fax: (31) 209-2925
Email: studycentre1@freemail.absa.co.za

SYNAGOGUES

Orthodox
Durban United Hebrew Congregation The Great Synagogue
Cnr. Essenwood & Silverton Roads, PO Box 50044,
Musgrave Road 4062   (31) 201-5177
Fax: (31) 202-8925
Email: shul@duhc.org.za

The Vryheid Memorial Shul
Cnr. Old Fort & Platfair Rds   (31) 201-5177
Fax: (31) 202-8925

Progressive
Durban Progressive Jewish Congregation
369 Ridge Road   (31) 208-6105
Fax: (31) 209-2429

Umhlanga

CONTACT INFORMATION

Chabad of Umhlanga
POBox 474 4320   (31) 561-2487
Fax: (31) 561-5845
Web site: www.chabadonline.com/kwazulu-natal
Open all hours. Regular minyanim especially Shabbat and Yomim Tovim. Ladies' mikvah twenty minutes away. Kosher hospitality. For kosher tours in Southern Africa contact Shlomo on the above numbers.

NORTHERN CAPE

Kimberley

SYNAGOGUES

Orthodox
Griqualand West Hebrew Congregation
20 Synagogue Street 8301   (53) 832-5652
Fax: (53) 832-3632
Email: ahorwitz@lantic.net

WESTERN CAPE

Cape Town

Cape Town has approximately 17,000 Jews. A visit to the Campus comprising the Gardens Synagogue (160 years old), the South African Jewish Museum, the Albow Centre – housing the Holocaust Museum and the Gitlin Library – and the Cafe Riteve, is a must for Jewish visitors.

BAKERIES
Checkers
Gallaria Centre, Regent Road, Sea Point (21) 439-6159
Supervision: Cape Beth Din

BUTCHERS
Claremont Kosher Butchers and Deli
150 Main Road, Corner Oliver Sea Point,
Claremont 7800   (21) 439-6909
Fax: (21) 439-6920
Email: adlercaz@hixnet.co.za
Supervision: Cape Beth Din
Can deliver to your door.

Pick 'N Pay
Constantia Village   (21) 794-5960
Supervision: Cape Beth Din

Main Road, Claremont   (21) 683-2724
Supervision: Cape Beth Din
Prepacked with Beth Din sign only.

Adelphi Centre, Main Road, Sea Point (21) 434-8987
Supervision: Cape Beth Din

COMMUNITY ORGANISATIONS
Cape Town Jewish Community Centre
87 Hatfield Street, Gardens 8001   (21) 464-6700
Fax: (21) 461-5805
Email: sajbd2@ctjc.co.za

DELICATESSEN
Goldies Nosh Bar
64 Regent Road, Sea Point 8001   (21) 434-1116
Fax: (21) 438-3851
Supervision: Cape Beth Din
Sit-down deli and take-away. Meat and pareve.
Hours: Sunday to Thursday, 7 am to 8 pm; Friday, to 5 pm.

GROCERIES
Pick 'N Pay
Centre Point Milnerton   (21) 552-2057
Supervision: Cape Beth Din
Prepacked with Beth Din sign only.

Spar
Regent Road, Sea Point   (21) 439-0913
Supervision: Cape Beth Din
Prepacked with Beth Din sign only.

HOTELS
Kosher
The Belmont Shareblock
3 Holmfirth Road, Sea Point 8005   (21) 439-1155
Fax: (21) 434-9451
Supervision: Cape Beth Din
Breakfast and Lunch only.

LIBRARIES
Jacob Gitlin Library
Albow Centre, 88 Hatfield Street 8001
(21) 462-5088
Fax: (21) 465-8671
Email: gitlib@netactive.co.za

MIKVAOT
Arthur's Road Synagogue, Sea Point
(21) 434-3148; 439-8787

MUSEUMS
Cape Town Holocaust Centre
88 Hatfield Street, Gardens 8001   (21) 462-5553
Fax: (21) 462-5554
Email: ctholocaust@mweb.co.za
Web site: www.museums.org.za/ctholocaust
Sunday to Thursday: 10.00 am - 5.00 pm. Friday: 10.00 am - 1.00 pm.

South African Jewish Museum
88 Hatfield Street, Gardens 8001   (21) 465-1546
Fax: (21) 465-0284
Email: info@sajewishmuseum.co.za
Web site: www.sajewishmuseum.co.za
Open Sunday - Thursday 10.00am - 5.00pm; Fridays 10.00am - 2.00pm. Museum shop and café.

RESTAURANTS
Dairy
Café Riteve
88 Hatfield Street, Gardens   (21) 465-1594
Fax: (21) 465-5980
Supervision: Cape Beth Din

Meat
Avron's Place Restaurant & Grill
307 Main Road, Sea Point 8005   (21) 439-7610
Fax: (21) 439-7599
Email: avronsplace@netactive.co.za
Supervision: Cape Beth Din
Delivery within 5km radius.

Goldies Bakery & Deli
66 Regent Road, Sea Point   (21) 439-0628
Supervision: Cape Beth Din

Kaplan Student Canteen
University of Cape Town   (21) 650-2688
Fax: (21) 650-3064
Supervision: Cape Beth Din
Lunches, take-away and orders. Meat and pareve.
Open Monday to Friday. Closed December/January for varsity holidays and during summer vacation.

Sylvlah's Restaurant
11 Regent Road, Sea Point   (21) 433-2303

SYNAGOGUES
Orthodox
Arthur's Road
31 Arthur's Road, Sea Point   (21) 434-8680
                                      Fax: (21) 434-8880

Camps Bay
Chilworth Road, Camps Bay   (21) 438-8082
                                      Fax: (21) 438-8082
                      Email: cbhc@netactive.co.za

Cape Town Hebrew Congregation
84 Hatfield Street, Gardens   (21) 465-1405
                                      Fax: (21) 461-7659
                        Email: cthc@isoft.co.za
                 Web site: www.gardensshul.org

Claremont Hebrew Congregation
Grove Avenue (at Morris Rd), P.O. Box 23035,
Claremont 7735   (21) 671-9006
                                      Fax: (21) 683-3011
                      Email: clarshul@iafrica.com

Constantia Hebrew Congregation
Old Kendal Road, Constantia 7806   (21) 713-1818
                                      Fax: (21) 715-3110
                  Email: mkornblum@herzlia.com
                  Web site: www.shul.org.za

Green & Sea Point Hebrew Congregation
10 Marais Road, Sea Point   (21) 439-7543
                                      Fax: (21) 434-3760
                      Email: gspheb@mweb.co.za

Milnerton
29 Fitzpatrick Road, Cambridge Estate 7441
                                      (21) 551-0442
                                      Fax: (21) 552-4285

Muizenberg
Camp Road, Muizenberg   (21) 788-1488
Sephardi Hebrew Congregation
Weizmann Hall, 85 Regent Road, Sea Point
                                      (21) 439-1962
                                      Fax: (21) 439-9620
                        Email: rabbi@yebo.co.za

Wynberg Hebrew Congregation
1 Mortimer Road, Wynberg 7806   (21) 797-5029
                                      Fax: (21) 797-5029

Reform
Temple Israel
Upper Portswood Road, Green Point   (21) 434-9721
                                      Fax: (21) 434-2400
                      Email: templect@iafrica.com

Oudtshoorn

SYNAGOGUES
United Hebrew Institutions
291 Buitenkant Street   (44) 272-3068
                                      Fax: (44) 272-3068
There is a Jewish section in the C.P. Nel Museum.

Paarl

SYNAGOGUES
New Breda Street   (21) 872-4087
For further information phone Mr. Kaufman (083)
325-6603.

SOUTH KOREA

Before the Korean War (1950-53) there were a handful of Jews in the country who had escaped from Russia. During the Korean War a larger community came to South Korea as US army soldiers. There is still an American detachment based in the country, and among them are some Jews. They have been joined by individuals coming to the country to work. Services are held at the US army base in Seoul, and the US army have their own Jewish chaplain in the country.

GMT +9 hours
Country calling code (82)
Emergency Telephone (Police – 112) (Fire – 119) (Ambulance – 119)

Total Population 46,858,000
Jewish Population 150
(Electricity voltage – 110/220)

Seoul

SYNAGOGUES
South Post Chapel
Building 3702, Youngsan Military Reservation
                                      (2) 793-3728
                                      Fax: (2) 796-3805
Civilians welcome to participate in all Jewish activities, inc. kosher le-Pesach sedarim, meals and services.

SPAIN

Spain has an ancient connection with the Jews, and the term 'Sephardi' originates from the Hebrew word for Spain. Beginning in Roman times, the Jews have suffered the usual cycle of acceptance and persecution, with a 'golden age' under the Islamic Moorish occupation, which began in 711. Great Jewish figures arose from the Spanish community, such as Ibn Ezra and the Ramban. However, the situation changed when the Christians gained the upper hand, and blood libels began. In 1492, almost 100 years after a particularly violent period of persecution, the Jews were expelled from Spain. Many thousands were baptised but practised Judaism in secret (the Conversos), and many were caught and burnt at the stake.

Jewish life began again in the nineteenth century. The Inquisition ended in 1834 and by 1868 Spain had promulgated religious tolerance. Synagogues could be built after 1909, and Spain accepted many thousands of Jewish refugees before and during the Second World War. Angel Sanz-Briz alone helped to save thousands of Hungarian Jews by issuing 'letters of protection' and entry visas.

There has been a recent immigration from North Africa, and the community today has a central body and synagogues in several towns (including Torremolinos and Malaga). Rambam's synagogue in Cordoba can be visited, and there are several other old synagogues throughout the country.

GMT +1 hour	**Total Population 39,270,000**
Country calling code (34)	**Jewish Population 14,000**
Emergency Telephone (Police – 092 or 091) (Fire – 080) (Ambulance – 092)	**(Electricity voltage – 220)**

Alicante

COMMUNITY ORGANISATIONS
Communidad Israelita
Apdo. 189, Playa de San Juan 03540   (96) 515-1572

SYNAGOGUES
Vila Carlota, 15 Urb Montivoli, Villajoyosa

Barcelona

The ancient community of the city lived in the area of the Calle (from the Hebrew Kahall) and the cemetery was in Montjuic (Mountain of the Jews). Most of the original tombstones are now in the Provincial Archaeological Museum.

BUTCHERS
Carniceria|
Porvenir 24   (93) 200-3375
Supervision: Barcelona Rabanut

COMMUNITY ORGANISATIONS
Communidad Israelita de Barcelona
Porvenir 24 08071   (93) 200 6148
                          Fax: (93) 200 6148

Community Centre
Porvenir 24 08071   (93) 200-6148 or 8513
Kosher meals are available on request

MIKVAOT
Porvenir 24 08071   (93) 200-6148, 8513

RESTAURANTS
Vegetarian
Comme Bio
Via Laietana 28 08003   (93) 319-8986
Gran Via 603 08007   (93) 301-0376

Self Naturista
Carrer de Santa Anna 11-17 08002   (93) 318 23 88
                          Fax: (93) 412 54 13

SYNAGOGUES
Orthodox
Communidad Israelita de Barcelona
Porvenir 24 08021   (93) 200-8513
The first synagogue to be built in Spain since the Inquisition.

Progressive
Comunitat Jueva ATID de Catalunya
Castanyer 27, bajos, izquierda 08022   (93) 417-3704
                          Fax: (93) 417-3704
                          Email: atid@arquired.es
                    Web site: www.atid.freeservers.com

TOURS OF JEWISH INTEREST
Urban Cultours Project
                          (93) 417-1191
                          Fax: (93) 417-1191
                    Web site: www.urbancultours.com
Walk of the Call (Jewish Quarter) by a Jewish American architect. Vsits to other places of Jewish interest in Catalonia can also be arranged.

TRAVEL AGENCIES
Jewish Travel Agency
Viajes Moravia, Consejo de Ciento 380 (93) 246-0300

Benidorm

KASHRUT INFORMATION
(96) 522-9360

Burgos

During the 13th century Burgos was the largest Jewish community in North Castile. The Juderia was in the area of the Calle Fernan Gonzalez.
There are no other specific locations of interest to travellers.

Cordoba

This is an ancient synagogue (declared as a monument). Nearby, a statue of Maimonides has been erected in the Plazuela de Maimonides. The entrance to the ancient Juderia is near the Almodovar Gate.

TOURIST SITE
Calle de los Judios 20
This is an ancient synagogue built in 1315 and one of only three pre-expulsion ones remaining. It was declared a national monument in 1985, Nearby, a statue of Maimonides has been erected in the Plaza de Tiberiades.(named to perpetuate the connection between his birthplace and where he is buried).

El Escorial

The library of the San Lorenzo Monastery contains a magnificent collection of medieval Hebrew Bibles and illuminated manuscripts. On the walls of the Patio of Kings, in the Palace of Philip II, are sculpted effigies of the six Kings of Judah.

LIBRARIES
San Lorenzo Monastry
The library of San Lorenzo Monastery contains a magnificent collection of medieval Hebrew Bibles and illuminated manuscripts. On the walls of the Patio of Kings, in the Palace of Philip II, are sculpted effigies of six Kings of Judah.

Estella

The Jewish community here was one of the most important in the kingdom of Navarre. The Santa Maria de Jus Castillo Church was once a synagogue.
There are no specific locations of interest to travellers.

Gerona

The Jewish quarter of Gerona, known as the Call (a name believed to originate from the Hebrew word kehilla or community), is located in the heart of the old town. Its main street exists today, and is known as Carrer de la Forca. The Jewish Quarter of Gerona is one of the best-preserved to be found in Europe today where the complex of rooms, courtyards and staircases are a slice of medieval Jewish life.

During the Middle Ages, the Jewish community of Gerona achieved considerable importance. It was there that the most important Cabbala school in Western Europe was developed, largely under the guidance of Rabbi Mossé ben Nahman, or Ramban, perhaps its best known representative.

In the municipal archives there is an important collection of fragments of Hebrew manuscripts dating from the thirteenth and fourteenth centuries. The Archaeological Museum contains more than twenty medieval gravestones with Hebrew inscriptions, found in the old Jewish cemetery.

ORGANISATIONS
Patronat Municipal Call De Girona
8, Forca Street 17004   (972) 21 67 61
Fax: (972) 21 67 61
Email: callgirona@grn.es
Web site: www.ajuntament.gi/el-call
Comprises: Museum of the History of the Jews and Nahmanides Institute for Jewish Studies.

Granada

Originally the Jewish community was one of the most important in Spain.

It is believed that the "lion fountain", in the courtyard of the Alhambra, was a gift from the Jews of the city and is based upon a fountain in King Solomon's palace.
There are no other specific locations of interest to travellers.

Hervas

This village in the Gredos Mountains, 150 miles west of Madrid, has a well-preserved Juderia, which has been declared a national monument. Its main street has been renamed Calle de la Amistad Judeo Cristiana.

Madrid

About 3,500 Jews live in Madrid. A new synagogue was completed in 1968, and there is a community centre providing kosher food. The Prado has a number of paintings of Jewish interest.

BUTCHERS

Elias Shoshanna
35 calle Viriato   (91) 446-7847
Supervision: Harav ben Dahan, rabbi of the community

COMMUNITY ORGANISATIONS

Community Centre
Calle Balmes 3   (91) 591-3131
                              Fax: (91) 594-1517
        Email: cjmsecretaria@terra.es

EMBASSY

Embassy of Israel
Calle Velasquez 150, 7th Floor 28002   (91) 411-1357

GIFT SHOP

Sefarad Handicrafts
Gran Via 54   (91) 548-2577, 547-6142
                              Fax: (91) 548-2577
        Email: sefaradgalleries@bravored.com
Jewish religious articles.

MIKVAOT

Calle Balmes 3   (91) 591-3131

MUSEUM

Museo Arquelogico
Calle de Serrano 13
Permanent exhibition of casts of Hebrew inscriptions from medieval buildings.

RESTAURANTS

Meat
Community Centre
Calles Balmes 3   (91) 591-3131
                              Fax: (91) 594-1517
        Email: cjmsecretaria@terra.es
For groups only.

Vegetarian
El Estragon
Pel de la Paja 10, Austrias 28005   (91) 365-8982

SYNAGOGUES

Calle Balmes 3   (91) 591-3131
                              Fax: (91) 594-1517
        Email: cjmsecretaria@terra.es
The capital's first synagogue since the expulsion of Jews in 1492 was opened in December 1968. The building also houses the Community Centre, as well as mikvah, library, classrooms, an assembly hall and the office of the community. Nearest underground station: Metro Iglesias.

Congregacion Bet El
Castello 77 28006   (91) 519-3227
                              Fax: (91) 662-3730
        Email: betel_es@hotmail.com
Web site: www.members.xoom.com/betelspain/

TOURS

Alex Benarroch
                                    (91) 558-529
    Email: www.puertademadrid.com/rentacellphone
Jewish sightseeing tours to Toledo, Kosher meals delivered to your hotel in Madrid.

Malaga

BUTCHERS

Carmiceria Kosher
Calle Somera 14 29001   (95) 260-4201

MIKVAOT
Calle Somera 12 29001

SYNAGOGUES
Alameda Principal, 47,20.B 29001   (95) 260-4094

TOURIST SITE
There is a statue of the eleventh-century Hebrew poet, Shlomo Ibn-Gabirol, a native of Malaga, in the gardens outside the Alcazaba Castle, in the heart of the city.

Marbella

COMMUNITY ORGANISATIONS
Community Centre
Paseo Maritima

GROCERIES
Hipercor
El Corte Ingles, Section No 16, Puerto Banus
Mrs Jacqueline Ohayon
    (95) 282-6649
Kosher Poultry and wine.

MEDIA
Periodicals
Edificio Marbella 2000
Paseo Maritima

Focus
PO Box 145 29600
Community Journal

SYNAGOGUES
Conservative
Beth El Synagogue
21 calle Jazmines, Urbanizacion El Real,
Km 184   (95) 277-9387
    Email: cimarbella@yahoo.es
About two miles from the town centre to the east. Services: Friday eve. (winter) 7.00pm, (summer) 8.30pm; Shabbat morning & all festivals 10am. Kosher meals on request (also take out). Mikveh on premises.

Salamanca

RESTAURANTS
Vegetarian
El Trigal
Calle Libreros 20

Saragossa

This city was once a very important Jewish centre. A mikvahh has been discovered in the basement of a modern building at 126-132 Calle del Coso
There are no other specific locations of interest to travellers.

Segovia

The Alcazar contains the 16-century 'Tower of the Jews'. Calle de la Juderia Vieja and Calle de la Juderia Nueva are the sites of the medieval Jewish quarters, where the former synagogue now houses the Corpus Christi Convent.

Seville

The first mention of a Jewish community in Seville was in the 4th century. In 1391 riots broke out and many synagogues were converted into churches. The most important of these and well worth visiting is the Church of Santa Maria la Blanca.

The Archives of the Indies holds an extensive collection of documents relating to both north and south America and include the account books of Luis de Santagel, a Converso, who financed Columbus and assisted Jews to leave the country in 1492. It is being currently restored and will reopen in 2003.

MUSEUMS
Casa de la Memoria
Ximenes de Encisco 28   (95) 560-670
    Email: memorias@teleline.es
A small museum which contains items from local pre-expulsion Jewish homes.

SYNAGOGUES
Comunidad Israelita de Sevilla
Calle Bustos Tavera 8 41003   (95) 427-5517

Tarragona

Tarragona Cathedral, Calle de Escribanias Viejas.
This has in its cloister a seventh-century stone inscribed in Latin and Hebrew. Some very old coins are preserved in the Provincial Archaeological Museum. The gate to the medieval Juderia still stands at the entrance to Calle de Talavera.
There are no other specific locations of interest to travellers.

Toledo

Though it now has no established community, Toledo is the historical centre of Spanish Judaism. Well worth a visit are two ancient former synagogues. One is the El Transito (in Calle de Samuel Levi), founded by Samuel Levi, the treasurer of King Pedro I, in the 14th century. It has been turned by the Spanish Government into a museum of Sephardi culture. The other, now the Church of Santa Maria la Blanca, is the oldest Jewish monument in Toledo, having been built in the 13th century. It stands in a quiet garden in what was once the heart of the Juderia, not far from the edge of the Tagus River. Also of interest is the house of Samuel Levi, in which El Greco, the famous painter, lived. The house is now a museum of his works.

Plaza de la Juderia, half-way between El Transito and Santa Maria la Blanca, was part of the cityís two ancient Jewish quarters, where many houses and streets are still much as they were 500 years ago.

JUDAICA
Casa de Jacob
Calle del Angel 15 45002   (925) 216-454
Fax: (925) 216-454
Email: libreria-judaica@casadejacob.com
Web site: www.casadejacob.com

Torremolinos

BAKERIES
Panaderia
c/Casablanca, 27 (Local 9B) 29620   (95) 374-975
Email: www.perso.wanadoo.es/k
Close to the synagogue

RESTAURANTS
Meat
Little Jerusalem
Calle San-Miguel 52, 2nd Floor 29620   (95) 205-3155

SYNAGOGUES
Beth Minzi
Calle Skal 13 29620   (95) 383952
Fax: (95) 237-0444
Calle Skal La Roca is a small street at the seaward end of the San Miguel pedestrian precinct, almost opposite the Police Station. Sephardi and Ashkenazi services are held on Sabbath morning at 9.30am and Friday evening services are held at 6.30pm in winter and 8.30pm in summer.

Tudela

The remains of the Juderia are near the cathedral. There is a memorial stone to the great Jewish traveller, Benjamin of Tudela author of Book of Travels (1172/3).
There are no other specific locations of interest to travellers.

Valencia

RESTAURANTS
Vegetarian
Buffet Chino Veg
Conde Altea 46   (96) 334-7061
La Lluna
San Ramon 23   (96) 392-214

SYNAGOGUES
Calle Asturias 7-4'   (96) 334-3416
Services: Friday eve. & festivals.

Conservative
La Javura
calle Uruguay 59, pta 13 46007   (96) 380-2129
Email: atoscano@arrakis.es
Web site: www.uscj.org/world/valencia
Tours of medieval Jewish quarter. The synagogue is a room in a private home.

Orthodox Sephardi
Comunidad Israelita de Valencia
Calle Ingeniero Joaquin Benlloch, 29
2nd Floor 46006   (96) 334-6848
Fax: (96) 352-7901
Email: civ@ctv.es

Vitoria

The monument on the Campo de Judimendi commemorates the ancient Jewish cemetery which, following the edict of expulsion in 1492, the town council undertook to take care of, and never to build over it.
There are no other specific locations of interest to travellers.

OVERSEAS REGIONS

Ceuta

KASHRUT INFORMATION
Calle Sargento Coriat 8

SYNAGOGUES
Calle Sargento Coriat 8

Melilla

KASHRUT INFORMATION
Calle General Mola 19   267-4057

SYNAGOGUES
Isaac Benarroch
Calle Marina 7

Jacob Almonznino
Calle Luis de Sotomayor 4

Salama
Calle Alfonso XII 6

Solinquinos
Calle O'Donnell

Yamin Benarroch
Calle Lopez Moreno 8

BALEARIC ISLANDS

Majorca

Majorca's Jewish population today numbers about 300, although fewer than 100 are registered with the community. Founded in 1971, it was the first Jewish community in Spain to be officially recognised since 1435. The Jewish cemetery is at Santa Eugenia, some 12 miles from Palma.

Palma Cathedral contains some interesting Jewish relics, including a candelabrum with 365 lights, which was originally in a synagogue. In the Tesoro room are two unique silver maces, over 6 feet long, converted from Torah rimonim brought from Sicily in 1493. The Santa Clara Church stands on the site of another pre-Inquisition synagogue. The Montezion Church was, in the 14th century, the Great Synagogue. In Calle San Miguel is the Church of San Miguel, which also stands on the site of a former synagogue. It is not far from the Calle de la Plateria, once a part of the Palma Ghetto.

COMMUNITY ORGANISATIONS
Communidad Israelita de Mallorca
Apartado Correos 389   (971) 283799

SYNAGOGUES
Orthodox
Communidad Israelita de Mallorca (Jewish Community of Mallorca)
Palma de Mallorca 07014   (971) 283-799
                                    Email: r_ajkatz@hotmail.com
                                    Web site:
www.fortunecity.com/victorian/coldwater/252
This synagogue was dedicated to the community in June 1987. Services are held on Fridays and Holy-days. A communal seder is also held. The community invites all congregants and guests to kiddush following the services.

CANARY ISLANDS

Las Palmas

SYNAGOGUES
Ap. Correos 2142 35080   (928) 823-1976

Tenerife

COMMUNITY ORGANISATIONS
Comunidad Israelita de Tenerife
                                    (922) 247296, 247246

KASHRUT INFORMATION
General Mola 4, Santa Cruz, Holdings 38006
                                    (922) 274157
Welcomes all Jewish visitors.

SYNAGOGUES
Ap. De Correos 939, Villalba Hervas 38001
                                    (922) 224-6013

SRI LANKA

Islamic and Samaritan legend relates that Adam came to the island after his expulsion from Eden and that Noah's Ark came to rest there. Solid evidence for Jewish settlement was recorded about 1,000 years ago by Muslim travellers. There was a small Jewish community when the Dutch took the island as a colony. This attracted Jews from southern India to the island because of the possibilities of trade.

There was a plan put forward when the island came under British rule for mass Jewish immigration. The Chief Justice, Sir Alexander Johnston appeared to consider the idea a serious one, but the British government did not act on it. A coffee estate was founded in 1841 near Kandy by Jews from Europe.

There is no communual organisation on the island. The Sri Lankans appear to be supportive of Israel, despite the government's official pro-Arab stance. Diplomatic relations with Israel were resumed in May 2000.

GMT +5 1/2 hours
Country calling code (94)
Emergency Telephone (Police – 43 3333) (Fire – 42 2222)
(Ambulance – 42 2222)

Total Population 18,552,000
Jewish Population Under 100
(Electricity voltage – 230/240)

Colombo

KASHRUT INFORMATION
82 Rosmead Place 7

(1) 695-642
Fax: (1) 74715-306

SURINAME

Suriname's Jewish community is very old. The first Jews settled here in the seventeenth century, escaping from persecution in Brazil. Later Jews came from Britain, after the country had passed into British hands. Suriname welcomed more Jewish refugees from the Caribbean and the country became a Dutch colony in 1668, bringing Sephardi Jews from Amsterdam. Eventually, half the white population in the country was Jewish, and there was a 'Joden Savanah' (Jewish savannah), where the Jews owned large sugar plantations. They called the plantations by Hebrew names and built a synagogue in 1685. The community began to decline in the nineteenth century. Recently, many have emigrated to Israel.

Today, there are two synagogues in Paramaribo, the capital. The Ashkenazi synagogue, like the one in Curacao, has a sandy floor, which is symbolic of the 40 years in the desert and was also said to have muffled the footsteps of the Conversos as they carried out their Judaism in secret.

GMT -3 hours
Country calling code (597)

Total Population 437,000
Jewish Population 200
(Electricity voltage – 110/220)

Paramaribo

KASHRUT INFORMATION
Commewijnestr. 21

400236
Fax: 471154

ORGANISATIONS
Suriname Jewish Community
Keizerstraat 82-84

400236/473896
Fax: 402380/471154

SYNAGOGUES
Ashkenazi
Neveh Shalom
Keizerstr. 82
Services are held every Shabbat in each synagogue alternately.

TOURIST SITE
Sights to see include Joden Savanah (Jewish savanah), one of the oldest Jewish settlements in the Americas.

Sedek Ve Shalom
Herenstr. 20
The entire contents of this eighteenth century synagogue are currently on 'long term loan' to the Israel Museum in Jerusalem. The building is now being used as an Internet café.

SWEDEN

Sweden was under the influence of the Lutheran church until the late eighteenth century and was opposed to Jewish settlement. Aaron Isaac from Mecklenburg in Germany, a seal engraver, was the first Jew admitted into the country, in 1774. The emancipation of Jews in Sweden was a slow process; Jews had limited rights, as they were designated a 'foreign colony'. After a gradual lifting of restrictions in the nineteenth century, Jews were fully emancipated in 1870, although the right to hold ministerial office was closed to them until 1951.

The emancipation heralded the growth of the community, and many eastern European Jews found refuge in Sweden at the beginning of the twentieth century. The initial refusal to accept Jews fleeing the Nazis changed to sympathy as evidence for the Holocaust mounted, and in 1942 many Jews and other refugees were allowed into the country, followed, in 1943, by almost all of Danish Jewry. Sweden also accepted Hungarian, Czechoslovakian and Polish Jews after the war.

There is an Official Council of Jewish Communities in Sweden, and many international Jewish groups are represented. There are three synagogues in Stockholm, including the imposing Great Synagogue built in 1870. There are synagogues in other large towns. Although shechita is forbidden, kosher food is imported, and there are some kosher shops.

GMT +1 hour	Total Population 8,847,000
Country calling code (46)	Jewish Population 16,000
Emergency Telephone (Police – 112) (Fire – 112) (Ambulance – 112)	(Electricity voltage – 220)

Boras

COMMUNITY ORGANISATIONS
Jewish Community of Boras & Synagogue
Varbergsvagen 21, Box 46 50305   (33) 124892
Email: s. rytz@vertextrading.se

Gothenburg

COMMUNITY ORGANISATIONS
Jewish Community Centre and Community Offices
Ostra Larmgatan 12 S-411 07   (31) 177245
Fax: (31) 7119360
Email: kansli@judforsgot.o.se

GROCERIES
Dr. Allards
gata 4   (31) 741-1545

MEDIA
Radio

Thursdays at 9pm on 94.4 MHz.

SYNAGOGUES
Conservative
Ostra Larmgatan 12 S-411 07   (31) 177245
Fax: (31) 711-9360
Email: kansli@judforsgot.o.se

Orthodox
Beilh Tefilah
Storgatan 5   (31) 711-7872
Web site: www.welcome.to/minyan

Helslingborg

COMMUNITY ORGANISATIONS
Jewish Centre
Springpostgranden 4

Lund

SYNAGOGUES
Orthodox
Winstrupsgatan 1   (46) 148052
Services on festivals and High Holy-days only.

Malmo

COMMUNITY ORGANISATIONS
Jewish Community Centre
Kamrergatan 11, Box 4198 20313
(40) 611 6460; 8860; 976043 (Rabbi)
Fax: (40) 234-469
Email: rabeli@alfa.telenordia.se

MIKVAOT
Kamrergatan 11   (40) 118860

SYNAGOGUES
Orthodox
Foreningsgatan
The Moorish style building celebrates its centenary during 2003.

Stockholm

Stockholm has a number of Jewish facilities. In addition the Raoul Wallenberg Park is worth a visit.

COMMUNITY ORGANISATIONS

Jewish Community Centre
Judaica House, Nybrogatan 19,
PO Box 5053 102 42   (8) 5878-5867
Fax: (8) 5878-5870
Email: info@jf-stockholm.org
Web site: www.jf-stockholm.org

Jewish Community of Stockholm
Wahrendorffsgatan 3, PO Box 7427 103 91
(8) 5878-5800
Fax: (8) 5878-5858
Email: info@jf-stockholm.org
Web site: www.jf-stockholm.org
Open Monday to Thursday 9am-5pm Friday 9am-
4pm (closed for lunch noon-1pm).

EMBASSY

Embassy of Israel
Torstenssongatan 4, PO Box 14006 104 40
(8) 663-1465
Fax: (8) 662-5301
Email: israel.embassy.swipnet.se

GIFT SHOP

Menorah: Community Centre Shop
Judaica House, Nybrogatan 19, PO Box 5053 102 42
(8) 663-6580

GROCERIES

Kosherian Blecher & Co
Nybrogatan 19, PO Box 5053 102 42   (8) 663-6580
Fax: (8) 663-6580
Kosher groceries. Also offers cooked meals such as
burgers, sausages, meat sandwiches etc. Delivery to
groups, hotels etc.

KASHRUT INFORMATION

Rabbi Meir Horden
Community House, Wahrendorffsgatan 3B,
PO Box 7427   (8) 5878-5800
Fax: (8) 5878-5850
Email: info@judiskacentret.a.se
Rabbi Meir Horden supervises kashrut in Stockholm.
Look at www.jf-stockholm.org/kosher for the latest
updated information.

LIBRARIES

The Jewish Library
Wahrendorffsgatan 3, PO Box 7427 103 91
(8) 587-858 34
Fax: (8) 587-858 51
Email: judiska.biblioteket@jf-stockholm.org
The Raoul Wallenberg Room is also on the premises.
It is named after the Swedish diplomat who saved
scores of thousands of Hungarian Jews from the
Nazis, was arrested by the Russians in Budapest in
1945 and disappeared.

MEDIA

Periodical
Judisk Kronika
PO Box 5053 102 42   (8) 660-3872
Fax: (8) 660-3892
Email: judisk.kronika@swipnet.se

Menorah
PO Box 5053 102 42   (8) 667-6770
Fax: (8) 663-7676
Email: kh-uia@swipnet.se
Web site: www.menorah-sweden.com

MIKVAOT

Community Centre
Judaica House, Nybrogatan 19 102 42   (8) 5878-5867
Fax: (8) 5878-5870
Email: info@jf-stockholm.org
Web site: www.jf-stockholm.org
The Mikva is located in the Judaica House.

MONUMENT

The Holocaust Monument
Wahrendorffsgatan 3
The monument was opened in 1998 by King Carl XVI
Gustaf of Sweden, and records the over 8,500
holocaust victims who are relatives of Jews residing in
Sweden.

MUSEUM

Jewish Museum
Halsingegatan 2   (8) 318 404
Fax: (8) 318404
Email: info@judiska-museet.a.se
Web site: www.judiska-museet.a.se
The only one of its kind in the Nordic countries.
Arranges exhibitions about the history of Swedish
Jewry and is open every day, except Saturday,
between noon and 4 pm.

RESTAURANTS

Community Centre
Nybrogatan 19 102 42   (8) 663-6580
Email: info@jf-stockholm.org
Kosher lunches under Rabbi Meir Horden's
supervision at the Community Centre are available
during the summer. Dinners can also be arranged at
the Community Centre for groups. Contact Mr Ike
Tankus. Tel: 647-4475.

Lao Wai
Luntmakargatan 74   (8) 673-7800
Supervision: Rabbi Meir Honden

Mino's Café
Tegnergatan 36   (8) 30 77 42
Jewish North African Cuisine. All meat is said to be
kosher but there is no kosher licence.

SYNAGOGUES

Masorti
Great Synagogue
Wahrendorffsgatan 3, PO Box 7427 103 91
(8) 5878-5800
Fax: (8) 5878-5850
Email: kansli@jf-stockholm.org
Web site: www.jf-stockholm.org
The interior originally comes from a synagogue in
Hamburg which survived the Kristallnacht in
Germany. Services: Monday, Thursday morning,
Friday evenings & Saturday morning. Open to tourists
Monday - Friday from 10am till 2pm.

Orthodox
Adat Jeshurun
Riddargatan 5, PO Box 5053 102 42   (8) 679-2900
Fax: (8) 663-6580
Daily services: Weekdays 7.45 am, Shabat 9 am,
Sunday 8.30 am.

Adat Jisroel
St. Paulsgatan 13   (8) 679-2900
Situated in an 18th century building it was renovated
some 20 years ago. Daily Services: weekdays 7.30am,
Shabbat 9.00am, Sunday 8.15am

Uppsala

ORGANISATIONS
Jewish Students Club.
Dalgatan 15   (8) 125453

SWITZERLAND

Swiss Jewry originated in medieval times and their history followed the standard course of medieval European Jewry: working as money-lenders and pedlars, attacked by the local population, who accused them of causing the Black Death, then resettling a few years afterwards, only to be subsequently expelled.

By the late eighteenth century, when the Helvetic Confederation was formed, there were three small communities. Freedom of movement was allowed, and full emancipation was granted in 1866. Theodor Herzl held the first World Zionist Conference in Basle in 1897.

Although Switzerland accepted some refugees from Nazism, many were refused, and most of the new refugee Jewish population emigrated soon after the war. The community today has a central body, and is made up of various factions, from ultra-Orthodox to Reform. The major towns have synagogues, and kosher meat is imported. There are several hotels with kosher facilities. Over half of the community live in the German-speaking area, the French-speaking area has the second largest number, and a small population is found in the southern, Italian-speaking area.

Switzerland has elected its first Jewish (and first female) president, Ruth Dreifuss.

In 2001 it was reported that evidence had been found of an early Jewish presence in the country, being a ring bearing images of a menorah and a ram's horn and dating from 200CE.

GMT + 1 hour	**Total Population 7,085,000**
Country calling code (41)	**Jewish Population 18,000**
Emergency Telephone (Police – 117) (Fire – 118) (Ambulance – 144)	**(Electricity voltage – 220)**

Arosa

HOTELS
Levin's Hotel Metropol
(81) 377-4444
Fax: (81) 377-2100
Mikva on premises. Own kosher bakery.

Baden

KOSHER FOOD
Atrium Hotel Blume
Kurplatz 4 5400   (56) 222-5569
Fax: (56) 222-4298
Email: info@blume-baden.ch
Web site: www.blume-baden.ch
Prepacked kosher meals on request

SYNAGOGUES

Israelitische Kultusgemeinde Baden
Parkstrasse 17 5400 (56) 221-5128
Fax: (56) 222-9447
Email: ikgb@dplanet.ch
Friday nights: Winter 18.30; Summer 19.30. Shabbat and Festivals: mornings 8.45am.

Basle

The Jewish community dates back to the beginning of the 12th century. This lasted for some two hundred years until the Jews had to flee from persecution.

They returned in the 16th century and Basle became a centre for Jewish printing.

Basle is of course famous for the first Zionist Conference of 1897. A plaque on the wall of the Concert Hall commemorates this event.

BAKERIES

Bakery Schmutz
Austrasse 53 (61) 272-4765

BOOKSELLERS

Victor Goldschmidt
Mostackerstrasse 17 4051 (61) 261 61 91
Fax: (61) 261 61 23

BUTCHERS

Juedische Genossenschafts-Metzgerei
Friedrichstrasse 26 4055 (61) 301-3493
Fax: (61) 301-6882
Supervision: Both Basel Rabbinates
Also sells groceries and wine. Open 7.30am-12.00 noon, 3pm-6.00. Closed Friday afternoon.

HOTELS

Hotel Euler
Centralbahnplatz 14 4002 (61) 275-8000
Fax: (61) 275-8050
Offers kosher meals on request. Has a synagogue and Mikvah on the premises.

MIKVAOT

Eulerstr. 10 4051 (61) 301-6831
Thannerstrasse 60 (61) 301-2220

MUSEUM

Jewish Museum of Switzerland
Kornhausgasse 8 4051 (61) 261-9514
Hours: Monday and Wednesday, 2 pm to 5 pm; Sunday, 11 am to 5 pm. Free entrance.

RESTAURANTS

Holbein Cafe
Leimenstrasse 67 4051 (61) 270-6868
Fax: (61) 270-6810
Email: info@holbeinhof.ch
Supervision: Basle Rabbinate
Serves both meat and dairy.

Restaurant Topas
Leimenstrasse 24 4051 (61) 206-9500
Fax: (61) 206-9501
Email: info@restaurant-topas.ch
Web site: www.restaurant-topas.ch
Supervision: Under the supervision of local rabbinical authority.
Hours: 11:30 am to 2 pm Sunday to Friday. 6:30 pm to 9 pm Sunday to Thursday. Friday night, Shabbat lunch and holidays by reservation before 2 pm of preceding day.

Vegetarian Kosher
Falafel- & Pitahaus
Oberwilerstasse 46 4102 (61) 423-7575
Fax: (61) 423-7575
Email: info@falafel-und-pitahaus.ch
Web site: www.falafel-und-pitahaus.ch

SYNAGOGUES

Israelitische Religionsgesellschaft
Ahornstrasse 14 (61) 301-4898
Rabbi, Tel: 41-61-302-1434.

Orthodox
Israelitische Gemeinde Basel
Leimenstrasse 24 4003 (61) 279-9850
Fax: (61) 279-9851
Email: igb@igb.ch

Bern

EMBASSY

Embassy of Israel
Alpenstrasse 32 3006 (31) 356-3500
Fax: (31) 356-3556
Email: info@emb.israel.ch

SYNAGOGUES

Conservative Traditional
Synagogue & Community Center
Kapellenstrasse 2 (31) 381-4992
Fax: (31) 382-3861
Email: info@jgb.ch
Web site: www.jgb.ch
Rabbiner Dr Michael Leipziger, Tel: 41-31 381-7303.

Biel/Bienne

SYNAGOGUES

Ruschlistrasse 3 (32) 342-3670

Bremgarten / Aargau

CONTACT INFORMATION
Israelitische Cultusgemeinde
Werner Meyer-Moses, Ringstrasse. 37 CH-5620
(56) 633-6626
Fax: (56) 633-6626

Endingen

CONTACT INFORMATION
J. Bloch
Buckstr. 2 5304 (56) 242-1546
Visits to the old synagogue and cemetery can be arranged.

Engelberg

HOTELS
Hotel Marguerite
6390 Engelberg (41) 637-2522
Fax: (41) 637-2926
Supervision: Agudas Achim, Zurich
Mikva on premises.

Fribourg

SYNAGOGUES
9 avenue de Rome (26) 322-1670

Geneva

Originally Jews were not allowed to settle in Geneva itself but only the surrounding district. They had come in 1182 from France. In 1490 they were expelled.

After Geneva's annexation by France, at the end of the 18th century, Jews were allowed back in. They were not allowed civic rights however until 1841.

BAKERIES
Pouly
Rue des Eaux Vives 72
Ask for kosher bread.

BUTCHERS
Boucherie Kosher
Biton 21, rue de Montchoisi (22) 736-3168

EMBASSY
Permanent Mission of Israel to the United Nations
9 Chemin Bonvent, Cointrin 1216

MEDIA
Periodicals
Israelitsches Wochenblatt/Revue Juive
Avenue du Mail 5 1205 (22) 800-1026
Fax: (22) 800-1028

MIKVAOT
(22) 346-9732
Fax: (22) 736-9632

RESTAURANTS
Restaurant Le Neguev
Rue de la Servette 20 1201 (22) 740-4070
Supervision: Rabbi A Y Schlesinger
Near to the town centre and 200 yards from the railway station.

Meat
Le Jardin Rose
10, rue St-Leger (22) 317-8910
Fax: (22) 317-8990
Only open for lunch but arrangements can be made so that lunches and dinners can be delivered to any hotel downtown.

R.Liebermann
Av. Jules Crosnier 4 1206 (22) 346-0892
Fax: (22) 346-0830
Supervision: Machsike Hadas

SYNAGOGUES
Orthodox
Beth Habad
12 rue du Lac (22) 736-3682
Machsike Hadass
2 place des Eaux Vives 1207 (22) 786-2589
The Geneva Synagogue (Ashkenazi)
Place de la Synagogue
Sephardi
Hekhal Haness
54 ter route de Malagnou (22) 736-9632

Kreuzlingen

CONTACT INFORMATION
Louis Hornung
Schulstr. 7 (71) 671-1630

La-Chaux-de-Fonds

SYNAGOGUES
Rue de Parc 63 2300 (39) 231-794
Jews first came to the town from Alsace in 1777. The synagogue was built in 1896. It has been recently refurbished.

Lausanne

COMMUNITY ORGANISATIONS

Communauté Israélite de Lausanne
3 avenue Georgette 1001 (21) 341-7240
Fax: (21) 341-7241
Email: secretariat.cil@vtx.ch

GROCERIES

Kolbo Shalom
7 avenue Juste-Olivier (21) 312-1265

MIKVAOT

1 avenue Juste-Olivier (21) 617-5818

RESTAURANTS

Community Centre
3 avenue Georgette 1003 (21) 341-7242
Serves lunch only, from 12 pm to 2 pm.

SYNAGOGUES

Orthodox
1 avenue Juste-Olivier (21) 320-9911
Cnr J. Olivier and av. Florimont.

Lengnau

CONTACT INFORMATION

(56) 241-1203
For visits to the old synagogue and cemetery.

Lucerne

BUTCHERS

Judische Metzgerei
Bruchstrasse 26 (41) 240-2560

MIKVAOT

Bruchstrasse 51 (41) 320-4750

SYNAGOGUES

Bruchstrasse 51 (41) 240-6400

Lugano

GROCERIES

Koschere Lebensmittel erhaltlich bei
Frutor SA via Bagutti 4 (91) 922-8522

HOTELS

Hotel Dan
Via Fontana 1 6902 (91) 985-7030
Fax: (91) 985-7031
Email: danlugano@yahoo.com
Web site: pibt.de/l/dan.htm
Kashrut under the supervision of the rabbinat
Lugano's Jewish Community.

MIKVAOT

Via Maderno 11 (91) 923-8952

SYNAGOGUES

Via Maderno 11 (91) 923-5698

Neukirch-Egnach

CENTRAL ORGANISATION

Vegetarian society
Schweizerische Vereinigung fur Vegetarismus (SVV)
Bahnhofstr 52 9315 757-1586
Fax: 757-2819
Email: svv@vegetarismus.ch
Web site: www.vegetarismus.ch
Can supply information on those who wish to eat
vegetarian in Switzerland.

St Gallen

SYNAGOGUES

Frongartenstrasse 18 (71) 223-5923

St Moritz

HOTELS

Bermann's Hotel Edelweiss
(81) 836-5555
Fax: (81) 833-5556

Vevey

RESTAURANTS

Les Bergers du Leman
923-5355
Fax: 922-5923

Winterthur

SYNAGOGUES

Rosenstrasse 5 (52) 232-8136

Yverdon

CONTACT INFORMATION

Dr Maurice Ellkan
1400 Cheseaux-Noreaz (24) 425-1851

Zug

RESTAURANTS

Restaurant Glashof
Baarerstr. 41 6301 (42) 221-248
Prepared kosher meals are available.

Zurich

Jews first arrived in Zurich in 1273. Over the following two centuries Jews were repeatedly expelled and allowed to return. There are five stained glass Chagall windows in the Fraumunster Church (located at Munsterhof Square) of which four are on themes from the Hebrew Bible.

BAKERIES
Ruben Bollag
Waffenplatzstrasse 5, (near Bahnhof Enge)
8002   (1) 202-3045
Brauerstrasse 110 8004   (1) 242-8700
                                  Fax: (1) 291-4684

BOOKSELLERS
Morascha
Seestrasse 11 8002   (1) 201.11.20
                                  Fax: (1) 201.31.20
                        Email: morascha@bluemail.ch
                        Web site: www.morascha.com

BUTCHERS
Zukom
8 Aemtlerst   (1) 451-8384
                                  Fax: (1) 451-8386
Supervision: Judische Gemeinde Aguda Achim and Israelitsche Religionsgellschaft.

GROCERIES
Jelmoli Department Store
Bahnhofstrasse
Has a kosher section.

Pick and Pay
Lavaterstrasse
Has a kosher section.

HOTELS
Hotel International
                                        (1) 311-4341
Offers kosher meals on request.

MEDIA
Periodical
Jewish City Guide of Switzerland
Spectrum Press International, Im Tannegg 1,
Friesenbergstrasse 221 8055 (1) 462-6411; 462-6412
                                  Fax: (1) 462-6462
                        Email: info@jewishguide.ch
                        Web site: www.jewishguide.ch
Published quarterly in English and German, a guide to Jewish communities throughout Switzerland.

Tachles
Rudigerstr 10, Postfach 8027   (1) 206-4200
                                  Fax: (1) 206-4210
                        Email: redaktion@tachles.ch
                        Web site: www.tachles.ch
Weekly magazine.

MIKVAOT
Freigutstrasse 37   (1) 201-7306
Appointment by phone between 9am & 11am.

RESTAURANTS
Restaurant Schalom
G. van Dijk Lavaterstrasse 33-37 8002   (1) 283-2233
                                  Fax: (1) 283-2234
                Email: catering.schalom@bleuwin.ch
Supervision: Rabbi Rothschild.

Dairy
Fein & Schein
Schontalstrasse 14, Corner/Ecke
Hallwylstrasse   (1) 241-3040
                                  Fax: (1) 241-2112
Supervision: IRGZ Rabbi Daniel Levy

Meat
Club Savjon
G. van Dijk-Neufeld., Lavaterstr. 33   (1) 201-1476
                                  Fax: (1) 201-1496
                Email: catering.schalom@bluewin.ch
Supervision: Rabbi Rothschild

SYNAGOGUES

Beth Hamidrash, Chasidei Gur

(1) 242-3899

Chabad Minjan Esra

(1) 386-8403

Israel, Religionsgesellschaft
Freigutstrasse 37 8002   (1) 201-6746

Israelitische Cultusgemeinde Zurich
Lavaterstrasse 33 8002   (1) 283-2222
Fax: (1) 283-2223
Email: info@icz.org

Judische Gemeinde Agudas Achim
Erikastrasse 8 8003   (1) 463-5798
Orthodox
Minjan Machsikei Hadass
Anwandstrasse 60   (1) 241-3759
Fax: (1) 241-2668
Rabbi Schmerler: 01-242-9046

Minjan Wollishofen
Etzelstrasse 6 8038   (1) 286-5010
Fax: (1) 286-5018
Email: minjan.wollishofen@schweiz.ch
Contact: Dr. Sigmund Pugatsch

TAIWAN

The US Army brought the first Jews to Taiwan in the 1950s, when an American base, now closed, was set up in the country. In the 1970s, some Jewish businessmen began to work on the island, serving two- or three-year contracts with their companies. Most are Americans, although there are some Israelis and other nationalities. Services are held on Shabbat in a hotel, and there is a Jewish community centre.

GMT +8 hours	**Total Population 21,854,000**
Country calling code (886)	**Jewish Population Under 100**
Emergency Telephone (Police – 110) (Fire – 119) (Ambulance – 119)	**(Electricity voltage – 110)**

Taipei

COMMUNITY ORGANISATIONS

Taiwan Jewish Community Centre
No 1, Lane 61, Teh Hsing East Road,
Shihlin   (2) 396-0159
Fax: (2) 396-4022
Services are held on most Friday evenings at 7.30pm.
Visitors should check in advance. All Holy Days and
major festivals are celebrated.

RESTAURANTS
Meat
Y.Y.'s Steakhouse
Chungshan North Road, Section 3, cnr. The Huei St.
There are no supervised kosher restaurants in Taipei,
but this steakhouse has a separate kitchen and dining
room, where kosher meat meals are served on
separate crockery, with separate cutlery. No milk
products are available in this section.

SYNAGOGUES
Orthodox
Ritz Landis Hotel
41 Min Chuan East Road   (2) 2597-1234
Fax: (2) 2596-9223
Email: ritz@theritz-taipei.com
Shabbat and festival services are held here, when a
minyan is available, Weekday Services.

TAJIKISTAN

One of the former Soviet Republics, Tajikistan has a small Jewish population but, after the fall of the Soviet Union, many Jews emigrated to Israel. The community is a mix of 40 per cent Bokharans and 60 per cent Soviet Jews from other parts of the former USSR who migrated to Tajikistan during the Second World War. The Bokharan Jews are believed to be descendants of Persian Jewish exiles. Dushanbe, the capital, and Shakhrisabz are provided with synagogues, and Dushanbe also has a library.

GMT +5 hours
Country calling code (7)

Total Population 5,513,000
Jewish Population 1,500
(Electricity voltage – 220)

Dushanbe

SYNAGOGUES
Ashkenazi
Proletarsky Street

Bokharan
Nazyina Khikmeta Street 26

Shakhrisabz

SYNAGOGUES
23 Bainal Minal Street

THAILAND

Although the first confirmed presence of Jews in Thailand was in 1890, Thai Jewry really began with Jews escaping Russia and eastern Europe in the 1920s and 1930s although most of them emigrated after 1945.

The present community arrived in the post-war period of the 1950s and 1960s. They came from Syria and Lebanon, and also from Europe and America. Some Israelis also came, and jewellery is an important source of trade with Israel. Another relatively large influx came in 1979 as Jews left Iran after the fall of the Shah.

Bangkok has Ashkenazi, Sephardi and Lubavitch synagogues. The community centre is based in the Ashkenazi synagogue. The Lubavitch synagogue offers several communual activities, including Seders at Passover, which have a large attendance.

GMT +7 hours
Country calling code (66)

Total Population 60.206,000
Jewish Population 250
(Electricity voltage – 220)

Bangkok

COMMUNITY ORGANISATIONS
Jewish Community of Thailand
Beth Elisheva Building, 121 Soi Sai, Nam Thip 2,
Sukhumvit Soi 22   (2) 663-0244
                     Fax: (2) 663-0245
Email: ykantor@ksc15.th.com
Web site: www.jewishthailand.com
Friday night and Shabbat services with Kiddush &
Shabbat meal. Holidays services. Call to confirm.

EMBASSY
Embassy of Israel
'Ocean Tower II' 25th floor, 75 Sukhumvit Soi 19,
Asoke Road 10110   (2) 204-9200
                     Fax: (2) 204-9255
Email: consul.bkk@israelfm.org

KASHRUT INFORMATION
                     (2) 318-1577
                     (2) 234-0606
                     (2) 237-1697

MIKVAOT
Jewish Community of Thailand
Beth Elisheva Building, 121 Soi Sai, Nam Thip 2,
Sukhumvit Soi 22   (2) 663-0244
                     Fax: (2) 663-0245
Email: ykantor@ksc15.th.com
Web site: www.jewishthailand.com

RESTAURANTS

Ohr Menachem - Chabad House
96 Ram Buttri Rd., Kaosarn Road, Banglampoo

(2) 282-6388
Fax: (2) 629-1153

Supervision: Rabbi Y. Kantor
Open 12 noon to 9 pm daily. Bakery and Store. Tel 629-2944/5.

SYNAGOGUES

Orthodox
Beth Elisheva
121 Soi Sai, Nam Thip 2, Sukhumvit Soi 22

(2) 663-0244
Fax: (2) 663-0245
Email: ykantor@ksc15.th.com

Close to: Imperial Queens Park, Jade Pavilion, Rembrandt, and Sheraton Grande Hotels. Friday night service at candle lighting time followed by Shabbat meal. Shabbat services 10.00am with Kiddush & Shabbat meal. Call to confirm.

Even Chen
The Bossotel Inn 2nd floor, 55/12-14 Soi Charoenkrung, 42/1 New Road (Silom Road area)

(2) 630-6120
Fax: (2) 237-3225

Daily morning service. Regular Friday evening and Shabbat morning, afternoon and evening services. Light kosher meal after Shabbat service, by advance reservation.

Ohr Menachem - Chabad House
96 Ram Buttri Rd., Kaosarn Road, Banglampoo

(2) 282-6388
Fax: (2) 629-1153
Email: chabadbangkok@yahoo.com

Daily services, Friday evenings at sundown with Shabbat meal, attracts young Jewish travellers.

TUNISIA

There is written proof of ancient Jewish settlement in Carthage in the year 200CE, when the region was under Roman control. The community was successful and was left in peace. Under the Byzantine Empire, conditions for the Jews did worsen, but after the Islamic conquest, the 'golden age' of Tunisian Jewry occurred. There was prosperity and many centres of learning were established. This did not continue into the Middle Ages, as successive Arab and Spanish invasions led to discrimination. Emancipation came from the French, but the community suffered under the Nazi-influenced Vichy government. After the war, many emigrated to Israel or to France and the community is currently shrinking.

There are several synagogues in the country, together with kindergartens and schools. Tunisia is not as extreme in its attitude towards Israel as some Arab states, and there has been communication between the two countries at a high level. An Israeli Interest Bureau in Tunis acts as an unofficial embassy. The Bardo Museum in Tunis has an exhibition of Jewish ritual objects.

GMT +1 hour
Country calling code (216)

Total Population 9,215,000
Jewish Population 1,500
(Electricity voltage – 220)

Jerba

There are Jews in two villages on this small island off the Tunisian coast.

Each year a traditional Lag B'Omer celebration is held. Following the terrorist attack in 2001 attendance dropped from 7000 to 800. Jewish silversmiths are prominent in Hournt souk on rue Bizerte.

The community in Jerba is possibly the oldest continuous one outside Israel. There are two small Jewish towns; Hara Saghira and Hara Kebira. Most of the Jews live in Hara Kebira, where there is the Al Ghriba "extraordinary" synagogue which has a multicoloured interior and is a site of pilgrimage.
There are no other specific locations of interest to travellers.

Sfax

SYNAGOGUES

Azriah
71 rue Habib Mazoun
Near the Town Hall.

Tunis

COMMUNITY ORGANISATIONS

Community Offices
15 rue de Cap Vert
(1) 282469, 287153

KASHRUT INFORMATION

26 rue de Palestine
(1) 282406; 283540

SYNAGOGUES

Beth Yacob
3 rue Eve, Nohelle   (1) 348964

Grande
43 Av. de la Liberte

Lubavitch Yeshiva
73 rue de Palestine   (1) 791429

TURKEY

There have been Jews in Turkey since at least the fourth century BCE, making Turkey one of the earliest Jewish communities. The fifteenth and sixteenth centuries were periods of major prosperity for the Jews of Turkey.

After the Expulsion of the Jews from Spain in 1492, at a time when Jews were not tolerated in most of the Christian countries of Western Europe, what was then the Ottoman (Turkish) Empire was their principal land of refuge. The Sultan was reported to have said of the Spanish King: 'By expelling the Jews, he has impoverished his country and enriched mine'.

During the Second World War Turkey was neutral and accepted those Jews able to enter it.

GMT +2 hours	**Total Population 63,745,000**
Country calling code (90)	**Jewish Population 20,000**
Emergency Telephone (Police – 155) (Fire – 110) (Ambulance – 11)	**(Electricity voltage – 220)**

Ankara

EMBASSY

Embassy of Israel
Mahatma Gandhi Sok 85, Gaziosmanpasa
     (312) 446-3605
Fax: (312) 446-8071

SYNAGOGUES

Birlik Sokak
Samanpazari   (312) 311-6200
This synagogue is not easy to find. Off Anafartalar Caddesi in Samanpazari, there is a stairway down at the right of the TC Ziraat Bankasi. The synagogue is several buildings along the street on the left, behind a wall. Services every morning. Sabbath morning services begin at 7 or 7.30 am depending on the time of year.

Balat

A coastal town about 20 miles west of Istanbul which has a 500-year- old synagogue. Now closed, the keys are with the mosque next door.
There are no other specific locations of interest to travellers.

Bursa

SYNAGOGUES

Gerush Synagogue
Kurucesme Caddesi   (224) 368-636
Services on Friday evening, Shabbat morning and festivals. This synagogue is in the old Jewish quarter.

Istanbul

In the 12th century Benjamin Tudela said of the city "There is no city like her except Baghdad". At that time it was one of the most important Jewish centres in the world.

Since 1949 the Jewish community has had autonomy in its own affairs.

COMMUNITY ORGANISATIONS

Buyuk Hendek
Sokak No 61, Galata   (212) 293-7566
Secretary General: Lina Filiba

EMBASSY

Consul General of Israel
Valikonag Caddesi No 73   (212) 255-1040
Fax: (212) 225-1048
Email: isrcon@comnet.com.tr

MUSEUM

Zulfari Museum
     (212) 274-2607
Fax: (212) 274-2607
The museum contains material relating to the Jewish members of the Ottoman Parliament, physicians at the Imperial Court, diplomats, academicians, police officers and civil servants. Contact Mr H Ojalvo (212-275-3944) for further information.

RELIGIOUS ORGANISATIONS

Chief Rabbinate
Yemenici Sokak 23, Beyoglu, Tunel 80050
     (212) 293-8794/5
Fax: (212) 244-1980

RESTAURANTS

Levi Restaurant
Tustempasamah Kalcin Sok, Cavustasa Han
(2nd floor)   (212) 512-1196
Meat

Karne Restaurant
Muallim Naci Cad. 41   (212) 260-8424

Robelyu
Omerpasa Cad 38/1   (212) 385-7181
Supervision: Istanbul Rabbinate

SYNAGOGUES

Askenazi Synagogue
Yuksekkaldinm Sok No 37, Galata   (212) 252-2157
                          Fax: (212) 244-2975
          Email: eskenazivakli@superonline.com

Beth Israel
Efe Sok No 4, Sisli   (212) 240-6599
Every day.

Caddesbostan Synagogue
Tasmektep Sok, Goztepe   (212) 356-5922
Every day.

Etz Ahayim Synagogue
Muallim Naci Cad No 40 & 41, Ortakoy
                                 (212) 260-1896
Every day.

Hemdat Israel Synagogue
Izettin Sok No 65, Kadikoy   (212) 336-5293
Every day.

Hesed Leavraam Synagogue
Pancur Sok No 15, Buyukada   (212) 382-5788
June-September including High Holy days.

Italian Synagogue
Sair Ziya Pasa Yokusu No 27, Karakoy,
Galata   (212) 293-7784

Neve Shalom Buyuk Hendek Sok
No 61, Galata   (212) 293-7566
Saturdays only.

Izmir

BUTCHERS

Kosher Meat
                                 (232) 148-395
Tuesday and Thursday. Enquire at the synagogue.

COMMUNITY ORGANISATIONS

Jewish Community Council
Azizler Sokak 920/44, Guzelyurt   (232) 421-12-90
                          Fax: (232) 463-52-25
          Email: isakalaluf@superonline.com.tr

SYNAGOGUES

Beth Israel
265 Mithatpasa Street, Karatas, Kanamursil District

Shaar Ashamayan
1390 Sokak 4/2, Bikur Holim

UKRAINE

The Ukraine has had a long and complicated history, with areas of the present country being under the rule of a number of other countries, from Austria to Romania. The history of the Jews who live in the modern-day, independent Ukraine is both long and tragic. From settlement in Kiev in the tenth century, before the concept of a Ukrainian national identity had been formed, the Jewish community grew and was joined by many Jews from central Europe. The Chmielnicki massacre of 1648, in which up to 100,000 were killed, was the worst event to befall the Jews before the Holocaust, and much destruction occurred in the west of the country.

Throughout the nineteenth century, the Ukraine was mainly under Russian domination. After 1918, the Ukraine attempted to become independent, and many Jews were killed in the fighting. The Ukraine absorbed some of south-eastern Poland in 1939 and, after the German invasion of the Soviet Union, the Jewish community suffered terrible losses in the Holocaust.

The community today remains fairly large, and is slowly emerging from the atheist Soviet times. Most Jews live in towns, and Kiev (the capital) is a major centre. There are now Jewish schools, and kosher food can be obtained. In a similar way to Belarus, there are many interesting places to visit. Graves of famous Hassidic masters and the monument to the Babi Yar massacre (near Kiev) are frequent destinations. There have been memorials erected (mainly after the fall of Communism) all over the country to events which happened during the Holocaust.

GMT +2 hours	**Total Population 50,800,000**
Country calling code (380)	**Jewish Population 180,000**
Emergency Telephone (Police – 02) (Fire – 01) (Ambulance – 03)	**(Electricity voltage – 220)**

Berdichev

MIKVAOT
4 Dzherzhinskaya Street   (4143) 23938 / 20222

SYNAGOGUES
4 Dzherzhinskaya Street   (4143) 23938 / 20222
Kosher kitchen on premises.

Beregovo

SYNAGOGUES
17 Sverdlov Street

Bershad

SYNAGOGUES
25 Narodnaya Street

Chernigov

SYNAGOGUES
34 Kommunisticheskaya Street

Chernovtsy

SYNAGOGUES
24 Lukyana Kobylitsa Street   54878

Chmelnitsy

SYNAGOGUES
58 Komminnestnaya Street

Dnepropetrovsk

SYNAGOGUES
Synagogue of Dnepropetrovsk
7 Kotsubinskovo St. 320030   (56) 2342-120
Fax: (56) 2342-137
Email: dnepr@jewcom.dp.ua
Web site: www.jew.dp.ua

Donetsk

SYNAGOGUES
Synagogue of Donetsk
36 Oktabriskaya Street 340000   (62) 2357-725
Fax: (62) 2938-155

Ivano-Frankivsk

SYNAGOGUES
Synagogue of Ivano-Frankivsk
Strachenyh 7 284000   (34) 22- 23029
Fax: (34) 325-367
Rabbi Rolesnik (22-34894) is prepared to assist those doing historical or genealogical research in the Western Ukraine (Galicia).

Kharkov

SYNAGOGUES
48 Kryatkovskaya Street
Web site: www.kharkovejewish.com
Orthodox Union Project Reunite
Surnskaya 45 (572) 408-378
Fax: (572) 439-209
Synagogue of Kharkov
12 Pushkinskaya Street 310057 (572) 126-526
Fax: (572) 452-140
Email: chabad@kharkov.com

Kherson

SYNAGOGUES
Synagogue of Kherson
27 Gorkovo Street 325025 (552) 223-334
Fax: (552) 325-367

Kiev

Kiev's central position as a crossroad of Western Europe and central Asia attracted Jewish settlers as early as the eighth century. The unfortunate usual cycle of persecution and resettlement then began.

In 1911 Kiev was the location of a modern blood libel case "the Beilis affair".

EMBASSY
Embassy of Israel
Lesi Ukrainki 34, GPE-S 252195

SYNAGOGUES
Aish Ha-Torah Ukraine
Verhniy Val 18 (44) 417-2213
Central Synagogue of Kiev
29 Shchekovitzkaya Street (44) 417-3583
Reform
Reform Congregation
7 Nemanskaya Street (44) 296-3961
Fax: (44) 295-9604

Korosten

SYNAGOGUES
8 Shchoksa Street

Kremenchug

SYNAGOGUES
50 Sverdlov Street

Lviv

Situated on the edge of shifting imperial boundaries, this city has been under Austrian, Polish and Soviet control. It has had as many names as its number of rulers among them Lwów in Polish and Lemberg in German. Now called Lviv in Ukrainian, there are 6,000 Jews in the city, once a major Jewish centre in Galicia. A couple of synagogues are still functioning, and a number of monuments have been erected commemorating the Holocaust. Many Jews on 'heritage tours' use the town as a base to explore the region, and guides (generally Yiddish-speaking) are available.

SYNAGOGUES
Beis A'aron V'Yisroel
4 Brativ Michnovskich Street 79018 (322) 978-955
Fax: (322) 333-535
Email: bald@link.lviv.ua
Restaurant orders must be placed in advance. Tourist information.

Nikolayev

SYNAGOGUES
Synagogue of Nikolayev
13 Karl Libknechta Street 327001 (512) 358-310
Fax: (512) 353-072

Odessa

SYNAGOGUES
Main Synagogue
Corner of ul.Evreiskaya and ul. Richlieu
Synagogue of Odessa
21 Osipovo St. 270011 (482) 218-890
Fax: (482) 247-296

Simferopol

JEWISH CENTER
Mironova 24, Crimea 95001 (52) 510-773
Email: chabadcrimea@cris.crimea.ua

SYNAGOGUES
Orthodox
Krasna Znamyonaya 78
Also has a mikvah. Information on kosher matters is available from the main office.

Slavuta

SYNAGOGUES
Kuzovskaya Street 2 (447) 925-452
The first edition of Tanya was printed here by the Shapira family whose tombs are in the cemetery.

Uman

Each year followers of the Breslau Chassidic sect visit the grave of Rabbi Lachman of Breslau its founder for Rosh Hashana. In 2000 there were a reported 13,000 visitors.
There are no specific locations of interest to travellers.

Zaparozhe

SYNAGOGUES
Synagogue of Zaparozhe
22 Turgeneva Street. 330063 (612) 642-961

Zhitomir

SYNAGOGUES
59 Lubarskaya Street (412) 373-468
Reb Ze'ev Wolf, disciple of Dov Baer, is buried in the Smolanka cemetery.

Synagogue of Zhitomire
7 M. Berdishevskaya St. 262001 (412) 226-608
Fax: (412) 373-428

UNITED KINGDOM

There were probably individual Jews in England in Roman and (though less likely) in Anglo-Saxon times, but the historical records of any organised settlement start after the Normal Conquest of 1066. Jewish immigrants arrived early in the reigh of William the Conqueror and important settlements came to be established in London (at a site still known as Old Jewry), Lincoln and many other centres. In 1190 massacres of Jews occured in many cities, most notably in York. This medieval settlement was ended by Edward I's expulsion of the Jews in 1290, after which date, with rare and temporary exceptions, only converts to Christianity or secret adherents of Judaism could live in the country.

After the expulsion of the Jews from Spain in 1492 a secret Converso community became established in London, but the present Anglo-Jewish community dates in practice from the period of the Commonwealth. In 1650 Menasseh ben Israel, of Amsterdam, began to champion the cause of Jewish readmission to England, and in 1655 he led a mission to London for this purpose. A conference was convened at Whitehall and a petition was presented to Oliver Cromwell. Though no formal decision was then recorded, in 1656 the Spanish and Portuguese Congregation in London was organised. It was followed towards the end of the seventeenth century by the establishment of an Ashkenazi community, which increased rapidly inside London as well as throwing out offshoots before long to a number of provincial centres and seaports. The London community, howeve, has always comprised the largest section of Anglo-Jewry.

Although Jews in Britain had achieved a virtual economic and social emancipation by the early nineteenth centur, they had not yet gained 'political emancipation'. Minor Jewish disabilities were progressively removed and Jews were admitted to municipal rights and began to win distinction in the professions.

During the nineteenth century British Jews diversified from those callings which had hitherto been regarded as characteristic of the Jews.

There has always been a steady stream of immigration into Britain from Jewish communities in Europe, originally from the Iberian Peninsula and northern Italy, later from western and central Europe. The community was radically transformed by the large influx of refugees which occured between 1881 and 1914, the result of the intensified persecution of Jews in the Russian Empire. The Jewish population rose from about 25,000 in the middle of the nineteenth century to nearly 350,000 by 1914. It also became far more dispersed geographically.

From 1933 a new emigration of Jews commenced, this time from Nazi persecution, and again many settled in this country. Since the end of the Second World War and notably since 1956, smaller numbers of refugees have come from Iran, Arab countries and eastern Europe.

Counties are currently being restructured into Counties and Unitary Authorities. The new designations are not yet in common use and for this year the 'old' County names and areas have been retained.

GMT +0 hours	**Total Population 58,500,000**
Country calling code (44)	**Jewish Population 280,000**
Emergency Telephone (Police – 999) (Fire – 999) (Ambulance – 999)	**(Electricity voltage – 240)**

ENGLAND

AVON

Bristol

Bristol was one of the principal Jewish centres of medieval England. Even after the Expulsion from England in 1290 there were occasional Jewish residents or visitors. A community of Conversos lived here during the Tudor period. The next Jewish settlement in Bristol was around 1754 and its original synagogue opened in 1786. The present building dates from 1871 and incorporates fittings from the earlier building.

DELICATESSEN
British Hebrew Congregation

(117) 970-6938

Open alternate Sundays at 10 am.

ORGANISATIONS
Hillel House
45 Oakfield Road, Clifton BS8 2BA   (117) 946-6589

RESTAURANTS
Vegetarian
Cherries
122 St Michaels Hill, BS2 8BU   (117) 929-3675

Millwards Vegetarian Restaurant
40 Alfred Place, Kingsdown BS2 8HD (117) 924-5026

SYNAGOGUES
Bristol Hebrew Congregation
9 Park Row BS1 5LP   (117) 927-3334
Email: simon770@aol.com
Services: Friday night at 183 Bishop Road BS7
Summer 7.45 pm, Winter 7 pm. Saturday at
synagogue 9.45 am

Progressive
Bristol & West Progressive Jewish Congregation
43 Bannerman Road, Easton BS5 0RR   (117) 954-1937
Email: webmaster@bwpjc.org
Web site: www.bwpjc.org
Secretary: 973-8744

BEDFORDSHIRE

Luton

SYNAGOGUES
PO Box 215 LU1 1HW   (1582) 25032
Fri night and Sabbath morning. services. Office open
9.30am to 12.30pm on Sundays.

BERKSHIRE

Maidenhead

SYNAGOGUES
Reform
Synagogue
Grenfell Lodge, Ray Park Road SL6 8QX
(1628) 673012

Fax: (1628) 625536
Email: mheadsyn@aol.com
Services: Friday 8.30pm; Saturday 10.30am

Reading

SYNAGOGUES
Orthodox
Goldsmid Road RG1 7YB   (118) 9571018
Email: secretary@rhc.org.uk
Web site: www.rhc.org.uk

Progressive
Thames Valley Progressive Jewish Community
6 Church Street   (118) 781971

BUCKINGHAMSHIRE

Milton Keynes

BUTCHERS
Gilbert's Kosher Foods
Kestrel House, Mount Avenue MK1 1LJ
(1908) 646-787
Fax: (1908) 646-788
Supervision: London Board of Shechita

CAMBRIDGESHIRE

Cambridge

COMMUNITY ORGANISATIONS
Cambridge University Jewish Society
33 Thompson's Lane CB5 8AQ   (1223) 354783
Email: soc-cujs@lists.cam.ac.uk
Web site: www.cam.ac.uk/societies.cujs
The Cambridge University CULanu Centre
33 Bridge Street CB2 1UW   (1223) 366338
Fax: (1223) 366338
Email: sae23@cam.ac.uk
The CULanu Centre organises, with the Cambridge
University Jewish Society a programme of education
events, debates and socials. There are regular Friday
night meals.

GROCERIES
(1223) 352145
There is a kosher canteen during term time serving
lunch most weekdays and Friday night and Shabbat
meals.

KOSHER FOOD
Derby Stores
Derby Street   (1223) 354391
Stocks a range of kosher food and wine; fresh bread
products each Thursday lunchtime. Can purchase
goods to order.

SYNAGOGUES
Orthodox
Cambridge Synagogue
Syn/Student Centre, 3 Thompsons Lane
CB5 8AQ   (1223) 354783 or 368346 answer phone
Email: ctjcorguk@aol.com
Web site: www.ctjc.org.uk
Daily morning and evening service during term time.
Friday evening and Saturday morning during
vacations, other services by arrangement.

Reform
Beth Shalom Reform Synagogue
(1223) 365614

CUMBRIA

Grasmere

HOTELS
Vegetarian
Lancrigg Vegetarian Country House Hotel
Easedale LA22 9QN   (1539) 435317

DEVON

Exeter

In pre-Expulsion times, Exeter was an important Jewish centre. Jews were first mentioned in 1181, After the resettlement a community was again established in 1728.

SYNAGOGUES
Hebrew Congregation
Synagogue Place, Mary Arches Street EX4 3BA
                                    (1392) 251529
                        Fax: (1392) 01363-772338
                Email: fjg@exetersynagogue.org.uk
        Web site: www.exetersynagogue.org.uk
The synagogue was built in 1763, and the cemetery in Magdalen Road dates from 1757. The synagogue, a Grade II* listed building, has just had a major refurbishment.

Plymouth

The congregation was founded in 1752 and a synagogue erected ten years later. This is now the oldest Ashkenazi synagogue building in England still used for its original purpose. It is a scheduled historical monument. In 1815 Plymouth was one of the most important provincial centres of Anglo-Jewry.

LIBRARIES
Holcenberg Collection
Plymouth Central Library, Drake Circus PL4 8AL
                                    (1752) 305907/8
                        Fax: (1752) 305905
                Email: ref@plymouth.gov.uk
        Web site: www.plymouthlibraries.info
A Jewish collection of fiction and non-fiction books, mainly lending copies.

RESTAURANTS
Vegetarian
Plymouth Arts Centre Vegetarian Restaurant
38 Looe Street PL4 0EB   (1752) 202-616
Hours: lunch, Monday to Saturday, 12 pm to 2 pm; dinner, Tuesday to Saturday, 5 pm to 8 or 8.30 pm.

SYNAGOGUES
Orthodox
Plymouth Hebrew Congregation
Catherine Street PL1 2AD   (1752) 301955
                Email: info@plymouthsynagogue.co.uk
Services: Fri., 6pm; Sat., 9:30am. The congregation offers free use of minister's modern flat as holiday accommodation in return for conducting Orthodox Friday evening and Saturday morning services.

Torquay

SYNAGOGUES
Old Town Hall, Abbey Road TQ1 1BB (1803) 607197
Covering also Brixham and Paignton. Services first Sabbath of every month and festivals, 10.30am.

DORSET

Bournemouth

The Bournemouth Hebrew Congregation was established in 1905, when the Jewish population numbered fewer than 20 families. Today, the town's permanent Jewish residents number 3,500 out of a total population of some 15,000. During the holiday season, however, there are many more Jews in Bournemouth, for it is an extremely popular resort, with kosher hotels, guest houses and other holiday accommodation.

COMMUNITY ORGANISATIONS
Bournemouth Jewish Representative Council
                                    (1202) 762101

DELICATESSEN
Louise's Butchers & Deli
164 Old Christchurch Road BH1 1NU
                                    (1202) 295-979
                        Fax: (1202) 295-979

HOTELS
Kosher
New Ambassador Hotel
Meyrick Road, East Cliff BH1 3DP   (1202) 555-453
                        Fax: (1202) 311-077
                Email: sales@newamb.co.uk
                Web site: www.newamb.com
Supervision: London Beth Din
112 rooms, all with bathroom en suite.

Normandie Hotel
Manor Road, East Cliff BH1 3HL   (1202) 552-246
                        Fax: (1202) 291-178
                Email: thenormandiehotel@aol.co.uk
Supervision: Kedassia
71 rooms.

MIKVAOT
Bournemouth Hebrew Congregation
Synagogue Chambers, Wootton Gardens
BHI IPW   (1202) 557-443

SYNAGOGUES
Orthodox
Synagogue Chambers, Wootton Gardens BHI IPW
                    (1202) 557-433
                    Fax: (1202) 557-578
                    Email: bhc.1@virgin.net

Reform
Bournemouth Reform Synagogue
53 Christchurch Road BHI 3PN   (1202) 557736

Colchester

SYNAGOGUES
Independent
**Colchester and District Jewish Community
Synagogue**
Fennings Chase, Priory Street COI 2QG
                    (1206) 545-992
                    Email: tanenb@essex.ac.uk
Services every Friday at 8pm, on the High Holydays
and most festivals.

Harlow

SYNAGOGUES
Reform
Harlow Jewish Community
Harberts Road CM20 4DT   (1279) 432503

Chigwell

SYNAGOGUES
Orthodox
Limes Avenue, Limes Farm Estate IG7 5NT
                    (208) 8500-2451

Loughton

SYNAGOGUES
Orthodox
Loughton Synagogue
Borders Lane IG10 1TE   (020) 8508-0303
          Email: loughtonsynagogue@line-one.net
Friday evening. 7.00pm; Saturday morning 9.00am

Redbridge

BAKERIES
Golan Bakery
388 Cranbrook Road, Ilford   (020) 8554-8202
Supervision: London Beth Din

BUTCHERS
N. Goldberg
12 Claybury Broadway, Redbridge IG
                                  (020) 8551-2828
Supervision: London Board of Shechita

DELICATESSEN
Deli on the Lane
13 Beehive Lane, Redbridge   (202) 8554-5008
Supervision: Beth Din of the Federation of
Synagogues

GROCERIES
Brownstein's
24a Woodford Avenue, Gants Hill   (020) 8550-3900
            Email: deli@brownsteins.co.uk
          Web site: www.brownsteins.co.uk
Supervision: London Beth Din

MIKVAOT
Ilford Mikvah Federation of Synagogues
463 Cranbrook Road, Ilford IG
          (020) 8554-2551 (Evenings: 8554-8532).
Correspondence to 367 Cranbrook Road, Ilford.

Southend-on-Sea

BOOKSELLERS
Dorothy Young
21 Colchester Road SS2 6HW   (1702) 331218
           Email: dorothy@dorothyyoung.co.uk
          Web site: www.dorothyyoung.co.uk
Religious articles, Israeli giftware, etc., also stocked.
Jewish software ordered. Call for appointment.

COMMUNITY ORGANISATIONS
Southend & District Representative Council
                                  (1702) 343192

HOTELS
Redstone's Hotel
Pembury Road, Westcliff SS0 8DS   (1702) 348-441
Supervision: Unsupervised

SYNAGOGUES
Southend and Westcliff Hebrew Congregation
Finchley Road SS0 8AD   (1702) 344900
                             Fax: (1702) 391131
                         Email: swhc@btclick.com
                       Web site: www.swhc.org.uk
Southend Reform Synagogue
851 London Road, Westcliff SS0   (1702) 75809

GLOUCESTERSHIRE

Cheltenham

The congregation was established in 1824 and the
present synagogue opened in 1839. However,
after two generations, the congregation declined
and the synagogue was closed in 1903. At the
outbreak of the Second World War, the synagogue
was re-opened following the influx of Jewish
newcomers to the town.

RESTAURANTS
Vegetarian
The Orange Tree
317 High Street GL50 3HW   (1242) 234232
                             Fax: (1242) 234232
          Email: shaipateluk@yahoo.co.uk
Strictly vegan & vegetarian cuisine. Fully licensed with
selection of organic wines & beers.

SYNAGOGUES
Cheltenham Hebrew Congregation
St James Square GL50 5PU   (1242) 578893
                             Fax: (1242) 578893
Services every Friday at 7.00pm and High Holydays as
advised.

HAMPSHIRE

Portsmouth & Southsea

The Portsmouth community was founded in
1746. Its first synagogue was in Oyster Row, but
the congregation moved to a building in Whiteís
Row which it continued to occupy for almost two
centuries. A new building was erected in 1936.
The cemetery is in a street which was once
known as Jews Lane.

SYNAGOGUES

Synagogue Chambers
The Thicket, Southsea PO5 2AA   (23) 9282 1494

Southampton

LIBRARIES

Hartley Library
University of Southampton SO17 1BJ   (23) 592721
Fax: (23) 593007
Email: archives@soton.ac.uk
Houses both the Parkes Library and the Anglo-Jewish Archives.

SYNAGOGUES

Moordaunt Road, The Inner Avenue SO2 0GP
Services Sat. morn 10am

HERTFORDSHIRE

Bushey

BUTCHERS

J.D Glass & Co
100 High Road, Bushey Heath, Bushey
WD2 3JE   (20) 8420-4443
Supervision: London Board of Shechita

SYNAGOGUES

Orthodox
Bushey and District
177 Sparrows Herne WD23 1AJ   (20) 8950-7340
Fax: (20) 8421-8267
Email: administrator@busheyus.org

Hemel Hempstead

SYNAGOGUES

Morton House
Midland Road HD1 1RP   (1923) 232007

St Albans

SYNAGOGUES

Masorti
St Albans Masorti Synagogue
PO Box 23 AL1 4PH   (1727) 860642
Email: sams@masorti.org.uk
Orthodox
Oswald Road AL1 3AQ   (1727) 825925

Watford

SYNAGOGUES

Orthodox
16 Nascot Road WD17 3RE   (1923) 222755
Covers also Abbots Langley Carpenters Park, Croxley Garden, Garston, Kings Langley and Rickmansworth.

Welwyn Garden City

SYNAGOGUES

Orthodox
Barn Close, Handside Lane AL8 6ST   (1707) 890575
Email: floradora@hotmail.com

HUMBERSIDE

Grimsby

SYNAGOGUES

Sir Moses Montefiore Synagogue
Heneage Road DN32 9DZ   (1472) 351-404
Services every Friday 7:00pm and all major festivals.

Hull

In Hull, as in other English port towns, a Jewish community was formed earlier than in inland areas. The exact date is unknown, but it is thought to be the early 1700s. There were enough Jews in Hull to buy a former Roman Catholic chapel, damaged in the Gordon Riots of 1780, and turn it into a synagogue. Hull was then the principal port of entry from northern Europe, and most Jewish immigrants came through it. Both the Old Hebrew Synagogue in Osborne Street and the Central Synagogue in Cogan Street were destroyed in air raids during the Second World War.

MUSEUM

Hull Synagogue Museum
Linnaeus Street HU3 2PD   (1482) 217153
Fax: (1482) 216565
Email: jcsc@exobus.org
Correspondence to: Old Synagogue, Linnaeus Street, HU3 2PD.

SYNAGOGUES

Orthodox
Hull Hebrew Congregation
30 Pryme Street, Anlaby HU10 6SH   (1482) 653242
Reform
Reform Synagogue
Great Gutter Lane, West Willerby HU10 7JT
(1482) 658312
Fax: (1482) 342836
Email: iansugarman@isa.karoo.co.uk

KENT

Canterbury

TOURIST SITE
The Old Synagogue
King Street CT
The Old Synagogue, an Egyptian-style building of
1847, stands in King Street and is now used by the
Kings School for recitals.

Margate

SYNAGOGUES
Godwin Road, Cliftonville CT9 2HA   (1843) 223219

Ramsgate

SYNAGOGUES
Montefiore Endowment
Hereson Road

Montefiore Mausoleum & Synagogue
33 Luton Avenue, Broadstairs   (1843) 862507

Rochester

SYNAGOGUES
Magnus Memorial Synagogue
366 High Street ME1 1DJ   (1634) 847665
Grade 2, listed building known as The Chatham
Memorial Synagogue.

LANCASHIRE

Blackpool

DELICATESSEN
The Deli
6 Station Road, Lytham St Annes   (1253) 735861

SYNAGOGUES
Orthodox
United Hebrew Congregation
Synagogue Chambers, Leamington Road FY1 4HD
                                    (1253) 28164

Reform
Reform Jewish Congregation
40 Raikes Parade FY1 4EX   (1253) 623-687

Lancaster

BED AND BREAKFAST
Lancaster University Jewish Society
Interfaith Chaplaincy Centre, University of Lancaster,
Bailrigg Lane LA1 4YW   (1524) 594075
Jewish rooms and kosher kitchen. Contact Rev
Malcolm Wiseman.

St Annes On Sea

SYNAGOGUES
Orthodox
Orchard Road FY8 1PJ   (1253) 721831
Services 7.30am and 8pm

LEICESTERSHIRE

Leicester

There has been a Jewish presence here since the
Middle Ages, but the first record of a ëJewsí
Synagogueí dates from 1861 in the Leicester
Directory. In 2001 the Leicester City Council
finally renounced a ban on Jews living in the city
which was originally imposed in 1731.

LIBRARIES
Jewish Library and Bookshop
Community Hall, Highfield Street LE2 0NQ
                                    (116) 212-8920

MIKVAOT
Synagogue Building, Highfield Street LE2 0NQ
                                    (116) 270-6622
                               Fax: (116) 270-8796
        Email: stanley.lidiker@btopenworld.com

RESTAURANTS
Vegetarian
The Good Earth
19 Free Lane LE1 1JX   (116) 262-6260

SYNAGOGUES
Progressive Jewish Congregation
24 Avenue Road LE   (116) 271-5584
                               Fax: (116) 271-7571
          Email: jeffrey@kaufmans.co.uk

Orthodox
Synagogue
Highfield Street LE2 0NQ   (116) 254-0477
Mikva on premises.

LINCOLNSHIRE

Lincoln

Lincoln was one of the centres of medieval Jewry. One of England's oldest stone houses in the city is known as Aaron the Jew's House. The site of Old synagogue is remembered now at Jews' Court. In the cathedral is a recent token of ecclesiastical apology for the thirteenth-century incident of the "blood libel", retold in Chaucer. Jews returned to the area in the nineteenth century. The current community is of very recent date.

COMMUNITY ORGANISATIONS

Lincolnshire Jewish Community
3 West End Road, Ulceby   (1469) 588951

TOURIST SITE

Aaron the Jew's house
47 Steep Hill
Believed to be the home of Aaron of Lincoln (c1123-1186) the most prominent Anglo-Jewish financier of the time. A Grade I listed building.

Jew's Court
2 Steep Hill
Site of the pre-expulsion synagogue. A Grade I listed building.

LONDON (GREATER)

London

Jews came to London with the Normans following their conquest of the country in 1066. A Jewish area in London is first mentioned in 1128 it was known as 'the Jewish quarter' and was situated around Old Jewry, a street in the City of London close to the Bank of England. Nearby to the west is the church of St Lawrence Jewry and about one mile to the east is Jewry Street. The community expanded and until 1177 had the only Jewish cemetery in the country. Although there is now no evidence of early Jewish life, the remains of a mikveh were found in October 2001 in Milk Street, close to Old Jewry. It is one of the earliest pieces of physical evidence of Jews in Europe and is the only identifiable structure that has survived from the then Jewish community. It is intended that it be dismantled and moved to the Bevis Marks synagogue.

The community flourished as arrivals including a number of scholars came into the country. In 1194 it contributed a large sum towards the levy raised to ransom Richard I.

In due course, anti-Jewish feeling developed and Jews were expelled from the whole country in 1290. At that time the population was estimated to be around 500.

Until the resettlement the only Jews in London, apart from converts to Christianity who lived in the Domus Conversorum, a home established for that purpose in New Street, now Chancery Lane, were rare occasional visitors. After the expulsion from Spain in 1492, however, services were held in the city in secret by groups of crypto-Jews.

In December 1656, with resettlement, the approximately 20 families then living in the country established a synagogue in Creechurch Lane (a plaque now commemorates this just under one mile east of the original settlement), and in the following year a cemetery was acquired.

Following the accession of William of Orange to the throne, the number of Spanish and Portuguese Jews arriving from Holland increased. Included among these were merchants and brokers. As a result, in 1697 'Jew Brokers' were allowed to trade on the Royal Exchange. In due course, Ashkenazi settlers arrived, establishing their own community in 1690.

During the 19th century both communities expanded. In 1835 David Salomons (1797-1873) was elected a sheriff of the city. In 1847 he became the first Jewish alderman and in 1855 the first Jewish lord mayor of the City of London. In 1851 he had been elected a member of parliament but was unable to take his seat as he refused to take the oath of allegiance 'on the true faith of a Christian'. After the oath was amended in 1858, he sat as a member from 1859 until his death. The first Jew to take his seat, however, was Lionel de Rothschild, some months earlier in 1858.

From the 1880's until controls on immigration were established by the 1905 Aliens Act, around 100,000, generally poor, Jews arrived from Russia, Poland and other eastern European countries both to avoid pogroms and as 'economic migrants'.

A Reform community was established in 1840. Jews College (now London School of Jewish Studies) was established in 1855 and the Board of Guardians for the Relief of the Jewish Poor in 1859.

Jewish London is split into a number of areas. Central, the East End and the city, the traditional home of immigrants into England; North London, which contains Stamford Hill, the most Orthodox area; and the North-West where the majority of London Jews now live. The remaining parts of London, the South and the

East, have communities but offer little interest to a visitor.

Central London
The Hebrew section of the British Library, situated in Euston, has a large collection of interest to all Jewish visitors to the city. There is a Holocaust Memorial Garden in Hyde Park in the centre of London.

The East End and the City.
There is little remaining of Jewish life apart from the historical Jewish sites. Of particular interest is Bevis Marks Synagogue, which was built in 1701 and is almost a duplicate of the Spanish and Portuguese Great Synagogue in Amsterdam. It is the oldest synagogue in the country (some of the oak benches come from the original synagogue in Creechurch Lane). It is still almost exactly the same now as it was 300 years ago, even being lit by candles. Also worth a visit is the Spitalfields Heritage Centre, devoted to the history of immigration into the country. It is on the site of Princelet Street synagogue, which itself was originally a Huguenot family house.

North London
Stamford Hill is the centre of London Jewish hassidic life. It is full of shteibels and small Jewish shops. Also in Stamford Hill is the Jewish Military Museum. Nearby in Camden Town is the Ben Uri Art Gallery and the Jewish Museum dealing with Jews in Britain and throughout the world. The Jewish Museum further north in Finchley covers the social history of London Jewry itself. It is in the grounds of the Sternberg Centre for Judaism, which also includes Leo Baeck College.

North-West
Apart from two restaurants in the West End of London this is the place to go if one wishes to eat kosher. The area around Golders Green and Edgware abounds in restaurants of varying cuisine and quality. There is also an abundance of Jewish shops of many kinds.

South London
Visitors to London should endeavour to go to the Holocaust Exhibition at the Imperial War Museum in Lambeth. In addition to the exhibition itself, the Imperial War Museum has much of interest
    Currently, around three-quarters of the approximate 300,000 Jews living in Britain live in London.

BAKERIES
Carmelli Bakeries Ltd
126-128 Golders Green Road, Golders Green
NW11   (020) 8455-2074
                           Fax: (020) 8455-2789
Supervision: London Beth Din and Kedassia

Crème de la Crème
5 Temple Fortune Parade, Bridge Lane
NW11 1QN   (020) 8458-9090
Supervision: Kedassia

Daniel's Bagel Bakery
12-13 Hallswelle Parade, Finchley Road, Golders
Green NW11 0DL   (020) 8455-5826
                           Fax: (020) 8455-5826
Supervision: London Beth Din

David Bagel Bakery
38 Vivian Avenue, Hendon NW4 3XP
                                  (020) 8203-9995
Supervision: London Beth Din & Kedassia

Dinos Bakeries
11 Edgwarebury Lane, Edgware HA8 8LH
                                  (020) 8958-1554
                           Fax: (020) 8958-2554
Supervision: London Beth Din & Kedassia
106 Brent Street, Hendon NW4 2HH
                                  (020) 8203-6623
Supervision: London Beth Din and Kedassia

Grodzinski
9 Northways Parade NW3   (020) 8722-4944
Supervision: London Beth Din

Hendon Bagel Bakery
55-57 Church Road, Hendon NW4 (020) 8203-6919
                           Fax: (020) 8203-8843
Supervision: Kedassia

M & D Grodzinski
223 Golders Green Road, Golders Green NW119ES
                                  (020) 8458-3654
                           Fax: (020) 8905-5382
Supervision: Kedassia & London Beth Din

Parkway Patisserie Ltd.
30a North End Road, Golders Green NW11
                                  (020) 8455-5026
Supervision: London Beth Din and Kedassia

204 Preston Road, Wembley HA9   (020) 8904-7736
Supervision: London Beth Din and Kedassia

Parkway Patisseries Ltd.
326-328 Regents Park Road, Finchley N3
                                  (020) 8346-0344
Supervision: London Beth Din and Kedassia

The Cake Company
2 Sentinel Square, Hendon NW4 2EL
                                  (020) 8202-2327
                           Fax: (020) 202-8058
                  Email: cakes@thecakecompany.co.uk
               Web site: www.thecakecompany.co.uk
Supervision: London Beth Din & Kedassia

Woodberry Down Bakery
47 Brent Street, Hendon NW4   (020) 8202-9962
Supervision: London Beth Din & Kedassia

BED AND BREAKFAST

Harold Godfrey Hillel House
25 Louisa Street, Stepney E1 4NF   (020) 7790-9557
Summer accommodation in London. Twenty-three rooms, self-catering separate meat and milk kitchens. Very close to Stepney Green tube station with easy access to all London attractions. Please contact the warden at the above address for more information or to book a room.

Kacenberg's Guest House
1 Alba Gardens, Near Alba Court, Golders Green
NW11 9NS   (020) 8455-3780
Fax: (020) 8381-4250
Shabbat meals available. "Strictly Orthodox".

BOOKSELLERS

Boreham Wood Judaice
11 Croxdale Road, Boreham Wood WD6 4QD
(020) 8381-5559

Jewish Memorial Council and Bookshop
25 Enford Street W1H 2DD   (020) 7724-7778
Fax: (020) 7706-1710
Email: jmcbookshop@btinternet.com
Web site: www.jmcouncil.org

Steimatzky Hasifria
46 Golders Green Road NW11 8LL (020) 8458-9774
Fax: (020) 8458-3449
Email: hasifria@hotmail.com
Web site: www.hasifria.com

Torah Treasures
4 Sentinel Square, Brent Street, Hendon
NW4 2EL   (020) 8202-3134
Fax: (020) 8202-3161
Email: torahtreasures@btinternet.com
Seforim, Judaica and gifts.

BOOKSELLERS AND JUDAICA

Carmel Gifts
62 Edgware Way, Middx   (020) 8958-7632
Fax: (020) 8958-6226
Email: info@carmelgifts.co.uk
Web site: www.carmelgifts.co.uk

Hebrew Book and Gift Centre
24 Amhurst Parade, Amhurst Park N16 5AA
(020) 8802-0609
Fax: (020) 8802-0609

J. Aisenthal
11 Ashbourne Parade, Finchley Road, Temple Fortune
NW11 0AD   (020) 8455-0501
Email: infor@aisenthal.co .uk
Web site: www.aisenthal.co.uk

Jerusalem the Golden
146a Golders Green Road, Golders Green
NW11 8HE   (020) 8455-4960
Fax: (020) 8203-7808

Menorah Book and Gift Centre
16 Russell Parade, Golders Green Road
NW11 9NN   (020) 8458-8289
Fax: (020) 8731-8403

BUTCHERS

A. Perlmutter & Son
1-2 Onslow Parade, Hampden Square, Southgate
N14 5JN   (020) 8361-5441/2
Fax: (020) 8361-5442
Supervision: London Board of Shechita

Frohwein's
1095 Finchley Road, Temple Fortune NW11
(020) 8455-9848
Supervision: Kedassia
Deli and cooked food available for weekends and Shabbat.

Golders Green Kosher
132 Golders Green Road, Golders Green
NW11 8HB   (020) 8381-4450
Fax: (020) 8731-6450

Greenspans
9-11 Lyttelton Road N2 0DW   (020) 8455-9921
Fax: (020) 8455-3484
Supervision: London Board of Shechita

Jack Schlagman
112 Regents Park Road, Finchley N3 (020) 8346-3598
Supervision: London Board of Shechita

La Boucherie
4 Cat Hill, East Barnet EN4 8JB   (020) 8449-9215
Fax: (020) 8441-1848
Supervision: London Board of Shechita

Louis Mann
23 Edgwarebury Lane, Edgware HA8
(020) 8958-3789
Supervision: London Board of Shechita

M. Lipowicz
9 Royal Parade, Ealing W5 (020) 8997-1722
Fax: (020) 8997-0048
Supervision: London Board of Shechita

Menachem's
15 Russell Parade, Golders Green Road, Golders
Green NW11 (020) 8201-8629
Fax: (020) 8201-8629
Supervision: London Board of Shechita

R. Wolff
84 Edgware Way, Edgware HA8 8JS (020) 8958-8454
Supervision: London Board of Shechita

BUTCHERS & DELICATESSENS

Mehadrin Meats
19 Russell Parade, Golders Green NW11 9NN
(020) 8455-9992
Fax: (020) 8455-3777/8599 0984
Supervision: Kedassia

25 Belfast Road, Stamford Hill N16 (020) 8806-0000
Fax: (020) 8880-0500
Supervision: Kedassia

COMMUNITY ORGANISATIONS

Board of Deputies of British Jews
6 Bloomsbury Square WC1A 2LP (020) 7534-5400
Fax: (020) 7534-0010
Email: info @bod.org.uk
Web site: www.bod.org.uk

The Sephardi Centre
2 Ashworth Road, Maida Vale W9 1JY
(020) 7266-3682
Fax: (020) 7289 5957
Email: sephardicentre@easynet.co.uk

CONTACT INFORMATION

Jewish Community Information (JCI)
6 Bloomsbury Square WC1A 2LP (020) 7543-5421
Fax: (020) 7543-0100
Email: jci@bod.org.uk
The basic information service for all aspects of the
Jewish Community in Britain. Available Monday to
Friday throughout the year, 10.00am to 4.30pm
(1.30pm on Fridays) excluding Public and Jewish
Holidays.

The International Jewish Vegetarianism Society
Bet Teva, 855 Finchley Road NW11 8LX
(020) 8455-0692
Fax: (020) 8455-1465
Email: ijvs@yahoo.com
The International Jewish Vegetarian Society was
formed 35 years ago to promote vegetarianism from
a Jewish perspective.

DELICATESSEN

Kosher King
293 Hale Lane, Edgware HA8 7AX   (020) 8281-1656
Supervision: London Beth Din

Munch Box
41 Greville Street EC1   (020) 7242-5487
Supervision: London Beth Din

EMBASSY

Consul General of Israel
15a Old Court Place, Kensington W8 4QB
(020) 7957-9500
Fax: (020) 957-9577
Web site: www.israel-embassy.org.uk/london
Nearest tube station: High Street Kensington.
Consular office hours: Monday to Thursday, 10 am to
1 pm; Friday, 10 am to 12 pm. Postal address:
Consulate Section, Embassy of Israel, 2 Palace Green,
London W8 4QB.

Embassy of Israel
2 Palace Green, Kensington W8 4QB
(020) 7957-9500
Fax: (020) 7957-9555
Email: info-assist@london.mfa.gov.il
Web site: www.israel-embassy.org.uk/london/

FISHMONGERS

Leveyuson
47a Brent Street, Hendon NW4   (020) 8202-7834
Supervision: London Beth Din

Sam Stoller
28 Temple Fortune Parade, Finchley Road, Golders
Green NW11 0QS   (020) 8455-1957; 8458-1429
Fax: (020) 8445-1957
Supervision: Sephardi Kashrut Authority

GROCERIES

B Kosher
91 Bell Lane, Hendon NW4   (020) 8202-1711
Opposite Vincent Court.

Carmel Fruit Shop
40 Vivian Avenue, Hendon NW4   (020) 8202-9587
Fresh fruit and vegetables as well as a good supply of
kosher products, cakes and biscuits.

Great Foods
5 Canons Corner HA8 8AE   (020) 8958-9446
                                  Fax: (020) 8905-4700
                        Email: stephen@mrbutler.biz
                        Web site: www.mrbutler.biz
Supervision: London Beth Din

Kosher Corner
42, St. George's Rd, Wimbledon SW19 4ED
                                  (020) 8944-1581
                        Email: Lubwdon@aol.com

Kosher King
223 Golders Green Road, Golders Green
NW11 9ES   (020) 8455-1429
                                  Fax: (020) 8201-8924
                Email: kosherking@compuserve.com
Supervision: London Beth Din

Kosher Paradise
10 Ashbourne Parade, Finchley Road,
Temple Fortune NW11 0AD   (020) 8455-2454
                                  Fax: (020) 8731-6919

Maxine's
20 Russell Parade, Golders Green Road, Golders
Green NW11   (020) 8458-3102
                                  Fax: (020) 8455-3632
Kedassia Deli. Deliveries.

Pelter Stores
82 Edgware Way, Edgware HA8   (020) 8958-6910
Supervision: Beth Din of the Federation of
Synagogues

Yarden
123 Golders Green Road, Golders Green
NW11   (020) 8458-0979
Free delivery on orders over £25. Hours: Sunday,
Wednesday, Thursday, 8 am to 10 pm; Monday,
Tuesday, 8 am to 9 pm; Friday, 8 am.

GUEST HOUSE

Sharon Guest House
7 Woodlands Close, Golders Green (020) 8458-8531
                        Email: jlazenga@aol.com
Although not officially supervised it is said to be
Shomer Shabbat Dati.

HOTELS

Central Hotel
35 Hoop Lane, Golders Green NW11 8BS
                                  (020) 8458-5636
                                  Fax: (020) 8455-4792
Private bathrooms and parking.

Croft Court Hotel
44 Ravenscroft Avenue, Golders Green
NW11 8AY   (020) 8458-3331
                                  Fax: (020) 8455-9175

King Solomon Palace Hotel
155-159 Golders Green Road NW11 9BX
(020) 8201-9000
Fax: (020) 8201-9853
Kosher
Kadimah Hotel
146 Clapton Common, Stamford Hill E5 9AG
(020) 8800-5960
Fax: (020) 8800-6237
Supervision: Kedassia

KASHRUT INFORMATION
Federation of Synagogues Kashrus Board - KF
65 Watford Way, Hendon NW4 3AQ
(020) 8202-2263
Fax: (020) 8203-0610
Email: info@kfkosher.org
Web site: www.kfkosher.org

Joint Kashrus Committee-Kedassia (Union of Orthodox Hebrew Congregations)
140 Stamford Hill, Stamford Hill N16 6QT
(020) 8800 6833
Fax: (020) 8809-7092

London Beth Din
735 High Road, Finchley N12 0US
(020) 8343-6255 (Kashrut hotline: 8343-6333)
Fax: (020) 8343-6254
Email: info@kosher.org.uk
Web site: www.kosher.org.uk
Publishes 'The Really Jewish Food Guide', which contains a list of all the establishments it certifies as well as guidance for the shopper in buying general consumer products.

National Council of Shechita Boards
Elscot House, Arcadia Avenue, Finchley N3 2JU
(020) 8349-9160
Fax: (020) 8346-2209
Email: shechita@tiscali.co.uk

Sephardi Kashrut Authority
2 Ashworth Road, Maida Vale W9 1JY
(020) 7289-2573
Fax: (020) 7289-7663
Email: dvsteinhof@onetel.net.uk

LIBRARIES
British Library, Asia, Pacific and Africa Collections - Hebrew Section
96 Euston Road NW1 2DB
(020) 7412-7646
Fax: (020) 7412-7641/7870
Email: ilana.tahan@bl.uk
Web site: www.bl.uk/collections/hebrew.html
The Hebrew section contains over 70,000 printed books, 3,000 manuscripts and some 10,000 Genizah fragments. Oriental reading room open to holders of readers' passes: Monday 10.00am-5.00pm; Tuesday-Saturday 9.30am-5.00pm. Hebrew manuscripts on permanent display. The Golden Haggadah is included in the electronic "Turning the Pages" programme.

Institute of Contemporary History and Wiener Library
4 Devonshire Street W1W 5BH
(020) 7636-7247
Fax: (020) 7436-6428
Email: info@wienerlibrary.co.uk
Web site: www.wienerlibrary.co.uk
The world's oldest institution dedicated to the documentation of Nazi Germay and the Holocaust. The collection includes 60,000 books and pamphlets, periodicals, documents, videos and photographs as well as extensive press cuttings from 1933 onwards. Other subjects include twentieth-century Jewish history, anti-semitism, refugees, minorities, fascism, citizenship, etc.

The Jewish Studies Library
University College London Library, Gower Street WC1E 6BT
(020) 7679-2598
Fax: (020) 7679-7373
Email: library@ucl.ac.uk
In addition to materials purchased for the College's Department of Hebrew Studies it incorporates the Mocatta Library, Altmann Library, William Margulies Yiddish Library and the Library of the Jewish Historical Society of England. Applications to use or view the collections should be made in advance in writing to the Librarian.

MEDIA
Directory
Jewish Year Book
Vallentine Mitchell, Crown House, 47 Chase Side, Southgate N14 5BP
(020) 8920-2100
Fax: (020) 8447-8548
Email: jyb@vmbooks.com
Annual directory of all information relating to the British Jewish Community.

Internet
Brijnet
11 The Lindens, Prospect Hill, Waltham Forest E17 3EJ
(020) 8520-3531
Email: info@brijnet.org
Web site: www.brijnet.org

Listings
The Diary
32 Bell Lane NW4 2AD
(020) 8922-5437
Fax: (020) 8922-8709

Newspapers
Essex Jewish News
Crown House, 47 Chase Side, Southgate N14 5BP
(020) 8920-2100
Fax: (020) 8447-8548
Quarterly publication serving East London and Essex.

Hamodia
149 Kyverdale Road N16 6PS
(020) 8806 7577
Fax: (020) 8806 1222
Email: Post@Hamodia.demon.co.uk

Jewish Chronicle
25 Furnival Street EC4A 1JT
(020) 7415-1500
Fax: (020) 7405-9040
Email: editorial@thejc.com
Established 1841. Weekly publication.

London Jewish News
28 St Albans Lane, Golders Green
NW11 7QE　　　　　　(020) 8731-8031
　　　　　　　　Fax: (020) 8381-4033

Mikvaot

Adath Yisroel Synagogue Mikvah
40a Queen Elizabeth's Walk, cnr. 28 Gazebrook Rd.,,
Stamford Hill N16 0HH　　　(020) 8802-2554

Craven Walk Mikvah
72 Lingwood Road, Stamford Hill N16
　　　　　　　　(020) 8800-8555
Evening Telephone number: 020-8809-6279.

Edgware & District Communal Mikvah
Edgware United Synagogue Grounds, 22 Warwick
Avenue Drive, Edgware HA8　　(020) 8958-3233
　　　　　　　Fax: (020) 8958-4004
　　　　　　Email: estrin@clara.co.uk

North West London Communal Mikvah
10a Shirehall Lane, Hendon NW4
　　(020) 8202-1427 (Evenings:8202-8517/5706).

Satmar Mikvah
62 Filey Avenue, Stamford Hill N16　(020) 8806-3961

South London Mikvah
42 St Georges Road, Wimbledon SW19 4ED
　　　　　　　　(020) 8944-7149
　　　　　　　Fax: (020) 8944-7563
　　　　　　Email: lubwdon@aol.com

Stamford Hill and District Mikvah
Margaret Road, Stamford Hill N16　(020) 8806-3880
Other Telephone numbers: 020-8809-4064 or 020-
8800-5119.

The New Central London Mikveh
21 Andover Place NW6 5ED　　(020) 7372-7237
By appointment only.

The Sternberg Centre for Judaism
80 East End Road, Finchley N3 2SY　(020) 8349-5640
　　　　　　　Fax: (020) 8349-5699
　　　　Email: admin@reformjudaism.org.uk
　　　　　　Web site: www.refsyn.org.uk
Hours: 9.30 - 5.30 Monday to Thursday, Friday 9.30 -
3.30 /4.

Union of Orthodox Hebrew Congregations
140 Stamford Hill, Stamford Hill N16 6QT
　　　　　　　　(020) 8802-6226
　　　　　　　Fax: (020) 8809-7097

Museums

Ben Uri Art Society & Gallery
126 Albert Street NW1 7NE　　(020) 7482-1234
　　　　　　　Fax: (020) 7482-1414
　　　　　　Email: benuri@ort.org
The aim of the Society, which is a registered charity
founded 1915, is to promote Jewish art as part of the
Jewish cultural heritage. The Gallery provides a
showcase for exhibitions of contemporary art as well
as for the Society's own collection of over 800 works
by Jewish artists, including David Bomberg, Mark
Gertler, Jacob Epstein, Reuven Rubin and Leon
Kossof. Open Monday-Thursday 10-4, Sunday
afternoons during exhibitions 2pm-5pm. Closed
Jewish Holy-days and Bank Holidays.

Jewish Military Museum and Memorial Room
AJEX House, East Bank, Stamford Hill N16 5RT
　　　　　　　　(020) 8800-2844
　　　　　　　Fax: (020) 8800-1117
　　　　　　Email: ajexuk@talk21.com
　　　　　　Web site: www.ajex.org.uk
Memorabilia, artefacts, medals, letters, documents,
pictures and uniforms all illustrating British Jewry's
contribution to the Armed Forces of the Crown from
the Crimea to the present day. By appointment,
Sunday to Thursday, 11 am to 4 pm.

The Holocaust Exhibition
Imperial War Museum, Lambeth Road SE1 6HZ
　　　　　　　　(020) 7416-5320
　　　　　　　Fax: (020) 7416-5374
　　　　　　Email: khogan@iwm.org.uk
　　　　　　Web site: www.iwm.org.uk
The Exhibition covers two floors and uses original
artefacts, film, documents and photographs to tell the
story of the Nazis' genocidal programme. It brings to
the UK for the first time rare and important historical
material, some lent by former concentration and
extermination camps. Special talks can be arranged
for groups visiting the exhibition.

Museum of Immigration
19 Princelet Street E1   (020) 7247-5352
A museum devoted to the history of immigration into
Great Britain. Included in the site is Princelet street
Synagogue, a 1870 synagogue built onto a Grade II*
listed Georgian town house.

The Jewish Museum
The Sternberg Centre, 80 East End Road, Finchley
N3 2SY   (020) 8349-1143
                    Fax: (020) 8343-2162
        Email: enquiries@jewishmuseum.org.uk
        Web site: www.jewishmuseum.org.uk
Permanent exhibitions trace history of London Jewry
with reconstructions of a tailoring and a furniture
workshop. Holocaust education is also a major
feature of the Museum's work and the Museum's
displays include a moving exhibition on London-born
Holocaust survivor, Leon Greenman. Open Monday
to Thursday: 10.30am - 5.00pm, and Sunday 10.30am
to 4.30pm. Closed Jewish festivals and Public
Holidays and 25 December to 5 January.

Raymond Burton House, 129-131 Albert Street,
Camden NW1 7NB   (020) 7284-1997
                    Fax: (020) 7267-9008
        Email: admin@jmus.org.uk
        Web site: www.jewishmuseum.org.uk
The Museum's attractive premises include a History
Gallery, Ceremonial Art Gallery and a Temporary
Exhibitions gallery offering a varied programme of
changing exhibitions. The Museum has been awarded
Designated status by the Museums and Galleries
Commission in recognition of its outstanding
collections of Jewish ceremonial Art, which are
amongst the finest in the world. Open Monday to
Thursday 10am - 4pm, and Sunday 10am to 5pm.
Closed Jewish festivals and Public Holidays. Group
visits by prior arrangement. Admission charge.

RELIGIOUS ORGANISATIONS

**With more than 200 synagogues in the London
area alone, not counting independent
synagogues and 'shtieblach', we recommend
that you contact one of these organisations to
find the synagogue of your choice nearest you,
along with minyan times.**

Assembly of Masorti Synagogues
1097 Finchley Road, Golders Green NW11 0PU
                    (020) 8201-8772
                Fax: (020) 8201-8917
        Email: office@masorti.org.uk
        Web site: www.masorti.org.uk

Federation of Synagogues
65 Watford Way, NW4 3AQ   (020) 8203-3363
                                 (020) 8203-0610

Reform Synagogues
The Sternberg Centre for Judaism, 80 East End Road,
Finchley N3 2SY   (020) 8349-5640
                    Fax: (020) 8343-5699
        Email: admin@reformjudaism.org.uk
        Web site: www.reformjudaism.org.uk

Spanish & Portuguese Jews' Congregation
2 Ashworth Road, Maida Vale W9 1JY
                    (020) 7289-2573
                Fax: (020) 7289-2709
        Email: howard@sandpsyn.demon.co.uk

Union of Liberal and Progressive Synagogues
The Montagu Centre, 21 Maple Street W1T 4BE
                    (020) 7580-1663
                Fax: (020) 7436-4184
        Email: montagu@ulps.org
        Web site: www.ulps.org

Union of Orthodox Hebrew Congregations
140 Stamford Hill, Stamford Hill N16 6QT
                    (020) 8802-6226
                Fax: (020) 8809-7902

United Synagogue
Adler House, 735 High Road, Finchley N12 0US
                    (020) 8343-8989
                Fax: (020) 8343-6262
        Web site: www.unitedsynagogue.org.uk

RESTAURANTS
Dairy
Art 2 Heart
109a Golders Green Road, London NW11
                    (020) 8201-9991
Supervision: London Beth Din

Bon Baggeute
122 Golders Green Road NW11 8HB
                    (020) 8209-0232
Supervision: London Beth Din

Café Dan
14 Halleswelle Parade, Finchley Road NW11 8HB
                    (020) 8455-3731
Supervision: London Beth Din

Café on the Green
122 Golders Green Road, Golders Green NW11 8HB
                    (020) 8209-0232
Supervision: London Beth Din
Chalav Yisrael. Open Motzei Shabbat in winter.

Cassit
225 Golders Green Road, Golders Green NW11 9PN
                    (020) 8455-8195
                Fax: (020) 8458-4837
Supervision: Beth Din of the Federation of
Synagogues

Isola Bella Café
63 Brent Street, Hendon NW4 2EA (020) 8203-2000
Supervision: Beth Din of the Federation of
Synagogues & Sephardi Kashrut Authority

Milk n' Honey
124 Golders Green Road, Golders Green NW11 8HB
                    (020) 8455-0664
Supervision: Kedassia
Vegetarian/dairy restaurant/coffee shop/air-
conditioned. Menus in English and Hebrew. Also
take-away available.

Orli Cafe
96 Brent Street, Hendon NW4 2HH (020) 8203-7555
Supervision: Kedassia

108 Regents Park Road, Finchley N3 3JG
(020) 8371-9222
Supervision: Kedassia

295 Hale Lane, Edgware HA8 7AX   (020) 8958-1555

Taboon
17 Russell Parade, Golders Green Road
NW11 9NN   (020) 8455-7451
Supervision: Sephardi Kashrut Authority & Kedassia

Tasti Pizza
252 Golders Green Road, Golders Green NW11
(020) 8209-0023
Supervision: London Beth Din and Kedassia

Tasty Pizza
23 Amhurst Parade, Amhurst Park,
Stamford Hill N16 5AA   (020) 8802-0018
Supervision: London Beth Din and Kedassia

Meat

Amor
8 Russell Parade, Golders Green NW11
(020) 8458-4221
Supervision: Kedassia

Aviv
87 High Street, Edgware   (020) 8952-2484
Fax: (020) 8952-0200
Email: info@avivrestaurant.com
Web site: www.avivrestaurant.com
Supervision: Beth Din of the Federation of
Synagogues

Blooms Restaurant
130 Golders Green Road, Golders Green
NW11 8HB   (020) 8455-1338
Fax: (020) 8455-1338
Supervision: London Beth Din
Free delivery service, air-conditioned. Open until
1.00am Sunday to Thursday; Friday lunchtime and
Saturday nights 1 hour after Shabbos until 4.00am.

Dizengoff
118 Golders Green Road, Golders Green
NW11 8HB   (020) 8458-7003
Fax: (020) 8381-4902
Email: shurkin@btopenworld.com
Supervision: Sephardi Kashrut Authority
Hours: Sunday to Thursday, 11 am to midnight;
Friday, to 4 pm; Saturday night, winter only.

Folman's Restaurant
134 Brent Street NW4   (020) 8202-5592
Supervision: London Beth Din

Kaifeng
51 Church Road, Hendon NW4 4DU
(020) 8203-7888
Fax: (020) 8203-8263
Web site: www.kaifeng.co.uk
Supervision: London Beth Din
Chinese restaurant with take-away and delivery
service. Free delivery with minimum order of £25.
Hours: Sunday to Thursday, 12:30 pm to 2:30 pm, 6
pm to 11 pm; Open Saturday evening, September to
April.

Kinneret
313 Hale Lane HA8 7AX   (020) 8958-4955
Supervision: Beth Din of the Federation of
Synagogues

La Fiesta
239 Golders Green Road NW11 9PN
(020) 8458-0444
Fax: (020) 8455-2003
Supervision: London Beth Din

Lemonade
87 Brent St. NW4   (020) 8201-5222
Supervision: Sephardi Kashrut Authority

Marcus's
5 Hallswelle Parade, Finchley Road, Golders Green
NW11 0DL   (020) 8458-4670
Web site: www.marcuss.co.uk
Supervision: London Beth Din

Reubens
79 Baker Street W1M 1AJ   (020) 7486-0035
Fax: (020) 7486-7079
Supervision: Sephardi Kashrut Authority
Open daily except for Shabbat; open Friday until two
hours before sundown.

Sami's Restaurant
157 Brent Street, Hendon NW4 4DJ (020) 8203-8088
Fax: (020) 8203-1040
Supervision: Beth Din of the Federation of
Synagogues
Glatt kosher Middle Eastern cuisine.

Six-13
19 Wigmore Street W1   (020) 7629-6133
Web site: www.six13.com
Supervision: London Beth Din

Solly's
148a Golders Green Road, Golders Green NW11
(020) 8455-0004
Supervision: London Beth Din

Solly's Exclusive
146-150 Golders Green Road, Golders Green NW11
(020) 8455-2121
Supervision: London Beth Din

Tavlin
1-4 Belmont Parade, Finchley Road NW11 6XP
(020) 8458-1999
Fax: (020) 8458-2999

The White House Restaurant
10 Bell Lane, Hendon NW4   (020) 8203-2427
Supervision: Beth Din of the Federation of
Synagogues & Sephardi Kashrut Authority

Uncle Shloime's
204 Stamford Hill, Stamford Hill N16
(020) 8802-9355
Supervision: Kedassia

Snack Bar
Sue Harris Student Centre
B'nai B'rith-Hillel Foundation,
1-2 Endsleigh Street WC1H 0DS   (020) 7388-0801
Fax: (020) 7916-3973
Email: info@hillel.co.uk
Web site: www.hillel.co.uk
Supervision: London Beth Din
Hours: Monday to Thursday. Please phone for details
of summer months opening. Re-opens for students
and all other visitors mid-September.

TRAVEL AGENCIES
Goodmos Tours
Dunstan House, 14a St Cross Street EC1N 8XA
(020) 7430-2230
Fax: (020) 7405-5049

LestAir Services
80 Highfield Ave, Golders Green NW11 9TT
(020) 8455-9654
Fax: (020) 455-9654
Email: family.schleimer@ukgateway.net
Promoting Jewish Heritage Tours to the Czech
Republic, Poland, Hungary, Byelorus, Latvia and
Lithuania and can be contacted for detailed
information and guidance.

Longwood Travel
182 Longwood Gardens, Ilford IG5 0EW
(020) 8551-4466
Fax: (020) 8551-5588
Peltours
70 Edgware Way, Edgware HA8 8JS   (020) 8958-3188
Fax: (020) 8958-8898
11-19 Ballards Lane, Finchley N3 1UX
(020) 8346-9144
Fax: (020) 8343-0579
Email: sales@peltours.com
Web site: www.peltours.com
Sabra Travel Ltd.
9 Edgwarebury Lane, Edgware HA8 8LH
(020) 8958-3244-7
Travelink Group Ltd.
50 Vivian Avenue NW4 3XH   (020) 8931-8000
Fax: (020) 8931-8877
Email: info@travelinkuk.com
Web site: www.travelinkuk.com

MANCHESTER (GREATER)

Cheadle

BUTCHERS
Hymark Kosher Meat Ltd
39 Wilmslow Road, Cheadle, Cheshire SK
(161) 428-3400
Supervision: Manchester Beth Din
Meat department only.

DELICATESSEN
Hyman's Delicatessen
41 Wilmstow Road, Cheadle M   (161) 491-1100
Fax: (161) 491-1100
Supervision: Manchester Beth Din

SYNAGOGUES
Orthodox
Yeshurun Hebrew Congregation
Coniston Road, Gatley-Cheadle, Cheshire
SK8 4AP   (161) 428-8242
Fax: (161) 491-5265
Email: yeshurun@btinternet.com

Hale Barns

BUTCHERS
Hymark of Hale
The Square, Hale Barns, Cheshire   (161) 980-2836
Supervision: Manchester Beth Din

MIKVAOT
Naomi Greenberg South Manchester Mikvah
Hale Synagogue, Shay Lane, Hale Barns M
(161) 904-8296
Use is by appointment only.

RESTAURANTS
Aviv Restaurant
18 The Square, Hale Barns   (161) 980-0009
Supervision: Manchester Beth Din

SYNAGOGUES
Orthodox
Hale & District Hebrew Congregation
Shay Lane, Hale Barns, Cheshire WA15 8PA
(161) 980-8846
Fax: (161) 980-1802

Manchester

The Manchester Jewish community is the second
largest in the United Kingdom, numbering about
35,000. There was no organised community until
1780. The present Great Synagogue claims to be
the direct descendant of this earliest community.
The leaders of Manchester Jewry in those early
days came from the neighbouring relatively
important Jewish community of Liverpool. In
1871 a small Sephardi group from North Africa
and the Levant drew together and formed a
congregation, which extended to fill two
handsome synagogues. One has now been turned
into a Jewish museum.

BAKERIES
State Fayre Bakeries
Unit 1, Empire Street M3   (161) 832-2911
Supervision: Manchester Beth Din

BUTCHERS
J.A. Hyman (Titanic) Ltd
123/9 Waterloo Road M8   (161) 792-1888
Supervision: Manchester Beth Din
Suppliers of meat and poultry, cooked meats and
delicatessen products.

Lloyd Grosberg (J. Kreger)
102 Barlow Moor Road M20   (161) 445-4983
Supervision: Manchester Beth Din

GROCERIES
State Fayre
77 Middleton Road M8   (161) 740-3435
Supervision: Manchester Beth Din

KASHRUT INFORMATION
Manchester Beth Din
435 Cheetham Hill Road M8 0PF   (161) 740-9711
                           Fax: (161) 721-4249
Contact them to ensure that the establishment is still
certified.

LIBRARIES
Central Library
St Peter's Square M2 5PD   (161) 234-1983; 1984
                           Fax: (161) 234-1927
Email: socsci@libraries.manchester.gov.uk
Large collection of Jewish books for reference and
loan, including books in Hebrew. Contact the Social
Sciences Library.

MUSEUM
Manchester Jewish Museum
190 Cheetham Hill Road M8 8LW
               (161) 834-9879; 832-7353
                           Fax: (161) 834-9801
Email: info@manchesterjewishmuseum.com
Web site: www.manchesterjewishmuseum.com
Exhibitions, Heritage trails, Demonstrations & Talks.
Details of events available on request. Educational
visits for schools and adult groups must be booked in
advance. Open Monday-Thursday, 10.30am to 4pm
Sundays 10.30am to 5pm. Admission charge. Contact
Don Rainger.

RESTAURANTS
Antonio's Restaurant
JCLC, Corner Bury Old Road & Park Road
                           (161) 795-8911
                           Fax: (161) 795-8911
Supervision: Manchester Beth Din
Open Monday-Thursday 5.00pm-11.00pm ; Sunday
1.00pm to 11.00pm. In winter 1 1/2 hours after
Shabbat until 2.00 am.

SYNAGOGUES
Orthodox
Cheetham Hebrew Congregation
Jewish Cultural Centre, Bury Old Road
M7 4QY
                           (161) 740-7788

Heaton Park Hebrew Congregation
Ashdown, Middleton Road M8 6JX   (161) 740-4766

United Synagogue
Meade Hill Road M8 4LR   (161) 740-9586

Reform
**Cheshire Reform Congregation Menorah
Synagogue**
Altrincham Road M22 4RZ   (161) 428-7746
                           Fax: (161) 428-0937
Email: office@menorah.org

Manchester Reform Synagogue
Jackson's Row M2 5NH   (161) 834-0415
                           Fax: (161) 834-0415

TRAVEL AGENCIES
ITS: Israel Travel Service
427/430 Royal Exchange, Old Bank Street
M2 7EP   (161) 839-1111
                           Fax: (161) 839-0000
Email: all@itstravel.co.uk
Web site: www.itstravel.co.uk
Freephone 0800 0181 839

Peltours Ltd
27-29 Church Street M4 1QA   (161) 834-3721
                           Fax: (161) 832-9343

Prestwich

BAKERIES
Swiss Cottage Patisserie
118 Rectory Lane, Prestwich M25   (161) 798-0897
                           Fax: (161) 798-8212
Supervision: Manchester Beth Din

BOOKSELLERS

B. Horwitz
20 King Edwards Buildings, Bury Old Road,
Prestwich M7 4QJ   (161) 740-5897
Open 9.30am-5.30pm Monday to Friday; 10.00am-
1.00pm Sunday; 9.00am-2.00pm Fridays during
winter.

B. Horwitz Judaica World
2 Kings Road, Prestwich M25 0LE   (161) 773-4956
Fax: (161) 773-4956
Email: horbroom@aol.com

BUTCHERS

Kosher Foods
49 Bury New Road, Prestwich M25   (161) 773-1308
Supervision: Manchester Beth Din
Sells groceries as well.

Kosher Supreme
61 Bury Old Road, Prestwich M25   (161) 773-2020
Supervision: Manchester Beth Din

Vidal's Kosher Meats
75 Windsor Road, Prestwich M25   (161) 740-3365
Supervision: Manchester Beth Din

DELICATESSEN

Deli King
Kings Road, Prestwich M25 8LQ   (161) 798-7370
Fax: (161) 798-5654
Supervision: Manchester Beth Din
Hours: Sunday to Friday, 8:30 am to 6 pm.

Haber's
8 Kings Road, Prestwich M25 0LE   (161) 773-2046
Fax: (161) 773-9101
Supervision: Manchester Beth Din

MEDIA

Newspaper
Jewish Telegraph
Telegraph House, 11 Park Hill, Bury Old Road,
Prestwich M25 0HH   (161) 740-9321
Fax: (161) 740-9325
Email: manchester@jewishtelegraph.com
Web site: www.jewishtelegraph.com

MIKVAOT

Manchester & District Mikva (Machzikei Hadass)
Sedgley Park Road, Prestwich M25
(161) 773-1537; 795-2223

RESTAURANTS

Asher's
5 Kings Road, Prestwich   (161) 773-1414
Supervision: Manchester Beth Din

Meat
J.S. Kosher Restaurant
7 Kings Road, Prestwich M25 0LE   (161) 798-7776
Supervision: Manchester Beth Din
Glatt kosher.

SYNAGOGUES

Orthodox
Higher Prestwich
445 Bury Old Road, Prestwich M25 1QP
(161) 773-4800
Fax: (161) 773-4800

Holy Law South Broughton Congregation
Bury Old Road, Prestwich M25 0EX
(161) 792-6349/721-4705
Fax: (161) 720-6623
Email: office@holylaw.org.uk

Prestwich Hebrew Congregation
Bury New Road M25 9WN   (161) 773-1978
Fax: (161) 773-7015

Sedgley Park (Shomrei Hadass)
Park View Road, Prestwich M25 5FA
(161) 773-4828/740-1969
Email: laurencemiller@hotmail.com

Sale

SYNAGOGUES

Orthodox
Sale & District Hebrew Congregation
14 Hesketh Road, Sale M33 5AA   (161) 973-2172

Salford

BAKERIES

Brackman's
45 Leicester Road, Salford M7   (161) 792-1652
Supervision: Manchester Beth Din

BOOKSELLERS

Hasefer Book Store
18 Merrybower Road, Salford M7   (161) 740-3013
Fax: (161) 721-4649

J. Goldberg
11 Parkside Avenue, Salford M7 0HB (161) 740-0732

Jewish Book Centre
25 Ashbourne Grove, Salford M7 4DB
(161) 792-1253
Fax: (161) 661-5505
Hours: Sunday to Thursday, 9 am to 9 pm;
Friday, 9.00am-1.00pm.

BUTCHERS

Halberstadt Ltd
55 Leicester Road, Salford M7 4AS   (161) 792-1109
Supervision: Manchester Beth Din
Open full day Tuesday, Wednesday, and Thursday.
Open half day Sunday, Monday and Friday. Only Glatt
Beth Yosef Meat-Mehadrin Poultry. Electric
doors/disable ramp.

GROCERIES

Halperns Kosher Food Store
57-59 Leicester Road, Salford M7 4DA
(161) 792-1752 Office 792-2992
Fax: (161) 708-8881
Email: halperns.kosherfood@virgin.net
Supervision: Manchester Beth Din

HOTELS

Fulda's Hotel
144 Old Bury Road, Salford M7 4QY   (161) 740-4551
Fax: (161) 795-5920
Web site: www.here.at/fuldas.com
Supervision: Manchester Beth Din
Four-star hotel open all year. Glatt kosher. Within
easy access of motorways, and uniquely placed in the
heart of the Manchester Jewish community in
Broughton Park. Within easy walking distance of
numerous synagogues and shopping facilities.

MIKVAOT

Manchester Communal Mikvah
Broome Holme, Tetlow Lane, Salford M7 0BU
(161) 792-3970
During opening hours only. For appointments for
Friday night and YomTov evenings: 740-4071; 740-
5199. For tevilat kelim, 795-2272.

RESTAURANTS

Dairy
Brackman's Bakery & Coffee Shop
45 Leicester Road   (161) 792-1652
Supervision: Manchester Beth Din

SYNAGOGUES

Orthodox
Adass Yeshurun
Cheltenham Crescent, Salford M7 0FE
(161) 792-1233

Adath Yisroel Nusach Ari
Upper Park Road, Salford M7 0HL   (161) 740-3905

**Central & North Manchester (incorporating
Hightown Central and Beth Jacob)**
Leicester Road, Salford M7 4GP   (161) 740-4830

Congregation of Spanish and Portuguese
18 Moor Lane, Kersal, Salford M7 4WX
(161) 792-7406
Fax: (161) 792-3471
Email: ahodari@antonyhodari.co.uk
Web site: www.18moorlane.freeserve.co.uk

Higher Crumpsall & Higher Broughton
Bury Old Road, Salford M7 4PX   (161) 740-1210

Kahal Chassidim
62 Singleton Road, Salford M7 4LU   (161) 740-1629

Machzikei Hadass
17 Northumberland Street, Salford M7 0FE
(161) 792-1313

Manchester Great & New Synagogue
Stenecourt, Holden Road, Salford M7 4LN
(161) 792-8399
Fax: (161) 792-1991

North Salford
2 Vine Street, Salford M7 0NX   (161) 792-3278

Ohel Torah
132 Leicester Road, Salford M7 0EA   (161) 740-2568
Fax: (161) 745-8876

TRAVEL AGENCIES

Goodmos Tours (Man) Ltd.
23 Leicester Road, Salford M7 0AS   (161) 792-7333
Fax: (161) 792-7336
Email: goodmos836@aol.com

Whitefield

BUTCHERS

Park Lane Kosher Meats
142 Park Lane, Whitefield M45 7PX   (161) 766-5091
Supervision: Manchester Beth Din
Hours: Sunday 8.30am - 1.00pm; Monday & Friday
8.00am - 1.00pm; Tuesday, Wednesday & Thursday
8.00am - 6.00pm.

DELICATESSEN

Cottage Deli
83 Park Lane, Whitefield M   (161) 766-6216
Supervision: Manchester Beth Din

MIKVAOT

Whitefield Mikvah
Park Lane, Whitefield M45 7PB   (161) 796-1054
Fax: (161) 767-9453
Ansaphone. Evenings only: 773-7830. Use is by
appointment only.

SYNAGOGUES

Orthodox
Hillock Hebrew Congregation
Beverley Close, Ribble Drive, Whitefield M45
(161) 959-5663
Mailing address is 13 Mersey Close, Whitefield,
Manchester, M45 8LB

Whitefield Hebrew Congregation
Park Lane, Whitefield M45 7PB   (161) 766-3732
Fax: (161) 767-9453

Reform
**Sha'arei Shalom North Manchester Reform
Synagogue**
Elms Street, Whitefield M45 8GQ   (161) 796-6736
Fax: (161) 796-6736

MERSEYSIDE

Liverpool

There is evidence of an organised community before 1750, believed to have been composed of Sephardi Jews and to have had some connection with the West Indies and with Dublin, although some authorities believe they were mainly German Jews. The largely Ashkenazi community, who arrived later, were to some degree intending emigrants for the USA and the West Indies who changed their minds and stayed in Liverpool. By 1807 the community had a building in Seel Street, the parent of today's synagogue in Princes Road, one of the handsomest in the country.

BOOKSELLERS AND JUDAICA
Liverpool Jewish Book & Gift Centre
Harold House, Dunbabin Road L15 6XL
(151) 475-5671
Fax: (151) 475-2212
Full range of Jewish books, artefacts and gifts.
Sundays 11.00am to 1.00pm.

COMMUNITY ORGANISATIONS
Merseyside Jewish Representative Council
433 Smithdown Road L15 3JL   (151) 733-2292
Fax: (151) 734-0212
Email: mjrcshifrin@hotmail.com

KASHRUT INFORMATION
Liverpool Kashrut Commission (inc. Liverpool Shechita Board)
c/o Shifrin House, 433 Smithdown Road L15 3JL
(151) 733-2292
Fax: (151) 734-0212

MEDIA
Newspaper
Jewish Telegraph
Harold House, Dunbabin Road L15 6XL
(151) 475-6666
Fax: (151) 475-2222
Email: liverpool@jewishtelegraph.com
Web site: www.jewishtelegraph.com

MIKVAOT
Childwall Hebrew Congregation
Dunbabin Road L15 6XL   (151) 722-2079
Fax: (151) 722-2079

RESTAURANTS
JLGB Centre
(151) 475-5825; 475-5671
Open Sun, Tues., Thurs. 6.30-11.00pm. Licensed bar. Out-of-town visitors welcome. Also take-away service.

Kosher
Harold House Youth and Community Centre
Dunbabin Road L15 6XL   (151) 475-5825/5671
Fax: (151) 475-2212
Email: info@liverpooljewish.com
Web site: www.liverpooljewish.com
Supervision: Liverpool Kashrut Commission
Also does take-away.

Vegetarian
Munchies Eating House
Myrtle Parade   (151) 709-7896

SYNAGOGUES
Orthodox
Allerton Hebrew Congregation
cnr. Mather & Booker Avenues, Allerton
L18 9TB   (151) 427-6848

Childwall Hebrew Congregation
Dunbabin Road L15 6XL   (151) 722-2079
Fax: (151) 722-2079

Greenbank Drive Hebrew Congregation
Greenbank Drive L17 1AN   (151) 733-1417
Fax: (151) 733-3862

Old Hebrew Congregation
Princes Road L8 1TG   (151) 709-3431
Fax: (151) 709-4187
Grade II Listed Building. Guided talks available during the week daily. Pre-booking essential. Other times by special arrangement.

Progressive
Liverpool Progressive Synagogue
28 Church Road North L15 6TF   (151) 733-5871

Southport

COMMUNITY ORGANISATIONS
Southport Jewish Representative Council
(1704) 540704
Fax: (1704) 540704

SYNAGOGUES
Orthodox
Southport Hebrew Congregation
Arnside Road PR9 0QX   (1704) 532964
Fax: (1704) 514002
Mikvah on premises.

Reform
New (Reform) Synagogue
Portland Street PR8 1LR   (1704) 535950
Email: snewsyn@aol.com

MIDDLESEX

Staines

SYNAGOGUES
Orthodox
Staines & District Synagogue
Westbrook Road, South Street TW18 4PR
(1784) 254604
Fax: (1784) 254604
Email: staines.synagogue@btinternet.com
Includes Slough and Windsor.

NORFOLK

Norwich

Norwich is the site of the first recorded "blood libel" in Europe when in 1144 William of Norwich was found murdered. At that time Jews were connected with the woollen and worsted trades for which the city was at that time famous. Resettlement took place in the early 18th century and the present community was established in 1813.

SYNAGOGUES
3a Earlham Road NR2 3RA (1603) 503434
Progressive Jewish Community of East Anglia
c/o Frimette Carr NR (1603) 714162

NORTHAMPTONSHIRE

Northampton

SYNAGOGUES
Overstone Road BB1 3JW (1604) 33345
Services on Friday night.

NOTTINGHAMSHIRE

Newark

HOLOCAUST MEMORIAL CENTRE
Bet Shalom
Laxton, Newark, Notts NG22 0PA (1623) 836627
Fax: (1623) 836647
Beth Shalom Holocaust Memorial Centre was conceived as a place where some of the implications of the Holocaust can be faced. It is an education centre where Jews and non-Jews work together to forge a united front against the perils of anti-Semitism and racism in society today.

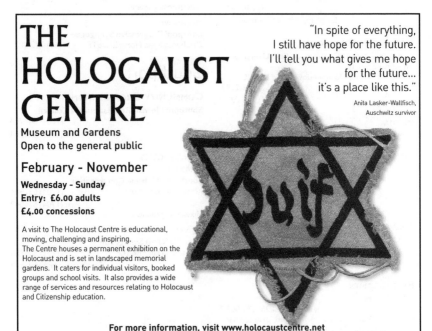

Nottingham

Jews settled in Nottingham as early as medieval times, and centres of learning and worship are known to have existed in that period. The earliest known record of an established community dates from 1822 when a grant of land for burial purposes was made by the Corporation.

The synagogue in Shakespeare Street originally a Methodist Church is a Grade II listed building.

RESTAURANTS
Vegetarian
Maxine's Salad Table
56 Upper Parliament Street NG1 2AG
(115) 947-3622

SYNAGOGUES
Orthodox
Shakespeare Street NG1 4FQ (115) 947-2004

Progressive
Nottingham Progressive Jewish Congregation
Lloyd Street, Sherwood NG5 4BP (115) 962-4761
Email: npjc@ulps.org
Web site: www.npjc.org.uk

Oxford

There was an important medieval community, and the present one dates back to 1842. The Oxford Synagogue and Jewish Centre, opened in 1974, serves both the city and the university. It is available for all forms of Jewish worship.

COMMUNITY ORGANISATIONS
L'Chaim Society
Albion House, Little Gate OX (1865) 794-462

SYNAGOGUE
The Synagogue and Jewish Centre
21 Richmond Road OX1 2JL (1865) 553042
Email: information@oxford-synagogue.org.uk
Regular Orthodox, Masorti and Progressive Services. Wide range of communal activities. A kosher meals service operates during term-time. Phone or email for information.

Stoke On Trent

SYNAGOGUES
Birch Terrace, Hanley ST1 3JN (1782) 616417

Guildford

SYNAGOGUES
Orthodox
Guildford & District Synagogue
York Road GU1 4DR (1483) 576470
Email: gould.harry@net.ntl.com
Web site: www.geocities.com/guildfordjewishcommunity
Correspondence: Mrs B. Gould, Lynwood, Hillier Road, Guildford, Surrey, GU1 2JG.

TOURIST SITE
Enquiries about the important discovery in 2000 of a medieval synagogue in the town may be addressed to the Guildford Museum.

Brighton and Hove

The first known Jewish resident of Brighton lived here in 1767. The earliest synagogue was founded in Jew Street in 1789. Henry Solomon, vice-president of the congregation, was the first Chief Constable of the town. His brother-in-law, Levi Emanuel Cohen, founded the Brighton Guardian, and was twice elected president of the Newspaper Society of Great Britain. The town's Jewish population today is about 8,000.

COMMUNITY ORGANISATIONS
Lubavitch Chabad House
15 The Upper Drive BN3 6GR (1273) 321-919
Fax: (1273) 821-518

DELICATESSEN
Cantor's of Hove
20 Richardson Road, Hove BN3 5BB (1273) 723-669

MEDIA
Newspaper
Sussex Jewish News
PO Box 2178 BN3 3SZ (1273) 330-550
Fax: (1273) 504-455
Email: doris@sussexjewishnews.com
Web site: www.sussexjewishnews.com

MIKVAOT
Prince Regent Swimming Pool Complex, Church Street BN1 1YA (1273) 321-919

ORGANISATIONS

Hillel House
18 Harrington Road BN1 6RE   (1273) 503-450
Closed during summer vacation. Friday evening meals
available.

RELIGIOUS ORGANISATIONS

Brighton and Hove Joint Kashrus Committee
c/o B.H.H.C., 31 New Church Road,
Hove BN3 4AD   (1273) 888855
          Fax: (1273) 888810

RESTAURANTS

Vegetarian
Food for Friends
17-18 Prince Albert Street, The Lanes(1273) 202-310
          Fax: (1273) 774-171
          Email: simon@foodies.freeserve.co.uk
          Web site: www.foodforfriends.com

Vegetarian
Wai Kika Moo Kau Limited
42 Meeting House Lane   (1273) 323-824

SYNAGOGUES

Orthodox
Brighton & Hove Hebrew Congregation
Middle Street Synagogue, 66 Middle Street
BN1 1AL   (1273) 888855
          Fax: (1273) 888810
The synagogue, which was built in 1874 when
Brighton was very fashionable, has an elaborate
Victorian interior. It is a Grade II listed building.

Hove Hebrew Congregation
79 Holland Road, Hove BN3 1JN   (1273) 732035

West Hove Synagogue
31 New Church Road, Hove BN3 4AD
          (1273) 888855
          Fax: (1273) 888810
          Email: bhhc@breathemail.net

Progressive
Progressive Synagogue
6 Landsdowne Road BN3 1FF   (1273) 737223
9.30am to 1pm

Reform
New (Reform)
Palmeira Avenue BN3 3GE   (1273) 735343
          Fax: (1273) 734-537

Eastbourne

SYNAGOGUES

Orthodox
22 Susans Road BN21 3TJ   (1323) 640441

Hastings

CONTACT INFORMATION

Alfred Ross
PO Box 74, Bexhill on Sea   (1424) 848344

TYNE & WEAR

Gateshead

A community with many schools, yeshivot and
other training institutions.

BAKERIES

Stenhouse
215 Coatsworth Road NE8 1SR   (191) 477-2001

BOOKSELLERS

J. Lehmann
28-30 Grasmere Street NE8 1TS   (191) 477-3523
          Fax: (191) 430-0555
          Email: info@lehmanns.co.uk
Also has wholesale and mail order, Unit E, Viking
Industrial Park, Rolling Mill Road, NE32 3DP. Tel:
0191 430-0333

BUTCHERS

K.L. Kosher Butcher
83 Rodsley Avenue NE8   (191) 477-3109
Kosher.

MIKVAOT

180 Bewick Road NE8 1UF   (191) 477-3552

SYNAGOGUES

138 Whitehall Road NE8 1TP   (191) 477-3012
180 Bewick Road NE8 1UF   (191) 477-0111

Newcastle upon Tyne

The community was established before 1831,
when a cemetery was acquired. Jews have lived in
Newcastle since 1775. There are about 1,200
Jews in the city today.

GROCERIES

Zelda's Delicatessen
Unit 7 Kenton Park Shopping Centre,
Gosforth NE3 4RU   (191) 213-0013
          Fax: (191) 213-0013
          Email: zeldasdeli@aol.com
Supervision: Newcastle Kashrus Committee, Rabbi
Yehuda Black

KASHRUT INFORMATION
Kashrus Committee
Lionel Jacobson House, Graham Park Road,
Gosforth NE3 4BH (191) 284-0959

MEDIA
Newspapers
The North-East Jewish Recorder
24 Adeline Gardens NE3 4JQ (191) 285-1253
Fax: (191) 242-1316
Email: clivando@hotmail.com

MIKVAOT
Graham Park Road NE3 4BH (191) 284-0959

RELIGIOUS ORGANISATIONS
Representative Council of North-East Jewry
(191) 215-6253
Fax: (191) 215-6080

RESTAURANTS
Vegetarian
The Supernatural
2 Princess Square NE1 8ER (191) 261-2730

SYNAGOGUES
Orthodox
United Hebrew Congregation
Graham Park Road NE3 4BH (191) 284-0959
Mikva on premises.

Reform
Newcastle Reform Synagogue
The Croft, off Kenton Road NE3 4RF (191) 284-8621

Sunderland

MIKVAOT
11 The Oaks East, Ryhope Road SR2 8EX
(191) 565-0224

SYNAGOGUES
Orthodox
Sunderland Hebrew Congregation
Ryhope Road SR2 7EQ (191) 565-8093
This building has been given Grade II listed status.

WEST MIDLANDS

Birmingham

This Jewish community is one of the oldest in the Provinces, dating from at least 1730. Birmingham was a centre from which Jewish pedlars covered the surrounding country week by week, returning home for Shabbat.

The first synagogue of which there is any record was in The Froggery in 1780. There was a Jewish cemetery in the same neighbourhood in 1730. The synagogue of 1780 was extended in 1791, 1809 and 1827. A new and larger synagogue, popularly known as 'Singers Hill', opened in 1856. Today's Jewish population stands at about 2,300.

BOOKSELLERS
Lubavitch Bookshop
95 Willows Road B12 9QF (121) 440-6673
Fax: (121) 446-4199

DELICATESSEN
Gee's Butchers Ltd
75 Pershore Road B5 7NX (121) 440-2160
Kosher butcher, baker and deli.

INFORMATION AND RESOURCE CENTRE
Israel Information Centre for the Midlands
Singers Hill, Ellis Street B1 1HL (121) 643-2688
Fax: (121) 643-2688
Email: rjacobs@iicmids.u-net.com
Hours of opening: 10am-4pm Monday, Tuesdays, Thursdays or by appointment.

KASHRUT INFORMATION
Shechita Board
Singers Hill, Ellis Street B1 1HL (121) 643-0884

MIKVAOT
Birmingham Central Synagogue
133 Pershore Road B5 7PA (121) 440-4044
Fax: (121) 440-5405

SYNAGOGUES
Liberal
Progressive Synagogue
4 Sheepcote Street B16 8AA (121) 643-5640
Fax: (121) 633-8372
Email: bps@uips.org
Web site: www.bps-pro-syn.co.uk
Orthodox
Bimingham Hebrew Congregation
Singer's Hill, Ellis Street B1 1HL (121) 643-0884
Fax: (121) 643-5950

Central Synagogue
133 Pershore Road, Edgbaston B5 7PA
(121) 440-4044
Fax: (121) 440-5405

Coventry

SYNAGOGUES
Orthodox
Coventry Hebrew Congregation
Barras Lane CV1 3BW   (24) 7622-0168
The Jewish presence in Coventry dates back to 1775,
if not earlier.

Reform
Coventry Jewish Reform Community
(24) 7667-2027

Solihull

SYNAGOGUES
Orthodox
Solihull & District Hebrew Congregation
3 Monastery Drive B91 1DW   (121) 707-5199
Fax: (121) 706-8736
Email: rabbiypink@compuserve.com
Web site: www.solihullshul.org
Services: Friday evening 6.30pm winter, 8.00 pm
summer; Saturday 9.45am, Sunday 9am

Harrogate

SYNAGOGUES
Orthodox
Harrogate Hebrew Congregation
St Mary's Walk   (1423) 871713
Fax: (1423) 879143
Email: philip.morris@ukgateway.net
Services: Saturday 9.30 am. First Friday evening in
month - Winter 6 pm. / Summer 7 pm.

York

TOURS OF JEWISH INTEREST
Yorkwalk
3 Fairway, Clifton Y030 5QA   (1904) 622303
Fax: (1904) 656244
Email: admin@yorkwalk.fsnet.co.uk
Web site: www.yorkwalk.co.uk
Introduced new walk called 'The Jewish Heritage
Walk', recalling the Jewish contribution to York's
history. The walk finishes at Clifford's Tower, the site
of a dreadful massacre in 1190.

Sheffield

SYNAGOGUES
Orthodox
Sheffield Jewish Congregation and Centre
Kingfield Synagogue, Brincliffe Crescent
S11 8UX   (114) 255-2296
There is a mikveh in the building. There is also a
kosher restaurant and butcher on Tursdays only.

Reform
Sheffield & District Reform Jewish Congregation
PO Box 675 S11 8TE   (114) 209259
Fax: (114) 236-2982
Web site: www.shef-ref.co.uk
Service alternate Friday evenings and Saturday
mornings, and high Holy Days

Bradford

The Jewish community, although only about 140
years old, has exercised much influence on the
city's staple industry: wool. Jews of German
descent developed the export trade of wool yarns
and fabrics.

SYNAGOGUES
Orthodox
Bradford Hebrew Congregation
Springhurst Road, Shipley BD18 3DN (1274) 581189
Fax: (1274) 01422-374101
Services 10am monthly on Shabbat Mevorachim,
High Holy Days & certain festivals.

Reform
Bradford Synagogue
Bowland Street, Manningham Lane
BD1 3BW   (1274) 728925
Service Sat 11am; Festivals, 6pm & 11am. A Grade II
listed building, built in the 1873 in the Moorish style.

Leeds

The Leeds Jewish community is the second largest
in the provinces, and numbers about 12,000. The
community dates only from the 1820's, although a
few Jews are known to have lived there in the
previous half-century. The first synagogue was
built in 1860.

The population which peaked at around 20,000
in the 1920's and was possibly the city where the
largest population of Jews in the Country is now
less than 8000.

BAKERIES

Chalutz Bakery
378 Harrogate Road LS17 6PY   (113) 269-1350
Supervision: Leeds Beth Din
Hours: Monday to Thursday, 8 am to 6 pm; Friday, to
one hour before Shabbat; Saturday, from one hour
after Shabbat to 2 pm Sunday.

BUTCHER AND DELICATESSEN

Fisher's Deli
391 Harrogate Road LS17 6DJ   (113) 268-6944
Supervision: Leeds Beth Din
Butcher and deli.

Gourmet Foods
Sandhill Parade, 584 Harrogate Road
LS17 8DP   (113) 268-2726
Supervision: Leeds Beth Din
Butcher and deli.

COMMUNITY ORGANISATIONS

Leeds Jewish Representative Council
c/o Shadwell Lane Synagogue LS17   (113) 269-7520
Fax: (113) 237-0851
Publishes Year Book.

DELICATESSEN

The Kosherie
410 Harrogate Road LS17 6PY   (113) 268-2943
Fax: (113) 269-6979
Supervision: Leeds Beth Din

HOTELS

Beegee's Guest House
18 Moor Allerton Drive, off Street Lane,
Moortown LS17 6RZ   (113) 293-5469
Fax: (113) 275-3300
Near all synagogues.

LIBRARIES

Jewish Library
Porton Collection; Leeds Central Library,
Municipal Buildings LS1 3AB   (113) 247-8282
Fax: (113) 247-8426
Web site: www.leeds.gov.uk

MEDIA

Newspaper
Jewish Telegraph
1 Shaftesbury Avenue LS8 1DR   (113) 295-6000
Fax: (113) 295-6006
Email: leeds@jewishtelegraph.com
Web site: www.jewishtelegraph.com

MIKVAOT

411 Harrogate Road LS17 7BY
(113) 237-1096 (answerphone)

RELIGIOUS ORGANISATIONS

Beth Din
Etz Chaim Synagogue LS17 6BY   (113) 269-6902
Fax: (113) 237-0893
Information about kosher food and accommodation
may be obtained here.

RESTAURANTS

Hansa's Gujarati Restaurant
72 North Street LS2 7PN   (113) 244-4408
Web site: www.hansasrestaurant.co.uk
Indian Vegetarian restaurant.

SYNAGOGUES

Orthodox
Beth Hamidrash Hagadol
399 Street Lane LS17 6HQ   (113) 269-2181
Fax: (113) 237-0113
Email: office@bhhs.freeserve.co.uk

Chassidishe
c/o Donisthorpe Hall, Shadwell Lane LS17 6AW

Etz Chaim
411 Harrogate Road LS17 7BY   (113) 266-2214

Queenshill Synagogue
26 Queenshill Avenue LS17 6AX   (113) 2687364
Email: sabrah2936.aol.com

**Shadwell Lane Synagogue (United Hebrew
Congregation)**
151 Shadwell Lane LS17 8DW   (113) 269-6141
Fax: (113) 269-6165

Shomrei Hadass
368 Harrogate Road LS17 6QB   (113) 268-1461
Reform
Sinai
Roman Avenue, off Street Lane LS8 2AN
(113) 266-5256
Fax: (113) 266-1539
Email: synagogue@sinaileeds.freeserve.co.uk

SCOTLAND

FIFE

Dundee

SYNAGOGUES
St Mary Place DD1 5RB   (1382) 223557

Dunoon

SYNAGOGUES
Argyll & Bute Jewish Community
(1369) 705118

St Andrews

CONTACT INFORMATION
Jewish Student's Society
c/o Sec., Students' Union, University of St Andrews
KY16 9UY

GRAMPIAN

Aberdeen

RESTAURANTS
Vegetarian
Lemon Tree Café
5 West North Street AB24 5AT   (1224) 621610
Fax: (1224) 630888
Email: bar@lemontree.org
12 noon to 4.00pm Tuesday - Sunday.

SYNAGOGUES
74 Dee Street AB11 6DS   (1224) 582135

LOTHIAN

Edinburgh

The Town Council and Burgess Roll minutes of 1691 and 1717 record applications by Jews for permission to live and trade in Edinburgh.

BUTCHERS
3 Oxgangs Road   (131) 445-3437
Regular meat deliveries from suppliers in Glasgow and Manchester. Further information from Hon. Sec. W. Simpson.

KASHRUT INFORMATION
Rabbi D Sedley
(131) 667-9360

RESTAURANTS
Vegetarian
Black Bo's
Blackfriars Street EH   (131) 557-6136

Henderson's
94 Hanover Street EH2 1DR   (131) 225-2131
Fax: (131) 220-3542
Email: mail@hendersonsofedinburgh.co.uk
Web site: www.hendersonsofedinburgh.co.uk
Hours 8.00am - 10.30pm, closed on Sundays.
Adjoining Bistro is also vegetarian, (Open on Sunday).

Kalpna Restaurant
2/3 St Patrick Sq. EH8 9EZ   (131) 667-9890
Fax: (131) 443-8782
Email: kalpnarestaurant@yahoo
Web site: www.kalpna.co.uk
Hours: Lunch 1100am to 2.00pm. Dinner 5.30pm to 11.00pm.

SYNAGOGUES
Orthodox
4 Salisbury Road EH16 5AB   (131) 667-3144
Fax: (131) 0132-461-3750
Email: ray.taylor@lineone.net

STRATHCLYDE

Glasgow

The Glasgow Jewish community dates back to 1823. The oldest synagogue building is the Garnethill Synagogue, now also the home of the Scottish Jewish Archives, which opened in 1879. The community grew rapidly from 1891 with many Jews settling in the Gorbals. In recent years the community has gradually spread southwards and is now mainly situated in the Giffnock and Newton Mearns areas.

BOOKSELLERS
J & E Levingstone
47/55 Sinclair Drive G42 9PT   (141) 649-2962
Fax: (141) 649-2962
Religious requisites also stocked.

Well of Wisdom
Giffnock Synagogue G46   (141) 577-8260
Fax: (141) 620-0823

COMMUNITY ORGANISATIONS
Jewish Community Centre
222 Fenwick Road G46 6UE   (141) 577-8200
Fax: (141) 577-8202
Email: glasgow@j-scot.org
Web site: www.j-scot.org/glasgow

DELICATESSEN
Hello Deli
200 Fenwick Road G46   (141) 638-8267
Fax: (141) 621-2290

Marlenes Kosher Deli
2 Burnfield Road G46 7QB   (141) 638-4383

Michael Morrison and Son
52 Sinclair Drive G42 9PY   (141) 632-0998
Email: kosher@talk21.com
Not under official supervision. Stockist of many glatt kosher items.

HOTELS
Giffnock Guest House
10 Forres Avenue G46 6LJ
(141) 638-5554 (mobile: 07801 666-864)
Fax: (141) 571-9301
Email: stay@giffnockguesthouse.co.uk
Web site: www.giffnockguesthouse.co.uk
Not kosher. 5 minute walk to Synagogue.

Guest House
26 St Clair Avenue G46 7QE   (141) 638-3924
Kosher, but not supervised.

KOSHER FOOD

Mindelicious
Unit 2, Block 8, Thornliebank Industrial Estate
G77 5PZ   (141) 620-0787
Fax: (141) 638-4411
Email: chef@mindelicious
Web site: www.mindelicious.com
Delivers to hotels.

MEDIA

Newspaper
Jewish Telegraph
May Terrace, Giffnock G46 6DL   (141) 621-4422
Fax: (141) 621-4333
Email: glasgow@jewishtelegraph.com
Web site: www.jewishtelegraph.com

MIKVAOT

Giffnock & Newlands Synagogue
Maryville Avenue G46 7NE   (141) 577-8269
Fax: (141) 577-8252

SYNAGOGUES

Orthodox
Garnethill
129 Hill Street G3 6UB   (141) 322-4151
Shabbat services 10am. Yomtov services 9.45 am.

Giffnock & Newlands Hebrew Congregation
Maryville Avenue G46 7NE   (141) 577-8250
Fax: (141) 577-8252
Email: rabbimrubin@talk21.com

Langside
125 Niddrie Road G42 8QA   (141) 423-4062

Netherlee & Clarkston
Clarkston Road at Randolph Drive G44
(141) 637-8206/639-7194
Fax: (141) 616-0743

Newton Mearns
14 Larchfield Court G77 5BH   (141) 639-4000
Fax: (141) 639-4000
Email: nmhc@btconnect.com

Reform
Glasgow New Synagogue
147 Ayr Road, Newton Mearns G77 6RE
(141) 639-4083
Fax: (141) 639-4083
Email: shul@gns.org.uk
Web site: www.gns.org.uk

WALES

GLAMORGAN (SOUTH)

Cardiff

MIKVAOT
Wales Empire Pool Building, Wood Street
CF1 1PP   (29) 2038-2296

RESTAURANTS
Vegetarian
Munchies Wholefood Co-op
60 Crwys Road, Cathays CF2 4NN   (29) 2039-9677

SELF-CATERING
Hillel House CF2 5NR   (29) 2022-8845
Self catering for students.

SYNAGOGUES
Orthodox
Cardiff United Synagogue
Brandreth Road, Penylan CF
(29) 2047-3728/2048-7377
Fax: (29) 2047-3728
Email: rabbi@cardiffunited.org.uk
Web site: www.cardiffunited.org.uk
Reform
Cardiff New Synagogue
Moira Terrace CF24 0EJ   (29) 2049-1689
Email: info@cardiffnewsyn.org

GLAMORGAN (WEST)

Swansea

RESTAURANTS
Vegetarian
Chris's Kitchen
The Market SA1 3PE   (1792) 643455
8.30am to 5.30pm Mon.-Sat

SYNAGOGUES
Ffynone
17 Ffynone Drive SA1 6DB   (1792) 473333

GWENT

Newport

SYNAGOGUES
Newport Mon Hebrew Congregation
Risca Road NP9 5HH   (1633) 262308
                        Fax: (1633) 266362
Communication: 45 St Marks Crescent, Newport, S.
Wales, NP20 5HE.

GWYNEDD

Llandudno

HOTELS
Vegetarian
Plas Madoc Vegetarian Guesthouse
60 Church Walks LL30 2HL   (1492) 876514
        Email: plasmadoc@vegetarianguesthouse.com
        Web site: www.vegetarianguesthouse.com
Synagogue 100 yards away.

SYNAGOGUES
28 Church Walks LL30 2HL   (1492) 572549
No resident minister, but visiting ministers during
summer months. Friday night services held
throughout year, 6.15pm (winter) and 8pm
(summer).

NORTHERN IRELAND

Belfast

There were Jews living in Belfast in the year 1652,
but the present community was founded in 1869.

ORGANISATIONS
Vegetarian & Vegans Charity
66 Ravenhill Gardens BT6 8GQ   (28) 9028-1640

RESTAURANTS
Jewish Community Centre
49 Somerton Road BT15 3LH   (28) 9077-7974
Open Sunday 6.30 pm to 9.30 pm. Phone ahead as
the centre closing during the summer. Both Meat and
Dairy.

SYNAGOGUES
Orthodox
49 Somerton Road BT15 3LH   (28) 9077-7974
Services: Saturday, Sunday, Monday, & Thursday; am.
Friday pm.

CHANNEL ISLANDS

ALDERNEY

Longy

MEMORIAL
Corblets Road
There is a memorial to the victims of the Nazis during
their occupation of the Channel Islands during the
Second World War. It bears plaques in English,
French, Hebrew and Russian.

JERSEY

St Brelade

CONTACT INFORMATION
16 La Rocquaise, La Route des Genets
St Brelade JE3 8HY   (1534) 742-819
                        Fax: (1534) 747-554
Honorary secretary of the Jersey Jewish
Congregation.

SYNAGOGUES
Jersey Jewish Congregation
La Petite Route des Mielles, St Brelade JE3 8FY
                            (1534) 865-333
                        Fax: (1534) 861-431
Shabbat morning service, 10:30 am; Holy days, 7 pm
and 10 am.

ISLE OF MAN

Douglas

SYNAGOGUES
Hebrew Congregation
                            (1624) 24214
There are more than seventy Jews on the island.

UNITED STATES OF AMERICA

The first Jews came to what is now the United States of America in 1654. The ship had come from the West Indies and included 23 Jews from Brazil, attempting to escape the arrival of the Inquisition following Portugal's recapture of Brazil from the Dutch earlier that year. It is believed that they thought they were travelling to Amsterdam in the Netherlands rather than to New Amsterdam as New York was then called. Within ten years, however, the commuity was moribund. The surrender of New Amsterdam to the British in 1664 brought substantial changes to the Jewish settlement as some restrictions to both civil and religious rights were lifted. In a few colonies they were even granted the right to vote.

Following the English takeover communities were established along the eastern coast, and by 1700 there were between 200 and 300 Jews in the country. At the time of the Revolution there were between 1,500 and 2,000 Jews and they served both in the Militia (which was compulsory) and as officers and soldiers. In the decades immediately before the Civil War the Jewish population rose from 15,000 to 150,000 as a result of emigration, mainly from German areas. During that war Jews served on both sides with their respective communities.

Immigration was at its peak between 1880 and 1925 (when free emigration ended) and during this period the Jewish population grew from 280,000 to 4,500,000. Unfortunately, during the 1930s only a small number of the Jewish refugees trying to escape from Germany were able to enter the USA. America's numerical position in world Jewry has declined, with its population being in 1948 as much as ten times the population of Israel, to its current approaching parity. The largest concentration by far has always been in New York.

Each of the main religious groups has its own association of synagogues and rabbis and, unlike many other countries, there is no central religious organisation. There is therefore no central supervision of kashrut. Instead there are many hashgachot issued by both individual local communal organisations and rabbis, as well as by companies who issue such certificates on a commercial basis. Travellers may always check with a local rabbi to ascertain the appropriate supervisory body in a relevant location.

Travellers should also be aware that, following a decision in the Brooklyn (New York) District Court in July 2000, discussions are under way in several other jurisdictions to prepare for the eventuality that New York's kosher laws may be rendered unconstitutional on appeal.

Country calling code (1)	**Total Population 274,520,000**
Emergency Telephone (Police – 911) (Fire – 911) (Ambulance – 911)	**Jewish Population 5,200,000**
	(Electricity voltage – 110/220)

ALABAMA

Birmingham

COMMUNITY ORGANISATIONS
Birmingham Jewish Federation
3966 Montclair Road 35213   (205) 803-0416
                               Fax: (205) 803-1526

CONTACT INFORMATION
Rabbi Avraham Shmidman
3225 Montevallo Road 35223   (205) 879-1664
                               Fax: (205) 879-5774
                     Email: kicongreg@aol.com
Visitors requiring information about kashrut, temporary accommodation, etc., should contact Rabbi Shmidman.

DELICATESSEN
Browdy's
2607 Cahaba Road 35223   (205) 879-6411

MIKVAOT
Knesseth Israel
3225 Montevallo Rd 35213   (205) 879-1464
Supervision: (O)

SYNAGOGUES
Conservative
Beth-El
2179 Highland Avenue 35205   (205) 933-2740
                               Fax: (205) 933-2747

Orthodox
Knesseth Israel
3225 Montevallo Road 35223   (205) 879-1464
                               Fax: (205) 879-5774

Reform
Emanu-El
2100 Highland Avenue 35205   (205) 933-8037

Huntsville

SYNAGOGUES
Conservative
Etz Chayim
7705 Bailey Cove Road 35802   (256) 882-2918
Fax: (256) 881-6160

Mobile

SYNAGOGUES
Reform
Spring Hill Avenue Temple
1769 Spring Hill Avenue 36607   (334) 478-0415

Montgomery

COMMUNITY ORGANISATIONS
Jewish Federation
PO Box 20058 36120   (334) 277-5820
Fax: (334) 277-8383

SYNAGOGUES
Conservative
Agudath Israel
3525 Cloverdale Road 36111   (334) 281-7394
Mikvah attached.

Orthodox
Etz Ahayem (Sephardi)
725 Augusta Road 36111   (334) 281-9819

Reform
Beth Or
2246 Narrow Lane 36106

ALASKA

Anchorage

GROCERIES
Carr's Market
Diamond Boulvevard and Seward Hwy
(907) 341-1020
Market has a kosher section.

SYNAGOGUES
Orthodox
Congregation Shomrei Ohr
1210 E. 26th 99508   (907) 279-1200
Fax: (907) 279-7890
Email: lubavitchofak@gci.net
The centre offers full Shabbat meals featuring
homemade dishes.

Reform
Beth Sholom
7525 E. Northern Lights Blvd 99504   (907) 338-1836
Fax: (907) 337-4013
Email: sholom@alaska.net

Denali National Park

GROCERIES
PS Kosher Food Services
P.O. Box 240, Mile 248.5 Parks Highway,
Healy 99743   (907) 683-1560
Fax: (907) 683-4026
Email: psfood@juno.com
Kitchens located at Denali North Star Inn. Open in
the summer only.

Juneau

SYNAGOGUES
Reform
Juneau Jewish Community
(907) 463-4333

ARIZONA

Phoenix

COMMUNITY ORGANISATIONS
Jewish Federation of Greater Phoenix
32 W. Coolidge, Suite 200 85013   (602) 274-1800

Orthodox Rabbinical Council of Greater Phoenix
515 E. Bethany Home Road 85012   (602) 277-8858
Fax: (602) 274-0713

KASHRUT INFORMATION
Rabbi David Rebibo
Phoenix Vaad Hakashruth, 515 E. Bethany
Home Rd. 85012   (602) 277-8858
Fax: (602) 274-0713
Email: bethjoseph515@hotmail.com
Visitors requiring kashrut information should contact
Rabbi Rebibo.

MEDIA
Newspapers
Jewish News of Greater Phoenix
1625 E. Northern Ave., Suite 106 85020
(602) 870-9470
Fax: (602) 870-0426
Email: editor@jewishaz.com
Web site: www.jewishaz.com

Shalom Arizona
32 W. Coolidge, Suite 200 85013   (602) 274-1800

RESTAURANTS
King Solomon's Pizza
4810 N. 7th Street   (602) 870-8655
Meat
Segal's New Place
4818 N. 7th Street   (602) 285-1515

SYNAGOGUES
Conservative
Beth El Congregation
1118 W. Glendale 85021   (602) 944-3359
Email: bethelarizona@aol.com

Temple Beth Sholom
3400 N Dobson Road, Chandler 85224
(602) 897-3636
Fax: (602) 897-3633
Email: templebethsholom@aol.com
Web site: www.templebethsholomaz.org

Orthodox
Congregation Beth Joseph
515 E. Bethany Home Road 85012   (602) 277-8858
Fax: (602) 274-0713
Email: bethjoseph515@hotmail.com

Congregation Shaarei Tzedek
7608 N. 18th Avenue 85021   (602) 944-1133

Young Israel of Phoenix
745 E Maryland Avenue, Ste.120 85014
(602) 265-8888
Fax: (602) 265-8867
Email: cnsil5@home.com

Reform
Temple Beth Ami
4545 N. 36th Street, No. 211 85018   (602) 956-0805

Temple Chai
4545 East Marilyn Rd 85032   (602) 971-1234

Scottsdale

MUSEUM
Sylvia Plotkin Judaica Museum
10460 N. 56th St, Scottsdale 85253   (480) 951-0323
Fax: (480) 951-7150
Email: museum@templebethisrael.org
Web site: www.sylviaplotkinjudaica.org
Hours: Most Sundays 12am-3pm, Tuesday-
Friday10am-3pm, Friday evenings after services.
Advanced notice required for groups of ten or more.

SYNAGOGUES
Conservative
Beth Emeth of Scottsdale
5406 E. Virginia Avenue 85254   (480) 947-4604

Beth Joshua Congregation
6230 E. Shea Blvd. 85254   (480) 991-5404

Har Zion
5929 E. Lincoln Drive 85253   (480) 991-0720

Orthodox
Chabad of Scottsdale
10215 North Scottsdale Road 85253   (480) 998-1410
Web site: www.chabadofscottsdale.org

Reform
Temple Kol Ami
15030 N. 64th Street 85254   (480) 951-9660
Fax: (480) 951-5231
Email: templekolami@aol.com

Temple Solel
6805 E. MacDonald Drive 85253   (480) 991-7414
Fax: (480) 451-0829
Email: mleano@templesolel.org
Web site: www.templesolel.org

Sierra Vista

SYNAGOGUES
Reform
Temple Kol Hamidbar
PO Box 908 Sierra Vista 85636
(520) 458-8637 (Ans. phone only)
Email: tkh85636@hotmail.com
Web site: www.uahcweb.org/congs/az/tkh/
Location is 228 North Canyon Drive

Sun City

SYNAGOGUES
Conservative
Beth Emeth of Sun City
13702 Meeker Blvd., 85373   (602) 584-1957

SYNAGOGUES
Reform
Beth Shalom of Sun City
12202 101st Avenue 85351   (623) 977-3240
Fax: (623) 977-3214
Email: tbsaz@goodnet.com

Tempe

COMMUNITY ORGANISATIONS
Tri-City Jewish Community Center
1965 E. Hermosa Drive 85282   (602) 897-0588

SYNAGOGUES
Orthodox
Chabad-Lubavitch Center
23 W. 9th Street 85281   (602) 966-5163

Reform
Temple Emanuel
5801 Rural Road 85283   (602) 838-1414

Tucson

BAKERIES
Nadine's Pastry Shoppe
4553 Broadway Blvd.   (520) 326-0735

BUTCHERS & DELICATESSENS
Feig's Kosher Market & Deli
5071 E. 5th Street 85711   (520) 325-2255
     Fax: (520) 325-2978
Supervision: Rabbi R. Eisen.
Fresh glatt beef, lamb and veal, full service deli, groceries. Hours: Monday to Thursday, 8 am to 5:45 pm; Friday, to 3:45 pm; Sunday, to 1:45 pm.

COMMUNITY ORGANISATIONS
Jewish Federation of Southern Arizona
3822 E. River Rd. 85718   (520) 577-9393
     Fax: (520) 577-0734
     Email: stumellan@jon.cjfny.org

SYNAGOGUES
Conservative
Congregation Bet Shalom
3881 E. River Road 85718   (520) 577-1171
     Fax: (520) 577-8903
     Email: cbs3881@juno.com
Supervision: Rabbi Leo M Abrami
Kosher (dairy) kitchen, operated by Sisterhood.

Orthodox
Congregation Chofetz Chayim
5150 E. 5th Street 85711   (520) 747-7780
     Fax: (520) 745-6325
     Email: ewbecker@flash.net

Young Israel of Tucson
2443 E 4th Street 85710   (520) 326-8362

ARKANSAS

El Dorado

SYNAGOGUES
Reform
Beth Israel
1130 E. Main Street

Helena

SYNAGOGUES
Reform
Temple Beth-El
406 Perry Street 72342   (501) 338-6654
Founded 1875.

Hot Springs

SYNAGOGUES
Reform
House of Israel
300 Quapaw Avenue. 71901   (501) 623-5821
     Fax: (501) 622-3500
     Email: houseofi@direclynx.net
Hot Springs is known for its curative waters. The Leo Levi Memorial Hospital (for joint disorders, such as arthritis) was founded by B'nai B'rith, as was the adjacent Levi Towers, a senior citizen housing project.

Little Rock

BAKERIES
Andre's
11121 Rodney Parham Rd 72212

COMMUNITY ORGANISATIONS
Jewish Federation of Arkansas
425 N. University Ave., Little Rock 72205
     (501) 663-3571
     Fax: (501) 663-7286
     Email: jfalr@aristotle.net
Monday to Thursday 9.00am to 5.00pm. Friday 9.00am to 4.00pm.

SYNAGOGUES
Orthodox
Agudath Achim
7901 W. 5th St. 72205   (501) 225-1683
Mikva on premises.

Reform
B'nai Israel
3700 Rodney Parham Rd. 72212   (501) 225-9700
     Fax: (501) 225-6058
     Email: elevy@snider.net

CALIFORNIA

As the general population of California continues to increase, the Jewish community is growing as well. Places of worship abound, from Eureka in the north to San Diego in the south, but the major part of the community lives in the Los Angeles metropolitan area.

Alameda

SYNAGOGUES
Reform
Temple Israel
3183 Mecartney Road 94502   (510) 522-9355
Fax: (510) 522-9356
Email: tialameda@prodigy.net

Arleta

SYNAGOGUES
Reform
Temple Beth Solomon of the Deaf
13580 Osborne Street 91331   (818) 899-2202
Fax: (818) (TDD) 896-6721

Bakersfield

SYNAGOGUES
Conservative
B'nai Jacob
600 17th Street 93301   (661) 325-8017

Reform
Temple Beth El
2906 Loma Linda Drive 93305   (661) 322-7607
Fax: (661) 322-7807
Email: kernjew@aol.com

Berkeley

MIKVAOT
Mikvah Taharas Israel
2520 Warring St. 94704-3111   (510) 848-7221
Fax: (510) 217-3596
Email: vaad@flash.net
Available by appointment only. (Women 510-848-7221; daytime: men 510-548-8729)

MUSEUM
The Magnes Museum
2911 Russell St. 94705   (510) 591-8800
Fax: (510) 591-8815
Email: info@magnesmuseum.org
Web site: www.magnesmuseum.org
Presents artistic expressions of Jewish culture through contemporary and historic exhibitions. Call or visit website for up to date information on exhibition dates and hours, special events and public programs.

RESTAURANTS
Dairy
Noah's Bagels
1883 Solano Avenue   (510) 525-4447
Supervision: The Vaad Kakashrus of Northern California

SYNAGOGUES
Conservative
Netivot Shalom
1841 Berkeley Way 94708   (510) 549-9447
Fax: (510) 549-9448
Email: administrator@netivotshom.org
Web site: www.netivotshalom.org
Weekly Shabbat/Holy Day services at 1414 Walnut Street.

Egalitarian
Berkeley Hillel Foundation
2736 Bancroft Way 94704   (510) 845-7793
Fax: (510) 845-7753
Traditional egalitarian services on Friday evening/student programmes.

Jewish Renewal
Aquarian Minyan
c/o Goldfarb, 2020 Essex 94703

Kehilla
PO Box 3063 94703

Orthodox
Chabad House
2643 College Avenue 94704   (510) 540-5824

Congregation Beth Israel
1630 Bancroft Way 94703   (510) 843-5246
Fax: (510) 843-5058
Email: office@beth-israel.berkeley.ca.us
Web site: www.beth-israel.berkeley.ca.us

Reform
Congregation Beth El
2301 Vine Street 94708   (510) 848-3988
Fax: (510) 848-9434
Email: frontoffice@bethelberkeley.org

Bonita

SYNAGOGUES
Orthodox
Beth Eliyahu Torah Center
5012 Central Avenue, Bonita 91902   (619) 472-2144
Fax: (619) 472 0718

Burlingame

SYNAGOGUES
Reform
Peninsula Temple Sholom
1655 Sebastian Drive 94010   (415) 697-2266
Fax: (415) 697-2544

Carmel

SYNAGOGUES
Reform

Congregation Beth Israel
5716 Carmel Valley Road 93923   (831) 624-2015
Fax: (831) 624-4786
Email: shalomcbi@aol.com
Services: Friday night 8.00 pm and Saturday 11.00 am.

Castro Valley

SYNAGOGUES
Reform
Shir Ami
4529 Malabar Avenue 94546   (415) 537-1787

Chula Vista

SYNAGOGUES
Conservative
Temple Beth Sholom
208 Madrona Street, Chula Vista 91910
(619) 420-6040
Email: bethsholomcv@aol.com
Web site: www.ascj.org/pacsw/chulavista/1ntel.

Costa Mesa

COMMUNITY ORGANISATIONS
Jewish Federation of Orange County
250 E. Baker Street, Suite #A 92626
(714) 755-5555 ext 241
Fax: (714) 755-0307
Email: info@jfoc.org
Web site: www.jewishorangecounty.org

GIFT SHOP
The Golden Dreidle
1835 Newport Blvd. #A111 92627   (714) 645-3878
Fax: (714) 646-5081

Daly City

SYNAGOGUES
Conservative
B'nai Israel
1575 Annie Street 94015   (415) 756-5430

Davis

SYNAGOGUES
Reform
Davis Jewish Fellowship
1821 Oak Avenue 95616   (916) 758-0842

Encinitas

SYNAGOGUES
Reform
Temple Solel
552 S.Camino Real, Encinitas 92024   (760) 436-0654
Fax: (760) 436-2748
Email: info@templesolel.net

Eureka

SYNAGOGUES
Reform
Beth El
Hodgson & T Streets, PO Box 442 95502
(707) 444-2846

Fresno

COMMUNITY ORGANISATIONS
Jewish Federations Office
1340 W. Herndon, Suite 103 93711

SYNAGOGUES
Conservative
Beth Jacob
406 W. Shields Avenue 93705   (209) 222-0664
Orthodox
Chabad House
6735 N. ILA 93711   (209) 432-2770
Reform
Temple Beth Israel
6622 N. Maroa Avenue 93704   (209) 432-3600
This temple has its own etrog tree, planted from a
sprig brought to the USA from Israel.

La Jolla

RESTAURANTS
Meat
Western Glatt Kosher & N.Y. Deli
7739 Fay Avenue, La Jolla 92037   (619) 454-6328

SYNAGOGUES
Conservative
Congregation Beth El
8660 Gilman Drive, La Jolla 92037   (619) 452-1734
Fax: (619) 452 5578
Email: congregationbethel.com

Orthodox
Congregation Adat Yeshurun
8625 La Jolla Scenic Dr., N. 92037   (619) 535-1196
Fax: (619) 535-0037
Email: info@adatyeshurun.org
Web site: www.adatyeshurun.org
8950 Villa La Jolla Drive, Suite 1224,
La Jolla 92037   (619) 535-1196
Fax: (619) 535-0037
Email: adatyeshurun.org
adatyeshurun.org

La Mesa

MEDIA
Newspapers
San Diego Jewish Times
4731 Palm Avenue, La Mesa 91941   (619) 463-5515
Fax: (619) 463-1309
Email: jewishtimes@earthlink.net

Laguna Hills

DELICATESSEN
The Kosher Bite
23595 Moulton Parkway 92653   (949) 770-1818
Fax: (949) 770-5321
Email: kosherbite.com
Supervision: Rabinical Council of Orange County
Monday, Tuesday, Thursday 9am to 5pm. Wednesday
9 am to 7 pm. Friday 9am-3pm.

Lakewood

SYNAGOGUES
Conservative
Temple Beth Zion Sinai
6440 Del Amo Blvd. 90713   (310) 429-0715
Fax: (310) 429-0715
Email: tbzs@jps.net

LOS ANGELES (GREATER)

Anaheim

RESTAURANTS
Disneyland
Kosher meals are available at the Blue Bayou
restaurant, adjacent to the Pirates of the Caribbean.
Place orders at least one hour in advance.

SYNAGOGUES
Conservative
Temple Beth Emet
1770 W. Cerritos Avenue 92804   (714) 772-4720
Fax: (714) 772-4710
Email: tbe-anaheim@tea-house.com

Arcadia

SYNAGOGUES
Conservative
Congregation Shaarei Torah
550 S. 2nd Avenue 91006   (818) 445-0810

Beverly Hills

SYNAGOGUES
Orthodox
Beth Jacob
9030 Olympic Boulevard 90211   (310) 278-1911
Fax: (310) 278-9186

Young Israel of Beverly Hills
8701 Pico Blvd 90035   (310) 275-3020

Young Israel of North Beverly Hills
9350 Civic Center Drive, North Beverly Hills
90210   (310) 203-0170

Orthodox Sephardi
Magen David
322 N. Foothill 90210

Burbank

SYNAGOGUES
Conservative
Temple Emanu-El
1302 N. Glenoaks Avenue, Burbank 91504
(818) 845-1734

Reform
Beth Emet
320 E. Magnolia Blvd, Burbank 91502

Downey

SYNAGOGUES
Reform
Temple Ner Tamid
10629 Lakewood Boulevard 90241   (310) 861-9276

Encino

SYNAGOGUES
Conservative
Valley Beth Shalom
15739 Ventura Blvd, Encino 91316   (818) 788-6000

Orthodox
Chabad House
4915 Hayvenhurst, Encino 91346

Reform
Shir Chadash
17000 Ventura Blvd, Encino

Gardena

SYNAGOGUES
Conservative
Southwest Temple Beth Torah
14725 S. Gramercy Place 90249   (310) 327-8734

Granada Hills

COMMUNITY ORGANISATIONS
North Valley Center
16601 Rinaldi Street, Granada Hills 91344

Hollywood

KASHRUT INFORMATION
Kosher Information Bureau
15365 Magnolia Blvd, Sherman Oaks 91403
(818) 762-3197 & 262-5351
Fax: (818) 766-8537
Email: eeidlitz@kosherquest.org
Web site: www.kosherquest.org

Long Beach

BAKERIES
Fairfax Kosher Market & Bakery
11196-98 Los Alamitos Blvd 90720   (562) 828-4492

COMMUNITY ORGANISATIONS
**Jewish Federation of Greater Long Beach & W.
Orange County**
3801 E. Willow St. 90815   (562) 426-7601

MEDIA
Newspapers
Jewish Community Chronicle
3801 E. Willow St. 90815 1791

MIKVAOT
3847 Atlantic Avenue 90807

SYNAGOGUES
Orthodox
Congregation Lubavitch
3981 Atlantic Avenue 90807   (562) 596-1681

Young Israel of Long Beach
PO Box 7041 90807-0041   (562) 527-3163

Reform
Temple Beth David
6100 Hefley Street, Westminster

Temple Israel
338 E. 3rd Street 90812

Los Angeles

Los Angeles is America's, and the world's, second largest Jewish metropolis, with a Jewish population of around 600,000. Fairfax Avenue and Beverly Blvd together form the crossroads of traditional Jewish life, while a growing Orthodox enclave centers around Pico and Robertson Blvds.

Important note: Area telephone codes have recently been split to 310 and 213 for central Los Angeles. We have endeavoured in all cases to correct our information, but cannot guarantee the accuracy of those who did not send in updates.

BAKERIES
Noah's New York Bagels
1737 Santa Rita Road #400, Pleasanton 94566
(213) 485-1921
Email: noah@noahs.com
Supervision: California Rabbinical Council
All stores in Southern California are under RCC supervision; for the location of a store near you, call the above number.

Schwartz Bakery
441 N. Fairfax Ave. 90036   (213) 653-1683
Fax: (213) 653-6142
Supervision: RCC

8616 W. Pico Blvd   (213) 854-0592
Fax: (213) 653-6142
Supervision: RCC

BOOKSELLERS
House of David
9020 W. Olympic Blvd, Beverly Hills 90211
(213) 276-9414
Probably the most complete selection of books of Jewish interest can be found here.

COMMUNITY ORGANISATIONS
Board of Rabbis of Southern California
6505 Wilshire Blvd, Suite 415 90048 (213) 761-8600
Fax: (213) 761-8603

Jewish Federation of Greater Los Angeles
6505 Wilshire Blvd 90048   (213) 761-8000
Fax: (213) 761-8123
Web site: www.jewishla.org

Los Angeles West Side Community Center
5870 W. Olympic Blvd 90036   (213) 938-2531
Fax: (213) 954-9175
Email: westsidejcc@jcc-gla.org

DELICATESSEN
Pico Kosher Deli
8826 W. Pico Blvd 90035   (213) 273-9381
Fax: (213) 273-8476
Supervision: RCC
Hours: Sunday to Thursday, 10 am to 9 pm; Friday, 9 am to 3 pm. Glatt.

EMBASSY

Consul General of Israel
Suite 1700, 6380 Wilshire Blvd 90048   (213) 852-5523
Fax: (213) 852-5555
Email: israinfo@primenet.com
Web site: www.israelemb.org/la

GROCERIES

PS Kosher Food Services
9760 W. Pico Blvd 90035   (213) 553-8804
Fax: (213) 275-3031
Email: psfood@juno.com
Web site: www.pskosherfood.com
Kitchens located at Yeshiva University of Los Angeles,
and Young Israel of Beverly Hills.

HOSPITAL

Cedars Sinai Hospital
8700 Beverly Blvd   (213) 855-4797
Supervision: RCC

KASHRUT INFORMATION

Rabbi Bukspan
6407 Orange Street 90048   (213) 653-5083

Rabbinical Council of California
1122 S. Robertson Blvd 90035   (213) 271-4160
Fax: (213) 271-7147

MEDIA

Newspapers
Heritage Southwest Jewish Press
Weekly publication, coming out on Fridays.

Jewish Journal
Weekly publication, coming out on Fridays.

MIKVAOT

Los Angeles Mikva
9548 W. Pico Blvd., 90035   (213) 550-4511

MUSEUM

Museum of Tolerance (Beit Hashoah)
9786 West Pico Blvd 90035   (213) 553-8403
Fax: (213) 553-4521
Email: information@wiesenthal.net
Web site: www.wiesenthal.com/library
High-tech, hands-on museum that focuses on two
themes through interactive exhibits: the dynamics of
racism and prejudice, and the history of the
Holocaust – the ultimate example of man's
inhumanity to man. Hours Monday - Thursday
11.30am - 4.00pm, Friday 11.30am to 3.00pm April
to October, 1.00am November to March, Sunday
11.00am to 5.00pm.

ORGANISATIONS

Jewish Social Action Organisation
Simon Wiesenthal Center, 1399 South
Roxbury Dr. 90035   (213) 553-9036
Fax: (213) 553-4521
Email: information@wiesenthal.net
Web site: www.wiesenthal.com

RESTAURANTS

Dairy
Fish Grill
7226 Beverly Blvd   (213) 937-7162

Fish Place Restaurant
9340 W. Pico Blvd   (213) 858-8737
Supervision: Kehila Kosher

Milk & Honey
8837 W. Pico Blvd   (213) 858-8850

Pizza Delight
435 N. Fairfax Avenue   (213) 655-7800

Pizza World
368 S. Fairfax Ave   (213) 653-2896

Meat
Chick 'N Chow
9301 W. Pico Blvd   (213) 274-5595

Cohen Restaurant
316 E. Pico Blvd 90015   (213) 742-8888
Fax: (213) 742-0066
Supervision: RCC

Glatt Hut
9303 W. Pico Blvd   (213) 246-1900

Jeff's Gourmet Sausage Factory
8930 W. Pico Blvd.   (213) 858-8590

Magic Carpet
8566 W. Pico Blvd 90035   (213) 652-8507
Fax: (213) 652-3568
Supervision: Kehillah of Los Angeles

Simon's La Glatt
446 N. Fairfax Avenue   (213) 658-7730

Pizzerias
Pizza Delight
435 N. Fairfax Avenue 90036   (213) 655-7800
Fax: (213) 655-1142
Supervision: Kehillah of Los Angeles
Chalav Yisrael.

Shalom Pizza
8715 W. Pico Blvd   (213) 271-2255
Email: shalompizza@la.com
Supervision: RCC

SYNAGOGUES

Conservative
Adat Shalom
3030 Westwood Blvd 90034   (213) 475-4985

Sinai Temple
10400 Wilshire Blvd 90024   (213) 474-1518
Fax: (213) 474-6801

Temple Beth Am
1039 S. La Cienega Blvd 90035   (213) 652-7353
Fax: (213) 652-2384
Email: betham@tbala.org
Web site: www.tbala.org

Orthodox
Breed St. Shule
247 N. Breed St. 90033
This synagogue, the oldest still standing in Los
Angeles, is of historial interest.

Chabad House
741 Gayley Avenue, West Los Angeles 90025

Etz Jacob Congregation
7659 Beverly Blvd 90036   (213) 938-2619
Fax: (213) 930-2373
Email: office@etzjacob.org

Ohel David
7967 Beverly Blvd

Young Israel of Century City
9317 West Pico Blvd, Century City 90035
(213) 273-6954
Fax: (213) 273-7103
Email: shuloffice@yicc.org
Web site: www.yicc.org

Young Israel of Hancock Park
225 South La Brea   (213) 931-4030
Fax: (213) 935-3819

Young Israel of Los Angeles
660 N. Spaulding Avenue 90036   (213) 655-0300
Fax: (213) 655-0322

Orthodox Sephardi
Kahal Joseph
10505 Santa Monica Blvd 90025   (213) 474-0559

Temple Tifereth Israel
10500 Wilshire Blvd 90024   (213) 475-7311
Fax: (213) 470-9238

Reconstructionist
Kehillat Israel
16019 Sunset Blvd, Pacific Palisades 90272
(213) 459-2328
Fax: (213) 573-2098
Email: kihome@aol.com
Kehillat Israel has a modern sanctuary in the round. It
is the largest reconstructionist synagogue in the
United States.

Reform
Leo Baeck Temple
1300 N. Sepulveda Blvd 90049   (213) 476-2861

Stephen S. Wise Temple
15500 Stephen S. Wise Drive, Bel Air 90024
(213) 476-8561
Fax: (213) 476-3587

Temple Akiba
5249 S. Sepulveda Blvd, Culver City 90230
(213) 398-5783
Fax: (213) 398-1637
Web site: www.temakiba

Temple Isaiah
10345 W. Pico Blvd 90064

University Synagogue
11960 Sunset Blvd 90049   (213) 472-1255
Fax: (213) 476-3237

Wilshire Blvd Temple
3663 Wilshire Blvd 90010   (213) 388-2401
Fax: (213) 388-2595

North Hollywood

Kashrut Information
The Kashrus Information Bureau
12753 Chandler Blvd, N. Hollywood 91607
(818) 762-3197 & 262-5351
Fax: (818) 766-8537
Email: eeidlitz@kosherquest.org
Web site: www.kosherquest.org

MIKVAOT

Teichman Mikvah Society
12800 Chandler Blvd, N. Hollywood 91607
(818) 506-0996

RESTAURANTS

Meat
Drexler's Kosher Restaurant
12519 Burbank Blvd, N. Hollywood   (818) 984-1160

Flora Falafel
12450 Burbank Blvd, N. Hollywood   (818) 766-6567
Supervision: RCC

SYNAGOGUES

Orthodox
Adat Ari El Synagogue
5540 Laurel Canyon Blvd, N. Hollywood
91607   (818) 766-9426
There are eleven beautiful stained-glass windows,
designed by Mischa Kallis, depicting significant dates
in the religious calendar.

Shaarey Zedek
12800 Chandler Blvd, N. Hollywood 91607
(818) 763-0560
Fax: (818) 763-8215

Northridge

SYNAGOGUES

Conservative
Temple Ramat Zion
17655 Devonshire Avenue, Northridge
(818) 360-1881

Orthodox
Young Israel of Northridge
17511 Devonshire Street 91325   (818) 368-2221
Fax: (818) 360-5754
Email: rebbe@idt.net

Reform
Temple Ahavat Shalom
11261 Chimineas Avenue, Northridge

Pasadena

SYNAGOGUES

Conservative
Pasadena Jewish Temple and Center
1434 North Altadena Drive 91107   (626) 798-1161

San Fernando Valley

BAKERIES

Continental Kosher Bakery
12419 Burbank Blvd   (818) 762-5005

RESTAURANTS

Apropo Falafel
6800 Reseda Blvd   (818) 881-6608

Hadar Restaurant and Catering
12514 Burbank Blvd 91607   (818) 762-1155
Supervision: RCC

Dairy
Orly Dairy Restaurant & Pizza
12454 Magnolia Blvd   (818) 508-5570

Meat
Falafel Express
5577 Reseda Bl   (818) 345-5660

Sportsman Lodge
Sherman Oaks   (818) 984-0202

Pizzerias
La Pizza
12515 Burbank Blvd   (818) 760-8198

Pacific Kosher Pizza
12460 Oxnard   (818) 760-0087

SYNAGOGUES

Conservative
Beth Meier Congregation
11725 Moorpark, Studio City   (818) 769-0515

Temple B'nai Hayim
4302 Van Nuys Blvd, Sherman Oaks   (818) 788-4664

Sherman Oaks

RESTAURANTS

Dairy
Fish Grill
13628 Ventura Blvd   (818) 788-9896

Tarzana

BOOKSELLERS

Steimatzky
19566 Ventura Blvd, Tarzana 91356   (818) 708-2347
Fax: (818) 708-2319
Email: stmla@earthlink.net

SYNAGOGUES

Reform
Temple Judea
5429 Lindley Avenue, Tarzana

Tustin

SYNAGOGUES

Conservative
Congregation B'nai Israel
655 S. "B" St 92680   (714) 259-0655

Van Nuys

COMMUNITY ORGANISATIONS
Valley Cities Center
13164 Burbank Blvd., Van Nuys 91401

Venice

SYNAGOGUES
Orthodox
Jewish Pacific Center
505 Ocean Front Walk & 720 Rosa Avenue
90291   (310) 392-8749
Email: office@pjcenter.com
Web site: www.pjcenter.com
Mikva and an elementary day school with summer
camp facilities for visitors. It also offers a full range of
kosher food, bakery products and meat, as well as
accommodation.

**National Council of Young Israel West Coast
Regional Office**
1050 Indiana Avenue 90291   (310) 396-3935
Fax: (310) 581-0904
Email: ncyi.west@youngisrael.org

West Hills

COMMUNITY ORGANISATIONS
West Valley Center
22622 Vanowen Street, West Hills 91307

SYNAGOGUES
Conservative
Shomrei Torah
7353 Valley Circle, West Hills 73531   (818) 346-0811

Oakland

COMMUNITY ORGANISATIONS
Berkeley/Richmond JCC
1414 Walnut St.,, Berkeley 94709   (510) 848-0237
Fax: (510) 848-0170
Email: brjcc-office@eb.jfed.org
Web site: www.brjcc.org

Jewish Federation of the Greater East Bay
401 Grand Avenue #500 94610

DELICATESSEN
Holy Land Restaurant
677 Rand Avenue 94610   (510) 272-0535
Glatt kosher.

MIKVAOT
Beth Jacob Synagogue
3778 Park Blvd 94610
(510) 482-1147
Fax: (510) 482-2374
Email: bjc-office@eb.jfed.org

SYNAGOGUES
Conservative
Beth Abraham
327 MacArthur Blvd. 94610   (510) 832-0936
Beth Sholom
642 Dolores, San Leandro 94577
Independent
B'nai Israel of Rossmoor
c/o Fred Rau, 2601 Ptarmigan #3, Walnut Creek
94595
Beth Chaim
PO Box 23632, Pleasant Hill 94523
Orthodox
Beth Jacob Synagogue
3778 Park Blvd 94610   (510) 482-1147
Fax: (510) 482-2374
Email: bjc-office@eb.jfed.org
Reform
Beth Emek
PO Box 722, Livermore 94550
Beth Hillel
801 Park Central, Richmond 94803
Temple Beth Torah
42000 Paseo Padre Pkwy 94539   (510) 656-7141
Temple Isaiah
3800 Mt. Diablo Blvd., Lafayette 94549
Temple Sinai
2808 Summit 94609   (510) 451-3263
Fax: (510) 465-0603
Email: templeoffice@oaklandsinai.org

Palm Springs

COMMUNITY ORGANISATIONS
Jewish Federation of Palm Springs Desert Area
611 S. Palm Canyon Drive 92264   (760) 325-7281

SYNAGOGUES
Conservative
Temple Isaiah
332 W. Alejo Road 92262   (760) 325-2281
Fax: (760) 325-3235
Jewish community centre is at this location.
Orthodox
Chabad of Palm Springs
425 Avenue, Ortega   (760) 325-0774
Daily Services

Desert Synagogue
1068 N. Palm Canyon Drive 92262   (760) 327-4848
Fax: (760) 322-5238
Web site: www.desertshul.org
Daily minyan: January through Purim (call shul to
confirm).

Palo Alto

COMMUNITY ORGANISATIONS
Albert L. Schultz Community Center
655 Arastradero Road 94306   (650) 493-9400

GROCERIES
Garden Fresh
1245 W. El Camino Road, Mount View 94040
    (650) 961-7795

SYNAGOGUES
Orthodox
Chabad of Greater South Bay
3070 Louis Road 94303   (650) 424-9800
    Fax: (650) 493-3425
    Email: chabad@jewish.org
Palo Alto Orthodox Minyan
260 Sheridan Avenue 94306   (650) 948-7498

Poway

SYNAGOGUES
Orthodox
Chabad of Poway
16934 Chabad Way 92064   (858) 451-0455
    Fax: (858) 673-0299

Reform
Temple Adat Shalom
15905 Pomerado Road, Poway 92064 (858) 451-1200
    Fax: (858) 451 2409

Ramona

SYNAGOGUES
Reform
Etz Chaim
PO Box 1138, Ramona 92065   (760) 789-7393

Sacramento

COMMUNITY ORGANISATIONS
Jewish Federation of Sacramento
2351 Wyda Way 95825   (916) 486-0906
    Fax: (916) 486-0816
    Email: jfed@juno.com
    Web site: www.jewishsac.org

MIKVAOT
1024 Morse Ave 95864   (916) 481-1158

RESTAURANTS
Meat
Bob's Butcher Block
6436 Fair Oaks Blvd., Carmichael Oaks
Shopping Ctr   (916) 482-6884

SYNAGOGUES
Conservative
Mosaic Law
2300 Sierra Blvd. 95825   (916) 488-1122
    Fax: (916) 488-1165
    Web site: www.mosaiclaw.org
Orthodox
Kenesset Israel Torah Center
1165 Morse Avenue 95864   (916) 481-1159
    Fax: (916) 481-2096
    Email: itc1159@earthlink.net
    Web site: www.kitsacramento.org
Reform
B'nai Israel
3600 Riverside Blvd. 95818   (916) 446-4861
Beth Shalom
4746 El Camino Avenue 9608   (916) 485-4478
    Fax: (916) 485-0776
    Email: office@cbshalom.org
    Web site: www.cbshalom.org

San Bernardino

SYNAGOGUES
Reform
Emanu El
3512 N. E Street 92405   (909) 886-4818
    Fax: (909) 883-5892
    Email: cee@emanuelsb.org
This congregation is the oldest in southern California. The 'Home of Eternity' cemetery, 8th St. & Sierra Way, presented by the Mormons, is one of the oldest Jewish cemeteries in western USA.

San Carlos

ACCOMMODATION INFORMATION
Jewish Travel Network
PO Box 283 94070   (650) 368-0880
    Fax: (650) 599-9066
    Email: info@jewishtravelnetwork.com
    Web site: www.jewishtravelnetwork.com/
International hospitality exchange. Bed and breakfast and home exchanges.

San Diego

BAKERIES
Sheila's Café & Bakery
4577 Clairemont Drive 92117   (619) 270-0251
    Fax: (619) 274-5797
    Email: SheilasSanDiego@hotmail.com
    Web site: www.sheilascafe.com
Full time Shomer Shabbos Mashgiach on the premises.

COMMUNITY ORGANISATIONS
United Jewish Federation of San Diego County
4950 Murphy Canyon 92123-4325   (619) 571-3444
Fax: (619) 571-0701
Email: outreach@ujfsd.org
Web site: www.jewishinsandiego.org
Hours of opening: 8.30am.

DELICATESSEN
Eva's Fresh & Natural
6717 El Cajon Blvd 92115   (619) 462-5018
Fax: (619) 453-5659
Supervision: Vaad of San Diego
Dairy and vegetarian food. Meat dinners are available
to go only upon request in advance.

MEDIA
Newspapers
San Diego Jewish Press Heritage
PO Box 19363   (619) 265-0808
Fax: (619) 265-0850
Email: sdheritage@cox.net

MIKVAOT
(619) 546-1563
Call to arrange an appointment.

RESTAURANTS
Dairy
Aarons Glatt Kosher Market
4488 Convoy Street 92111   (619) 636-7979
Fax: (619) 636-7980
Web site: www.kosherfooddelivery.com
Lang's
6165 El Cajon Blvd 92115
(619) 287-7306; 800-60-LANGS
Fax: (619) 582-1545
Email: sales@kosherbread.com
Web site: www.kosherbread.com
Supervision: Vaad HaRabbanim of San Diego
Kosher pareve bakery, dairy deli and foods.

Sababa, Kosher Restaurant
7520 El Cajon Blvd.   (619) 337-1880
Fax: (619) 523-9963
Shmoozers Vegetarian & Pizzeria
6366 El Cajon Blvd 92115   (619) 583-1636
Fax: (619) 583 1635
Email: shmoozers1@aol.com
Supervision: Vaad HaRabbanim of San Diego
Hours: Sunday to Thursday, 11:30am to 9pm; Friday,
to 2pm; Saturday, Motzei Shabbat to 11pm.

Meat
Sheila's Café & Bakery
4577 Clairemont Dr. 92117   (619) 270-0251
Fax: (619) 274-5797
Email: SheilasSanDiego@hotmail.com
Web site: www.sheilascafe.com
Hours: Monday to Thursday 11.00 am - 9.00 pm,
Friday 11.00 am - 2.30 pm, and Sunday 2.00 pm -
9.00 pm. The restaurant does Shabbat take-aways
which must be ordered in advance.

SYNAGOGUES
Conservative
Congregation Beth Am
5050 Black Mtn. Road 92130   (619) 481-8454
Fax: (619) 481-6068
Email: betham@betham.com
Ner Tamid
16770 West Bernardo Drive, Suite A 92127
(619) 592-9141
Fax: (619) 592-4889
Email: nertamid@altavista.com
Tifereth Israel Synagogue
6660 Cowles Mountain Blvd 92119   (619) 697-6001
Fax: (619) 697 1102
Email: tiferethisrael.com

Orthodox
Beth Jacob Synagogue
4855 College Avenue 92115   (619) 287-9890
Fax: (619) 287-0578
Chabad House
6115 Montezuma Road 92115   (619) 265-7700
Fax: (619) 265 0346
Chabad of La Jolla
3813 Governor Drive, Suite N 92122 (619) 455-1670
Fax: (619) 451 1443
Ohr Shalom
1260 Morena Blvd, Suite 100 92100 (619) 275-9299
Fax: (619) 275-2078
Young Israel of San Diego
7291 Navajo Road, Suite 102 92119 (619) 589-1447

Reconstructionist
Congregation Dor Hadash
4858 Ronson Court, Suite A 92111   (619) 268-3674
Fax: (619) 794 4087

Reform
Congregation Beth Israel of San Diego
9001 Towne Centre Drive 92122   (619) 535-1111
Fax: (619) 535-1130
Email: bmiller@cbisd.org
Web site: www.cbisd.org
Temple Emanu-El
6299 Capri Drive 92120   (619) 286-2555
Fax: (619) 286 3176

San Francisco

BAKERIES
Noahs Bagels
3519 California Street, Willow Glen   (415) 387-3874

COMMUNITY ORGANISATIONS
**Jewish Com. Fed. of San Francisco, the
Peninsula, Marin & Sonoma Counties**
121 Steuart St. 94105   (415) 777-4545
Fax: (415) 495-6635
Email: jewishNfo@sfjcf.org
Web site: www.jewishfed.org
Publishes 'Resource guide to Jewish life in Bay Area'.

EMBASSY
Consul General of Israel
Suite 2100, 456 Montgomery Street 94104

GROCERIES
Jacob's Kosher Meats
2435 Noriega Street 94122   (415) 564-7482

Kosher Meats Israel & Cohen Kosher Meats
5621 Geary Blvd 94121   (415) 752-3064

Kosher Nutrition Kitchen
Montefiore Senior Center, 3200 California Av.,
Supervision: Orthodox Rabbinical Council

Tel Aviv Strictly Kosher Meats
2495 Irving Street 94122   (415) 661-7588
                                  Fax: (415) 661-8258
Supervision: Orthodox Rabbinical Council

LIBRARIES
Holocaust Library & Research Center
601 14th Avenue 94118   (415) 751-6040

MIKVAOT
Mikva
3355 Sacramento Street 94118   (415) 921-4070

MUSEUM
The Magnes Museum
121 Steuart St 94105   (415) 591-8800
                                  Fax: (415) 591-8815
                     Email: info@magnesmuseum.org
                  Web site: www.magnesmuseum.org
Presents artistic expressions of Jewish culture
through contemporary and historic exhibitions. Call
or visit website for up to date information on
exhibition dates and hours, special events and public
programs.

RESTAURANTS
Meat
Red Ox
1271 South Carolina Blvd, Walnut Creek
                                  (415) 256-6500
Supervision: Glatt kosher

Sabra
419 Grant Avenue, Chinatown   (415) 982-3656
                                  Fax: (415) 982-3650
Supervision: Vaad Hakashrus of Northern CA
Bishul Yisrael, Pat Yisrael and Mashgiach Temidi.
Israeli mediterranean cuisine. Catering available.

This Is It
430 Geary Street 94210   (415) 749-0201
Middle Eastern cuisine.

SYNAGOGUES
Conservative
B'nai Emunah
3595 Taraval Street 94116   (415) 664-7373
                                  Fax: (415) 664-4209
                        Email: emuna@jps.net
               Web site: www.bnaiemunahsf.org

Beth Israel-Judea
625 Brotherhood Way 94132   (415) 586-8833

Beth Sholom
14th Avenue & Clement Street 94118 (415) 221-8736
                                  Fax: (415) 221-3944
                      Email: cbsholom@aol.com

Ner Tamid
1250 Quintara Street 94116   (415) 661-3383

Orthodox
Adath Israel
1851 Noriega Street 94122   (415) 564-5565

Anshey Sfard
1500 Clement Street 94118   (415) 752-4979

Chabad House
11 Tillman Place 94108   (415) 956-8644

Chevra Thilim
751 25th Avenue 94121   (415) 752-2866

Keneseth Israel
873 Sutter Street 94109   (415) 771-3420
A downtown synagogue offering meals over Shabbat.

Torat Emeth
768 27th Avenue 94121   (415) 386-1830

Young Israel of San Francisco
1806 A Noriega Street 94122   (415) 387-1774

Reform
Emanu-El
Arguello Blvd. & Lake Street 94118 (415) 751-2535
                                  Fax: (415) 751-2511
                      Email: mail@emanuelsf.org

Sha'ar Zahav
290 Dolores Street 94103   (415) 861-6932
                                  Fax: (415) 841-6081
                  Email: office@shaarzahav.org

Sherith Israel
2266 California Street 94115   (415) 346-1720
                                  Fax: (415) 673-9439
                  Email: ed@sherithisrael.org

Sephardi
Magain David
351 4th Avenue 94118   (415) 752-9095

TOURIST INFORMATION
Jewish Community Information & Referral
121 Steuart St 94105   (415) 777-4545
                                  Fax: (415) 495-4897
                     Email: jewishNfo@sfjcf.org
                  Web site: www.jewishfed.org
Local toll free within the Bay Area 877/777-JCIR
(5247).

San Jose

BOOKSELLERS
Alef Bet Judaica
14103-0 Winchester Blvd, Los Gatos 95032
                                  (408) 370-1818
                                  Fax: (408) 725-8269
                      Email: nurit@best.com

COMMUNITY ORGANISATIONS

Jewish Federation of Greater San Jose
14855 Oka Road, Los Gatos 95030   (408) 358-3033
Fax: (408) 356-0733

RESTAURANTS

Meat
Willow Glen Kosher Market
1185 Lincoln Avenue 95125   (408) 297-6604
Email: kosher@visto.com
Supervision: Va'ad Hakashrus San Jose
Glatt kosher. Will deliver to local hotels.

SYNAGOGUES

Conservative
Congregation Beth David
19700 Prospect Road, Saratoga 95070
(408) 257-3333
Fax: (408) 257-3338
Email: admin@beth-david.org

Congregation Emeth
PO Box 1430, Gilroy 95021   (408) 847-4111

Orthodox
Ahavas Torah
1537-A Meridian Avenue 95125   (408) 266-2342
Fax: (408) 264-3139
Web site: www.ahava.org

Almaden Valley Torah Center
1281 Juli Lynn Drive 95120   (408) 997-9117

Am Echad Community
1504 Meridian Avenue 95125   (408) 267-2591
Email: info@amechad.org
Web site: www.amechad.org
Orthodox community offering Shabbos hospitality,
shiurium and daily minyonim. Mailing address: P O
Box 5101, San Jose, California 95150.

Reform
Congregation Shir Hadash
16555 Shannon Road, Los Gatos 95032
(408) 358-1751
Fax: (408) 358-1753
Web site: www.shirhadash.org

Temple Beth Sholom
2270 Canoas Garden Avenue 95125   (408) 978-5566

Temple Emanu-El
1010 University Avenue 95126   (408) 292-0939

Traditional
Congregation Sinai
1532 Willowbrae Avenue 95125-4450
(408) 264-8542
Fax: (408) 264-4316
Email: sinai_sj@juno.com

San Rafael

SYNAGOGUES

Reform
Rodef Sholom
170 N. San Pedro Rd 94903   (415) 479-3441

Santa Barbara

SYNAGOGUES

Orthodox
Chabad of S. Barbara
6047 Stow Canyon, Fairview 93117   (805) 683-1544
Fax: (805) 683-1545
Email: rabbi@sbchabad.org

Young Israel of Santa Barbara
1826 C Cliff Drive 93109   (805) 966-4565

Reform
Congregation B'nai B'rith
1000 San Antonio Creek Road 93111   (805) 964-7869
Fax: (805) 683-6473
Email: cbbrav@aol.com

Santa Monica

SYNAGOGUES

Orthodox
Chabad House
1428 17th Street 90404

Young Israel of Santa Monica
21 Hampton Avenue   (310) 399-8514
Mailing address is: PO Box 5725, 90405.

Reform
Beth Sholom
1827 California Avenue 90403   (310) 453-3361

Santa Rosa

SYNAGOGUES

Conservative
Beth Ami
4676 Mayette Avenue 95405   (707) 545-4334
Dairy kitchen on premises.

Reform
Congregation Shomrei Torah
1717 Yulupa Avenue, . 95405   (707) 578-5519
Fax: (707) 578-3967
Email: shomrei@pacbell.net

Stockton

Stockton is one of the oldest communities west of
the Mississippi River, founded in the days of the
California Gold Rush. Temple Israel was founded
as Congregation Ryhim Ahoovim in 1850 and
erected its first building in 1855.

SYNAGOGUES

Reform
Temple Israel
5105 N. El Dorado St. 95207   (209) 477-9306

Thousand Oaks

SYNAGOGUES
Conservative
Temple Etz Chaim
1080 E. Janss Rd 91360   (805) 497-6891
                               Fax: (805) 497-0086
Kosher catering. Synagogue contains unique artistic
Aron Kodesh and Holocaust memorial.

Tiburon

SYNAGOGUES
Conservative
Congregation Kol Shafar
215 Blackfield Dr 94920   (415) 388-1818

Vallejo

SYNAGOGUES
Unaffiliated
Congregation B'nai Israel
1256 Nebraska St. 94590   (707) 642-6526

Ventura

COMMUNITY ORGANISATIONS
Jewish Community Centre
259 Callens Road   (805) 658-7441

SYNAGOGUES
Reform
Temple Beth Torah
7620 Foothill Road 93004   (805) 647-4181

Walnut Creek

COMMUNITY ORGANISATIONS
Contra Costa JCC
2071 Tice Valley Blvd. 94595   (925) 938-7800
                               Fax: (925) 937-0765

SYNAGOGUES
Conservative
B'nai Shalom
74 Eckley Lane 94596   (925) 934-9446
                             Fax: (925) 934-9450
                  Email: office@bshalom.org
          Web site: www.jfed.org/bnaishalom

Contra Costa Jewish Community Center
2071 Tice Valley Blvd 94595

Orthodox
Chabad of Contra Costa
1530 South Main Street 94596   (925) 937-4101

Reform
Congregation B'nai Tikvah
25 Hillcroft Way 94595   (925) 933-5397

Whittier

SYNAGOGUES
Conservative
Beth Shalom Synagogues Center
14564 E. Hawes Street 90604   (310) 914-8744

COLORADO

Boulder

ORGANISATIONS
Lubavitch of Boulder County
4900 Sioux Drive 80303   (303) 494-1638
                               Fax: (303) 938-8350
                  Email: lubavbldr@cs.com
          Web site: www.lubavitchofboulder.org
Offering home hospitality.

RESTAURANTS
JCC
3800 Kalmia Avenue 80304

SYNAGOGUES
Hillel Foundation
2795 Colorado Avenue, University of Colorado
                               (303) 442-6571
Conservative
Congregation Bonai Shalom
1527 Cherryvale Rd, 80303   (303) 442-6605
                               Fax: (303) 442-7545
                  Email: bonaishalom@aol.com
          Web site: www.bonaishalom.org
Offering home hospitality.
Orthodox
Chabad
4900 Sioux Drive 80303   (303) 494-1638
                  Email: lubofbldr@juno.com
Reform
Congregation Har Hashem
3950 Baseline Road 80303   (303) 499-7077
Jewish Renewal Community of Boulder
5001 Pennsylvania 80303   (303) 271-3541
Meets third Friday of each month.

Colorado Springs

SYNAGOGUES
Conservative & Reform
Temple Shalom
1523 E. Monument Street 80909   (719) 634-5311
   Fax: (719) 447-9385
   Email: Tshalom@qwest.net
   Web site: www.Templeshalom.com
Reform services are held on Fri. evening &
Conservative services on Saturday morning. Minyan
at 7.00am Thursday mornings.

Orthodox
Chabad House
3465 Nonchalant Circle 80909   (719) 596-7330

Denver

BAKERIES
The Bagel Store
942 South Monaco 80224   (303) 388-2648
Supervision: Vaad Hakashrus of Denver

COMMUNITY ORGANISATIONS
Allied Jewish Federation of Colorado - Israel Office
300 S. Dahlia Street 80246   (303) 321-3399
   Fax: (303) 322-8328
   Email: mgardenswartz@ajfcolorado.org
   Web site: www.jewishcolorado.org
Jewish Family & Children's Service
1355 S. Colorado Blvd 80222   (303) 759-4890
   Fax: (303) 759-5998
   Email: jfs@jewishfamilyservice.org
   Web site: www.jewishfamilyservice.org

GROCERIES
Auerbach's
4810 Newport St.   (303) 289-4521

Cub Foods
1985 Sheridan Blvd, Edgewater   (303) 232-8972
With kosher section.

King Soopers
890 S.Monaco Parway   (303) 333-1535
With kosher section.

6470 East Hampden Avenue   (303) 758-1210
With kosher section.

Safeway
7150 Leetsdale drive (& Quebec)   (303) 377-6939
With kosher section.

6460 E. Yale (& Monaco)   (303) 691-8870
With kosher section.

KASHRUT INFORMATION
Scoll K Vaad Hakashrus of Denver
1350 Vrain 80204   (303) 595-9349
   Fax: (303) 629-5159

MEDIA
Newspaper
Intermountain Jewish News
1275 Sherman Avenue, Suite 214 80203
   (303) 861-2234
   Fax: (303) 832-6942
   Email: email@ijn.com
Weekly American Jewish newspaper of the
intermountain region

MIKVAOT
Mikvah of Denver
1404 Quitman 80204   (303) 893-5315
   Fax: (303) 825-5810

RELIGIOUS ORGANISATIONS
Synagogue Council of Greater Denver
PO Box 102732 80250   (303) 759-8484

RESTAURANTS
Dairy
Mediterranean Health Cafe
2817 East 3rd Avenue 80206   (303) 399-2940
Supervision: Vaad Hakashrus of Denver
Kosher/dairy/vegetarian food. Chalav Yisrael and Pat
Yisrael available. Hours: Sunday, 12 pm to 8 pm;
Monday to Thursday, 11 am to 8 pm; Friday, to 2 pm.

Meat
East Side Kosher Deli
5475 Leetsdale Drive 80246   (303) 322-9862
   Fax: (303) 331-3290
   Email: eskd1@aol.com
Supervision: Vaad Hakashrus of Denver
Glatt kosher. Deli, restaurant, grocer, butcher shop
and caterer. Closed on Saturday and Friday
afternoon.

Jeff's Diner
731 Quebec Street 80220   (303) 333-4637
Pizzeria
Pete's Kosher Pizza
5606 E. Cedar Avenue 80204   (303) 355-5777

SYNAGOGUES
Conservative
Beth Shalom
2280 East Noble Place, Littleton 80121
   (303) 794-6643
A congregation serving the southern metropolitan
area. Provides religious services religious school
(weekend and afternoon) social and educational
activities, and rabbinic services.

Hebrew Educational Alliance (HEA)
3600 South Ivanhoe St. 80237   (303) 758-9400
   Fax: (303) 758-9500
   Email: info@headenver.org

Rodef Shalom
450 S. Kearney 80224   (303) 399-0035
   Fax: (303) 399-7623
   Email: crsoffice@aol.com

Orthodox
Aish/Ahavas Yisroel; A Center for Jewish Learning
9550 E Belleview Ave,
Greenwood Village 80111   (303) 220-7200
                                 Fax: (303) 290-9191
                            Email: ymeyer@aish.com

Bais Medrash Kehillas Yaakov
295 S. Locust Street 80222   (303) 377-1200
                                 Fax: (303) 355-6010
                        Email: tai@jewishpeople.com

Congregation Zera Abraham
1560 Winona Court 80204   (303) 825-7517
Over 100 year old Orthodox Congregation. Two
morning Minyanim, Mincha and Maariv every day. Call
for Davening times. Mikvah, Eruv, nationally
recognized Vaad HaKashrus. "We are a very warm,
welcoming community that looks forward to every
opportunity to welcome guests and assist visitors."

Reform
Beth Shalom
2280 E. Noble Place 80121   (303) 794-6643

Congregation Emanuel
51 Grape Street 80231   (303) 388-4013
                                 Fax: (303) 388-6328
         Email: bronitsky@congregationemanuel.com
            Web site: www.congregationemanuel.com

Temple Micah
2600 Leyden Street 80207   (303) 388-4239
                                 Fax: (303) 773-0321
                 Email: office@micahdenver.org
            Web site: www.micahdenver.org
A small but long-established Reform Jewish
congregation, style is warm blending tradition with
progressive thought. Encourages members
participation and welcomes visitors.

Temple Sinai
3509 South Glencoe Street 80237   (303) 759-1827
                                  Fax: (303) 759-2519
                  Email: mail@sinaidenver.org
             Web site: www.sinaidenver.org

Traditional
B.M.H.-BJ Congregation
560 S. Monaco Pkwy. 80224   (303) 388-4203
                                 Fax: (303) 388-4210

Evergreen

SYNAGOGUES
Liberal
Congregation Beth Evergreen
2931 Evergreen Parkway 80439   (303) 670-4294
                                 Fax: (303) 836-6470
           Email: shalom@bethevergreen.org
           Web site: www.bethevergreen.org

Pueblo

SYNAGOGUES
Conservative
United Hebrew Congregation
106 W. 15th Street 81003   (719) 544-6448
Reform
Temple Emanuel
1325 Grand Avenue 81003   (719) 544-6448
                    Email: pavisilva@earthlink.net

CONNECTICUT

Bridgeport

COMMUNITY ORGANISATIONS
**Jewish Center for Community Services of
Eastern Fairfield County**
4200 Park Avenue 06604   (203) 372-6567
                                  Fax: (203) 374-0770
                       Email: info@jccs.org
Serving Bridgeport, Easton, Fairfield, Monroe,
Shelton, Stratford, Trumbull and Westport.

MEDIA
Radio
WVOF Radio
c/o Fairfield University, Fairfield 06430
                                  (203) 254-4111
Jewish public affairs show on Sundays at 7pm on
88.5FM

MIKVAOT
Mikveh Israel
1326 Stratfield Road, Fairfield 06432

RELIGIOUS ORGANISATIONS
Va'ad of Fairfield County
1571 Stratfield Road, Fairfield 06432 (203) 372-6529
                                  Fax: (203) 373-0467
                     Email: rbaun64732@aol.com

RESTAURANTS
Cafe Shalom
c/o Abel, Community Center   (203) 372-6567

SYNAGOGUES
Conservative
B'nai Torah
5700 Main St., Trumbull 06611
Rodeph Sholom
2385 Park Avenue 06604   (203) 334-0159
                                   Fax: (203) 334-1411
           Email: cong.rodeph.sholom@suet.net
           Web site: www.rodephsholom.com

Orthodox
Agudas Achim
85 Arlington Street 06606

Bikur Cholim
Park & Capitol Avenues 06604   (203) 336-2272
     Email: jbm@ou.org
     Web site: www.ou.org

Shaare Torah Adath Israel
3050 Main Street 06606

Reconstructionist
Congregation Shirei Shalom
PO Box 372, Monroe 06468

Reform
Temple B'nai Israel
2710 Park Avenue 06604   (203) 336-1858
     Fax: (203) 367-7889
     Email: welcome@congregationbnaiisrael.org

Danbury

COMMUNITY ORGANISATIONS
Jewish Federation
105 Newtown Road 06810   (203) 792-6353
     Fax: (203) 748-5099
Issuing monthly publication.

SYNAGOGUES
Conservative
Congregation B'nai Israel
193 Clapboard Ridge Road 06811   (203) 792-6161
     Fax: (203) 792-8315
     Email: cbi193clab@juno.com

Orthodox
Chabad
9 Golden Heights Road 06811   (203) 790-4700
     Email: lgurkov@juno.com

Reform
United Jewish Center
141 Deer Hill Avenue 06810   (203) 748-3355

Fairfield

BAKERIES
Carvel Ice Cream Bakery
1838 Black Rock Turnpike   (203) 384-2253
Supervision: Vaad Hakashrus of Fairfield County
Ice cream, cakes & novelties. All products in the store
are under supervision, except for those Snapple
drinks not marked with an "OK".

SYNAGOGUES
Conservative
Congregation Beth El
1200 Fairfield Woods Rd, Fairfield 06825
     (203) 374-5544
     Fax: (203) 374-4962
     Email: congbethel@aol.com
     Web site: www.uscj.org/ctvalley/fairfield
Kosher facility.

Orthodox
Congregation Ahavath Achim
1571 Stratfield Road, Fairfield 06432   (203) 372-6529
     Fax: (203) 373-0647
     Email: rbaum64732@aol.com
     Web site: 222.ahavathachim.org
Home hospitality, mikveh, youth programs, adult
education.

Hartford

COMMUNITY ORGANISATIONS
Jewish Federation of Hartford
333 Bloomfield Avenue 06117   (860) 232-4483
Publishes 'All Things Jewish'.

KASHRUT INFORMATION
Kashrut Commission
162 Brewster Road 06117   (860) 563-4017

MEDIA
Guide
All Things Jewish
333 Bloomfield Avenue 06117   (860) 232-4483

MIKVAOT
Mikva
61 Main Street 06119

SYNAGOGUES
Conservative
Beth El
2626 Albany Avenue, West Hartford 06117

Beth Tefilah
465 Oak St, East Hartford 06118

Congregation B'nai Sholom
26 Church St, Newington 06111   (860) 667-0826
     Fax: (860) 667-0827
     Email: cbsnewington@aol.com

Emanuel Synagogue
160 Mohegan Dr, West Hartford 06117
     (860) 236-1275
     Fax: (860) 231-8890
     Email: emansyn@ziplink.net

Orthodox
Agudas Achim
1244 N. Main St, West Hartford 06117

Beth David Synagogue
20 Dover Road, West Hartford 06119   (860) 236-1241
     Fax: (860) 232-8272
     Email: rabbi@bethdavidwh.org

Chabad House of Greater Hartford
798 Farmington Avenue 06119
Contact for kosher meal & Shabbat arrangements.

Teferes Israel
27 Brown St, Bloomfield 06002

United Synagogue of Greater Hartford
840 N. Main St, West Hartfordv 06117

Reform
Beth Israel
701 Farmington Avenue, West Hartford 06119
(860) 233-8215
Fax: (860) 523-0223
Temple Sinai
41 W. Hartford Road, Newington 06011

Manchester

SYNAGOGUES
Conservative
Temple Beth Sholom
400 Middle Turnpike E 06040　　(860) 643-9563
Fax: (860) 643-9565
Email: riplavin@prodigy.net
Web site: www.uscj.org/ctvalley/manchestertbs
Services seven days a week. Call for times.

Meriden

SYNAGOGUES
Conservative
B'nai Abraham
127 E. Main St 06450　　(203) 235-2581

Middletown

SYNAGOGUES
Conservative
Adath Israel
48 Church St 06457　　(860) 346-4709

New Britain

SYNAGOGUES
Conservative
B'nai Israel
265 W. Main St 06051　　(860) 224-0479
Orthodox
Tephereth Israel
76 Winter Street 06051

New Haven

COMMUNITY ORGANISATIONS
Jewish Federation of Greater New Haven
360 Amity Road, Woodbridge Ct. 06525
(203) 387-2424

CONTACT INFORMATION
Young Israel House at Yale University
c/o Joseph Slifka Center, 80 Wall Street 06510
(203) 432-1134
Fax: (203) 776-4212
Email: Rabbiisaacs@cs.com
Web site: www.yale.edu/hillel/orgs/yihy.html
Hours vary daily; call for updated information.
Orthodox kashrut supervision.

DELICATESSEN
The Westville
1460 Whalley Avenue 06515　　(203) 397-0839
Fax: (203) 387-4129
Email: pweinb@aol.com
Zackey's
1304 Whalley Avenue 06515　　(203) 387-2454

GROCERIES
Westville Kosher Meat Market
95 Amity Road 06525　　(203) 389-1723

LIBRARIES
Center Cafe & Jewish Library
360 Amity Road 06525　　(203) 387-2424

MIKVAOT
86 Hubinger Street 06511　　(203) 387-2184

RESTAURANTS
Dairy
**Claire's Gourmet Vegetarian Restaurant &
Caterer**
1000 Chapel Street 06510　　(203) 562-3888
Supervision: Young Israel of New Haven

SYNAGOGUES
Conservative
Beth-El Keser Israel
85 Harrison Street 06515　　(203) 389-2108
Orthodox
Beth Hamedrosh Westville
74 West Prospect Street 06515　　(203) 389-9513
Congregation Bikur Cholim Sheveth Achim
112 Marvel Road 06515　　(203) 387-4699
Yeshiva of New Haven
765 Elm Street, New Haven 06511　　(203) 977-2200
Fax: (203) 777-7198
Email: info@yeshivanewhaven.org
Web site: www.yeshivanewhaven.org

New London

COMMUNITY ORGANISATIONS
Jewish Federation of Eastern Connecticut
28 Channing Street 06320　　(203) 442-8062

Norwalk

COMMUNITY ORGANISATIONS
Jewish Federation of Greater Norwalk
Shorehaven Road 06855　　(203) 853-3440

Norwich

SYNAGOGUES
Orthodox
Brothers of Joseph
Broad & Washington Avs. 06360　　(203) 887-3777
Mikva attached.

Stamford

COMMUNITY ORGANISATIONS
United Jewish Federation
1035 Newfield Avenue 06905   (203) 321-1373

DELICATESSEN
Delicate-Essen at the JCC
1035 Newfield Avenue 06902   (203) 322-0944
                                    Fax: (203) 322-5160
Supervision: Vaad Hakashrus of Fairfield County
Glatt kosher sit down café serving hot and cold
sandwiches, soups and grilled items.

GROCERIES
Delicate-Essen
111 High Ridge Road 06905   (203) 316-5570
                                    Fax: (203) 316-5573
                    Email: bhert2b111@aol.com
Supervision: Vaad Hakashrus of Fairfield County
Full selection of grocery items. Glatt kosher butcher
and take-out products available. Open six days a
week.

SYNAGOGUES
Orthodox
Young Israel of Stamford
69 Oak Lawn Avenue 06905   (203) 348-3955

Waterbury

COMMUNITY ORGANISATIONS
Jewish Communities of Western CT, Inc.
73 Main Street, South Woodbury 06798
                                    (203) 263-5121
                                    Fax: (203) 263-5143
                    Email: jfedwtby@aol.com

West Hartford

BOOKSELLERS
The Judaica Store
31 Crossroads Plaza 06117   (860) 236-9956
                                    Fax: (860) 236-9956

SYNAGOGUES
Orthodox
Young Israel of West Hartford
2240 Albany Avenue 06117   (860) 233-3084
                                    Fax: (860) 232-6417
                    Email: westhartfordrav@aol.com
                    Web site: www.youngisraelwh.org

Westport

SYNAGOGUES
Orthodox
215 Post Road West 06880   (203) 226-6901

Woodbridge

LIBRARIES
Department of Jewish Education Library
360 Amity Road 06525   (203) 387-2424 ext. 330
                                    Fax: (203) 387-1818
                    Email: library@jewishnewhaven.org
Judaic library and media center serving adults and
children of all ages. Open to all.

DELAWARE

Dover

SYNAGOGUES
Conservative
Congregation Beth Sholom of Dover
PO Box 223 19903   (302) 734-5578

Newark

SYNAGOGUES
Reconstructionist
Temple Beth El
101 Possum Park Rd 19711   (302) 366-8330

Wilmington

COMMUNITY ORGANISATIONS
Jewish Community Center
101 Garden of Eden Road 19803   (302) 478-5660
                                    Fax: (302) 478-6068
                    Email: jccinfo@jccdelaware.org

SYNAGOGUES
Conservative
Beth Shalom
18th St. and Baynard Blvd 19802
Orthodox
Adas Kodesh Shel Emeth
Washington Blvd & Torah Drive 19802
                                    (302) 762-2705
                                    Fax: (302) 762-3236
                                    Web site: www.akse.org

Reform
Beth Emeth
300 W. Lea Blvd. 19802   (302) 764-2393
                                    Fax: (302) 764-2395

DISTRICT OF COLUMBIA

Washington

DELICATESSEN

Hunan Deli
"H" Street   (202) 833-1018

Posins Bakery & Deli
5756 Georgia Avenue   (202) 726-4424
Bakery is under Conservative hashgacha.

EMBASSY

Embassy of Israel
3514 International Drive 20008   (202) 364-5500
                           Fax: (202) 364-5423

GALLERIES

The National Portrait Gallery
"F" Street between 7th & 8th Sts.
Houses more than 100,000 portraits including amongst others Albert Einstein, Golda Meir and George Gershwin.

KASHRUT INFORMATION

Rabbinical Council of Greater Washington
7826 Eastern Avenue 20012   (202) 291-6052
                           Fax: (202) 291-5377
                  Email: capitalkdc@ad.org
                  Web site: www.capitolk.org

MUSEUMS

B'nai B'rith Klutznick National Jewish Museum
1640 Rhode Island Av. 20036   (202) 857-6583
                           Fax: (202) 857-1099
                  Email: eberman@bnaibrith.org
                  Web site: www.BBInet.org
Hours 10.00am to 5.00pm, Sunday through Friday and early close on Fridays in winter.

Lillian & Albert Small Museum
701 3rd Street N. W. 20001   (202) 789-0900
                           Fax: (202) 789-0485
                  Email: info@jhsgw.org
Hidden within the nation's capital is the Washington area's oldest surviving synagogue, Adas Israel, built in 1876.

National Museum of American Jewish Military History
1811 R. Street N.W. 20009   (202) 265-6280
                           Fax: (202) 462-3192
                  Email: mnmajmh@nmajmh.org
                  Web site: www.nmajmh.org
The National Museum of American Jewish Military History, under the auspices of the Jewish War Veterans of the USA, documents and preserves the contributions of Jewish Americans to the peace and freedom of the United States, educates the public concerning the courage, heroism and sacrifices made by Jewish Americans who served in the armed forces, and works to combat anti-Semitism. The Museum includes exhibitions, a library, a chapel and a Study Center. Hours: 9 am to 5 pm Monday to Friday and 1 pm to 5 pm on Sundays.

Smithsonian Institute
The Natural History Building, 10th & Constitution Avs N.W. 20001
Contains a collection of Jewish ritual articles.

The Isaac Polack Building
2109 Pennsylvania Av. N.W.
Built in 1796, The Isaac Polack Building was the home of the first Jew to settle in Washington.

United States Holocaust Memorial Museum
100 Raoul Wallenberg Place S.W. 20024-2150
                                (202) 488-0400
                           Fax: (202) 488-2606
                  Email: group_visit@ushmm.org
                  Web site: www.ushmm.org
Hours: 10.00am to 5.30pm. The Museum is accessible to people with disabilities. The permanent exhibition recommended for visitors eleven years and older, presents a comprehensive history of the Holocaust through artefacts photographs films and eyewitness testimonies. There are other changing special exhibitions and an exhibition designed for children eight years and older.

ORGANISATIONS

Jewish Historical Society of Greater Washington
701 3rd Street N. W. 20001-2624 (202) 789-0900
                           Fax: (202) 789-0485
                  Email: info@jhsgw.org
Also the Lillian & Albert Small Jewish Museum. Hours: Sunday-Thursday 12am-4pm.

RESTAURANTS
Meat
Jewish Community Centre
1529 16th Street NW   (202) 518-9400
Supervision: Va'ad Hakashrut of Washington

SYNAGOGUES
Orthodox
Kesher Israel
208 N. Street NW   (202) 333-2337
Conservative
Tifereth Israel
7701 16th Street NW   (202) 882-1605
Reform
Tempke Micah
2829 Wisconsin Avenue NW   (202) 342-9175

TOURIST SITE
John F. Kennedy Center
2700 "F" Street
Israeli lounge donated by the people of Israel

FLORIDA

Boca Raton

COMMUNITY ORGANISATIONS
Jewish Federation of South Palm Beach County
9901 Donna Klein Blvd 33428-1788 (561) 852-3100

JUDAICA
Holyland Judaica
Del Mar Shopping Village, 7080 Beracasa Way
(561) 367-8277

MIKVAOT
Boca Raton Synagogue
7900 Montoya Circle 33433   (561) 394-5854

RESTAURANTS
Dairy
Campus Café
Cultural Arts Building, 9801 Donna Klein Blvd
3428-1788   (561) 852-3200 ext. 4103
Fax: (561) 852-3282
Breakfast - dairy; Lunch - meat. Jewish Federation of
South Palm Beach County on the Richard and Carole
Siemens Campus.

Eilat Café
6853 SW 18th Street, Wharfside Shopping
Center 33428-1788   (561) 368-6880

Jon's Place
22191 Powerline Road, (southwest corner Palmetto
& Powerline)   (561) 338-0008
Meat
Café Haifa
2901 N. Federal Highway 33431   (561) 955-8500

City Grill
Delmar Shopping Village, 7158 N. Beracasa Way
33434   (561) 417-8936

Jerusalem Grill
19635 US Highway 411, Boca Plaza Greens 33428
(561) 470-1120

SYNAGOGUES
Conservative
Beth Ami Congregation
1401 N.W. 4th Avenue 33432   (561) 347-0031
Fax: (561) 393-5326
Email: bethamicong@aol.com
Orthodox
Boca Raton Synagogue
7900 Montoya Circle 33433   (561) 394-5732
Fax: (561) 394-0180
Email: www.brsweb.org

Young Israel of Boca Raton
7200 Palmetto Circle Blvd 33433   (561) 391-3235
Fax: (561) 391-5509
Email: yiboca@bellsouth.net

Reform
Congregation B'nai Israel
2200 Yamato Road 33431   (561) 241-8118
Fax: (561) 241-8118

Clearwater

COMMUNITY ORGANISATIONS
Jewish Federation of Pinellas County
13191 Starkey Road, Suite 8, Largo 33773-1438
(727) 530-3223
Fax: (727) 531-0221
Email: pinellas@jfedpinellas.org

SYNAGOGUES
Conservative
Beth Shalom
1325 S. Belcher Road 33764   (727) 531-1418
Fax: (727) 531-0798

Orthodox
Young Israel of Clearwater
2385 Tampa Road, Suite 1, Palm Harbor 34684
(727) 789-0408

Reform
B'nai Israel
1685 S. Belcher Road 34624   (727) 531-5829

Temple Ahavat Shalom
1575 Curlew Road, Palm Harbor 34683
(727) 785-8811
Fax: (727) 785-8822
Email: rabgar@tampabay.rr.com

Daytona Beach

COMMUNITY ORGANISATIONS
Jewish Federation of Volusia & Flagler Counties
733 S. Nova Road, Ormond Beach 32174
(904) 672-0294
Fax: (904) 673-1316

SYNAGOGUES
Conservative
Temple Israel
1400 S. Peninsula Drive 32118   (904) 252-3097
Reform
Temple Beth El
579 N. Nova Road, Ormond Beach 32174
(904) 677-2484

Deerfield Beach

SYNAGOGUES
Orthodox
Young Israel of Deerfield Beach
1880 W. Hillsboro Blvd 33442   (954) 421-1367
Fax: (954) 426-9127

Delray Beach

GROCERIES
Meat Market
Oriole Kosher Market, 7345 West Atlantic Ave., 33446

SYNAGOGUES
Conservative
Temple Anshei Shalom of West Delray
Oriole Jewish Center, 7099 W. Atlantic Avenue
3446   (561) 495-1300
Temple Emeth
5780 W. Atlantic Avenue 33446   (561) 498-3536
Orthodox
Anshei Emuna
16189 Carter Road 33445   (561) 499-9229
Reform
Temple Sinai
2475 W. Atlantic Avenue 33445   (561) 276-6161
                            Fax: (561) 276-3485
                        Email: sinai1@juno.com

Fort Lauderdale

COMMUNITY ORGANISATIONS
Jewish Federation of Greater Fort Lauderdale
8358 W. Oakland Park Blvd 33321   (954) 748-8400
                            Fax: (954) 748-6332

DELICATESSEN
East Side Kosher Restaurant & Deli
6846 W. Atlantic Blvd, Margate 33063

KOSHER FOOD
Meat
Galt Kosher Market
3515 Galt Ocean Drive 33308   (954) 563-2026

RESTAURANTS
Amore' Ristorante
8067 West Oakland Park Blvd, Sunrise
                            (954) 749-6888
Supervision: Glatt kosher

SYNAGOGUES
Orthodox
Temple Ohel B'nai Raphael
4351 West Oakland Park Boulevard 33313
                            (954) 733-7684
Sephardi
B'nai Sephardim
3670 Stirling Rd, Ft Lauderdale

Fort Meyers

SYNAGOGUES
Reform
Temple Beth El
16225 Winkler Road Ext 33908   (941) 433-0018

Fort Pierce

SYNAGOGUES
Reform
Temple Beth-El Israel
4600 Oleander Drive 34982   (407) 461-7428

Hollywood & Vicinity

COMMUNITY ORGANISATIONS
Jewish Federation of South Broward
2719 Hollywood Blvd 33020   (954) 921-8810

JUDAICA
Holyland Judaica
5650 Stirling Road, Hollywood   (954) 964-4288

KOSHER FOOD
Ilana's Cookies
5650 Stirling Road, Hollywood   (954) 963-6130

MIKVAOT
Mikveh/Young Israel of Hollywood - Ft. Lauderdale
3291 Stirling Road, Fort Lauderdale 33312
                            (954) 963-3952
                            Fax: (954) 962-5566

RESTAURANTS
Dairy
Sara's
3944 N. 46th Avenue 33021   (954) 986-1770
                            Fax: (954) 986-2602
Meat
Pita King
5650 Stirling Road 33021   (954) 985-8028
Pizzerias
Jerusalem Pizza
5650 Stirling Road 33021   (954) 964-6811
                            Fax: (954) 964-2911

SYNAGOGUES
Conservative
B'nai Aviv
1410 Indian Trace, Weston 33326
Century Pines Jewish Center
13400 S.W. 10 St., Pembroke Pines 33027
                            (954) 431-3300

Hallandale Jewish Center
416 N.E. Eighth Ave., Hallandale 33009
(954) 454-9100

Temple Beth Ahm Israel
9730 Stirling Rd 33024 (954) 431-5100

Temple Judea of Carriage Hills
6734 Stirling Rd, Hollywood

Temple Sinai of Hollywood
1400 N. 46 Avenue, Hollywood 33021
(954) 987-0026

Orthodox
Chabad Ocean Synagogue
4000 S. Ocean Drive, Hallandale (954) 458-7999

Chabad of Southwest Broward
11251 Taft St., Pembroke Pines

Congregation Ahavat Shalom
315 Madison St., Hollywood 33022 (954) 922-4544

Congregation Levi Yitzchok-Lubavitch
1295 E. Hallandale Beach Blvd,
Hallandale 33009 (954) 458-1877
Fax: (954) 458-1651
Email: chai@dialisdn.com

Young Israel of Hollywood/Ft Lauderdale
3291 Stirling Road, Ft Lauderdale 33312
(954) 966-7877
Fax: (954) 962-5566
Email: yih@bellsouth.net

Young Israel of Pembroke Pines
13400 S.W. 10 St., Pembroke Pines

Reform
Temple Beth El
1351 S. 14 Av, Hollywood 33020 (954) 920-8225

Temple Beth Emet
4807 South Flamingo Road, Cooper City,
Pembroke Pines (954) 680-1882
Email: bethemet@aol.com

Temple Solel
5100 Sheridan St., Hollywood 33021 (954) 989-0205

Jacksonville

COMMUNITY ORGANISATIONS

Jacksonville Jewish Federation
8505 San Jose Blvd 32217 (904) 448-5000

MIKVAOT

Etz Chaim
10167 San Jose Blvd 32257 (904) 262-3565

ORGANISATIONS

Kosher Nutrition Center
5846 Mt Carmel Terrace. 32216 (904) 737-9075

SYNAGOGUES

Orthodox
Eitz Chaim Synagogue
10167 San Jose Boulevard 32217 (904) 262-3565

Kendall

SYNAGOGUES

Orthodox
Young Israel of Kendall
7880 SW 112th Street 33156 (305) 232-6833
Email: yikendall@aol.com

Key West

SYNAGOGUES

Conservative
B'nai Zion
750 United Street 33040-3251 (305) 294-3437

Lakeland

SYNAGOGUES

Conservative
Temple Emanuel
600 Lake Hollingsworth Drive 33803 (813) 682-8616

Melbourne

GROCERIES

Brevard Kosher Zone
416N Harbor City Blvd., 1/4 mile south of
Eau Gallie (321) 752-8000
Fax: (321) 752-8000
Email: bkz1@mindspring.com

Miami/Miami Beach

BOOKSELLERS

Jerusalem Judaica
459 41st Street 33140 (305) 535-8888

EMBASSY

Consul General of Israel
Suite 1800, 100N Biscayne Blvd 33132

GROCERIES

Kosher World-Fine Food Market
514 W. 41st Street 33140 (305) 532-2210
Fax: (305) 532-8816
Supervision: Delivers to all hotels in the Miami Beach
area.

HOTELS

Saxony Hotel
3201 Collins Avenue, Miami Beach 33140
(305) 538-6811
Fax: (305) 672-3721
Supervision: National Kashruth

MEDIA

Directory
Jewish Life in Dade County
4200 Biscayne Blvd 33137
(305) 576-4000
Fax: (305) 573-8115
Web site: www.jewishmiami.org
Radio
Shalom South Florida (WAXY 790 AM)
Covers South Florida's Jewish community.

MIKVAOT

B'nai Israel & Greater Miami Youth Synagogue Mikveh
16260 S. W. 288th Street, Naranja 33033
(305) 264-6488

Congregation and Mikvah Adas Dej
225 37th Street 33140
(305) 538-0070

Daughters of Israel
2530 Pinetree Drive 33140
(305) 672-3500

Mikveh Blima of North Dade, Inc.,
1054 N.E. Miami Gardens Drive 33179
(305) 949-9650

Rabbi Meisel's Mikveh
Washington Av. & 2nd Street 33139
(305) 673-4641
For men only.

Shul of Bal Harbour Mikvah
9540 Collins Avenue, Surfside 33154
(305) 868-1411
Email: info@theshul.org

MUSEUM

Jewish Museum of Florida
301 Washington Avenue, Miami Beach
33139-6965
(305) 672-5044
Fax: (305) 672-5933
Email: mzerivitz@aol.com
Web site: www.jewishmuseum.com
Open Tuesday to Sunday 10.00am to 5.00pm. Closed Mondays and Jewish holidays.

RELIGIOUS ORGANISATIONS

Young Israel Southern Regional Office
173575 NE 7th Avenue 33162
(305) 770-3993
Fax: (305) 770-3993
Email: ncyi.south@youngisrael.org

RESTAURANTS

Dairy
Bagel Time
3915 Alton Road 33140
(305) 538-0300
Supervision: Star-K
Eat in or take-out. Hours: Sunday to Friday, 6:30 am to 4 pm.

Gitty's Hungarian Kitchen
6565 Collins Avenue, Sherry Frontenac Hotel
33141
(305) 865-4893

Milky Way
530 41st Street
(305) 534-4144
Meat
Embassy Peking Tower Suite
4101 Pine Tree Drive, Tower 41 33140
(305) 538-7550
Fax: (305) 538-7570
Supervision: NK

Jerusalem Peking
4299 Collins Avenue, Miami Beach
(305) 522-2263

Mexico Bravo
16850 Collins Avenue, Sunny Isles Beach
(305) 945-1999
Fax: (305) 949-5560
Supervision: Star-K Supervision

Original Pita Hut
530-41st St.
(305) 534-4144

Shalom Tokyo Steak house
5101 Collins Avenue, Miami Beach
(305) 866-6039
Pizzeria
Shemtov's Pizza
514 41st Street 33140
(305) 538-2123
Fax: (305) 534-4213
Supervision: Star-K
Cholov Yisroel. Sunday-Thursday 11am-10pm, Friday 11am-3pm, Saturday - Motzei Shabbos - 1am
Pizzerias
Yonnie's Kosher Pizza
19802 W. Dixie Hwy. 33180
(305) 932-1961

SYNAGOGUES

Conservative
Beth Raphael
1545 Jefferson Avenue 33139
(305) 538-4112
This synagogue is dedicated to the six million martyrs of the Holocaust. On an outside marble wall, a large six-light menorah burns every night in their memory. Six hundred names, representing each city, have been inscribed on the marble. There is also a notable Holocaust Memorial at Dade Av., and Meridian Av.;

Orthodox
National Council of Young Israel Southern Regional Office
1035 NE 170th Terrace 33162
(305) 770-3993
Email: ncyi.south@youngisrael.org

The Shul of Bal Harbor, Bay Harbor & Surfside
9540 Collins Avenue 33154
(305) 868-1411
Email: info@theshul.org

Young Israel of Miami Beach
4221 Pine Tree Drive 33140
(305) 538-9462

North Miami / North Miami Beach

RESTAURANTS
Dairy
The Noshery
Saxony Hotel, 3201 Collins Ave., 33140
(305) 538-6811
Seasonal.

Meat
China Kikar Tel Aviv
5005 Collins Avenue 33140 (305) 866-3316

Giuliani's Café
3439 NE 163rd Street, North Miami Beach
(305) 940-8141

Kosher World
514 - 41st. (305) 532-2263

Mexico Bravo
16850 Collins Avenue, Sunny Isles Beach
(305) 945-1999

Pita Plus
20103 Biscayne Blvd 33180 (305) 935-0761

Shalom Haifa
18533 W. Dixie Hwy, Aventura (305) 936-1800
Fax: (305) 936-1811

Subrific
1688 NE Strret (305) 949-7811

Tani Guchi's Place
2224 N.E. 123rd St, North Miami (305) 892-6744
Fax: (305) 892-1035
Supervision: Glatt Kosher

Wing Wan II
1640 N.E, 164 Street 33162 (305) 945-3585

Pizzerias
Jerusalem Pizza
761 N.E. 167th Street 33162 (305) 653-6662

Sarah's Kosher Pizza
2214 N.E. 123 Street 33181 (305) 891-3312
1127 N. E. 163 Street 33162 (305) 948-7777

SYNAGOGUES
Orthodox
Young Israel of Greater Miami
990 NE 171st Street, North Miami Beach
33162 (305) 651-3591

Young Israel of Sky Lake
1850 NE 183rd Street, North Miami Beach 33179
(305) 945-8712/8715

Young Israel of Sunny Isles
17395 North Bay Road, North Miami Beach 33160
(305) 935-9095

Orlando

COMMUNITY ORGANISATIONS
Jewish Federation of Greater Orlando
851 N. Maitland Avenue, Maitland 32751
(407) 645 5933
Fax: (407) 645 1172
Email: postmaster@orlandojewishfed.org

DELICATESSEN
Market Place Deli, Hyatt Orlando
6375 W. Irlo Bronson Highway (407) 396-1234
Has frozen kosher food only.

GROCERIES
Amira's Catering and Specialty
1351 E. Altamonte, Altamonte Springs
(407) 767-7577
Cold cuts, side dishes, frozen meals, groceries.

Kosher Korner
8464 Palm Parkway, Vista Center 32836
(407) 238-9968
Fax: (407) 238-2008
Supervision: Florida Kosher Services
Complete kosher grocery and take-out. Packaged
frozen glatt meat. Will deliver to hotels. Two minutes
from downtown Disney.

HOTELS
Quality Inn Kosher Hotel
4944 W. 192 Orlando-Kissimmee 34746
(407) 787-3400
Fax: (407) 397-1116
Web site: www.kosher-korner.com

MIKVAOT
Mikvah Yisrael
8 Lake Howell Road 32751 (407) 644-2362

RESTAURANTS
Kinneret Kitchens
517 South Delany (407) 422-7205
Senior Citizens' dining room. Meals: d, Mon.-Fri at
5pm. Call at least twenty-four hours in advance to
reserve a meal.

The Lower East Side Restaurant
8548 Palm Parkway 32836 (407) 465-0565
Fax: (407) 238-6427
Supervision: Florida Kosher Services
There is a shul next door to the restaurant.

Meat
Kosher Korner
Vista Center, 8464 Palm Pkwy. 32836 (407) 238-9968
Fax: (407) 238-2008
Glatt kosher.Dine in, take-out and delivery.

SYNAGOGUES
Conservative
Congregation Beth Shalom
13th & Center Streets, Leesburg 32748
(407) 742-0238

Congregation Ohev Shalom
5015 Goddard Avenue 32804   (407) 298-4650

Congregation Shalom Aleichem
PO Box 424211, Kissimmee 34742-4211

Congregation Shalom (Williamsburg)
c/o Sydney Ansell, 11821 Soccer Lane 32821-7952

Southwest Orlando Jewish Congregation
11200 S. Apopka-Vineland Road 32836
Web site: www.sojc-orlando.org
The closest Synagogue to Walt Disney world (one mile away).

Temple Israel
4917 Eli Street 32804   (407) 647-3055
Orthodox
Cong. Ahavas Yisrael/Chabad
708 Lake Howell Road, Maitland 32751
(407) 644-2500
Fax: (407) 644-7763
Email: rabbidubov@aol.com

Reform
Congregation of Liberal Judaism
928 Malone Drive 32810   (407) 645-0444

Palm Beach

SYNAGOGUES
Conservative
Temple Emanu-el
190 N. County Road 33480   (561) 832-0804
Orthodox
Palm Beach Orthodox Synagogue
120 North County Road 33480   (561) 838-9002
Fax: (561) 838-5356
Web site: www.pbos.org
Mailing address: PO Box 1028

Palm City

SYNAGOGUES
Conservative
Treasure Coast Jewish Center-Congregation Beth Abraham
3998 S.W. Leighton Farms Avenue 34990
(407) 287-8833

Palm Coast

SYNAGOGUES
Conservative
Temple Beth Shalom
40 Wellington Drive, POB 350557 32135-0557
(904) 445-3006

Pembroke Pines

SYNAGOGUES
Orthodox
Young Israel of Pembroke Pines
13400 SW 10th Street 33027   (954) 433-8666

Pensacola

SYNAGOGUES
Conservative
B'nai Israel
1829 N. 9th Avenue, PO Box 9002 32513
(805) 433-7311
Fax: (805) 435-9597
Reform
Beth El
800 N. Palafox Street 32501   (805) 438-3321

Rockledge

COMMUNITY ORGANISATIONS
Jewish Federation of Brevard
108A Barton Avenue   (321) 636-1824
Fax: (321) 636-0614
Email: jfbrevard@aol.com

Sarasota

COMMUNITY ORGANISATIONS
Sarasota-Manatee Jewish Federation
580 S. McIntosh Road 34232-1959   (941) 371-4546
Fax: (941) 378-2947
Email: smjf@jon.cjfny.org

SYNAGOGUES
Conservative
Temple Beth Shalom
1050 South Tuttle Avenue 34237   (941) 955-8121

St Augustine

SYNAGOGUES
Orthodox
The First Congregation Sons Of Israel
161 Cordova Street 43084

St Petersburg

GROCERIES
Jo-El's Specialty Foods
2619 23rd Avenue N. 33713   (727) 321-3847
Fax: (727) 327-0682
Also has delicatessen and butcher shop. Hours: Tuesday to Thursday, 9 am to 5 pm; Friday, to 4 pm; Sunday, to 1 pm.

SYNAGOGUES
Conservative
B'nai Israel
300 58th Street North 33710   (727) 381-4900
                                     Fax: (727) 344-1307
          Email: rabbissec@cbistpete.org

Beth Shalom
1844 54th Street S. 33707   (727) 321-3380

Reform
Beth-El
400 Pasadena Avenue S. 33707   (727) 347-6136

Tallahassee

SYNAGOGUES
Conservative
Congregation Shomrei Torah
4858 Kerry Forest Parkway 32308   (850) 893-9674
          Email: shomreitorah@aol.com

Tamarac

SYNAGOGUES
Orthodox
Young Israel of Taramac
8565 W McNab Road 33321   (954) 726-3586

Tampa

COMMUNITY ORGANISATIONS
Tampa Jewish Federation
13009 Community Campus Drive 33625-4000
                                     (813) 264-9000
                               Fax: (813) 265-8450
                        Email: tjfjcc@aol.com

DELICATESSEN
Jo-El's
11727 N Dale Mabry 33618   (813) 964-9299
Also has bakery and groceries. Hours Monday to
Thursday 10 am to 7.30 pm; Friday 10 am to 3.30 pm
and Sunday 9 am to 2.30 pm.

MIKVAOT
Bais Tefilah
14908 Pennington Road 33624   (813) 963-2317
Mikva, Orthodox pre-school on premises.

SYNAGOGUES
Conservative
Kol Ami
3919 Moran Road 33618   (813) 962-6338

Rodeph Shalom
2713 Bayshore Blvd. 33629   (813) 837-1911

Temple David
2001 Swann Avenue 33606   (813) 254-1771

Orthodox
Hebrew Academy
14908 Penington Road 33624   (813) 963-0706
Young Israel of Tampa
3721W Tacon Street 33629   (813) 832-3018
Reform
Schaarai Zedek
3303 Swann Avenue 33609   (813) 876-2377

Vero Beach

SYNAGOGUES
Reform
Temple Beth Shalom
365 43rd Avenue 32968   (772) 569-4700
                                Fax: (772) 569-4701
                          Email: tbsoff@aol.com
Mailin address: PO Box 2113, Vero Beach, Florida
32961.

West Palm Beach

COMMUNITY ORGANISATIONS
Chabad House
4800 23rd St. N 33407   (561) 640-8111
Jewish Federation of Palm Beach County
4601 Community Drive 33417   (561) 478-0700
                                Fax: (561) 478-9696

DELICATESSEN
Mr Glatt Mart
4869 Okeechobee Blvd 33417   (561) 689-6267
                                Fax: (561) 689-2595
                        Email: rav613@hotmail.com

GEORGIA

Athens

SYNAGOGUES
Reform
Congregation Children Of Israel
Dudley Drive 30606   (404) 549-4192

Atlanta

BED AND BREAKFAST
Bed & Breakfast Atlanta
1608 Briarcliff Road, Suite 5 30306   (404) 875-0525
                                 Fax: (404) 875-8198
          Web site: www.bedandbreakfast.com
Kosher and Shomer Shabbat accommodation.

COMMUNITY ORGANISATIONS

Jewish Federation
1753 Peachtree Road, NE 30309   (404) 873-1661
Fax: (404) 874-7043
Publishes an annual community guide.

DELICATESSEN

Chai Peking
2205 La Vista Road, N.E. 30329   (404) 327-7810
Fax: (404) 327-7811
Web site: www.chaipeking.com
Supervision: Atlanta Kashruth Commission
Inside Kroger Supermarket. Authentic glatt kosher
Chinese cuisine.

EMBASSY

Consul General of Israel
Suite 440, 1100 Spring Street, NW 30309-2823

KASHRUT INFORMATION

Atlanta Kashrut Commission
1855 La Vista Road, N.E. 30329   (404) 634-4063
Fax: (404) 634-4254
Email: akc613@usa.com
A non-profit organisation dedicated to promoting
kashrut through education, research and supervision.
Publishes a monthly kashrut newsletter.

RESTAURANTS

Dairy
Broadway Café
2166 Briarcliff Road 30329   (404) 329-0888
Fax: (404) 329-9888
Supervision: Atlanta Kashrut Commission
Seafood, vegetarian, and vegan foods.

CJ's Café
5825 Glenridge Drive, Bldg 2,
Suite 115 30342   (404) 705-9100

Wall Street Pizza
2470 Briarcliff Road, 30329   (404) 633-2111
Supervision: Atlanta Kashrut Commission
Delivery available.

Meat
Quality Kosher
2153 Briarcliff Road 30329   (404) 636-1114
Fax: (404) 636-8675
Supervision: Atlanta Kashrut Commission

SYNAGOGUES

Conservative
Ahavath Achim
600 Peachtree Battle Avenue   (404) 355-5222

Orthodox
Anshi S'Fard
1324 North Highland Avenue,
N.E. 30306   (404) 874-4513
Email: greggbrenner@aol.com

Congregation Beth Jacob
1855 La Vista Road NE 30329   (404) 633-0551
Fax: (404) 320-7912
Email: cbj@mindspring.com
Web site: www.toll-free.com/bethjacob
Mikveh on premises.

Young Israel of Toco Hills
2074 La Vista Road, Toco Hills 30329 (404) 315-1417
Fax: (404) 315-1417
Email: info@yith.org
Web site: www.yith.org

Reform
Temple Sinai
5645 Dupree Drive, N.W. 30327   (404) 252-3073

The Temple
1589 Peachtree Road   (404) 873-1731
Sephardi
Ner Hamizrach
1858 La Vista Road, N.E. 30329   (404) 315-9020

Augusta

BAKERIES

Sunshine Bakery
1209 Broad Street 30902

DELICATESSEN

Parti-Pal
Daniel Village 30904

Strauss
965 Broad Street 30902

SYNAGOGUES

Orthodox
Adas Yeshuron
935 Johns Road, Walton Way 30904   (404) 733-9491

Columbus

SYNAGOGUES

Conservative
Shearith Israel
2550 Wynnton Road 31906   (706) 323-1443
Reform
Temple Israel
1617 Wildwood Avenue 31906   (706) 323-1617

Decatur

RESTAURANTS

Meat
Twelve Oaks Barbecue
1451 Scot Blvd.   (404) 377-0120

TOURS OF JEWISH INTEREST

Kosher Expeditions
2932 Westbury Drive, Suite 100   (404) 441-2545
                                    Fax: (404) 234-5170
                    Email: dl@kosherexpeditions.com
                    Web site: www.kosherexpeditions.com
World wide kosher travel organisers.

Macon

SYNAGOGUES

Conservative
Sha'arey Israel
611 First Street 31201   (478) 745-4571
                                    Fax: (478) 745-5892
                        Web site: www.csimacon.org

Reform
Beth Israel
892 Cherry Street 31201   (478) 745-6727

Savannah

COMMUNITY ORGANISATIONS

Savannah Jewish Federation
5111 Abercorn Street 31405   (912) 355-8111
                                    Fax: (912) 355-8116
                        Email: sharon@savj.org

CONTACT INFORMATION

Rabbi Avigdor Slatus
5444 Abercorn Street 31405   (912) 354-2359
                                    Fax: (912) 354-5272
Visitors requiring information about kashrut,
temporary accommodation, etc., should contact
Rabbi Slatus.

GUEST APARTMENTS

Buckingham South
5450 Abercorn Street 31405   (912) 355-5550
                                    Fax: (912) 353-9393
                Email: information@buckinghamsouth.com
Supervision: Rabbi Avigdor Slatus
Glatt kosher meals available on request. Next door to
Orthodox synagogue, minyan available.

SYNAGOGUES

Conservative
Agudath Achim
9 Lee Blvd. 31405   (912) 352-4737

Orthodox
B'nai B'rith Jacob
5444 Abercorn Street 31405   (912) 354-7721
                                    Fax: (912) 354-9923

Reform
Mickve Israel
Bull & Gordon Sts. 31401   (912) 233-1547
The oldest synagogue in Georgia, having been
founded before 1790, is currently being renovated
and is reopening this year. Mailing address: PO Box
816, Savannah, Georgia, 31402-0816.

HAWAII

HAWAII

Hilo

SYNAGOGUES

Unaffiliated
Temple Beth Aloha
PO Box 96720
Services once a month.

Kona

SYNAGOGUES

Reform
Kona Beth Shalom Kailua-Kona
                            (808) 322-4192 or 322-6004

MAUI

Kihei

SYNAGOGUES

Jewish Congregation of Maui
PO Box 6101, Maui 96732   (808) 243-2499

Reform
Congregation Gan Eden
PO Box 555, Kihei Road 96753   (808) 879-9221
                                    Fax: (808) 874-8570

OAHU

Honolulu

COMMUNITY ORGANISATIONS

Jewish Federation of Hawaii
44 Hora Lane 96813   (808) 941-2424

GROCERIES

Down To Earth
King's Street, Near University Av.,

Foodland Supermarket Beretania
1460 S. Beretania St.

SYNAGOGUES
Conservative
Congregation Sof Ma'arav
2500 Pali Highway 96817   (808) 595-3678
Orthodox
Chabad of Hawaii
2nd floor conference room, 1777 Ala Moana Blvd.,
96822   (808) 735-8161
    Fax: (808) 735-4130
Reform
Temple Emanu-El
2550 Pali Highway 96817   (808) 595-7521
Temple Emanu-El is the oldest congregation in
Hawaii, the only one in its own building and the only
congregation with its own full-time rabbi.

Waikiki

SYNAGOGUES
Orthodox
Chabad
Hawaiian Monarch Hotel, Nieu St   (808) 735-8161

IDAHO

Boise

SYNAGOGUES
Conservative
Ahavath-Beth Israel
1102 State Street 83702   (208) 343-6601
The oldest continually functioning synagogue in the
western USA.

ILLINOIS

Champaign-Urbana

COMMUNITY ORGANISATIONS
Champaign-Urbana Jewish Federation
503 E. John St 61820   (217) 367-9872
    Fax: (217) 344-1540
    Email: cujf@shalomcu.org
    Web site: www.shalomcu.org

SYNAGOGUES
Reform
Sinai Temple
3104 Windsor Road 61821   (217) 352-8140

Chicago

Chicagoland (Greater Chicago) consists of the
City of Chicago and the collar counties of Cook,
Dupage, Kane, Lake and McHenry. The Jewish
community is spread throughout Chicagoland,
with the main concentrations being in West
Rogers Park (City of Chicago), Skokie (Cook
County), Buffalo Grove and Highland Park (Lake
County).

Greater Chicago has a Jewish population of
about 260,000. For a history of the Jews of
Chicago see: I. Cutter, 'The Jews of Chicago:
From Shtetl to Suburbs'.
There are three basic divisions in Chicagoland:
a. City of Chicago (telephone area code 312 and
773) includes West Rogers Park.
b. North and Northwest Suburbs (includes Cook,
Lake and McHenry counties; telephone area
codes 773, 815 and 847) includes Buffalo Grove,
Deerfield, Evanston, Highland Park, Northbrook,
and Skokie;
c. South and West Suburbs (includes DuPage and
Kane counties' telephone area codes 630 or 708)
includes Flossmoor and Olympia Fields.
Chicago below covers area a. The areas b and c
are listed under the respective town name where
appropriate.

For more information see the Jewish Chicago
website at www.jewishchicago.com. This site is
however currently being revised.

BOOKSELLERS
Chicago Hebrew Book Store
2942 W. Devon 60659   (773) 973-6636
    Fax: (773) 973-6465

Rosenblum's World of Judaica, Inc.
2906 W. Devon Ave 60659   (773) 262-1700
    Fax: (773) 262-1930
    Email: avi@alljudaica.com
    Web site: www.alljudaica.com
Toll free 800-626-6535.

The Bariff Shop at the Spertus Museum
618 S. Michigan Avenue 60605   (312) 322-1740
    Fax: (312) 922-6406
    Email: bariff_shop@spertus.edu
    Web site: www.bariff.org
Hours: Sunday to Wednesday 10.00am to 5.00pm.
Thursday 10.00am to 7.00pm (5.00pm in January and
February). Friday 10.00am to 3.00pm. Closed
Saturday. Toll free (888) 322-1740.

DELICATESSEN
Romanian Kosher Sausage
7200 N. Clark 60625   (773) 761-4141
Supervision: Orthodox Union

EMBASSY

Consul General of Israel
Suite 1308, 111 East Wacker Drive 60601

MIKVAOT

Bnei Ruven
(773) 743-4282

MUSEUM

Spertus Museum
Spertus Institute of Jewish Studies,
618 S. Michigan Avenue 60605   (312) 322-1747
Fax: (312) 922-3934
Email: musm@spertus.edu
Web site: www.spertus.edu
Hours: 10.00 am-5.00 pm Sunday to Wednesday.
10.00 am-7.00 pm Thursday. 10.00 am-3.00 pm
Friday. Closed Saturday.

RESTAURANTS

Dairy
Jerusalem Kosher Restaurant
3014 W. Devon 60659   (773) 262-0515
Supervision: OK

Meat
Great Chicago Food & Beverage Co.
3149 W. Devon 60659   (773) 465-9030
Fax: (773) 465-9011
Email: gcfbken@aoi.com
Supervision: Chicago Rabbinical Council

Mi Tsu Yun Kosher Chinese Rest.
3010 W. Devon 60659   (773) 262-4630
Fax: (773) 262-4835
Supervision: Chicago Rabbinical Council
Sunday-Thursday 12.00pm-9.00pm.

Shallots
2324 N. Clark St. 60614   (773) 755-5205
Web site: www.shallots-chicago.com

SYNAGOGUES

Conservative
Anshe Emet Synagogue
3760 N. Pine Grove 60613   (773) 281-1423
Fax: (773) 281-2813
Web site: ansheemet.org

Orthodox
K.I.N.S of West Rogers Park
2800 W. North Shore Avenue 60645   (312) 761-4000
Fax: (312) 761-4959
Email: congkins@cs.com

Lake Shore Drive Synagogue
70 E. Elm street 60611   (773) 337-6811

Loop Synagogue
16 S Clark street 60603

Young Israel of Chicago
4931 North Kimball Street 60625   (773) 338-6380

Young Israel of West Rogers Park
2706 West Touhy Avenue 60645   (773) 743-9400

Highland Park

DELICATESSEN

Best's Kosher Outlet Store
1630 Deerfield Rd. 60035   (847) 831-9435
Fax: (847) 831-9440

Now we're cooking grill
710 Central 60035   (847) 432-7310
Fax: (847) 432-8352
Supervision: Chicago Kashrut Association Inc
Eat in and take-out.

SYNAGOGUES

Conservative
North Surburban Synagogue Beth El
1175 Sheriden Road 60035   (847) 432-8900

Northbrook

SYNAGOGUES

Orthodox
Young Israel of Northbrook
3545 Walters Road 60062   (847) 480-9462
Fax: (847) 205-1967

Peoria

COMMUNITY ORGANISATIONS

Jewish Federation
Town Hall Building, 5901 N. Prospect Road
61604   (309) 689-0063

SYNAGOGUES

Orthodox
Agudas Achim
5614 N. University 61614   (309) 692-4848
Fax: (309) 692-7255

Reform
Anshai Emeth
5614 North University Street 61614   (309) 691-3323
Email: rariel@aol.com

Rock Island

COMMUNITY ORGANISATIONS

Jewish Federation of the Quad Cities
209 18th Street 61201   (309) 793-1300
Fax: (309) 793-1345

Rockford

COMMUNITY ORGANISATIONS
Jewish Federation of Greater Rockford
1500 Parkview Avenue 61107   (815) 399-5497
Fax: (815) 399-9835
Email: rockfordfederation@juno.com

SYNAGOGUES
Conservative
Ohave Sholom
3730 Guildford Road 61107   (815) 226-4900

Reform
Temple Beth El
1203 Comanche Drive 61107   (815) 398-5020

Skokie

JUDAICA
Hamakor Gallery Ltd.
4150 Dempster 60076   (847) 677-4150
Fax: (847) 677-4160
Email: gallery@jewishsource.com
Web site: www.jewishsource.com

MEDIA
Newspaper
Chicago Jewish Star
PO Box 268 60076   (847) 674-7827
Fax: (847) 674-0014
Email: chicago-jewish-star@mcimail.com

RESTAURANTS
Dairy
Bagel Country
9306 Skokie Blvd, Skokie, IL 60077   (847) 673-3030
Fax: (847) 673-4040
Email: bcskokie@aol.com
Supervision: Chicago Rabbinical Council

Da'Nali's
4032 W. Oakton 60076   (847) 677-2782
Supervision: Chicago Rabbinical Council

Meat
Bugsy's Charhouse
3355 W. Dempster 60076   (847) 679-4030
Fax: (847) 835-3354
Email: gcfbken@aol.com
Supervision: Chicago Rabbinical Council

Hy Life
4120 W. Dempster, Skokie 60076   (847) 674-2021
Supervision: Chicago Rabbinical Council

Ken's Diner
3353 W. Dempster 60076   (847) 679-4030
Fax: (847) 835-3354; 3835- Deli
Email: gcfbken@aoi.com
Supervision: Chicago Rabbinical Council

Vegetarian
Mysore Woodlands
2548 Devon Avenue 60659   (847) 338-8160
Fax: (847) 338-8162
Supervision: CKA

SYNAGOGUES
Orthodox
Young Israel of Skokie
3740 W Dempster 60076   (847) 329-0990
Shul is located in the Timber Ridge School, Samoset
and Davis. P.O. Box 857

Springfield

SYNAGOGUES
Conservative
Temple Israel
1140 West Governor Street 62704   (217) 546-2841
Fax: (217) 726-9857
Email: templeisrael@springnet1.com

INDIANA

Bloomington

SYNAGOGUES
Orthodox
Chabad House
516 E. 17th Street 47408   (812) 332-6784

Reform
Congregation Beth Shalom
3750 E. Third 47401   (812) 334-2440

East Chicago

SYNAGOGUES
Orthodox
B'nai Israel
3517 Hemlock Street 46312

Evansville

SYNAGOGUES
Conservative
Temple Adath B'nai Israel
3600 E. Washington Avenue 47715   (812) 477-1577
Fax: (812) 477-1577
Email: tabi@evansville.net

Reform
Tempe
Washington Avenue Temple, 100 Washington
Avenue 47714

Fort Wayne

SYNAGOGUES
Conservative
B'nai Jacob
7227 Bittersweet Moors Drive 46814 (219) 672-8459
Fax: (219) 672-8928

Reform
Achduth Vesholom
5200 Old Mill Road 46807 (219) 744-4245
Fax: (219) 744-4246
Email: TempleCAV@aol.com

Gary

SYNAGOGUES
Reform
Temple Israel
601 N. Montgomery Street 46403 (219) 938-5232

Hammond

SYNAGOGUES
Conservative
Beth Israel
7105 Hohman Avenue 46324 (219) 931-1312

Reform
Temple Beth-El
6947 Hohman Avenue 46324 (219) 932-3754

Highland

COMMUNITY ORGANISATIONS
Jewish Federation of North West Indiana
2939 Jewett Street, Highland 46322 (219) 972-2251
Fax: (219) 972-4779
Serving Lake Porter and LaPorte Counties.

Indianapolis

COMMUNITY ORGANISATIONS
Jewish Federation of Greater Indianapolis
6705 Hoover Road 46260 (317) 726-5450
Fax: (317) 205-0307
Email: hnadler@jewishinindy.org

SYNAGOGUES
Conservative
Shaarey Tefilla Congregation
5879 Central Avenue 46220-2509 (317) 253-4591
Fax: (317) 253-8529
Email: execdir@shaareytefilla.org
Web site: www.shaareytefilla.org

Conservative/Reconstructionist
Beth-El Zedeck
600 W. 70th Street 46260 (317) 253-3441
Fax: (317) 259-6849
Email: bez613@bez613.org

Orthodox
B'nai Torah
6510 Hoover Road 46260 (317) 253-5253
Fax: (317) 253-5459
Email: scrandall@iqvest.net

Etz Chaim Sephardic Congregation
826 West 64 Street 46260 (317) 251-6220

Reform
Indianapolis Hebrew Congregation
6501 N. Meridian Street 46260 (317) 255-6647

Lafayette

SYNAGOGUES
Orthodox
Sons of Abraham
661 N. 7th Street 47906 (317) 742-2113
Email: retrovir@bragg.bio.purdue.edu

Michigan City

SYNAGOGUES
Reform
Sinai Temple
2800 S. Franklin Street 46360 (219) 874-4477

Muncie

SYNAGOGUES
Reform
Temple Beth El
525 W. Jackson Street, cnr. Council Street 47305
(317) 288-4662

South Bend

COMMUNITY ORGANISATIONS
Jewish Federation of St. Joseph Valley
3202 Shalom Way 46615 (574) 233-1164
Fax: (574) 288-4103
Email: mgardner@jon.cjfny.org

CONTACT INFORMATION
Rabbi Y. Gettinger
Hebrew Orthodox Congregation, 3207 S. High
Street 46614 (574) 291-4239
Fax: (574) 291-9490
Visitors requiring information about kashrut,
temporary accommodation, etc., should contact
Rabbi Gettinger or Michael Lerman, 1-800-348-2529.
Ext. 137.

KASHRUT INFORMATION
Hebrew Orthodox Congregation
3207 S. High Street 46614   (574) 291-4239
     Fax: (574) 291-9490

MIKVAOT
     (574) 291-6240

SYNAGOGUES
Conservative
Sinai
1102 E. Laselle Street 46617   (574) 234-8584
     Fax: (574) 234-6856
     Email: sinai@michiana.org
     Web site: www.uscj.org/midwest/southbend

Orthodox
Hebrew Orthodox Congregation
3207 S. High Street 46614   (574) 291-4239
     Fax: (574) 291-9490

Reform
Beth-El
305 W. Madison Street 46601   (574) 234-4402

Terre Haute

DELICATESSEN
Kosher Meat & Sandwiches
410 W. Western Avenue 47807

Valparaiso

SYNAGOGUES
Conservative
Temple Israel
PO Box 2051 46383

West Lafayette

SYNAGOGUES
Reform
620 Cumberland Street 47906   (765) 463-3455
     Fax: (765) 463-9309
     Email: temple@nlci.com

Whiting

SYNAGOGUES
Orthodox
B'nai Judah
116th Street & Davis Avenue 46394   (219) 659-0797

IOWA

Cedar Rapids

SYNAGOGUES
Reform
Temple Judah
3221 Lindsay Lane S.E. 52403   (319) 362-1261

Davenport

SYNAGOGUES
Reform
Temple Emanuel
12th Street & Mississippi Avenue 52803
Davenport is part of the Rock Island, Illinois area, which is divided by the Mississippi River. See the Rock Island (Illinois) entry.

Des Moines

COMMUNITY ORGANISATIONS
Jewish Federation of Greater Des Moines
910 Polk Blvd 50312   (515) 277-6321

DELICATESSEN
The Nosh
800 First Street 50265

SYNAGOGUES
Conservative
Tifereth Israel
924 Polk Blvd 50312   (515) 255-1137

Orthodox
Beth El Jacob
954 Cummins Parkway 50312   (515) 274-1551
     Fax: (515) 274-1552
     Email: rav613@hotmail.com
     Web site: www.cyberconnect.com/bej
Vaad Hakashrut of Des Moines offer information on Kosher establishments & home hospitality. Contact rabbi. Mikvah available by appointment.

Reform
Temple B'nai Jeshurun
5101 Grand Avenue 50312   (515) 274-4679
     Fax: (515) 274-2072
     Email: arptbj@aol.com
     Web site:
www.shamash.org/reform/uahc/congs/ia/ia001

Dubuque

SYNAGOGUES
Reform
Beth El
475 W. Locust Street 52001   (563) 583-3483

Fort Dodge

SYNAGOGUES
Conservative
501 N. 12th Street 50501   (515) 572-8925

Iowa City

SYNAGOGUES
Conservative & Reform
Agudas Achim
602 E. Washington Street 52240   (319) 337-3813
Fax: (319) 337-6764
Email: agudasachim@aol.com

Postville

SYNAGOGUES
Orthodox
440 South Lawlor Street   (319) 863-3013

Sioux City

COMMUNITY ORGANISATIONS
Jewish Federation
525 14th Street 51105   (712) 258-0618

SYNAGOGUES
Conservative
Congregation Beth Shalom
815 38th Street 51104   (712) 255-1990
Fax: (712) 258-0619
Email: drosen4005@aol.com
Orthodox
United Orthodox
Nebraska & 14th Street 51105   (712) 255-4455

KANSAS

Lawrence

SYNAGOGUES
Lawrence Jewish Community Center
917 Highland Drive 66046   (913) 841-7636
Email: ljcc@grapevine.net
Web site: www.grapevine.net/~ljcc

Overland Park

BUTCHERS
Jacobsons Strictly Kosher Foods
5200 West 95th Street 66207   (913) 648-3880

SYNAGOGUES
Orthodox
Congregation Beth Israel Abraham & Voliner
9900 Antioch 66212   (913) 341-2444
Fax: (913) 341-2467

Kehilath Israel Synagogue
10501 Conser 66212   (913) 642-1880
Fax: (913) 642-7332

Reform
Congregation Beth Torah
6100 W 127th Street 66209   (913) 498-2212
Fax: (913) 498-1071

Prairie Village

SYNAGOGUES
Conservative
Ohev Sholom
5311 W. 75th Street 66208   (913) 642-6460
Fax: (913) 642-6461
Email: rabbidanny@aol.com
Conservative Egalitarian.

Topeka

COMMUNITY ORGANISATIONS
Topeka Lawrence Jewish Federation
4200 Munson Street 66604

SYNAGOGUES
Reform
Beth Sholom
4200 SW Munson Avenue 66604-1818
(785) 272-6040

Wichita

GROCERIES

Dillon's
Foodbarn Woodlawn & Central Sts 67208
21st Street & Rock Road 67208
13th Street & Woodlawn Street 67208

The Bread Lady
20205 Rock Road, #80 2607

SYNAGOGUES
Orthodox
Hebrew Congregation
1850 N. Woodlawn 67208   (316) 685-1139

Reform
Congregation Emanu-El
7011 E. Central Street 67206   (316) 685-5148

KENTUCKY

Lexington

COMMUNITY ORGANISATIONS
Central Kentucky Jewish Federation
340 Romany Road 40502   (859) 268-0672
Fax: (859) 268-0775
Email: ckjf@jewishlexington.org

SYNAGOGUES
Conservative
Lexington Havurah
685 Shasta Circle 40503   (859) 223-1299

Ohavay Zion
2048 Edgewater Ct. 40502   (859) 266-8050
Fax: (859) 268-3357
Email: ozslex@gte.net
Web site: www.ozs.org

Reform
Adath Israel
124 N. Ashland Avenue 40502   (859) 269-2979
Fax: (859) 269-7347

Louisville

COMMUNITY ORGANISATIONS
Jewish Community Federation
3630 Dutchman's Lane 40205   (502) 451-8840
Fax: (502) 458-0702
Email: jfed@iglou.com

SYNAGOGUES
Conservative
Adath Jeshurun
2401 Woodbourne Avenue 40205   (502) 458-5359

Knesseth Israel
2531 Taylorsville Road 40205   (502) 459-2780

Orthodox
Anshei Sfard
3700 Dutchman's Lane 40205   (502) 451-3122
Mikvah attached.

Reform
Temple Shalom
4615 Lowe Road 40220   (502) 458-4739
Fax: (502) 451-9750
Email: rsmiles@pipeline.com

The Temple
5101 Brownsboro Road 40241   (502) 423-1818
Fax: (502) 423-1835
Email: gronkin@thetempleaibs.org
Web site: www.uahcweb.org/ky/thetemple

Paducah

SYNAGOGUES
Reform
Temple Israel
330 Joe Clifton Drive 42001

LOUISIANA

Alexandria

CONTACT INFORMATION
Jewish Welfare Federation
          (318) 445-4785

GROCERIES
Dr & Mrs B Kaplan
100 Park Place 71301   (318) 445-9367
Fax: (318) 445-9369
Kosher food by arrangement.

LIBRARIES
Meyer Kaplan Memorial Library (Judiaca)
c/o B'nai Israel, 1908 Vance Street 71301

SYNAGOGUES
Conservative
B'nai Israel
1907 Vance Street 71301   (318) 455-9367

Reform
Gemiluth Chassodim
2021 Turner Street 71301   (318) 455-3655

Baton Rouge

COMMUNITY ORGANISATIONS

Jewish Federation of Greater Baton Rouge
PO Box 80827 70898   (504) 291-5895

SYNAGOGUES

Reform

B'nai Israel
3354 Kleinert Avenue 70806   (504) 343-0111

Beth Shalom
9111 Jefferson Highway 70809   (504) 924-6773

Lafayette

SYNAGOGUES

Reform

Temple Sholom
603 Lee Avenue, PO Box 53711 70505
     (318) 234-3760
There is a fine Judaica library at the University of Southwestern Louisiana.

New Orleans

COMMUNITY ORGANISATIONS

Jewish Federation of Greater New Orleans
3500 N. Causeway Blvd., #1240,
Metairie 70002   (504) 828-2125
     Fax: (504) 828-2827

DELICATESSEN

Kosher Cajun Deli & Grocery
3519 Severn St, Metairie 70002   (504) 888-2010
     Fax: (504) 888-2014
     Web site: www.koshercajun.com
Glatt N.Y. Deli - Dine in or take-out. Challah, wine, large selection of kosher grocery items. Under strict rabbinical supervision. Hours: Monday - Thursday, 10 am to 7 pm; Friday and Sunday, 10am to 3 pm. We also deliver to hotels.

GROCERIES

Casablanca
3030 Seven Avenue, Metrairie 70002-4826
     (504) 888-2209

Touro Infirmary
1401 Foucher Street 70115   (504) 897-8246
Glatt kosher meals available

GUEST HOUSE

2405 St. Charles Avenue   (504) 581-5858
     Fax: (504) 891-5626
     Email: paulag@sunshinebrokers.com
Guest House around the corner from Anshe Sfard Synagogue.

MEDIA

Newspaper

The Jewish News
3500 N. Causeway Blvd, #1240,
Metairie 70002   (504) 828-2125
     Fax: (504) 828-2827
     Email: jewishnews@jewishnola.com

MIKVAOT

Beth Israel
7000 Canal Blvd 70124   (504) 283-4366

RESTAURANTS

Meat

Casablanca
3030 Severn Avenue, Metairie   (504) 888-2209
     Fax: (504) 888-5605
     Web site: www.kosherneworleans.com
Supervision: Lubavitch Shechita & Chabad.

Creole Kosher Kitchen
115 Chartres Street   (504) 529-4120
Supervision: Beth Israel Congregation

SYNAGOGUES

Orthodox

Anshe Sfard
2230 Carondelet Street 70130   (504) 522-4714

Chabad House
7037 Freret Street   (504) 866-5164

Shreveport

COMMUNITY ORGANISATIONS

Jewish Federation
2032 Line Avenue 71104   (318) 221-4129

SYNAGOGUES

Conservative

Agudath Achim
9401 Village Green Drive 71115   (318) 797-6401
     Fax: (318) 797-6402

Reform

B'nai Zion
245 Southfield Road 71105   (318) 861-2122

MAINE

Auburn

COMMUNITY ORGANISATIONS

Lewiston-Auburn Jewish Federation
74 Bradman Street 04210   (207) 786-4201
     Fax: (207) 786-4202
     Email: temple6359@aol.com

SYNAGOGUES
Conservative
Congregation Beth Abraham
Main Street & Laurel Avenue 04210   (207) 783-1302

Temple Shalom
74 Bradman Street 04210   (207) 786-4201
                                               Fax: (207) 786-4202
                                  Email: temple6359@aol.com

Augusta

SYNAGOGUES
Reform
Temple Beth El
PO Box 871, Woodlawn Street 04330 (207) 622-7450

Bangor

RESTAURANTS
Bagel Central
33 Central Street 04401   (207) 947-1654
Supervision: Beth Abraham Rabbi Fred Neble

SYNAGOGUES
Conservative
Congregation Beth Israel
144 York Street 04401   (207) 945-3433
                                               Fax: (207) 945-3840

Orthodox
Beth Abraham
145 York Street 04401   (207) 942-8093
                                  Email: rabbi@jewishbangor.com
                             Web site: www.jewishbangor.com

Old Orchard Beach

KASHRUT INFORMATION
Eber Weinstein
187 E. Grand Avenue 04064   (207) 934-7522

SYNAGOGUES
Orthodox
Beth Israel
49 E. Grand Avenue 04064   (207) 934-2973
                                               Fax: (207) 934-5800
Daily minyan, May 28 to Yom Kippur; Shabbat & Yom Tov minyan all year round.

Portland

BUTCHERS
Penny Wise Super Market
182 Ocean Avenue 04130
Take-out counter at a local supermarket.

COMMUNITY ORGANISATIONS
Jewish Fed.-Com. Council of Southern Maine
57 Ashmont Street 04103   (207) 773-7254

MIKVAOT
Shaarey Tphiloh
76 Noyes Street 04103   (207) 773-0693

SYNAGOGUES
Conservative
Temple Beth El
400 Deering Avenue 04103   (207) 774-2649
                                               Fax: (207) 774-7518
                          Email: office@templebethel-maine.org
U.S.C.J.

Orthodox
Shaarey Tphiloh
76 Noyes Street 04103   (207) 773-0693
Mikvah & Hebrew Day School on premises.

Rockland

SYNAGOGUES
Conservative
Adas Yoshuron
Willow Street   (207) 594-4523

MARYLAND

Annapolis

SYNAGOGUES
Conservative
Congregation Kol Ami
1909 Hidden Meadow Lane 21401   (410) 266-6006
                                  Email: kolami2@toadmail.toad.net

Reform
Temple Beth Shalom
1461 Baltimore-Anaapolis Blvd., 21012

Baltimore

There are more than 50 synagogues in the Baltimore metropolitan area. Visitors are advised to contact one of the community organizations in the area to find the synagogue nearest to them.

Although the first Jew Benjamin Levy is recorded as arriving in 1773 a synagogue was not established until 1830. Jews arrived from eastern Europe in large numbers during the 1880's and the population now amounts to around 100,000. It was apparently known at one time as "the Jerusalem" of America.

Possibly Baltimore's most important personality was Henrietta Szold daughter of Rabbi Benjamin Szold who arrived in 1859.

The Temple Oheb Shalom at 7310 Park Avenue, designed by Walter Gropius is well worth visiting.

BAKERIES

Alder's Bakery
1860D Reisterstown Road   (410) 653-1119

Dunkin Donuts
1508 Reisterstown Road 21208   (410) 653-8182
Supervision: Rabbi Salfer

7000 Reisterstown Road 21215   (410) 764-6846
Supervision: Rabbi Salfer

Goldman's Kosher Bakery
6848 Reisterstown Road, Farstaff Shopping
Center 21215   (410) 358-9625
    Fax: (410) 358-5859
    Email: mcohn@comcast.net
Star-K Certified.

Pariser's Kosher Bakery
6711 Reisterstown Road 21215   (410) 764-1700

Schmell & Azman Kosher Bakery
    (410) 484-7343

Schmell-Azman
7006 Reisterstown Road 21215   (410) 484-7373
Supervision: Star K

BUTCHERS

Shlomo Meat & Fish Market
4135 Amos Ave., (Menlo Industrial Park)
21215   (410) 358-9633

Wasserman & Lemberger
7006-D Reisterstown Road 20208   (410) 486-4191

COMMUNITY ORGANISATIONS

Associated Jewish Community Federation of Baltimore
101 W. Mount Royal Avenue 21201   (410) 727-4828

Jewish Information and Referral Service
5750 Park Heights Avenue 21215   (410) 466-4636
    Fax: (410) 664-0551
    Email: jirs@jfs.org
Open Monday - Thursday 9.00am to 5.00pm, Friday 9.00am to 3.00pm.

DELICATESSEN

Knish Shop
508 Reisterstown Road 21208   (410) 484-5850
Conservative supervision

Liebes Kosher Deli Carry Out
607 Reisterstown Road 21208   (410) 653-1977
Only glatt kosher meats. Hours: Sunday to Wednesday, 8:30am to 6pm; Thursday, late night Friday, to one hour before sundown. Specialising in party trays.

GROCERIES

Seven Mile Market
4000 Seven Mile Lane 21208   (410) 653-2000; 2002
Supervision: Star-K
Items sold in the Fresh Meat, Fresh Fish, Fresh Bakery, Fresh Deli, Fresh Dairy, Hot Prepared Foods & Salad Departments are approved by the Vaad Hakashrus of Baltimore, when so stated on sign or label.

Shlomo Meat & Fish
506 Reisterstown Road 21215   (410) 358-9633

Wasserman & Lemberger
7006-D Reisterstown Road 21208   (410) 486-4191

KASHRUT INFORMATION

Star-K Kosher Certification
122 Slade Avenue, Suite 300 21208   (410) 484-4110
    Fax: (410) 653-9294
    Email: star-k@star-k.org
    Web site: www.star-k.org
Also issues Worldwide Kashrut Certification.

MIKVAOT

Mikva of Baltimore Inc.,
3207 Clarks Lane 21215   (410) 764-1448
    Fax: (410) 578-0018

MUSEUM

The Jewish Museum of Maryland
15 Lloyd Street 21202   (410) 732-6400
    Fax: (410) 732-6451
    Email: info@jewishmuseummd.org
    Web site: www.jewishmuseummd.org
This newly- enlarged complex of museum buildings is unlike anything else in the United States, comprising two historic synagogues (Lloyd Street Synagogue, built in 1845, and B'nai Israel, built in 1876) and an adjoining research center and museum featuring two exhibition galleries, library and gift shop. Opening hours: Tuesday, Wednesday, Thursday and Sunday 12am-4pm.

RESTAURANTS

Café Shalom
2401 West Belvedere Avenue
    (410) 601-5000 ext 3971
Supervision: Star-K
Serves both Meat and Dairy

Goldberg's Bagels
708 Reisterstown Road   (410) 415-7001
Supervision: Star-K

Krispy Kremes
10021 Reisterstown Road (nr Painters Mill Rd).
    (410) 356-2655
Supervision: Star-KD

Mama Leah's Pizza
1852 Reisterstown Road   (410) 653-7600
Supervision: Star-K

Dairy
Caramel's Pizza & Ice Cream
700 Reisterstown Road   (410) 486-2365
Supervision: Star-K

Milk and Honey Bistro
Commercecentre, 1777 Reisterstown Road
    (410) 484-3544
Supervision: Star-K

Meat
David Chu's China Bistro
7105 Reistertown Road 21215   (410) 602-5008
Supervision: Star-K

Kosher Bite
6309 Reistertown Road 21215   (410) 358-6349
Supervision: Star-K

Royal Restaurant
7006 Reistertown Road 21208   (410) 484-3544
Supervision: Star-K

Szechuan Dynasty
1860C Reistertown Road   (410) 602-1817

The Brasserie
Pomona Square Shopping Center, 1700 Reistertown
Rd 21208   (410) 484-0476
Supervision: Star-K

Pizzeria
Tov Pizza
6313 Reistertown Road   (410) 358-5238

TOURS OF JEWISH INTEREST
Holocaust Memorial
Gay & Lombard Sts   (410) 542-4850
    Fax: (410) 542-4834
    Email: mtishler@aea-bal.tjc.org

Cumberland

SYNAGOGUES
Conservative
Beth Jacob
1 Columbia Street 21502   (301) 777-3717

Reform
B'Er Chayim
107 Union Street 21502   (301) 722-5688
    Web site: www.berchayim.org

GREATER WASHINGTON

Bethesda

COMMUNITY ORGANISATIONS
**United Jewish Appeal Federation of Greater
Washington**
7900 Wisconsin Avenue 20814   (301) 652-6480

Bowie

SYNAGOGUES
Conservative
Nevey Shalom
12218 Torah Lane 20715   (301) 262-9020
    Fax: (301) 262-9015
    Email: neveyshalom@maxinter.net

Reform
Temple Solel
2901 Mitchelville Road 20716   (301) 249-2424

Chevy Chase

SYNAGOGUES
Conservative
Ohr Kodesh
8402 Freyman Drive 20815   (301) 589-3880
    Fax: (301) 495-4801
    Email: okcjmm@erols.com

Reform
Temple Shalom
8401 Grubb Road 20815   (301) 587-2273

Gaithersburg

SYNAGOGUES
Conservative
Kehilat Shalom
9915 Apple Ridge Road 20886   (301) 869-7699
    Fax: (301) 977-7870
    Email: mail@kehilatshalom.org
    Web site: www.kehilatshalom.org

Greenbelt

SYNAGOGUES
Conservative
Mishkan Torah
Westway and Ridge Road 20770   (301) 474-4223

Kemp Mill

SYNAGOGUES
Kemp Mill Synagogue
11910 Kemp Mill Road   (301) 593-0966

Kensington

SYNAGOGUES
Reform
Temple Emanuel
10101 Connecticut Avenue 20895   (301) 942-2000
    Fax: (301) 942-9488

Olney

SYNAGOGUES
Conservative
B'nai Shalom
18401 Burtfield Drive 20832   (301) 774-0879

Potomac

RESTAURANTS
Meat
Hunan Gourmet
350 Fortune Terrace   (301) 424-0191

SYNAGOGUES
Conservative
Har Shalom
11510 Falls Road 20854   (301) 299-7087
Email: shalom@harshalom.org
Web site: www.harshalom.org
Orthodox
Beth Sholom Congregation and Talmud Torah
11825 Seven Locks Road 20854   (301) 279-7010
Fax: (301) 279-5815
Email: bethsholom.org
Young Israel Ezras Israel of Potomac
11618 Seven Locks Road 20854   (301) 299-2827
Web site: www.yieip.org

Rockville

GROCERIES
Katz Supermarket
4860 Boiling Brook Parkway   (301) 468-0400

RESTAURANTS
Dairy
Siena's
Nicholson Road   (301) 770-7474
Across the road from the White Flint Shopping Center.

Meat
Royal Dragon
4840 Boiling Brook Parkway   (301) 468-1922
Meat and Dairy
Kat'z Kafe
4860 Boiling Brook Parkway   (301) 468-0400

SYNAGOGUES
Conservative
B'nai Israel
6301 Montrose Road 20852   (301) 881-6550
Fax: (301) 881-6221

Tikvat Israel
2200 Baltimore Road 20851   (301) 762-7338
Fax: (301) 424-4399
Orthodox
Magen David Sephardic Congregation
11215 Woodglen Drive, Rockville, MD 20852
     (301) 770-6818
Fax: (301) 881-0498
Reform
Temple Beth Ami
14330 Travilah Road 20850   (301) 340-6818
Fax: (301) 738-0094
Email: cgs@bethami.org

Silver Spring

BAKERIES
Kosher Pastry Oven
2521 Ennalls Avenue   (301) 946-0159
Schmell and Azman
Kemp Mill Shopping Center, Arcola Avenue
     (301) 593-4785

BOOKSELLERS
Lisbon's Hebrew Books & Gifts
2305 University Blvd West, Wheaton 20902
     (301) 933-1800
Fax: (301) 933-7466
Email: slisbon@idsonline.com
The Jewish Bookstore
11252 Georgia Avenue 20902   (301) 942-2237
Fax: (301) 933-5464

GROCERIES
Shalom
2309 University Blvd 20902   (301) 946-6500
Fax: (301) 946-1041

MIKVAOT
Mikva
8901 Georgia Avenue 20910   (301) 565-3737

RESTAURANTS
Dairy
Ben Yehuda Pizza
Kemp Mill Shopping Center, off Arcola Avenue
The Nut House
11419 Georgia Avenue 20902   (301) 942-5900
Meat
Max's
2309 University Blvd   (301) 949-6297

SYNAGOGUES
Conservative
Har Tzeon-Agudath Achim
1840 University Blvd. W 20902
Shaare Tefila
11120 Lockwood Drive 20901   (301) 593-3410
Fax: (301) 593-3860
Email: brwagschal@aol.com
Temple Israel
420 University Blvd. E 20901   (301) 439-3600
Orthodox
Silver Spring Jewish Center
1401 Arcola Avenue 20902   (301) 649-4425
Fax: (301) 649-1274

South-East Hebrew Congregation
10900 Lockwood Drive 20902

Woodside Synagogue Ahavas Torah
9001 Georgia Avenue 20910   (301) 587-8252
Email: president@wsat.org
Web site: www.wsat.org
Shabbat Hospitality 301-585-8080

Young Israel of White Oak
PO Box 10613, White Oak 20914   (301) 369-1531

Young Israel Shomrai Emunah of Greater Washington
1132 Arcola Avenue 20902   (301) 593-4465
Fax: (301) 593-2330
Email: yise@erols.com

Hagerstown

DELICATESSEN
Celebrity Deli
6700 Adelphi Road 20782   (301) 927-5525

SYNAGOGUES
Reform
B'nai Abraham
53 E. Baltimore Street 21740   (301) 733-5039

Hyattsville

SYNAGOGUES
Conservative
Beth Torah Congregation
6700 Adelphi Road 20782   (301) 927-5525

Laurel

SYNAGOGUES
Reconstructionist
Oseh Shalom
8604 Briarwood Drive 20708   (301) 498-5151

Lexington Park

SYNAGOGUES
Conservative
Beth Israel Congregation
PO Box 1683, 21780 Bunker Hill Drive 20653
(301) 862-2021
Email: bethisraelsyna@geocities.com
Web site: www.geocities.com/bethisraelsyna

Pocomoke

SYNAGOGUES
Conservative
Temple Israel
3rd Street 21851

Salisbury

SYNAGOGUES
Conservative
Beth Israel
Camden Avenue & Wicomico Street 21801
(410) 742-2564

Temple Hills

SYNAGOGUES
Conservative
Shaare Tikva
5405 Old Temple Hills Road 20748   (301) 894-4303

MASSACHUSETTS

Acton

SYNAGOGUES
Independent
Beth Elohim
10 Hennessy Drive 07120   (978) 263-8610

Amherst

SYNAGOGUES
Independent
Jewish Community
742 Main Street 01002   (413) 256-0160
Fax: (413) 256-1588
Email: JCA.info@verizon.net
Web site: www.j-c-a.org

Andover

SYNAGOGUES
Reform
Temple Emanuel
7 Haggett's Pond Road 01810   (978) 470-1356
Fax: (978) 470-1783

Athol

SYNAGOGUES
Conservative
Temple Israel
107 Walnut Street 01331   (978) 249-9481

Attleboro

SYNAGOGUES
Reconstructionist
Agudas Achim Congregation
901 N. Main Street 02703 (508) 222-2243
Email: agudasachim@netzero.net
Web site: www.shamash.org/jrf/agudasma

Ayer

SYNAGOGUES
Independent
Congregation Anshey Sholom
Cambridge Street 01432 (508) 772-0896

Belmont

SYNAGOGUES
Reform
Beth El Temple Center
2 Concord Avenue 02478 (617) 484-6668
Fax: (617) 484-6020
Web site: www.uahc.org/ma/betc

Beverly

SYNAGOGUES
Conservative
B'nai Abraham
200 E. Lothrop Street 01915 (978) 927-3211
Fax: (978) 922-5281
Email: TBA200East@cs.com

Boston

COMMUNITY ORGANISATIONS
Jewish Community Relations Council of Greater Boston
1 Lincoln Plaza, Suite 308 02111 (617) 330-9600
Represents thirty-four community organisations in the area.

EMBASSY
Consul General of Israel
1020 Statler Office Blvd 02116

KASHRUT INFORMATION
Synagogue Council of Massachusetts
1320 Centre Street, Newton Centre 02459-2400
(617) 244-6506
Fax: (617) 964-7055
Email: info@synagoguecouncil.org
The Kashruth Commission
177 Tremont Street 02111 (617) 426-2139
Fax: (617) 426-6268
Email: kvh613@aol.com

MEDIA
Guide
Jewish Guide to Boston and New England
15 School Street 02108 (617) 367-9100
Fax: (617) 367-9310
Email: thejewishadvocate@thejewishadvocate.com
Newspapers
Boston Jewish Times
15 School Street 02108 (617) 267-9100
Fax: (617) 367-9310

The Jewish Advocate
15 School Street 02108 (617) 367-9100
Fax: (617) 367-9310
Email: thejewadv@aol.com
Web site: www.thejewishadvocate.com

RELIGIOUS ORGANISATIONS
Rabbinical Council of New England
177 Tremont Street 02111 (617) 426-2139
Fax: (617) 426-6268

RESTAURANTS
Dairy
50 Milk Street (617) 542-FOOD
Fax: (617) 451-5FAX
Supervision: Orthodox Rabbinic Council of Greater Boston
Hours: Monday to Friday, 7 am to 3 pm.

SYNAGOGUES
Orthodox
Chabad House
491 Commonwealth Avenue 02215 (617) 424-1190
Fax: (617) 266-5997
Email: chabad@peoplepc.com

The Boston Synagogue (at Charles River Park)
55 Martha Road 02114 (617) 523-0453
Fax: (617) 723-2863
Administrator: Rebecca Sussman. Services: Friday evening, Saturday 9.15am.

Zvhil-Mezbuz Beis Medrash
15 School Street 02108 (617) 227-8200
Fax: (617) 227-8420
Web site: www.rebbe.org
Reform
Temple Israel
Longwood Ave & Plymouth Street 02215
(617) 566-3960
Fax: (617) 731-3711
Web site: www.tisrael.org

Braintree

SYNAGOGUES
Conservative
Temple Bnai Shalom
41 Storrs Avenue 02184 (781) 843-3687

Brighton

MIKVAOT

Daughters of Israel
101 Washington Street, Brighton 02135
(617) 782-9433

SYNAGOGUES

Conservative
Temple B'nai Moshe
1845 Commonwealth Avenue, Brighton 02135
(617) 254-3620
Fax: (617) 254-3620
Email: templebnaimoshe.org

Orthodox
Chai Odom
77 Englewood Av 02135
(617) 734-5359
Web site: www.netcom/~coriat/chaidom

Congregation Kadimah-Toras Moshe
113 Washington Street, Brighton 02135
(617) 254-1333

Lubavitch Shul of Brighton
239 Chestnut Hill Avenue, Brighton 02135
(617) 782-8340

Talner Congregation Beth David
64 Corey Road 02135
(617) 232-2349

Brockton

SYNAGOGUES

Conservative
Temple
479 Torres Street 02401
(508) 583-5810

Orthodox
Agudas Achim
144 Belmont Avenue 02301
(508) 583-0717

Reform
Temple Israel
184 W. Elm Street 02401
(508) 587-4130

Brookline

BAKERIES

Catering by Andrew
402 Harvard Street 02446
(617) 731-6585
Fax: (617) 232-3788
Email: cbandrew@aol.com
Supervision: Vaad Harabonim of Massachusetts
Shomer Shabbat.

Kupel's
421 Harvard Street
(617) 566-9528

GROCERIES

Beacon Kosher
1706 Beacon Street
(617) 734-5300

RESTAURANTS

Dairy
Café Eilat
420 Harvard Street 02446
(617) 277-7770

Meat
Rami's
324 Harvard Street 02446
(617) 738-3577

Rubin's Kosher Deli and Restaurant
500 Harvard Street, Brookline 02146
(617) 731-8787

Ruth's Kitchen
401 Harvard Street
(617) 734-9810

Shalom Hunan
92 Harvard Street 02445-46
(617) 731-9778
Fax: (617) 731-9760

Taam China
423 Harvard Street
(617) 264-7274

SYNAGOGUES

Conservative
Kehillath Israel
384 Harvard St 02146
(617) 277-9155

Orthodox
Beth Pinchas (Bostoner Rebbe)
1710 Beacon Street 02146
(617) 734-5100
Fax: (617) 739-0163
Email: rofeh@world.std.com

Congregation Lubavitch
100 Woodcliff Road 02167
(617) 469-0088
Fax: (617) 469-0089

Young Israel of Brookline
62 Green Street 02446
(617) 734-0276
Fax: (617) 734-7195
Email: yibrookline@yahoo.com
Web site: www.yibrookline.org

Reform
Ohabei Shalom
1187 Beacon St 02446
(617) 277-6610
Email: dberman@ohabei.org
Web site: www.ohabei.org

Temple Sinai
50 Sewall Av, Coolidge Corner 02146
(617) 277-5888

Sephardi
Sephardic Congregation
1566 Beacon St 02146
(617) 566-8171

Burlington

SYNAGOGUES

Reform
Temple Shalom Emeth
14-16 Lexington Street 01803
(781) 272-2351

Cambridge

KASHRUT INFORMATION

Harvard Hillel
Harvard University, 52 Mt. Auburn St 02138
(617) 495-4696
Fax: (617) 864-1637
Email: linda@hillel.harvard.edu
Kosher meals are obtainable during the school year
(September - May). Reservations are required for
Shabbat meals and can be made by calling Linda at
extension 310.

RESTAURANTS

52 Mt Auburn Street 02138
(617) 495-4695
Fax: (617) 864-1637
Email: linda@hillel.harvard.edu
Web site: www.hillel.harvard.edu

Meat
M.I.T. Hillel
40 Massachusetts Avenue 02139
(617) 253-2982
Fax: (617) 253-3260
Email: hillel@mit.edu
Supervision: Vaad Harabonim of Massachusetts

SYNAGOGUES

Conservative
Temple Beth Shalom of Cambridge
8 Tremont Street 02139
(617) 864-6388
Fax: (617) 864-0507
Email: office@tremontstreetshul.org

Orthodox
Chabad
38 Banks Street 02138
(617) 547-6124
Email: rebharvard@aol.com

Harvard Hillel
52 Mt Auburn Street 01238
(617) 495-4695
Fax: (617) 864-1637
Email: linda@hillel.harvard.edu
Web site: www.hillel.harvard.edu

Canton

SYNAGOGUES

Conservative
Beth Abraham
1301 Washington Street 02021
(781) 828-5250

Reform
Temple Beth David of the South Shore
1060 Randolph Street 02021
(781) 828-2275
Fax: (781) 821-3997
Email: info@templebethdavid.com
Web site: www.templebethdavid.com

Cape Cod

SYNAGOGUES

Orthodox
Beth Israel
cnr. of Onset Avenue & Locust Street, PO Box 24,
Onset 02558
(508) 295-9185
Email: capeshul@att.net
Web site: www.home.att.net/capeshul
Services three times daily from last Saturday in June
to Labor Day. Services are also held on the Holy
Days. Apartments available near synagogue. Further
information from Burt Parker.

Chelmsford

SYNAGOGUES

Reform
Congregation Shalom
Richardson Road 01824
(978) 251-8090

Clinton

SYNAGOGUES

Independent
Shaarei Zedeck
Water Street 01510
(978) 365-3320

East Falmouth

SYNAGOGUES

Reform
Falmouth Jewish Congregation
7 Hatchville Road 02536
(508) 540-0602
Fax: (508) 540-8094
Web site: www.falmouthjewish.org

Easton

SYNAGOGUES

Traditional
Temple Chayai Shalom
238 Depot Street 02334
(508) 238-6385
Mail address: PO Box 404, N. Easton 02356

Everett

SYNAGOGUES

Traditional
Tifereth Israel
34 Malden Street 02149
(617) 387-0200

Fall River

COMMUNITY ORGANISATIONS
Fall River Jewish Community Council
Room 327, 56 N. Main St 02720   (508) 673-7791
                 Fax: (508) 673-7791

SYNAGOGUES
Conservative
Beth El
385 High Street 02720   (508) 674-9761

Orthodox
Adas Israel
1647 Robeson Street 02720   (508) 674-9761
                 Fax: (508) 678-3195

Fitchburg

SYNAGOGUES
Independent
Agudas Achim
40 Boutelle Street 01420   (978) 342-7704

Framingham

RESTAURANTS
Meat
Rami's of Framington
341 Cochituate Rd 01701   (508) 370-3577

SYNAGOGUES
Conservative
Temple Beth Sholom
50 Pamela Road 01701   (508) 877-2540
                 Fax: (508) 877-8278
        Web site: www.beth-sholom.org

Orthodox
Chabad House
74 Joseph Road 01701   (508) 877-5313
                 Fax: (508) 877 5313

Reform
Beth Am
300 Pleasant Street 01701   (508) 872-8300
                 Fax: (508) 872-9773
      Email: tempbetham@aol.com

Gloucester

SYNAGOGUES
Conservative
Ahavat Achim
86 Middle Street 01930   (978) 281-0739
                 Fax: (978) 281-0739

Greenfield

SYNAGOGUES
Conservative
Temple Israel
27 Pierce Street 01301   (413) 773-5884

Haverhill

SYNAGOGUES
Orthodox
Anshe Sholom
427 Main Street 01830   (508) 372-2276
Reform
Temple Emanu-El
514 Main Street 01830   (508) 373-3861

Hingham

SYNAGOGUES
Reform
Congregation Sha'aray Shalom
1112 Main Street 02043   (781) 749-8103
                 Fax: (781) 740-1480
      Email: cssadm@aol.com

Holbrook

SYNAGOGUES
Conservative
Temple Beth Shalom
95 Plymouth Street 02343   (617) 767-4922

Holliston

SYNAGOGUES
Conservative
Temple Beth Torah
2162 Washington Street 01746   (508) 429-6268
                 Fax: (508) 429-7729
      Email: tbt@bethtorah.org

Holyoke

SYNAGOGUES
Conservative
Sons of Zion
378 Maple Street 01040   (413) 534-3369
Orthodox
Rodphey Sholom
1800 Northampton Street 01040   (413) 534-5262

Hull

SYNAGOGUES
Conservative
Temple Beth Sholom
600 Nantasket Avenue 02045   (617) 925-0091
Fax: (617) 925-9053

Temple Israel of Nantasket
9 Hadassah Way 02045   (617) 925-0289
Summer only.

Hyannis

SYNAGOGUES
Reform
Cape Cod Synagogue
145 Winter Street 02601   (508) 775-2988

Hyde Park

SYNAGOGUES
Conservative
Temple Adas Hadrath Israel
28 Arlington Street 02136   (617) 364-2661

Lawrence

COMMUNITY ORGANISATIONS
Jewish Com. Council of Greater Lawrence
580 Haverhill Street 01841   (508) 686-4157

SYNAGOGUES
Orthodox
Anshai Sholum
411 Hampshire Street 01843   (508) 683-4544

Leominster

SYNAGOGUES
Conservative
Congregation Agudat Achim
268 Washington Street 01453   (508) 534-6121

Lexington

SYNAGOGUES
Conservative
Temple Emunah
9 Piper Road 02421   (781) 861-0300
Fax: (781) 861-7141
Email: rholmes@emunahlex.org
Web site: www.templeemunah.org

Orthodox
Chabad Center
9 Burlington Street 02173   (781) 863-8656

Reform
Temple Isaiah
55 Lincoln Street 02173   (781) 862-7160

Longmeadow

MIKVAOT
Mikveh Association
1104 Converse, Long. MA 01106   (413) 567-1607

SYNAGOGUES
Conservative
B'nai Jacob
2 Eunice Dr 01106   (413) 567-3163
Orthodox
Beth Israel
1280 Williams St 01106   (413) 567-3210
Lubavitcher Yeshiva Synagogue
1148 Converse St 01106   (413) 567-8665

Lowell

MIKVAOT
Mikvah
48 Academy Drive   (978) 970-2008

SYNAGOGUES
Conservative
Temple Beth El
105 Princeton Blvd. 01851   (978) 453-7744
Orthodox
Montefiore Synagogue
460 Westford Street 01851   (978) 459-9400
Reform
Temple Emanuel of Merrimack Valley
101 W. Forest Street 01851   (978) 454-1372

Lynn

SYNAGOGUES
Orthodox
Ahabat Sholom
151 Ocean Street 01902   (617) 593-9255
Fax: (617) 593-9255
Email: ahabat@juno.com
Web site: www.ahabatsholom.org
Houses the Eliot Feuerstein Library.

Anshai Sfard
150 South Common Street 01905   (617) 599-7131
Chevra Tehilim
12 Breed Street 01902   (617) 598-2964

Malden

SYNAGOGUES
Conservative
Ezrath Israel
245 Bryant Street 02148   (781) 322-7205

Orthodox
Congregation Beth Israel
10 Dexter Street 02148   (781) 322-5686
Fax: (781) 322-6678
Email: congbi@aol.com

Young Israel of Malden
45 Holyoke Street 02148   (781) 961-9817

Reform
Tifereth Israel
539 Salem Street 02148   (781) 322-2794

Traditional
Agudas Achim
160 Harvard Street 02148   (781) 322-9380

Marblehead

SYNAGOGUES
Conservative/Masorti
Temple Sinai
1 Community Road 01945   (617) 631-2763
Fax: (617) 631-2244
Email: Tmpsinai@gis.net

Orthodox
Orthodox Congregation of the North Shore
4 Community Road 01945   (617) 598-1810

Reform
Temple Emanu-El
393 Atlantic Avenue 01945   (617) 631-9300

Marlboro

SYNAGOGUES
Conservative
Temple Emanuel
150 Berlin Road 01752   (508) 485-7565

Medford

SYNAGOGUES
Conservative
Temple Shalom
475 Winthrop Street 02155   (781) 396-3262

Melrose

SYNAGOGUES
Reform
Temple Beth Shalom
21 E. Foster Street 02176   (617) 665-4520

Milford

SYNAGOGUES
Conservative
55 Pine Street 01757   (508) 473-1590
Web site: www.templebethshalom.com

Millis

SYNAGOGUES
Conservative
Ael Chunon
334 Village Street 02054   (508) 376-5984
Fax: (508) 533-3802
Email: TNULB@mediaone.net

Milton

SYNAGOGUES
Conservative
Temple Shalom
180 Blue Hill Avenue 02186   (617) 698-3394
Fax: (617) 696-9265
Email: templeshalom@yahoo.com
Web site: www.uscj.org/neweng/milton

Orthodox
B'nai Jacob
100 Blue Hill Parkway 02187   (617) 698-0698

Natick

SYNAGOGUES
Conservative
Temple Israel
145 Hartford Street 01760   (508) 650-3521
Fax: (508) 655-3440
Web site: www.tiofnatick.org

Orthodox
Chabad Lubavitch Center
2 East Mill Street 01760   (508) 650-1499

Needham

SYNAGOGUES
Conservative
Temple Aliyah
1664 Central Avenue 02492   (781) 444-8522
Fax: (781) 449-7066
Web site: www.templealiyah.com

Reform
Temple Beth Shalom
670 Highland Avenue 02494   (781) 444-0077
Fax: (781) 449-3274
Email: tbshalom@fcl-us.net

New Bedford

COMMUNITY ORGANISATIONS
Jewish Federation of Greater New Bedford
467 Hawthorn Street, N. Dartmouth 02747
(508) 997-7471

SYNAGOGUES
Conservative
Tifereth Israel
145 Brownell Avenue 02740 (508) 997-3171
Fax: (508) 997-3173

Orthodox
Ahavath Achim
385 County Street 02740 (508) 994-1760
Fax: (508) 994-8186
Email: rabbibarry@aol.com
Web site: www.members.aol.com/rabbibarry

Newburyport

SYNAGOGUES
Conservative
Congregation Ahavas Achim
Washington & Olive Streets 09150 (508) 462-2461

Newton

COMMUNITY ORGANISATIONS
Jewish Community Center of Greater Boston
333 Nahanton Street 02159 (617) 558-6522
Kosher snack bar provided.

RESTAURANTS
Julie's Kitchen
34 Langley Road 02459 (617) 965-6368

Rosenfeld Bagels
1280 Centre Street, Newton Center 02459
(617) 527-8080

SYNAGOGUES
Orthodox
Beth El Ateret Israel
561 Ward Street 02459 (617) 244-7233

Congregation B'nai Jacob (Zvhil-Mezbuz Rebbe)
955 Beacon Street (617) 227-8200
Fax: (617) 227-8420
Web site: www.rebbe.org

Shaarei Tefilla
35 Morseland Avenue 02459 (617) 527-7637

North Adams

SYNAGOGUES
Conservative
Congregation Beth Israel
265 Church Street 01247 (413) 663-5830
Fax: (413) 663-5830
Email: cbi@bcn.net

Northampton

SYNAGOGUES
Conservative
B'nai Israel
253 Prospect Road 01060 (413) 584-3593

Norwood

SYNAGOGUES
Conservative
Temple Shaare Tefilah
556 Nichols Street 02062 (781) 762-8670
Fax: (781) 762-8670
Web site: www.uscj.org/neweng/norwood

Onset

HOTELS
Bridge View Hotel
12 S. Water Street 02558 (508) 295-9820
Welcomes Jewish guests. Self-catering flatlets
available. Kosher meat and other products available.

Peabody

SYNAGOGUES
Conservative
Temple Ner Tamid
368 Lowell Street 01960 (508) 532-1293
Fax: (508) 532-0101
Email: audrey368@aol.com
Web site: www.templenertamid.org

Independent
Congregation Tifereth Israel
Pierpont Street 01960 (508) 531-8135

Reform
Beth Shalom
489 Lowell Street 01960 (508) 535-2100
Fax: (508) 536-3115

Traditional
Congregation Sons of Israel
Park & Spring Streets 01960 (508) 531-7576

Pittsfield

COMMUNITY ORGANISATIONS

Jewish Federation of the Berkshires
235 East Street 01201 (413) 442-4360
Kosher meals served Monday, Tuesday and Thursday
at noon.

Plymouth

SYNAGOGUES
Reform
Congregation Beth Jacob
Synagogue on Pleasant Street, Community Center on
Court Street, PO Box 3284 02361 (508) 746-1575
Email: cbethjacob@juno.com

Quincy

SYNAGOGUES
Conservative
Adas Shalom
435 Adams Street 02169 (617) 471-1818
Email: adasshalom@aol.com

Temple Beth El
1001 Hancock Street 02169 (617) 479-4309

Orthodox
Beth Israel
33 Grafton Street, PO Box 690388 02269-0388
(617) 472-6796

Randolph

BOOKSELLERS
Davidson's Hebrew Book Store
1106 Main Street 02368 (781) 961-4929

SYNAGOGUES
Conservative
Temple Beth Am
871 N. Main Street 02368 (781) 963-0440
Fax: (781) 963-0536
Email: TempleBethAm@attbi.com
Web site: www.uscj.org/neweng/randolph
Orthodox
**Young Israel - Kehillath Jacob of Mattapan &
Randolph**
374 N. Main Street, PO Box 880 02368
(781) 986-6461
Email: Youngisrael@Juno.com

Revere

DELICATESSEN
Myer's Kosher Kitchen
168 Shirley Avenue 02151

SYNAGOGUES
Independent
Temple B'nai Israel
1 Wave Avenue 02151 (617) 284-8388
Orthodox
Ahavas Achim Anshei Sfard
89 Walnut Way 02151 (617) 289-1026

Tifereth Israel
43 Nahant Avenue 02151 (617) 284-9255

Salem

COMMUNITY ORGANISATIONS
Jewish Federation of the North Shore
21 Front Street 01970 (508) 745-4222
Fax: (508) 741-7507
Email: mail@jfns.org

SYNAGOGUES
Conservative
Temple Shalom
287 Lafayette Street 01970 (508) 741-4880
Fax: (508) 741-4882
Web site: www.templeshalomsalem.org

Sharon

BED AND BREAKFAST
Sharon Woods Inn
80 Brook Road 02067 (781) 784-9401
Fax: (781) 784-5162
Email: kctova@yahoo.com

MIKVAOT
Chevrat Nashim
9 Dunbar Street 02067 (781) 784-7444
Operated by the Mikvah Organisation of the South
Shore, Chevrat Nashim Mikvah

RELIGIOUS ORGANISATIONS
Eruv Society
(781) 784-6112
Eruv maintained by Sharon County Eruv Society.

SYNAGOGUES
Conservative
Adath Sharon
18 Harding Street 02067 (781) 784-2517
Temple Israel
125 Pond Street 02067 (781) 784-3986
Fax: (781) 784-0719
Orthodox
Chabad Center
101 Worcester Road 02067 (781) 784-8167
Young Israel of Sharon
100 Ames Street 02067 (781) 784-6112
Fax: (781) 784-7758
Web site: www.yisharon.org

Reform
Temple Sinai
25 Canton Street 02067 (781) 784-6081
Fax: (781) 784-2616
Email: office@temple-sinai.com

Somerville

SYNAGOGUES
Independent
B'nai B'rith of Somerville
201 Central Street 02145 (617) 625-0333
Email: tbb@templebnaibrith.org

Springfield

COMMUNITY ORGANISATIONS
Jewish Community Center
1160 Dickinson Street 01108 (413) 739-4715
Fax: (413) 739-4747

GROCERIES
Waldbaum's Food Mart
355 Belmont Avenue 01108 (413) 732-3866

RESTAURANTS
Kosher Coffee Corner
Jewish Federation of Greater Springfield, 1160
Dickinson Street 01108 (413) 737-4313

SYNAGOGUES
Orthodox
Congregation Kodimoh
124 Sumner Avenue, Springfield 01108
(413) 781-0171
Fax: (413) 737-8002
Email: kodimoh@TheSpa.com
The largest Orthodox congregation in New England.

Kesser Israel
19 Oakland Street 01108 (413) 732-8492
Reform
Temple Sinai
1100 Dickinson Street 01108 (413) 736-3619

Stoughton

BAKERIES
Ruth's Bake Shop
987 Central Street 02072 (781) 344-8993
Supervision: Vaad Harabonim of Massachusetts

SYNAGOGUES
Conservative
Adhavath Torah Congregation
1179 Central Street 02072 (781) 344-8733
Fax: (781) 344-4315

Sudbury

SYNAGOGUES
Independent
Congregation B'nai Torah
Woodside Road 01776 (978) 443-2082
Reform
Congregation Beth El
105 Hudson Road 01776 (978) 443-9622
Fax: (978) 443-9629
Email: secretary@bethelsudbury.org
Web site: www.bethelsudbury.org

Swampscott

SYNAGOGUES
Conservative
Beth El
55 Atlantic Avenue 01907 (617) 599-8005
Fax: (617) 599-1860

Temple Israel
837 Humphrey Street 01907 (781) 595-6635
Fax: (781) 595-0033
Web site: www.templeisraelswampscott.org

Vineyard Haven

SYNAGOGUES
Reform
Martha's Vineyard Hebrew Center
Center Street 02568 (508) 693-0745

Wakefield

SYNAGOGUES
Conservative
Temple Emmanuel
120 Chestnut Street 01880 (781) 245-1886
Web site: www.geocities.com/temple_emanuel

Waltham

SYNAGOGUES
American Jewish Historical Society (Brandeis University campus)
2 Thornton Road 02154 (617) 891-8110
Fax: (617) 899-9208

Conservative
Beth Israel
25 Harvard Street 02154 (617) 894-5146

Wayland

SYNAGOGUES
Reform
Templr Shir Tikva
141 Boston Post Road 01778   (508) 358-5312

Wellesley Hills

SYNAGOGUES
Reform
Beth Elohim
10 Bethel Road 02181   (617) 235-8419

West Roxbury

SYNAGOGUES
Conservative
Hillel B'nai Torah
120 Corey St, W. Roxbury 02132   (617) 323-0486

Westboro

SYNAGOGUES
Reform
B'nai Shalom
117 E. Main Street, PO Box 1019 01581-6019
    (508) 366-7191

Westwood

SYNAGOGUES
Reform
Beth David
40 Pond Street 02090   (617) 769-5270

Winchester

SYNAGOGUES
Reform
Temple Shir Tikvah
PO Box 373 01890   (617) 792-1188

Winthrop

SYNAGOGUES
Orthodox
Tifereth Abraham
283 Shirley Street 02152   (617) 846-5063

Tifereth Israel
93 Veteran's Road 02152   (617) 846-1390

Worcester

COMMUNITY ORGANIZATIONS
Jewish Federation
633 Salisbury Street 01609   (508) 756-1543
    Fax: (508) 798-0962
    Email: bluks@jfcm.org
    Web site: www.jfcm.org

CONTACT INFORMATION
**Agudath Israel of America Hachnosas Orchim
Committee**
69 S. Flagg Street 01602   (508) 754-3681
Contact Rabbi Reuven Fischer.

Rabbi Hershel Fogelman
22 Newton Avenue   (508) 752-5791
Visitors requiring information about kashrut,
temporary accommodation, etc., should contact
Rabbi Fogelman.

MIKVAOT
Mikva
Huntley Street 01602   (508) 755-1257

SYNAGOGUES
Orthodox
Young Israel of Worcester
889 Pleasant Street 01602   (508) 754-3681

MICHIGAN

Ann Arbor

COMMUNITY ORGANISATIONS
Jewish Federation of Washtenaw County
2939 Birch Hollow Drive 48108   (734) 677-0100
    Fax: (734) 677-0109
    Email: info@jewishannarbor.org

MIKVAOT
Chabad House
715 Hill 48104   (734) 995-3276
    Fax: (734) 996-2479
    Email: chabad@jewmich.com

SYNAGOGUES
Orthodox
Ann Arbor Orthodox Minyan
1429 Hill Street 48104   (734) 994-5822

Benton Harbor

SYNAGOGUES
Conservative
Temple B'nai Shalom
2050 Broadway 49022   (616) 925-8021

Detroit

With tens of synagogues in the Bloomfield, Oak Park and Southfield areas, visitors are recommmended to contact one of the local religious organizations listed for the nearest synagogue.

COMMUNITY ORGANISATIONS
Jewish Federation of Metr. Detroit
Telegraph Road, Bloomfield Hills 48303

DELICATESSEN
Sarah's Glatt Kosher Deli
15600 W. Ten Mile Road, Southfield 48075
      (313) 443-2425

GROCERIES
Sperber's Kosher Karry-Out
25250 W. Ten Mile Road, Oak Park 48237
      (313) 443-2425

KASHRUT INFORMATION
Council of Orthodox Rabbis of Greater Detroit
16947 W. Ten Mile Road, Southfield 48075
      (313) 559-5005/6
      Fax: (313) 559-5202
      Email: cordetroit@hotmail.com

MEDIA
Newspaper
Jewish News
Franklin Road, Southfield 48034

MIKVAOT
Mikvah Israel
15116 W. Ten Mile Road, Oak Park 48237
      (313) 967-5402
      Fax: (313) 967-5403

ORGANISATIONS
Machon L'Torah (The Jewish Network of Michigan)
W. 10 Mile Road 48237

RELIGIOUS ORGANISATIONS
Council of Orthodox Rabbis of Detroit (Vaad Harabonim)
16947 W. Ten Mile Road, Southfield 48075
      (313) 559-5005/06
      Fax: (313) 559-5202

Jewish Community Center of Metr. Detroit
6600 W. Maple Road, W. Bloomfield 48322
      (313) 661-1000
      Fax: (313) 661-3680

RESTAURANTS
Dairy
Jerusalem Pizza
26025 Greenfield, Southfield 48034   (313) 552-0088
      Fax: (313) 552-0087

La Difference
7295 Orchard Lake Road   (313) 932-8934
      Fax: (313) 932-8942
Supervision: Orthodox Rabbis of Greater Detroit

Meat
Unique Kosher
25270 Greenfield, Southfield   (313) 967-1161

East Lansing

SYNAGOGUES
Conservative & Reform
Shaarey Zedek
1924 Coolidge Road 48823

Flint

COMMUNITY ORGANISATIONS
Flint Jewish Federation
619 Wallenberg Street 48502   (810) 767-5922
      Fax: (810) 767-9024
      Email: fjf@tm.net

SYNAGOGUES
Conservative
Congregation Beth Israel
5240 Calkins Road 48532   (810) 732-6310
      Fax: (810) 732-6314
      Email: cbiflint@tir.com
      Web site: www.uscj.org/michigan/flint/
Orthodox
Chabad House
5385 Calkins 48532   (810) 230-0770
Reform
Temple Beth El
501 S. Ballenger Highway 48532   (810) 232-3138

Grand Rapids

SYNAGOGUES
Conservative
Congregation Ahavas Israel
2727 Michigan Street N.E. 49506   (616) 949-2840
      Fax: (616) 949-6929
      Email: davkrishef@aol.com
      Web site: www.members.aol.com/ahvavsisri

Orthodox
Chabad House of Western Michigan
2615 Michigan Street N.E. 49506 (616) 957-0770

Reform
Temple Emanuel
1715 E. Fulton Street 49503 (616) 459-5976

Jackson

SYNAGOGUES
Reform
Temple Beth Israel
801 W. Michigan Avenue 49202 (601) 784-3862

Kalamazoo

SYNAGOGUES
Conservative
Sons of Moses
2501 Stadium Drive 49008 (616) 342-5463

Lansing

SYNAGOGUES
Reconstructionist
Kehillat Israel
2014 Forest Road 48910 (517) 882-0049
Fax: (517) 882-9270
Email: kilori@msu.edu

Saginaw

SYNAGOGUES
Conservative
Temple B'nai Israel
1424 S. Washington Avenue 48601 (517) 753-5230

Reform
Congregation Beth El
100 S. Washington Avenue 48607 (517) 754-5171

South Haven

SYNAGOGUES
Orthodox
First Hebrew Congregation
249 Broadway 49090 (616) 637-1603

Southfield

SYNAGOGUES
Orthodox
Young Israel of Southfield
27705 Lahser Road 48034 (248) 358-0154
Fax: (248) 358-0154
Email: rabg@aol.com

West Bloomfield

MUSEUM
Holocaust Memorial Center
6602 W. Maple Road 48322-3005 (248) 661-0840
Fax: (248) 661-4204
Email: info@holocaustcenter.org
Web site: www.holocaustcenter.org
First free-standing holocaust museum in USA.
Consists of museum, library-archive, garden.
Services include tours, lectures, oral history program,
exhibits, speakers' bureau. No admission fee.

SYNAGOGUES
Orthodox
Young Israel of West Bloomfield
6111 West Maple Road, Suite 408 48322
(248) 661-4182

MINNESOTA

Duluth

COMMUNITY ORGANISATIONS
Jewish Federation & Com. Council
1602 E. 2nd Street 55812 (218) 724-8857

SYNAGOGUES
Conservative & Reform
Temple Israel
1602 E. 2nd Street 55812 (218) 724-8857

Orthodox
Adas Israel
302 E. Third Street 55802 (218) 722-6459

Minneapolis

COMMUNITY ORGANISATIONS
Sabes Jewish Community Center
4330 Cedar Lake Rd S., 55416 (612) 381-3410
Fax: (612) 381-3401
Email: jschachtman@jccminneapolis.org

GROCERIES
Fishman's Kosher Market
4100 Minnetonka Blvd, St Louis Park 55416
(612) 926-5611
Glatt butcher, deli, bakery and eat-in/ take-out
certified by the local Orthodox Vaad.

MIKVAOT
Knesseth Israel
4330 W. 28th Street, St Louis Park 55416
(612) 926-3829
Fax: (612) 920-2184
Email: office@kenessethisrael.org

RESTAURANTS
Dairy
Calypso Coffee Co.
3238 W. Lake St. 55416   (612) 929-6245
Restaurant, coffee, and ice cream certified by the
local Orthodox Vaad. (Chalav Yisrael)

SYNAGOGUES
Orthodox
Congregation Bais Yisroel
4221 Sunset Blvd 55416   (612) 924-0654
Fax: (612) 926-2936
Email: BaisLine@mninter.net
Web site: www.baisyisroel.org

Kenesseth Israel
4330 W. 28th Street, St Louis Park 55416
(612) 920-2183
Fax: (612) 920-2184
Email: rabbi@kenessethisrael.org
Web site: www.kenessethisrael.org

Rochester

HOME HOSPITALITY
Lubavitch Bais Chaya Moussia Hospitality Center
730 2nd Street S.W. 55907   (716) 288-7500
Fax: (716) 286-9329
Email: rabbigreene@charter.net
Also provides Shabbat dinners and hospital visitations.
Mikva on premises.

SYNAGOGUES
Reform
B'nai Israel Synagogue
621 SW 2nd Street 55902   (716) 288-5825
Email: bnairsrael@aol.com

St Paul

GROCERIES
L'chaim
655 Snelling Avenue 55116

RESTAURANTS
Dairy
Old City Cafe
1571 Grand Avenue   (612) 699-5347
Supervision: Upper Midwest Kashrus
Dairy/vegetarian. Hours: Sunday, 10 am to 9 pm;
Monday to Thursday, 11 am to 9 pm; Friday, to 2 pm.
Corner of Grand and Snelling Avenues, both of which
are buslines.

MISSISSIPPI

Greenville

SYNAGOGUES
Reform
Hebrew Union Congregation
504 Main Street 38701   (662) 332-4153

Greenwood

SYNAGOGUES
Orthodox
Ahavath Rayim
Market & George Streets,
PO Box 1235 38935-1235   (662) 453-7537
Only services on the first Friday of each month.

Jackson

SYNAGOGUES
Reform
Congregation Beth Israel
5315 Old Canton Road 39211   (601) 956-6215
Email: bic5315@mindspring.com

Natchez

SYNAGOGUES
Reform
B'nai Israel
Washington & S. Commerce Streets,
PO Box 2081 39120
Oldest synagogue in Mississippi.

Tupelo

SYNAGOGUES
Conservative
Marshall & Hamlin Streets 38801   (601) 842-9169

MISSOURI

Jefferson City

SYNAGOGUES
Reform
Temple Beth El
238 East High Street 65101   (573) 635-8727

Kansas City

RESTAURANTS
Sensations
1148 W. 103 Street 64114

SYNAGOGUES
Conservative
Congregation Beth Shalom
9400 Wornall road 64114   (816) 361-2990
Fax: (816) 361-4495
Reform
Temple B'nai Jehudah
712 E. 69th Street 64131   (816) 363-1050
Fax: (816) 363-8610

The New Reform Temple
7100 Main 64114   (816) 523-7809
Fax: (816) 523-2454
Email: nrt7100@aol.com

St Joseph

SYNAGOGUES
Conservative
Temple B'Nai Sholem
615 S. 10th Street 64501   (816) 279-2378
Fax: (816) 361-4495

St Louis

BAKERIES
Schnuck's Nancy Ann Bakery
Olive & Mason   (314) 434-7323

BUTCHERS
Diamant's Kosher Meat Market
618 North & South Road   (314) 721-9624
S. Kohn's
10405 Old Olive St. Road 63141   (314) 569-0727
Fax: (314) 569-1723
Sol's Kosher Meat Mart
8627 Olive Street   (314) 993-9977

COMMUNITY ORGANISATIONS
Jewish Federation of St Louis
12 Millstone Campus Drive 63146   (314) 432-0020
Fax: (314) 432-1277
Email: jfedstl@jfedstl.org
Web site: www.jewishinstlouis.org
The Jewish Federation of St. Louis can provide
information on tours of Jewish interest in the city. For
more information visit their web site.

GROCERIES
Lazy Suzan Imaginative Catering
110 Millwell Drive   (314) 291-6050

Simon Kohn's Kosher Meat & Deli
10405 Old Olive Street   (314) 569-0727
Fax: (314) 569-1723
Complete kosher deli & meat market. Seating
available. Fresh cold & hot selections available daily.
Pizza available for carry-out.

LIBRARIES
The Brodsky Jewish Community Library
12 Millstone Campus Drive 63146

MIKVAOT
Mikva
4 Millstone Campus 63146   (314) 569-2770

MUSEUM
Holocaust Museum and Learning Center
12 Millstone Campus Drive   (314) 432-0020
Fax: (314) 432-1277
Email: dreich@jfedstl.org
Web site: www.hmlc.org

RELIGIOUS ORGANISATIONS
The Vaad Hoeir (United Orthodox Jewish
Community of St Louis)
4 Millstone Campus 63146   (314) 569-2770
Fax: (314) 569-2774
Recognised Orthodox religious authority for the city.

RESTAURANTS
Meat
Diamant's
618 North & South Rd.   (314) 712-9624
Simon Kohn's
10405 Old Olive Street   (314) 569-0727
The Empire Steak Building
8600 Olive Blvd., just off McKnight   (314) 993-9977
Fax: (314) 993-6647
Web site: www.chef2-go.com

SYNAGOGUES
Orthodox
Young Israel of St Louis
8101 Delmar Blvd 63130   (314) 727-1880
Fax: (314) 727-2177
Email: yi-stl@juno.com

MONTANA

Billings

SYNAGOGUES
Reform
Congregation Beth Aaron
1148 N. Broadway 59101   (406) 248-6412

Great Falls

SYNAGOGUES
Reform
Aitz Chaim
PO Box 6192 59406-6192   (406) 468-2073
      Email: aaron@weissman.com

Missoula

SYNAGOGUES
Har Shalom
PO Box 7581 59807   (406) 523-5671

NEBRASKA

Lincoln

SYNAGOGUES
Conservative
Congregation Tifereth Israel
3219 Sheridan Blvd. 68502   (402) 423-8569
      Fax: (402) 423-0178

Reform
South Street Temple B'nai Jeshurun
20th & South Streets 68502   (402) 435-8004

Omaha

COMMUNITY ORGANISATIONS
Jewish Federation of Omaha
333 S. 132nd Street   (402) 334-8200
      Fax: (402) 334-1330
      Email: pmonsk@top.net
      Web site: www.jewishomaha.org

MIKVAOT
Com. Mikva
323 S. 132nd Street 68154   (402) 334-8200

SYNAGOGUES
Conservative
Beth El
14506 California Street 68154   (402) 492-8550

Orthodox
Beth Israel
1502 N. 52nd Street 68104   (402) 556-6288

Beth Israel Synagogue
1502 North 52nd Street 68104   (402) 556-6288
      Email: bethisrael@novia.net

Reform
Temple Israel
7023 Cass Street 68132   (402) 556-6536

NEVADA

Las Vegas

DELICATESSEN
Casba Glatt Kosher
2845 Las Vegas Blvd   (702) 791-3344

Jerusalem Kosher Restaurant & Deli
1305 Vegas Valley 89109   (702) 791-3668

Rafi's Place
6135 West Sahara 89102   (702) 253-0033

Sara's Place
4972 S. Maryland

KASHRUT INFORMATION
Community Relations
      (702) 732-0556

MIKVAOT
1260 S. Arville   (702) 259-0770 ext 8

RESTAURANTS
Meat
Haifa Restaurant
855 E. Twain   (702) 791-1956
      Fax: (702) 791-2966

Jerusalem Glatt Kosher Restaurant
1305 Vegas Valley Dr., 89109   (702) 696-1644
      Fax: (702) 696-0919

Las Vegas Kosher Deli
3317 L.V. Blvd S.   (702) 892-9080

Shalom Hunan
4850 W Flamingo Road   (702) 871-3262
      Fax: (702) 871-3083
      Email: yosstheboss@earthlink.net
Supervision: Chabad of Southern Nevada

SYNAGOGUES
Conservative
Midbar Kodesh Temple
1940 Paseo Verde, Henderson   (702) 454-4848
      Fax: (702) 454-4847
      Email: MidbarkodeshT@aol.com
Shabbat Services: weekly, Friday 7:30pm, Saturday
9:00am and all holidays. Special services.

Temple Emanu-El
4925 South Torrey Pines Drive 89118   (702) 254-3270
Orthodox
Chabad of Southern Nevada
1261 S. Arville   (702) 259-0770
      Fax: (702) 877-4700
      Email: chabadlv@aol.com
      Web site: www.chabadlv.org

Congregation Or-Bamidbar
2991 Emerson Ave.   (702) 369-1175
Shabbat service: Monday-Friday 7:00am; Saturday
8:30am; Sunday 9:00am; Mincha & Ma'ariv daily at
sunset. Education: Hebrew School, Sunday 12-2pm;
Judaism Class, Wednesday 8pm.

Young Israel of Las Vegas
9590 West Sahara 89117   (702) 360-8909
Fax: (702) 360-9627
Email: ywyne@aish.com
Web site: www.aish.combranches/las_vegas
Shabbat service: Saturday 9am, Sunday 9am.
Beginners minyon for ages 10-15. Radio-talk show:
1230AM, Tuesday at 8pm.

Reform
Adat Ari El
3310 S. Jones Blvd.   (702) 221-1230
Fax: (702) 221-1385
Email: info@adatariel.com
AAE Event Hotline: (702) 390-8142. Shabbat service:
Friday 7:30pm.

Congregation Ner Tamid
2761 Emerson Ave.   (702) 733-6292
Fax: (702) 733-8553
Email: info@lvnertamid.org
Web site: www.lvnertamid.org
CNT Event Hotline: (702) 263-5960. Shabbat service:
Friday. 7:30pm.

Temple Bet Emet
St. Andrew Lutheran Church, 8901 Del Webb Blvd.,
Sun City   (702) 243-5781
Shabbat service: first & third Friday 7:30pm.

Temple Beth Am
9001 Hillpointe Road   (702) 254-5110
Fax: (702) 254-0997
Shabbat service: Friday 7:30pm; Saturday 10:30am;
Saturday Torah Study 9:30am.

Traditional
Chabad of Summerlin
2620 Regatta Dr. #117   (702) 259-0770
Fax: (702) 242-4318
Shabbat service: Friday 6:00pm; Saturday 10:00am.
Special children's service, 11:00am; Sunday 8:30am is
the B-L-T service (Bagels, Lox, Tefillah).

Reno

SYNAGOGUES
Reform
Temple Sinai
3405 Gulling Road 89503   (775) 747-5508
Fax: (775) 747-1911
Email: temple.sinai@juno.com

NEW HAMPSHIRE

Bethlehem

HOTELS
Arlington Hotel
     (603) 869-3353
The hotel which is only open in the summer has a
mikvah and synagogue. For information during other
periods phone (718) 486-6367.

MIKVAOT
Machzikei Hadas
Lewis Hill Road 03574   (603) 869-3336

SYNAGOGUES
Conservative
Bethlehem Hebrew Congregation
Strawberry Hill 03574   (603) 869-5465
Orthodox
Machzikei Hadas
Lewis Hill Road 03574   (603) 869-3336

Concord

SYNAGOGUES
Reform
Temple Beth Jacob
67 Broadway 03301   (603) 228-8581
Email: tbjconcord@aol.com

Manchester

COMMUNITY ORGANISATIONS
Jewish Federation of Greater Manchester
698 Beech Street 03104   (603) 627-7679
Fax: (603) 627-7963

MEDIA
Newspaper
The Reporter
698 Beech Street 03104   (603) 627-7679
Fax: (603) 627-7963
Lists further communities in Amherst, Concord,
Derry, Dover, Durham, Hanover, Keene, Laconia and
Nashua.

SYNAGOGUES
Orthodox
Lubavitch
7 Camelot Drive 03104   (603) 647-0204
Reform
Adath Yeshurun
152 Prospect Street 03104   (603) 669-5650

Portsmouth

SYNAGOGUES
Conservative
Temple Israel
200 State Street 03801   (603) 436-5301

NEW JERSEY

Aberdeen

SYNAGOGUES
Orthodox
Bet Tefilah
479 Lloyd Road 07747   (732) 583-6262

Atlantic City

RESTAURANTS
Meat
Jerusalem
6410 Ventnor Ave, Ventnor 08406   (609) 822-2266
Supervision: Rabbi Abraham Spacirer

SYNAGOGUES
Conservative
Beth El
500 N. Jerome Ave, Margate 08402
     Fax: (609) 823-1810

Beth Judah
700 N Swarthmore Avenue, Ventnor 08406
     (609) 822-7116
     Fax: (609) 822-4654
     Email: congbethjudah@aol.com

Chelsea Hebrew Congregation
4001 Atlantic Av 08401   (609) 345-0825

Community Synagogue
Maryland & Pacific Avs 08401   (609) 345-3282
Orthodox
Rodef Shalom
3833 Atlantic Av 08401   (609) 345-4580
Reform
Beth Israel
2501 Shore Rd, Northfield 08225   (609) 641-3600

Temple Emeth Synagogue
8501 Ventnor Av, Margate 08402   (609) 822-4343

Bayonne

COMMUNITY ORGANISATIONS
Jewish Community Centre
1050 Kennedy Blvd 07002   (201) 436-6900

SYNAGOGUES
Conservative
Temple Emanuel
735 Kennedy Blvd 07002   (201) 436-4499
Orthodox
Ohab Sholom
1016-1022 Ave. C 07002

Ohav Zedek
912 Ave. C 07002   (201) 437-1488
Uptown Synagogue
49th St. & Ave. C 07002
Reform
Temple Beth Am
111 Ave. B 07002   (201) 858-9052

Belmar

SYNAGOGUES
Orthodox
Sons of Israel Congregation
PO Box 298 07719   (973) 681-3200

Bergenfield

BUTCHERS
Glatt World
89 Newbridge Road   (201) 439-9675
     Fax: (201) 439-0342
Supervision: RCBC

DELICATESSEN
Foster Village Kosher Delicatessen & Catering
469 S. Washington Avenue 07621   (201) 384-7100
     Fax: (201) 384-0303
Supervision: Quality Kashrut Supervisory Service

SYNAGOGUES
Conservative
Congregation Beth Israel of Northern Valley
169 N. Washington Avenue 07621   (201) 384-3911
     Fax: (201) 384-3738
     Email: cbitemple@juno.com
     Web site: www.uscj.org/njersey/bergenfield

Bradley Beach

SYNAGOGUES
Orthodox
Congregation Agudath Achim
301 McCabe Avenue 07720   (973) 774-2495

Bridgeton

SYNAGOGUES
Conservative
Congregation Beth Abraham
330 Fayette Street 08302

Burlington

SYNAGOGUES
Conservative
B'nai Israel
212 High Street 08332 (609) 386-0406

Cherry Hill

BAKERIES
Pastry Palace Kosher Bakery
State Highway 70 08034 (856) 429-3606

BUTCHERS
Cherry Hill Kosher Market
907 W. Marlton Pike 08002 (856) 428-6663
Fax: (856) 216-0752

DELICATESSEN
Leo's Deli
J.C.C. 1301 Springdale Road (856) 424-4444 Ext 158
Supervision: Tri-County Vaad

MIKVAOT
Sons of Israel
720 Cooper Landing Road 08002 (856) 667-3515
Email: Tasha.flecha@verizon.net

RESTAURANTS
Meat
Maxim's Restaurant
404 Route 70 (856) 428-5045

SYNAGOGUES
Conservative
Beth El
2901 W. Chapel Avenue 08002 (856) 667-1300
Beth Shalom
1901 Kresson Road 08003 (856) 751-6663
Congregation Beth Tikva
115 Evesboro-Medford Road, Marlton
Orthodox
Congregation Sons of Israel
720 Cooper Landing Road 08002 (856) 667-9700
Fax: (856) 667-9765
Email: Tasha.flecha@verizon.net
Daily minyan.

Reform
Congregation M'kor Shalom
850 Evesham Road (856) 424-4220
Fax: (856) 424-2890

Temple Emmanuel
1101 Springdale Road

Cinnaminson

SYNAGOGUES
Conservative
Temple Sinai
2101 New Albany Road 08077 (609) 829-0658
Fax: (609) 829-0310
Email: tsoffice@snip.net
Web site: www.uscj.org/njersey/cinnaminson

Clark

SYNAGOGUES
Conservative
Temple Beth O'r
111 Valley Road 07066 (732) 381-8403
Fax: (732) 381-8403

Clifton

COMMUNITY ORGANISATIONS
Jewish Federation of Greater Clifton-Passaic
199 Scoles Avenue 07012 (973) 777-7031
Fax: (973) 777-6701
Email: planned.giving@verizon.net

MEDIA
Newspaper
Jewish Community News
199 Scoles Avenue 07012

RESTAURANTS
Jerusalem II Pizza
224 Brook Avenue 07055 (973) 778-0960

SYNAGOGUES
Conservative
Clifton Jewish Center
18 Delaware Street 07011 (973) 772-3131
Reform
Beth Shalom
733 Passaic Avenue 07012 (973) 773-0355

Colonia

SYNAGOGUES
Conservative
Ohev Shalom
220 Temple Way 07067 (908) 388-7222

Cranbury

SYNAGOGUES
Conservative
Jewish Congregation of Concordia
c/o Club House 08512   (609) 655-8136

Cranford

CONTACT INFORMATION
Rabbi Hoffberg
                                        (908) 276-9231
Contact for kosher hospitality.

SYNAGOGUES
Conservative
Temple Beth El Mekor Chayim
338 Walnut Avenue 07016   (908) 276-9231
                              Fax: (908) 276-6570
      Web site: www.uscj.org/njersey/cranfotb

Deal

RESTAURANTS
Pizzerias
Jerusalem II Pizza
106 Norwood Avenue 07723   (732) 531-7936

SYNAGOGUES
Orthodox
128 Norwood Avenue 07723   (732) 531-3200
Ohel Yaacob Congregation
6 Ocean Avenue, PO Box 225 07723
                      (732) 531-0217/531-2405

East Brunswick

BUTCHERS
East Brunswick Kosher Meats
1020 State Highway 18 08816   (908) 257-0007

SYNAGOGUES
Conservative
E. Brunswick Jewish Center
511 Ryders Lane 08816   (908) 257-7070
Reform
Temple B'nai Shalom
Old Stage Road & Fern Road 08816   (908) 251-4300

Edison

BUTCHERS
Edison Kosher Meats
State Highway 27, and Evergreen Rd   (732) 549-3707

COMMUNITY ORGANISATIONS
Jewish Community Center of Middlesex County
1775 Oak Tree Road 08820   (732) 494-3232
                              Fax: (732) 548-2850

SYNAGOGUES
Conservative
Beth El
91 Jefferson Blvd 08817   (732) 985-7272

Elizabeth

MIKVAOT
Mikvah Tomor Deborah
35 North Avenue 07208   (908) 352-5048
                              Fax: (908) 289-5245

RESTAURANTS
Dairy
Dunkin' Donuts
186 Elmora Avenue 07202
Meat
New Kosher Special
163 Elmora Avenue 07202   (908) 353-1818
Pizzerias
Jerusalem Restaurant
150 Elmora Avenue 07202   (908) 289-4810

SYNAGOGUES
Orthodox
Adath Israel
1391 North Avenue 07208   (908) 355-4850
Bais Yitzchak
153 Bellevue Street 07202   (908) 354-4789

Elmwood Park

COMMUNITY ORGANISATION
Elmwood Park Jewish Center
100 Gilbert Ave.,   (201) 797-7320/797-9749

Englewood

GROCERIES
Kosher By the Case & Less
255 Van Nostrand Avenue 07631   (201) 568-2281
                              Fax: (201) 568-5681
Supervision: RCBC

MIKVAOT
Mikva
89 Huguenot Avenue   (201) 567-1143

RESTAURANTS
Dairy
The Fish Grill
16 W. Palisade Avenue   (201) 227-6182
Supervision: RCBC

Meat
Sol & Sol
34 E Palisade Avenue 07631   (201) 541-6880
                                    Fax: (201) 541-6883
Supervision: Kashrut Committee of Bergen County

SYNAGOGUES
Conservative
Temple Emanu-El
147 Tenafly Road 07631   (201) 567-1300
                                Fax: (201) 569-7580

Orthodox
Ahavath Torah
240 Broad Avenue 07631   (201) 568-1315
                                Fax: (201) 568-2991
                Email: egorlyn@ahavathtorah.org
                Web site: www.ahavathtorah.org
Shomrei Emunah
89 Huguenot Avenue 07631   (201) 567-9420
Daily morning services, and mikva.

Fair Lawn

BAKERIES
New Royal Bakery
19-09 Fair Lawn Avenue 07410   (201) 796-6565
                                      Fax: (201) 796-8501
Supervision: RCBC

BUTCHERS
Food Showcase
24-28 Fair Lawn Avenue 07410   (201) 475-0077
                                      Fax: (201) 794-6728
Supervision: RCBC
Sells food provisions as well.

RESTAURANTS
Dairy
J.C. Pizza of Fairlawn
14-20 Plaza Road 07410   (201) 703-0801
Supervision: RCBC

SYNAGOGUES
Orthodox
Bris Arushon
2204 Fairlawn Ave.,   (201) 791-7200

Fort Lee

BUTCHERS
Blue Ribbon Self-Service Kosher Meat Market
1363 Inwood Terr. 07024   (201) 224-3220
                                 Fax: (201) 224-7281
                Email: koshercomida@msn.com

DELICATESSEN
Al's Kosher Deli
209 Main Street 07024   (201) 461-3044
                               Fax: (201) 461-7188
Supervision: Quality Kashrut Supervisory Service

SYNAGOGUES
Conservative
Jewish Community Center of Fort Lee
1449 Anderson Avenue 07024   (201) 947-1735
                                    Fax: (201) 947-1530
                     Email: aschafer@jcc.org

Orthodox
Young Israel of Fort Lee
1610 Parker Avenue 07024   (201) 592-1518
                                  Fax: (201) 592-8414

Freehold

RESTAURANTS
Fred and Murry's
Pond Road Shopping Center, Route 9 07728
                                    (732) 462-3343
            Web site: www.fredandmurrys.com
Not glatt kosher or shomer Shabbat, but has
Conservative supervision.

SYNAGOGUES
Orthodox
Agudath Achim/Freehold Jewish Center
Broad & Stokes Streets 07728   (732) 462-0254
                                      Fax: (732) 462-0217
Traditional congregation with daily minyans.

Hackensack

COMMUNITY ORGANISATIONS
Jewish Federation of Community Services of Bergen County
170 State Street 07601

SYNAGOGUES
Conservative
Temple Beth El
280 Summit Avenue 07601   (201) 342-2045

Haddonfield

BUTCHERS
Sarah's Kosher Kitchen
63 Ellis Road

Hasbrouck Heights

SYNAGOGUES
Reform
Temple Beth Elohim
Bourlevard & Charlton Aves   (201) 393-7707

Highland Park

GROCERIES
Berkley Bakery
405 Raritan Avenue 08904   (732) 220-1919

Dan's Deli & Meat Market
515 Raritan Avenue 08904

Kosher Catch
239 Raritan Avenue   (732) 572-9052

MIKVAOT
Park Mikva
112 S. 1st Avenue 08904   (732) 249-2411

SYNAGOGUES
Conservative
Highland Park Conservative Temple & Center
201 S. 3rd Ave. 08904   (732) 545-6482
Fax: (732) 246-3100

Orthodox
Congregation Ahavas Achim
(732) 247-0532
Fax: (732) 247-6739
Email: aa613@juno.com
Congregation Etz Ahaim (Sephardi)
230 Denison St 08904   (732) 247-3839
Fax: (732) 545-3191
Email: etzahaim@earthlink.net
Web site: www.home.earthlink.net/~etzahaim
Congregation Ohav Emeth
415 Raritan Avenue 08904   (732) 247-3038
Fax: (732) 247-1438
Email: office@ohavemeth.org

Hillside

SYNAGOGUES
Conservative
Shomrei Torah Ohel Yosef Yitzchok
910 Salem Avenue 07205   (908) 289-0770

Orthodox
Congregation Sinai Torath Chaim
1531 Maple Avenue 07205   (908) 923-9500

Hoboken

SYNAGOGUES
Conservative
United Synagogue of Hoboken
830 Hudson Street & 115 Park Avenue 07030
(201) 659-2614
Fax: (201) 659-7944

Jamesburg

SYNAGOGUES
Rossmoor Jewish Congregation Meeting Room
(609) 655-0439

Jersey City

SYNAGOGUES
Orthodox
Congregation Mount Sinai
128 Sherman Avenue 07307   (201) 659-4267
Fax: (201) 659-4267
Email: congmtsinai@netzero.net
Web site: www.mtsinai.net
Offers shabbat hospitality for travellers.

Lakewood

BAKERIES
Gelbsteins Bakery
415 Clifton Avenue 08701   (562) 363-3636
Supervision: Orthodox supervision

Lakewood Heimishe Bakeshop
225-2nd St 08701   (562) 905-9057
Supervision: Orthodox supervision

BOOKSELLERS
Torah Treasures
254-2nd St. 08701   (562) 901-1911
Fax: (562) 905-6482

BUTCHERS
Shloimy's Kosher World
23 E. County Line Road 08701   (562) 363-3066

COMMUNITY ORGANISATIONS
Ocean County Jewish Federation
301 Madison Avenue 08701   (562) 363-0530
Fax: (562) 363-2097
Email: ocjf@optonline.net

KASHRUT INFORMATION
KCC - Cashrus Council of Lakewood
(562) 901-1888

MIKVAOT
Congregation Mikvah Tahara
1101 Madison Avenue 08701 (562) 370-1666
Call to schedule appointment.

RESTAURANTS
Dairy
Bagel Nosh
380 Clifton Avenue 08701 (562) 363-1115
Fax: (562) 363-5745

Meat
R. & S. Kosher Restaurant and Deli
416 Clifton Avenue 08701 (562) 363-6688
Glatt kosher meat only. Hours: Sunday to Thursday,
12:30 pm to 9 pm; Friday, 8 am to 2:30 pm. On
Friday, take-out only.

Yum Mee Glatt
116 Clifton Avenue 08701 (562) 886-9688
Chinese and American.

Pizzeria
Pizza Plus
241 4th St 08701 (562) 367-0711
Supervision: Orthodox supervision

SYNAGOGUES
Conservative
Ahavat Shalom
Forest Avenue & 11th Street 08701 (562) 363-5190
Fax: (562) 363-5225
Email: ahavat_shalom_nj@netzero.com
Web site: www.uscj.org/njersey/lakewood

Orthodox
Kol Shimshon
323 Squamkum Road 08701 (562) 901-6680

Lakewood Yeshiva
Private Way & 6th Street 08701 (562) 367-1060

Sons of Israel
Madison Avenue & 6th Street 08701 (562) 364-2230

Reform
Beth Am
Madison Avenue & Carey Street 08701
(562) 363-2800

Lawrenceville

SYNAGOGUES
Orthodox
Young Israel of Lawrenceville
2556 Princeton Pike 08648 (609) 883-8833
Web site: www.yiol.com

Linden

SYNAGOGUES
Conservative
Mekor Chayim Suburban Jewish Center
Deerfield Road & Academy Terrace 07036
(908) 925-2283

Orthodox
Congregation Anshe Chesed
100 Orchard Terrace at St George Ave. 07036
(908) 486-8616

Livingston

RESTAURANTS
Dairy
Jerusalem Restaurant
99-101 West Mt Pleasant Avenue 07039
(973) 533-1424
Fax: (973) 533-9275
Supervision: Vaad Hakashrus of the Council of
Orthodox Rabbis Metrowest

Meat
Moshavi
515 S. Livingston Avenue 07039 (973) 740-8777
Supervision: Vaad Hakashrus of the Council of
Orthodox Rabbis Metrowest

SYNAGOGUES
Conservative
Temple Beth Shalom
193 E. Mt Pleasant Ave. 07039 (973) 992-3600

Independent
Temple B'Nai Abraham
300 East Northfield Court 07039 (973) 994-2290
Fax: (973) 994-1838
Email: lwold@tbanj.org
Web site: www.tbanj.org

Orthodox
Etz Chaim Synagogue
304 Mt Pleasant Avenue 07039 (973) 597 1655

Synagogue of the Suburban Torah Center
85 W. Mount Pleasant Avenue 07039
(973) 994-0122; 994-2620
Fax: (973) 535-3898
Email: execdirector@suburbantorah.org
Web site: www.suburbantorah.org

Reform
Temple Emanu-el of West Essex
264 W. Northfield Rd 07039 (973) 992-5560

Mahwah

SYNAGOGUES
Reform
Temple Beth Haverim
280 Remjo Valley Road (201) 512-1983

Maplewood

BOOKSELLERS

Rabbi L. Sky Hebrew Book Store
1923 Springfield Avenue, Maplewood 07040
(973) 763-4244/5
Fax: (973) 763-1412

Metuchen

SYNAGOGUES
Conservative
Neve Shalom
250 Grove Avenue 08840 (732) 548-2238
Fax: (732) 603-7976
Email: neveshal@webspan.net

Millville

SYNAGOGUES
Conservative
Beth Hillel
3rd Avenue & Oak Street 08332 (609) 825-8672

Morris Plains

DELICATESSEN
Jonathan's Deli Restaurant
2900 Route 10 West 07950 (973) 539-6010
Fax: (973) 539-6011

Morristown

KASHRUT INFORMATION
Congregation Ahavath Yisrael
9 Cutler Street 07960 (973) 267-4184
Fax: (973) 898-1711
Email: sofernj@aol.com
This synagogue operates a kosher food buying service for the community, dealing only in strictly kosher products.

Rabbinical College of America
226 Sussex Avenue 07960 (973) 267-9404
Fax: (973) 267-5208
Email: rca226@aol.com

MIKVAOT
Mikvah Bais Chana, Sarah Esther Rosenhaus Mikvah Institutue
93 Lake Road 07960 (973) 292-3932

SYNAGOGUES
Conservative
Morristown Jewish Center
177 Speedwell Avenue 07960 (973) 538-9292

Orthodox
Congregation Levi Yitzchok
226 Sussex Avenue 07960 (973) 984-6326

New Brunswick

SYNAGOGUES
Conservative
Congregation B'nai Tikvah
1001 Finnegans Lane 08902 (732) 297-0696
Fax: (732) 297-2673
Email: administrator@bnaitikvah.org
Web site: www.bnaitikvah.org
Orthodox
Chabad House Friends of Lubavitch
8 Sicard St 08901 (732) 828-9191
Reform
Anshe Emeth Memorial Temple
222 Livingston Av 08901 (732) 545-6484
Fax: (732) 745-7448
Email: temple@aemt.net
Web site: www.aemt.net
Unaffiliated
Congregation Poile Zedek
145 Neilson St. 08901 (732) 545-6123

Old Bridge

SYNAGOGUES
Conservative
Ohav Shalom
3018 Bordertown Avenue 08859 (201) 727-4334

Paramus

BUTCHERS
Harold's Self-Service Kosher Meat
67-A E. Ridgewood Avenue 07652 (201) 262-0030

COMMUNITY ORGANISATIONS
Jewish Center of Paramus
304 Midland Ave., (201) 262-7691

SYNAGOGUES
Conservative
Jewish Community Center of Paramus
E-304 Midland Ave., 07652 (201) 262-7691
Fax: (201) 262-6516
Email: jccparam@mail.idt.net
Web site: www.uscj.org/njersey/paramus

Parsipanny

DELICATESSEN
Arlington Kosher Deli, Restaurant & Caterers
Arlington Shopping Center,
744 Route 46W 07054 (973) 335-9400

Passaic

DELICATESSEN
B&Y Kosher Korner Inc.,
200 Main Avenue 07055 (973) 777-1120

RESTAURANTS
Meat
Main-Ly Chow
227 Main Avenue 07055 (973) 777-4900

SUPERMARKET
Kosher Konnection
200 Main Avenue 07055 (973) 777-1120
Fax: (973) 777-4991

SYNAGOGUES
Orthodox
Young Israel of Passaic-Clifton
200 Brook Avenue 07055 (973) 778-7117

Paterson

SYNAGOGUES
Conservative
Temple Emanuel
151 E. 33rd Street 07514 (973) 684-5565

Perth Amboy

SYNAGOGUES
Conservative
Beth Mordechai
224 High Street 08861 (732) 442-2431

Orthodox
Shaarey Teflioh
15 Market Street 08861 (732) 826-2977

Piscataway

SYNAGOGUES
Reform
B'nai Shalom
25 Netherwood Avenue 08854 (908) 885-9444

Plainfield

SYNAGOGUES
Orthodox
United Orthodox Synagogue
526 W. 7th Street 07060 (908) 755-0043
Reform
Temple Sholom
815 W. 7th Street 07063 (908) 756-6447

Princeton

SYNAGOGUES
Traditional
Jewish Center
435 Nassau Street 08540 (609) 921-0100
Fax: (609) 921-7531
Email: JCenter@thejewishcenter.org

Rahway

SYNAGOGUES
Conservative
Temple Beth Torah
1389 Bryant Street 07065 (609) 576-8432

Randolph

SYNAGOGUES
Orthodox
Mount Freedom Jewish Center
1209 Sussex Turnpike 07970 (781) 895-2100

Ridgewood

SYNAGOGUES
Conservative
Temple Israel
475 Grove Street (201) 444-9320

River Edge

SYNAGOGUES
Reform
Temple Sholom
385 Howland Avenue 07661 (201) 489-2463
Fax: (201) 489-0775
Web site: www.uahcweb.org/nj/tsholomre/

Roselle

MEDIA
Guide Book
Shalom Book
843 St Georges Avenue 07203 (908) 298-8200
Fax: (908) 298-8220

Rumson

SYNAGOGUES
Conservative
Congregation B'nai Israel
Hance & Ridge Roads 07760   (908) 842-1800

Scotch Plains

COMMUNITY ORGANISATIONS
Jewish Federatiuon of Central New Jersey
1391 Martine Avenue 07076   (908) 889-5335

SYNAGOGUES
Conservative
Congregation Beth Israel
1920 Cliffwood Street 07076   (908) 889-1830
                                   Fax: (908) 889-5523

Short Hills

SYNAGOGUES
Reform
B'Nai Jeshurun
1025 South Orange Ave. 07078   (973) 379-1555
                                    Fax: (973) 379-4345
                                 Email: info@tbj.org

Somerset

SYNAGOGUES
Conservative
Temple Beth El
1945 Amwell Road 08873   (201) 873-2325

South Orange

GROCERIES
Zayda's Super Value Meat Market & Deli
309 Irvington Avenue 07079   (973) 762-1812

SYNAGOGUES
Conservative
Oheb Shalom Congregation
170 Scotland Rd 07079   (973) 762-7067
Reform
Temple Sharey Tefilo-Israel
432 Scotland Rd 07079   (973) 763-4116

South River

COMMUNITY ORGANISATIONS
Jewish Federation of Greater Middlesex County
230 Old Bridge Turnpike, South River,
Middlesex County 08882   (732) 432-7711
                               Fax: (732) 432-0292
                    Email: middlesexfed@aol.com

SYNAGOGUES
Traditional
Congregation Anshe Emeth of South River
88 Main Street 08882   (732) 257-4190
                            Fax: (732) 254-8819
Web site: www.members.home.net/ebweiss

Spotswood

SYNAGOGUES
Reform
Monroe Township Jewish Center
11 Cornell Avenue 08884   (201) 251-1119

Teaneck

BAKERIES
Butterflake Bake Shop
448 Cedar Lane 07666   (201) 836-3516
                             Fax: (201) 836-3056

Supervision: RCBC
Pat Yisrael.

Sammy's New York Bagels
1443 Queen Anne Road 07666   (201) 837-0515
                                   Fax: (201) 837-9733
Supervision: Kof-K
Pat Yisrael.

BOOKSELLERS
Zoldan's Judaica Center
406 Cedar Lane 07666   (201) 907-0034

BUTCHERS
Glatt Express
1400 Queen Anne Road 07666   (201) 837-8110
                                   Fax: (201) 837-0084
Supervision: RCBC
Sells food provisions as well.

DELICATESSEN
Chopstix
172 West Englewood Avenue 07666   (201) 833-0200
                                   Fax: (201) 833-8326
Supervision: RCBC
Glatt kosher Chinese take-out. Hours: Sunday to
Thursday, 11:30 am to 10 pm; Friday, closing times
vary – please call.

MIKVAOT
Mikveh
1726 Windsor Road 07666   (201) 837-8220

RESTAURANTS
Dairy
Jerusalem Pizza
496 Cedar Lane 07666   (201) 836-2120
                             Fax: (201) 836-2261
Supervision: RCBC

Plaza Pizza & Restaurant
1431 Queen Anne Road 07666   (201) 837-9500
Fax: (201) 836-2261
Supervision: RCBC

Shelly's
482 Cedar Lane 07666   (201) 692-0001
Fax: (201) 692-1890
Email: shellys@noahsark.net
Supervision: RCBC
Cholov Yisrael. Hours: Monday to Thursday, 10:30
am to 9:30 pm; Sunday, 10 am to 9 pm. Ten minutes
from the George Washington Bridge.

Meat
Grill Street
184 West Englewood Avenue 07666   (201) 833-0001
Fax: (201) 833-8030
Supervision: RCBC

Hunan Teaneck
515 Cedar Lane 07666   (201) 692-0099
Fax: (201) 692-1907
Supervision: RCBC
Glatt kosher Chinese and American cuisine. Eat in or
take-out. Mashgiach temidi. Hours: Sunday to
Thursday, 11:30 am to 9:45 pm; Friday, to 3 pm;
Saturday night, after Shabbat until midnight.

Noah's Ark
493 Cedar Lane 07666   (201) 692-1200
Fax: (201) 692-1890
Email: info@noahsark.net
Supervision: RCBC
Chassidishe shechita meats. Hours: Monday to
Thursday, 10:30 am to 10:30 pm; Friday, 8 am to 4
pm; Sunday, 9:30 am to 10:30 pm; Saturday during
winter, after Shabbat to midnight. Ten minutes from
the George Washington Bridge.

SYNAGOGUES
Conservative
Congregation Beth Sholom
354 Maitland Avenue 07666   (201) 833-2620
Fax: (201) 833-2323
Email: bsteaneck@aol.com
Web site: www.uscj.org/njersey/teaneckcbs

Jewish Center of Teaneck
70 Sterling Place 07666   (201) 833-0515
Fax: (201) 833-0511
Email: execdir@aol.com

Orthodox
Congregation Beth Aaron
950 Queen Anne Rd 07666   (201) 836-6210
Fax: (201) 836-0005
Email: mail@bethaaron.org
Web site: www.bethaaron.org

Congregation Bnai Yeshurun
641 W. Englewood Avenue 07666   (201) 836-8916
Fax: (201) 836-1888

Rinat Yisrael
389 W. Englewood Av 07666   (201) 837-2795
Fax: (201) 837-7881
Email: office@rinat.org

Roemer Synagogue
Whittier School, W. Englewood Av., 07666
Reform
Congregation Beth Am
510 Claremont Av 07666   (201) 836-5752
Fax: (201) 836-5760

Temple Emeth
1666 Windsor Rd 07666   (201) 833-1322
Fax: (201) 833-4831
Email: temple@emeth.org
Web site: www.emeth.org

Tenafly

SYNAGOGUES
Reform
Temple Sinai of Bergen County
1 Engle Street 07670   (201) 568-3035
Fax: (201) 568-6095
Email: temsinai@idt.net
Web site: www.uahc.org/congs.nj/nj009

Trenton

COMMUNITY ORGANISATIONS
Jewish Federation of Mercer & Bucks Counties
999 Lower Ferry Road 08628   (609) 883-5000

Union

COMMUNITY ORGANISATIONS
Jewish Federation of Central New Jersey
Green Lane 07083   (908) 351-5060

SYNAGOGUES
Conservative
Beth Shalom
2046 Vauxhall Road 07083   (908) 686-6773

Temple Israel
2372 Morris Avenue 07083   (908) 686-2120

Vineland

COMMUNITY ORGANISATIONS
Jewish Federation of Cumberland County
1063 East Landis Avenue, Suite B 08360-3785
(856) 696-4445
Fax: (856) 696-3428
Email: jfedcc@aol.com
Also serves the Bridgeton & Cumberland County
areas.

SYNAGOGUES
Conservative
Beth Israel
1015 E. Park Avenue 08630   (856) 691-0852
Orthodox
Ahavas Achim
618 Plum Street 08360   (856) 691-2218
Sons of Jacob Congregation
321 Grape Street 08360   (856) 692-4232
   Fax: (856) 691-4985
Monday to Friday 6.45 am. Saturday 9.00 am. Sunday 7.30 am. For evening service, please call synagogue.

Warren

COMMUNITY ORGANISATIONS
Jewish Federation of Central New Jersey
Suburban Services Office, 150 Mt. Bethel Rd
07059   (908) 647-0232
   Fax: (908) 647-3115

SYNAGOGUES
Reform
Mountain Jewish Community Center
104 Mount Horeb Road 07060   (908) 356-8777

Washington Township

SYNAGOGUES
Reform
Temple Beth Or
56 Ridgewood Rd   (201) 664-7422

Wayne

COMMUNITY ORGANISATIONS
Jewish Federation of New Jersey
1 Pike Drive 07470   (973) 595-0555

SYNAGOGUES
Conservative
Shomrei Torah
30 Hinchman Avenue 07470   (973) 694-6274
Reform
Temple Beth Tikvah
950 Preakness Avenue 07470   (973) 595-6565
   Fax: (973) 595-8192

West New York

SYNAGOGUES
Orthodox
Congregation Shaare Zedek
5308 Palisade Avenue 07093   (201) 867-6859

West Orange

DELICATESSEN
David's Deco-Tessen
555 Passaic Avenue 07006   (973) 808-3354
   Fax: (973) 808-5806
Supervision: Rabbi Herman Savitz (Conservative)
Open 7 days, 8 am to 7pm and Mondays 9am to 3pm.

GROCERIES
Gourmet Galaxy
659 Eagle Rock Avenue 07052   (973) 736-0060
Supervision: Vaad Hakashrus of the Council of Orthodox Rabbis Metrowest
Dairy and meat available.

JUDAICA
Lubavitch Center of Essex County
456 Pleasant Valley Way 07052   (973) 731-0770
   Fax: (973) 731-6821
Books, gifts, Judaica and all Chabad Outreach activities.

RESTAURANTS
Meat
Eden Wok
478 Pleasant Valley Way 07052   (973) 243-0115
   Fax: (973) 243-1332
Supervision: Vaad Hakashrus of the Council of Orthodox Rabbis Metrowest
Chinese food, also a sushi bar.

Pleasantdale Kosher Meat
470 Pleasant Valley Way 07052   (973) 731-3216

SYNAGOGUES
Conservative
B'Nai Shalom
300 Pleasant Valley Way 07052   (973) 731-0160
   Fax: (973) 731-1160
   Email: bnai@aol.com
Orthodox
Congregation Ahawas Achim B'nai Jacob and David
700 Pleasant Valley Way 07052   (973) 736-1407
   Fax: (973) 736-8006
   Email: shul.aabjdmail@verizon.com

Westfield

SYNAGOGUES
Reform
Temple Emanu-El
756 E. Broad Street 07090   (908) 232-6770
   Fax: (908) 233-3959
   Email: shantee@aol.com

Whippany

COMMUNITY ORGANISATIONS
United Jewish Federation of Metrowest
901 Route 10 07981   (973) 884-4800
Fax: (973) 884-7361

MEDIA
Newspaper
The New Jersey Jewish News
901 Route 10 07981   (973) 887-8500
Fax: (973) 887-4152
Email: njjewnews@aol.com
Weekly publication owned by United Jewish Fed. of
Metrowest; also publishes a weekly edition in
arrangement with the Jewish Federation of Central
New Jersey. Bl-Weekly edition with the Jewish
Federation of Middlesex County; and monthly edition
with the Jewish Federation of Princeton Mercer Bucks.

Willingboro

SYNAGOGUES
Reform
Adath Emanu-El
299 John F. Kennedy Way 08046   (609) 871-1736

Woodbridge

SYNAGOGUES
Conservative
Adath Israel
424 Amboy Avenue 07095   (732) 634-9601
Fax: (732) 634-1593
Email: lina1330@bellatlantic.net

Wyckoff

SYNAGOGUES
Reform
Temple Beth Rishon
585 Russell Ave   (201) 891-4466
Fax: (201) 891-0508
Email: bethrish@bellatlantic.net

NEW MEXICO

Albuquerque

COMMUNITY ORGANISATIONS
Jewish Federation of Greater Alberquerque
5520 Wyoming Blvd N.E. 87109   (505) 821-3214
Fax: (505) 821-3351
Email: andrew@jewishnewmexico.org
Web site: www.jewishnewmexico.org

KASHRUT INFORMATION
JFGA
(505) 821-3214

MEDIA
Newspaper
The Link
5520 Wyoming Blvd 87109   (505) 821-3214
Fax: (505) 821-3351

SYNAGOGUES
Conservative
Conservative B'nai Israel
4401 Indian School Road 87110   (505) 266-0155
Orthodox
Chabad of New Mexico
4000 San Pedro 87110   (505) 880-1181

Las Cruces

SYNAGOGUES
Reform
Temple Beth El
702 Parker Road, at Melendres 88004 (505) 524-3380
Fax: (505) 521-3737
Email: rabbikane@cs.nmsu.edu
Web site: www.uahc.org/nm/nm002/

Los Alamos

SYNAGOGUES
Conservative
Los Alamos Jewish Center
2400 Canyon Road 87544   (505) 662-2440

Rio Rancho

SYNAGOGUES
Reform
Rio Rancho Jewish Center
2009 Grande Blvd 87124   (505) 892-8511

Santa Fe

CONTACT INFORMATION
(505) 986-2091
For information about home hospitality, Shabbat and
mikva.

SYNAGOGUES
Orthodox
Chabad Jewish Center
242 West S. Mateo (corner Galisteo) (505) 983-2000
Fax: (505) 983-2055
Email: ChabadSantaFe@aol.com
Web site: www.chabadsf.com
Friday night and Shabbat services. Call for reservation
to a community Shabbat dinner. Thursday morning
minyans at 8:00am. Kadish minyans. Kosher catering
and take-out.

Pardes Yisroel
1307 Don Diego Avenue 87505   (505) 986-1603
Email: shammes@pardes-yisroel.org
Web site: www.pardes-yisroel.org/py/
Shabbat home hospitality. Kosher meals.

Reform
Congregation Beit Tikvah
PO Box 2112 87504   (505) 820-2991
Fax: (505) 820-2991
Email: rap1818@aol.com
Web site: www.beittikva.org

Temple Beth Shalom
205 E. Barcelona Road 87505   (505) 982-1376
Fax: (505) 983-7746
Email: tbs@santafe-newmexico.com
Web site: www.santafe-newmexico.com/~tbs
Friday evening and Saturday morning services.

NEW YORK

New York City encompasses so much territory and so much activity that it can sometimes be easy to forget that there is also a whole state named New York. The Empire State stretches from New York City in the south to the Canadian border at Quebec and Ontario provinces in the north; from the New England border with Connecticut, Massachusetts and Vermont in the east to Pennsylvania and the Great Lakes of Erie and Ontario in the southwest and west.

Within this 50,000 square mile expanse lie metropolis, suburb, small town, large city, village, vast state parks and preserves, seashores, islands, high mountains and rolling foothills, and abundant natural wilderness.

To New York City residents, anything outside the five boroughs (Manhattan, Queens, Brooklyn, the Bronx, and Staten Island) is either upstate or Long Island. But within those areas are numerous large and thriving Jewish communities. The cities of Buffalo, Rochester, Binghamton, Syracuse, and Schenectady, the suburban counties of Westchester and Rockland, and the Long Island counties of Nassau and Suffolk count hundreds of thousands of Jews among their residents.

Jewish settlement began in New York in early September 1654 when twenty-three Sephardic and Ashkenazi Jews disembarked at the harbour of New Amsterdam from the French ship St Catherine. They had escaped the Spanish Inquisition in Recife, Brazil to settle in the Dutch colony. Though Governor Peter Stuyvesant forbade their admission to his jurisdiction, the travellers' protests to his bosses at the Dutch West India Company were accepted and the Jews were

allowed to settle. Ten years later, in 1664, four British men-of-war appropriated New Amsterdam in the name of King Charles II of England, who, in turn, made a gift of it to his brother, James, Duke of York. Hence the name, New York.

Jewish immigration was sparse for the next 150 years, but it increased dramatically, especially in New York City between 1880 and 1924, as more than two million Jews made their way to 'der goldene medinah' (the golden door) from eastern and central Europe.

From that original group of twenty-three Jews in 1654, some made their way up the Hudson River as far as Albany (now the state capital). Two of them, Asser Levy and Jacob de Lucena, became Hudson River traders and also dealt in real estate in the Albany and Kingston areas. South of Albany, in nearby Newburgh, Jewish merchants established a trading post in 1777, but no Jewish community existed there until 1848.

New York's first Jewish community outside of New York City was the town of Sholom in the Catskill mountains in Ulster county. Founded by twelve families, it no longer exists. The oldest existing community is Congregation Beth El, founded in 1838 in Albany and later merged with Congregation Beth Emeth.

Westchester (just north of New York City) county's present Jewish population of close to 150,000 dates from 1860.

Rockland
Southeast of the Catskills, in Rockland county just north of New York City, are a number of communities with large Hasidic and Orthodox populations. New Square, a corruption of the name Skvir, was founded by the Skvirer Hasidim and is incorporated as a separate village within the town of Ramapo. With such an administrative and legal designation, New Square has its own zoning rules, its own village council, its own mayor, etc., and is run on strictly orthodox precepts. Monroe, Monsey and Spring Valley have very large Orthodox and Hasidic communities. Though observant Jews are predominant, these communities are also home to non-Jews and less-observant Jews. There are a number of villages in the area which have been incorporated with the express purpose of keeping Orthodox and Hasidim out, through regulations such as zoning to prevent synagogues from being built too close to residences and through the prohibition of having a synagogue in one's house.

Albany

GROCERIES
Price Chopper Market
1892 Central Avenue 12205   (518) 456-2970
Supervision: Vaad Hakashruth
Full service kosher department.

JEWISH STUDENT CENTRE
Shabbos House
State University of New York, 316 Fuller Road
     (518) 438-4227
     Email: shabbos@albany.net
     Web site: www.shabboshouse.com
Is also a synagogue.

MIKVAOT
340 Whitehall Road   (518) 437-1303

SYNAGOGUES
Conservative
Ohav Shalom
New Krumkill Rd 12208   (518) 489-4706

Temple Israel
600 New Scotland Ave. 12208   (518) 438-7858

Orthodox
Beth Abraham-Jacob
380 Whitehall Rd 12208   (518) 489-5819; 489-5179
     Fax: (518) 489-5179
     Email: mbomzer@aol.com

Chabad-Lubavitch Center of the Capital District
122 S. Main Av 12208   (518) 482-5781
     Fax: (518) 482-3684
     Email: albanychabad@knick.net
     Web site: www.chabadonline.com/albany

Shomray Torah
463 New Scotland Av 12208   (518) 438-8981

Reform
B'nai Sholom
420 Whitehall Rd 12208   (518) 482-5283

Beth Emeth
100 Academy Rd 12208   (518) 436-9761
At this 160-year-old congregation, Rabbi Isaac Mayer Wise, founder of American Reform Judaism, served when he first arrived in the United States.

Daughters of Sarah Senior Community
180 Washington Avenue Extension 12203
     (518) 456-7831
     Fax: (518) 456-1563
     Email: info@daughtersofsarah.org
     Web site: www.daughtersofsarah.org
Traditional service, Saturday 9:15 am. Reform service, Friday 3 pm. Traveller's advisory and kosher facility.

Amsterdam

SYNAGOGUES
Conservative
Congregation of Sons of Israel
355 Guy Park Avenue 12010   (518) 842-8691

Beacon

SYNAGOGUES
Conservative
Hebrew Alliance
55 Fishkill Avenue 12508   (845) 831-2012

Binghamton

MIKVAOT
Beth David Synagogue
39 Riverside Drive 13905   (607) 722-1793
     Fax: (607) 722-7121
     Email: bethdavidrabbi@aol.com

SYNAGOGUES
Community Center
500 Clubhouse Road 13903   (607) 724-2417
     Fax: (607) 824-2311
     Email: JCC13850@AOL.com

Conservative
Temple Israel
Deerfield Place, Vestal 13850   (607) 723-7461

Reform
Temple Concord
9 Riverside Drive 13905   (607) 723-7355

Buffalo

COMMUNITY ORGANISATIONS
Jewish Federation of Greater Buffalo
787 Delaware Avenue 14209   (716) 886-7750
     Fax: (716) 886-1367

DELICATESSEN
Tops Kosher Deli
Cnr of North Bailey and Maple Road   (716) 615-0076

GROCERIES
Corner of North Bailey and Maple Road
     (716) 515-0075

MEDIA
Guide
Shalom Buffalo
787 Delaware Ave. 14209   (716) 886-7750
     Fax: (716) 886-1367

Newspaper
Buffalo Jewish Review
15 Mohawk Street 14203   (716) 854-2192

MIKVAOT
Mikva
1248 Kenmore Avenue 14216   (716) 632-1531

MUSEUMS
Benjamin & Dr. Edgar R. Cofeld Judaic Museum
805 Delaware Av. 14209   (716) 886-7150
                           Fax: (716) 831-1126
A collection of more than a thousand Judaic artifacts
dating from the tenth century to the present. There
are unique Ben Shahn stained glass windows in the
building.

SYNAGOGUES
Conservative
Hillel of Buffalo
Campus Center for Jewish Life, 520 Lee Entrance,
The Commons/Suite #204, Amherst,
NY 14228   (716) 639-8361
                           Fax: (716) 639-7817
Shaarey Zedek
621 Getzville Rd 14226   (716) 838-3232
Temple Beth El of Greater Buffalo
2368 Eggert Road, Tonawanda 14150 (716) 836-3762
                           Fax: (716) 836-3764
               Email: templebethel@juno.com
          Web site: www.uscj.org/empire/tonawatb/
Orthodox
B'nai Shalom
1675 N. Forest Rd 14221   (716) 689-8203
Beth Abraham
1073 Elmwood Av 14222   (716) 874-4786
Chabad House
3292 Main St., & N. Forest Rd 14214 &14068
                                (716) 688-1642
Saranac Synagogue
85 Saranac Avenue 14216   (716) 876-1284
                           Fax: (716) 833-7178
Daily Minyan.
Young Israel of Greater Buffalo
105 Maple Rd, Williamsville 14221 (716) 634-0212
Reconstructionist
Temple Sinai
50 Alberta Dr., Amherst 14226   (716) 834-0708
                           Fax: (716) 838-2597
               Email: templesinai@juno.com
Reform
Beth Am
4660 Sheridan Dr 14221   (716) 633-8877
                           Fax: (716) 633-8952
                 Email: rabbif@aol.com
Congregation Havurah
6320 Main St. 14221   (716) 874-3517

Temple Beth Zion
805 Delaware Avenue 14209   (716) 886-7150
                           Fax: (716) 831-1126
                  Email: zbt@webt.com
                Web site: www.tbz.org
Traditional
Kehilat Shalom
700 Sweet Home Rd 14226   (716) 885-6650

CATSKILLS

Ellenville

MIKVAOT
Congregation Ezrath Israel
Rabbi Herman Eisner Square 12428
                             (845) 647-4450/72
                        Fax: (845) 647-4472
              Email: ezrathisrael@cs.com
Mikvah - call for hours.

Fleischmanns

HOTELS
Kosher
Oppenheimer's Regis
PO Box 700, Fleischmanns 12430 (845) 254-5080
                           Fax: (845) 254-4399
                  Email: kurtopp@aol.com
Supervision: Rabbinate of K'hal Adas Jeshurun, NYC
Open from Pesach to Succos. Off-season: Fax 1-732-
367-5417.

Loch Sheldrake

RESTAURANTS
Meat
Kikar Tel Aviv
Vacation Village   (845) 434-0600

SYNAGOGUES
Orthodox
Young Israel of Vacation Village
PO Box 650 12759   (845) 436-8359

Monticello

HOTELS
Kutsher's Country Club
                                (845) 794-6000
                           Fax: (845) 794-0157
              Email: kutshers@warwick.net
Daily services.

MIKVAOT
Mikva
16 North Street 12701   (845) 794-6757
Summer: opens at sunset for two hours. Winter: by
appointment only.

SYNAGOGUES
Orthodox
Landfield Avenue Synagogue
18 Landfield Avenue 12701   (845) 794-8470
                    Fax: (845) 794-8478

Daily services.

Reform
Temple Sholom
Port Jervis & Dillon Roads 12701   (845) 794-8731
Daily services.

Sharon Springs

HOTELS
Yarkony's Adler Spa Hotel
PO Box 328 13459
            (845) 284-2285 or 1 800 448-4314
                  Fax: (845) 284-2215
Supervision: OU

Woodbourne

HOTELS
Chalet Hotel
                    (845) 434-5124
Supervision: Orthodox
Glatt kosher.

Woodridge

HOTELS
The Lake House Hotel
                    (845) 434-7800
Glatt kosher. Chalav Yisrael products only. Open
Pesach to Succot.

Clifton Park

SYNAGOGUES
Conservative
Beth Shalom
Clifton Park, Center Road 12065   (716) 371-0608

Delmar

SYNAGOGUES
Orthodox
Chabad House of Delmar
109 Elsmere Avenue 12054   (518) 439-8280
                    Fax: (518) 439-3226
      Email: DelmarChabadSimon@juno.com

Reconstructionist
**Reconstructionist Havurah of the Capital
District**
98 Meadowland Street 12054   (518) 439-5870

Elmira

SYNAGOGUES
Orthodox
Shomray Hadath
Cobbles Park 14905   (607) 732-7410

Reform
B'nai Israel
Water & Guinnip Streets 14905   (607) 734-7735

Geneva

SYNAGOGUES
Reform
Temple Beth El
755 South Main Street 14456   (315) 789-9710
           Email: rosenfield@hws.edu

Glens Falls

SYNAGOGUES
Conservative
Shaaray Tefila
68 Bay Street 12801   (518) 792-4945
                  Fax: (518) 792-5966
     Email: Shaarayt@localnet.com

Reform
Temple Beth El
3 Marion Avenue 12801   (518) 792-4364

Gloversville

SYNAGOGUES
Community Center
28 E. Fulton Street 12078

Conservative
Knesseth Israel
34 E. Fulton Street 12078   (518) 725-0649

Hudson

SYNAGOGUES
Conservative
Anshe Emeth
240 Jolsen Blvd. 12534   (518) 828-9040

Ithaca

SYNAGOGUES
Conservative
Temple Beth El
402 N. Tioga Street 14850   (607) 273-5775
           Email: tbe18@aol.com

Orthodox
Young Israel of Cornell
106 West Avenue 14850   (607) 272-5810

Lake Placid

SYNAGOGUES
Traditional
30 Saranac Avenue, PO Box 521 12946-0521
     (518) 523-3876
     Fax: (518) 891-2629

LONG ISLAND

NASSAU COUNTY

Baldwin

RESTAURANTS
Ben's Kosher Delicatessen
933 Atlantic Avenue   (516) 868-2072
     Fax: (516) 868-2062
     Email: info@bensdeli.net
     Web site: www.bensdeli.net
Supervision: Supervised

Cedarhurst

BAKERIES
Zomick's Bake Shop
444 Central Avenue, Cedarhurst   (516) 569-5520
Supervision: Vaad HaKashrus of the Five Towns

BOOKSELLERS
Judaica Plus
530 Central Avenue, Cedarhurst   (516) 295-4343

RESTAURANTS
Dairy
Ruthie's Kosher Dessert and Dairy Café
560A Central Avenue, Cedarhurst   (516) 569-1818
Supervision: Vaad HaKashrus of the Five Towns

Meat
Burger Express
140 Washington Ave   (516) 295-2040
Supervision: Supervised

K.D.'s El Passo BBQ
546 Central Avenue, Cedarhurst   (516) 569-2920
Supervision: Supervised

K Roasters
72 Columbia Avenue, Cedarhurst   (516) 791-5100
Supervision: Vaad HaKashrus of the Five Towns

King David Delicatessen
550 Central Avenue, Cedarhurst   (516) 569-2920
Supervision: Vaad HaKashrus of the Five Towns
Glatt kosher, Shomer Shabbat. Ten minutes from JFK
International Airport.

Wok Tov
594 Central Avenue, Cedarhurst   (516) 295-3843
     Fax: (516) 295-3865
Supervision: Vaad HaKashrus of the Five Towns

Great Neck

BUTCHERS
Great Neck Glatt
501 Middle Neck Road 11023   (516) 773-6328
     Fax: (516) 773-4694
Supervision: Vaad Harabonim of Queens

MEDIA
Newspapers
Long Island Jewish Week
98 Cutter Mill Road 11020   (516) 773-3679
Long Island Jewish World
115 Middle Neck Road 11021   (516) 829-4000

MIKVAOT
26 Old Mill Road 11023   (516) 487-2726

RESTAURANTS
Meat
Bistro Grill
132 Middle Neck Road   (516) 829-4428
     Fax: (516) 829-3320

Chattanooga
37 Cuttermill Road   (516) 487-4455
Colbeh
75 N. Station Plaza, Greatneck   (516) 466-8181
Supervision: Kof-K
Danny's
624 Middle Neck Road   (516) 487-6666
Hunan
507 Middle Neck Road, Greatneck   (516) 482-7912
Supervision: Vaad Rab. of Queens
Kings Kosher Pizza
605 Middle Neck Road   (516) 482-0400
Soprano's
113 Middle Neck Road   (516) 482-0000
     Fax: (516) 482-0560

Greenvale

RESTAURANTS
Meat
Ben's Kosher Delicatessen
140 Wheatley Plaza   (516) 621-3340
     Fax: (516) 621-2178
     Email: info@bensdeli.net
     Web site: www.bensdeli.net
Supervision: Supervised

Jericho

DELICATESSEN
437 No. Broadway   (516) 939-2367
Fax: (516) 939-2294
Email: info@bensdeli.net
Web site: www.bensdeli.net
Supervision: Supervised

Lawrence

BAKERIES
Tasty Heimish Bakery
343 Central Avenue, Lawrence   (516) 569-5551/5552

RESTAURANTS
Dairy
Dairy Review
143 Washington Avenue, Lawrence   (516) 295-7417
Supervision: Vaad HaKashrus of the Five Towns

Primavera
357 Central Avenue, Lawrence   (516) 374-5504
Fax: (516) 374-5589
Supervision: Supervised

Meat
Burger Express
140 Washington Avenue, Lawrence   (516) 374-1714
Supervision: Vaad HaKashrus of the Five Towns

Cho-Sen Island
367 Central Avenue, Lawrence 11559 (516) 374-1199
Fax: (516) 374-1459
Supervision: Vaad HaKashrus of the Five Towns

Traditions
302 Central Avenue   (516) 295-3630

Long Beach

MIKVAOT
Sharf Manor, 274 W. Broadway 11561   (516) 431-7758

SYNAGOGUES
Conservative
Beth Shalom of Long Beach and Lido
700 E. Park Ave 11561   (516) 432-7464

Orthodox
Temple Beth El
570 W. Walnut Street 11561   (516) 432-1678

New Hyde Park

KASHRUT INFORMATION
Long Island Commission of Rabbis
1300 Jericho Turnpike 11040   (718) 343-5993

Syosset

COMMUNITY ORGANISATIONS
Conference of Jewish Organisations of Nassau County
North Shore Atrium, 6900 Jericho Turnpike
11791   (516) 364-4477
Fax: (516) 921-5092

West Hempstead

MIKVAOT
775 Hempstead Avenue 11552   (516) 489-9358

RESTAURANTS
Meat
Wing Wan
248 Hempstead Avenue   (516) 482-7912

Woodbury

RESTAURANTS
Ben's Kosher Delicatessen
7971 Jericho Turnpike   (516) 496-4236
Fax: (516) 496-4354
Email: info@bensdeli.net
Web site: www.bensdeli.net
Supervision: Supervised

Woodmere

KASHRUT INFORMATION
Vaad HaKashrus of the Five Towns
859 Peninsula Blvd., Woodmere 11598
(516) 569-4536
Fax: (516) 295 4212

RESTAURANTS
Soprano's
1034 Broadway 11598   (516) 792-9800
Fax: (516) 792-0409

SYNAGOGUES
Orthodox
Young Israel of North Woodmere
634 Hungry Harbor Road, North Woodmere
11581   (516) 791-5099
Email: info@yinw.org

SUFFOLK COUNTY

Commack

COMMUNITY ORGANISATIONS
Suffolk Jewish Communal Planning Council
74 Hauppauge Road 11725   (516) 462-5826
Email: sjcpc@att.net
Web site: www.lijewishlinks.org
Publishes "Suffolk Jewish Directory".

RESTAURANTS
Meat
Pastrami 'N Friends
110a Commack Road 11725   (516) 499-9537

SYNAGOGUES
Orthodox
Young Israel of Commack
40 Kings Park Road 11725   (516) 543-1441

Dix Hills

TOURIST INFORMATION
Jewish Genealogy Society of Long Island
37 Westcliff Drive 11746-5627   (631) 549-9532
Email: jgsli@suffolk.lib.ny.us
Web site: www.jewishgen.org/jgsli
Offers assistance to Jewish travellers on their New York or US roots.

Westhampton Beach

CAFETERIA
Beach Bakery Café
112 Main Street 11978   (631) 288-6552
Supervision: Rabbi Jonathan Feldman

SYNAGOGUES
Orthodox
Hampton Synagogue
154 Sunset Avenue 11978   (631) 288-0534

Monroe

SYNAGOGUES
Conservative
Congregation Eitz Chaim
County Route 105 10950   (845) 783-7424
Reform
Monroe Temple of Liberal Judaism
314 N. Main Street 10950

Newburgh

KASHRUT INFORMATION
Agudas Israel
290 North Street 12550   (845) 562-5604
Fax: (845) 562-5622
Email: agudasisrael@aol.com

MUSEUM
Gomez Mill House
Millhouse Road, Marlboro 12542   (845) 236-3126
Fax: (845) 236-3365
Email: gomezmillhouse@juno.com
Web site: www.gomez.org
Oldest Jewish residence now maintained as a museum.

NEW YORK CITY

Nowhere in the United States is there a city richer in Jewish heritage than New York. From the city's beginnings as a Dutch trading post in the 17th century up to the present day, Jews have flocked to New York, made it their home, and left an indelible mark on the city's heritage, language, culture, physical structure, and day-to-day life. There are more Jews in the New York metropolitan area than in any other city in the world, and more than in any country except Israel. So, without a great deal of effort, just being in this largest urban Jewish community in history affords you the opportunity to be a tourist without concern about the ease of observing kashrut and Shabbat.

New York City is the largest Jewish community in the world outside Israel. The estimated Jewish population of New York City proper is just over one million. Another million or so live in the immediate suburbs, which include not only New York, but also New Jersey and Connecticut. Roughly one-third of American Jews live in and around New York City and virtually every national Jewish organization has its headquarters here.

New York City neighbourhoods with large Jewish populations are the upper west and upper east sides of Manhattan (modern Orthodox and secular Jewish), Borough Park, Williamsburg (Orthodox and Hasidic) and Brighton Beach (Russian) in Brooklyn, Forest Hills (Israelis and Russians), Kew Gardens, Kew Garden Hills (Orthodox) in Queens, Riverdale in the Bronx, and Staten Island.

In this largest urban Jewish community in history, the Jewish traveler is overwhelmed with choices of where to eat, where to find a minyan, what to see of Jewish interest and so on. And the variety of kosher restaurants makes choosing a pleasure: Chinese, Moroccan, Italian (both meat and dairy), traditional European, Indian, Japanese and seafood.

Though Jews from numerous countries of origin live together throughout New Yorkís Jewish communities, many groups tend to congregate in their own neighbourhoods or sections of neighbourhoods.

Ever since the fateful year of 1654 Jews have been coming to New York City. Sometimes a few, sometimes more, and sometimes by the boatload, as was the case between 1880 and 1924 when some two million Jews entered the United States. And though one might argue cause and effect, New York City is still the commercial, intellectual and financial center of the country.

Synagogues

Hundreds if not thousands of synagogues, chavurot and shtiblech lie within the city, representing the myriad expressions of Judaism: Orthodox, Hasidic, Conservative, Reform and Reconstructionist.

Complete lists of synagogues in all five boroughs can be obtained from the various umbrella organizations listed in the beginning of the section on the USA.

The 1,300-seat, Moorish-style Central Synagogue (Reform) at 652 Lexington Avenue in Manhattan reopened its doors in October 2001, three years after a devastating fire. It is the cityís oldest synagogue on an original site and is an official New York City landmark; the oldest Ashkenazi congregation, founded in 1825, is Bínai Jeshrun (Conservative) at 270 West 89th Street; Shearith Israel, the Spanish and Portuguese synagogue on Central Park West at 70th Street, is one of the oldest congregations in the United States and originated with those 23 refugees from the Spanish Inquisition in Brazil in 1654. The present building still has religious items from the earliest days of the congregation and its small chapel is representative of the American colonial period; Temple Emanu-El (Reform) at Fifth Avenue and 65th Street is not only the city's largest, but the worldís largest synagogue. The congregation was founded in 1848 and the building, built in 1929, can seat over 2,000 people; the Fifth Avenue synagogue at 5 East 62nd Street was, until early 1967, presided over by the then Rabbi Dr Immanuel Jakobovits, who later became the Chief Rabbi of Great Britain and the Commonwealth; the Park East synagogue at 163 East 67th Street, on the very fashionable Upper East Side, was founded in 1890 and is a historic landmark. Kehilath Jeshurun (Orthodox), 125 East

85th Street, is a popular option if you are on the Upper East Side. On the Upper West Side, Lincoln Square Synagogue (Orthodox), 200 Amsterdam Avenue at 69th Street, and Ohab Zedek (Orthodox), 118 West 95th Street, are both very popular options.

Visitors may be interested in a late 9 am minyan on the Upper West Side at 303 W.91st East between West End Avenue and Riversdale Drive.

Libraries, Museums, and Institutes of Learning

New York's newest educational research center and one of the country's most important resources for Jewish scholarship opened in October 2000 and is located at 15 West 16th Street. The center is a partnership of five major institutions of Jewish scholarship: American Jewish Historical Society, American Sephardi Federation, Leo Baeck Institute, Yeshiva University Museum and YIVO Institute for Jewish Research. The combined collections and the professional staff of these five institutions create an opportunity for an unparalleled comprehensive study of modern Jewish history.

The Jewish Museum (Fifth Avenue and 92nd Street, 212-423-3200) has been in existence since 1904. Under the auspices of the Conservative Jewish Theological Seminary, the museum has permanent and changing exhibits and programs and an excellent collection of Jewish ritual and ceremonial objects.

The library at the Jewish Theological Seminary (3080 Broadway at 122nd Street, 212-678-8000) houses one of the greatest collections of Judaica and Hebraica in the world. Its holdings include a rare manuscript by Maimonides (the Rambam).

Other libraries with large Judaica collections are at Yeshiva University (212-960-5400), the Judaica Collection at the New York Public Library (212-340-0849), New York University (212-998-1212), Columbia University (212-854-1754), the House of Living Judaism at Temple Emanu-El (212-744-1400) and the Leo Baeck Institute (212-744-6400). Inquire at each one individually as to availability of the collections.

One of New York's living museums is the Eldridge Street Synagogue (14 Eldridge Street, 212-219-0888). At over 100 years old, the Eldridge Street synagogue is a ghost of its former splendour. But, in its heyday at the turn of the century, it was among the busiest synagogues on the Lower East Side, and the first built for that purpose by New York's eastern European Jews. An official New York City landmark, and listed on the National Register of Historic Places, the synagogue is an ongoing restoration project. The synagogue functions as a museum and has a whole host of programs.

In the same neighbourhood and sociologically related is the Lower East Side Tenement Museum (97 Orchard Street, 212-431-0233). Contrary to popular opinion, the word tenement does not mean slum housing, but a particular building design devised to house the masses of immigrants who came to New York in the latter part of the 19th century. Tenements are five- or six-storey walk-up buildings distinguished by narrow entry halls and a central air shaft. Each floor contained four apartments. Toilet facilities, located in the hallway, were shared by all the residents. Baths were taken at numerous local public bath houses. The museum, located in a restored tenement built in 1863, shows visitors what tenement life was like via a model apartment. In addition, actors in period dress present 90-minute shows in a small theatre. This is how the vast majority of Jews lived when they first came to New York City.

Ellis Island National Monument (212-269-5755) was once the point of entry for Jews and other immigrants. Some five million Jews came to the United States between 1850 and 1948 and most were processed through immigration at Castle Garden (the present ferry ticket office) or, after 1890, Ellis Island.

Neighbourhoods and areas of historical interest

Manhattan

The Lower East Side has physically changed very little in over a century. Cramped tenements and crowded, dirty streets have always characterised the area. But for the absence of vendors calling out 'I cash clothes' one can get a pretty good idea of what life looked like for Jews newly arrived in New York City from eastern European countries, although it is difficult to imagine the strangeness of a new language or being away from home for the first time.

Although the Lower East Side is not as Jewish as it once was and many Jewish shops have closed, it is appropriate that historical jaunts in New York begin in its tangle of streets and alleys. For the ancestors of some 80 per cent of American Jews, this was the first piece of America they saw. Now other immigrant groups call the Lower East Side home. Settlement houses such as the Henry Street Settlement and the Educational Alliance on East Broadway once served the Jewish immigrant population in their need to learn English and become Americanised. Still in existence, they provide services to current residents, Jewish and non-Jewish alike.

Many Jews still do business in the neighbourhood and the area is full of historic buildings, Jewish shops, foodstores and stores selling all manner of ritual items (kipot, taliltot, tefilin, siddurim, etc.). Look along Essex, Orchard, Grand, Rivington, Hester and Canal streets.

One of the best guidebooks for this area (as well as the rest of New York City) is the 'AIA [American Institute of Architects] Guide to New York City' by Elliot Willensky and Norval White. An organization called Big Onion Walking Tours gives Lower East Side tours and they are worth a telephone call (212-439-1090).

You may notice that a number of churches on the Lower East Side used to be synagogues. They were re-consecrated as churches when the Jewish community dwindled. But in many cases you still can tell which were synagogues. Look for things like Stars of David on building cornerstones, darkened mezuzah shaped areas on doorposts, and shadows of Stars of David on building faÁades. They are quite evident if you look.

Synagogues of note in the area are the Bialystoker synagogue (7 Wilet Street); Beth Midrash HaGadol (60 Norfolk Street); First Roumanian American Congregation (89 Rivington Street); and the Eldridge Street Synagogue (14 Eldridge Street).

The only kosher winery in Manhattan is Schapiroís kosher Winery (126 Rivington Street, 674-4404), founded in 1899. Call for tour information.

Along Second Avenue below 14th Street you can still see the remnants of the scores of Yiddish theatres that once lined the street. Note particularly the movie theatre on Second Avenue at 12th Street, currently the City Cinemas Village East. In the upper level auditorium you can get an idea of what the place looked like when stars like Molly Picon and Boris Tomeshevsky held forth on the stage.

Forty-seventh Street between Fifth Avenue and Avenue of the Americas is the diamond center. Some 75 per cent of all the diamonds which enter the United States pass through here. As this is overwhelmingly a Jewish and Hasidic business, the street is bustling with diamond dealers concluding deals in the open market atmosphere that is pervasive. Most deals are made with a handshake. There are a number of kosher restaurants up and down the block and on the mezzanines of office buildings.

Historical Cemeteries
Manhattan
Shearith Israel Cemeteries
Vestiges of early Jewish settlement in New York can be gleaned from the remnants of the communityís first cemeteries. The following three are owned by New York's oldest congregation, Shearith Israel, the Spanish Portuguese Synagogue.

First: Shearith Israel Graveyard: 55 St. James Place (between Oliver and James St), the first Jewish cemetery in New Amsterdam, was consecrated in 1656 and was located near the present Chatham Square. Its remains were moved to this location. It contains the remains of Sephardic Jews who emigrated from Brazil.

Second: Cemetery of the Spanish and Portuguese Synagogue (1805ñ1829): 72-76 West 11th Street, just east of Sixth Avenue on the south side of the street.

Third: Cemetery of the Spanish and Portuguese Synagogue (1829-1851): 98-110 West 21st Street, just west of Sixth Avenue on the south side of the street.

Brooklyn
Green-Wood Cemetery (Fifth Avenue and Fort Hamilton Parkway, Brooklyn) contains the graves of many prominent Jewish figures.

Queens
Fourth Cemetery of the Spanish and Portuguese Synagogue: Cypress Hills Street and Cypress Avenue, Queens. The beautiful chapel and gate were built in 1885.

Arts and Entertainment
As American entertainment is largely a secular Jewish enterprise, one need not look very far for Jewish references in plays and musicals. However, there are some dedicated Jewish theatrical companies and venues: the Jewish Repertory Company (212-831-2000); the American Jewish Theater (212-633-1588); the YM & YWHA (212-427-6000) has several outstanding lecture series, some with specific Jewish themes. For other events of Jewish interest consult one of the weekly listings magazines such as Time Out New York or New York Magazine, or the Sunday Arts & Leisure section of the New York Times. Jewish newspapers with events listings are Jewish Week, Forward and Jewish Press, all available at most newsstands.

Jewish Neighbourhoods of Interest outside Manhattan
Brooklyn
Williamsburg was for many years the center of Hasidic life in New York City. But in the last decade many rebbes and their followers have moved to the suburbs, particularly Rockland county. However, a trip to Williamsburg is still worthwhile.

Boro Park is almost completely Orthodox and is a world apart from the rest of the city.

Crown Heights is populated by Hasidim of many sects, but particularly the Lubavitch, whose world headquarters is at 770 Eastern Parkway. The neighbourhood is not totally Jewish and there are often clashes (sometimes violent) between the Caribbean residents and Jewish residents.

New Jersey
Many towns in northern and central New Jersey are less than 40 minutes travel time by either car or public transport from Manhattan, and as such are part of metropolitan New York. They are: Bayonne, Clifton, Elizabeth, Englewood, Fairlawn, Hackensack, Hoboken, Jersey City, Newark, Passaic, Teaneck, Union and West New York.

Restaurants
By law in New York State, the selling of non-kosher food as kosher is a punishable fraud. Administered by the kosher Law Enforcement Section of the New York State Department of Agriculture, heavy penalties are imposed on violators. An Orthodox rabbi oversees the operation. Businesses selling kosher food must display proper signage, indicating under whose hashgacha they operate, and establishments which sell both kosher and non-kosher food must display that as well, with a sign in block letters no smaller than four inches high.

In July 2000 a Federal Judge ruled that this law violated the First Amendment. In September 2002 there was a further stay of this ruling pending appeal.

'The Kosher Directory', issued by the Union of Orthodox Jewish Congregations, lists foods and services which bear the symbol. It is available for a charge by calling 212-563-4000. Other reliable kashruth insignias also exist.

Note that kosher packaged foods, including bread, meat, fish, cake, biscuits and virtually anything you can think of, are widely available in supermarkets throughout the New York metropolitan area. Many foodstores, especially on the Upper West Side of Manhattan and in Jewish neighbourhoods in Brooklyn and Queens, sell fresh kosher prepared meals as well.

BRONX

RESTAURANTS

Second Helping
3532 Johnson Avenue 10463   (616) 548-1818
Supervision: Vaad Harabonim of Riverdale
Take-out food only; Glatt kosher.

Yeshiva University: Bronx Center
Eastchester Rd & Morris Park Avenue 10461
    (616) 430-2131
Dairy
Main Event
3708 Riverdale Avenue, Riverdale 10463
    (616) 601-6246
    Fax: (616) 601-0008
    Email: maineventc@aol.com
Supervision: Rabbi Jonathan Rosenblatt, Riverdale
Jewish Center

Meat
Riverdelight
3534 Johnson Avenue, Riverdale 10463
    (616) 543-4270
    Fax: (616) 543-7545
Supervision: Vaad Harabonim of Riverdale
Glatt kosher. Grill, deli and Middle-Eastern cuisine.
Take-out and catering.

BROOKLYN

HOTELS

Avenue Plaza Hotel
4624 13th Avenue 11219   (616) 552-3200
    Fax: (616) 552-3276
    Email: info@theavenueplaza.com
    Web site: www.theavenueplaza.com

Midwood Suites
1078 East 15 St. 11230   (616) 253-9535
    Fax: (616) 253-3269
    Email: shalom@midwoodsuites.com

Scharf's Ateret of Midwood
1410 East 10th Street 11230   (616) 998-5400
    Fax: (616) 645-8600
    Email: ateretavoth@aol.com
Daily Minyon. Under strict Hashgocha. Cholov
Yisroel/Glatt Kosher

The Crown Palace Hotel
570-600 Crown Street   (616) 604-1777
Glatt kosher.

LIBRARIES

Levi Yitzhak Library
305 Kingston Avenue 11213

MUSEUMS

The Chasidic Art Institute
375 Kingston Avenue

RESTAURANTS

Broadway's J-2 N.Y.C. Pizza
926 3rd Ave.   (616) 768-7437
Dairy
Bella Luna
557 Kings Highway   (616) 376-2999

Bernies Place
1287 Ave. J.   (616) 677-1515
Supervision: Rabbi Gornish

Chapp-u-Ccino
4815 12th Avenue   (616) 633-4377
Supervision: Rabbi Amrom Roth

Fontana Bella
2086 Coney Island Avenue   (616) 627-3904
Supervision: Rabbi Gornish

Gio Caffe
448 Avenue P   (616) 375-5437

Il Cup Caffe
1320 East 19th Street, off Avenue M in Midwood

Milk 'N Honey
5013 - 10 Ave.   (616) 871-4319
    Fax: (616) 871-4297
Supervision: Rabbi Friedlander

Sunflower Café
1223 Kings Highway, cor. E. 13th St.   (616) 336-1340
Supervision: Rabbi Gornish

Tea For Two Café
547 Kings Highway   (616) 998-0020
Supervision: Rabbi Gornish

Wendy's Plate
434 Avenue U   (616) 376-3125
    Fax: (616) 871-4297
Supervision: Rabbi Friedlander

Meat
1st Jerusalem Steak House
533 Kings Highway   (616) 336-5115

47th St. Kosher Restaurant
274 - 47th Street , (off 3rd Ave.)   (616) 492-2000
    Fax: (616) 492-4199

A-Kosher Delight
4600 13th Ave.   (616) 435-8500
    Fax: (616) 435-1669

Bamboo Garden
904 Kings Highway   (616) 375-8501
Supervision: Rabbi Yisroel P. Gornish

Cancun
448 Avenue P.   (616) 375-4916
Supervision: Vaad Harabonim of Flatbush

Chap-A-Nosh Plus
1424 Elm Avenue 11230   (616) 627-0072
    Fax: (616) 645-6336

China Glatt
4413 - 13th Ave   (616) 438-2576

Dougies
4310 18th Ave, Bet. McDonald Ave. & E. 2nd St, Off
Ocean Parkway   (616) 686-8080
Supervision: Udvar Kashruth of America

Essex on Coney
1359 Coney Island Ave   (616) 253-1002
Supervision: Vaad Harabonim of Flatbush

Fuji Hana
512 Av. U   (616) 336-3888
Supervision: Vaad Harabonim of Flatbush

Glatt-a-la-Carte
5502 18th Ave.   (616) 621-3697
Supervision: R'Yechiel Babad

Jerusalem Steak House II
1316 Ave. M   (616) 376-0680

Kaosan
1387 Coney Island Ave.   (616) 252-6969

Kineret Steak House
521 Kings Highway, Bet. E. 2nd - E. 3rd Sts
                                 (616) 336-8888
Supervision: Kehilah Kashruth

McFleishig's
5508 16th Avenue   (616) 435-2779
Supervision: Rabbi Babad, Tartikover

Nathan's Famous
825 Kings Highway, cor. E. 9   (616) 627-5252
Supervision: Kehilah Kashrus

Olympic Pita
1419 Coney Island Avenue, Bet. J & K (616) 258-6222
Supervision: Kehilah Kashrus

Shang-Chai
2189 Flatbush Ave.   (616) 377-6100

Tokyo of Brooklyn
2954 Ave. U., off Nostrand Ave. (616) 891-6221
Supervision: Kehilah Kashrus

Yunkee
1424 Elm Ave, (cor. E. 15th/St & Ave. M)
                                 (616) 627-0072
                        Fax: (616) 645-6336
Supervision: Rabbi Friedlander

SYNAGOGUES
Orthodox
Lubavitch Movement
770 Eastern Parkway 11213   (616) 221-0500
                        Fax: (616) 221-0985

MANHATTAN

There are of course a large number of synagogues
of all kinds in New York.

The major synagogues in Manhattan, and of
possible interest to visitors are the following:

Orthodox
Fifth Avenue Synagogue
5 East 62nd Street, NY, 1002   (212) 838-2122

Kehilath Jeshurun
125 East 85th Street, NY, 10028 (212) 427-1000

Lincoln Square
200 Amsterdam Avenue at 69th Street
NY 10023   (212) 874-6100

Ohab Zedeck
118 West 95th Street, NY 10025   (212) 749-5150

Park East
163 East 67th Street, NY 10021   (212) 737-6900

Sephardi
Shearith Israel
28 West 70th Street, NY 10023   (212) 873-0300

Reform
Central Synagogue
123 East 55th Street, NY 10022   (212) 838-5122

Temple Emanuel-El
1 East 65th Street, NY 10023   (212) 744-1400

Conservative
B'nai Jeshrun
270 West 89th Street, NY 10010   (212) 787-7600

Park Avenue Synagogue
50 East 87th Street, NY 10128   (212) 369-2600
                        Fax: (212) 410-7879

**Visitors wishing to ascertain details of other
synagogues in Manhattan or of synagogues in
outlying areas should contact the appropriate
central authority as detailed below.**

Orthodox
Agudat Israel World Organization
84 William Street, NY 10038   (212) 797-9600
                        Fax: (212) 269-2843

Lubavitch Movement
770 Eastern Parkway,Brooklyn, NY 11213
                                 (718) 221-0500
                        Fax: (718) 221-0985

National Council of Young Israel National Office
3 West 16th Street, NY 10011   (212) 929-1525
                        Fax: (212) 727-9526
                Email: nyci@youngisrael.org
                       www.youngisrael.org

**Union of Orthodox Jewish Congregations of
America**
333 Seventh Avenue, NY 10001   (212) 563-4000
                        Fax: (212) 613-8333

Conservative
United Synagogue of America
155 Fifth Avenue, NY 10010   (212) 533-7800
World Council of Synagogues can be found at the
same location.

Progressive
World Union for Progressive Judaism
838 Fifth Avenue, NY 10021   (212) 650-4090
                        Fax: (212) 650-4090
                Email: 5448032@mcimail.com

Reform
Union of America Hebrew Congregations
838 Fifth Avenue, NY 10021   (212) 650-4085
             Fax: (212) 650-4169

Sephardi
Union of Sephardi Congregations
8 West 70th Street, NY 10023   (212) 873-0300

BAKERIES
H & H / The Excellent Bagel
2239 Broadway 10024   (616) 595-8000
Supervision: Kof-K

BOOKSELLERS
J.Levine Judaica
5 West 30th Street   (616) 695-6888
         Web site: LevineJudaica.Com

EMBASSY
Consul General of Israel
800 Second Avenue 10017   (616) 499-5400
             Fax: (616) 499-5555

LIBRARIES
Butler Library of Colombia University
Broadway at 116th Street 10027
Has some 6,000 Hebrew books and pamphlets, plus 1,000 manuscripts and a Hebrew psalter printed at Cambridge University in 1685 and used by Samuel Johnson at the graduation of the first candidates for bachelor's degrees.

The Jewish Division of the New York Public Library
Fifth Avenue at 42nd Street 10018   (616) 930-0601
             Fax: (616) 642-0141
Has 125,000 volumes of Judaica and Hebraica, along with extensive microfilm and bound files of Jewish publications, one of the finest collections in existence.

MUSEUMS
Center for Jewish History
15 West 16th Street 10011   (616) 294-8301
          Fax: (616) 294-8302
          Email: cjh@cjh.org
         Web site: www.cjh.org
The Center has brought together the following five institutes to create the largest single repository for Jewish history in the Diaspora: American Jewish Historical Society, American Sephardi Federation, Leo Baeck Institute, Yeshiva University Museum and YIVO Institute for Jewish Research. It has over 500,000 volumes and over 100 million documents. A wide variety of exhibitions illustrate the diversity of Jewish art, history and culture. Tours are available and there is a kosher dairy cafe open Monday to Thursday 9.15 am to 4.30 pm and Sunday 11.00 am to 4.30 pm.

Jewish Theological Seminary of America
3080 Broadway at 122nd Street 10027
            (616) 678-8975
        Email: shmintz@jtsa.edu
The Library of the Jewish Theological Seminary is one of the world's premier research libraries of Judaica and Hebraica. More than a thousand years of written history are to be found within the library's 375,000 rare books, 40,000 Genizah fragments and thousands of rare documents and prints. The remarkable treasures represent scholarship in the areas of Bible, liturgy, rabbinics, kabbala, philosophy and history. Throughout the year, exhibitions featuring selected pieces from the collection, showcase the library's treasures. Sundays, 10am to 5pm; Monday through Thursday, 9am to 6pm; Fridays, 9am to 2pm; closed Saturday.

Lower East Side Tenement Museum
90 Orchard Street 10002   (616) 431-0233
            Fax: (616) 431-0402
         Web site: www.tenement.org
Housed in a 1863 structure, the Museum presents and interprets the variety of immigrant experience on Manhattan's Lower East side, "A gateway to America".

The House of Living Judaism
5th Avenue and 65th Street
Frequently shows paintings and ritual objects. Twelve marble pillars symbolise the Twelve Tribes.

The Jewish Museum
1109 Fifth Avenue 10128   (616) 423-3200
This is one of the outstanding museums in the city and a 'must' not just for Jewish visitors but for all interested in art. The permanent display consists of one of the finest collection of Jewish ritual and ceremonial art in the world, along with notable paintings and sculptures.

The Museum of Jewish Heritage
18 First Place, Battery Park City 10004
            (616) 509-6130
         Web site: www.mjhnyc.org
The Museum's core exhibition combines archival material with modern media as a living memorial to the Holocaust.

Theological Seminary of America
Fifth Avenue & 92nd Street 10028
An outstanding museum, with permanent displays of Jewish ritual and ceremonial art, along with notable paintings and sculptures.

ORGANISATIONS
UJA-Federation Resource Line
130 E. 59th Street 10022   (616) 753-2288
            Fax: (616) 888-7538
      Email: resourceline@ujafedny.org
         Web site: www.ujafedny.org

RESTAURANTS

Ben's Kosher Delicatessen
209 West 38th Street (616) 398-2367
Fax: (616) 398-3354
Email: info@bensdeli.net
Web site: www.bensdeli.net
Supervision: Supervised
Hours: 11am to 9.30 pm.

Deniz
400 East 57th 10022 (616) 486-2255

Yeshiva University: Main Center
500 W. 185th Street 10033-3201 (616) 960-5248
Fax: (616) 960-0070

Dairy
American Café
160 Broadway (616) 732-1426

Bagels & Co.
1428 York Ave., cnr. E. 76th St. (616) 717-0505
Supervision: New York Kosher

Broadway's Jerusalem 2
1375 Broadway, at 38th Street 10018 (616) 398-1475
Fax: (616) 212-398-6797
Email: n.y.pies@.com
Supervision: OU
Chalav Yisrael, Prs Yisruel. Home of the N.Y. Flying
Pizza Pies. Visit the 'Jewish Wall of Fame', 7.00 am to
12.00 pm. Saturday nights to 2.00 am.

Café 18
8 East 18th Street, Bet. 5th and Broadway
(616) 620-4182

Cafe 123
2 Park Avenue (616) 685-7117

Cafe Roma Pizzeria
175 W. 90th Street (616) 875-8972

Diamond Dairy Kosher Lunchonette
4 W. 47th Street 10036 (616) 719-2694
On the gallery overlooking the diamond & jewelry
exchange. Hours: Monday to Thursday, 7:30 am to 5
pm; Friday, to 2 pm.

Gusto va Mare
237 E. 53rd St. (616) 583-9300
Supervision: Organised Kashrut

JT Café
226 W. 72 St. (616) 724-2424

Mom's Bagels of NY
240 West 35th Street 10001 (616) 494-0440
Fax: (616) 494-0402
Email: info@momsbagelsnyc.com
Supervision: Kof-K
Chulov Yisruel

My Most Favorite Desert
120 West 45th Street (616) 997-5130
Fax: (616) 997 5046
Supervision: OU
Chalav Yisrael.

Provi, Provi
228 W. 72nd St., Bet. B'way and
West End Ave. (616) 875-9020
Supervision: Organised Kashrut

Va Bene
1589 Second Avenue 10028 (616) 517-4448
Fax: (616) 517-2258
Supervision: OU
Chalav Yisrael Italian restaurant.

Vegetable Garden
48 East 41st St., (Bet. Mad & Park) (616) 883-7668

Village Crown Italian
94 Third Avenue 10003 (616) 777-8816
Fax: (616) 388-9639
Email: info@villagecrown.com
Web site: www.villagecrown.com
Supervision: Kof-K/Cholev Israel

Kosher Vegetarian
Great American Health Bar
35 W. 57th Street (616) 355-5177
Web site: www.57thstreetkosher.com

Meat
A-Kosher Delight
1359 Broadway (616) 563-3366
Fax: (616) 268-9352

Abigael's Grill and Caterers
9 East 37th Street 10016 (616) 725-0130
Fax: (616) 725-3577
Supervision: Kof-K
Glatt kosher.

Abigael's on Broadway
1407 Broadway, at 39th Street 10016 (616) 575-1407
Fax: (616) 866-0666
Supervision: Kof-K
Glatt kosher. Lunch Monday-Friday 12pm-3pm.
Dinner Sun-Thursday 5pm-10pm.

Cafe Classico
35 West 57th Street (616) 355-5411
Email: www.57thstreetkosher.com
Glatt kosher.

Colbeh
43 West 39 St, (Mid Town) (616) 354-8181

Deli Kasbah
2553 Amsterdam Avenue (616) 568-4600

Domani Ristorante
1590 First Ave., Bet. 82nd-83rd St.
(616) 717-7575/7557
Supervision: Organised Kashrut

Dougies
222 West 72nd (616) 724-2222
Fax: (616) 724-3421
Web site: www.Dougiesbbq.com

Eden Wok
127 W. 72 Street 10023 (616) 787-8700
Fax: (616) 787-9801
Supervision: OU

Essex on Coney Downtown
17 Trinity Place   (616) 809-3000

Estihana
221 W. 79 St.   (616) 501-0393
                            Fax: (616) 501-0458
                    Web site: www.estihana.com
Japanese cuisine, glatt kosher

Glatt Dynasty
1049 Second Avenue, East 55th &
East 56th Street 10022   (616) 888-9119
                            Fax: (616) 888-9163
Supervision: Kof-K
Glatt kosher.

Haikara
1016 2nd Avenue 10022   (616) 355-7000
Supervision: OU

Hapisgah Steakhouse
147-25 Union Turnpike, Kew Gardens Hills
                                    (616) 380-4449

Il Patrizio
206 East 63rd St., Bet. 2nd and 3rd Aves
                                    (616) 980-4007
Supervision: OU

Jasmine
11 East 30 Street, between Madison and
5th Avenues   (616) 251-8884
Supervision: Vaad I'Kashrut Badatz Sepharadic
Glatt kosher Persian and Middle Eastern cuisine.
Open Sunday to Friday, for lunch and dinner.

Jerusalem Pita
212 E. 45th Street   (616) 922-0009
                            Fax: (616) 922-0018
Under Rabbinical Supervision

Jewish Theological Seminary Dining Hall
3080 Broadway at 122nd Street 10027
                                    (616) 678-8822
Open September through to July (closed August) for
breakfast and lunch: 7.30am to 10.00am; 11.00am to
2.00pm. Strictly kosher, Shomer Shabbat.

Kasbah Restaurant
251 W. 85th Street   (616) 496-1500
                            Fax: (616) 496-2273
Supervision: Circle K
Hours: Sunday to Thursday, 12 pm to 11 pm.
American and Mediterranean food.

Kosher Delight
1359 Broadway (37th Street)   (616) 563-3366

Kosher Deluxe
10 W. 46th St, (Off 5th Avenue)   (616) 869-6699

Le Marais
150 W. 46th Street 10036   (616) 869-0900
                            Fax: (616) 869-1016
Supervision: Circle K
Glatt kosher. Hours: Sunday to Thursday, 12 pm to 12
am; Friday, to 3 pm; Saturday, October to May, one
hour after sundown to 1 am.

Le Marais 2
15 John St   (616) 285-8585
                            Fax: (616) 791--3280
Supervision: Organised Kashrut

Levana
141 West 69th Street 10023   (616) 877-8457
                            Fax: (616) 595-7522
                    Email: info@levana.com
                    Web site: www.levana.com
Supervision: Orthodox Union
Glatt kosher.

Mendy's
Rockfeller Center, 30 Rockfeller Plaza (616) 262-9600

Mendy's West
208 West 70th Street 10023   (616) 877-6787
Supervision: OU

Mr Broadway
1372 Broadway, (Bet. 37 & 38 St)   (616) 921-2152

Penguin
258 W. 15th St., Bet. 7-8 Ave.   (616) 255-3601
Supervision: Vaad Hakashrus

Pita Express
1470 2nd Avenue (77th Street)   (616) 249-1300
Glatt kosher.

Prime Grill
60 East 49th St.   (616) 692-9292
                            Fax: (616) 883-8752

Second Avenue Delicatessan-Restaurant
156 2nd Avenue, cnr. 10th Street   (616) 677-0606
                            Fax: (616) 477-5327
                Email: 2ndavedeli@quicklink.com
Hours - Sunday-Thursday 7.30am-12.00pm. Friday &
Saturday 7.30am-3.00am.

Shallots
550 Madison Avenue, New York 10022
                                    (616) 833-7800
                    Email: shallotsny.com
In the Sony Plaza Atrium. Between 55th and 56th Sts

Tevere "84"
155 E. 84 St.

Tuscan Grill
228 West 72nd Street, (Bet. Bway & West End)
                                    (616) 875-9020

Village Crown Moroccan
96 Third Avenue 10003   (616) 674-2061
                            Fax: (616) 388-9639
                Email: info@villagecrown.com
                Web site: www.villagecrown.com

Wolf & Lamb Steakhouse
10 E. 48th St., Nr Rockefeller Ctr., Between 5th &
Madison 10017   (616) 317-1950
                            Fax: (616) 317-0159
Supervision: Organised Kashrut

Organic
Caravan of Dreams
405 East 6th Street, Bet. 1st Ave. & Ave. A
(616) 254-1613
Email: angel@caravanofdreams.net
Supervision: Orthodox Rabbinical Supervision

Vegetarian
Maharani Restaurant
156 W. 29 St, (Bet. 6 & 7 Ave.)   (616) 868-0707/2211

Quintessence
566 Amsterdam Ave.
(616) 501-9700 or (646)-654-1823

Saffron (Indian Vegetarian Cuisine)
81 Lexington Avenue 10016   (616) 696-5130
Fax: (616) 696-5146

SYNAGOGUES
Orthodox
Union of Orthodox Jewish Congregations of America
333 Seventh Avenue 10001   (616) 563-4000
Fax: (616) 613-8333

THEATRE
Jewish Repertory Theatre
c/o Midtown YMHA, 344 E. 14th Street
(616) 505-2667; 674-7200

VINEYARD
Kosher
Shapiro's Wine Company
124 Rivington Street   (616) 475-7383
In business since 1899. Providing free tours on telephone call.

QUEENS

Flushing

DELICATESSEN
Meal Mart
72-10 Main Street, Flushing 11367   (718) 261-3300
Fax: (718) 261-3435
Supervision: Vaad Harabonim of Queens
Catering and take out.

RESTAURANTS
Meat
Cho-Sen Garden
64-43 108th Street, Forest Hills 11375
(718) 275-1300
Supervision: Vaad Harabonim of Queens
Chinese food.

Colbeh
68-34 Main Street, Flushing   (718) 268-8181
Supervision: Kof-K

Pita House
98-102 Queens Blvd, Bet. 66-67th Ave.
(718) 897-4829
Supervision: Rabbi David Katz

Pizzerias
Dan Carmel Ice Cream and Pizza
98 Queens Blvd, Forest Hills 11375   (718) 544-8530
Supervision: Vaad Harabonim of Queens

Vegetarian
Budda Bodai
42-96 Main Street, Flushing   (718) 939-1188
Supervision: Rabbi Mayer Steinberg

Forest Hills

DELICATESSEN
Berso Foods
64-20 108th Street, Forest Hills 11375
(718) 275-9793
Supervision: Vaad Harabonim of Queens
Take-out only.

RESTAURANTS
Meat
Da Mikelle II
102-39 Queens Blvd   (718) 997-6166

Dougie's
73-27 Main Street, Kew Gardens Hills   (718) 793-4600
Fax: (718) 793-9003
Supervision: Vaad Harabonim of Queens

Glatt Kosher International Restaurant
JFK Airport, Terminal 4, 3rd floor   (718) 751-4787
Email: erwin7@nyc.rr.com
Supervision: Vaad Harabonim of Queens

La France
111-08 Queens Blvd   (718) 520-6488

Hillcrest

BUTCHERS
Herskowitz Glatt Meat Market
164-08 69th Avenue, Hillcrest 11365   (718) 591-0750
Fax: (718) 591-0750
Supervision: Vaad Harabonim of Queens

RESTAURANTS
Dairy
Habustan Mediterranean Cuisine
188-202 Union Turnpike, Jamaica Estate

Jamaica

RESTAURANTS
Meat
Glatt Wok Express
190-11 Union Turnpike, Flushing 11366
(718) 740-1675
Supervision: Vaad Harabonim of Queens
Chinese food. Take-away service available.

Kew Garden Hills

RESTAURANTS
Dairy
Kosher Corner Dairy
73-01 Main Street   (718) 263-1177

Meat
Burger Nosh
69-48 Main Street   (718) 520-1933

Hapisgah Steakhouse
147-25 Union Turnpike   (718) 380-4449

Little Neck

RESTAURANTS
Dairy
Zen Pavillion
251-15 Northern Blvd   (718) 281-1500

Rego Park

RESTAURANTS
Ben's Best Deli Restaurant
96-40 Queens Blvd, Rego Park 11374 (718) 897-1700
                        Fax: (718) 997-6503
          Email: bensbest@worldnet.att.net

STATEN ISLAND

KASHRUT INFORMATION
Directories
Organised Kashrus Laboratories
PO Box 218, Brooklyn   (616) 851-6428
Including the Circle K trademark.

Niagara Falls

COMMUNITY ORGANISATIONS
Jewish Federation of Niagara Falls
c/o of Beth Israel   (716) 284-4575

SYNAGOGUES
Conservative
Beth Israel
College & Madison Avenues 14305   (716) 285-9894

Reform
Beth El
720 Ashland Avenue 14301   (716) 282-2717
Call for time of services.

Poughkeepsie

COMMUNITY ORGANISATIONS
Jewish Community Center of Dutchess County
110 Grand Avenue 12603   (845) 471-0430

SYNAGOGUES
Conservative
Temple Beth El
118 Grand Avenue 12603   (845) 454-0570
                        Fax: (845) 454-7257
          Web site: www.uscj.org/empire/poughktb

Orthodox
Shomre Israel
18 Park Avenue 12603   (845) 454-2890

Reform
Vassar Temple
140 Hooker Avenue 12601   (845) 454-2570

Rochester

BAKERIES
Brighton Donuts
Monroe Avenue   (716) 271-6940

COMMUNITY ORGANISATIONS
Jewish Community Federation
441 E. Avenue 14607   (716) 461-0490

DELICATESSEN
Brownstein's Deli and Bakery
1862 Monroe Avenue 14618

Fox's Kosher Restaurant and Deli
3450 Winton Place 14623

MEDIA
Newspaper
Jewish Ledger
2525 Brighton-Henrietta Town Line R 14623

RESTAURANTS
Meat
Jewish Home of Rochester Cafeteria
2021 S. Winton Road 14618

SYNAGOGUES
Conservative
Temple Beth Hamedrash-Beth Israel
1369 East Avenue 14610   (716) 244-2060

Orthodox
Congregation Beth Sholom
1161 Monroe Avenue 14620   (716) 473-1625

ROCKLAND COUNTY

Haverstraw

SYNAGOGUES
Orthodox
Congregation Sons of Jacob
37 Clove Avenue 10927   (845) 429-4644

Monsey

BAKERIES
Bubba's Bagels
Wesley Hills Plaza, Wesley Hills 10952(845) 362-1019
Fax: (845) 362-0549
Supervision: Va'ad Harabonim of Greater Monsey

DELICATESSEN
Sammy's Bagels
421 Route 59 10952   (845) 356-3030

RESTAURANTS
Dairy
Al di La
455 Route 306, Wesley Hills 10952   (845) 354-2672
Supervision: Va'ad Harabonim of Greater Monsey
Italian/Dairy. Cholov Yisrael.

Chai Pizza
94 Route 59 10952   (845) 356-2135

Jerusalem Pizza & Restaurant
190 Route 59 10952   (845) 426-1500

Kol Tov Pizza
118 Rte 59   (845) 356-5455

Meat
Fleigals Restaurant
43 Route 59 10952   (845) 352-4200
Glatt kosher.

Glat Wok
106 Rte 59   (845) 426-3600

Kyo Sushi and Steak
419 Rte 59   (845) 371-5855

Pulkies
455 Route 306, Wesley Hills 10952   (845) 362-7855
Glatt kosher.

SYNAGOGUES
Orthodox
Young Israel of Monsey and Wesley Hills Inc
58 Parker Blvd 10952   (845) 362-1838

New City

DELICATESSEN
Steve's Deli-Bake
179 South Main Street 10956   (845) 634-8749

GROCERIES
M&S Kosher Meats
191a South Main Street 10956   (845) 638-9494

SYNAGOGUES
Conservative
New City Jewish Center
47 Old Schoolhouse Road 10956   (845) 634-3619
Fax: (845) 634-3481
Email: ncjc@j51.com
Web site: www.uscj.org/metny/newcity/index.html

Reform
Temple Beth Sholom
228 New Hempstead Road 10956   (845) 638-0770
Fax: (845) 638-1696
Web site: www.tbs-nc.org

Orangeburg

SYNAGOGUES
Conservative
Orangetown Jewish Center
8 Independence Avenue 10962   (845) 359-5920

Spring Valley

DELICATESSEN
GPG Deli
Main Street 10977

HOME HOSPITALITY
Mendel & Margalit Zuber
32 Blauvelt Road, Monsey 10952   (845) 425-6213
The Zuber's write 'Anyone wishing to spend a
Shabbat or Yom Tov with us is more than welcome.
We are Lubavitch Chasidim, glatt kosher.'

RESTAURANTS
Eli's Bagel Shop
58 N. Myrtle Avenue 10977   (845) 425-6166
Hours: Sunday - Thursday 6.30am-5.00pm. Friday
6.30am-2.00pm. Open Motzei Shabbos from after
Succos until Pesach. Catering and Platters for all
occasions. Under the Hashgocha of Rabbi B.
Gruber/Yoshen.

Mehadrin Restaurant
82 Route 59, Monsey 10952

Dairy
Sheli's Café and Pizza
126 Maple Avenue 10977   (845) 426-0105
Fax: (845) 362-5004
Email: shely@ucs.net
Supervision: Rabbi Breslaver

SYNAGOGUES
Orthodox
Young Israel of Spring Valley
23 Union Road 10977   (845) 356-3363

Suffern

SYNAGOGUES
Orthodox
Bais Torah
89 West Carlton Road 10901   (845) 352-1343
Fax: (845) 352-0841
Email: yhaber@ou.org

Saratoga Springs

SYNAGOGUES
Conservative
Shaare Tefilah
84 Weibel Avenue 12866   (518) 584-2370
Orthodox
Congregation Mikveh Israel
26 Lafayette Street 12866   (518) 584-6338
Services in July & August. Kosher food available.

Orthodox Minyan
510 1/2 Broadway 12866   (518) 437-1738

Schenectady

SYNAGOGUES
Conservative
Agudat Achim
2117 Union Street 12309   (518) 393-9211
Orthodox
Beth Israel
2195 Eastern Parkway 12309   (518) 377-3700
Reform
Gates of Heaven
852 Ashmore Avenue 12309   (518) 374-8173

Syracuse

SYNAGOGUES
Orthodox
Young Israel Shaarei Torah of Syracuse
4313 E. Genesee Street 13214   (315) 446-6194
    Fax: (315) 446-7936

Troy

MIKVAOT
Troy Chabad Center
2306 15th Street 12180   (518) 274-5572

SYNAGOGUES
Conservative
Temple Beth El
411 Hoosick Street 12180   (518) 272-6113
Reform
Congregation Berith Shalom
167 3rd Street 12180   (518) 272-8872
    Fax: (518) 272-8984

Utica

COMMUNITY ORGANISATIONS
Jewish Community Federation of the Mohawk Valley
2310 Oneida Street, Utica, NY 13501 (315) 733-2343
    Fax: (315) 733-2346
    Email: jcci@borg.com
The Federation supports the Jewish Community Center.

SYNAGOGUES
Conservative
Temple Beth El
1607 Genesee Street 13501   (315) 724-4751
Orthodox
Congregation Zvi Jacob
112 Memorial Parkway 13501   (315) 724-8357
Reform
Temple Emanu-El
2710 Genesee Street 13502   (315) 724-4177

Vestal

COMMUNITY ORGANISATIONS
Jewish Federation of Broome County
500 Clubhouse Road 13850   (607) 724-2332
    Fax: (607) 724-2311

MEDIA
Newspaper
The Reporter
500 Clubhouse Road 13850   (607) 724-2360
    Fax: (607) 724-2311
    Email: treporter@aol.com

WESTCHESTER COUNTY

Harrison

SYNAGOGUES
Orthodox
Young Israel of Harrison
207 Union Avenue 10528   (914) 777-1236

Mount Vernon

SYNAGOGUES
Orthodox
Brothers of Israel
116 Crary Avenue 10550   (914) 667-1302
    Fax: (914) 667-0278

Fleetwood
11 East Broad Street 10552   (914) 664-5581
    Fax: (914) 699-6954
    Email: rabbi@fleetwoodsynagogue.org
    Web site: www.fleetwoodsynagogue.org

New Rochelle

RESTAURANTS
Eden Wok
1327 North Avenue 10804   (914) 637-9363
    Fax: (914) 637-9371
Supervision: Vaad of Westchester

SYNAGOGUES
Conservative
Bethel
Northfield Road

Orthodox
Cong. Anshe Sholom
50 North Avenue, New Rochelle, NY 10805
(914) 632-9220
Fax: (914) 632-8182
Email: asnewroch@aol.com
Young Israel of New Rochelle
1228 North Avenue 10804 (914) 777-1236
Contact Rabbi on 835-5581

Reform
Temple Israel
1000 Pine Brook Blvd. 10804

Peekskill

SYNAGOGUES
Conservative
First Hebrew Congregation
1821 E. Main Street 10566 (914) 739-0500
Fax: (914) 739-0684

Port Chester

RESTAURANTS
Vegetarian
Green Symphony
427 Boston Post Road 10573 (914) 937-6537

Vegetarian Kosher
427 Boston Post Road (914) 937-6537

SYNAGOGUES
Conservative
Kneses Tifereth Israel
575 King Street 10573 (914) 939-1004
Fax: (914) 939-1086

Scarsdale

SYNAGOGUES
Orthodox
Young Israel of Scarsdale
1313 Weaver Street 10583 (914) 636-8686
Fax: (914) 636-1209

Orthodox Sephardi
Magen David Sephardic Congregation
1225 Weaver Street, P O B 129H 10583
(914) 633-3728
Fax: (914) 636-0608
Email: mitchser@aol.com

White Plains

SYNAGOGUES
Conservative
Temple Israel Center
280 Old Mamaroneck Road, at Miles Avenue
10605 (914) 948-2800
Fax: (914) 948-4755

Orthodox
Hebrew Institute of White Plains
20 Greenridge Avenue 10605 (914) 948-3095
Fax: (914) 949-4676
Email: hebinst@idt.com
Young Israel of White Plains
135 Old Mamaroneck Road, NY 10605
(914) 683-YIWP
Email: yiwp.org
Web site: www.yiwp.org

Reconstructionist
Bet Am Shalom
295 Soundview Avenue 10606 (914) 946-8851
Reform
Jewish Community Center
252 Soundview Avenue 10606 (914) 949-4717

Yonkers

SYNAGOGUES
Conservative
Agudas Achim
21 Hudson Street 10701

Lincoln Park Center
323 Central Park Avenue 10704 (914) 965-7119

Orthodox
Rosh Pinah
Riverdale Avenue 10705

Reform
Temple Emanu-El
306 Rumsey Road 10705 (914) 963-0575

West Point

SYNAGOGUES
United States Military Academy Jewish Chapel
Building 750 10096 (845) 938-2766
Fax: (845) 446-7706
With a local community of over 200 the Chapel was designed by the firm responsible for the United Nations building and the Lincoln Center.

NORTH CAROLINA

Asheville

SYNAGOGUES
Conservative
Congregation Beth Israel
229 Murdock Avenue 28804   (704) 252-8431
Fax: (704) 252-3882
Email: bethisrael@buncombe.main.nc.us

Reform
Beth Ha-Tephila
43 N. Liberty Street 28801   (704) 253-4911
Email: tephila@worldnet.att.net

Charlotte

COMMUNITY ORGANISATIONS
Jewish Federation
5007 Providence Road 28226   (704) 366-5007

DELICATESSEN
The Kosher Mart & Delicatessen
Amity Gardens Shopping Center, 3840 E.
Independence Blvd 28205   (704) 563-8288
Fax: (704) 532-9111
Email: koshermartusa@mindspring.com
Web site: www.koshermartusa.com
Sandwiches and deli department are glatt kosher.
Groceries also sold here. Hours: Monday to
Wednesday, 10 am to 6 pm; Thursday, to 7 pm; Friday
to 3 pm; Sunday, to 3:30 pm; Shabbat, closed.

LIBRARIES
Speizman Jewish Library
5007 Providence Road 28226

MEDIA
Newspaper
Charlotte Jewish News
     (704) 366-5007

MIKVAOT
Chabad House
6619 Sardis Road 28270   (704) 366-3984
Fax: (704) 362-1423

SYNAGOGUES
Conservative
Temple Israel
4901 Providence Road   (704) 362-2796
Fax: (704) 362-1098
Email: templeisraelnc.org

Orthodox
Chabad House
6619 Sardis Road 28270   (704) 366-3984
Fax: (704) 362-1423
Email: sardis@earthlink.net

Reform
Temple Beth El
5101 Providence Road 28207   (704) 366-1948

Durham

COMMUNITY ORGANISATIONS
**Durham-Chapel Hill Jewish Federation and
Community Council**
205 Mt. Bolus Road, Chapel Hill 27514
     (919) 967-6916

KASHRUT INFORMATION
Leon Dworsky
1100 Leon Street, Apt. 28 27705

SYNAGOGUES
Conservative
Beth El
1004 Watts Street 27701   (919) 682-1238
Reform
Judea Reform Congregation
1955 Cornwallis Road 27705   (919) 489-7062
Fax: (919) 489-0611
Email: infobox@judeareform.org

Fayetteville

SYNAGOGUES
Conservative
Beth Israel Congregation
2204 Morganton Road 28303   (910) 484-6462

Greensboro

COMMUNITY ORGANISATIONS
Greensboro Jewish Federation
5509 C West Friendly Avenue 27410-4211
     (336) 852-5433
Fax: (336) 852-4346
Email: mfcgsonc@jon.cjfny.org

SYNAGOGUES
Conservative
Beth David
804 Winview Drive 27410   (336) 294-0006
Fax: (336) 294-7011
Email: info@bethdavidsynagogue.org

Hendersonville

SYNAGOGUES
Conservative
Agudas Israel Congregation
328 N. King Street, PO Box 668 28793

Raleigh

COMMUNITY ORGANISATIONS
Wake County Jewish Federation
3900 Merton Drive 27609   (919) 751-5459

GROCERIES
Eshel Kosher Market
5540 Atlantic Springs Road   (919) 872-7757

MIKVAOT
Congregation of Sha'arei Israel
7400 Falls of the Neuse Road 27615   (919) 847-8986

SYNAGOGUES
Conservative
Beth Meyer
504 Newton Road 27615   (919) 848-1420

Orthodox
Congregation of Sha'arei Israel - Lubavitch
7400 Falls of the Neuse Road 27615   (919) 847-8986
                                Fax: (919) 847-3142

Reform
Temple Beth Or
5315 Creedmoor Road 27612   (919) 781-4895
Pre-school.

Wilmington

SYNAGOGUES
Conservative
Beth Jacob
1833 Academy Street 27101

Reform
Temple Emanuel
201 Oakwood Drive 27103   (302) 722-6640

NORTH DAKOTA

Bismark

SYNAGOGUES
Reform
Bismark Hebrew Congregation
703 North Fifth Street 58103   (701) 258-3572

Fargo

SYNAGOGUES
Orthodox
Fargo Hebrew Congregation
901 S. 9th Street 58103   (701) 237-5629

Reform
Temple Beth El
809 11th Avenue S. 58103   (701) 232-0441

OHIO

Akron

COMMUNITY ORGANISATIONS
Jewish Community Board of Akron
750 White Pond Drive 44320   (330) 869-2424
                                Fax: (330) 867-8498
                        Web site: www.jewishakron.org

MIKVAOT
                                (330) 867-6798

SYNAGOGUES
Conservative
Beth El
464 S. Hawkins Avenue 44320   (330) 864-2105

Orthodox
Anshe Sfard Synagogue
646 N.Revere Road 44333   (330) 867-7292
                                Fax: (330) 867-7719

Reform
Temple Israel
133 Merriman Road 44303   (330) 762-8617
                                Fax: (330) 762-8619
                        Email: rabbi@neo.rr.com

Canton

COMMUNITY ORGANISATIONS
Jewish Community Federation
2631 Harvard Avenue 44709   (330) 452-6444

SYNAGOGUES
Conservative
Shaaray Torah
423 30th Street N.W. 44709   (330) 492-0310

Orthodox
Agudas Achim
2508 Market Street N. 44704   (330) 456-8781

Reform
Temple Israel
333 25th Street N.W. 44709   (330) 455-5197

Cincinnati

BAKERIES
Just Desserts
6964 Plainfield Road 45236   (513) 793-6627

COMMUNITY ORGANISATIONS
Community Center
1580 Summit Road 45237   (513) 761-7500
Fax: (513) 761-0084

Jewish Federation
1811 Losantiville, Suite 320 45237   (513) 351-3800

DELICATESSEN
Bilkers
7648 Reading Road 45237

GROCERIES
Pilder's Kosher Foods
7601 Reading Road 45237

LIBRARIES
The Hebrew Union College-Jewish Institute of Religion
3101 Clifton Avenue 45220   (513) 221-1875
Fax: (513) 221-0519
Email: klau@cn.huc.edu
One of the largest Jewish libraries in the world. It is also has an art gallery of artefacts, and houses a collection Jewish 'objets d'art' and religious and ceremonial appurtenances as well as rare books and manuscripts.

MEDIA
Newspaper
American Israelite
906 Main Street 45202
Oldest Anglo-Jewish weekly in the US.

MIKVAOT
Kehelath B'nai Israel
1546 Beaverton Avenue 45237   (513) 761-5260

RESTAURANTS
Dairy
Dunkin' Donuts
9385 Colerain Avenue 45231   (513) 385-0930

Meat
Pilder's Deli
4070 East Galbraith Road 45236   (513) 792-9961
Fax: (513) 792-9605

SYNAGOGUES
Conservative
Northern Hills Synagogue - Congregation B'nai Avraham
715 Fleming Road 45231   (513) 931-6038
Fax: (513) 931-6147
Email: berniceu@fuse.net
Web site: www.nhs-cba.org

Orthodox
Downtown Synagogue
Bartlett Building, 36 E. Fourth, 7th Floor 45202
(513) 241-3576

Golf Manor Synagogue
6442 Stover Avenue 45237   (513) 531-6654

Sephardic Beth Shalom
Manss Avenue, PO Box 37431 45222 (513) 793-6936

Reform
Isaac M. Wise Temple
8329 Ridge Road 45236   (513) 793-2556

Cleveland

BAKERIES
Breadsmith
9708 Kenwood Road, Blue Ash 45242   (216) 791-8817

BUTCHERS
Tibor's Glatt Meat Market
2185 S. Green Road, S. Euclid 44121   (216) 381-7615
Fax: (216) 381-5215

COMMUNITY ORGANISATIONS
Jewish Community Federation of Cleveland
1750 Euclid Avenue 44115   (216) 566-9200
Fax: (216) 861-1230
Email: info@jcfcleve.org
Web site: www.jewishcleveland.org
With literally dozens of synagogues of each demonination, it is advisable to contact the local religious organisation for specific details.

DELICATESSEN
Unger's Kosher Market and Bakery
1831 S. Taylor Road, Cleveland Heights 44118
(216) 321-7176
Fax: (216) 321-0777

LIBRARIES
The Temple Museum of Religious Art Library.
University Circle, Silver Park 44106
Houses the Abba Hillel Silver Archives. (Jewish art objects, religious & ceremonial treasures, rare books and manuscripts.)

MEDIA
Newspaper
Cleveland Jewish News
3645 Warrensville Center Road, Suite 230 44122

MIKVAOT
Cleveland Heights   (216) 387-1040
Charlotte Goldberg Community Mkvah of the Park Synagogue
3300 Mayfield Road, Cleveland Heights 44118
(216) 371-2244 ext 198
Fax: (216) 321-0639

K'hal Yereim Synagogue
1771 S. Taylor Road, Cleveland Heights 44118
(216) 321-5855

MUSEUM
Park Synagogue
3300 Mayfield Road 44118
Holding a collection of Jewish art and sculpture.

RESTAURANTS
Dairy
Issi's Place
14100 Cedar Road, Waterstone Medical Bldg.,
University Heights 44121   (216) 291-4251

Marx Hot Bagels
9701 Kenwood Road, Blue Ash 45242 (216) 891-5542
Fax: (216) 891-1063

Meat
Abba's Market and Grille
13937 Cedar Road, S. Euclid 44121   (216) 321-5660
Fax: (216) 321-4135

Contempo Cuisine
13898 Cedar Road, University Heights 44118
(216) 397-3520
Fax: (216) 397-3523

Empire Kosher Kitchen
2234 Warrensville Center Road,
University Heights   (216) 691-0006

Ruchama's Singapore
2172 Warrensville Center Road,
University Heights 44118   (216) 321-1100
Fax: (216) 321-1485

SYNAGOGUES
Orthodox
Congregation Shomre Shabbos
1801 S. Taylor Road, Cleveland Heights 44118
(216) 371-0033

K'hai Yereim
1771 S. Taylor Road, Cleveland Heights 44118
(216) 321-6855

Young Israel of Beachwood
2463 South Green Road 44122   (216) 691-9007

Columbus

RESTAURANTS
Dairy
Sammy's New York Bagels
40 N. James Road 43213   (614) 237-2444
Fax: (614) 235-4177
Supervision: Vaad Ho-ir of Columbus
Deli as well.

SYNAGOGUES
Orthodox
Agudas Achim Synagogue
2767 E. Broad Street 43209   (614) 237-2747

Congregation Ahavas Sholom
2568 E. Broad Street 43209   (614) 252-4815
Fax: (614) 252-1316
Email: ahavas@beol.net
Web site: www.ahavas-sholom.org
Nusach sefard; daily and Shabbat minyan.

Dayton

BAKERIES
Rinaldo's Bakery
910 West Fairview Avenue 45406   (937) 274-1311
Supervision: Rabbi Hillel Fox, Beth Jacob
Congregation.
Certain products only, please ask for certificate.

COMMUNITY ORGANISATIONS
Jewish Federation of Greater Dayton
4501 Denlinger Road 45426   (937) 854-4150

HOME HOSPITALITY
Shomrei Emunah
1706 Salem Avenue 45406   (937) 274-6941
Fax: (937) 274-7511
Email: shomrei@earthlink.net
Please contact to arrange for accommodations.

MEDIA
Newspapers
Dayton Jewish Observer
4501 Denlinger Road 45426   (937) 854-4150
Fax: (937) 854-2850
Email: dayjobs@aol.com

The Dayton Jewish Advocate
(937) 854-4150 ext. 118
Published by the Jewish Federation of Greater
Dayton by Marshall Weiss, editor.

MIKVAOT
556 Kenwood Avenue 45406   (937) 275-1436

SYNAGOGUES
Orthodox
Beth Jacob Congregation
7020 North Main Street 45415   (937) 274-2149
Fax: (937) 274-9556
Email: bethjacob1@aol.com
Web site: www.bethjacobcong.org
Supervision: Rabbi Hillel Fox, Beth Jacob
Congregation

Shomrei Emunah/Young Israel of Dayton
1706 Salem Avenue 45406   (937) 274-6941
                            Fax: (937) 274-6941
Rabbi's study: (937)-277-4626. Shachris daily:
6:45am. Sundays and National holidays 8:30am.
Shabbos and Yom Tov 9:15am. Mincha and Maariv at
sunset, call for details.

Lorain

SYNAGOGUES
Conservative
Agudath B'nai Israel
1715 Meister Road 44053   (216) 282-3307

Toledo

SYNAGOGUES
Conservative
B'nai Israel
2727 Kenwood Blvd. 43606   (419) 531-1677

Orthodox
Congregation Etz Chayim
3852 Woodley Road 43606   (419) 473-2401

Reform
The Temple-Congregation Shomer Emunium
6453 Sylvania Avenue 43560   (419) 883-3341

Youngstown

COMMUNITY ORGANISATIONS
Youngstown Area Jewish Federation
505 Gypsy Lane 44501   (330) 746-3251

MIKVAOT
Children of Israel
3970 1/2 Logan Way 44505   (330) 759-2167

SYNAGOGUES
Conservative
Beth Israel Temple Center
2138 E. Market Street, Warren 44483-6104
                                 (330) 395-3877
                            Fax: (330) 394-5918
                  Email: bethisrael1@juno.com

Ohev Tzedek-Shaarei Torah
5245 Glenwood Avenue 44512   (330) 758-2321

Temple El Emeth
3970 Logan Way 44505   (330) 759-1429

Reform
Rodef Sholom
Elm Street & Woodbine Avenue 44505
                                 (330) 744-5001

OKLAHOMA

Oklahoma City

BAKERIES
Ingrid's Kitchen
2309 N.W. 36th Street 73112

COMMUNITY ORGANISATIONS
Jewish Federation of Greater Oklahoma City
3022 N.W. Expressway, Suite 116 73112
                                 (405) 949-0111

KASHRUT INFORMATION
Chabad House
6401 Lenox Avenue, Oklahoma City 73116
                                 (405) 810-1770
                            Fax: (405) 810-1772

SYNAGOGUES
Conservative
Emanuel Synagogue
900 N.W. 47th Street 73106   (405) 528-2113

Reform
Temple B'nai Israel
4901 N. Pennsylvania Avenue 73112 (405) 848-0965

Tulsa

COMMUNITY ORGANISATIONS
Jewish Federation
2021 E. 71st Street 74136   (918) 495-1100
                            Fax: (918) 495-1220
                  Email: federation@jewishtulsa.org

KASHRUT INFORMATION
Chabad House
6622 S. Utica Avenue 74136
                         (918) 492-4499; 493-7006
                            Fax: (918) 492-4499
Hospitality for travellers. Services: Shabbat and
Sunday 9:00 am and by arrangement (Kaddish,
Yarziet, etc.).

MEDIA
Newspaper
Tulsa Jewish Review
2021 E. 71st Street 74136   (918) 495-1100

MIKVAOT
Congregation B'nai Emunah
1719 S. Owasso 74120   (918) 583-7121
                            Fax: (918) 747-9696
              Email: thenicepeople@tulsagogue.com
                    Web site: www.tulsagogue.com
Open 8.00 am to 6.00 pm daily.

Mikva Shoshana - Chabad
6622 So. Utica Avenue 74136   (918) 493-7006
Ask for Etel Weg

MUSEUM
The Sherwin Miller Museum of Jewish Art
Box 52188 74152   (918) 294-1366
                                Fax: (918) 294-8338
                    Email: jewishmuseum@webzone.net
Largest Judaica collection in the Southwest.

RESTAURANTS
Congregation B'nai Emunah
1719 S. Owasso 74120   (918) 583-7121
                                Fax: (918) 747-9696
                    Email: thesynagogue@bnaiemunah.com
Open 8.00am to 6.00pm daily.

SYNAGOGUES
Conservative
1719 S. Owasso 74120   (918) 583-7121
                                Fax: (918) 747-9696
                    Email: thesynagogue@bnaiemunah.com
Orthodox
Chabad House
6622 S Utica Avenue 74136
                            (918) 492-4499; 493-7006
                                Fax: (918) 492-4499
Services: Shabbat and Sunday 9.00 am and by
arrangement (Kaddish, Yarziet, etc.).

Reform
Temple Israel
2004 E. 22nd Place 74114   (918) 747-1309
                                Fax: (918) 747-3564
                       Email: templeis@ionet.net

OREGON

Ashland

SYNAGOGUES
Reform
**Temple Emek Shalom-Rogue Valley Jewish
Community**
1081 East Main St   (541) 488-2909
                                Fax: (541) 488-2814
                    Email: TEShalom@emekshalom.org
                    Web site: www.emekshalom.org
Office hours 10.00am-3.00pm Monday-Friday.
Mailing address: PO Box 1107, Ashland, Oregon
97520. Call for schedule of services.

Eugene

SYNAGOGUES
Conservative
Temple Beth Israel
42 W. 25th Avenue 97405   (541) 485-7218

Portland

COMMUNITY ORGANISATIONS
Jewish Federation of Portland
6680 S.W. Capitol Highway 97219   (503) 245-6219
                                Fax: (503) 245-6603
                    Email: federation@jewishportland.org
                    Web site: www.jewishportland.org

GROCERIES
Albertson's
5415 SW Beaverton Hillsdale Highway 97221
                                     (503) 246-1713

MIKVAOT
Ritualarium
1425 S.W. Harrison Street 97219   (503) 224-3409

MUSEUM
Oregon Jewish Museum
310 NW Davis Street 97209   (503) 226-3600
                                Fax: (503) 226-1800
The museum was founded in 1989 by a volunteer
group committed to providing Oregon with a
museum dedicated to Jewish art and history.

RESTAURANTS
**Mittleman Jewish Community Center
(Kosher restaurant)**
6651 S. W. Capitol Highway 97219   (503) 244-0111

SYNAGOGUES
Orthodox
Ahavath Achim
3225 S.W. Barbur Blvd 97201   (503) 775-5895

Kesser Israel
136 S.W. Meade Street 97201   (503) 222-1239

Shaare Torah
920 N.W. 25th Avenue 97210   (503) 226-6131
                                Fax: (503) 226-0241
                    Email: info@shaarietorah.org
                    Web site: www.shaarietorah.org
Reform
Neveh Shalom Synagogue
2900 SW Peaceful Lane 97239   (503) 246-8831
                                Fax: (503) 246-7553
                    Email: frothstein@nevehshalom.org
                    Web site: www.nevehshalom.org

Temple Beth Israel
1972 NW Flanders 97209   (503) 222-1069

Salem

SYNAGOGUES
Reconstructionist
Beth Shalom
1795 Broadway NE 97303   (503) 362-5004

Temple Beth Shalom
1795 Broadway, NE 97303   (503) 362-5004

PENNSYLVANIA

Allentown

COMMUNITY ORGANISATIONS
Jewish Federation
702 22nd Street 18104   (610) 821-5500

MIKVAOT
1834 Whitehall Street 18104   (610) 776-7948

RESTAURANTS
Meat
Glatt Kosher Community Center
702 N. 22nd Street 18104   (610) 435-3571
Since opening hours vary according to season, it is
advisable to call before visiting.

SYNAGOGUES
Conservative
Temple Beth El
1702 Hamilton Street 18104   (610) 435-3521

Orthodox
Congregation Agudas Achim
625 North Second Street 18102   (610) 432-4414

Congregation Sons of Israel
2715 Tilghman Street 18104   (610) 433-6089
Fax: (610) 433-6080
Email: rabbi@att.net
Web site: www.sonsofisrael.net

Reform
Congregation Keneseth Israel
2227 Chew Street 18104   (610) 435-9074
Email: congki@enter.net

Bensalem

MIKVAOT
Bucks County Mikveh
2454 Bristol Road 19020   (215) 891-5565

Bethlehem

SYNAGOGUES
Conservative
Congregation Brith Sholom
Macada & Jacksonville Roads 18017   (610) 866-8009

Orthodox
Agudath Achim
1555 Linwood Street 18017   (610) 866-8891
Contact person: Gerald Wekberger. 1-610-838-0767.

Easton

SYNAGOGUES
Conservative
B'nai Abraham
16th & Bushkill Streets 18042   (610) 258-5343
Established 1888.

Reform
Temple Covenant of Peace
1451 Northampton Street 18042   (610) 253-2031
Fax: (610) 253-7973
Email: tcp@ fast.net
Established 1839.

Elkins park

TOURIST SITE
Beth Sholom
8231 Old York Park 19027   887-1342
Conservative. The only synagogue designed by the
eminent architect Frank Lloyd Wright. Tours are
available.

Erie

COMMUNITY ORGANISATIONS
Jewish Community Council
Suite 405, Professional Building, 161 Peach St.,
16501   (814) 455-4474
Fax: (814) 455-4475

SYNAGOGUES
Conservative
Brith Sholom Jewish Center
3207 State Street 16508   (814) 454-2431
Fax: (814) 452-0790

Reform
Temple Anshe Hesed
930 Liberty Street 16502   (814) 454-2426
Fax: (814) 454-2427
Email: anshhsd@velocity.net

Harrisburg

COMMUNITY ORGANISATIONS
United Jewish Community of Greater Harrisburg
100 Vaughn Street 17110   (717) 236-9555

GROCERIES
Bakeries Giant Food Store and Weis Market
Linglestown Road

Quality Kosher
7th Division Street 17110

KOSHER FOOD
Norman Gras Catering
3000 Green Street 17110-1234   (717) 234-2196
         Fax: (717) 234-3943
         Email: normangras@aol.com
Glatt kosher. Offers catering for groups. Stocks kosher vending machines at the JCC, 3301 N Front St. Tel: 717-236-9555 ext. 3105.

SYNAGOGUES
Conservative
Beth El
2637 N. Front Street 17110   (717) 232-0556
         Fax: (717) 232-6240

Chisuk Emuna
5th & Division Streets 17110   (717) 232-4851
         Fax: (717) 232-7950
         Email: muroff@juno.com

Orthodox
Kesher Israel
2945 N. Front Street 17110   (717) 238-0763

Reform
Ohev Sholom
2345 N. Front Street 17110   (717) 233-6459
         Fax: (717) 236-7844

Hazelton

SYNAGOGUES
Conservative
Agudas Israel
77 N. Pine Street 18201   (717) 455-2851

Reform
Beth Israel
98 N. Church Street 18201   (717) 455-3971

Hershey

SNACK BAR
Meat
Central PA's Kosher Mart
Hershey Park   (717) 392-1503

Johnstown

COMMUNITY ORGANISATIONS
United Jewish Federation of Johnstown
700 Indiana Street 15905   (814) 536-0647

SYNAGOGUES
Conservative
Beth Sholom Congregation
700 Indiana Street 15905   (814) 536-0647

Lancaster

COMMUNITY ORGANISATIONS
Jewish Federation
2120 Oregon Pike 17601   (717) 597-7354

SYNAGOGUES
Conservative
Beth El
1836 Rohrerstown Road 17601   (717) 581-7891
         Fax: (717) 581-7870
         Email: templebethel@dejazzd.com

Orthodox
Degel Israel
1120 Columbia Avenue 17603   (717) 397-0183
         Fax: (717) 509-6188
         Email: ourkehilla@mail.com

Reform
Temple Shaarei Shomayim
N. Duke & James Streets 17602   (717) 397-5575

McKeesport

SYNAGOGUES
Conservative
Tree of Life-Sfard
Cypress Avenue 15131   (412) 673-0938

Orthodox
Gemilas Chesed
1400 Summit Street, White Oak 15131
         (412) 678-9859

Reform
B'nai Israel
536 Shaw Avenue 15132   (412) 678-6181
         Fax: (412) 678-6908
         Email: tbi536@juno.com or tbi536@aol.com

Philadelphia

BAKERIES
Arthur's Bakery
Academy Plaza, Red Lion and Academy Roads
19114   (215) 637-9146
Supervision: Rabbinical Assembly

Best Cake Bakery
7594 Haverford Avenue 19151 (215) 878-1127
Email: rugalach@aol.com
Supervision: Orthodox Vaad of Philadelphia
Closed Shabbat and holidays. Intersection Route 1
and Haverford Avenue (close to Route 3).

Buy the Dozen
219 Haverford Avenue, Narberth 19072
(215) 667-9440
Supervision: Orthodox Vaad of Philadelphia
Wholesale croissant bakery open to the public.

Dante's Bakery
Richboro Centre, Bustleton and
Second Street Pikes, Richboro 18954 (215) 357-9599
Supervision: Rabbinical Assembly

Hesh's Eclair Bake Shoppe
7721 Castor Avenue 19152 (215) 742-8575
Supervision: Vaad Hakashruth
Closed on Shabbat.

Hutchinson's Classic Bakery
13023 Bustleton Pike 19116 (215) 676-8612
Supervision: Rabbinical Assembly

Kaplan's New Model Bakery
901 North 3rd Street 19123 (215) 627-5288
Supervision: Rabbi Solomon Isaacson

Lipkin and Sons Bakery
8013 Castor Avenue 19152 (215) 342-3005
Supervision: Rabbi Abraham Novitsky

Michael's
6635 Castor Avenue 19149 (215) 745-1423
Supervision: Rabbi Dov Brisman

Moish's Addison Bakery
10865 Bustleton Avenue 19116 (215) 469-8054
Supervision: Rabbinical Assembly

Rilling's Bakery
2990 Southampton Road 19154 (215) 698-6171
Supervision: Rabbinical Assembly

The Village Baker
2801 South Eagle Road, Newton 18940
(215) 579-1235
Supervision: Rabbinical Assembly

Viking Bakery
39 Cricket Avenue, Ardmore 19003 (215) 642-9227
Supervision: Rabbi Joshua Toledano

Weiss Bakery
6635 Castor Avenue 19149 (215) 722-4506
Supervision: Rabbi Dov Brisman
Closed on Shabbat.

Zach's Bakery
6419 Rising Sun Avenue 19111 (215) 722-1688
Supervision: Rabbinical Assembly

BOOKSELLERS
Gratz College
Old York Road and Melrose Avenue,
Melrose Park 19027 (215) 635-7300
Fax: (215) 635-7320
Email: gratzinfo@aol.com

Jerusalem Israeli Gift Shop
7818 Castor Avenue 19152 (215) 342-1452
Rosenberg Hebrew Book Store
409 Old York Road, Jenkintown 19046
(215) 884-1728; 800-301-8608
Fax: (215) 884-6648
6408 Castor Avenue 19149

BUTCHERS
Aries Kosher Meats
6530 Castor Avenue 19149 (215) 533-3222
Supervision: Vaad Hakashruth

Best Value Kosher Meat Center
8564 Bustleton Avenue 19152 (215) 342-1902
Fax: (215) 342-5775
Supervision: Rabbi Dov Brisman

Bustleton Kosher Meat Market
6834 Bustlton Avenue 19149 (215) 332-0100
Supervision: Rabbi Shalom Novoseller

Glendale Meats
7730 Bustleton Avenue 19152 (215) 725-4100
Supervision: Vaad Hakashruth

Main Line Kosher Meats
75621 Haverford Avenue 19151 (215) 877-3222
Supervision: Vaad Hakashruth

Simons Kosher Meats and Poultry
6926 Bustleton Avenue 19149 (215) 624-5695
Supervision: Vaad Hakashruth

Wallace's Krewstown Kosher Meat Market
8919 Krewstown Road 19115 (215) 464-7800
Supervision: Vaad Hakashruth

CONTACT INFORMATION
Jewish Information and Referral Service
2100 Arch Street, 7th Floor 19103 (215) 832-0821
Fax: (215) 832-0833
Email: lyouman@philafederation.org
A free confidential service that provides answers to
questions about Jewish organisations, institutions,
community services and events as well as various
subjects of Jewish interest in the five-county Greater
Philadelphia area.

EMBASSY
Consul General of Israel
230 South 15th Street 19102 (215) 546-5556
Fax: (215) 545-3986
Email: info.ph@israelfm.org
Web site: www.israelemb.org/pa

GROCERIES
Best Value Kosher Meat Center
8564 Bustleton Avenue 19152 (215) 342-1902
Supervision: Rabbi Dov Brisman

Milk and Honey
7618 Castor Avenue 19152 (215) 342-3224
Supervision: Vaad Hakashruth

HISTORIC SITE

Congregation Beth T'fillah of Overbrook Park
7630 Woodbine Avenue 19151   (215) 477-2415
Fax: (215) 477-2417
Conservative synagogue with a ten-foot high replica
of the Western Wall in its lobby.

Mikveh Israel Cemetery
8th and Spruce Streets 19107   (215) 922-5446
One of the oldest Jewish cemeteries in the United
States, with graves dating from 1740. Interred here
are Haym Solomon, Rebecca Gratz, and twenty-one
veterans of the American Revolution.

The Frank Synagogue
Albert Einstein Medical Center, Old York
and Tabor Roads 19141   (215) 456-7890
Modelled after first- and second-century synagogues
discovered in the Galilee region of north central
Israel, this small, historically certified synagogue was
originally dedicated in 1901

JUDAICA

Bala Judaica Center
222 Bala Avenue, Bala Cynwyd 19004   (215) 664-1303
Fax: (215) 664-4319
Email: jewishwedding@erols.com

KASHRUT INFORMATION

Board of Rabbis of Greater Philadelphia
2100 Arch Street - 3rd Floor 19103   (215) 832-0675
Fax: (215) 832-0689
Email: info@brdavphila.com

Ko Kosher Service
5871 Drexel Road 19131   (215) 696-0408
Fax: (215) 696-9249
Email: ko_kosher_service@msm.com
Web site: www.ko-kosher-service.org

Orthodox Vaad of Philadelphia
7505 Brookhaven Road 19151   (215) 473-0951
Fax: (215) 473-6220
Rabbi Shlomo Caplan (610) 658-1967 Rabbi Aaron
Felder (215) 745-2968 Rabbi Yehoshua Kaganoff
(215) 742-8421

Rabbinical Assembly
United Synagogue of Conservative, Judaism,
1510 Chestnut Street 19102   (215) 563-8814

Rabbinical Council of Greater Philadelphia
44 North 4th Street, Philadelphia 19106
(215) 922-5446
Fax: (215) 922-1550
Supervision: (O)

Vaad Hakashruth and Beth Din of Philadelphia
1147 Gilham Street, Philadelphia 19111
(215) 725-5181
Fax: (215) 725-5182
Supervision: (O)

LIBRARIES

Annenberg Research Institute
420 Walnut Street 19106   (215) 238-1290
Approximately 180,000 books and thousands of
periodicals with emphasis on Judaic and Near Eastern
studies. Rare book collection archives of American
Judaica particularly that of Philadelphia.

Philadelphia Jewish Archives Center
Balch Institute for Ethnic Studies,
18 South 7th Street 19106   (215) 925-8090
Jewish community archives containing records of
agencies synagogues and community organisations
personal and family papers autobiographies and
memoirs and a photograph collection Open to the
public.

Reconstructionist Rabbinical College Library
Church Road and Greenwood Avenue,
Wyncote 19095   (215) 576-0800
The Kaplan Library serves rabbinical students and the
general public 33,000 books and periodicals in
English, Hebrew, and other languages The Kaplan
Archives house documents of the Reconstructionist
movement.

Talmudical Yeshivah Library
6063 Dexel Road 19131   (215) 477-1000
Fax: (215) 477-5065
Library of Sefarim (Hebrew books on the Bible the
Talmud Responsa etc.) Open for in-library work to
the general public by appointment.

Temple University
Paley Library, 13th Street and Berks
Mall 19122   (215) 787-8231
Large collection of Judaica Hebraica and Talmudic
studies and literature in Hebrew and in translation.
Main stacks are open Borrowing can be arranged
through inter-library loan

The Free Library of Philadelphia
Central Library, Logan Square 19103   (215) 686-5392
Fax: (215) 563-3628
Web site: www.library.phila.gov
3,000-volume Moses Marx Collection of Judaica and
Hebraica in the Central Library, covers history liturgy,
printing and bibliography with some books on
philosophy, religion, the Bible, the Talmud, and
Passover haggadahs. Open to the public. Russian-
language collection available at the Northeast
Regional Library.

Tuttleman Library
Gratz College, Mandell Education Campus,
7605 Old York Road, Melrose Park 19027
(215) 635-7300 ext. 169
Fax: (215) 635-7320
Email: libraryinfo@gratz.edu
Specialised library of Judaic and Hebraic studies.
Multilingual collection of approximately 100,000
books, periodicals, music and audio-visual materials.
Special collections include a rare book room, a music
library, and a Holocaust oral history archive.

University of Pennsylvania
Van Pelt Library, 3420 Walnut Street 19104
(215) 898-7556
Large collection of biblical studies rabbinics Jewish
history and medieval and modern Hebrew language
and literature. Stacks and seminar rooms open to the
public.

MEDIA
Newspapers
Jewish Exponent
Jewish Publishing Group, 2100 Arch Street,
Philadelphia 19103   (215) 832-0700
Fax: (215) 832-0786
Email: dalpher@jewishexponent.com
Weekly newspaper covering world news of Jewish
interest and detailed information on local activities
including Jewish Federation of Greater Philadelphia
meetings and events. Special sections include
community and health calendars singles and campus
activities a Russian-language column and synagogue
activities.

Jewish Post
P.O.Box 442, Yardley 19067   (215) 321-3443
Monthly newspaper serving Bucks County Pa and
Mercer County N.J.

Jewish Times
Jewish Publishing Group, 103A Tomlinson Road,
Huntingdon Valley 19006   (215) 938-1177
Weekly newspaper covering issues and programmes
of interest to area Jewish residents of the greater
Northeast and Bucks County including Jewish
Federation of Greater Philadelphia meetings and
events. Special sections include synagogue senior
adult singles and campus activities.

Mir
P.O. Box 6162, Philadelphia 19115   (215) 934-5512
Local weekly Russian-language newspaper

Periodicals
Inside Magazine
Jewish Publishing Group, 2100 Arch Street
19103   (215) 893-5797
Fax: (215) 546-3957
Email: rleiter@jewishexponent.com
Quarterly magazine of Jewish life and style. Sold at
news-stands and sent to all "Jewish Exponent" and
"Jewish Times" subscribers.

Jewish Quarterly Review
420 Walnut Street 19106   (215) 238-1290
Email: jqroffice@sas.upenn.edu
Scholarly journal of the Center for Advanced Judaic
studies published four times a year.

Shofar Magazine
P.O. Box 51591 19115   (215) 676-8304
Russian-language monthly magazine

Radio
Meridian
(215) 962-8000
Russian language program Saturdays 10 am to 10.30
am

Radio & TV
Barry Reisman Show
(215) 365-5600
WSSJ (1310AM) Jewish music in Yiddish and
Hebrew, and English and Jewish news. Mondays
through Fridays 3.30 to 5.30pm Sundays 9.30 am to 1
pm.

Bucks County Jewish Life
(215) 949-1490
WBCB (1490AM) Rabbi Allan Tuffs hosts this weekly
Sunday morning radio program at 10 am

Comcast Cablevision of Philadelphia
4400 Wayne Avenue 19140   (215) 673-6600
Channel 66 (Cable Television) Half-hour program on
Jewish culture shown twice a week in the evening
usually midweek and Sundays See local listings for
exact time.

Pulse
WSSJ, Camden   (215) 365-5600
WSSJ (1310AM) Russian-language news and music
program Sundays 9.30 to 10.30 am.

MEMORIAL
Monument to the Six Million Jewish Martyrs
16th Street and the Benjamin,
Franklin Parkway 19103
This memorial sculpture was the first public
Holocaust monument in the United States.

MIKVAOT
Mikveh Association of Philadelphia (Ardmore)
Torah Academy, Wynnewood and
Argyle Roads, Ardmore 19003   (215) 642-8679

Mikveh association of Philadelphia (Northern)
7525 Loretto Avenue, Philadelphia 19111
(215) 745-3334

MUSEUMS
Balch Institute for Ethnic Studies
18 South 7th Street 19106   (215) 925-8090
Documents and interprets American multi-
culturalism Research library has a Yiddish collection.
Houses the Jewish Archives Center.

Borowsky Gallery
Jewish Community Centers of Greater,
Philadelphia, 401 South Broad Street 19147
(215) 545-4400
Email: www.gershmany.org
Continuing exhibits of special interest to the Jewish
community.

Fred Wolf Jr Gallery
Jewish Community Centers of Greater,
Philadelphia, 10100 Jamison Avenue 19116
(215) 698-7300
Continuing exhibits of special interest to the Jewish
community

Holocaust Awareness Museum
Gratz College, Mandell Education Campus,
7601 Old York Road, Melrose Park 19027
(215) 635-6480
Previously known as the Jewish Identity Center, the
Holocaust Awareness Museum contains donations
form Holocaust survivors and concentration camp
liberators. The collection documents and teaches the
facts of genocide and dangers of ethnic hatred and
bigotry.

National Museum of American Jewish History
55 North 5th Street, Independence Mall
East 19106-2197
(215) 923-3811
Fax: (215) 923-0763
Email: nmajh@nmajh.org
Web site: www.nmajh.org
Presents programmes and experiences that preserve,
explore and celebrate the history of Jews in America.
Award-winning gift shop.

Philadelphia Congregation Rodeph Shalom
615 North Broad Street 19123
(215) 627-6747
Nationally recognised for exhibits of contemporary
Jewish art and history. Permanent collection of
twentieth-century Jewish art and photographs.

Rosenbach Museum & Library
2010 Delancey Place 19103
(215) 732-1600
Fax: (215) 545-7529
Email: info@rosenbach.org
The collection includes the first Haggadah printed in
America and letters, portraits and furniture of the
Gratz family of Philadelphia. Access to books is by
appointment only. Also home to the earliest printing
of the Pentateuch in Hebrew of which complete
copies are known.

Temple Judea Museum of Keneseth Israel
8339 Old York Road, Elkins Park, PA 19027
(215) 887-2027; 887-8700
Fax: (215) 887-1070
Email: tjmuseum@aol.com
This synagogue museum has four changing exhibitions
of Judaica and Jewish art each year. The synagogue
sanctuary has ten magnificent stained glass windows
by Jacob Landau. Group tours available by request.

RESTAURANTS
Irv's Place
(Kosher Dining at Univ. of Pennsylvania),
4051 Irving Street 19104
(215) 573-7596
Hours of operation are for lunch and dinner during
the school year.

Dairy
Cherry Street Chinese vegetarian
1010 Cherry Street 19107
(215) 923-3663
Supervision: Rabbinical Assembly

Meat
Sim's Place
300 Levering Mill Road, Bela Cynwyd
(215) 949-9420

Pizzaeria
Shalom Pizza
7598a Haverford Avenue
(215) 878-1500
Email: shalom2u@rcn.com
Supervision: Orthodox Vaad of Philadelphia
Vegetarian, Middle - Eastern. Open 11.00 am to 9.00
pm daily. Friday closed at 4.00 pm (winter at
2.00pm). Closed Shabbat. Cholov Israel and Pas
Israel.

Pizzeria
Holyland Pizza
8010 Castor Avenue
(215) 725-7444

SYNAGOGUES
Conservative
Congregation Beth El
21 Penn Valley Road, Fallsington,
Levittown 19054
(215) 945-9500

Ohev Shalom
2 Chester Road, Wallingford 19086
(215) 874-1465
Web site: www.uscj.org/delvlly/wallingford
The synagogue vestibule contains twelve stained-glass
panes (designed and executed by Rose Isaacson),
each depicting a Jewish holiday. In the main lobby is an
additional stained-glass panel erected as an Holocaust
memorial.

Tiferet Bet Israel
1920 Skippack Pike, Blue Bell 19422
(215) 275-8797
Orthodox
Congregation Rodeph
615 North Broad Street
(215) 627-6747
The congregation is the oldest Ashkenazi one in the
United States having been founded in 1795.

Young Israel of Elkins Park
7715 Montgomery Avenue, Elkins Park 19027
(215) 635-3152
Email: host@yiep.org
Web site: www.yiep.org

Young Israel of Oxford Circle
6427 Large Street 19149
(215) 725-7087
With dozens of synagogues of the various
demoninations in the area, travellers are advised to
contact a local religious organisation for specific
details.

Young Israel of the Main Line
PO Box 117 19004
(215) 667-3255
Orthodox Sephardi
Congregation Mikveh Israel
44 North 4th Street 19106
(215) 922-5446
Fax: (215) 922-1550
Web site: www.mikvehisrael.org
Spanish-Portuguese synagogue founded in 1740.
Located on Independence Mall. Entrance is shared
with the National Museum of American Jewish
History. Daily and Shabbat services are still conducted
using historic artifacts and tradition.

Reform
Temple Shalom
Edgley Road, off Mill Creek Pkwy.,
Levittown 19057   (215) 945-4154

THEATRE
Theatre Ariel/Habima Ariel
PO Box 0334, Merion Station 19066   (215) 567-0670
Theatre productions, readings workshops mini-
performances and speakers all dedicated to exploring
the Jewish theatrical experience.

TOURS OF JEWISH INTEREST
American Jewish Committee Historic Tour
117 South Seventeenth Street, Suite 1010
                         (215) 665-2300
                    Fax: (215) 665-8737
Tours, run by Simmi Hurwitz, may be arranged to suit
personal or group interests or needs.

Pittsburgh

BAKERIES
Pastries Unlimited
2119 Murray Avenue 15217   (412) 521-6323

BOOKSELLERS
Pinskers Judaica Center
2028 Murray Avenue 15217   (412) 421-3033;
                  1- 800-JUDAISM (1-800-583-2476)
                    Fax: (412) 421-6103
                Email: info@judaism.com
               Web site: www.judaism.com

COMMUNITY ORGANISATIONS
United Jewish Federation of Greater Pittsburgh
234 McKee Place 15213   (412) 681-8000
                    Fax: (412) 681-3980
                Email: enaveh@ujf.net
               Web site: www.ujf.net
Houses all administrative offices of the Federation
and commission on Public Affairs.

GROCERIES
Brauner's Emporium
2023 Murray Avenue 15217

Koshermart
2121 Murray Avenue 15217

MEDIA
Newspaper
Pittsburgh Jewish Chronicle
5600 Baum Blvd   (412) 687-1000
                    Fax: (412) 687-5119
                Email: pittjewchr@aol.com

MIKVAOT
2326 Shady Avenue 15217   (412) 422-8010

MUSEUM
**Holocaust Center of the United Jewish
Federation of Greater Pittsburgh**
5738 Darlington Road 15217   (412) 421-1500
                    Fax: (412) 422-1996
                Email: lhurwitz@ujf.net
               Web site: www.ujfhc.net
Serves as a living memorial by providing educational
resources, sponsoring community activities, housing
archives and cultural materials related to the
Holocaust.

RESTAURANTS
Dairy
Yaacov's
2109 Murray Ave. 15217   (412) 421-7208
Meat
Greenberg's Kosher Poultry
2223 Murray Avenue 15217

Platters Restaurant
2020 Murray Avenue 15217   (412) 422-3370

Prime Kosher
1916 Murray Avenue 15217   (412) 421-1015

SYNAGOGUES
Conservative
Ahavath Achim
500 Chestnut St., Carnegie 15106   (412) 279-1566

Beth El of South Hills
1900 Cochran Rd 15220   (412) 561-1168

Beth Shalom
Beacon & Shady Avs 15217   (412) 421-2288
                    Fax: (412) 421-5923
               Web site: www.bethshalom-pgh-org

New Light
1700 Beechwood Blvd. 15217   (412) 421-1017

Parkway Jewish Center
300 Princeton Dr. 15235   (412) 823-4338
                    Fax: (412) 823-4338

Tree of Life
Wilkins & Shady Avs 15217   (412) 521-6788
                    Fax: (412) 521-7846
                Email: tolpon@aol.com

Orthodox
B'nai Emunoh Congregation
4315 Murray Av. 15217   (412) 521-1477
                    Fax: (412) 521-1762
                Email: drmaimon@netzero.net

B'nai Zion
6404 Forbes Av. 15217   (412) 521-1440

**Beth Hamedrash Hagodol - Beth Jacob
Congregation**
1230 Colwell St. 15219   (412) 471-4443
                    Fax: (412) 281-1965

Bohnei Yisroel
6401 Forbes Av. 15217   (412) 521-6047

Kether Torah
5706 Bartlett St. 15217   (412) 521-9992

Poale Zedeck
6318 Phillips Avenue 15217   (412) 421-9786
                                 Fax: (412) 421-3383
                                 Email: mil313@aol.com
                                 Web site: www.pzonline.com

Shaare Tefillah
5741 Bartlett St. 15217   (412) 521-9911

Shaare Torah
2319 Murray Av. 15217   (412) 421-8855

Torath Chaim
728 N. Negley Av. 15206   (412) 362-7736; 362-0036
                           Email: joeberger1@juno.com
Contact person is Arnie Schwartz at 362-0036.

Young Israel of Greater Pittsburgh
5831 Bartlett Street 15217-1636   (412) 421-7224

Reconstructionist
Dor Hadash
6401 Forbes Av. 15217

Reform
Rodef Shalom
4905 5th Av. 15213   (412) 621-6566
                                 Fax: (412) 621-5475
                                 Email: herzog@rodefshalom.org

Temple David
4415 Northern Pike, Monroeville 15146

Temple Emanuel of South Hills
1250 Bower Hill Rd. 15243   (412) 279-2600
                                 Fax: (412) 279-7628
Hours: M-Th 9.00 to 5.00. Friday 9.00 to 4.00.

Temple Sinai
5505 Forbes Av. 15217   (412) 421-9715

Pottstown

SYNAGOGUES
Conservative
Congregation Mercy & Truth
575 N. Keim Street 19464   (610) 326-1717

Reading

COMMUNITY ORGANISATIONS
Jewish Federation
1700 City Line St 19604   (610) 921-2766
                                 Fax: (610) 921-2766
                                 Email: sramati@epix.net

SYNAGOGUES
Conservative
Kesher Zion
Eckert & Perkiomen Streets 19602   (610) 374-1763

Orthodox
Shomrei Habrith
2320 Hampden Blvd. 19604   (610) 921-0881

Reform
Reform Congregation Oheb Sholom
555 Warwick Drive, Wyomissing 19610
                                 (610) 375-6034
                                 Fax: (610) 375-6036
                                 Email: office@ohebsholom.org
                                 Web site: www.ohebsholom.org

Scranton

BUTCHERS
Blatt's Butcher Block
420 Prescott Avenue 18510   (570) 342-3886
                                 Fax: (570) 342-9711
Supervision: Rabbi Fine and Rabbi Herman of
Scranton Rabbinate
Glatt kosher meat, poultry, delicatessen and
groceries. Also meat restaurant.

COMMUNITY ORGANISATIONS
Jewish Federation of Northeastern Pennsylvania
601 Jefferson Avenue 18510   (570) 961-2300
                                 Fax: (570) 346-6147
                                 Email: jfednepa@epix.net

MUSEUM
Houdini Museum Tour and Magic Show
1433 N. Main 18508   (570) 342-5555
                                 Email: magicusa@microserve.net
                                 Web site: www.houdini.org
The only museum totally devoted to Harry Houdini
(Eric Weiss born in Budapest, the son of Rabbi Mayer
Samuel Weiss).

SYNAGOGUES
Conservative
Temple Israel
Gibson Street & Monroe Avenue 18510
                                 (570) 342-0350
                                 Fax: (570) 342-7250
                                 Email: tiscran@epix.net

Orthodox
Beth Shalom
Clay Avenue at Vine Street 18510   (570) 346-0502
                                 Fax: (570) 346-8800
Daily service. Close to motels & hotels.

Congregation Machzikeh Hadas
cnr. Monroe & Olive 18510   (570) 342-6271

Ohev Zedek
1432 Mulberry Street 18510   (570) 343-2717

Reform
Temple Hesed
Lake Scranton 18505   (570) 344-7201

Sharon

SYNAGOGUES
Reform
Temple Beth Israel
840 Highland Road 16146   (724) 346-4754
                                 Fax: (724) 981-4424

Wilkes-Barre

COMMUNITY ORGANISATIONS
Jewish Federation of Greater Wilkes-Barre &
Community Center
60 S. River Street   (570) 822-4146
                                 Fax: (570) 824-5966

SYNAGOGUES
Conservative
Temple Israel
236 S. River Street 18702   (570) 824-8927

Orthodox
Ohav Zedek
242 S. Franklin Street 18701   (570) 825-6619
                                 Fax: (570) 825-6634
                                 Email: info@ohavzedek.org

Reform
B'nai B'rith
408 Wyoming Street, Kingston 18704

Williamsport

SYNAGOGUES
Conservative
Ohev Sholom
Cherry & Belmont Streets 17701   (717) 322-4209
Reform
Beth Ha-Sholom
425 Center Street 17701   (717) 323-7751

RHODE ISLAND

Barrington

SYNAGOGUES
Reform
Temple Habonim
165 New Meadow Road 02806   (401) 245-6536

Bristol

SYNAGOGUES
Conservative
United Brothers
215 High Street 02809   (401) 253-3460

Cranston

SYNAGOGUES
Conservative
Temple Torat Yisrael
330 Park Avenue 02905   (401) 785-1800
Reform
Temple Sinai
30 Hagan Avenue 02920   (401) 942-8350

Middletown

SYNAGOGUES
Conservative
Temple Shalom
223 Valley Road 02842   (401) 846-9002
                                 Fax: (401) 682-2417

Narragansett

SYNAGOGUES
Conservative
Congregation Beth David
Kingstown Road 02882   (401) 846-9002

Newport

BED AND BREAKFAST
Admiral Weaver Inn
28 Weaver Avenue 02840   (401) 849-0051
                                 Fax: (401) 847-5902
                                 Email: olgat@gis.net
            Web site: www.kosherbedandbreakfast.com
Kosher: Located only minutes away from the Touro
Synagogue, the oldest synagogue in North America.

TOURS OF JEWISH INTEREST
Touro Synagogue
85 Touro Street 02840   (401) 847-4794
                                 Fax: (401) 847-8121
The synagogue, designed by Peter Harrison and
dedicated in 1763, is one of the finest examples of
eighteenth-century Colonial architecture. It has been
named as the National Trust for Historic
Preservation's first religious historic site. The Jewish
cemetery, the second oldest in the US, dates back to
1677 and was immortalised in Longfellow's poem
'The Jewish Cemetery of Newport'. Judah Touro is
buried here.

Providence

COMMUNITY ORGANISATIONS
Jewish Federation of Rhode Island
130 Sessions Street 02906   (401) 421-4111

DOCUMENTATION CENTRE
Rhode Island Jewish Historical Association
(401) 863-2805
Has a vast amount of material regarding Colonial
Jewry.

KASHRUT INFORMATION
Brown University-RISD Hillel
80 Brown Street 02906   (401) 863-2805
Fax: (401) 863-1591
Email: spf@brown.edu

Vaad Hakashrut
(401) 621-9393
Fax: (401) 331-9393
Email: bethshalom1@juno.com

MEDIA
Periodical
L'Chaim
130 Sessions Street 02906   (401) 421-4111

MIKVAOT
401 Elmgrove Avenue 02906   (401) 751-0025

MUSEUM
Rhode Island Holocaust Memorial Museum
401 Elmgrove Avenue 02906   (401) 861-8800
The state memorial to the victims of the Holocaust.
Many survivors now living in Rhode Island have
donated memorabilia and personal mementoes.
There is also a garden of remembrance.

SYNAGOGUES
Conservative
Temple Emanu-El
99 Taft Avenue 02906   (401) 331-1616

Orthodox
Beth Sholom
275 Camp Avenue 02906   (401) 621-9393
Fax: (401) 331-9393
Email: bethsholom1@hotmail.com

Congregation Sons of Jacob
24 Douglas Avenue 02908   (401) 274-5260

Mishkon Tfiloh
203 Summit Avenue 02906   (401) 521-1616

Shaare Zedek
688 Broad Street 02907   (401) 751-4936

Reform
Beth El
70 Orchard Avenue 02906   (401) 331-6070

Warwick

SYNAGOGUES
Conservative
Temple Am David
40 Gardiner Street 02888   (401) 463-7944

Westerly

SYNAGOGUES
Orthodox
Congregation Shaare Zedek
Union Street 02891   (401) 596-4621

Woonsocket

SYNAGOGUES
Conservative
Congregation B'nai Israel
224 Prospect Street 02895   (401) 762-3651
Fax: (401) 767-5243
Email: cbi_synagogue@juno.com

SOUTH CAROLINA

Charleston

BAKERIES
Ashley Bakery
1662 Savannah Highway 29407   (843) 763-4125

Cookie Bouquet
280 W. Coleman Road   (843) 881-0110

Great Harvest Bread Company
975 Savannah Highway 29407   (843) 763-2055

COMMUNITY ORGANISATIONS
Jewish Federation and Community Center
1645 Raoul Wallenberg Blvd,
PO Box 31298 29416   (843) 571-6565
Fax: (843) 556-6206

DELICATESSEN
Nathan's Deli
1836 Ashley River Road 29407   (843) 556-3354

West Side Market and Deli
1300 Savannah Highway 29407   (843) 763-9988
Fax: (843) 763-4476
Kosher market, restaurant and catering. Open
Sunday to Friday.

SYNAGOGUES
Orthodox
Brith Sholom Beth Israel
182 Rutledge Avenue   (843) 577-6599
Fax: (843) 577-6699
Email: sholomsc@aol.com
Web site: www.bs-bi.com

Reform
Beth Elohim
86 Hasell Street 29401 (843) 723-1090
Fax: (843) 723-0537
Email: office@kkbe.org
Web site: www.kkbe.org
Dating from 1749, it is the birthplace of Reform Judaism in the United States, the Second oldest synagogue building in the country, and the oldest surviving Reform Synagogue in the world. It has been designated as a national historic landmark. A museum is housed in the administration building next door.

Columbia

COMMUNITY ORGANISATIONS
Columbia Jewish Federation
4540 Trenholm Road, Cola 29206 (803) 787-2023

DELICATESSEN
Groucho's
Five Points 29205

SYNAGOGUES
Conservative
Beth Shalom
5827 North Trenholm Road 29206 (803) 782-2500
Fax: (803) 782-5420
Email: bethshalom@bellsouth.net
Web site:
www.midnet.sc.edu/beth_shalom/index.htm
Reform
Tree of Life
6719 Trenholm Road 29206 (803) 787-2182
Fax: (803) 787-0309

Georgetown

CEMETERIES
Old Cemetery
Although there are now very few Jews in Georgetown, and there is no synagogue, there is a very old Jewish cemetery, which is maintained by the city.

Myrtle Beach

RESTAURANTS
Jerusalem Kosher
1007 Withers Dr. (803) 946-6650

SYNAGOGUES
Orthodox
Beth El
401 Highway 17 N., 56th Avenue 29577
(803) 449-3140

Chabad Lubavitch
2803 N. Oak Street (803) 448-0035
Fax: (803) 626-6403
Services every day.

SOUTH DAKOTA

Aberdeen

SYNAGOGUES
Conservative
Congregation B'nai Isaac
202 North Kline Street 57401 (605) 225-7360
Email: beapre@iw.net

Rapid City

SYNAGOGUES
Reform
Synagogue of the Hills
417 N. 40th Street 57702 (605) 348-0805
Email: bhshul@rapidnet.com
Affiliated with UAHC. Services Friday evenings at 7.30

TENNESSEE

Chattanooga

COMMUNITY ORGANISATIONS
Jewish Community Federation
5326 Lynnland Terrace 47311 (423) 894-1317
Fax: (423) 894-1319

SYNAGOGUES
Conservative
B'nai Zion
114 McBrien Road 37411 (423) 894-8900
Orthodox
Beth Sholom
20 Pisgah Avenue 37411 (423) 894-0801
Reform
Mizpah Congregation
923 McCallie Avenue 37403 (423) 267-9771
Fax: (423) 267-9773
Email: admmizpahcong@juno.com
Siskin Museum of Religious Artifacts
1 Siskin Plaza 37403 (423) 267-9771
Fax: (423) 634-1717

Memphis

COMMUNITY ORGANISATIONS
Jewish Federation and Community Center
6560 Poplar Avenue 38138   (901) 767-7100

DELICATESSEN
Kroger Kosher Deli
540 S. Mendenhall   (901) 683-8846

Schnuck's Kosher Deli
799 Truse Parkway   (901) 682-2989

KASHRUT INFORMATION
Vaad Hakehilloth of Memphis
Memphis Orthodox Jewish Community Council, PO
Box 41133 38104   (901) 767-2263
                         Fax: (901) 761-3788

MIKVAOT
Anshei Sphard
120 E. Yates Rd.   (901) 682-6302

Baron Hirsch Congregation
369 Winter Oak Lane 38119   (901) 683-7485

SYNAGOGUES
Conservative
Beth Sholom
482 S. Mendenhall Ave. 38117   (901) 683-3591

Orthodox
Anshei Sephard-Beth El Emeth
120 E.Yates Road N. 38117   (901) 682-1611

Baron Hirsch Cong.
369 Winter Oak   (901) 683-7485

Kesser Torah
531 S. Yates   (901) 761-6060

Reform
Temple Israel
1376 E. Massey Road   (901) 761-3130

Nashville

COMMUNITY ORGANISATIONS
**Jewish Federation of Nashville and Middle
Tennessee**
801 Percy Warner Blvd. 37205   (615) 356-3242
                                      Fax: (615) 352-0056

MIKVAOT
Sherith Israel
3600 West End Avenue 37205   (615) 292-6614
                                    Fax: (615) 463-8260
                          Email: SylvL@AOL.com

SYNAGOGUES
Conservative
West End Synagogue
3814 West End Avenue 37205   (615) 269-4592
                                    Fax: (615) 269-4695
             Email: office@westendsyn.org or
exec@westendsyn.org

Reform
The Temple
5015 Harding Road 37205   (615) 352-7620
                                 Fax: (615) 352-9365

Oak Ridge

SYNAGOGUES
Conservative
Jewish Congregation of Oak Ridge
101 W. Madison Lane 37830   (423) 482-3581

TEXAS

Amarillo

SYNAGOGUES
Reform
Temple B'nai Israel
4316 Albert Street 79106   (806) 352-7191

Arlington

MEDIA
Newspaper
Texas Jewish Post
3120 South Freeway , Ft. Worth 76110
                                  (817) 927-2831
                          Fax: (817) 429-0840
        Email: news@texasjewishpost.com
Weekly Newspaper in circulation since 1947.

SYNAGOGUES
Reform
Congregation Beth Shalom
1210 Thannisch Drive 76011   (817) 860-5448
                          Email: bethshalom.org

Austin

COMMUNITY ORGANISATIONS
**Jewish Federation and Community Center of
Austin**
7300 Hart Lane 78731   (512) 331-1144
                              Fax: (512) 331-7059

SYNAGOGUES
Conservative
Agudas Achim
4300 Bull Creek Road 78731   (512) 459-3287

Congregation Beth El
8902 Mesa Drive 78759   (512) 346-1776
                               Fax: (512) 233-004
            Email: difriedman@aol.com

Reform
Temple Beth Israel
3901 Shoal Creek Blvd. 78756   (512) 454-6806

Baytown

SYNAGOGUES
Unaffiliated
K'nesseth Israel
100 W. Sterling, PO Box 702 77522   (281) 424-8765

Beaumont

SYNAGOGUES
Reform
Temple Emanuel
1120 Broadway 7740   (409) 832-6131

Corpus Christi

SYNAGOGUES
Conservative
B'nai Israel
3434 Fort Worth Street 78411   (361) 855-7308
Fax: (361) 855-7309
Email: CGDK@aol.com

Reform
Temple Beth El
4402 Saratoga Street 78413   (361) 857-8181

Dallas

The Dallas Jewish community was founded in the decade following the Civil War by predominantly German Jews. The social importance of German Jewish ancestry can still be seen in the Temple Emanu-El cemetery which is home to scores of 19th-century headstones bearing German regional names for eastern European birth places.

The JCC sponsors a prestigious Jewish Arts Festival each August along with concerts and gallery exhibitions. A Holocaust Museum has served as a regional focal point for preserving the memory of the Shoah. For more information, see the Dallas Virtual Jewish Community website at www.dvjc.org.

COMMUNITY ORGANISATIONS
Jewish Federation of Greater Dallas and Community Center
7800 Northaven Road 75230   (214) 369-3313
Fax: (214) 369-8943
Email: contact@jfgd.org
Web site: www.jewishdallas.org
The Campus houses the Dallas Holocaust Center and the Dallas Jewish Historical Society. There is a kosher café on Sundays and lunch service on some weekdays during the fall and winter months (under the supervision of the Vaad Hakashrus of Greater Dallas)

HOTELS
The Westin Galleria, Dallas
13340 Dallas Parkway   (214) 934-9494
Fax: (214) 851-2869
Email: galas@westin.com
Lock-up kosher kitchens under the supervision of the Vaad Hakashrus of Dallas.

MIKVAOT
Mikvah Association
5640 McShan 75230   (214) 776-0037

RELIGIOUS ORGANISATIONS
Dallas Area Torah Association (Kollel)
5840 Forest Lane 75230   (214) 987-3282
Fax: (214) 987-1764
Email: data@datanet.org
Web site: www.datanet.org

SITE
Zaide Reuven's Esrog Farm
    (214) 931-5596
Fax: (214) 931-5476
Email: zrsesrog@aol.com
Web site: www.members.aol.com/arsesrog
Dallas' only Esrog tree farm is open by appointment.

SYNAGOGUES
Orthodox
Chabad of Dallas
7008 Forest Lane 75230   (214) 361-8600
Fax: (214) 361-8680
Email: shull@airmail.net
Web site: www.chabadcenters.com/dallas
Ohr HaTorah
12800 Preston Road   (214) 404-8980
Shaare Tefilla
6131 Churchill Way, off Preston Road 75230
    (214) 661-0127
Fax: (214) 661-0150
Email: shaaretefilla@juno.com
Reform
Temple Emanu-El
8500 Hillcrest Road 75230   (214) 706-0000
Fax: (214) 706-0025
Web site: www.tedallas.org

Sephardi
Magen David Congregation
7314 Campbell Road, Dallas, Texas 75248
    (214) 386-7166

El Paso

COMMUNITY ORGANISATIONS
Chabad House
6515 Westwind 79912   (915) 584-8218
Web site: www.chabadelpaso.com
Also has a mikva.

MUSEUM

El Paso Holocaust Museum and Study Center
401 Wallenberg Drive 79912   (915) 833-5656
Fax: (915) 833-9523
Email: epholo@flash.net
Web site: www.flash.net/~epholo.com
The museum features an impressive collection of artifacts, dramatic displays, pictures and posters depicting the chronological history of Europe during the Nazi era. Open Sunday and Tuesday 1pm-4pm or by appointment.

SYNAGOGUES

Conservative
B'nai Zion
805 Cherry Hill Lane 79912   (915) 833-2222
Also has a mikva.

Reform
Sinai
4408 N. Stanton Street 79902   (915) 532-5959

Houston

BAKERIES

Kroger's
S. Post Oak 77096   (713) 721-7691
Supervision: Houston Kashruth Association

New York Bagel Shop
9724 Hillcroft 77096   (713) 723-5879
Supervision: Houston Kashruth Association

Randall's Bakery
Supervision: Houston Kashruth Association
Can be found at eight locations including : Clear Lake, Sugar Land, Highway 6 & Memorial, Fondren & Bissonnet, W. Bellfort & S. Post Oak, Gessner & W. Bellfort, and Holcombe & Kirby.

Three Brothers Bakery
4036 S. Braeswood 77025   (713) 666-2551
Supervision: Houston Kashruth Association

BUTCHERS

Albertson's
S. Braeswood   (713) 271-1180
Supervision: Houston Kashruth Association

Kroger's
S. Post Oak 77096   (713) 721-7691
Supervision: Houston Kashruth Association

COMMUNITY ORGANISATIONS

Jewish Federation of Greater Houston
5603 S. Braeswood Blvd. 77096   (713) 729-7000
Fax: (713) 721-6232
Web site: www.houstonjewish.org

EMBASSY

Consul General of Israel
Suite 1500, 24 Greenway Plaza 77046

GROCERIES

Albertson's
S. Braeswood   (713) 271-1180
Supervision: Houston Kashruth Association

KASHRUT INFORMATION

Houston Kashrut Association
9001 Greenwillow 77096   (713) 723-3850
Fax: (713) 723-3852

TORCH - Torah & Outreach Resource Center of Houston
7000 Westview, Suite 121 77055   (713) 721-6400
Fax: (713) 721-6900
Email: ypolatsek@torchweb.com
Web site: www.torchweb.com

MIKVAOT

Chabad Lubavitch Center
10900 Fondren Road 77096   (713) 777-2000

United Orthodox Synagogues
4221 S. Braeswood Blvd., 77096   (713) 723-3850

RESTAURANTS

Dairy
Saba's Mediterranean
9704 Fondren   (713) 270-7222
Supervision: Houston Kashruth Association

Meat
Nosher's at the Jewish Community Centre
5601 S. Braeswood 77096   (713) 729-3200
Supervision: Houston Kashruth Association

Vegetarian
Madras Pavilion
3910 Kirby Drive 77098   (713) 521-2617
Supervision: Houston Kashruth Association

Wonderful Vegetarian Restaurant
7549 Westheimer 77063   (713) 977-3137
Supervision: Houston Kashruth Association

SYNAGOGUES

Conservative
B'rith Shalom
4610 Bellaire Blvd. 77401   (713) 667-9201

Beth Am
1431 Brittmore Rd. 77043   (713) 461-7725
Fax: (713) 461-7773
Email: ebbe@earthlink.net
Web site: www.bethamtx.org
One room and board is available to anyone attending services.

Beth Yeshurun
4525 Beechnut St. 77096   (713) 666-1881
Fax: (713) 666-7767
Email: arthur@bethyeshurun.org
Web site: www.bethyeshurun.org

Congregation Shaar Hashalom
16020 El Camino Real 77062   (713) 488-5861
Fax: (713) 488-3561
Email: Ferderow@blkbox.com
Web site: www.uscj.org.sowest/houstosh

Orthodox
Chabad Lubavitch of Houston
10900 Fondren Road 77096   (713) 777-2000

Congregation Beth Rambam
11333 Braesridge Blvd. 77071   (713) 723-3030
Fax: (713) 726-8737
Email: gez@flash.net
Web site: www.flash.net/~bentzion/br.htm
Home hospitality available. Office hours Monday -
Friday, 9am to 2 pm.

United Orthodox Synogogues
9001 Greenwillow 77096   (713) 723-3850
Web site: www.uosh.org
Mikva on premises. Daily minyan and Shabbat
services.

Young Israel of Houston
7823 Ludinton Road 77071   (713) 729-0719
Web site: www.youngisraelofhouston.org

Reform
Beth Israel
5600 N. Braeswood Blvd. 77096   (713) 771-6221
Fax: (713) 771-5705
Web site: www.Beth-Israel.org

Congregation Emanu El
1500 Sunset Blvd. 77005   (713) 529-5771
Fax: (713) 529-0703
Email: emanuelhouston.org
Web site: www.emanuel.org

Congregation for Reform Judaism
801 Bering Dr. 77057   (713) 782-4162
Fax: (713) 782-4167

Jewish Community North
5400 Fellowship Lane 77379   (713) 376-0016
Fax: (713) 251-1033
Email: jcn@wt.net

Temple Sinai
783 Country Place Dr. 77079   (713) 496-5950
Fax: (713) 496-1537

Lubbock

GROCERIES
Albertson's
(806) 794-6761

Lowe's Supermarket
82nd & Slide Rd

SYNAGOGUES
Reform
Congregation Shaareth Israel
6928 3rd Street 79424   (806) 794-7517
Mailing address: PO Box 93594, 79493-3594.

San Antonio

COMMUNITY ORGANISATIONS
Jewish Federation
8434 Ahern Drive 78216   (210) 341-8234

DELICATESSEN
Delicious Food
7460 Callaghan Road 78229   (210) 366-1844

MUSEUMS
Holocaust Memorial
12500 N W Military Highway 78231   (210) 302-6807
Fax: (210) 408-2332
Email: cohenm@jfstx.org

SYNAGOGUES
Conservative
Agudas Achim
1201 Donaldson Avenue 78228   (210) 734-4216

Orthodox
Rodfei Sholom
3003 Sholom Drive 78230   (210) 493 3558
Fax: (210) 492 0629
Email: rodfei@world-net.net
Web site: www.ou.org
Mikvah on premises.

Reform
Beth El
211 Belknap Place 78212

Waco

SYNAGOGUES
Conservative
Agudath Jacob
4925 Hillcrest Drive 76710   (254) 772-1451
Fax: (254) 772-2471
Email: Agudath@stonemedia.com
Web site: www.agudath-jacob.org

Reform
Rodef Sholom
1717 N. New Road 76707   (254) 754-3703
Fax: (254) 754-5538

UTAH

Salt Lake City

COMMUNITY ORGANISATIONS
United Jewish Federation of Utah
2416 East, 1700 South 84108   (801) 581-0102
Fax: (801) 581-1334

DELICATESSEN
Kosher on the Go
1575 S. 1100 East   (801) 463-1786

SYNAGOGUES
Orthodox
Chabad Lubavitch of Utah
1433 South 1100 East 84105   (801) 467-7777
Fax: (801) 486-7526
Email: chabadutah@aol.com
Web site: www.chabadutah.com
For Mikvah appointment call Mrs Sharonne Zippel,
Tel: (801) 582-0220.

Reconstructionist
Chavurah B'yachad
Jubilee Center, 309 East 100 South 84111
(801) 596-8996
Email: byachad@aol.com

Reform
Congregation Kol Ami
2425 E. Heritage Way 84109   (801) 484-1501
Fax: (801) 484-1162
Email: clyon@conkolami.org
Web site: www.conkolami.org

VERMONT

Burlington

SYNAGOGUES
Conservative
Ohavi Zedek
188 N. Prospect Street 05401   (802) 864-0218
Fax: (802) 864-0219
Email: www.ohavizedek.com

Orthodox
Ahavath Gerim
cnr. Archibald & Hyde Streets 05401   (802) 862-3001

Reform
Temple Sinai
500 Swift Street 05401   (802) 862-5125

Montpelier

SYNAGOGUES
Congregation Beth Jacob
10 Harrison Avenue 05602   (802) 229-9429

VIRGINIA

Alexandria

SYNAGOGUES
Conservative
Agudas Achim
2908 Valley Drive 22302   (703) 998-6460
Reform
Beth El Hebrew Congregation
3830 Seminary Road 22304   (703) 370-9400
Fax: (703) 370-7730
Email: bethelhc@erols.com

Arlington

SYNAGOGUES
Conservative
Arlington-Fairfax Jewish Congregation
2920 Arlington Blvd. 22204   (703) 979-4466
Fax: (703) 979-4468
Email: office@arfax.net
Web site: www.arfax.org
Daily minyan and Shabbat services. Includes areas
known as Crystal City, Rosslyn and Skyline.

Charlottesville

SYNAGOGUES
The Hillel Jewish Center
The University of Virginia, 1824 University
Circle 22903   (804) 295-4963
Reform
Congregation Beth Israel
301 E. Jefferson Street 22902   (804) 295-6382
Fax: (804) 296-6491
Email: office@www.cbicville.org

Danville

SYNAGOGUES
Reform
Temple Beth Sholom
Sutherlin Avenue   (804) 792-3489
This building is 95 years old, one of oldest synagogues
in the South. Friday evening and holiday services.

Fairfax

SYNAGOGUES
Conservative
Congregation Olam Tikvah
3800 Glenbrook Road 22031   (703) 425-1880
Fax: (703) 425-0835
Two miles from Beltway Exit 6W.

Falls Church

SYNAGOGUES
Reform
Temple Rodef Shalom
2100 Westmoreland Street 22043   (703) 532-2217
Email: trsfcva@erols.com

Hampton

SYNAGOGUES
Conservative
Rodef Sholom
318 Whealton Road, Hampton 23666 (757) 826-5894
Email: rabbirst@erols.com

Traditional
B'nai Israel
3116 Kecoughtan Road, Hampton 23661
(757) 772-0100

Newport News

BAKERIES
Brenner's Warwick Bakery
240 31st Street, Newport News 23607
Supervision: Va'ad Hakashrut

COMMUNITY ORGANISATIONS
United Jewish Community of the Virginia Peninsula
2700 Spring Road, Newport News 23606
(757) 930-1422

MIKVAOT
Adath Jeshurun
12646 Nettles Drive, Newport News 23606
(757) 930-0820
Email: adathjeshurun@juno.com
Mikvah: On premises. Please call the shul as much in advance as possible.

SYNAGOGUES
Reform
Temple Sinai
11620 Warwick Blvd., Newport News 23601
(757) 596-8352

Norfolk

COMMUNITY ORGANISATIONS
United Jewish Federation of Tidewater
5029 Corporate Woods Drive, Suite 225,
Virginia Beach 23462   (757) 671-1600
Fax: (757) 671-7613

GROCERIES
The Kosher Place
738 W. 22nd Street   (757) 623-1770
Fax: (757) 623-2237
Web site: www.kosherplacecafe.com
Supervision: Vaad Hakashrus of Tidewater
Meats, deli, prepared foods. Hours: Monday to Thursday, 9 am to 6 pm; Friday, to 3 pm; Sunday, 10 am to 4 pm. Close to colonial Williamsburg and Virginia Beach.

HOTELS
Sheraton Norfolk Waterside Hotel
777 Waterside Drive 23510   (757) 622-6664
Supervision: Va'ad

KASHRUT INFORMATION
Vaad Hakashrus of Tidewater
PO Box 11082 23517   (757) 627-7358
Fax: (757) 627-8544
Email: mostsky1@hotmail.com

MIKVAOT
B'nai Israel Congregation
420 Spotswood Avenue 23517   (757) 627-7358
Fax: (757) 627-8544
Email: office@bnaiisrael.org
Web site: www.bnaiisrael.org

SYNAGOGUES
Conservative
Beth El
422 Shirley Av. 23517   (757) 625-7821
Fax: (757) 627-4905
Email: office@bethelnorfolk.com

Temple Israel
7255 Granby St. 23505   (757) 489-4550

Orthodox
B'nai Israel
402 Spotswood Avenue 23517   (757) 627-7358

Reform
Ohef Sholom
Stockley Gdns at Raleigh Av. 23507 (757) 625-4295

The Commodore Levy Chapel
Frazier Hall, Building C-7 (inside Gate 2),
Norfolk US Navy Station   (757) 444-7361
Fax: (757) 444-7362
Email: chaplain@nsn.cmar.navy.mil
The US Navy's oldest synagogue. Visitors welcome for tour or Erev Shabbat services. Contact Jewish chaplain for Base Pass first.

Richmond

COMMUNITY ORGANISATIONS

Jewish Community Federation
5403 Monument Avenue 23226 (804) 288-0045
Fax: (804) 282-7507
Email: www.jewishrichmond.org

HOTELS

The Farbreng-Inn Kosher Retreat Center
1800 SEE Virginia 23233
(804) 740-2000/800-733-8474
Fax: (804) 750-1341
Email: info@chabadofva.org
Kosher retreat center open year round. Under the
Hashgacht of Lubavitch of Virginia.

MIKVAOT

Young Israel
4811 Patterson Avenue 23226 (804) 353-3831
Fax: (804) 288-4381
Email: adere@juno.com

MUSEUM

Beth Ahabah Museum & Archive
1117 W. Franklin Street 23220 (804) 353 -0268
Also housing Jewish archives, which are of great
historical interest.

SYNAGOGUES

Conservative
Or Atid
501 Parham Road 23229 (804) 740-4747
Orthodox
Keneseth Beth Israel
6300 Patterson Avenue 23226 (804) 288-7953
Fax: (804) 673-9558
Email: kbi6300@erols.com

Young Israel of Richmond
4811 Patterson Avenue 23226 (804) 353-5831
Email: yosefb@juno.com

Reform
Or Ami
9400 N. Huguenot Road 23235 (804) 272-0017

Virginia Beach

MEDIA

Newspapers
Southeastern Virginia Jewish News
5029 Corporate Woods Drive,
Suite 225 23462 (757) 671-1600
Fax: (757) 671-7613
Email: news@ujft.org
Web site: www.jewishva.org
Published every two weeks.

Periodical
Renewal Magazine
5029 Corporate Woods, Suite 225 23462
(757) 671-1600
Fax: (757) 671-7613
Email: news@ujft.org
Web site: www.jewishva.org
Published three times per year.

SYNAGOGUES

Conservative
Kempsville Conservative
952 Indian Lakes Blvd. 23464 (757) 495-8510
Web site: www.uscj.org/seabd/virginiabeach/

Temple Emanuel
25th Street 23451 (757) 428-2591
Orthodox
Chabad Lubavitch
533 Gleneagle Drive 23462 (804) 499-0507
Reform
Beth Chaverim
3820 Stoneshore Road 23452-7965 (757) 463-3226
Fax: (757) 463-1134
Email: bethchaverim@ddaccess.com

WASHINGTON

Aberdeen

SYNAGOGUES

Conservative
Temple Beth Israel
1219 Spur Street 98520 (206) 533-3784

Mercer Island

COMMUNITY ORGANISATIONS

**Stroum Jewish Community Center of Greater
Seattle**
Mercer Island Facility, 3801 E. Mercer Way
98040 (206) 232-7115
Fax: (206) 232-7119
Email: info@sjcc.org
Web site: www.sjcc.org

Olympia

SYNAGOGUES

Progressive
Temple Beth Hatfiloh
802 South Jefferson, SE 98057 (206) 754-8519

Seattle

BAKERIES
Bagel Deli
340 15th Ave. E. (206) 322-2471

COMMUNITY ORGANISATIONS
Jewish Federation of Greater Seattle
2031 3rd Avenue 98121 (206) 443-5400
Stroum Jewish Community Center of Greater Seattle
Northend Facility, 8606 35th Avenue NE 98115
(206) 526-8073
Fax: (206) 526-9958
Email: NeReception@sjcc.org
Web site: www.sjcc.org
Washington Association of Jewish Communities
2031 3rd Avenue 98121

JEWISH STUDENT/YOUNG ADULT CENTER
Hillel, Foundation for Jewish Campus Life at the University of Washington
4745 17th Av. N.E. 98105 (206) 527-1997
Fax: (206) 527-1999
Email: mail@hilleluw.org
Web site: www.hilleluw.org
Programs, services, occasional kosher meals for students & young adults, 18-30.

KASHRUT INFORMATION
Va'ad HaRabanim of Greater Seattle
5100 South Dawson Street,
Suite 102 98118-2100 (206) 760-0805
Fax: (206) 725-0347
Email: vaad@w-link.net
The Va'ad HaRabanim was organised in 1993. In addition to providing kosher meat, the board provides kosher supervision for many restaurants, bakeries, retail outlets and catering facilities in the Seattle area. For further questions and information, please contact David Grashin at the number above.

MEDIA
Periodicals
The Jewish Transcript
2031 3rd Avenue 98121 (206) 441-4553
Fax: (206) 441-2736
Email: jewishtran@aol.com

MUSEUM
Community Center
3801 E. Mercer Way, Mercer Island 98040
(206) 232-7115
A Holocaust memorial with a bronze sculpture by Gizel Berman has been dedicated here.

RESTAURANTS
Dairy
Leah's Deli
65 St. between 21st and 22nd (206) 524-3870
Take Out

Panini Grill
2118 NE 65 St. (206) 522-2730
Vegetarian
Bamboo Garden
364 Roy Street, near Seattle Center 98109
(206) 282-6616
Fax: (206) 284-2775
Email: bamboogarden@aol.com
Web site: www.bamboogarden.net
Supervision: Va'ad HaRabanim of Greater Seattle

Teapot Vegetarian House
125 E. 15th Ave (206) 325-1010

Spokane

COMMUNITY ORGANISATIONS
Jewish Community Council
North 221 Wall, Suite 500, Spokane 99201
(509) 838-4261

SYNAGOGUES
Conservative
Temple Beth Shalom
1322, 30th Street 99203 (509) 747-3304

WEST VIRGINIA

Charleston

SYNAGOGUES
Reform
Temple B'nai Israel
2312 Kanawha Boulevard 25311 (304) 342-5852
Traditional
Congregation B'nai Jacob
1599 Virginia Street 25317 (304) 344-4167

Huntington

SYNAGOGUES
Conservative & Reform
B'nai Sholom
949 10th Avenue 25701 (304) 522-2980

WISCONSIN

Madison

COMMUNITY ORGANISATIONS
Madison Jewish Community Council
6434 Enterprise Lane 53179   (608) 278-1808
Fax: (608) 278-7814
Email: mjcc@mjcc.net
Web site: www.jewishmadison.org

SYNAGOGUES
Conservative
Beth Israel Center
1406 Mound Street 53711   (608) 256-7763
Fax: (608) 256-9434
Email: office@bethisraelcenter.org
Web site: www.bethisraelcenter.org
Orthodox
Chabad House
1722 Regent Street 53705   (608) 231-3450
Fax: (608) 231-3790
Reform
Beth El
2702 Arbor Drive 53711   (608) 238-3123

Milwaukee

COMMUNITY ORGANISATIONS
Coalition for Jewish Learning
6401 North Santa Monica Boulevard 53217
(414) 962-8860
Fax: (414) 962-8852

MEDIA
Directory
Milkwaukee Jewish Federation
1360 N. Prospect Avenue 53202   (414) 271-2992
Newspapers
Wisconsin Jewish Chronicle
1360 N. Prospect Avenue 53202   (414) 390-5888
Fax: (414) 271-0487
Email: milwaukeej@aol.com

RESTAURANTS
Meat
Kosher Meat Klub
4731 West Burleigh 53210   (414) 449-5980
Fax: (414) 449-5985
Meat sandwiches, delicatessen and kosher groceries
are available.

SYNAGOGUES
Orthodox
Agudas Achim Chabad
2233 West Mequon Road, Mequon 53092
(414) 242-2235
Fax: (414) 242-2268
Email: chabadmequon@aol.com
Web site: www.chabadmequon.org
Also has a mikvah.

Beth Jehudah
3100 North 52nd Street 53216   (414) 442-5730
Fax: (414) 442-6171
Email: bethjehudah@juno.com
Web site: www.bethjehudah.org

Congregation Anshai Leibowitz
2415 West Mequon Road 53092   (414) 512-1195
Fax: (414) 512-1695

Sheboygan

SYNAGOGUES
Traditional
Temple Beth El
1007 North Avenue 53083   (920) 452-5828
Email: bethelsheboygan@juno.com

WYOMING

Casper

SYNAGOGUES
Reform
4105 S. Poplar, PO Box 3534 82602   (307) 237-2330

Cheyenne

SYNAGOGUES
Conservative
Mount Sinai
2610 Pioneer Avenue 82001   (307) 634-3052
Gift shop and mikvah by appointment.

Laramie

SYNAGOGUES
Reform
Laramie JCC
PO Box 202 82073   (307) 760-9275
Email: www.uahc.org/wy/wy001

URUGUAY

After the Conversos in the sixteenth century, there was no known Jewish community in Uruguay until the late nineteenth century, when the country served as a stop-over on the way to Argentina. The Jewish population rose in the twentieth century, with immigration from the Middle East and eastern Europe. A synagogue was opened by 1917. Despite restrictive immigration laws imposed against European Jews fleeing Nazism, 2,500 Jews managed to enter the country between 1939 and 1940. Further Jewish immigration followed, from Hungary and the Middle East, in the post-war period.

There are many Jewish organisations functioning in Uruguay, including Zionist and women's organisations. Kosher restaurants exist in Jewish institutions, and there are a number of synagogues.

GMT -3 hours	Total Population 3,221,000
Country calling code (598)	Jewish Population 25,000
Emergency Telephone (Police – 999) (Fire – 999) (Ambulance – 999)	(Electricity voltage – 220)

Montevideo

With approximately 10,000 families in the capital of Uruguay, Montevideo contains almost all of the countryís Jewish community. There is a Museum of the Holocaust in Montevideo, and near the Teatro Solis opera house stands a Golda Meir monument. An Albert Einstein monument can be found in Rodo Park.

COMMUNITY ORGANISATIONS

Centro Lubavitch
Av. Brasil 2704, CP 11300   (2) 709-3444; 708-5169
Fax: (2) 711-3696
Email: shemtov@chasque.apc.org

Comite Central Israelita Del Uruguay
Rio Negro 1308, P. 5 11100   (2) 903-0464
Fax: (2) 900-6562
Email: cciu@adinet.com.uy

EMBASSY

Embassy of Israel
Bulevar Artigas 1585-89   (2) 400-4164
Fax: (2) 409-5821
Email: emisuyur@adlnet.com.uy

GROCERIES

Yavne
Cavia 2800   (2) 908-7869
Fax: (2) 707-0866

MEDIA

Newspaper
Semanario Hebreo
Soriano 875/201   (2) 925-311
Spanish-language weekly. Editor also directs daily Yiddish radio programme.

MIKVAOT

Adat Yiereim
Durazno 1183   (2) 711-1686
Fax: (2) 711-7736

MUSEUM

Centro Recordatorio del Holocausto
Canelones 1084, P.3 11100   (2) 902-5750
Fax: (2) 902-5740
Email: centroshoa@conectate.com.uy
First Museum of the Shoah in South America

RESTAURANTS

Kasherissimo
Camacua 623   (2) 915-0128
Fax: (2) 208-1536
Supervision: Chief Rabbi Yosef Bitton
The restaurant is situated in the Hebraica Macabi building.

SYNAGOGUES

Comunidad Israelita Hungara
Durazno 972   (2) 900-8456
Fax: (2) 900-8456

Social Isralite Adat Yeshurun
Alarcon 1396
Ashkenazi
Comunidad Israelita de Uruguay
Canelones 1084, Piso 1   (2) 902-5750
Fax: (2) 902-5740
Email: kehila@adinet.com.uy

Conservative
Nueva Congregacion Israelita
Wilson Ferreira Aldunate 1168   (2) 902-6620
Fax: (2) 902-0589
Email: nci@adinet.com.uy

Orthodox
Vaad Ha'ir
Canelones 828   (2) 900-6106
Fax: (2) 711-7736
Email: marebis@com.uy

Sephardi
Comunidad Israelita Sefardi
Buenos Aires 234, 21 de Setiembre 3111 (2) 710-179

Templo Sefardi
de Pocitos L. Franzini 888

TOURIST SITE
"Memorial to Golda Meir"
Reconquista y Ciudadela

Email: cciu@adinet.com.uy

UZBEKISTAN

The ancient Jewish community in this central Asian republic is believed to have originated from Persian exiles in the fifth century. The Jews were subject to harsh treatment under the various rulers of the region, but still managed to become important traders in this area, which straddled the route between Europe and China and the Far East. In the late Middle Ages Jewish weavers and dyers were asked to help in the local cloth industry, and Bukhara became a key Jewish city after it became the capital of the country in the 1500s. Once the area had been incorporated into the Russian Empire in 1868, many Jews from the west of the Empire moved into Uzbekistan. A further influx occurred when Uzbekistan was used to shelter Jews during the Nazi invasion of the Soviet Union – many subsequently set up home there.

The original Bukharan Jews are generally more religious than the Ashkenazim who entered the area in the nineteenth and twentieth centuries. There are Jewish schools in the area, and although there is no central Jewish organisation, there are many Jewish bodies operating on separate levels for the Ashkenazim and the Bukharans.

GMT +5 hours
Country calling code (7)
Emergency Telephone (Police – 03) (Fire – 03) (Ambulance – 03)

Total Population 21.206,000
Jewish Population 15,000
(Electricity voltage – 220)

Andizhan

SYNAGOGUES
7 Sovetskaya Street

Bukhara

SYNAGOGUES
20 Tsentralnaya Street

Katta-Kurgan

SYNAGOGUES
1 Karl Marx Alley

Kermine

SYNAGOGUES
36 Narimanov Street

Kokand

SYNAGOGUES
Dekabristov Street, Fergan Oblast

Margelan

SYNAGOGUES
Turtkilskaya Street, Fergan Oblast

Navoy

SYNAGOGUES
36 Narimanov Street

Samarkand

3,000 Jews live in Samarkand. Many are Bukharan, and live in the special mahala, the quarter designated to Jews.

SYNAGOGUES
18 Esayva Street

Tashkent

EMBASSY
Embassy of Israel
16A Shakhrisabz Street, 5th floor   (71) 152911
Fax: (71) 1521378
Email: isremb@online.ru

SYNAGOGUES
Gorbunova Street 62   (71) 1525978
Fax: (71) 1525978
Email: jewish@bcc.com.uz
Web site: www.jewish.uz

9 Chkalov Street

Ashkenazi
77 Chempianov Street

Sephardi
3 Sagban Street   (71) 40-0768

VENEZUELA

Settlement in Venezuela began in the early nineteenth century from the Caribbean. The Jews were granted freedom early (between 1819 and 1821), which encouraged more settlement. The community at that time was not religious. At the beginning of the twentieth century, some Middle Eastern Jewish immigrants organised a central committee for the first time. The powerful influence of the Catholic Church meant few Jews were accepted as immigrants in the pre-war rush to escape Nazi Europe.

After the war, however, the community began to expand, with arrivals from Hungary and the Middle East. The successful oil industry and the excellent Jewish education system attracted immigrants from other South American countries.

Today most Jews live in Caracas, the capital. Fifteen synagogues serve the country. The Lubavitch movement is present and maintains a yeshivah. Caracas has a Jewish bookshop and a weekly Jewish newspaper. Venezuela has an expanding Jewish community, in contrast to many of its South American neighbours. The oldest Jewish cemetery in South America, in Coro, with tombstones dating from 1832, is still in use today.

Note: (Dr. – 02 483 7021)
GMT -4 hours
Country calling code (58)
Emergency Telephone (Ambulance – 545 4545)

Total Population 22,777,000
Jewish Population 22,000
(Electricity voltage – 220)

Caracas

The first real Jewish settlement in the city dates from 1880 only although there is mention of them being in the territory in the early 18th century. The present community is basically Sephardi.

BAKERIES
Le Notre
Avenida Andres Bello   (2) 782-4448
Pasteleria Kasher
Avenida Los Proceres   (2) 515-086

BOOKSELLERS
Libreria Cultural Maimonides
Av Altamira Edif. Carlitos PB,
(near Av. Galapen), San Bernardino   (2) 551-6356
                              Fax: (2) 552-9127
                    Email: judaico@tecel.net.ve

CONTACT INFORMATION
Chabad-Lubavitch Centre
Apartado 5454 1010A   (2) 523-887

DELICATESSEN
La Belle Delicatesses
Av. Bogotá, Edif Santa María, Local 2,
Los Caobos   (2) 781-7204
                              Fax: (2) 781-7182
Kosher delicatessen and mini-market, restaurant and take-away.

EMBASSY
Embassy of Israel
Avenida Francisco de Miranda, Centro Empresarial Miranda, 4 Piso Oficina 4-D, Apartado Postal Los Ruices 70081   (2) 239-4511; 239-4921
                              Fax: (2) 239-4320

GROCERIES
Mini Market
Avenida Los Caobas   (2) 781-7204
Take-away.

MEDIA
Newspaper
Nuevo Mundo Israelita
Av Marques del Toro 9, Los Caobos

MIKVAOT
Shomrei Shabbat Association Synagogue
Av Anauco, San Bernardino   (2) 517-197

**Union Israelita de Caracas Synagogue &
Community Centre**
Av Marques del Toro 9, San Bernardino   (2) 552-8222
                              Fax: (2) 552-7628
                    Email: rabino@brener@eldish.net

SYNAGOGUES
Ashkenazi
Great Synagogue of Caracas
Av Francisco Javier Ustariz, San Bernardino
                                        (2) 511-869

Shomrei Shabbat Assoc. Synagogue
Av Anauco, San Bernardino   (2) 517-197

Union Israelita de Caracas Synagogue & Community Centre
Av Marques del Toro 9, San Bernardino (2) 552-8222
Fax: (2) 552-7628
Email: rabino@brener@eldish.net
If notified in advance, they can arrange kosher lunches. There is also a meat snack bar open in the evening.

Sephardi
Bet El
Av Cajigal, San Bernardino (2) 522-008

Keter Tora
Av Lopez Mendez, San Bernardino

Shaare Shalom
Av Bogota, Quinta Julieta, Los Caobos

Tiferet Yisrael
Av Mariperez, Los Caobos (2) 781-1942

Maracaibo

COMMUNITY ORGANISATIONS
Associación Israelita de Maracaibo
Calle 74 No 13-26 (61) 70333

Porlamar

SYNAGOGUES
Or Meir
Calle Carnevali, Margarita Island (95) 634-433
Mikva on premises.

VIRGIN ISLANDS (USA)

Jews first began to settle on the island in 1655, taking advantage of liberal Danish rule. They were mainly traders in sugar cane, rum and molasses, and by 1796 a synagogue had been founded. The Jewish population of 400 in 1850 made up half of the islands' white community. There have been three Jewish governors; one being Gabriel Milan, the first governor who was appointed by King Christian of Denmark.

The community began to shrink after the Panama Canal was opened in 1914, and by 1942 only 50 Jews remained. Since 1945, the community has expanded again, with families arriving from the US mainland.

GMT -4 hours
Country calling code (1 340)

Total Population 115,000
Jewish Population 300

St Thomas

SYNAGOGUES
Hebrew Congregation of St. Thomas
PO Box 266 00804 (340) 774-4312
Fax: (340) 774-4312
Email: hebrewcong@islands.vi
Web site: www.onepaper.com/synagogue
This synagogue built in 1833, was restored in 2000

Orthodox
Khal Hakodesh
(340) 779-2000

YUGOSLAVIA

(Yugoslavia at present comprises Serbia and Montenegro.) The history of Serbian Jewry is both long and comparatively happy, with initial settlement occurring in Roman times. Afte the onset of Turkish domination in 1389, the community continued to thrive and also prospered under Austrian rule in the eighteenth century. The nineteenth century saw some measures being taken against the Jews after Serbia became independent, but these were quickly redressed in 1889, following the Treaty of Berlin.

After 1918, Serbia was united with Croatia, Slovenia and the other south Slavic states into one country, known as Yugoslavia. The community suffered heavily under Nazi domination. The Jews were active among the Yugoslav partisans and, after liberation, many who had hidden or fought with the partisans began to return to their homes. Before the break-up of Yugoslavia, the Jews were allowed contact with other communities, including Israel. Since the civil war, some Jews have remained in the country, and there is a synagogue and a Talmud Torah school in Belgrade.

GMT + 1 hour	Total Population 10,597,000
Country calling code (381)	Jewish Population 2,500
Emergency Telephone (Police – 92) (Fire – 93) (Ambulance – 94)	(Electricity voltage – 220)

Belgrade

Some 2,000 Jews now live in the capital of Serbia, compared with hardly any during the latter stages of World War Two. There is an Ashkenazi synagogue which follows Sephardi tradition (or nusach), and there is a community centre, although kosher food is not available.

COMMUNITY ORGANISATIONS

Federation of Jewish Communities
7 Kralja Petra Street 71a/111,
PO Box 841 11001   (11) 624-359/621-837
Fax: (11) 626-674
Email: savezjev@infosky.net

MUSEUMS

Jewish Historical Museum
Kralja Petra Street 71a/1 11001   (11) 622-634
Fax: (11) 626-674
Email: muzej@eunet.yu
Web site: www.jim-bg.org
Open daily from 10.00 to 12.00.

SYNAGOGUES

Birjuzova Street 19
Services are held Friday evenings and Jewish holidays.

TOURIST SITE

Jewish Cemetery
There are monuments here to fallen fighters and martyrs of Fascism, fallen Jewish soldiers in the Serbian army in the First World War. In 1990 a new monument to Jews killed in Serbia was erected by the Danube, in the pre-War Jewish quarter Dorcol.

Novi Sad

COMMUNITY ORGANISATIONS

Community Offices
Jevrejska 11   (21) 613-882

TOURIST SITE

Jewish Cemetery
There is a monument to the Jews who fell in the War and the victims of Fascism. The synagogue here is no longer open but it's reported to be extremely beautiful, and is currently being converted to a concert hall.

Subotica

COMMUNITY ORGANISATIONS

Community Offices
Dimitrija Tucovica Street 13   28483

TOURIST SITE

The Subotica Synagogue built in 1901 and considered one of the finest Art Nouveau buildings in Europe is currently being restored.

ZAMBIA

The Jewish community began in the early twentieth century, with cattle ranching being the main attraction for Jewish immigrants. The community grew, and the copper industry was developed largely by Jewish entrepreneurs. With refugees from Nazism and a post-war economic boom, the Jewish community in the mid-1950s totalled 1,200. The community declined after independence in 1964.

Today, the Council for Zambian Jewry (founded in 1978) fulfils the role of the community's central body.

GMT +2 hours
Country calling code (260)
Emergency Telephone (Police – 999) (Fire – 999) (Ambulance – 999)

Total Population 9,715,000
Jewish Population Under 100
(Electricity voltage – 220)

Lusaka

COMMUNITY ORGANISATIONS
Council for Zambian Jewry
P O Box 30089 10101   (1) 229-556
Fax: (1) 223-798
Email: galaun@zamnet.zm

SYNAGOGUES
Lusaka Hebrew Congregation
Chachacha Road, POB 30020   (1) 229-190
Fax: (1) 221-428
Email: galaun@zamnet.zm

ZIMBABWE

Jews were among the earliest pioneers in Zimbabwe (formerly Rhodesia). The first white child born there (April 1894) was Jewish. The first synagogue in Zimbabwe (formerly Rhodesia) was set up in 1894, in a tent in Bulawayo. In 1897 a Jew was elected as the first mayor of Bulawayo. The first Jews came from Europe (especially Lithuania), and they became involved in trade and managing hotels. They were joined in the 1920s and 1930s by Sephardis from Rhodes. Some senior politicians in the country were Jewish, including one prime minister.

The 1970s saw the turbulent transition to Zimbabwe and many Jews emigrated to escape the unrest. The community is now mainly Ashkenazi, with an important Sephardi component. Harare has both an Ashkenazi and a Sephardi synagogue; Bulawayo has a Ashkenazi synagogue. There are community centres in both the towns, and schools, although the latter have many local, non-Jewish pupils.

GMT +2 hours
Country calling code (263)
Emergency Telephone (Police – 999) (Fire – 999) (Ambulance – 999)

Total Population 12,294,000
Jewish Population 900
(Electricity voltage – 220/240)

Bulawayo

SYNAGOGUES
Bulawayo Hebrew Congregation
Jason Moyo Street, PO Box 337   (9) 237-335

Harare

COMMUNITY ORGANISATIONS
Zimbabwe Jewish Board of Deputies
PO Box 1954   (4) 702-507
Fax: (4) 702-506
Email: cazo@zol.co.zw
Hours of opening 8.30 am. to 12 noon

SYNAGOGUES
Harare Hebrew Congregation
Milton Park Jewish Centre, Lezard Avenue,
PO Box 342   (4) 727-576

Sephardi Congregation
54 Josiah Chinamano Avenue, PO Box 1051
   (4) 722-899

International Access Dialling Codes

In order to phone from one country to another one must use the appropriate International Access Dialling Code.

Most International Access Dialling Codes are 00. The following however are the exceptions.

Australia	0011
Bahamas	11
Belarus	810
Canada	011
Colombia	9
Finland	varies
Hong Kong	1
Israel	varies
Japan	varies
Lithuania	810
Mexico	98
Russia	810
Singapore	1
South Africa	09
South Korea	varies
Taiwan	2
Thailand	1
Ukraine	810
United States of America	011
Uzbekistan	810
Yugoslavia	99

The procedure is as follows:

FIRST dial the International Access Code for the country you are calling from (as shown above).

SECOND dial the country calling code (as shown on the appropriate page of this guide) for the country you are dialling to.

THIRD dial the area code for the location you are dialling to (some countries do not require an area code).

FOURTH dial the local phone number.

Kosher Fish in Europe

CYPRUS

Antzouva (Anchovy)
Bacceliaos (Cod)
Barbouni (Pike)
Cephalos (Perch)
Glossa (Sole)
Lavraki (Bass)
Sardella (Pilchard)
Scoumbri (Mackerel)
Tonos (Tuna)
Tsipoura (Bream)

CZECH REPUBLIC

Ancovicka (Anchovy)
Belicka (Roach)
Kambala (Brill)
Kapr (Carp)
Lin (Tench)
Losos (Salmon)
Makrela (Mackerel)
Okoun (Perch)
Parmice (Mullet)
Platejs (Dab)
Platyz (Plaice)
Plotice (Sole)
Prazama (Bream)
Pstruh (Trout)
Sardinka (Sardine)
Sled (Herring)
Sprota (Sprat)
Stika (Pike)
Treska (Haddock)
Tunak (Tuna)

DENMARK

Aborre (Perch)
Ansjos (Anchovy)
Bars (Bass)
Brasen (Bream)
Brisling (Sprat)
Gedde (Pike)
Helleyflynder
    (Halibut)
Hvilling (Whiting)

Ising (Dab)
Karpe (Carp)
Knurhane (Gunard)
Kuller (Haddock)
Kulmule (Hake)
Laks (Salmon)
Lange (Ling)
Lubbe (Pollack)
Makrel (Mackerel)
Multe (Mullet)
Orred (Trout)
Rodspaette (Plaice)
Sardin (Sardine)
Sild (Herring)
Skalle (Roach)
Skrubbe (Flounder)
Slethvarre (Brill)
Suder (Tench)
Torsk (Cod)
Tun fisk (Tuna)
Tunge (Sole)

FRANCE

Aiglefin (Haddock)
Anchois (Anchovy)
Bar Commun (Bass)
Barbue (Brill)
Breme (Bream)
Brochet (Pike)
Cabillaud (Cod)
Carpe (Carp)
Carrelet (Plaice)
Daurade (Bream)
Epirlan (Smelt)
Flet (Flounder)
Fletan (Halibut)
Gardon (Roach)
Grondin (Gunard)
Hareng (Herring)
Lieu Jaune (Pollack)
Limande (Dab)
Lingue (Ling)
Maquereau
    (Mackerel)

Merlan (Whiting)
Merlu (Hake)
Mulet (Mullet)
Perche (Perch)
Pilchard (Pilchard)
Plie (Plaice)
Sardine (Sardine)
Saumon (Salmon)
Sole (Sole)
Sprat (Sprat)
Tanche (Tench)
Thon (Tuna)
Truite (Trout)

GERMANY

Barsch (Perch)
Brasse (Bream)
Flunder (Flounder)
Forelle (Trout)
Glattbutt (Brill)
Hecht (Pike)
Heilbutt (Halibut)
Hering (Herring)
Kabeljau (Cod)
Knurrhahn (Gunard)
Lachs (Salmon)
Leng (Ling)
Makrele (Mackerel)
Meerasche (Mullet)
Pilchard (Pilchard)
Plotze (Roach)
Pollack (Pollack)
Sardelle (Anchovy)
Sardine (Sardine)
Scharbe (Dab)
Schellfisch (Haddock)
Schlei (Tench)
Scholle (Plaice)
Seebarsch (Bass)
Seehecht (Hake)
Seezunge (Sole)
Sprotte (Sprat)
Thun (Tuna)
Weissfisch (Carp)

Wittling (Whiting)

GREECE

Antjuga (Anchovy)
Bakaliaros (Cod)
Chematida
    (Flounder)
Chromatida (Dab)
Gados (Haddock)
Giavros (Anchovy)
Glinia (Tench)
Glossa (Sole)
Glossaki (Plaice)
Hippoglossa
    (Halibut)
Kaponi (Gunard)
Kephalos (Mullet)
Kyprinos (Carp)
Lavraki (Bass)
Lestia (Bream)
Papalina (Sprat)
Pentiki (Ling)
Perca chani (Perch)
Pestropha (Trout)
Pissi (Brill)
Regha (Herring)
Romvos (Brill)
Sardella (Pilchard)
Sardine (Sardine)
Scoumbri (Mackerel)
Solomos (Salmon)
Tonnos (Tuna)
Tourna (Pike)
Tsironi (Roach)

ITALY

Acciuga (Anchovy)
Aringa (Herring)
Asinello (Haddock)
Brama (Bream)
Carpa (Carp)
Cefalo (Mullet)
Halibut (Halibut)
Limanda (Dab)

Luccio (Pike)
Maccerello
  (Mackerel)
Merlano (Whiting)
Merluzzo Bianco
  (Cod)
Merluzzo Giallo
  (Pollack)
Molva (Ling)
Nasello (Hake)
Passera (Plaice)
Passera Pianuzza
  (Flounder)
Pesce (Perch)
Pesce Capone
  (Gunard)
Rombo Liscio (Brill)
Salmone (Salmon)
Sardina (Sardine)
Sogliola (Sole)
Spigola (Bass)
Spratto (Sprat)
Tinca (Tench)
Tonno (Tuna)
Triotto (Roach)
Trota (Trout)

NETHERLANDS
Aaldoe (Mullet)
Ansjovis (Anchovy)
Baars (Perch)
Blankvoorn (Roach)
Bot (Flounder)
Brasem (Bream)
Forel (Trout)
Griet (Brill)
Harder (Mullet)
Haring (Herring)
Heek (Hake)
Helibot (Halibut)
Kabeljauw (Cod)
Karper (Carp)
Leng (Ling)
Makree (Mackerel)
Pelser (Sardine)
Poon (Gunard)

Salm (Salmon)
Sardien (Sardine)
Schar (Dab)
Schelvis (Haddock)
Schol (Plaice)
Snoek (Pike)
Sprot (Sprat)
Tong (Sole)
Tonijn (Tuna)
Wijting (Whiting)
Witte koolvis
  (Pollack)
Zeebaars (Bass)
Zeelt (Tench)

PORTUGAL
Alabote (Halibut)
Anchova (Anchovy)
Arenque (Herring)
Arinca (Haddock)
Atum (Tuna)
Bacalhau (Cod)
Badejo (Pollack)
Biqueirao (Anchovy)
Carpa (Carp)
Donzela (Ling)
Espadilha (Sprat)
Linguado (Sole)
Lucio (Pike)
Perca (Perch)
Pescada (Hake)
Petruca (Flounder)
Robalo (Bass)
Rodovalho (Brill)
Ruivaca (Roach)
Ruivo (Gunard)
Salmao (Salmon)
Sarda (Mackerel)
Sardinha (Sardine)
Sargo (Bream)
Solha (Plaice)
Solhao (Dab)
Tainha (Mullet)
Tenca (Tench)
Truta (Trout)

SPAIN
Abadejo (Pollack)
Anchoa (Anchovy)
Arenque (Herring)
Atun (Tuna)
Bacalao (Cod)
Bermejuela (Roach)
Boqueron (Anchovy)
Caballa (Mackerel)
Carpa (Carp)
Eglefino (Haddock)
Espadin (Sprat)
Halibut (Halibut)
Lenguado (Sole)
Limanda (Dab)
Lisa (Mullet)
Lubina (Bass)
Lucio (Pike)
Maruca (Ling)
Merlan (Whiting)
Merluza (Hake)
Perca (Perch)
Platija (Flounder)
Remol (Brill)
Rubios (Gunard)
Salmon (Salmon)
Sardina (Sardine)
Solla (Plaice)
Tenca (Tench)
Trucha (Trout)

TURKEY
Alabalik (Trout)
Bakalyaro (Whiting)
Berlam (Hake)
Caca (Sprat)
Civisiz kalkan (Brill)
Derepissi (Flounder)
Dil baligi (Sole)
Gelincik (Ling)
Hamsi (Anchovy)
Kadife baligi
  (Tench)
Kefal (Mullet)
Kirlangic (Gunard)
Kizilgoz (Roach)

Levrek (Bass)
Morina (Cod)
Palatika (Sprat)
Pisi baligi (Dab)
Ringa (Herring)
Sardalya (Sardine)
Sardayalo (Pilchard)
Sazan (Carp)
Som baligi (Salmon)
Tahta baligi (Bream)
Tatlisu levregi
  (Perch)
Ton baligi (Tuna)
Turna baligi (Pike)
Uskumru (Mackerel)

**UNITED
  KINGDOM**
Anchovy
Barbel
Bass
Bloater
Bonito
Bream
Brill
Brisling
Buckling
Carp
Coalfish
Cod
Coley
Dab
Dace
Flounder
Fluke
Grayling
Gurnard
Haddock
Hake
Halibut
Herring
Hoki
John Dory
Keta Salmon
Kipper
Ling

Mackerel
Megrim
Mock Halibut
Mullet Grey
Mullet Red
Norway Haddock
Parrot Fish
Perch
Pike

Pilchard
Plaice
Pole
Pollack
Redfish
Roach
Saithe
Salmon
Sardine

Shad
Sild
Smelt
Snapper
Snoek
Sole Dover
Sole Lemon
Sprat
Tench

Tilapia
Trout
Tuna (Tunny)
Whitebait
Whiting
Witch

Kosher Fish outside Europe

AUSTRALIA
Anchovy
Baramundi
Barracouta
Barracuda
Blue Eye
Blue Grenadier
Bream
Butterfly-fish
Cod
Coral Perch
Duckfish
Flathead
Flounder
Garfish
Groper
Gurnard
Haddock
Hake
Harpuka
Herring
Jewfish
John Dory
Lemon Sole
Mackerel
Morwong
Mullet
Murray Cod
Murray Perch
Orange Roughy
Perch

Pike
Pilchard
Red Emperor
Redfin
Salmon
Sardine
Sea Perch
Shad
Sild
Snapper
Tailor
Tasmanian
   Trumpeter
Terakiji
Trevally
Trout
Tuna:
   Albacore, Bluefin
   North bluefin
   South bluefin
   Skipjack (striped)
   Yellowfin
Whiting
Yellowtail

CANADA
Albacore
Anchovy
Bass
Boston Bluefish
Carp

Cisco
Cod
Flounder
Goldeye
Haddock
Hake
Halibut
Herring
Mackerel
Orange Roughy
Perch
Pickerel
Pike
Pollock
Pompano
Salmon
Sardine
Silverside
Smelt
Snapper
Sole
Sunfish
Tarpon
Trout
Tuna

CARIBBEAN
Bonito
Grouper
Kingsish
Mullet

Muttonfish
Pompano
Roballo
Smelt
Snapper Red/Yellow
Spanish Mackerel
Trout
Tuna

HONG KONG
Anchovy
Bigeyes
Carp
Crevalles
Croakers
Giant Perch
Grey Mullet
Grouper
Japanese Sea Perch
Leopard Coral Trout
Pampano
Pilchard
Red Sea Bream
Round Herring
Sardine
Scad
Whitefish

NEW ZEALAND
Hoki
John Dory

Kingfish
Mackerel
Mullet
Orange Roughy
Perch
Piper
Salmon
Smooth Black
Snapper
Sole
Southern Whiting
Terakihi
Trevally
Trout

SOUTH AFRICA

Albacore Tuna
Anchovies
Butterfish
Carp
Euthynnus Tuna
Haddock
Hake
Herring
Kabeljou
Kingklip
Maas Banker
Mackerel
Pilchards

Red Roman
Salmon
Sardines
Seventy Four
Skipjack Tuna
Snoek
Sole
Steembras
Stock Fish
Stump Nose
Tongol Tuna
Trout
Yellowfin Tuna

UNITED STATES OF AMERICA

Albacore
Alewife
Amberjack
Anchovies
Angelfish
Barb
Barracouta
Barracuda
Bass
Bigeyes
Black Cod
Blackfish
Blueback

Bluefish
Bluegill
Bonito
Bream
Brill
Capelin
Carp
Cero
Char
Chub
Cisco
Coalfish
Cod
Crevalle
Dab
Flounders
Fluke
Gag
Grayling
Grouper
Haddock
Hake
Halibut
Herrings
John Dory
Kingfish
Mackerel
Mahi Mahi
Merluccio

Mullet
Parrot Fish
Perch
Pike
Pilchard
Plaice
Pollock
Pomfrets
Red Snapper
Roach
Saithe
Salmon
Sardine
Shad
Sierra
Skipjack
Smelts
Snapper
Sole
Sprat
Tench
Tilapia
Trout
Tuna
Wahoo
Whitefish
Whiting
Yellowtail

Jewish Calendar

2003 (5763-5764)

Fast of Esther	Monday	March 17th
Purim	Tuesday	March 18th
First Day Pesach	Thursday	April 17th
Second Day Pesach	Friday	April 18th
Seventh Day Pesach	Wednesday	April 23rd
Eighth Day Pesach (Yizkor)	Thursday	April 24th
Holocaust Memorial Day	Tuesday	April 29th
Israel Independence Day	Wednesday	May 7th
Lag B'Omer	Tuesday	May 20th
First Day Shavout	Friday	June 6th
Second Day Shavout (Yizkor)	Saturday	June 7th
Fast of Tammuz	Thursday	July 17th
Fast of Av	Thursday	August 7th
First Day Rosh Hashanah	Saturday	September 27th
Second Day Rosh Hashanah	Sunday	September 28th
Fast of Gedaliah	Monday	September 29th
Yom Kippur (Yizkor)	Monday	October 6th
First Day Succot	Saturday	October 11th
Second Day Succot	Sunday	October 12th
Shemini Atseret (Yizkor)	Saturday	October 18th
Simchat Torah	Sunday	October 19th
First Day Chanutah	Saturday	December 20th

2004 (5764-5765)

Fast of Esther	Thursday	March 4th
Purim	Sunday	March 7th
First Day Pesach	Tuesday	April 6th
Second Day Pesach	Wednesday	April 7th
Seventh Day Pesach	Monday	April 12th
Eighth Day Pesach (Yizkor)	Tuesday	April 13th
Holocaust Memorial Day	Sunday	April 18th
Israel Independence Day	Monday	April 26th
Lag B'Omer	Sunday	May 9th
First Day Shavout	Wednesday	May 26th
Second Day Shavout (Yizkor)	Thursday	May 27th
Fast of Tammuz	Tuesday	July 6th
Fast of Av	Tuesday	July 27th
First Day Rosh Hashanah	Thursday	September 16th
Second Day Rosh Hashanah	Friday	September 17th
Fast of Gedaliah	Sunday	September 19th
Yom Kippur (Yizkor)	Saturday	September 25th
First Day Succot	Thursday	September 30th
Second Day Succot	Friday	October 1st
Shemini Atseret (Yizkor)	Thursday	October 7th
Simchat Torah	Friday	October 8th
First Day Chanukah	Wednesday	December 8th

Index

Berkeley	253	Brakpan	188	Canton (OH)	343
Berlin	95	Brantford	39	Cape Cod	296
Bermuda	24	Brasov	178	Cape Town	193
Bern	205	Bratislava	186	Caracas	370
Bershad	214	Braunschweig	96	Cardiff	247
Besancon	64	Brazil	27	Carmel	254
Bethesda	291	Bremen	96	Carpentras	85
Bethlehem (NH)	309	Bremgarten / Aargau	206	Casablanca	156
Bethlehem (PA)	348	Brest (Belarus)	20	Casale Monferrato	136
Beverly	294	Brest (France)	69	Casper	367
Beverly Hills	255	Bridgeport	267	Castro Valley	254
Beziers	85	Bridgeton	311	Catskills	324
Bialystok	173	Brighton (MA)	295	Cavaillon	86
Biel/Bienne	205	Brighton and Hove (UK)	241	Cayman Islands	46
Bielsko-Biala	173	Brisbane	8	Cedar Rapids	285
Billings	307	Bristol (RI)	356	Cedarhurst	326
Binghamton	323	Bristol (UK)	217	Celle	97
Birkirkara	151	Brno	54	Ceuta	199
Birmingham (AL)	249	Brockton	295	Chalkis	105
Birmingham (UK)	243	Brookline	295	Chalons-sur-Marne	65
Birobidjan	181	Brussels	22	Chalon-sur-Saone	65
Bischeim-Schiltigheim	69	Bryansk	182	Chambery	65
Bishkek	146	Bucharest	179	Champaign-Urbana	281
Bismark	343	Budapest	109	Champigny	78
Bitche	64	Buenos Aires	2	Charenton-le-Pont	78
Blackpool	223	Buffalo	323	Charleroi	24
Blida	1	Bukhara	369	Charleston	357
Bloemfontein	188	Bulawayo	37	Charleston	366
Bloomington	283	Bulgaria	33	Charlotte	342
Bobigny	78	Burbank	255	Charlottesville	363
Bobruisk	20	Burgos	196	Chateauroux	69
Boca Raton	272	Burlingame	253	Chatham	39
Bochum	96	Burlington (MA)	295	Chattanooga	358
Bogota	50	Burlington (NJ)	311	Cheadle	235
Boise	281	Burlington (VT)	363	Chelles	78
Bolivia	25	Burma see (Myanmar)		Chelmsford	296
Bologna	135	Bursa	212	Cheltenham	221
Bombay see Mumbai		Bushey	222	Chemnitz	97
Bondy	78	Bussum	163	Chernigov	214
Bonita	253			Chernovtsy	214
Bonn	96	**C**		Cherry Hill	311
Boras	202			Chevy Chase	291
Bordeaux	91	Caen	69	Cheyenne	367
Borisov	20	Caesarea	119	Chicago	281
Boskovice	54	Cairo	60	Chigwell	220
Bosnia-Hercegovina	26	Calcutta see Kolkata		Chile	46
Boston	294	Calgary	34	Chimkent	145
Botosani	178	Cali	50	China	48
Boulay	64	Caluire- et- Cuire	85	Chisinau	154
Boulder	265	Cambridge (MA)	296	Chmelnitsy	214
Boulogne sur Seine	78	Cambridge (UK)	218	Choisy-le-Roi	78
Boulogne-sur-Mer	65	Campinas	30	Christchurch	166
Bournemouth	219	Campos	28	Chula Vista	254
Bouzonville	65	Canada	34	Cincinnati	344
Bowie	291	Canberra	6	Cinnaminson	311
Bradford	244	Cannes	85	Clark	311
Bradley Beach	310	Canterbury	223	Clearwater	272
Braintree	294	Canton (MA)	296	Clermont-Ferrand	86

Cleveland	344	Daugavpils	146	Edison	312
Clichy-sur-Seine	78	Davenport	285	Edmonton	34
Clifton	311	Davis	254	Egypt	60
Clifton Park	325	Dayton	345	Eilat	120
Clinton	296	Daytona Beach	272	Eindhoven	164
Cluj Napoca	179	Dead Sea	120	Eisenstadt	14
Coblenz (Koblenz)	97	Deal	312	Ekaterinburg	182
Cochabamba	25	Deauville	69	El Dorado	252
Cochin	111	Decatur	279	El Escorial	196
Colchester	220	Deerfield Beach	272	El Jadida	156
Colmar	65	Degania Alef	120	El Paso	360
Cologne	97	Delft	164	El Salvador	61
Colombia	50	Delmar	325	Elbeuf	69
Colombo	201	Delray Beach	273	Elizabeth	312
Colonia	311	Denali National Park	250	Elkins park	348
Colorado Springs	266	Denmark	57	Ellenville	324
Columbia	358	Denver	266	Elmira	325
Columbus (GA)	279	Derbent	182	Elmwood Park	312
Columbus (OH)	345	Des Moines	285	Emmendingen	98
Commack	328	Detroit	304	Encinitas	254
Compiegne	65	Dieuze	65	Encino	255
Concord	309	Dijon	65	Endingen	206
Concordia	5	Dix Hills	328	Engelberg	206
Constanta	179	Dnepropetrovsk	214	Enghien	79
Copenhagen	57	Dominican Republic	59	Englewood	312
Cordoba (Argentina)	5	Donetsk	214	Enschede	164
Cordoba (Spain)	196	Dorohoi	179	Epernay	65
Corfu	106	Dortmund	97	Epinal	65
Cork	114	Douglas	248	Epinay	79
Cornwall	39	Dover	270	Erechim	29
Corpus Christi	360	Downey	255	Erfurt	98
Corsica	92	Dresden	97	Erie	348
Costa Mesa	254	Druskininkai	147	Ernakulam	111
Costa Rica	51	Dublin	114	Esch-Sur-Alzette	149
Coventry	244	Dubrovnik	52	Essaouira	
Cracow	173	Dubuque	286	(formerly Mogador)	156
Cranbury	312	Duluth	305	Essen	98
Cranford	312	Dundee	245	Essingen	98
Cranston	356	Dunedin	166	Estella	196
Créteil	78	Dunkirk	65	Estonia	61
Croatia	52	Dunoon	245	Ethiopia	62
Cuba	53	Durban	192	Eugene	347
Cuernavaca	152	Durham	342	Eureka	254
Cumberland	291	Dushanbe	210	Evansville	283
Cuneo	136	Dusseldorf	98	Everett	296
Curaçao	165			Evergreen	267
Curitiba	28	**E**		Evian	86
Cyprus	54			Exeter	219
Czech Republic	54	East Brunswick	312	Eze-Village	86
		East Chicago	283		
D		East Falmouth	296	**F**	
		East Lansing	304		
Dallas	360	East London	188	Fair Lawn	313
Daly City	254	Eastbourne	242	Fairfax	364
Dan	120	Easton (MA)	296	Fairfield	268
Danbury	268	Easton (PA)	348	Fall River	297
Danville	363	Ecuador	59	Falls Church	364
Darmstadt	97	Edinburgh	246	Fargo	343

Faulquemont-Crehange	65	Glens Falls	325	Hampton	364
Fayetteville	342	Gliwice	174	Hanita	123
Ferrara	136	Gloucester	297	Hanover	99
Fez	156	Gloversville	325	Haon	123
Fiji	62	Golan Heights	121	Harare	373
Finland	63	Gold Coast	9	Harlow	220
Fitchburg	297	Gomel	20	Harrisburg	349
Fleischmanns	324	Gori	93	Harrison	340
Flint	304	Gorizia	137	Harrogate	244
Florence	136	Gothenburg	202	Hartford	268
Flushing	337	Granada	196	Hasbrouck Heights	314
Fontainebleau	79	Granada Hills	256	Hastings	242
Fontenay aux Roses	79	Grand Cayman	46	Havana	53
Fontenay sous Bois	79	Grand Rapids	304	Haverhill	297
Forbach	65	Grasmere	219	Haverstraw	338
Forest Hills	337	Graz	14	Hazelton	349
Fort Dodge	286	Great Falls	308	Hazorea	123
Fort Lauderdale	273	Great Neck	326	Heidelberg	99
Fort Lee	313	Greater Rio de Janeiro	28	Helena	252
Fort Meyers	273	Greece	105	Helsinki	63
Fort Pierce	273	Greenbelt	291	Helslingborg	202
Fort Wayne	284	Greenfield	297	Hemel Hempstead	222
Framingham	297	Greensboro	342	Hendersonville	343
France	64	Greenvale	326	Herford	99
Frankfurt	98	Greenville	306	Hershey	349
Fredericton	38	Greenwood	306	Hervas	196
Freehold	313	Grenoble	86	Herzlia	123
Freeport	18	Grimsby	222	Highland	284
Freiburg	98	Grodno	20	Highland Park (IL)	282
Frejus	86	Groningen	164	Highland Park (NJ)	314
Fresno	254	Grosbliederstroff	65	Hildesheim	99
Fribourg	206	Guadalajara	152	Hillcrest	337
Friedberg	99	Guadeloupe	92	Hillside	314
Fulda	99	Guaruja	30	Hilo	280
Furth	99	Guatemala	107	Hilversum	164
		Guelph	39	Hingham	297
G		Guildford	241	Hiroshima	144
		Gush Etzion	122	Hobart	9
Gaithersburg	291			Hoboken	314
Galanta	186	**H**		Hof	99
Galati	180			Holbrook	297
Galilee	121	Haarlem	164	Holesov	55
Gardena	256	Hackensack	313	Holliston	297
Garges-les-Gonesse	79	Haddonfield	314	Hollywood (CA)	256
Gary	284	Hadera	122	Hollywood & Vicinity (FL)	273
Gateshead	242	Hagen	99	Holyoke	297
Gelsenkirchen	99	Hagerstown	293	Honduras	108
Geneva (NY)	325	Hagondange	66	Hong Kong	48
Geneva (Switzerland)	206	Haguenau	66	Honolulu	280
Genoa	137	Haifa	122	Hornbaek	58
Georgetown	358	Haiti	107	Hot Springs	252
Georgia	93	Hale Barns	235	Houston	361
Germany	94	Halifax	38	Hudson	325
Gerona	196	Halle	99	Hull (MA)	298
Ghent	24	Hamburg	99	Hull (UK)	222
Gibraltar	104	Hamilton (Bermuda)	24	Hungary	109
Glace Bay	38	Hamilton (Canada)	39	Huntington	366
Glasgow	246	Hammond	284	Huntsville	250

Le Kremlin-Bicetre	80	Lubeck	100	McKeesport	349
Le Mans	69	Lublin	174	Meaux	80
Le Perreux Nogent	80	Lucerne	207	Medellin	50
Le Raincy	80	Lugano	207	Medford	299
Le Vesinet	80	Lund	202	Meknes	157
Leeds	244	Luneville	66	Melbourne (Australia)	10
Leghorn	137	Lusaka	373	Melbourne (FL)	274
Legnica	174	Luton	218	Melilla	200
Leicester	223	Luxembourg	149	Melrose	299
Leiden	164	Luxembourg City	149	Melun	81
Leipzig	100	Lviv	215	Memphis	359
Lengnau	207	Lynn	298	Menton	89
Leominster	298	Lyons	87	Merano	137
Les Lilas	80			Mercer Island	365
Lethbridge	35	**M**		Meriden	269
Levallois Perret	80			Merlebach	66
Lexington (KY)	287	Maagan	129	Metuchen	316
Lexington (MA)	298	Maastricht	164	Metz	66
Lexington Park	293	Maayan Harod	129	Meudon-La-Foret	81
Liberec	55	Macedonia	150	Mexico	152
Libourne	91	Macon (France)	88	Mexico City	152
Liège	24	Macon (GA)	280	Miami/Miami Beach	274
Liepaja	146	Madison	367	Michelstadt	101
Lille	66	Madrid	197	Michigan City	284
Lima	171	Magdeburg	100	Middletown (CT)	269
Limoges	91	Mahanayim	129	Middletown (RI)	356
Lincoln (NE)	308	Mahwah	315	Mikulov	55
Lincoln (UK)	224	Maidenhead	218	Milan	137
Linden	315	Mainz	100	Milford	299
Linz	15	Maisons-Alfort	80	Millis	299
Lisbon	176	Majorca	200	Millville	316
Lithuania	147	Makhachkala	182	Milton	299
Little Neck	338	Malaga	197	Milton Keynes	218
Little Rock	252	malaysia	150	Milwaukee	367
Liverpool	239	Malden	299	Minden	101
Livingston	315	Malmo	202	Minneapolis	305
Ljubljana	187	Malta	151	Minsk	20
Llandudno	248	Manaus	27	Mississauga	40
Loch Sheldrake	324	Manchester (CT)	269	Missoula	308
Lod	129	Manchester (NH)	309	Mobile	250
Lodz	174	Manchester (UK)	236	Modena	138
Lohamei Hagetaot	129	Manila	172	Moghilev	20
London (Canada)	40	Mannheim	100	Mogi Das Cruzes	30
London (UK)	224	Mantua	137	Moldova	154
Long Beach (CA)	256	Maplewood	316	Monaco	155
Long Beach (NY)	327	Maputo	158	Monchengladbach	101
Long Island	326	Maracaibo	371	Moncton	38
Longmeadow	298	Marbella	198	Monroe	328
Longy	248	Marblehead	299	Mons	24
Lorain	346	Marburg an der Lahn	100	Monsey	339
Lorient	69	Margate	223	Montauban	91
Los Alamos	321	Margelan	369	Montbeliard	66
Los Angeles	256	Marignane	88	Monte Carlo	155
Los Angeles (Greater)	255	Marlboro	299	Monterrey	154
Loughton	221	Marrakech	157	Montevideo	368
Louisville	287	Marseilles	88	Montgomery	250
Lowell	298	Martinique	92	Monticello	324
Lubbock	362	Massy	80	Montpellier (France)	89

Montpelier (VT)	363	Bronx	332	Olympia	365
Montreal	43	Brooklyn	332	Omaha	308
Montreuil	81	Manhattan	333	Onni	93
Montrouge	81	Queens	337	Onset	300
Moose Jaw	45	Staten Island	338	Oporto	177
Morocco	156	New Zealand	166	Oradea	180
Morris Plains	316	Newark (DE)	270	Orangeburg	339
Morristown	316	Newark (UK)	240	Orlando	276
Moscow	182	Newburgh	328	Orleans	69
Moshav Shoresh	129	Newburyport	300	Orsha	20
Mount Vernon	340	Newcastle	6	Oshawa	40
Mozambique	158	Newcastle upon Tyne	242	Osijek	52
Mulheim	101	Newport (RI)	356	Oslo	168
Mulhouse	66	Newport (UK)	248	Osnabruck	101
Mumbai	112	Newport News	364	Ostend	24
Muncie	284	Newton	300	Ottawa	40
Munich	101	Niagara Falls (Canada)	40	Oudtshoorn	194
Myanmar	159	Niagara Falls (NY)	338	Oujda	157
Myrtle Beach	358	Nice	89	Overland Park	286
		Nicosia	54	Owen Sound	41
N		Nikolayev	215	Oxford	241
		Nimes	90		
Nagasaki	144	Niteroi	29	**P**	
Nahariya	129	Nizhny Novgorod	183		
Nairobi	145	Noisy Le Sec	81	Paarl	194
Nalchik	183	Norfolk	364	Paderborn	102
Namibia	159	North Adams	300	Padua	138
Nancy	66	North Bay	40	Paducah	287
Nantes	69	North Hollywood	258	Palm Beach	277
Naples	138	North Miami /		Palm City	277
Narragansett	356	North Miami Beach	276	Palm Coast	277
Nashville	359	Northampton (MA)	300	Palm Springs	260
Nassau	18	Northampton (UK)	240	Palo Alto	261
Nassau County	326	Northbrook	282	Panama	169
Natchez	306	Northridge	259	Panama City	169
Natick	299	Norwalk	269	Panevezys	147
Navoy	369	Norway	168	Pantin	81
Nazareth	130	Norwich (CT)	269	Paraguay	170
Needham	299	Norwich (UK)	240	Paramaribo	201
Negev	130	Norwood	300	Paramus	316
Nepal	160	Nottingham	241	Paravur	112
Netanya	130	Novi Sad	372	Parma	138
Netherlands	160	Novosibirsk	183	Parsipanny	317
Neuilly	81			Pasadena	259
Neukirch-Egnach	207	**O**		Passaic	317
Neustadt	101			Passo Fundo	29
New Bedford	300	Oak Ridge	359	Paterson	317
New Britain	269	Oakland	260	Pau	91
New Brunswick	316	Oakville	40	Peabody	300
New City	339	Obernai	67	Peekskill	341
New Delhi	112	Odenbach	101	Pelotas	29
New Haven	269	Odessa	215	Pembroke	41
New Hyde Park	327	Offenbach	101	Pembroke Pines	277
New London	269	Oklahoma City	346	Pensacola	277
New Orleans	288	Old Bridge	316	Penza	183
New Rochelle	340	Old Orchard Beach	289	Peoria	282
New York (State)	322	Olney	291	Perigueuex	91
New York City (NY)	328	Olomouc	55	Perm	183

Perpignan	90	**Q**		Rockville	292
Perth	13			Roissy-En-Brie	82
Perth Amboy	317	Qatzrin	131	Romania	178
Peru	171	Quebec City	45	Rome	139
Perugia	138	Quincy	301	Rosario	5
Petach Tikva	131	Quito	59	Roselle	317
Peterborough	41			Rosh Hanikra	131
Petropolis	29	**R**		Rosh Pina	132
Phalsbourg	67			Rosny-Sous-Bois	82
Philadelphia	349	Ra'anana	131	Rostov-na-Donu	183
Philippines Republic	172	Rabat	157	Rotterdam	164
Phoenix	250	Radauti	180	Rouen	70
Piatra Neamt	180	Rahway	317	Rousse	33
Piestany	186	Raleigh	343	Rueil-Malmaison	82
Pilsen	55	Ramat Gan	131	Rumson	318
Pisa	139	Ramat Hanegev	131	Russian Federation	181
Piscataway	317	Ramat Yohanan	131	Rzeszow	174
Pittsburgh	354	Ramona	261		
Pittsfield	301	Ramsgate	223	**S**	
Plainfield	317	Rancagua	46		
Plovdiv	33	Randolph (MA)	301	Saarbrucken	102
Plymouth (MA)	301	Randolph (NJ)	317	Sachkhere	183
Plymouth (UK)	219	Rapid City	358	Sacramento	261
Pocomoke	293	Reading (PA)	355	Safed	132
Poitiers	91	Reading (UK)	218	Safi	157
Poland	173	Rechitsa	20	Saginaw	305
Polna	55	Recife	28	Saint Germain	82
Ponta Delgada	177	Redbridge	221	Saint John	38
Porlamar	371	Regensburg	102	Saint-Avold	67
Port au Prince	107	Regina	45	Saint-Denis	82
Port Chester	341	Rego Park	338	Saint-Die	67
Port Elizabeth	188	Rehovot	131	Saint-Etienne	90
Portland (ME)	289	Reims	67	Saint-Fons	90
Portland (OR)	347	Rennes	70	Saint-Laurent-du-Var	90
Porto Alegre	29	Reno	309	Saint-Leu-La-Foret	82
Portsmouth (NH)	310	Reunion	92	Saint-Louis	67
Portsmouth & Southsea		Revere	301	Saint-Ouen-L'Aumône	82
(UK)	221	Rezhitsa	146	Saint-Quentin	67
Portugal	176	Rhodes	106	Salamanca	198
Postville	286	Riccione	139	Sale	237
Poti	93	Richmond (Canada)	35	Salem (MA)	301
Potomac	292	Richmond (VA)	365	Salem (OR)	348
Potsdam	102	Richmond Hill	41	Salford	237
Pottstown	355	Ridgewood	317	Salisbury	293
Poughkeepsie	338	Riga	147	Salonika	106
Poway	261	Rijeka	52	Salt Lake City	363
Prague	55	Rio Rancho	321	Salvador	27
Prairie Village	286	Ris-Orangis	82	Salzburg	15
Prestwich	236	River Edge	317	Samara	183
Pretoria	191	Roanne	90	Samarkand	369
Princeton	317	Rochester (MN)	306	San Antonio	362
Providence	356	Rochester (NY)	338	San Bernardino	261
Pueblo	267	Rochester (UK)	223	San Carlos	261
Puerto Rico	177	Rock Island	282	San Diego	261
Pune	113	Rockford	283	San Fernando Valley	259
		Rockland	289	San Francisco	262
		Rockland County	338	San Jose (CA)	263
		Rockledge	277	San Jose (Costa Rica)	51

San Juan-Santurce	177	Sicily	140	Stamford	270
San Pedro Sula	108	Siena	140	St-Brice-Sous-Foret	83
San Rafael	264	Sierra Vista	251	Ste. Agathe des Monts	45
San Salvador	61	Sighet	180	Stockholm	202
Santa Barbara	264	Silver Spring	292	Stockton	264
Santa Cruz	25	Simferopol	215	Stoke On Trent	241
Santa Fe	321	Singapore	185	Stoughton	302
Santa Monica	264	Sioux City	286	Strasbourg	67
Santa Rosa	264	Skokie	283	Straubing	102
Santiago	46	Skopje	150	Stuttgart	102
Santo Andre	30	Slavuta	216	Subotica	372
Santo Domingo	59	Slovakia	186	Suceava	180
Santos	30	Slovenia	187	Sudbury (Canada)	41
Sao Caetano do Sul	30	Sofia	33	Sudbury (MA)	302
Sao Jose dos Campos	30	Solihull	244	Suffern	339
Sao Paulo	30	Somerset	318	Suffolk County	328
Saragossa	198	Somerville	302	Sukhumi	93
Sarajevo	26	Sopron	110	Sun City	251
Sarasota	277	Sorocaba	32	Sunderland	243
Saratoga Springs	340	Sosua	59	Surami	93
Saratov	183	South Africa	188	Suriname	201
Sarcelles	82	South Bend	284	Surrey	35
Sardinia	140	South Haven	305	Suva	62
Sarrebourg	67	South Korea	194	Swampscott	302
Sarreguemines	67	South Orange	318	Swansea	247
Sartrouville	83	South River	318	Sweden	202
Saskatoon	45	Southampton	222	Switzerland	204
Satu Mare	180	Southend-on-Sea	221	Sydney (Australia)	6
Savannah	280	Southfield	305	Sydney (Canada)	39
Saverne	67	Southport	239	Syosset	327
Savigny sur Orge	83	Spain	195	Syracuse	340
Scarsdale	341	Speyer	102	Szczecin	174
Schenectady	340	Spezia	140		
Schwerin	102	Split	52	**T**	
Scotch Plains	318	Spokane	366		
Scottsdale	251	Spotswood	318	Tahiti	92
Scranton	355	Spring Valley	339	Taipei	209
Seattle	366	Springfield (IL)	283	Taiwan	209
Sedan-Charleville	67	Springfield (MA)	302	Tajikistan	210
Segovia	198	Springs	192	Tallahassee	278
Selestat	67	Sri Lanka	201	Tallinn	61
Senigallia	140	St Albans	222	Tamarac	278
Sens	67	St Andrews	246	Tampa	278
Seoul	194	St Annes On Sea	223	Tangier	158
Seville	198	St Augustine	277	Tarbes	91
Sevran	83	St Brelade	248	Tarragona	198
Sfax	211	St Catharine's	41	Tarzana	259
Shakhrisabz	210	St Gallen	207	Tashkent	369
Shanghai	49	St Joseph	307	Tbilisi	93
Sharon (MA)	301	St Louis	307	Teaneck	318
Sharon (PA)	356	St Moritz	207	Tegucigalpa	108
Sharon Springs	325	St Paul	306	Tehran	113
Sheboygan	367	St Petersburg (FL)	277	Tel Aviv	132
Sheffield	244	St Petersburg (Russia)	183	Teleneshty	155
Sherman Oaks	259	St Thomas	371	Tempe	251
Shiauliai	148	St. John's	38	Temple Hills	293
Short Hills	318	Staines	240	Temuco	47
Shreveport	288	Stains	83	Tenafly	319

Tenerife	200		
Teplice	57		
Terezin	57		
Terre Haute	285		
Tetuan	158		
Thailand	210		
Thane	113		
The Hague	164		
Thiais	83		
Thionville	68		
Thornhill	41		
Thousand Oaks	265		
Thunder Bay	42		
Tiberias	134		
Tiburon	265		
Tijuana	154		
Timisoara	181		
Tirana	1		
Tiraspol	155		
Tirgu Mures	181		
Tokyo	144		
Toledo (OH)	346		
Toledo (Spain)	199		
Topeka	286		
Toronto	42		
Torquay	219		
Torremolinos	199		
Toul	68		
Toulon	90		
Toulouse	91		
Tours	70		
Trappes	83		
Trenton	319		
Trier	102		
Trieste	141		
Trikkala	106		
Trnava	187		
Trondheim	168		
Troy	340		
Troyes	68		
Tshelyabinsk	184		
Tshkinvali	93		
Tskhakaya	93		
Tucson	252		
Tucuman	5		
Tudela	199		
Tula	184		
Tulburg	165		
Tulsa	346		
Tunis	211		
Tunisia	211		
Tupelo	306		
Turin	141		
Turkey	212		
Turku	63		
Tushnad	181		
Tustin	259		

U

Ukraine	214
Uman	216
Umhlanga	192
Union	319
United Kingdom	217
Channel Islands	248
England	217
Isle of Man	248
Northern Ireland	248
Scotland	245
Wales	247
United States of America	249
Uppsala	204
Urbino	141
Uruguay	368
Utica	340
Utrecht	165
Uzbekistan	369

V

Valdivia	47
Valence	90
Valencia	199
Valenciennes	69
Vallejo	265
Valletta	151
Valparaiso (Chile)	47
Valparaiso (IN)	285
Van Nuys	260
Vancouver	36
Vani	93
Vatra Dornei	181
Veitshochheim	103
Venezuela	370
Venice (CA)	260
Venice (Italy)	141
Venissieux	90
Ventura	265
Vercelli	142
Verdun	69
Vero Beach	278
Verona	142
Versailles	83
Vestal	340
Vevey	207
Viareggio	142
Vichy	90
Victoria	37
Vienna	15
Villejuif	83
Villeneuve-la-Garenne	83
Villiers Sur Marne	83
Villiers-le-Bel-Gonesse	83
Vilnius	148
Vincennes	84

Vineland	319
Vineyard Haven	302
Virgin Islands (USA)	371
Virginia Beach	365
Vitoria	199
Vitry-sur-Seine	84
Vittel	69
Vladikavkaz	184
Volgograd	184
Volos	106

W

Waco	362
Waikiki	281
Wakefield	302
Walnut Creek	265
Waltham	302
Warren	320
Warsaw	174
Warwick	357
Washington	271
Washington (Greater)	291
Washington Township	320
Wasselonne	69
Waterbury	270
Waterloo	24
Watford	222
Wayland	303
Wayne	320
Wellesley Hills	303
Wellington	167
Welwyn Garden City	222
West Bloomfield	305
West Hartford	270
West Hempstead	327
West Hills	260
West Lafayette	285
West New York	320
West Orange	320
West Palm Beach	278
West Point	341
West Roxbury	303
Westboro	303
Westerly	357
Westfield	320
Westhampton Beach	328
Westport	270
Westwood	303
Whippany	321
White Plains	341
Whitefield	238
Whiting	285
Whittier	265
Wichita	287
Wiesbaden	103
Wilkes-Barre	356
Williamsport	356

Index to Advertisers

Please complete and return Jewish Travel Guide form to us by 1 September 2003

Please reserve the following advertising space in

Jewish Travel Guide 2004:

☐ Full Page   £475   181 x 115 mm

☐ Half Page   £245   91 x 115 mm

☐ Quarter Page   £145   45 x 115 mm

(UK advertisers please note that the above rates are subject to VAT)
Special positions by arrangement

☐ **Please insert the attached copy (If setting is required a 10% setting charge will be made.)**

☐ **Copy will be forwarded from our Advertising Agents (*see below*)**

Contact Name: _____

Advertisers Name: _____

Address for invoicing: _____

_____

Tel: _____ Fax: _____

Signed: _____ Title: _____

VAT No: _____

Date: _____

Agency Name (if applicable): _____

Address: _____

_____

Tel: _____ Fax: _____

All advertisements set by the publisher will only be included if they have been signed and approved by the advertiser.

To the Advertising Department
Jewish Travel Guide
Vallentine Mitchell & Co. Ltd.
Crown House, 47 Chase Side, Southgate, London N14 5BP
Fax: + 44(0)20-8447 8548. E-mail: jtg@vmbooks.com

Update for Jewish Travel Guide 2004

PUBLISHER'S REQUEST

Readers are asked kindly to draw attention to any omissions or errors. If errors are discovered, it would be appreciated if you could give appropriate up-to-date information, referring to the appropriate page, and send this form to the Editor at the address given below.

Alternatively, you can email us.

With reference to the following entry:

Page:

Country:

Entry should read:

Signed: _____ Date:_____

Name (BLOCK CAPITALS) _____

Address: _____

_____

Telephone:_____

SEND TO:

The Editor
Jewish Travel Guide
Vallentine Mitchell & Co. Ltd.
Crown House, 47 Chase Side,
Southgate, London N14 5BP
Fax: + 44(0)20-8447 8548. E-mail: jtg@vmbooks.com